Islam and the Politics of Secularism

This book examines the process of secularization in the Middle East in the late 19th and early 20th centuries through an analysis of the transformation and abolition of Islamic Caliphate. Focusing on debates in both the center of the Caliphate and its periphery, the author argues that the relationship between Islam and secularism was one of accommodation, rather than simply conflict and confrontation, because Islam was the single most important source of legitimation in the modernization of the Middle East.

Through detailed analysis of both official documents and the writings of the intellectuals who contributed to reforms in the Empire, the author first examines the general secularization process in the Ottoman Empire from the late 18th century up to the end of the 1920s. He then presents an in-depth analysis of a crucial case of secularization: the demise of Islamic Caliphate. Drawing upon a wide range of secondary and primary sources on the Caliphate and the wider process of political modernization, he employs discourse analysis and comparative-historical methods to examine how the Caliphate was first transformed into a "spiritual" institution and then abolished in 1924 by Turkish secularists. Ardıç also demonstrates how the book's argument is applicable to wider secularization and modernization processes in the Middle East.

Deriving insights from history, anthropology, Islamic law and political science, the book will engage a critical mass of scholars interested in Middle Eastern studies, political Islam, secularization and the near-global revival of religion as well as the historians of Islam and late-Ottoman Empire, and those working in the field of historical sociology and the sociology of religion as a case study.

Nurullah Ardıç is an assistant professor of sociology at Istanbul Şehir University, Turkey. His research focuses on religion and politics in the Middle East, Ottoman-Turkish modernization, social theory, and globalization, using historical-comparative and discourse analysis methods.

SOAS/Routledge studies on the Middle East
Series Editors
Benjamin C. Fortna, SOAS, University of London
Ulrike Freitag, Freie Universität Berlin, Germany

This series features the latest disciplinary approaches to Middle Eastern Studies. It covers the Social Sciences and the Humanities in both the pre-modern and modern periods of the region. While primarily interested in publishing single-authored studies, the series is also open to edited volumes on innovative topics, as well as textbooks and reference works.

1 **Islamic Nationhood and Colonial Indonesia**
The Umma below the winds
Michael Francis Laffan

2 **Russian-Muslim Confrontation in the Caucasus**
Alternative visions of the conflict between Imam Shamil and the Russians, 1830–1859
Thomas Sanders, Ernest Tucker and G.M. Hamburg

3 **Late Ottoman Society**
The intellectual legacy
Edited by Elisabeth Özdalga

4 **Iraqi Arab Nationalism**
Authoritarian, totalitarian and pro-Fascist inclinations, 1932–1941
Peter Wien

5 **Medieval Arabic Historiography**
Authors as actors
Konrad Hirschler

6 **The Ottoman Administration of Iraq, 1890–1908**
Gökhan Çetinsaya

7 **Cities in the Pre-Modern Islamic World**
The urban impact of religion, state, and society
Amira K. Bennison and Alison L. Gascoigne

Islam and the Politics of Secularism

The Caliphate and Middle Eastern modernization in the early 20th century

Nurullah Ardıç

Routledge
Taylor & Francis Group

LONDON AND NEW YORK

First published 2012
by Routledge
2 Park Square, Milton Park, Abingdon, Oxon OX14 4RN

Simultaneously published in the USA and Canada
by Routledge
711 Third Ave, New York, NY 10017

Routledge is an imprint of the Taylor & Francis Group, an informa business

British Library Cataloguing in Publication Data
A catalogue record for this book is available from the British Library

Library of Congress Cataloging in Publication Data
Ardıç, Nurullah.
   Islam and the politics of secularism: the Caliphate and Middle Eastern
   modernization in the early 20th century/Nurullah Ardıç.
   p. cm. – (SOAS/Routledge studies on the Middle East; 16)
   Includes bibliographical references and index.
   1. Caliphate–History–20th century. 2. Islam and politics–Turkey.
   3. Turkey–Politics and government–1909–1918. 4. Secularism–Turkey–
   History–20th century. I. Title.
   BP166.9.A73 2011
   297.2′72095609041–dc23
                                                        2011028858

ISBN: 978-0-415-67166-8 (hbk)
ISBN: 978-0-203-13773-4 (ebk)

Typeset in Times
by Wearset Ltd, Boldon, Tyne and Wear

To Asuman, my wife,
and Rabia and Haluk who
grew up along with the book

Contents

Figures and tables

Figures

Tables

Preface

This book examines the process of secularization in the Middle East in the early 20th century through an analysis of the debates over the transformation and abolition of Islamic Caliphate. It argues that the relationship between Islam and secularism was one of accommodation, rather than simply conflict and confrontation, because Islam was the single most important source of legitimation in the modernization process of the Middle East. It uses the comparative-historical method to examine how the Caliphate was first transformed into a "spiritual" institution and then abolished in 1924 by Turkish secularists, and draws on both secondary and primary sources (official documents, parliament records, political speeches, periodicals, and intellectuals' writings) on the Caliphate and the wider process of political modernization in both the "center" (Turkey) and the "periphery" (the Arabian Peninsula, North Africa, and India) of the Caliphate. It also demonstrates, with the discourse analysis method, that virtually all actors representing different groups involved in the debates, including "traditionalists," "modernists" and "secularists," made use of a similar Islamic discourse through a number of "discursive strategies" and "discursive techniques" in order to legitimize their politico-ideological positions. It also shows how this Islamic discourse was secularized by both Islamists and secularists during this period. It thus tries to demonstrate the interaction between discourse and action by examining how the (Islamic) discourse both shaped, and was shaped by, the political and military developments in the Middle East during the late 19th and early 20th centuries.

Acknowledgments

I completed writing the book in four different institutional settings: UCLA's Sociology Department and Center for European and Euroasian Studies (CEES), Istanbul Şehir University, and the Foundation for Sciences and Arts in Istanbul, Turkey. I thank their staff members for their support. In the early phases of this project, my two academic advisors at UCLA, Michael Mann and Gail Kligman, have been very helpful and supportive. My thanks and gratitude go to them for their guidance not only in the process of researching and writing my dissertation but also during my graduate study at UCLA as a whole. I should also mention Andreas Wimmer and Gabriel Piterberg, my other committee members, who provided useful comments and suggestions on my project. I did much of the research for this project in Turkey where I received help from some colleagues; I would like to thank particularly İsmail Kara and Sami Erdem for opening their personal archives to me. Also, I thank Ali Akyıldız, Suat Mertoğlu, and Bahattin Öztuncay for allowing me publish some of the pictures in their archives. I would also like to thank my colleagues Hızır M. Köse, Gökhan Çetinsaya, and Abdülhamit Kırmızı as well as Routledge's two anonymous reviewers for reading and commenting on the manuscript. Last but not least, I would like to mention my wife, Asuman Ardıç, and my other friends in Los Angeles and Istanbul, whose generous social support has been very helpful; my thanks and appreciation also go to them.

Abbreviations

BOA	*Başbakanlık Osmanlı Arşivleri* (The Prime Ministerial Ottoman Archives)
CDA	Critical Discourse Analysis
CHP	*Cumhuriyet Halk Partisi* (Republican People's Party)
CUP	Committee of Union and Progress
DRA	Department of Religious Affairs
FAP	Freedom and Alliance Party
GNA	Grand National Assembly
JMI	*Jamia Millia Islamia* (Islamic National University)
LBKTB	*Lozan Barış Konferansı, Tutanak-Belgeler* (Lausanne Peace Conference, Records and Documents)
PP	People's Party
RPP	Republican People's Party
SM	*Sırat-ı Müstakim*
TBMM	*Türkiye Büyük Millet Meclisi* (Turkish Grand National Assembly)
TBMMZC	*Türkiye Büyük Millet Meclisi Zabıt Ceridesi* (GNA Records)
UPP	Union and Progress Party

1 Islam, politics, and secularization

There is no authority without men,
and there are no men/army without money,
and there is no money without cultivation,
and there is no cultivation without
justice and good governance
                            The "Circle of Justice"[1]

The current Turkish Prime Minister, Tayyip Erdoğan, was tried and convicted of "inciting religious hatred" in 1998. He was sentenced to ten months imprisonment, of which he served four between March and July 1999, in addition to a ban from politics that delayed his coming to the office in 2004. The reason for his arrest was the fact that he had recited a poem on December 12, 1997 at a public meeting in Siirt in southeastern Turkey, titled "Prayer of the Soldier" and written by a well-known intellectual-poet Ziya Gökalp, who was an ideologue of (early) Kemalist laicism. The poem included the following lines:

Mosques are our barracks,
domes our helmets,
minarets our bayonets,
believers our soldiers
       (Gökalp 1989[1912])

Though, according to some historians, these lines were not included in Gökalp's original poem (Davison 2006), in the rest of the poem, Islam was still as dominant a theme. This story on the Turkish secular establishment's – ultimately unsuccessful – attempt to ban an "Islamist" politician (he himself calls his party "conservative democrat") who recited a poem written by a leading ideologue of secularism in Turkey, might give a hint as to how puzzling the religion-politics relationship can get in a Muslim society. This book examines the complex and paradoxical relationship between Islam and secularism (and the wider modernization process) in the Middle East with a particular focus on the first quarter of the 20th century. It takes the most important political institution in Islam, the Caliphate, and its demise as a crucial "site" to examine the complexity of the relationship between Islam and modernity.

Alan Taylor remarks that for Turkey Islam "is more than a doctrine, more than a private belief or worship. It is also a culture and an institutional framework governing all aspects of interpersonal relations" (1988: 32). This study is based on the assumption that what Taylor observed towards the end of the 20th century about contemporary Islam in Turkey was also true (and even more so) for early-20th century Turkey and the wider Middle East. Therefore, the main argument of this study is that the relationship between Islam and secularism in the Middle East was one of accommodation rather than confrontation during much of its modernization process that started in the late 18th century.

In a sense, then, my study is a critique of the idea of a fundamental incompatibility of Islam and modernity. Among the recent theories based on this dichotomous assumption is the infamous "clash of civilizations" thesis, which was first formulated by Samuel Huntington (1993) and then enthusiastically received by some neo-conservative intellectuals such as Bernard Lewis as well as by many hawkish politicians in the US and Europe. According to a more recent application of the thesis, the "Muslim rage" against the West is shaped by the centuries-long conflict between progressive-democratic Christian and reactionary-despotic Muslim civilizations (B. Lewis 2002). This view is based on the essentialist (and wrong) assumption that there is only one form of modernity and that Islam and modernity are two separate, incompatible worldviews and lifestyles. It argues that the Muslim failure to harmonize the two has led to a clash between the West and Islam. For Lewis, as Western civilization produced modernity during the last three centuries, Islamic civilization first rejected modernity because of its Christian nature and then failed to emulate it despite recognizing its superiority, which is "what went wrong" in Muslim society.

Lewis's study on Turkish modernization (1961), too, is a narrative of an essential conflict between pro-Western modernists and anti-Western traditionalists. This ideological narrative was taken up by the Turkish official view of history as well – though this view does not accept his emphasis on the continuity of Ottoman and Turkish modernizations. Interestingly, Lewis's idea of an eternal conflict between Islam and the West has also been accepted by many Muslim intellectuals during the 20th century. As Aydın observes:

> there have been numerous Islamist intellectuals who have perceived the relationship with Western civilization as a zero-sum game of conflict and competition. Yet this convergence of the clash of civilizations paradigm shared by Islamists on the one hand and Western scholars on the other hand is itself proof of the global circulation of ideas and mutual influences rather than the actual reality of civilizational conflict.
>
> (Aydın 2006: 460)

The Muslim world is large enough to contain cases of both conflict and co-operation between Islamic and Western institutions. The clash of civilizations approach loses much of its explanatory power in the face of some recent developments and exemplary models (such as Turkey and Malaysia) where Islam seems to be compatible with modernity and democracy. A purpose of this study is to illuminate the historical background of this reconciliatory situation, which might also help understand the conflictual cases in the Muslim world as well as the potential problems that diasporic Muslim communities in the US and Europe might face.

Locating secularization in the Middle Eastern context

Sociologist José Casanova, in his study on the global revitalization of religion during the 20th century, remarks that

> religions are likely to continue playing important public roles in the ongoing construction of the modern world [which] compels us to rethink systematically the relationship of religion and modernity and, more important, the possible roles religions may play in the public sphere of modern societies
>
> (Casanova 1994: 6)

Following this logic, this study tries to explore the following fundamental (and paradoxical) question: What role did Islam play in Middle Eastern modernization and, in particular, how did discursive Islamization accompany institutional secularization during the late 19th and early 20th centuries? The basic hypothesis of this study is that a heavy use of Islamic discourse to legitimize secular projects informed, as indicated by the the Caliphate's transformation and abolition in this period, the content and direction of secularization, an important part of the wider modernization process. Though secularization has usually been posed as a confrontation between religion and politics, for a long time it did not take the form of an open attack on Islam in the Middle East. Instead, we observe that political actors often resorted to Islam as the fundamental framework of political culture and the only source of legitimacy, and drew on the discourse of serving God and of "saving" Islam. Therefore, it seems that Middle Eastern modernization involved a different kind of secularization, which was based on the redefinition of religion in the public sphere rather than a direct confrontation with it.

Islam is still too strong in social life to openly challenge, and the dominant "secularist" discourse in the public sphere is still similar: that of protecting the authenticity of religion from corrupt politics. Focusing on both the wider modernization process and that of the transformation of the Caliphate – the most important political institution in Islam – during 1908–1924, this study will hopefully contribute to the understanding of the present as well as the past political conditions of the Muslim world, and particularly the role played by religion in political life. It will also contribute to the existing literature on "multiple" or "alternative modernities" (Eisenstadt 2000; Taylor 2001; Goankar 2001) by demonstrating that modernization of the Middle East did not have to follow the model produced in Western Europe – which is also demonstrated by the "Arab spring" ongoing as at this writing. It thus provides a critique of classical sociological view of the development of modernity as espoused by Marx, Durkheim, and Weber, who all assumed that the basic cultural and institutional forms created by Western modernity would "ultimately take over in all modernizing and modern societies; with the expansion of modernity, they would prevail throughout the world" (Eisenstadt 2000: 1; see also Delanty 2006).

The originating question of this research stems from an attempt to understand the peculiarities of Middle Eastern modernization during the late-Ottoman era. This is a period where there was a series of gradual yet quite significant socio-economic and political developments. For many, proponents and opponents of modernization alike, these changes marked a "civilizational" transformation. And it still continues today. So, how did this sea change take place in that period? Was it merely a replica of what had happened in Western societies, as modernization theorists of various kinds would suggest, despite the presence of Islam as a major social and political force? Or was it a dialectical process of political and ideological struggles along with major economic and military developments? In particular, what role did Islam play in this period of immense social change? Hence, the research question mentioned above: How and why did discursive Islamization accompany institutional secularization? This research attempts to account for this interesting phenomenon, which characterized the great struggle between Islamists and secularists in the first quarter of the 20th century. I hypothesize that the main reasons for the dominance of an Islamic discourse include:

- a fundamental concern for legitimacy by different actors;
- Islam's crucial role for social mobilization, avoiding – on the part of secularists – criticism by Islamist actors; and
- the lack of an alternative "language" and a framework (such as a secular-nationalist, or radical working-class or peasant movement) that could contain the reform attempts in a Muslim society.

The specifying questions of this study, which constitute the subsets of my main research question, include the following:

- Can we talk about a *variation* within the evolution of this discourse? In other words, what forms did it take as a result of its interaction with differing socio-political developments in different geographical and institutional contexts (such as in the caliphal center vs. its periphery) and at different times?
- What, then, are the implications of temporal and spatial comparisons for the interaction between Islamic discourse and secularism in the Muslim world?
- What social groups take what positions regarding religion and politics during this period, and how did the social and political aims of actors and intellectuals affect their respective positions?
- Finally, was the discourse of saving Islam and the state through a series of reforms a genuine argument or a strategy instrumentally employed by different actors to implement their political agenda?

My research takes the Caliphate as its case and focuses on the debates over it during its transformation and eventual abolition, a crucial cornerstone of the broader secularization process, in the post-*Meşrutiyet* era (1908–1924), a period when social and political change was most intense. I hypothesize that the development of secularism in the Middle East has a peculiar character in that for the most part it did not entail the conflict between religion and politics, which is reflected in the dominant discourse among the political and intellectual elite. A striking example of this discourse is provided by Abdullah Cevdet, a leading secularist intellectual of the late-Ottoman period, who wrote in 1905 that:

> Muslims can accept the advancements of civilization only if they come from a Muslim source.... Therefore we, who have taken it as their duty to inject a new blood into the Muslim vessel, should find those progressive principles that are abundant in Islam.
>
> (quoted in Hanioğlu 1981: 131)[2]

This was the common discourse in the major political projects both before and shortly after the establishment of the Turkish Republic in 1923. The main political actors in these two periods, the Committee of Union and Progress (CUP) that represented the ruling elite of the last decade of the Ottoman Empire (1908–1918), the Arab nationalist leaders such as King Hussein of *Hijaz* and King Fuad of Egypt as well as the Republican People's Party in Turkey, which was led by Kemal Atatürk who founded the Republic and ruled it for three decades, were rival to (and even the enemy of) each other, yet all of them extensively drew upon a similar Islamic discourse as they had the common goal of modernizing both state and society. In this sense, there is more continuity than rupture, unlike the conventional historiography based on the modernization theory holds, both temporally (from the Ottoman to post-Ottoman periods) and geographically (both in the center and the periphery of the Caliphate). For, although these rival modernizers came to power at different times and places, they all justified their secularizing reforms by reference to the discourse of serving and protecting the authentic Islam. Thus, the (secular) politics aimed at modernization was not necessarily situated against Islam in the late 19th and early 20th centuries. The Caliphate, on the other hand, proved to be an important institution to deal with in this period. Focusing on the process of its abolition, therefore, I examine the relationship between what Mann (1986) calls "ideological power" and "political power," taking them as two independent yet interrelated sets of power relations and applying them to the Islamic-Middle Eastern case. Given the Caliphate's importance for Islamic politics, it functions as a window through which one can examine the broader processes of secularization and modernization in the Middle East. My examination is thus a critique of the studies (especially in political science) that underestimate the significance of religion in terms of political development in the region (see, e.g., Berkes 1998; Lee 2009).

Accommodating politics and religion

The concept of the "Caliphate" lies at the center of the political philosophy in Islam. It is well known that religion and politics are not two separate domains in the Islamic political theory, which is already a branch of the *fiqh* that involves both theology and law. Islam thus exemplifies what Donald Smith (1970: 13) calls the "organic model" of religio-political system where there is the fusion of religious and political functions in one single body, unlike in Christianity which is characterized by the separation of those powers (i.e., the "church model").

There are three interrelated arguments for the inseparability of religion and politics in the Islamic political philosophy (see Davutoğlu 1994a: 98–105). First, the "meta-historical argument" is based on the parallelism between theocentric ontology and politics. It holds that the political organization of society is a reflection of the main ontological principle in Islam – that of the "differentiation of ontological levels" based on the concept of *tawhid* (unity of God), which implies the absolute authority of God over men. Furthermore, the clear separation between the realm of God and that of human beings prevents the emergence of any intermediary institution, i.e., the church, in Islam. For, even Prophet Muhammad, unlike Jesus Christ in Christianity, is seen only as a human being with no power to penetrate into the realm of Allah. Within this framework, the political organization of the relationships among human beings is said to be a reflection of the primordial meta-historical covenant between Allah and human beings where the latter declare to obey God unconditionally. The role given to the man in this relationship is to be the "Caliph of Allah." The usages of the term "Caliph" in the Qur'an also reinforce this image. It calls Adam, the first man and prophet, and King David, also a prophet for Muslims, the "Caliph of Allah" (2/30 and 38/27, respectively). The first usage is interpreted as referring to Adam's – and by extension, all human beings' – ontological status in relation to God, i.e., being his servant. The second usage, on the other hand, is usually interpreted as a socio-political title, i.e., the king who rules in the name of God (see al-Qadi [1988: 398–402] for different meanings of the term). Thus, the two semantic domains to which the term belongs are intermingled by Islamic scholars, creating a parallel between its "divine" and "this worldly" senses.

Second, the "logical argument" is based on an analogy between cosmology, micro-organism (the human body) and politics. Developed particularly by the two classical philosophers of Islam, al-Farabi and Ibn Rushd, this view holds that the organization of the polity in the "ideal state" is a reflection of the divine cosmic order ruled by the absolute justice of God. Also, just like the heart manages the operations of the human body, the just ruler (the Caliph) orchestrates the affairs of the Islamic *ummah*. This, together with protecting religion, is the main function of the ruler. Thus, the hierarchical organization of the universe based on the divine regulation is reflected in that of the "social body" as well as the human body.

Finally, the "historical argument" states a widespread assumption regarding the human nature among scholars: that of a need for and a natural tendency towards co-operation among men. Developed most clearly by al-Farabi and al-Tusi, this argument holds that the origins of polity lie in the social co-operation of individuals. The necessity of political authority as well as this assumption of human nature and its relation to political organization is common to all schools of thought in Islam (Davutoğlu 1994a: 102). Moreover, social co-operation is explained on the basis of "love," rather than mutual interest, which is also derived from "divine love" – the love of God for those He has created. Thus, the origins and functions of political authority are justified by Islamic scholars with reference to the ontological relationship between God and human beings: the latter is projected onto the this-worldly, hierarchical organization of the socio-political system. Hence the inseparability of religion and politics.

Significance of the Caliphate

The classical understanding of the Caliphate (e.g., al-Mawardī 1994; al-Taftazānī 1989) is, as mentioned, based on a hierarchical view of cosmology and world-view of which politics is a part. For the Caliph is the vicegerent of the Prophet, who in turn represents God:

> God, may His power be exalted, ordained for the community (*ummah*) a leader through whom He provided for the vicegerency of the prophet and through whom He protected the religion (*millah*), and He entrusted to him authority (*siyasah*) so that the management of affairs should proceed [on the basis of] legitimate religion,... and the Caliphate [*Imamate*] became the principle upon which the bases of the community were founded, by which the well-being of the community was regulated and affairs of general interest were made stable, and from which particular public functions (*al-wilayāt al-khassah*) emanated.
>
> (al-Māwardī 1994: 3; cf. al-Taftazānī 1989, V: 232)

For much of the Islamic history, except for a period of hiatus caused by the Mongolian invasions, this view both reflected and informed the historical practice, including the Ottoman political system (see Sanhoury 1926). Therefore, the abolition of the Caliphate meant the erosion of the classical view of hierarchical system based on "obedience" to the ruler in terms of the Islamic political philosophy.

Second, the Caliphate was both a source and a symbol of a universalistic political culture (as well as the political machinery itself) throughout much of Islamic history. For the first time in history, the Caliphate put in practice a universal political form of Abrahamic monotheism in a very short period of time (Yücesoy 2007: 88–93). Moreover, the near-global expansion of this *tawhid*-based political and aesthetic culture were achieved mostly in peaciful ways, such as trade and intellectual exchange, after military conquests (Fowden 1993: 138; Lombard 2003: 161ff.; Hodgson 1974). Such trans-regional and universalistic ideals of Islamic civilization (and Abrahamic tradition) as justice, which framed the emergence and expansion of the Caliphate, are best reflected in Islamic law, philosophy, and art (see Yücesoy 2007). Thus, its abolition also meant the end of the political culture based on such universalistic ideals in the Muslim world.

Third, the Caliphate is significant in terms of understanding the international political context in this period. European powers, including Britain, France, Italy, and Germany, had already had an interest in it during the 33-year reign of Abdülhamid II (1876–1909), for it was a matter of great concern for them. Since a lot of their colonial activities took place in the Muslim world, they continued to be interested in the Caliphate between the 1870s and the 1920s, especially in the Arab Middle East. Accordingly, it was quite significant for the emerging Arab nationalism as well. With the support especially of Britain, there emerged an intellectual and political movement, led by such intellectuals as al-Kawakibī, al-Afghani, and Rashid Rida, advocating the "return" of the Caliphate to Arabs. Sharif Hussein was the foremost political leader voicing this argument most ambitiously (Teitelbaum 1998; see also Chapter 5).

Finally, this institution is important in terms of understanding the domestic political context of the Ottoman Empire as well. During the reign of Abdülhamid II, the Caliphate was one of the central issues for the Young Turks in their quest for a parliamentary system. After they came to power in 1908, they were relatively stronger than any other group dominating the state until the end of the Great War in 1918. The Caliphate, however, was still significant in their attempts to modernize the state and the society (see Chapter 4). After the War, it was one of the most important issues for the nationalist movement, together with the problem of the Sultanate. Following the abolition in 1922 of the latter and with the establishment of the Turkish Republic in 1923, it became *the* most important problem for the secular(ist) elite of the new state (see Chapter 6). During this period, it was also the major topic of discussion in intellectual circles – not only, as mentioned, within the territories of the Empire but also abroad, especially in such capital cities of Europe as London, Paris, Berlin, and Rome, as well as Muslim capitals.

The Caliphate was one of the crucial "variables" that distinguished relative political-intellectual positions – which can roughly be classified as "Islamists" (with its "traditionalist" and "modernist" versions) vs. "secularists" – regarding the relationship between religion and politics in this period. For, just like the latter camp did not take a position against Islam, Islamists did not reject the "need for modernization" either. In fact, the dominant discourse among them was "to receive the science and technology from the West, but not their moral values" – simply because "Muslims did not need them." (This distinction itself was an indication at the ideological level of secularization, however.) For, perhaps as was the case with actors involved in the Russian transformation, modernization was essentially a *technical* problem/necessity for them, i.e., a question of power rather than a philosophical/ontological problem. Thus the two groups did not differ in terms of not situating modernization against religion. They did differ, however, on the Caliphate: on whether first to weaken its authority and then to abolish it. Whereas Islamist intellectuals were willing to keep the

Caliphate alive, though in different forms (see below), secularists tried to destroy it. The latter always (until 1924) insisted, however, that this was not to weaken the power of Islam in the public sphere, but to reinforce it! Even those on the extremities of the intellectual-political spectrum agreed on this basic position. For example, even Kemal Atatürk himself, the President of Turkey and the champion of secularism, said as late as in 1923:

> Our religion is the most reasonable and the most natural of all religions. It is for this reason that it is the last religion. For a religion to be natural, it should conform to reason, science, technology and logic. Our religion fully conforms to all of these.

> (quoted in Borak 1962: 34)

I hypothesize that this kind of Islamic discourse employed by secularist actors (as opposed to Islamists) had an *instrumental* character. They did see Islam as the major obstacle and a reactionary force in the way of secularization; however, they were *obliged* to adopt the Islamic stance in their discourses because they were aware that Islam was too powerful to challenge openly and that secularism had not been strongly implanted in the wider society. They had to resort to this discourse, as mentioned above, for the purpose of legitimation and social mobilization. I discuss this point in detail in Chapter 6.

I also hypothesize that the variation (spatial, temporal, and inter-group differentiation mentioned above) in the discourse over the Caliphate was part of a larger process of secularization and Islamization in the region. In other words, the divergence in the discourses employed by different groups signified (i.e., both reflected and reinforced/reproduced) the divergence that was emerging at the ontological level. For example, the "secularists" such as Gökalp and Atatürk had a problematic relationship with Islam due to their different (i.e., relatively secularized) world-views from Islamists; hence they adopted the instrumentalist discourse. The Islamists, on the other hand, were mostly "committed" as they wanted to restore and save Islam as well as the state. Most of them, however, did not see any conflict between Islam and modernity, though they differed in how they envisioned the Caliphate's future. Therefore, I argue, Islam was *the* single most important framework for any (secular or Islamic) political project, including those of modernizing reforms. In this context, the Caliphate is a case that allows us to see that the modernization process in the Middle East included the accommodation of secularization and Islam.

Accommodating secularization and Islamic politics

This study is located at the intersection of debates on the secularization process in the sociology of religion on the one hand, and those on the modernization of the Middle East in historical sociology, on the other. One needs to start out by noting that the relationship between the temporal and religious institutions has varied throughout history. The concept of secularism, which has a widespread currency in Protestant countries, is derived from the Latin word *saeculum*, and came to mean in Christian Latin "the temporal world" (Cox 1965: 18). Its synonym, "laicism," which is more widely used in the Catholic world – and in Turkey – has its roots in Greek *laikos* (the lay). (The same parallelism exists between the English word "secular" and the French word "*laique*.") "Secularization" is used to denote the process in which the politico-temporal realm (the state) is separated from the religious institution (the church), which took place in Europe and America as part of the modernization process. The relationship between the temporal and the religious constituted an important problem within the Western traditions of political thought and theology. The solution to this problem in Eastern Christianity was the submission of the church to the state that created a kind of state-church in Orthodox countries. Western Christianity, although earlier aspiring for a universal authority over various temporal authorities, finally found the solution in separating the two institutions after the Reformation in the 15th century. Struggles between Roman Catholics and Protestants were extremely vital in terms of leading to the separation of religion and politics, such as the French Wars of Religion in the 16th century and the Thirty Years' War (1618–1648), which led to the secular Westphalian order in international politics in the West. Also, it is possible to see Protestantism as a half-secular movement, with frequent subordination of religion to the state. However, the ways in which the separation of the state from the church took place varied in different polities: in Protestant countries maintaining the modus vivendi occurred more peacefully than in Catholic countries. Secularism within the processes of self-conscious modernization in such Catholic countries as France, Spain, and Austria took the form of a radical breakaway from religion limiting the authority of the Church to spiritual affairs and other-worldly matters. The Enlightenment had the notion of an open struggle against the power of the Church, in which the latter represented the image of darkness that was surrounded by such notions as irrationality, superstition, a reactionary attitude and lack of individual freedom (Martin 1978).

In light of the perceived widespread secularization in the West, the classical sociological theories of religion estimated that religion would fade away as modern institutions ensue in society. "From the start," observe Finke and Stark, "the social sciences have taken for granted the decline and eventual disappearance of religion. Perhaps no single social science thesis has come as close to universal acceptance as the belief that modernism dooms faith" (1988: 47). However, the resurgence of religion in the US especially in the 1960s[3] caused a change in the direction of the sociology of religion, which was previously based on the classical social theory. Recent developments in the sociology of religion embody two trends. First, since the 1960s they have involved a critique of the classical sociological understanding of Weber, Marx, Durkheim, and Parsons, which is based on evolutionary interpretive schemes. Second, they imply the rise of the phenomenological study of religion (Berger and Luckman 1966; Berger 1967), and of culturalist approaches to religion (Bellah 1970; Bell 1977; Wuthnow 1987), parallel with the rise of cultural sociology (Geertz 1966, 1973; Douglas 1970). These cultural-functionalist approaches attempt to redefine a social ground for religion, which survived the effects of secularization and modernity in the second half of the 20th century, unlike the predictions of the classical and evolutionary theories of religion.

Secularization theory and the West

Much of the literature on religion and secularism involves the idea of a fundamental conflict between politics and religion as the basic assumption. Based on this fundamental point, there have emerged two major paradigms in secularization theory. First, the above-mentioned classical and neo-classical paradigm is based on the argument that the significance of religion has decreased in modern times, as stated by Emile Durkheim: "If there is one truth that history has settled beyond all question, it is that religion embraces an ever-diminishing part of social life" (1947: 119). This perspective, also called the "secularization thesis," in turn involves two main variants: on the one hand, the "classics" focus on the disappearance (Comte 1969; Saint-Simon 1975[1832]) and decline (Weber 1963; Wilson 1966) of religious faith as a result of modernization and the development of science; on the other hand, phenomenological and cultural approaches emphasize the "retreat" and privatization of religion in modern society (Cox 1965, 1984; Luckmann 1967; Fenn 1978; Dobbelaere 1985; Smith 2003), its transformation into "secular" ideologies (Durkheim 1947; Parsons 1977; Bellah 1970, 1975; Gauchet 1997) or both privatization and transformation of it (Berger 1967). The underlying assumption of this paradigm is that of the increasing differentiation of religious institutions from other social and political institutions since the Middle Ages (Dobbelaere 1981; Tschannen 1991). Moreover, many of these approaches define religion only in institutional terms ignoring its other (individual and ontological) aspects, which are not necessarily affected to a great extent by the institutional decline of religion (Towler 1974; Glasner 1977).

Second, a recent critique of the classical and neo-classical paradigm from a rational-choice perspective, the "religious economies" approach, focuses on the effects of religion on aggregate levels of individual religiosity. It argues that religious participation (measured as church attendance) has in fact increased in modern era (since the 1780s) due to the "free market of religions" (absence of governmental regulation), competition among churches ("firms"), and the efforts of "religious entrepreneurs," especially in the US (Stark and Iannaccone 1993; Finke 1992; Finke and Iannaccone 1993; Warner 1993; Finke 1997; Iannaccone 1997; Stark and Finke 2000. For a critique of this paradigm, see Spickard 1998). Furthermore, unlike the mainstream view that sees urbanization and pluralism as among the principal causes of religious decline (e.g., Durkheim 1947; Berger 1967), the economic model posits that "urbanites are far more likely than rurals to *actively participate* in religion and that pluralism causes levels of activity and participation *to increase*" (Finke and Stark 1988: 41, emphases original).

The reason why these two paradigms reach opposite conclusions is related to their different definitions of secularization. The first paradigm defines it in institutional terms and the second one in terms of the religious participation of individuals. Thus, they exemplify the contradictory character of the sociology of secularization, aptly described by Budd (1973: 119):

> Like many other key concepts in sociology, its meaning has become so diffuse as to obscure rather than clarify so that, for example, both the full churches of the United States and the empty ones of England are pointed as evidence of its existence.

The latter approach assumes that the Middle Ages were a period of popular superstition whereas the first paradigm posits it as a time of universal faith (Finke and Stark 1988: 47). Hence, in modern times Western societies have become less Christian in the first view, and more Christian in the second. The recent literature suggests, however, that in the Middle Ages religion and superstition were more intermingled than opposite and that the process of secularization since then has entailed "rationalization" and individualization of the Christian faith rather than a "Christianization" of society (Gorski 2000). The way they "measure" the degree of secularization is also often inadequate as they focus heavily on some factors such as industrialization as the cause of the development of secularism, and ignore others such as the role of the state (Keddie 1997).

No matter how different their conclusions regarding the authority of Christianity, however, both perspectives share the assumption that the secularization process has involved a confrontation between religion and politics. While in fact there is no clear-cut separation between religion and politics even today in the non-Western world but also in the West (Keddie 1997: 23–24), Asad (1993: 28) recalls that "religion" as a bounded sphere of life, distinct from "politics" and "economics," is already a Western, secular idea. Thus, for him the very distinction between the religious and the secular is produced by the latter: "secularism" and "religion" in the privatized sense are two sides of the same phenomenon (2002: 193).

Moreover, many critical studies within the secularization literature focus on the Western/Christian world, and are therefore restricted in their scope. For example, Martin's (1978) Weberian-oriented "general theory of secularization" is attentive to variations among different regions in terms of the path taken towards secularization, which makes it a prominent study in the literature. However, it too entails the assumption that the process of secularization has basically involved a conflict and confrontation between the Church and the state. He identifies different patterns of secularization including the "American," "British," "French/Latin," "South American," "Russian," "Calvinist" and "Lutheran" patterns. He also juxtaposes these patterns with other modern trends such as pluralism and individualism, as well as with such other elements of modernization as Calvinism, Enlightenment, nationalism and cultural identity.

More recently, another refined "grand theory" of the "rise of secularity" has been provided by Charles Taylor's (2007) voluminous historical-philosophical rebuttal against "subtraction stories," i.e., various post-Enlightenment narratives of the radical and universal decline of religion, including the mainstream secularization theory. Taylor examines the profound change from a society in which belief in God was unchallenged to the modern one where it is only one of many options in two major phases. In the first one, he argues à la Weber that beginning in the early modern period European "social imaginary" dominated by Christian faith went through a process of disenchantment, passing through various stages, including (i) the emergence of the "buffered self" (i.e., "a new sense of the self and its place in the comos: not open and porous and vulnerable to a world of spirits and powers" [Taylor 2007: 27]), (ii) a conception of the nature as autonomous, (iii) the rise of religious individualism with the Reformation, and that of (iv) "Providential Deism" that led to a "buffered society" in the 18th century, and finally (v) dominance of rationality (epitomized by the Kantian phisolophy) as the basis of both science and morality. All these in turn led to the rise of what Taylor calls "exclusive humanism" as a new outlook of universe – as an alternative to Christianity – that marginalizes God and revelation. In the second phase, from the late 18th century on, this exclusive humanism had a "nova effect" that has resulted in the diversification of beliefs and practices that characterizes the contemporary "spiritual super-nova." Today's world of "an ever-widening variety of moral/spiritual options" (p. 299) is based also on an increasingly "expressive individualism" and an "ethic of authenticity" (the idea that every individual has the freedom to choose his/her own beliefs and morality), which have in turn created a this-worldy outlook, or an "immanent frame." This, however, does not necessarily mean the decline of religion:

> We have undergone a change in our condition, involving both an alteration of the structures we live within, and our way of imagining those structures. This is something we all share, regardless of our differences in outlook. But this cannot be captured in terms of a decline and marginalization of religion. What we share is … "the immanent frame"; the different structures we live in: scientific, social, technological, and so on, constitute such a frame in that they are part of a "natural" or "this-worldly" order which can be understood in its own terms, without reference to the "supernatural" or "transcendent."
>
> (Taylor 2007: 594)

As a result, he argues, the contemporary (Western) society is dominated by a plethora of moral positions in between the two extremes: religious and atheistic fanaticisms.

Like Martin's, then, Taylor's account is much richer than the simplistic narratives of "subtraction stories." Also, the fact that Martin takes into account the development of secularization in Russia expands the scope of his analysis. Yet, the fundamental conflict between Church and state, and the rejection of the authority and power of the former by the latter, remains in the core of his argument. Besides, Martin and Taylor's analyses, like others outlined above, focus only on the Christian world, assuming that the concept of secularism was initially an exclusively "Christian" phenomenon (Martin 1978: 2; Taylor 2007: 594). Likewise, the religious economies theory has not been applied to the Muslim world, either (for a small exception, see Introvigne 2006). Thus, all these approaches need to be expanded for the analysis of other religions, including Islam (see Warner *et al.* 2010 for various critiques of Taylor's account).

The assumption of secular universalism shared by most arguments in the classical secularization paradigm implies the incompatibility of religion with modern, industrial society. This assumption, however, has not been proved correct even in contemporary Western societies (Martin 1969: 28; see also Hill 1973; Casanova 1994; Taylor 2007), as demonstrated by the "religious economies" approach. Many empirical studies have shown that secularization has not been a global trend. For example, Sasaki and Suzuki (1987) have demonstrated, in their comparative study on aggregate data on the US, Holland and Japan, that secularization varies both generationally and culturally (in different social contexts). More recently, in his examination of the states' impact on religious organizations, Fox (2008) has shown, as the present study will try to do in Middle Eastern context, the co-existence of both secularization and sacralization on a global scale. By focusing on "government involvement ... in religious issues through legislation, policy or consistent action" (p. 63), and using data collected from 175 countries for the 1990 to 2002 period, Fox demonstrates that most states do not maintain the church-state separation, but rather utilize their resources to both promote and restrict religion.

The co-existence of the sacred and the secular is also true for the West, particularly American society that has been experiencing a process of "returning to the sacred" since the 1960s despite the official church-state separation. The rise of religion in the West has even led some of the leading figures within the neo-classical paradigm (e.g., Berger 1999a) to abandon the secularization thesis completely, identifying the phenomenon of "de-secularization" as the main trend in the whole world during the 20th century. Such leading sociologists of religion as David Martin, Grace Davie, Tu Weiming (all in Berger 1999a) and José Casanova (1994) as well as philosopher Charles Taylor (2007) have expressed doubts about the universality of the Western secularization theory. Thus, arguing that religious movements in many parts of the world have been experiencing a resurgence rather than decline, Berger (1999b: 2) states that "the assumption we live in a secularized world is false. The world today ... is as furiously religious as it ever was." However, Europe, China, and Russia seem to be exceptions: atheist communism has probably had an adverse effect on religiosity in the latter two; it is also true that European countries are much less religious than in the past (Davie 2000, 2002; Davie *et al.* 2008; Berger 1999b; Lambert 2004). The rise of Islam in Europe, which challenges the modern-European notion that religion should be banished from public life, further complicates the issue, however (see Asad 2002; Davie 2006; Jenkins 2007).

Secularization theory and the Middle East

The application in theory and practice of the concept of secularism to the Muslim world in particular has also been recently criticized, for it is seen as a product of Enlightenment thought and practice, which must be understood as a context-bound experience of Western societies. Esposito (2000: 13) observes, for example, that (t)he post-Enlightenment tendency to define religion as a system of belief restricted to personal or private life, rather than as a way of life, has seriously hampered our ability to understand the nature of Islam and many of the world's religions.

Similarly, Berger (2000) argues that the idea of the decline of religion at the individual and social level as a result of the development of secularism "has turned out to be wrong" in the Muslim world. Davutoğlu questions the universality of the concept of secularism, and argues that, being part of the "modernization package," it was identified with Westernization and imposed on the non-Western civilizations, revealing the "culture-bound exclusion made by the power structure of the hegemonic civilization" (2000: 172; see also Davutoğlu 1994b). Similarly, Tamimi (2000) observes that in the Arab world Westernization has been imposed as the only way of modernization. Keane (2000), on the other hand, notes the absence of a natural equivalent of the word "secular" in Arabic, for its literal translation (*la-diniyah*=non-religious) "would have been rejected by Muslims." Al-Ghannouchi (2000) draws attention to the difference between the Western experience where "secularism is associated with scientific progress, industrial revolution and democratic government" and modernization in the Middle East where the "pseudo-secularism ... has destroyed society and rendered it easy prey to a corrupt elite." He also argues that in this region secularism has become "a 'church' of the same type against which the West rebelled" (2000: 105). Hence, these critical approaches find the Western-centric perspectives narrow and often inadequate to explain the experiences of the Muslim world (see also Sayyid 2003).

Moreover, Euro-centric approaches often ignore, as Keddie (1997: 23) recalls, the fact that the state, especially in the non-Christian world including first and foremost Turkey, was the leading actor in the secularization process.[4] It is also true that in the Christian world, too, secular social movements challenged the authority of the Church, captured state power and used it to secularize society in the early modern period, as would later happen in Turkey – after 1923. Moreover, although in Christian Europe a similar religious discourse did exist up to the 18th century, which was accompanied by the emergence of various denominations, especially in Protestant countries, before it was replaced by the more familiar discourse positioning reason and science against religion and superstition; in the Middle East this was *the* distinctive character of the entire modernization process.

However, much of the literature on the modernization of the Middle East similarly holds the assumption that secularism is based on the conflict between the (secular) state and Islam (e.g., Engin 1955; Lerner 1958; B. Lewis 1961, 2002; Tunaya 1962; Jaschke 1972; Vatikiotis 1980; Keddie 1997).[5] Although the absence of an institutionally organized religion in the Muslim world preventing the state-church duality is acknowledged, the significance of this difference is often ignored in the literature. Secularism is thus seen by many as a conflict between two distinct forces: modernism versus tradition, progress vs. reaction,

Enlightenment vs. obscurantism. The conventional view usually holds it merely as a continuation of Renaissance and the Reformation as in Europe, and the abolition of the Caliphate as its natural consequence largely ignoring the unique character of the discourse of secularization. For instance, in his memoirs on Kemal Atatürk, General Charles Sherrill, then the US ambassador to Ankara, compares the abolition of the Caliphate with the separation of church and state in England, France, Italy, and the US. He also compares the Turkification of religious texts and worship (the prohibition of Arabic) with Martin Luther's attempts at translating the Bible, and ultimately with the Reformation (Sherrill 1934; cf. Edib 1930: 208–210; Engin 1955: 41–52; Öklem 1981). This view, which for a long time dominated the study of secularization in the Middle East, particularly in Turkey where the impact of Kemalist secularism has been heavily felt in academic circles, characterizes the conventional approach, which I call the "conflict paradigm."

The conflict paradigm

Influenced by the "modernization theory" that was dominant in the mid-20th century (see Lerner 1958) as well as nationalist secularism, or "Kemalism," of most post-colonial regimes in the Middle East, this paradigm conceives of Islam and modernity as incompatible with, and even the opposite of, each other. For this reason, it perceives their relationship in terms only of conflict and confrontation. The impact of this ideological stance is visible in the two leading figures in the study of the modernization of Ottoman Middle East: Tarık Zafer Tunaya and Bernard Lewis. In his comprehensive work, Tunaya (1952, 1962) fully adopted the discourse of "Islam as reaction," which was an ideological tool for the political and intellectual domination of the single-party regime in Turkey (1923–1945).[6] Tunaya, as an "organic intellectual," was engaged to this hegemonic discourse though the empirial data he collected do not easily permit such an interpretation. Similarly, despite the empirical depth of his research, Lewis's reductionist account (1961) describes the entire modernization process as a tension and struggle between the "modern(ist)s" and "reactionaries." It labels the opposition to different modernizing "reforms" as the "resistance by reactionary conservatives," paying little attention to their political and economic aspects. Lewis's impact is clearly seen in his pupil's recent account of the making of modern Turkey: Feroz Ahmad (1993) describes the history of Turkish modernization in terms of simplistic binary oppositions; he even asserts from a heavily ideological perspective that "nationalism was accepted by everyone except reactionaries" and "secularism was not opposed virtually by anyone" (1993: 63), missing the complexities of historical reality.

Another important problem with this view voiced by Lewis, Ahmad, and others is that of teleology: assuming that the "emergence" of modern Turkey (and this could be said of other modern states in the Middle East as well) was the ultimate and indispensible goal of an irreversible historical process, this view reduces the last preceding 200-year period of modernization to a "pre-historic" era whose only function was to prepare the *telos* that is the emergence of this new state. Based on the same teleological view, Tunaya (1952) sees Ottoman moderniza- tion, which was a much longer period than the Republican one, as a preparatory stage for the "emergence" of the new Turkey, and calls the dense modernization process of the Second Constitutional Period (1908–1918) the "political labora- tory" of the Republican period. He also asserts that Turkish secularism "achieved" to "end theocracy," "destroy the Ottoman order" and "fully embrace the Western civilization." His following remarks, which present the Ottoman modernization essentially as a "civilizational change," reflect his (and many others') engagement with Kemalism, which greatly affected their academic approaches:

> Western civilization is the dominant one; it is the only civilization.... Since it is strongest, and cannot be challenged, it is imperative to join it. [This] is a question of survival and development. It is an historical law to turn from the East towards the West. Therefore ... it is a matter of survival to enter Western civilization.
>
> (Tunaya 1981: 110–111)

Similarly, another leading (Kemalist) historian, Enver Ziya Karal, states that:

> A professor who wrote a book on this subject [the Ottoman Empire's col- lapse] gave us twenty-four causes. To my mind it is possible to reduce that number to one: the decline of the Empire was due to the fact that the Ottoman Moslems believed in the superiority of their institutions over those of Europe. But this belief was based on religious feeling, not on reason. The result was that independent thinking declined. The Ottoman Turks isolated themselves from European civilization, feeling that it was Christian and hence to be avoided.... The Ottomans were neither able to understand Euro- pean progress nor their defeat by European armies.
>
> (Lecture given at Stanford University, March 1959;
> quoted in Latimer 1960: 1–2)

This reductionist, dichotomous and teleological view is to be found among many scholars. Even the most prominent study on the Ottoman-Turkish secularization by Niyazi Berkes (1957, 1998[1964]), in line with this ideological view, takes it as a conflict between the "forces of tradition" of which Islam is a part, and those of "change." He describes the secularization process as a transition from a back- ward, ramshackle world dominated by the "Middle Ages mentality" to the modern world characterized by a "modern worldview," and as integration into the Western civilization that is the final stage of human development. Con- sequently, his teleological perspective conceives of the Middle Eastern seculari- zation as an irreversible one necessarily evolving towards the emergence of the modern nation-state. Thus, he treats the frequent incorporation of the Islamic elements in most attempts at modernization as residual, insignificant, and often instrumental. Also, despite the rich historical material gathered in his study,

Berkes indulges in simplistic and reductionist explanations based on a modernist ideology: he identifies many "reforms" that constituted different steps of Ottoman-Turkish modernization with different events that took place in Western Europe such as the Reformation; he also identifies Islam with "the tradition" that he locates vis-à-vis "the modern," presenting religion as part of the "Middle Ages worldview" that must be left behind:

> When, in the nineteenth century, the changes introduced were seen clearly to affect the existing order, two tendencies appeared and crystallized. One was to reject all innovations and cling to traditional institutions, which were identified with un-changeable religious values; the other was to extricate religious values from the vicissitudes of the changing world by narrowing the scope of tradition.
>
> (Berkes 1998[1964]: 508)

The traces of this Euro-centric, orientalist, and teleological view represented by Lewis, Tunaya, Karal and Berkes are found in more recent studies as well. For example, in her study on the abolition of the Caliphate, Akgün (2006) made precisely the same argument as Berkes about the status of the Caliphate without paying attention to the significance of Islam – and to those recent studies that did so! (In fact, there is no literature review in this study at all.) Based only on the survey of some newspapers and parliament records (that were published and studied before), this work is also insufficient in terms of analyzing primary sources, contributing little – if anything – to the literature in terms of empirical content and sociological interpretation. Moreover, the author defines the purpose of her research on the Caliphate as "demonstrating why this institution should not survive in the Turkish Republic that is based on national values, [and] the fact that the Caliphate was not a Turkish organization in terms of its roots" (Akgün 2006: 9, 11–12).

A survey of a sample of studies by leading older and younger generations within the conflict paradigm demonstrates, therefore, that this conventional view defines secularization on the basis of a fundamental conflict between religion and the state, and takes a normative position towards this conflict. It thus ignores the fact that virtually no "reform" attempt and no political movement during the modernization in the Middle East were positioned against religion, and that the fundamental source of justification in all modernizing reforms was almost always Islam, even for secularists such as Mustafa Kemal and Ziya Gökalp. Thus, based on an either Marxist or nationalist (or sometimes a mixture of both) ideological "baggage," this view often ignores the crucial role Islam plays in social processes and the Muslim subjects' lives, including their cultural practices and ideological orientations, which are directly related to religion.

Consequently, the conflict paradigm is, overall,

i *Euro-centric* because it assumes that secularization was experienced ideally in Western Europe and takes it as a model for the Islamic/Ottoman case, claiming that it has to go through the same process;

ii *teleological* in that it conceives of a 200-year period of modernization as a chain of events, as a linear and irreversible process and a preparatory stage ("labarotory") for the "emergence" of the modern nation-state in the 20th century;

iii it suffers from the methodological weakness of *functionalism*, which often identifies the consequences of a development/event with its causes;

iv it is also *orientalistic* in that it assumes that different geographical areas (defined with reference to nation-state boundaries) and time periods, such as the Ottoman and post-Ottoman stages, are mostly unrelated, homogenous, and static compact wholes, and thus ignores social change and historical dynamics;

v   for this reason, it tries to explain modernization and secularization processes from a *positivistic* perspective on the basis of static, binary oppositions such as "progress vs. reaction," "enlightenment vs. obscurantism," and "modern vs. pre-modern." For the same reason, it is also often *reductionist* and *one-dimensional*. Therefore, most studies within this paradigm are more ideological than scholarly. Finally,

vi most of them also suffer from *methodological nationalism*, i.e., taking nation-state boundaries as natural units of analysis coupled with a lack of comparative method that is essential to understand the dynamics of any part of the Middle East. This weakness is again based on an ideological assumption of the uniqueness of the country/region studied. However, this last problem is not confined to the conflict paradigm; many studies that fall in the alternative approach, which I call the "accommodation paradigm," also suffer from it.

The accommodation paradigm

This paradigm consists of studies that try to stay away from positivistic explanations and often simplistic and reductionist narratives of the conflict paradigm, seeing Ottoman/Middle Eastern modernization as a complex and dialectical process characterized by often contingent and dynamic power relations. The seeds of this view could be traced back to the 1940s (to Ülgener's work)[7] and the 1960s (to Mardin's work; see below), but it essentially rose in the 1980s and 1990s; its carriers are mostly those first-generation scholars who completed their PhDs in the US and Europe during the 1970s and 1980s, being affected by the theoretical and methodological currents of these periods, especially in history and the sociology of religion, as well as the younger generation of scholars who completed their education in the 1990s and 2000s. Staying away from the reductionism and Euro-centrism of the modernization theory, this view has produced more powerful explanations than both the official historiographies and the conflict paradigm. Moreover, in the case of religion-politics relations, this view emphasizes the concept of accommodation more than conflict, as a result of the careful attention to the intricacies of this relationship. For example, criticizing the one-sidedness of the conventional view, Rustow (1973: 103–104) refers to the fact that the actors who are often portrayed as "reactionary," such as Abdulhamid II, were also the leading proponents of modernization.

Similarly, Karpat points out that Abdulhamid II was not a reactionary, but a reformist sultan who believed in the compatibility of Islam and modernity: "[Sultan Abdulhamid] was crucial to the modernization process, and he prepared the ground for the rise of modern Turkey" (2001: vi). Karpat also draws attention to the notion that it was attempted to adapt Islam to modern conditions to save the Ottoman Empire, and argues that social and economic transformation in the last two Ottoman centuries produced a "new Muslim middle class," who in turn achieved a "popular revival of Islam." In this context, he contends that despite the rise of nationalism in the Ottoman territory during the 19th century and later, both Abdulhamid II and the Young Turks (who ruled the Empire after Abdulhamid) embraced an Islamist and Ottomanist policy and ideology, rather than Turkish nationalism, despite the efforts by such leading Turkist ideologues as Yusuf Akçura, Ziya Gökalp and Fuat Köprülü. Karpat also points out that in Turkey there was more continuity than a radical disconnect between the Ottoman and Republican periods, particularly in bureaucratic tradition, statist mentality and educational policies – for example, the Kemalist regime adopted ideological indoctrination as the basic purpose of education, just like Abdulhamid II and the CUP had done before (Karpat 2000).

Likewise, emphasizing the continuity argument, historian Erik Jan Zürcher (1984, 1993) contends that the Turkish Republic was simply a continuation of the Young Turk rule in the Second Constitutional Period (1908–1918). As an indication of this view, he calls the entire period between 1908 and 1950 the "Young Turk period," which de-emphasizes the regime change in Turkey with the proclamation of the Republic in 1923 (1993: 97–263). Moreover, he also pays attention to the continuity between the two periods in terms not only of the bureaucratic cadres that ran the state but also of their ideological positions, arguing that the Kemalist regime was inspired by the secularism and nationalism of the Young Turks, but of course taking them to extreme points (Zürcher 2000).

Similarly, Şerif Mardin's pioneering work draws attention to the elements of continuity between the Ottoman and post-Ottoman eras. Focusing on three major themes, including the relationships between the "center" and the "periphery," the opposition and civil society in Turkey, and the creation of the Turkish nation-state, it has made two important contributions to the understanding of Ottoman-Turkish modernization. First, Mardin (1962, 2003) criticizes the conventional-official historiography that sees a radical rupture between the Ottoman Empire and modern Turkey. His work goes beyond the continuity/discontinuity dichotomy that characterizes much of the literature. Second, from a sociology of religion perspective influenced by both Max Weber and the neo-classical paradigm, Mardin (1983b, 1983c, 1989, 1991a, 1991b, 2005) highlights the significance of Islam in terms of understanding political and everyday life in the Turkish society, arguing that religion has been a prominent social force underlying major socio-political developments in Turkey. Sensitive to the complexities of the Ottoman-Turkish modernization, he shows how understanding

Islam and Islamic movements is a requirement in understanding Turkish society. This is a direct critique of the mystification of religion by different groups, including many historians who subscribe to official historiography that usually disregards Islam and downplays its role. In this context, he argues that Kemalist secularism has failed to substitute an alternative to the role played by Islam in the "identity-constructing layers of culture" (1983b: 38; see also 1983c, 2003). Agreeing with Mardin, Mete Tunçay stresses, in his work on the single-party rule in Turkey, that due to its authoritarian and Jacobin character, the Kemalist modernization project has, on the one hand, caused the alienation of the elite minority from the masses' culture and lifestyle (despite the discourse of "populism"), but on the other hand, it has not tried to completely cleanse Islam from social life (Tunçay 2005).

As for the ideological/discursive aspect of secularization, the accommodation paradigm does not deny the fact that there may be a philosophical conflict between Islam and secularism. Rather, it argues that the potential conflict on the philosophical level may not necessarily be reflected in the political processes and cognitive effects of modernization. This discrepancy is reflected best in the discourses of intellectuals who try to make sense of modernizing changes in society. In fact, many studies have shown that in the Middle East an anti-religious discourse has never been strong enough to dominate the public sphere. Within this framework, Ahmet Davutoğlu (1994b, 2000) argues that institutional secularization did not necessarily lead to the secularization of individual consciousness at the ontological level in the Muslim world. He further contends that Islam has kept its power as a source of identity and civilizational "self-perception" (or consciousness), despite the fact that modernization has been presented as a project of civilizational change during the 20th century and that the "process of secularization has been seen as a direct threat to the self-perception of non-Western societies due to the fact that it has shaken their self-assertion through identifying man's existence with the historical existence of Western civilization" (Davutoğlu 2000: 188).

Also, intellectual historians İsmail Kara and Mümtaz'er Türköne, like Mardin, draw attention to Islam's role as a source of legitimation in the modernization process. In his study on the emergence of "Islamism" as a mass ideology in the mid-19th century, Türköne (1991) contends that in Ottoman society, where Islam had fully penetrated into social life, communication of ideas had to conform to the religion's images and style, and that Islam was the only basis for even modernist projects of the Ottoman revolutionary intellectuals who advocated freedom and democracy in the 1860s. Like Mardin and Türköne, Kara not only emphasizes the relationship of accommodation between religion and modernization, but he insists more on "Islamization" than secularization, arguing that modernization actually *increased* the significance and power of Islam in Turkey and that secular reforms were not intended to be against religion in the 19th and early 20th centuries (Kara 1998, 2001, 2003a). He points out that all modernist (intellectual and political) movements were also religious movements that reserved a lot of room for Islam in their respective projects. Thus, for him "modernization was at the same time Islamization in Turkey" (2003a: 29). Moreover, he analyzes the way secular elites in modern Turkey have always tried to make Islam a submissive and docile as well as a "national" religion, which for him implies that Turkish laicism has never meant a radical rupture from religion for the elites – nor for the masses (Kara 2008).

The accommodation paradigm, presented here with a snapshot of a few leading representatives, has also affected younger scholars who emphasize complexity and accommodation as main features of secularization in the Middle East, rather than simplification and confrontation. For example, Mertoğlu (2001) analyzes the ways in which the Qur'an was interpreted by intellectuals writing in the two important journals of the Second Constitutional Period, *Sırat-ı Müstakim* and *Sebilürreşad*, to justify the new social and political developments in the pre-war period, arguing that they used it as the fundamental framework for understanding social change. Likewise, Erdem (2003) analyzes the transformation of the legal system from this perspective and points to the revival of debates on the Islamic *sharia* in the first quarter of the 20th century.[8] He contends that the use and abuse of various concepts of the Islamic law, particularly the concept of *ijtihad* (legal reasoning), in accordance with the "exigencies of the time," was an important element in justifying the "need for modernization." On the other hand, in his analysis of the three influential journals of the Second Constitutional Period, *İctihad, Türk Yurdu* and *Sebilürreşad*, which represented secular, Turkish nationalist and Islamist perspectives, respectively, Gündüz (2007) demonstrates that although much of the literature labels these journals politically and ideologically different, even rival to each other, they actually agreed on a number of fundamental issues such as social change, education, language (and its "purification"), women, and the family. He thus argues that the leading intellectual representatives of the three competing ideologies did not much differ when it came to certain fundamental problems of the Ottoman society during this era. Finally, Şentürk (1996) describes the debates among intellectuals on the status of Islamic law and its relation to politics in this period showing how these debates were centered on the significance of Islam in political life. These studies imply that Islam was at the center of the attempts at modernization, shaping the form of various reforms and setting the agenda for the public debates among intellectuals that affected the direction of the modernization process in this period. The reasons for the centrality of Islam, in this view, include the need for legitimacy, the ease of social mobilization (an anti-Islamic project would not gain much support in society) and the difficulty of substituting other frameworks (e.g., nationalism) for Islam in political projects.

A distinctive feature of the younger generation of scholars is their critical approach to both nationalist and some liberal interpretations of Islam-secularism relationship. Moreover, completing their graduate education mostly during the 1990s and 2000s after critical theory had penetrated into different disciplines, these young scholars also question social and political developments themselves. In addition to the political context of this period, then, new developments in social theory, including the rise of post-structuralism, has influenced their view as well. For example, in his study on the Islamist discourses in Turkey in the post-Caliphate period, Aktay (1997) demonstrates how first- and second-generation Islamist intellectuals have tried to reconstruct the Islamic identity through a discourse of "diaspora" and "Islamic authenticity" based on the "text" (Islamic teachings) in response to the *ummah*'s "disembodiment" with the abolition of the Caliphate. Aktay (1999) also examines the other side of the religion-state relationship, i.e., how the Turkish state has tried to control religion during the post-Ottoman period. Building on such concepts in the post-structural literature as "deconstruction of dichotomies" and "multiple antagonisms," he questions how the "state" designed what is called the "Turkish Islam" as a political project and ideological invention in order to "Protestantize" Islam by turning it into a docile "official religion." Similarly, Silverstein (2008) looks at the relationships between Islamic subjectivity and daily practices on the one hand, and the mass communication media, on the other. Drawing on the Foucauldian concepts of "self," "discourse" and "discipline," he analyzes how a contemporary religious (Sufi) group (an Istanbul-based branch of the *Naqshibandiyya*) connects Islamic morality with the construction of self through the institution of *sohbet* (companionship-in-conversation), and how this institution has been transformed via the radio (representing modernity) today. Furthermore, assuming that the relationship between Islam and modernity cannot be adequately understood from a conflict perspective, Silverstein (2003) rightly argues that "Europe" itself, which is usually seen as the locus of modernity, must be problematized, because Ottoman modernization was not on the margins of the European transformation during the 18th and 19th centuries, but rather right at the center of it. Thus, for him, these two "models" cannot be understood as mutually exclusive entities. (After all, the Ottoman Empire was known, even at its deathbed, as the "sick man of *Europe*" and not of Asia or the Middle East.)

A recent post-structuralist critical re-reading of a relatively well-known topic has been provided by Andrew Davison (1998), who analyzes Ziya Gökalp's ideas from a Gadamerian hermeneutic perspective. His examination criticizes not only the previous studies on Gökalp but also the prevalence of binary oppositions, such as center/periphery and East/West, in the conventional view on the Turkish modernization. Finally, Tim Jacoby's recent study (2004), which applies sociologist Michael Mann's (1986, 1993) macro theory of power to the entire process of Ottoman-Turkish modernization, is closer to classical social theory with its organizational-structuralist perspective that represents a fresh look at this phenomenon within the literature.

As mentioned above, most studies in the accommodation paradigm, too, lack a comparative aspect: they are more historical than comparative.[9] Despite this, however, this paradigm, being sensitive to complexity and staying away from crude ideological assumptions, has produced many explanations that are in general more powerful than those put forward by the conflict paradigm. Furthermore, the critical and less Euro-centric trend within the former approach has the promise of transcending the positivist-nationalist conflict perspective, which implies a paradigmatic shift in the study of secularization and modernization in the Middle East as well as refining the accommodation paradigm itself, provided that this trend keeps growing among younger generations.

Now, each of the two paradigms I have discussed is in fact a model, an "ideal type" in the Weberian sense. As such, these models, like all theoretical constructions, lack the ability to perfectly represent the reality. Yet, as Weber (1949: 75) points out, we need those imperfect models to analyze social reality because without our theories and concepts, reality presents itself to us as a chaotic mess. Thus, I believe this categorization is useful to understand the nature of the existing "secularization literature" and the direction it takes. This classification should not be reified, however: there are also many studies that do not fit into either of these two models. For example, Karpat's work, which I included in the accommodation paradigm above, also contains elements of the conflict view. By exaggerating the development of capitalist production relations and of private property in 19th-century Ottoman society, Karpat largely ignores the role played by culture in general, and Islam in particular, in shaping political developments. From a purely materialist perspective, he often reduces them to "super-structural" elements used and abused by power holders and makes bold generalizations, such as: "Both constitutions and ideologies [during 1876–1945] must be viewed as the instruments through which particular social groups have tried to establish a new regime and to implement a predetermined policy" (Karpat 2004: 201). Similarly, in her analysis of the top-down ideology of secularism among the early Republican elite, Mert (1994) argues for the applicability of the classical Durkheimian and Weberian approach to secularization, which is based on the assumption of the decline of religion in modern society. Moreover, based on the assumptions of the secularization thesis, she claims, *contra* Mardin and others, that Kemalism has been successful in terms of both institutional re-arrangement and cultural-cognitive transformation. Unlike many proponents of Kemalist secularism, however, she is able to avoid the trap of ideological propaganda of Turkish laicism.

Despite such "ambiguous" examples, I believe that my two-tiered model of the literature is useful in understanding Middle Eastern modernization. Needless to say, here I side with the accommodation paradigm. I argue that during much of the modernization period (from the late 18th century to 1924) in the Middle East, the relationship between Islam and secularism was one of accommodation, rather than simply conflict and confrontation. I shall try to demonstrate this point, which is my main theoretical argument, throughout this study. Now, the post-1924 era is a different story. The fact that I end the accommodation period in 1924 already implies that the abolition of the Caliphate was a crucial turning point in the history of the Muslim world, particularly for the Caliphate's host country, Turkey. In this country, with which I am more familiar, what operated after 1924 was not, as conflict theorists would argue, the separation model: there was no state-mosque separation after the demise of the Caliphate. Rather, different models/paradigms have operated at different levels. At the discursive level, it was still the accommodation paradigm that was dominant: except for a short period (about 15 years) of hiatus, the state elite and intellectuals could never dare to confront Islam, but rather tried to resort to religion, among other things, as a source of legitimation. Though this accommodation relationship was not as strong as in the pre-1924 period, it has still been viable. This can still be seen in the discourses of army generals, supposedly the most secular group in Turkish society, as well in the rhetoric employed by virtually every politician, including members of the hard-Kemalist Republican People's Party.

At the level of state policy, on the other hand, what has been operating in Turkey since the mid-1920s is what I call the "domination" (or "control") paradigm. Instead of separating religion from the state, the Republican elite has been trying to control the religion by monopolizing the organization of mosques, seizing the property of religious organizations, banning certain religious groups and organizations (such as dervish lodges and Sufi communities), and even trying to control the content of religious teachings (such as Friday sermons). The state has been trying to dominate and monopolize the religious domain basically through the Department of Religious Affairs (DRA), which was founded on the day the Caliphate and Ministry of Religious Affairs were abolished in 1924 to replace them. However, the Kemalist project of dominating the religion, which is similar to the case in the Third French Republic (1871–1940), has failed: since its inception the Turkish state has not been able to fully control Islam, which has proven too strong to dominate, basically because masses of people have continued to remain more or less religious without losing their connection to traditional beliefs and practices in their daily lives. Also, various Sufi orders have secretly survived despite oppression by the state, and even the DRA has sometimes resisted the pressures from secular governments. Moreover, the Kemalist policy of bringing religion under state control has, ironically, undermined secularism: modern state structures (such as elections) have, particularly after 1950, provided religious groups and individuals with the opportunities to promote their values and influence politics in Turkey, as elsewere in the Middle East (e.g., Israel, and probably Egypt, Syria and Lebanon in the near future).

This does not mean, of course, that the Turkish society has not been secularized; but its secularization has remained limited, as indicated by the fact that over 70 percent of women in Turkey still wear the headscarf, and masses of people keep voting for the so-called "Islamist" parties (for example, the AK Party, the current ruling party, has won 49.9 percent of the vote in the most recent elections on June 12, 2011). Therefore, it is safe to argue that at the level of "practice," a mixture of accommodation, separation, and control characterizes the relationship between Islam and secularism in Turkey. Among these three, I would say the accommodation paradigm still has a bigger share than the other two because both an increase in religiosity *and* a secularization trend occur at the same time in contemporary Turkish society.

As for the other parts of the Muslim world, it is not possible to present a detailed analysis here, but suffice it to say that it is probably a mixture of accommodation and control processes that have dominated state-religion relations in many of them. In terms of the authoritarian state tradition, Algeria, Egypt, pre-1979 Iran, the Turkic Republics of Central Asia and to a certain extent Tunisia, Morocco and Syria have been similar to Turkey's hard-core secularism. While countries like Malaysia, Indonesia, India, Pakistan and Jordan have a more moderate relationship between Islam and the secular state, Saudi Arabia, Iran and the

Taliban Afghanistan present a reverse extreme model with their anti-secular authoritarianism, which is distinctly a modern phenomenon and closely related to their colonial past that produced dictatorships. (Many of the secular-authoritarian dictatorships in the Muslim world are also a legacy of European – and more recently, American – colonialism.) At the "societal" level, however, all top-down, Jacobin-like secularization projects have failed in the Muslim world because Islam has always been the most important social force in Muslim societies shaping much of the "content" of their cultural practices, institutions and meaning systems. In other words, as Mardin (1991b) notes for Ottoman society, Islam has been operating on three levels, as a societal "ideal" (ontological level), as a "language" or "idiom" (discursive level), and as an imaginative model of social action (practical level) for most Muslims, transcending their differences in terms of class, power, culture, etc. As such, it has also influenced the direction of social and political change in Muslim countries. Thus, social scientists must take Islam into consideration in understanding every major development in these societies, and policy makers must rethink their projects in light of the fact that religion constitutes the backbone of the "culture" of these countries.

The Caliphate in the literature

Studying the Caliphate presents a unique challenge for the researcher, as one has to transcend a great divide that has plagued the literature: most studies on the abolition of the Caliphate focus only on Turkey and on the last phase of this process (1922–1924), others on modernization in general isolating and ignoring Turkey. The reason for this is twofold: first, modernization of the Muslim world in general has usually been understood as a post-colonial experience; second, most studies on the modernization of the Middle East focus on the Arab world, which is in fact the periphery – not the center – of the Caliphate. Therefore, most researchers are not interested in the Ottoman Empire, though it was the strongest Muslim state and the center of Islamic world for about 500 years. Since Turkey was not formally colonized by Western powers (though for some it was "self-colonized"), much of the post-colonial literature does not pay much attention to it, causing a myopic view of the Middle East, which is a fundamental flaw in the study of the Islam-modernity relationship in the West. Thus, the Ottoman experience must be placed at the center of the modernization process of the Muslim world, rather than isolating this relationship both spatially and historically by focusing only on the Arab world. As Mardin (2005) and Silverstein (2003: 512) remark, the study of Islam and modernity must be rescued from the domination of the post-colonial literature.

Now, most studies on the abolition of the Caliphate also briefly present a history of it from different angles. Early orientalist studies on the Caliphate's history (Barthold 1912; Nallino 1917; Arnold 1965[1924]; Toynbee 1920, 1927) naturally do not discuss its abolition – except for Toynbee (1927). They were usually written by authors who worked for their governments (e.g., Toynbee, Arnold, and Morghani were advisors to the British Foreign Office, Nallino to the

Italian Foreign Ministry), and for the most part reflect the governments' opinions on the Caliphate. Others are detailed documentary surveys of the history of the Caliphate (e.g., Sanhoury 1926; Tyan 1954, 1956). Many of the later studies on it in the Middle East also adopt quite a partisan perspective – on both "Islamist" and "secularist" sides – lacking many academic standards and methodological rigor. Dilipak (1988), Albayrak (1992), Mısıroğlu (1993) and Gümüşoğlu (2004) from Turkey, and Mawdudi (1965) and Zallum (2002) from Pakistan and India represent the Islamic side in the partisan literature; Ökte (1968), Bozarslan (1969), Gologlu (1973), Öklem (1981), İnalcık (1998), and Akgün (2006) represent the secularist camp. Still on this side, Menteş (1969) and Önelçin (1970) are actually – very problematic – transliterations of a speech by the Minister of Justice Seyyid Bey at the Turkish Grand National Assembly on the day the Caliphate was abolished, which justified this secular reform in Islamic terms (see Chapter 6). They were published back-to-back in order to defend the official view of the Caliphate's history and abolition in the face of the increasing discussions on it in Turkey during the late 1960s with the impact of Islamic translations from the Arab world, particularly from the Muslim Brotherhood circles, which harshly criticized the Turkish government's move (see Kara 1991 for a discussion on these translations). The Kemalist-secularist literature has largely informed the official historiography on the Caliphate in Turkey. On the other hand, some of the "Islamist" studies (e.g., Mısıroğlu 1993) try to "disprove" one by one the official historiography's theological and historical arguments in order to break its domination – and to build up a counter-hegemony in this area.

Both the Islamic and secularist views in the partisan literature share the conflict paradigm's dichotomous assumption of confrontation between Islam and politics. An example of this ideological view based on the conflict paradigm is how secularist Hamza Eroğlu (1982) viewed the Caliphate in his textbook on the history of "Turkish Revolution." Trying to justify the Caliphate's abolition by Turkish authorities, like Berkes (1998[1964]), Akgün (2006) and others mentioned above, Eroğlu argues that the Caliphate belonged, like most other religious institutions, to the "Middle Ages" (assumed to be the universal dark ages) and could not have survived in modern Turkey: "The Caliphate is an institution based on the idea of the *ummah*. It was not possible that the new Turkey, which was based on the idea of national sovereignty and nationalism, could be compatible with this *Middle Age* institution" (Eroğlu 1982: 273).

As for the more academic-serious contemporary studies on the Caliphate – there are not many of them. An early example is Mohammad Sadiq's (1991) analysis of the abolition of the Caliphate in terms of Turkey's status in international relations. Sadiq argues that this event, which represents a turning point in the construction of the new Turkish Republic, negatively affected the Turkish position because by destroying the Caliphate, the Turks deprived themselves of the possibility of being the leader of a unified Islamic world. For him, the Caliphate would function as the center of Islamic unity, which would provide Turkey with the greatest political advantage it could have in the post-war period (Sadiq 1991: 28ff). On the other hand, Crone and Hinds's (2003) study presents a historical sketch of the early Caliphate from the beginning to the end of the Abbasids (1258), and explores the divergence of the Sunnis' conception of religious authority from the Shia view of the *imamate* (cf. Kennedy 2004; Yücesoy 2007).

More recently, Karpat (2001) has analyzed the modernization of the Ottoman Empire (reviewed above), in which he devoted a chapter to the Caliphate's functions in Ottoman foreign policy. While useful in some respects, such as detailing the Ottoman caliphal policy in Africa during the late-19th century, Karpat's examinations is both limited to the Hamidian era (1876–1909) only, and contains some errors. For example, he incorrectly claims that after Abdülhamid II, Islam and the Caliphate had no use and little influence on politics in the Ottoman Empire. Also, in his very short "literature review" he supposes that one of the transliterations of Seyyid Bey's parliamentary address discussed above (Menteş 1969) was actually written by the editor, which he calls "a partisan study."

Kara's important work (discussed above) on different aspects of the Ottoman-Turkish modernization contains useful, albeit scattered, discussions on Islamism's view of the Caliphate as well. While residually touching upon the Caliphate in his other writings, Kara (2001) specifically examines the views of the Islamist intellectuals and *ulema* on the Caliphate and the constitutional regime in the first volume of his work on the political ideas of Islamism in Turkey during the Second Constitutional Period. From a history of ideas perspective, he presents an analysis of the primary sources, mostly journal articles written by leading representatives of Islamism. Kara (2002–2005) has also led a team of researchers in uncovering, transliterating (into the Latin alphabet), translating, and publishing many primary sources (pamphlets, proclamations, books, articles) specifically on the Caliphate. In their ongoing project, they have so far published a series of five volumes, which is a great contribution to the study of not only the Caliphate but also the late-Ottoman Middle East in general. My study makes an extensive use of these data – being the first academic work to do it. One of the team members, Sami Erdem (1995) also discusses, in his pioneering study on Seyyid Bey, one of the most important – yet least known – figures in the transformation and abolition of the Caliphate, his ideas on the Caliphate and how they influenced Turkish political elites.

On the other hand, Özcan's (1997) extensive study on Ottoman-Indian relations focusing on the issue of "Panislamism" also examines the caliphal dimension during the 19th and early 20th centuries, containing many useful points and providing rich information. Similarly, Qureshi's (1999) work on the Indian Caliphate Movement naturally discusses the issue, especially in the context of the Movement's activities in Europe after World War I, documenting the details of the British and Indian efforts to undermine and preserve (respectively) the Ottoman Caliphate. More recently, Wegner's unpublished dissertation (2001) has focused on Egypt extensively discussing the post-1924 Caliphate debates and the failed Cairo Caliphate Congress (1926). This study successfully locates these events at the intersection of (i) the political context of the day (demonstrating the interplay between the political struggle among the *Ittihad*, *Ahrar*, and

Wafd parties as well as King Fuad's status and the British involvement in them), (ii) the religious controversy over Ali Abdur-raziq's anti-Caliphate views, which were comdemned by Al-Azhar *ulema*, and (iii) the centuries-long Sunni tradition of political theory, seeing the debates between 1924 and 1926 as a response to the modern challenge to this intellectual, religious and political tradition. Yıldırım's book (2004) on the same subject, whose title translates as *Debates on the Caliphate in the Islamic World during the 20th Century*, in fact only discusses the two alternative theories of the Caliphate by Seyyid Bey and Ali Abdur-raziq, without providing any original interpretation of them; it also describes the reactions to the Caliphate's abolition in 1924 from Egypt, particularly al-Azhar *ulema*'s negative reaction. The study contains no theoretical framework, nor a methodological discussion (needless to say, nor a literature review), which leads to many weak arguments as well as some contradictions (e.g., he claims on the same page [p. 71] both that the Caliphate was seen completely useless and powerless after 1922, and that many actors saw the Caliph as the head of the state during the same period). In terms of our specific discussion about the role of Islam in modernization, the author mentions in passing that a "language of religion" was used in the debates on the Caliphate's abolition (p. 14), but does not discuss it. On the other hand, Liebl's (2009) short piece on the Caliphate provides a good, albeit journalistic, overview of the post-1924 developments regarding this institution as well as discussing potential claimants for caliphate in the 21st century.

Finally, two studies on the Caliphate based on British archives are worth mentioning. First, Satan's recent study (2008) on the abolition of the Caliphate provides a useful description of the Caliphate's recent history and a detailed discussion on its abolition in its last few years. Though quite weak in terms of theoretical contribution and mostly remaining descriptive – rather than analytical – with few clear-cut empirical arguments, Satan's examination is nevertheless based on a detailed research on primary sources, particularly the press and the parliamentary records, as well as making use of the existing secondary literature. Its original contribution is its incorporation of rich British archives into the study of the Caliphate: the author provides a detailed account of secret British Foreign Office records and of the British press as well as Turkish sources, which makes it possible not only to compare the two sides but also to complement our lack of information on some crucial episodes, such as Sharif Hussein's claim for the Caliphate and the Lausanne Conference negotiations between Turkey and the Allies in 1922–1923. Similarly, Oliver-Dee's (2009) extensive study on British archives beginning in 1914 and going well into the Cold War is useful particularly in terms of seeing the intricacies of the evolution of how the Caliphate came to be understood by British government offices. The author well documents the details of conflicting accounts of different government branches, such as the Foreign Office, the Cairo Commission, and the Government of India, and how these differing views affected the political actors' policy choices. My study utilizes some of both Satan's and Oliver-Dee's descriptions based on their archival research.

Studying secularization: the historical-sociological perspective

Building on this body of work and on the accommodation paradigm, I examine the secularization process in the Middle East, paying particular attention to the debates over the Caliphate during 1908–1924, which proved to be most critical for secularization. I take the transformation of the Caliphate as a case where the evolution of the discourse of secularism and its relationship with Islam can be traced in the context of political and military developments of this period. My research methodology is inspired by the Weberian and Durkheimian notion that secularization as a concept cannot be understood without reference to some specific socio-historical context; for otherwise a reified concept of secularization carries the danger of being substituted for the empirical investigation itself. If, therefore, we treat secularization as an entity that exists in its own right, we might end up replacing it with our empirical analysis. My methodology is also inspired by the notion, voiced most clearly by the sociologist of religion Richard Fenn (1978), that secularization is primarily a battlefield in which different social groups struggle over the definition of religion and the boundaries of the sacred; therefore, we researchers should avoid imposing an a priori definition of religion and secularization on our subject matter.

In my case, the struggle was primarily on the definition of Islam's role in the public sphere. To examine this process, I analyze what forms this discourse took in different social groups (i.e., "secularists," "modernist Islamists" and "traditionalist Islamists"; see below) and how socio-political positions of actors affected their view of the Caliphate. For this I examine the views of leading intellectuals and political figures across the political spectrum. Moreover, I identify whether different actors (Islamists and secularists) employed the Islamic discourse genuinely or instrumentally, and how this relates to the political developments of the time. To this end, I employ a methodology that has two main dimensions: historical comparative focus and discourse analysis.

Historical-comparative analysis

Many historians (e.g., Thompson 1978) have criticized sociologists for paying insufficient attention to details of historical patterns whereas most sociologists think historians are unable to reach meaningful conclusions out of their painstaking investigations of archives due to the lack of an explicit theory with which to interpret the historical data. Historical sociology, which emerged as a subfield in the 1970s and early 1980s as a reaction to an over-emphasis on theory and under-emphasis on historical complexities in American sociology, have sought to bridge the gap between the two disciplines (Tilly 1981, 1984; Skocpol 1984; Calhoun 1987, 1998). However, there emerged a *methodenstreit* within the subfield in the 1990s between the proponents of "deduction from a general theory" and those of induction in historical-comparative research (for details, see *AJS* 1998). Inspired by Barrington Moore's work (1958), the first view (e.g., Kiser and Hechter 1991, 1998) holds that historical data should be used as a testing ground for a (falsifiable) general theory, from which the researcher must draw (through deduction) certain causal mechanisms and try to reach law-like generalizations. The goal here is to refine – if possible – the general theory through revision and/or falsification in light of historical analysis. Kiser and Hechter (1991), who criticize historical sociologists for acting too much like empiricist historians, suggest rational-choice theory as a good "general theory" to apply to historical phenomena. On the other hand, the "inductionists" (e.g., Somers 1998) argue that because general theories "do too much violence to the specifics of the historical patterns" (Calhoun 1998: 854), a proper analysis should proceed from empirical data and work through induction out of causal mechanisms or narratives toward more limited (as opposed to general) theoretical conclusions. This idea is based on the Weberian notion that human and social sciences are very different from natural sciences in that human nature and actions are culturally constructed and change over time, and that significant events occur very rarely unlike the repetitious patterns often found in nature; therefore, social action should be examined via an "interpretive understanding" (*verstehen*), rather than solely in terms of external causes (Weber 1949: 160).

Though leaning more toward the second view, this study is based on a methodological perspective that tries to find a middle ground in this *methodenstreit* between the two sides, and between deduction and induction, nomothetic and idiographic methods, explanation and understanding (*verstehen*). I try to go back and forth between my theoretical argument (secularization as accommodation) and historical data through different conceptual tools (e.g., "discursive technique" and "theological engineering" – see below) that I have drawn from the data. My goal is to both posit a (limited) theoretical argument by induction from the data *and* explain a historical process in light of this theoretical model. My examination thus derives inspiration from Stinchcombe's (1978) call for an emphasis on the complexity of historical patterns and comparisons among cases, rather than simply applying general theories.

An important aspect of my research is its historical-comparative focus, which has three dimensions: inter-group, spatial, and temporal comparisons. First, I divide the power actors whose views I discuss into three groups according to their ideological positions vis-à-vis the Caliphate. Their view of the Caliphate's nature and future constitutes the axis of this categorization: each group's position is determined in accordance with how it defined the Caliphate. I classify those politicians and intellectuals who defined the Caliphate as simply a "spiritual" institution (regardless of whether or not this is possible in terms of the Caliphate's history and theory) as "secularists," and those who defined it as strictly temporal/political as "modernists" (or modernist Islamists). The third group is the "traditionalists" (or traditional Islamists) who saw the Caliph as both a temporal and religious and/or "spiritual" leader. While the first group tried to destroy the Caliphate, the latter two tried to keep it alive. However, the second group (modernists), tried to weaken it by curbing its religious authority in the early years of the Second Constitutional Period, which was directly related to the domestic power struggles in the Ottoman capital (see below). Tragically, the same group then tried in vain to revive and strengthen it in its last phase (during 1920–1924) in the face of the Caliphate's demise and destruction, which the secularists eventually achieved. Though there were some ambiguities as to which actor was in what group at different points in time (for example, Seyyid Bey, the most important representative of the modernist group in the early years, later supported the secularists in the last moments of the Caliphate), this model is useful for understanding and analyzing the essentials of the power struggle around the Caliphate. What is interesting about these three groups is that despite their opposing positions vis-à-vis the Caliphate, they employed similar discourses (or "discursive strategies"), sometimes even the same ones, in order to achieve differing, even opposing political ends (see Chapter 3 for a detailed description of the three groups and their leading members whose ideas this study discusses). Moreover, since their view of the Caliphate was often incompatible with the classical understanding of it, the modernists and especially the secularists frequently resorted to a strategic intervention into Islamic theology and law. I call this form of "invention of tradition" (Hobsbawm 1992) "theological engineering," which I define as redefining key Islamic concepts on the basis of the exigencies of the modern historical context, and using the literature in legal and theological traditions to justify their own political claims and positions.

Second, in terms of spatial comparison, I examine modernization discourses (at the micro level) and political and military developments (at the macro level) that framed them focusing on both the center of the Caliphate (Turkey) and the caliphal periphery, including Egypt and North Africa, the Arabian Peninsula, and India. The analysis of the crucial variables found in different regions will enable us to examine spatial variation and the extent to which Islam, independent of local variations, was significant in terms of the nature of secularization in the region. We observe that the discourses used in debates in Istanbul involved different elements from those in Egypt and the Arabian Peninsula (both of which were then part of the Ottoman Empire, at least nominally), for European powers such as Britain and France had particular imperialistic interests in the destiny of the Caliphate and its impact on the Muslim world. On the other hand, Arab nationalism was an important factor shaping the discourses of many in the Arab world, which culminated into the emergence of an intellectual and political movement advocating an Arab caliphate. I thus look at how this discourse varied between the center and the periphery of the Caliphate.

Third, I also examine the variation within the evolution of the Islamic discourse in different periods as well as across different groups and regions. I examine the period of 1908–1924 in three phases. In the first phase (1908–1916), when the CUP seized power and greatly weakened the Caliphate in the center as a result of the 1908 Revolution, the power struggle was between the coalition of the Ottoman bureaucracy, represented by the CUP, and the modernist Islamists on the one hand, and that of the religious establishment and traditionalists, on the other. The bureaucracy won the battle and dominated the state; however, I hypothesize that in this phase the "modernist Islamist discourse" did not target

the Caliphate itself, but involved its transformation into strictly a temporal authority, isolating the Caliphate from its more powerful religious/spiritual basis, so that
it would be easier to abolish it later in 1924. In the second phase (1914–1920) I
look at the debates on the periphery over Muslim unity under the Ottoman
Caliphate and the alternative caliphate projects in Arabia and Morocco, in the
context of British and French colonialisms. I hypothesize that here the real power
struggle took place between the pro-Ottoman (Arab and Indian as well as Turkish)
actors, including both modernists and traditionalists, and the anti-Ottoman group
consisting mostly of Arab nationalists. Finally, in the third phase (1919–1924), I
go back to the center to examine the debates that were directly about the abolition
of the Caliphate, rather than the limits of its authority as was the case in the first
phase. The struggle in this phase occurred between modernists who tried to save
the Caliphate and the secularists who succeeded in destroying it. This, too, was
accomplished through a widespread justification with resort to Islam itself, rather
than an outright secularist discourse. Without this discursive practice, the most
important step in the way of secularism could not have been accomplished – at
least not as easily and peacefully. Therefore, I hypothesize that the incorporation
of Islamic elements in the discourse of secularism employed by political actors
was rather an integral part of secularization itself. This implies that the secularism
of the Middle Eastern modernization was based on the redefinition of the role of
the sacred in the public sphere, rather than simply a rejection of it. To demonstrate this argument, I apply the Foucaultian discourse analysis method.

Discourse analysis

Examining discourses is useful because they both affect, and are affected by,
social developments, thereby functioning as indicators of social change. That is,
they both reflect changes in social reality *and* help shape them, by making sense
of this very reality for individuals and groups, thereby informing their decisions,
actions, and reactions. For they provide cognitive and social lenses through
which to perceive one's social environment, which in turn influences the ranges
and angles of these lenses. Furthermore, discourses not only affect actors' dispo-
sitions, but also justify their positions – and undermine their opponents' – in
social struggles. Language can thus play significant roles in power relations by
helping actors create and impose a legitimate vision of the world that makes
division possible. As Bourdieu (1989: 20–21) observes, "the words, the names,
which construct social reality as much as they express it, are the stake par excellence of political struggle, which is a struggle to impose the legitimate principle
of vision and division." In other words, (dominant) discourses contribute greatly
to the "definition of the situation": as William Thomas famously put it, "if men
define things as real, they are real in their consequences" (Thomas 2002: 103).
Therefore, discourses (and language in general) often function as a "symbolic
capital" (or power source), which Bourdieu (1989: 23) defines as "a credit; [a]
power granted to those who have obtained sufficient recognition to be in a position to impose recognition." What Bourdieu calls the "theory effect" implies the

ability to define, classify, and determine things, that is, the capacity to order and shape social relations the way the power-holder wants. Moreover, this symbolic power of language makes formation of groups possible, for "a group, a class, a gender, a region, or a nation begins to exist as such ... only when it is distinguished ... from other groups, that is, through knowledge and recognition (*connaissance et reconnaissance*)" (ibid.).

The term "discourse" is understood and theorized in different ways depending on the disciplinary context in which it is used. In linguistics it is sometimes associated with spoken language and contrasted with "text," and sometimes it includes both spoken and written "texts." In cultural and literary theory, the meaning of discourse is derived from its Latin and French origins and its usage is influenced by Michel Foucault: it is understood as a domain of the production and circulation of various "statements" governed by certain rules (Mills 1997). For Bakhtin and Barthes, however, a particular discourse is taken as a "voice" within a text or a speech position (Hawthorn 1992). In social psychology, discourse is understood in relation to power relations and analyzed with a methodology derived from the early (linguistic) discourse analysis (Wilkinson and Kitzinger 1995). Critical approaches such as those of the "critical linguistics" (Fowler *et al.* 1979; Fairclough 1995, 2001a, 2003; Wodak and Meyer 2001) and of Pêcheux (1982), who draws upon Althusser's theory of ideology, are also concerned with how power relations are enacted in the production and consumption of utterances and texts. Fairclough suggests that a critical discourse analysis could be done focusing on three aspects of meaning in texts – "action and social relation," "representation" and "identification" – which "correspond to the categories of genres, discourses, and styles at the level of social practices" (Fairclough 2003: 38, see also 2001b). Thus, these latter approaches represent a fusion of linguistics and social theory under the impact of the Foucaultian approach.[10]

Foucault uses the term discourse in different meanings, but he basically means by it "a regulated practice that accounts for a number of statements" (Foucault 1972: 80). His "theory" of discourse is closely related to the notions of "truth," "power" and "knowledge," for it is because of these elements that it produces its effects. He is also critical of the "negative" understanding of power and of what he calls the "repressive hypothesis" – that power is always about prevention, constraint, and repression. His productive model implies on the contrary that power is dispersed throughout social relations and *produces* certain forms of behavior and thought as well as restricting others. This point is closely related to the production of *knowledge*: for Foucault there is no social relation, including the production of knowledge, that does not revolve around the notion of power. Thus, all knowledge produced and consumed is an effect of power struggles, and all power struggles need (and require) certain forms of knowledge. Hence the formulation of "power/knowledge" (Foucault 1979a, 1979b, 1979c). For him a proper textual analysis should be concerned with the "discursive formations" by which he means a set of rules concerning the formation of "objects" (of knowledge), "subject positions," "concepts" and "strategies." So it is the task of discourse analysis to specify the ways in which objects of knowledge, such as madness, nation, religion, and so on, are produced, transformed, and reproduced by different discursive formations. Moreover, discursive formations define concepts and strategies for their subjects. Like the formation of subjects and enunciative modalities, these concepts do not consist of a set of stable ones in well-defined relations with each other; rather it refers to shifting configurations of changing concepts (Foucault 1972: 57). These discursive activities occur in a historical context and an institutional setting, require a form of power/knowledge, and imply a subject position. This view of discourse assumes that discourse, hence language, not only "refers" to social reality, but also "signifies" it, in the sense that it not only "shows" but also contributes to the constitution of different dimensions of social reality (Fairclough 1992: 43). Thus, Foucault's approach in his "archaeological" studies (particularly Foucault 1972, 1979a) includes five major insights perceived by Fairclough (1992: 55–56) in terms of a systematic investigation of the relationship between discourse and social structure:

i   the constitutive nature of discourse, referring to the effect of discourse on social relations;
ii the primacy of intertextuality and interdiscursivity;
iii the political nature of discourse, implying that political struggle occurs both in and over discourse;
iv the discursive nature of power, implying that discourse is a significant element in power relations; and
v   the discursive nature of social change, referring to the fact that changing discursive practices are an important element in social change.

However, his model lacks a dialectical understanding of the relationship between discourse and social reality, which ignores the interaction between the pre-constituted dimensions of reality (social subjects, objects etc.) and the discourse that helps constitute them, overemphasizing the constitutive aspects of the latter.

I take the term "discourse" in a broad, Foucaultian sense ("a regulated practice that accounts for a number of statements") to account for the "language" of those texts that I analyze. I do not present here a full application of Foucaultian discourse analysis, but utilize some of his concepts as methodological tools, particularly his concept of "discursive strategy." Foucault (1972: 64ff.) calls the discursive organization of objects, concepts, and "enunciative modalities" a "discursive strategy," which involves different "theories" and – less coherent and stable – "themes." Finding this concept too general, I distinguish three levels of it. A "meta-discursive strategy" is the most general one, which consists of different discursive strategies that in turn contain a number of "discursive techniques" at the most specific level. Thus, for example, the discursive strategy of invoking the sacred texts of Islam for legitimation involves such techniques as abstracting Qur'anic verses and prophetic *hadith*s from their contexts, and emphasizing some concepts in them while ignoring others etc. This strategy in turn is part of the larger discursive "meta-strategy" of deriving justification from Islam, which I argue was the main pattern in the secularization of political institutions in the Middle East.

This Islamic justification in a sense constitutes what Michel de Certeau (1984, 1994) calls – though in a different context – a "strategy," and various discursive strategies and techniques the actors deployed during the period under study refer to "tactics." For de Certeau a strategy is "the calculus of force-relationships [producing] a subject of will and power [that] can be isolated from an environment," which makes it possible to transform the uncertainties of history into readable spaces (1994: 480, 1984: 36). As such, the strategy refers to various "forms of operations proper to the recomposition of a space by familial practices" whereas "tactics" refer to "negotiations and improvisation proper to ordinary language." As such, the latter "must constantly manipulate events in order to turn them into opportunities." Moreover, tactics operate mainly through rhetoric, "of which language can be both the site and the object; these manipulations are related to the ways of changing the will of another" (de Certeau 1994: 477–478, 480).

Thus, the three groups ("secularists," "modernist Islamists" and "traditionalist Islamists") I identify in my examination of Middle Eastern secularization used different discursive "tactics," which both modified and reproduced the dominant and hegemonic (i.e., legitimate) "strategy" (Islamic justification), in order to reinforce their own political positions and to undermine their opponents', as reflected in the documents examined.

The data

In my investigation, I analyze two sets of primary data: those on the Caliphate in particular and those on the Middle Eastern modernization in general. For the former, I heavily rely on the above-mentioned five-volume data, titled "Caliphate Pamphlets," edited by Kara and his teammates (2002–2005). It contains primary sources (pamphlets, books, parliamentary discussions etc.), some of them previously uncovered, written from 1876 to the mid-1920s in different geographic areas, from India to Britain and France, from Russia to Arabia and North Africa, as well as Turkey and Egypt. I am thankful to Professor İsmail Kara and his team for their hard work in presenting these valuable data to the service of academics.[11] I also use some primary sources not contained in this collection.

For my examination of the larger process of modernization, on the other hand I first examine documents embodying different elements of politico-legal reforms in the Middle East including the Constitutions of 1876, 1921, and 1924, and the discussions in the Parliament and the press. The discourse analysis of the debates in the media over the politico-legal processes that produced official documents enables us to contextualize the latter. I also analyze in a comparative manner the writings of important intellectuals from Turkey (including Ziya Gökalp who was the prominent ideologue of secularism, and others such as Elmalılı Hamdi, Seyyid Bey, İzmirli İ. Hakkı, and Hoca Şükrü, etc. as well as the speeches of Mustafa Kemal [Atatürk], the champion of secularism and the most important political actor in Turkish modernization after 1920), Arabia and North Africa (such as Sharif Hussein, Abdur-rahman al-Kawakibi, Rashid Rida, Ali Abdur-raziq, Abdulaziz Jawish and Ismail Safayihi) and from India (such as Syed Mahmud, Suleyman Nadvi, Hakim Ajmal Khan, Mukhtar Ahmed Ansari and Abul Kalam Azad, the leading members of the Indian "Caliphate Movement"). I emphasize the discursive strategies employed in the caliphal center by Seyyid Bey and Ziya Gökalp who were the intellectual fathers and ideologues of the political groups that were in power both before (Committee of Union and Progress) and after (Republican People's Party) the declaration of the Republic in 1923. This analysis will allow me to see the employment of the discourse of secularism in relation to Islam by a leading Islamic scholar (Seyyid Bey) and an influential intellectual (Gökalp) who played a crucial role in the secularization and destruction of the Caliphate. Gökalp also had a project of transforming the Islamic law, which represents, due to his being a follower of Durkheim, the embodiment of the Durkheimian sociology in Turkish politics. Finally, I also pay special attention on the ideas of Mustafa Kemal who was the leader the Turkish nationalist movement and later the Republic of Turkey. The evolution of his ideas represents a good example of the way the relationship between Islam and politics took different forms in different stages of the process of secularization.

On the periphery I emphasize, on the one hand, Rashid Rida and Sharif Hussein's ideas as they represent the anti-Caliphate movement in the Arab world, which also makes it possible to see the connections between the struggle for Caliphate and the rise of Arab nationalism as well as the impact of the British and French colonialism in the Middle East. I also focus on India where a traditionalist understanding of Islam and the Caliphate prevailed. The leaders of the Caliphate Movement, who would later found Pakistan, strongly supported the Ottoman Caliphate against both the European colonialism and Arab nationalists on the one hand, and Turkish secularists on the other. Part of the reason why they did this was to benefit from the Caliph's ideological and political power vis-à-vis Europeans, the British in particular, in order to save their land and people from British colonialism. Unlike many Turkish and Arab (modernist and secularist) actors, the Indian Muslim leaders saw the Caliph as both a temporal ruler and a spiritual leader for all Muslims.

Although my main method is discourse analysis, I present an extensive account of major developments in each chapter in order to provide the necessary contextual information on the historical background of the discursive struggles that took place on the Caliphate and the general modernization process in the Middle East. I relate ways in which the discourse of secularism is employed in the documents to the major social and political developments, considering the fact that discourse and practice are always tied together. The analysis of these texts might enable us to trace the evolution of the discourse of secularization – reflected in, and constructed by, these sources – within the context of political struggles and identify the main contours of political modernization in the region. The data are – mostly – in Ottoman Turkish, some in modern Turkish, Arabic,

English, and French (I have used the Turkish translations of some of the Arabic sources due to access problems; also, I could use only the sources originally published in Urdu available in Turkish and English.) The quotations from these sources are all my translations, except for the few that are already available in English (e.g., [Sharif] Hussein 1916; Syed Mahmud 1921). For the translations of Qur'anic verses, I have used Yusuf Ali's famous and widely cited translation, which can be easily accessed on the internet; I myself translated the prophetic *hadith*s that were cited but not translated in primary sources.

I analyze the extent to which texts embody or express a certain ideology taking these texts as the context where discourse is (re)produced and re-presented (Fowler 1996: 6). I thus present my specific arguments by frequent quotations from these texts; in interpreting them, I always take into account the socio-historical context in which these texts were produced in order to be able to present them without distorting their meanings and purposes. Since they document different aspects of the secularization process, which were always justified with reference to the Islamic *sharia*, their analysis will show how institutional secularization went hand in hand with the Islamization of public discourse in the Middle East in this period.

Organization of the book

As implied by the preceding explanation, my study is composed of two broad topics: the general secularization of the Middle East, and the Caliphate's transformation and demise as a case to analyze this process. I deal with the former in the following chapter, which aims to provide a foreground to my subsequent discussion on the Caliphate. Here I argue that what I call the accommodation relationship between Islam and modernity, which the debates over the Caliphate exemplify, is also true for the wider modernization process in the Middle East. Chapter 2 thus starts with a brief history of modernization in the Middle East, and then presents an examination of legal documents, reform decrees, and constitutions in particular, and discussions on them as well as a survey of the transformation of Islamic discourse in the Ottoman public sphere. This survey involves an account of the interaction between secularization and the press, and a discourse analysis of a sample of intellectuals to see how their discourse evolved with the transformation of the state in the Empire. It also includes specifically an analysis of Ziya Gökalp's (1876–1924) ideas, which exemplify a synthesis of secular social theory and Islamic legal discourse.

Chapter 3 functions as the opening section of my discussion specifically on the Caliphate. It starts with a brief history of the Caliphate, focusing particularly on the Ottoman period. Then it presents a description of my three groups of power actors and the main strategies they employ in their discourses in order to provide background information for my subsequent analysis of them. This chapter also provides the discursive context of the struggle between these groups by focusing on the common – and the most frequently used – discursive strategies, which all three groups employ. Here I discuss three main discursive strategies: invoking the sacred texts of Islam (the Qur'an and the prophetic traditions), invoking (early) Islamic history, and omitting contradictory evidence. This chapter aims to demonstrate that all three groups sometimes used the same strategies and techniques for their conflicting political purposes.

The following three chapters are organized in such a way as to comparatively analyze the power struggles among the three groups in different time periods and different geographical locations. Chapter 4 examines the struggle over the Caliphate and the state between the modernists and the traditionalists, that is, the "secular" bureaucratic elite vs. the religious establishment, including the Palace, in the *center* of the Caliphate (Turkey) during the early years of the Second Constitutional Period (1908–1916). More specifically, it analyzes two cases, the decline of the Caliph's authority with specific legal changes following the 1908 Young Turk Revolution, and that of the *Şeyhulislam* (the Caliph's religious dignitary), as the two cornerstones of the early transformation of the Ottoman Caliphate. Chapter 5 looks at the caliphal *periphery* to examine the political and ideological struggle between the supporters of the Ottoman Caliphate, including both traditionalist *and* modernist Islamists, and the anti-Caliphate groups, namely Arab nationalists, who were backed up by European powers. This struggle was conditioned heavily by World War I, the French and British projects of installing puppet-caliphs in Arabia and Northwest Africa, and the concern for Muslim unity these created on the part of the pro-Ottoman actors during the Great War. This chapter, too, analyzes two cases in particular: the French project of the "*Maghrib* Caliphate" and the British project of the "Arab Caliphate." Finally, Chapter 6 returns to the caliphal *center* in order to examine the struggle between the modernist Islamists and secularists, led by Mustafa Kemal, Turkey's first president. More specifically, this chapter examines two cases as well: the abolition of the Ottoman monarchy (1922) and that of the Caliphate itself (1924), which proved most crucial for the secularization of the political system in Turkey after World War I. It demonstrates that the secularists made extensive use of an Islamic discourse in destroying these two institutions, which paved the way for other radical secular reforms, for which Turkey is known today. The concluding chapter reviews my main theoretical and empirical arguments, and makes some suggestions for further research. This study thus aims to contribute to the understanding of both the nature of secularization (and, more broadly, modernization) in the Middle East, and to the refining of the secularization theory in the sociology of religion, which has been somewhat limited in its scope and unsophisticated in some of its central assumptions, particularly regarding the relationship between religion and politics.

2 Modernization, religion, and the Ottomans

Introduction

Since the Ottoman Empire dominated what we today call the Middle East from the 15th to the late 19th century, a historical account of the region during this period must be an account of Ottoman modernization. This chapter presents a (hi)story of Ottoman-Turkish modernization, from the late 18th century to the 1930s, and analyzes the role of Islamic discourse in the broader modernization process in order to provide a foreground to my subsequent examination on the Caliphate. It does not deal with the secularization process per se, but the wider modernization of political institutions in the Middle East. The subsequent chapters will deal with different aspects of the secularization process in particular in the case of the Caliphate. Drawing on both primary and secondary sources, the present chapter includes a survey of legal documents (reform decrees and constitutions, in particular) and the writings of intellectuals on topics – other than the Caliphate – of political significance. More specifically, I present a textual analysis of important documents that represent crucial turning points in Ottoman modernization, including the Reform Decree (1839), the Reform Edict (1856) and the constitutions of 1876, 1921 and 1924. I also discuss the views of Ziya Gökalp, the Kurdish/Turkish intellectual (mentioned in the previous chapter) and a leading figure among the "secularists," in order to show the prevalence of Islamic discourse even within this group. My discussion includes an analysis of an interesting debate, started by Gökalp, the founder of sociology in Turkey and a follower of Durkheim, on the "social bases of Islamic jurisprudence," a major attempt at secularizing Islamic law. I start with a historical sketch of the Middle Eastern modernization.

A brief history of modernization in the Middle East

The process of social and political modernization and secularization in the Middle East followed the period of intense transformation (often identified as "decline") in the Ottoman Empire starting in the latter half of the 17th century, which was marked by the Treaty of Karlowitz in 1699 when the Empire lost a portion of its lands for the first time.[1] Significant reforms in military and political institutions began during the time of Sultan Selim III (1789–1807), though Ottoman intellectuals such as Koçi Bey (1860[1631]) had for decades been calling for the restoration of the Ottoman system. The first reforms of the early 18th century had been characterized by an assumption of the superiority of Islam and the Ottoman state over the West, and the dominant view had seen nothing to gain from the "Franks" and little to fear from them. In Selim's time, however, given the relative "decline" in the empire's military power, they began to accept the West's technical superiority and to strive to "save the state and protect the religion." This view remained dominant until 1918 (Tanpınar 1997: 37–63; Karal 1940: 23–28).

In fact, modernization of the state had begun with Abdülhamid I, who had ruled before Selim III. In 1774, the former invited European experts to modernize the army and paved the way for the great reforms launched by the latter. Selim also started with military modernization, founding new military schools and creating a small model army, called *Nizam-ı Cedid* (literally, "the New Order"), based on Western military principles. He also attempted to modernize the state organization and education system, trying to decentralize the administration and founding new schools of higher education in addition to *medreses* (religious schools), such as engineering and medical schools.[2] His reforms created great discontent among the Janissaries, who then deposed and killed him. But the counter-revolution of his troops put his young nephew, Sultan Mahmud II, on the throne in 1807. Mahmud (1807–1839), who has been called "the Peter the Great of the Ottoman Empire" (Edib 1930: 66) – he was an enemy of long beards, too – further developed the reforms in the way of Westernization not only in military and educational institutions, but also in social and political life. In 1826 he abolished and massacred the rebellious Janissary army, which he saw as a fundamental threat not only to his reforms but also his life, and founded a new army, called the *Asakir-i Mansure-i Muhammediyye* (Victorious Soldiers of Muhammad), which was an entirely European-style army despite the clear religious reference in its title. He then centralized the bureaucracy and made his monarchy more powerful by abolishing the office of the all-powerful *sadrazam*, founding in its place a Western-style cabinet, and appointing a *başvekil* (chief minister) and *vekils* (ministers) to departments of government. (However, this would be a short-lived model, as the high-level bureaucracy would regain its power soon.) He also started the movement for mass primary education, founded new higher educational (military and civil) institutions, and invited foreign (especially French) teachers to teach in these schools, which further bifurcated the school system. He also changed the dress code, adopted the fez, the Greek headdress, and Western-style pants, coats, shirts, and shoes, and became the first sultan who dressed in Western style himself – which is how he came to be known as the "Infidel Sultan" among the public. He made fundamental changes in the legal system, aimed at creating equality for non-Muslims, and founded a new council to deal with judicial matters specifically outside the realm of the *sharia*. Finally, it was in his time that the first Turkish newspaper, *Takvim-i Vekayi* [*Calendar of Events*], was founded in 1836 as a government-sponsored publication (Tanpınar 1997: 64–73; Berkes 1998[1964]: 30–137; Edib 1930: 61–68; Lewis 1961: 73–104; Shaw 1971: 86ff.; Davison 1988: 67–78).

Thus, Mahmud's reforms paved the way for the *Tanzimat* (Reforms) period (1839–1876), which brought deeper and more lasting changes. The era opened with the Royal Decree of Gülhane, which was inaugurated by Abdülmecid I and established the equality of Muslims and non-Muslims before the law. This period was an era marked by the direct political and economic impact of the West. In education, new, non-religious primary (*ibtidai*) and secondary (*rüşdiye*) schools were established. In higher learning (*idadi*), in addition to the schools of engineering and medicine, new schools in the humanities that were modeled after the French *grandes écoles* were founded, including schools of mathematics and geography, the School of Political Science (*Mekteb-i Mülkiye*, 1859), the Lycée de Galatasaray (*Mekteb-i Sultani*, 1868), and the Law School (*Mekteb-i Hukuk*, 1880), in which French was the language of instruction. (The first modern, Western-style university, the Istanbul *Darülfunun*, would be founded in 1900.) Also, a Western-style taxation system was established; and with pressure from such European countries as Britain and France, the entire economic and financial system was revised to make it more suitable for foreign trade, and the capitalist market system began to enter the Ottoman lands, which negatively affected the traditional system of small producers in towns and peasants in rural areas (İnalcık and Quataert 1994: 761ff.; Genç 2000: 183–186; Çakır 2001: 24–98; Karpat 2001: 6–8; cf. Issawi 1966; Owen 1981). This era also witnessed the growth of urban population largely because of migrations from rural areas. With the development of the new school system, a new group of urban intellectuals called *münevver* ("the enlightened") emerged as opposed to the classical *ulema* of *medrese*s. On the other hand, the Reform Edict (*Islahat Fermanı*), which included important privileges for the non-Muslim subjects of the empire, was proclaimed in 1856, as a result of pressures from European countries, further extending the privileges of Christians in the empire (see below). Thus the *Tanzimat* and *Islahat* eras were characterized by the gradual emergence of citizenship and the extension of the privileges of non-Muslim and foreign individuals, more than the Turkish and Muslim subjects (*tebaa*) of the Empire, on the one hand, and by the rise of bureaucracy and a new group of intellectuals educated in Western style – and in the West – on the other (see Ortaylı 1983; Berkes 1998[1964]: 137–223; Edib 1930: 68–74; Quataert 1994: 761–776; Ahmad 1993: 15–30; Lewis 1961: 104–125; Akyıldız 2004: 15–30; Findley 1994; Somel 2001a; Çetinsaya 2001a: 54–56; Fortna 2002).

This new social group, which included such important figures as Şinasi, Namık Kemal, and Ziya Pasha, as well as such influential statesmen as Ali Pasha, Fuad Pasha, and, later, Midhat Pasha, many of whom had worked for the famous Translation Office, formed the core of the constitutional movement that in 1876 created the first parliament and written constitution in Ottoman history. Determined to modernize the state, these Tanzimat intellectuals formed a political group, known as the "Young Ottomans," and popularized the ideologies of, first, Ottomanism (the unification of all – Muslim and non-Muslim – peoples in the empire) and then *İttihad-ı İslam* (the rapproachment of Muslim peoples within and outside the empire), both of which were a reaction to the Russian-originated Pan-Slavism that threatened the Ottomans' Balkan territories (Somel 2001b: 88–97; Çetinsaya 2001b: 265–268). These intellectuals and politicians also helped the new sultan, Abdülhamid II (1876–1909), come to the throne and had him open the first parliament and proclaim the new constitution, which was drafted from the contemporary French constitution and represented a new milestone on the way of modernization. This, therefore, marked the beginning of what is called the First *Meşrutiyet* (Constitutional Monarchy) era. Although all ethnic and religious groups in the empire were represented in the parliament and a modern government was created and controlled by the Young Ottomans, the anti-constitutionalist sultan was still very powerful. Such disasters as the Serbian, Bulgarian, and Romanian uprisings, and especially the Turco-Russian War of 1877–1878 (in which the Ottoman Empire lost two-fifths of its territory and one-fifth of its population) gave Abdülhamid II the opportunity to abolish the constitution and close the parliament in 1878. He exiled Prime Minister Midhat Pasha, the "Father of the Constitution," and the Young Ottomans, and oppressed the opposition, censoring the press during his 33-year reign. He thus created enemies from different intellectual circles – Islamists and "secularists" alike. However, he continued with the modernizing reforms by reorganizing the Ministry of Justice to take control over all non-religious matters, improving secondary and higher education, establishing factories, and constructing modern forms of transportation (especially railways) and communication. He pursued a policy of "Islamic unity" (*İttihad-ı İslam*) within and without the Ottoman Empire[3] and successfully manipulated the tensions among European powers with this policy of balance forming the basis of his strategy. However, the Ottoman Empire lost some of its territories between 1876 and 1908, when Austria annexed Bosnia-Herzegovina and the sultan was obliged to restore the constitution and re-open the parliament by the Committee of Union and Progress (CUP) (Shaw and Shaw 1977: 172–271; Eraslan 1995; Kologlu 1998; Somel 2001a; Karpat 2002).

A coalition of different groups led by the Young Turks, who were inspired by the Young Italy (*Giovine Italia*) movement, and unified by their opposition to Abdülhamid II, the CUP was first founded as a student club in the Ottoman medical school and later developed into a (secret) political club organized outside the country. In its first phase (1889/1895–1902),[4] the CUP was led by Ahmed Rıza, who was in Paris in exile and published the CUP's influential newspaper, *Meşveret* (*Consultation*), there. Its second phase (1902–1918) had a more military character, as it overwhelmingly consisted of young officers led by Enver Pasha, Cemal Pasha and Talat Pasha. In both phases, however, the party's most important principles were Constitutionalism, Ottomanism (the idea that all ethnic and religious groups in the Ottoman lands should live together) and opposition to Abdülhamid II. Their ideas appealed to young students, staff officers, and army officials, and grew stronger at the turn of the new century. Finally, in 1908, they forced the sultan to restore the 1876 constitution and order elections (Tunaya 1952; Hanioğlu 1995, 2001; Toprak 1995; see also Chapter 4).

The second Ottoman Parliament met in Istanbul in January 1909, which marked the beginning of the Second *Meşrutiyet* era. However, an uprising by soldiers stationed in Istanbul and some religious groups, now known as the "March 31 Incident," took place very soon thereafter. It was severely repressed by the Unionist "Action Army," which came from Macedonia and subsequently deposed the sultan (see Chapter 4). Now, with a weak new sultan, Mehmed (Reşad) V, on the throne, the CUP was almost entirely sovereign in the empire, though there was a political opposition organized around the Freedom and Alliance Party (FAP). The years following the revolution witnessed unsuccessful wars with European states and Balkan countries that gained independence with the last blow of the First Balkan War in 1912. As a result, the Ottomans formed an alliance with Germany against Britain, France, Russia and Italy (see Ramsaur 1957; Mardin 1983a; Lewis 1961: 126–234; Davison 1988: 92–128; Shaw and Shaw 1997: 272–305; Sohrabi 1995).

Meanwhile, reforms continued, especially in the form of modernizing the army, the police, and mass education, and of Westernizing dress and manners. Also, the CUP continued the policy of Ottomanism, which was the Ottoman "official ideology" based on the idea of the Ottoman citizenship since the *Tanzimat* period, but this time it was blended with Turkish nationalism (Hanioğlu 2006: 19). In the cultural arena, too, Turkish nationalism flourished inside the country. Debates over Turkification in literature and education began and several nationalist societies, such as the *Türk Ocağı* (Turkish Hearth), were founded. Although there emerged a liberal movement that was organized under the FAP, which won several elections between 1911 and1918 (see Birinci 1990), Turkish nationalism gained much more political character, especially with the impact of the problems with Armenians and Arabs inside the country and with the European states outside. As a result, Pan-Turkism (or "Turanism") became the official state policy under the CUP after 1913 – though only for a short time (Arai 1992; Karpat 2000).

The loss of European territories was complemented by various tribal revolts in the Arab and Kurdish territories during the Second Constitutional Period. Though Istanbul was mostly successful in repressing such uprisings (with the exception of Yemen, which became practically autonomous after 1905), it could not prevent the eventual rise of Arab nationalism, which was backed by Britain and France. World War I created a perfect opportunity for Arab independence from the empire: Egypt, Libya, Algeria, and the rest of the *Maghrib* had already been occupied by Britain, Italy, France and Spain; the Ottomans also lost the Arabian Peninsula as a result of the Hashemite and Saudi revolts (1916–1918) and the Allied invasion during the war. The Ottoman palace and the CUP tried to use the Caliphate as a unifying force for Muslims, but the caliph, who had already been weakened by the Unionists, failed to fulfill any such function. Britain and France, on the other hand, tried to install their own puppet-caliphs in the *Hijaz* (Hashemite Sharif Hussein) and the *Maghrib* (Moroccan Sultan Yusuf), but gave up on their plans due to reactions from Muslim colonies and the abolition of the caliphate by Turkish secularists (Stoddard 1963; Trumpener

1968; Nevakivi 1969; Bayur 1983, vol. III; Kayalı 1997; Fromkin 2001; Goldschmidt 2005; see also Chapter 5).

World War I had brought a great disaster to the empire. An ally of Germany,
the Ottoman army simultaneously fought on several fronts (Western Turkey,
Eastern Anatolia, the Middle East and North Africa) and, together with
Germany, lost the war. The Allies invaded the Ottoman territories and imposed
an armistice in 1918, which gave them (particularly Britain) control over the
sultan and the government in Istanbul. The result was the formation of a new
nationalist movement in Anatolia under the leadership of some former members
of the CUP, among them Mustafa Kemal, who later became the leader of the
movement. An alternative parliament and a new government were instituted in
Ankara in 1920, which would form the core of the new Turkish Republic. The
movement waged a "War of Independence" against Greek occupation and the
Istanbul government, defeating them in 1922. Meanwhile the Allies left Turkey,
finding it unreasonable to keep invading. The victorious government abolished
the Ottoman monarchy (1922) and signed a peace agreement with the Allies at
Lausanne on July 24, 1923, and declared the Republic on October 29, 1923 (see
Zürcher 1984; Shaw and Shaw 1977: 306ff.).

The new Republic ruled by Mustafa Kemal's Republican People's Party
(RPP) quickly started the radical reforms that accelerated the modernization and
secularization process. Laws concerning the abolition of the Caliphate and of the
Ministry of *Sharia* and Pious Foundations (equal to the earlier office of the
Şeyhulislam) and the exile of the Ottoman dynasty were passed at one sitting on
March 3, 1924. Also, a new "Department of Religious Affairs" was founded in
place of the Ministry of *Sharia* and attached directly to the office of the prime
minister. The same day religious educational institutions (*medrese*s) were also
abolished with the law of the "Unification of Education." A few days later *sharia*
courts were abolished, ending the bifurcation and pluralism in the legal system.
Meanwhile, following the Kurdish revolt in 1925, all opposition was silenced
with the "Law of Maintenance of Order," and an era of iron rule reigned until
1929, which involved such reforms as the adaptation from Europe of new laws,
including the Trade Law and the penal and civil codes, and then the Latinization
of the alphabet (1928). Secularization of the constitutional basis for the Kemalist
regime was completed in 1928 with the elimination of the second article of the
constitution, which read, "The religion of the State is that of Islam," and was
later consolidated and given a formal expression in the revised Constitution in
1937, explicitly stating that "the Turkish Republic is a ... secular State" (see
Edib 1930: 158–237; Lewis 1961: 234–287; Heyd 1950: 88–94; Armstrong
1938; Dodd 1979: 83–85).

The puzzle: secularization of the state and Islamic discourse

Since it is impossible to cover all the data on the entire modernization process, in
this section I will analyze some important texts with the capacity to represent the
reforms that played significant roles in the secularization of Turkey. I will first

focus on two important reforms, the Reform Decree (1839) and the Reform Edict (1856), in terms of the way they reflect and construe the relationship between religion and the state. I will then proceed to the debates over the next significant reform, the 1876 Constitution, which are illustrative of the theme of this study. Third, I will analyze the constitutions of 1876, 1921, and 1924 in a comparative fashion, paying attention to the evolution of the discourse on the role of Islam in the public sphere. Then I will turn to an analysis of the Islamic discourse as reflected in the Ottoman press in its relation to the political and economic context of the late 19th and early 20th centuries. Finally, I will examine the ideas of an influential intellectual, Ziya Gökalp, who was a leading ideologue of secularism. Analyzing the evolution of his ideas might reveal important clues about the nature of the secularization process in the Ottoman Empire.

As mentioned above, I argue in this study that the relationship between Islam and secularism is one of accommodation as well as conflict, and that the nature of the process of secularization in the Middle East involves an extensive use of the discourse of "serving religion" or "protecting Islam." The traces of this discourse, which included many Islamic elements, can be found in the very first attempts at modernization in the Ottoman Empire in the late 18th century. An analysis of these first attempts, as well as the later cornerstones of modernization in the 19th century, the *Tanzimat Fermanı* and the *Islahat Fermanı*, shows that the *meta-discursive strategy* of justification with reference to the Islamic *sharia* was extensively applied in these reforms. The two *discursive strategies* most frequently employed in them were "invoking sacred Islamic texts" and "maintaining the superiority of the *sharia*." The main *discursive technique* employed in these texts was that of "renewing the existing institutions in accordance with *sharia* rules," which justified extensive reforms in the state system. When Selim III first started the modernization of the army by inviting European experts and founding a new, Western-style *Nizam-ı Cedid* army, he justified his attempts with reference to a famous *hadith* (saying of the prophet Muhammad), which says, "You can use your enemy's weapon." He maintained that there was nothing against the *sharia* in "defeating the infidels by using their weapons" (quoted in İnalcık 1968: 49). Similarly, when Mahmud II accelerated the reforms that had been started by his uncle, Selim, he resorted to the same discourse. For instance, in his speech in 1838 at the opening ceremony of the Royal Medical School (*Dar-ül Ulum-ı Hikemiyye ve Mekteb-i Tıbbiyye-i Şahane*), which would become a medium of change for futher modernization, the sultan referred to the "sacred duty" of protecting human health, which is one of the duties of the state and the legal system according to Islamic *sharia*, saying that he had "given precedence to this school because it [would] be dedicated to a sacred duty – the preservation of human health."[5] The sultan then went on to comment on the fact that the language of instruction would be French, and insisted that it was necessary to take medical knowledge from Europe instead of the Muslim world due to its obsolete character in the latter. The ultimate justification for the Westernization of education was to serve the cause of Muslims, according to Sultan Mahmud, who paved the way for the *Tanzimat* reforms.

The Reform Decree (1839) and the Reform Edict (1856)

The *Tanzimat* era was the second phase of Ottoman-Turkish modernization after the "New Order" of Selim III and Mahmud II. It was opened, as mentioned above, with the Royal Decree of Gülhane (*Tanzimat Fermanı*; sometimes called the "Gülhane Charter") on November 3, 1839, inaugurated by Sultan Abdülmecid I. It included several modernizing reforms, especially in the legal system, to ensure "a good administration." Partly a product of the pressures of European states, the decree, which proclaimed the principles of the *Tanzimat*, granted and guaranteed certain rights, called "the fundamentals" (*Mevadd-ı Esasiye*), such as the guarantee of life, property, and honor for all subjects of the sultan – non-Muslims as well as Muslims. Although the decree was aimed at formalizing certain rights of individuals and (civil) groups (implying the institution of "proto-citizenship"), it was filled with Islamic terminology and references to the Qur'an and the prophetic *Sunna*. The very first sentence stated the need for change in the state's institutions, which had been a widespread assumption – and discursive strategy – in all modernizing reforms since the late 18th century, and justified the reforms with reference to the "blessed *sharia*," which had not been obeyed properly, unlike earlier times, when "the orders of the Holy Qur'an and the rules of the *sharia* were observed perfectly." The decree then declared the sultan's order for a number of "new laws" (*kavanin-i cedide*) that would regulate the legal and financial system "relying on the help of the Almighty God and the spirit of the blessed prophet."[6]

Also, a Consultative Council prepared a protocol that stated the conditions upon which the *Tanzimat* Decree was built as follows:

a   the old disordered system has to be replaced by one based upon new laws,
b   these laws will be in accordance with the *sharia*,
c   they will be based on the inviolability of life, property, and honor as legal fundamentals,
d   they will be applicable to all Muslims and to the peoples of the *millet*s.[7]

Similarly, the decree itself specified the goals of the reform as follows:

1   "Security and protection of life, honor, dignity and property"
2   "Reforming the tax system"
3   "Reforming the levying of troops and duration of their service" (*Tanzimat Fermanı*, quoted in Alkan 2001: 449).

A basic presupposition in both the protocol and the decree was the idea that "the old disordered system has to be replaced by one based upon new laws," the necessity of a change, which was explicitly mentioned in article (a). What was implicit, however, was the direction of this change: the change in the governing structure would be towards the secular West. However, the claim that the "new laws" mentioned in the text and article (a) of the protocol would limit the authority and domain of the Islamic *sharia* and that of the sultan (Berkes 1998[1964]:

146) is highly exaggerated because the Decree, like any other *ferman*, was not binding for the sultan, nor was there any attempt at the institutionalization of law making in the European sense until 1876. (The first transfer of law from Europe occurred with the Commercial Code [*Ticaret Kanunnamesi*] adapted from the French Code in 1850.) Moreover, there was no direct indication of the authority of the *sharia* being undermined but rather the authors of the protocol and the decree explicitly referred to the *sharia* as the source of legitimization. However, it is also true that this had not been the standard procedure during the previous periods when the necessity for a law to be derived from *sharia* had been taken for granted and not mentioned in the legislative process, being part of the realm of "doxa" – a set of uncontested beliefs and ideas of which subjects are often unaware (Bourdieu 1984). Both this protocol and the charter itself positioned the *sharia* as a discursive object in a very high status – as a source of legitimacy in law making. However, its objectification would take a different form in later years, as its discursive status as the only source of legitimacy would shift to that of being in need of protection by the political-legal system. The Decree also maintained that laws would be produced by the councils of deliberation (*Mecalis-i Meşveret*) whose members would include the *Şeyhulislam*, the caliph's chief religious deputy, and other *ulema* as well as some "secular" bureaucrats. Though this was a new development, these councils were dominated by the religious establishment, and their decisions would still have to be approved by the Sultan. Moreover, as in the traditional practices of passing a law or issuing a decree, the proclamation of the decree was not accompanied by a *fatwa* (religious permit). Thus, the lack of a *fatwa* – as a discursive practice itself – does *not* signify (*contra* Berkes) the "first formal breach between 'the temporal' and 'the religious' in legislation" (Berkes 1998[1964]: 147); rather, the absence of a *fatwa* as a doxic element implied their "unity" as in previous periods. This is significant especially when we consider the fact that almost a century later secularist Mustafa Kemal and his friends *did* need a *fatwa* by the chief *Müfti* when they decided to abolish the Ottoman monarchy in 1922 (see Chapter 6).

Thus, the significance of these texts lies in the fact that they involved many Islamic elements in justifying an important step in political modernization. It is explicitly mentioned both in the decree and in article (b) that all new laws should be "in accordance with the *sharia*," acknowledging the superiority of Islamic law over the will of the sultan. Moreover, the basis of these proposed new laws, as stated in article (c), was again Islamic law. The principles of the "inviolability of life, property, and honor," together with that of "reason" and "generation," constitute what is known as the "five goals of *sharia*" (*maqâsid al-shari'ah*). According to Islamic *fiqh*, all rules and laws exist ultimately for the purpose of protecting these five elements of human life (Zaidan 1990). Because it is unthinkable that the *Tanzimat* statesmen who wrote the decree and its protocols could not have known one of the basic tenets of Islamic law, it is safe to conclude that they clearly wanted to draw on the unquestionable authority of the *sharia* itself to justify their actions and the reforms proposed by the royal decree.

A similar observation can be made for the subsequent Reform Edict (*Islahat Fermanı*), which was proclaimed on February 28, 1856, once again as a result of pressures by European countries to further extend the privileges of Christians living in Turkey, and granted important privileges to the non-Muslim subjects of the Empire.[8] This meant the creation of a whole new institution, modern *citizenship*, and a further step toward the formation of a modern state.[9] The edict included the reaffirmation of older rights and privileges as well as such further rights as guarantee of equal treatment to non-Muslims in matters of education, military service, the administration of justice, taxation, and appointments to governmental posts; the right of property ownership for foreigners; reform of judicial tribunals and penal and commercial codes; and representation for religious communities in the Supreme Council. The edict described the non-Muslim subjects of the empire as "the *emanet* trusted by the Almighty God," and granted equality for all subjects "who are related to each other with the sincere bonds of citizenship." There was, however, fewer references to the Islamic *sharia* in the edict compared to the *Tanzimat* Decree. Instead, the edict also employed another discourse: that of "catching up with contemporary civilization." It granted rights to non-Muslims with reference to the principle of the freedom of conscience, implying a further divergence from the classical Ottoman system, which was based exclusively on Islamic political philosophy (Davison 1963, I: 50). As a justification of the proposed regulations, it emphasized the need "to improve the conditions [of citizens] in accordance with the glory of our Sublime State and the eminent place it holds among the civilized nations." Therefore, the edict implied, as Berkes (1998[1964]: 153) observes, the coming of political, legal, religious, educational, and economic reforms; however, it was along with Islam that such notions as equality, freedom, material progress, and rationalism would form the "background" of these reforms (Mardin 2005).

What we see in these two reform projects, then, is an attempt at reforming bureaucracy and law in a modern style, which was made possible with the help of the discourse of renewing old institutions in accordance with the *sharia*. This technique of highlighting the inadequacy of the old institutions, including laws, and of the need to replace them with new ones would be repeated time and again in later reforms as well. Supported by these two reform projects, the political and economic developments that brought the Ottoman state closer to Europe in that era (see Davison 1963) paved the way for the first-ever constitution in Turkish history.

Debates on the first Constitution and parliament (1876)

The young Sultan Abdülhamid II came to power with a deal he made with the powerful Midhat Pasha, the leader of the *coup d'état* against Sultan Murad V, promising him to transition to a constitutional system. This would also be a proper response to European powers, including Russia, that were pressuring Istanbul for liberal (economic and political) reforms, which would open the Ottoman borders to European capitalists and further expand non-Muslims'

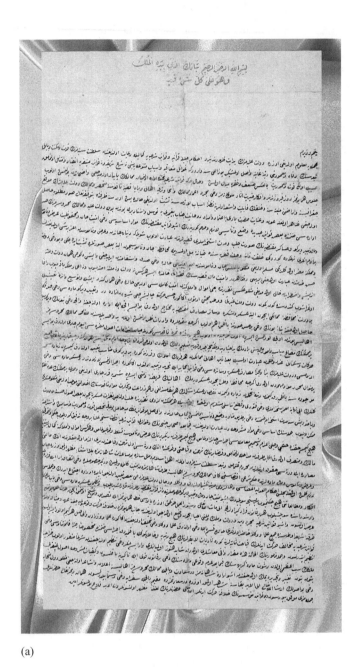

(a)

Figure 2.1 (a) The *Tanzimat* Decree (source: BOA, İrade, Mesail-i Mühimme, no. 24);
(b) The *Islahat* Decree (source: BOA, İrade, Meclis-i Mahsus, no. 245).

Note
I thank Ali Akyıldız for providing me with the illustrations.

(b)

Figure 2.1 Continued

economic and political privileges. The proclamation of the first Constitution (*Kanun-i Esasi*) and the institution of the first General Assembly (*Meclis-i Mebusan*) in 1876, which marked the beginning of the First *Meşrutiyet* era, were important developments for the modernization of the Ottoman state. For they signified a radical, though partial, change in the basis of the sovereignty of the state, assigning "the people" part of the ground for its legitimization and limiting the domain of the monarchy. In his royal decree, the sultan defined the purposes of the new General Assembly as follows:

> To guarantee the full enforcement of necessary laws; to make them *in accordance with the sharia* and the needs of the country and the people; to supervise the balance of the state's revenues and expenditures.[10]

Again we see here the same meta-discursive strategy employed in virtually all modernizing reforms in the pre-1924 era of Ottoman modernization. From the late 17th century on, most social, political, and legal changes were justified with reference to Islam. The theme of the congruence of the new laws with *sharia* had already been maintained in the *Tanzimat* decree. Here, too, there is a clear reference as a complementary discursive technique to the "implementation of the rules of the *sharia* in a more efficient way" in the institution of the new parliament, which marked a further step toward the formation of modern state. Within the intra-discursive realm, therefore, there is the relationship of what Foucault (1972) calls "presence" between the two texts: the discourse embodied in the earlier text(s) is present in the latter, too. Furthermore, within the sphere of inter-discursive relationships, although this discourse particle is seemingly characterized by a "relationship of opposition" to *secularism*, the strategy of helping Islam through new reforms involves a "relationship of complementarity" with the actual process of *modernization*, implying that in this period (unlike in the early 20th century) modernization was not necessarily based on secularism.

Moreover, Abdülhamid II was not happy with "secular" reforms; on the contrary, as mentioned above, he pursued a (domestic and foreign) policy of Islamic rapprochment during his reign. However, due to the delicate balance of power relations with European states and with the Young Ottomans, he had to co-operate with them in instituting the General Assembly and proclaiming the constitution, which he later abolished when he found the opportunity in 1878. The significance of this point lies in the fact that it was not only the reformers, but also the anti-Westernists (conservatives) themselves who resorted to the same discourse of serving Islam when attempting to promote modernizing changes in the political system.

A specific example illustrates this point even further. After the sultan's decree the issue was brought to the council of ministers and then to a larger convention where approximately two hundred persons, including ministers and the dignitaries of the civil, military, and *ulema* groups, discussed the institution of a parliament. Despite opposition by the majority of the high-ranking *ulema*, and the accusation that Midhat Pasha, the *sadrazam* (grand vizier) and a leading figure among the Young Ottomans who was called the "Father of the Constitution," behaved in an un-Islamic way by letting "infidel" (non-Muslim) deputies into the parliament, he succeeded in winning over the *ulema* (see Oktay 1991). He did this with the help of some members of the *ulema* themselves, the Constitutionalist members who justified the idea of a parliament with reference to the Qur'an. Among them, for example, Chief Justice (*Kadıasker*) Seyfeddin Efendi played an important role:

> Seyfeddin again explained at length, "by *akli* [rational] and *nakli* [textual] evidences," that *meşveret* [consultation, which he interpreted as "Parliament"] was "perfectly in accordance with Islam." To the delight of the constitutionalists who interpreted *meşveret* on their own way, Seyfeddin supported Midhat Pasha with a number of *hadith*s and the Qur'anic injunctions such as *washawir hum fi'l amri* and *wa ta'muru baynakum bi-ma'rufin* ("and consult with them upon the [conduct of] affairs" [III, 59]; and "and consult together in kindness" [LXV, 6]).[11]

In fact, this is another example of the situation we often see in which modernists apply the strategy of deriving justification for a reform (here, for a constitutional government) from the Qur'an by employing different discursive techniques, including the dissection of sacred texts; abstracting verses, sentences or even phrases from their context; and applying these to the solution of an emerging problem in terms of the lexicographical meaning of the selected phrases. Moreover, in the above quotation, Islam (or the Qur'an) still preserves its "object position" as being the primary source of legitimization for constitutional change. However, the verses that were cited by the speaker were being transformed through a brand new and, given the centuries-long tradition of *tafsir* (interpretation of the Qur'an) in Islam, unusual interpretation.[12] This is what I would like to call the "transformative technique," by which the meanings of verses as objects of knowledge were transformed. This technique would frequently be repeated and the new meanings attributed to these verses would thereby be reproduced in subsequent attempts at Westernizing political institutions and secularizing the political sphere. Furthermore, in the text the speaker put himself, and the other constitutionalists he represented, in a subject position where he had the authority to interpret the sacred text in an unusual way, and thus to bring change to a state institution in accordance with their political agenda. Finally, the non-discursive element that made Seyfeddin Efendi's discourse possible was the institutional position he occupied – his being the minister of justice and a member of the *ulema* class. His bureaucratic position and scholarly authority not only made it possible for him to perform this speech-act, but also to consolidate his subject position constituted in his speech by legitimizing his authority as an interpreter of the Qur'an based on his power/knowledge. This, then, is an instance of a situation where we can detect the interaction between discursive and non-discursive structures.

On the other hand, the fact that a member of the *ulema*, though a supporter of the constitutionalists, referred to the authority of the Qur'an and *hadith*s to prove the compatibility of a Western institution with Islam indicates again that important modernizing changes were often realized in both discursive and political spheres by resorting to Islam itself. In other words, we see in the extract above that the recurrent theme of the congruence of a reform with Islam appears again, though with a different technique. Although he encountered great opposition, Seyfeddin successfully integrated Islamic elements, which were supposed to belong to a different, even opposite, field of statements, into a discourse that he deliberately employed to make his case in the debates over the institution of parliament, lending life-saving support to Midhat and the constitutionalists.[13] This case is one of the early examples of a situation of the imbrication of power with knowledge where the "secularists," up until 1924, were often in desperate need of the support by the modernist *ulema* who were the only social group who could draw upon Islam for the justification of the secularizing reforms.

Constitutions and the formation of the modern state

The 1876 Constitution (Kanun-i Esasi)

The *Kanun-i Esasi* (Basic Law),[14] the first-ever constitution in Turkish history, included 119 articles and was more developed than the next (1921) constitution (*Teşkilat-ı Esasiye*), which was prepared in the midst of a war. The main discursive strategy employed in the former constitution was the inseparability of Islam and the caliph-sultan, and many of the articles contained in it expressed different techniques reflecting this main strategy. For example, the *Kanun-i Esasi* maintained first and foremost that both the sultanate and the caliphate belonged to the Ottoman dynasty (Article 3) and that the sultan was the protector of Islam and the ruler of the subjects of the Ottoman Empire (Article 4). The constitution also glorified the sultan, maintaining that "the blessed sultan himself is sacred and unaccountable" (Article 5). However, because Abdülhamid II abolished the constitution in 1878 and established himself as the absolute ruler until 1908, the constitution would later be amended by the ruling CUP in 1909 by adding a new sentence to the Article 3 requiring an oath by the sultan that he be loyal to the "blessed *sharia* and the rules of the Basic Law [the constitution]." Also, the Sultan's authority to abolish the Parliament (Article 73) was abrogated later in 1914 (see Chapter 4). Thus, the absolute ruler's authority was gradually limited through modifications of the articles of the constitution. In accordance with the earlier pattern, this was done by applying the same discursive strategy, "by reference to the *sharia*," as is evident in the requirement of the oath, which would also be in the name of God. Taking an oath in the name of God, which was required for both the sultan and deputies, and not only in this but also in the following two constitutions (1921, 1924) was a discursive practice that functioned as part of the larger strategy of seeking justification for a modern institution (the parliament) from Islam.

Moreover, the original version of the constitution itself limited the authority of the sultan and the *sharia*. For instance, the principle of the separation of powers was adopted, and separate sections were devoted to the executive branch,

‏﴿ ٤ ﴾

‏قانون اساسى

‏« ممالك دولت عثمانيه »

‏برنجى ماده   دولت عثمانيه ممالك وقطعات حاضره‌سى وايالات ممتازه‌يى محتوى وبكوجود اولمغله هيچ برزمانده هيچ برسببله تفريق قبول ايتمز

‏ايكنجى ماده   دولت عثمانيه‌نك پايتختى استانبول شهريدر وشهر مذكوره سائر بلاد عثمانيه‌دن آيرو اوله‌رق بركونه امتياز ومعافيتى يوقدر

‏اوچنجى ماده   سلطنت سنيهٔ عثمانيه خلافت كبراى اسلاميه‌يى حائز اوله‌رق سلاله آل عثماندن اصول قديمه‌سى وجهله اكبر اولاده‌مأندر

‏دردنجى ماده   ذات حضرت پادشاهى حسب الخلافه دين اسلامك حامى‌سى وبالجمله تبعهٔ عثمانيه‌نك حكمدار و پادشاهيدر

‏بشنجى ماده   ذات حضرت پادشاهينك نفس همايونى مقدس وغير مسؤلدر

‏التنجى ماده   سلاله آل عثمانك حقوق حريه واموال واملاك ذاتيه ومادام الحياة تخصيصات ماليه‌لرى تكافل عمومى تحتنده‌در

‏يدنجى ماده   وكلانك عزل و نصبى ورتبه و مناصب توجيهى ونشان اعطاسى وايالات ممتازه‌نك شرائط امتيازه‌لرينه توفقا اجراى توجيهاتى ومسكوكات ضربى وخطبه‌لرده نامنك ذكرى و دول اجنبيه ايله معاهدات عقدى و حرب وصلح اعلانى وقوهٔ بريه وبحريه‌نك قوماندانى وحركات عسكريه واحكام شرعيه وقانونيه‌نك اجراسى ودوائر اداره‌نك معاملاتنه متعلق نظامنامه‌لرك تنظيمى ومجازات قانونيه‌نك تخفيف وباعفوى ومجلس عموميك عقدو تعطيلى ولدى الاقتضا هيئت مبعوثانك اعضاسى يكيدن انتخاب اولنق شرطيله فسخى حقوق مقدسهٔ پادشاهى جمله‌سندندر

‏﴿ تبعهٔ دولت عثمانيه‌نك حقوق عموميه‌سى ﴾

‏سكزنجى ماده   دولت عثمانيه تابعيتنده بولنان افرادك جمله‌سنه هرقنغى دين (ومذهبدن)

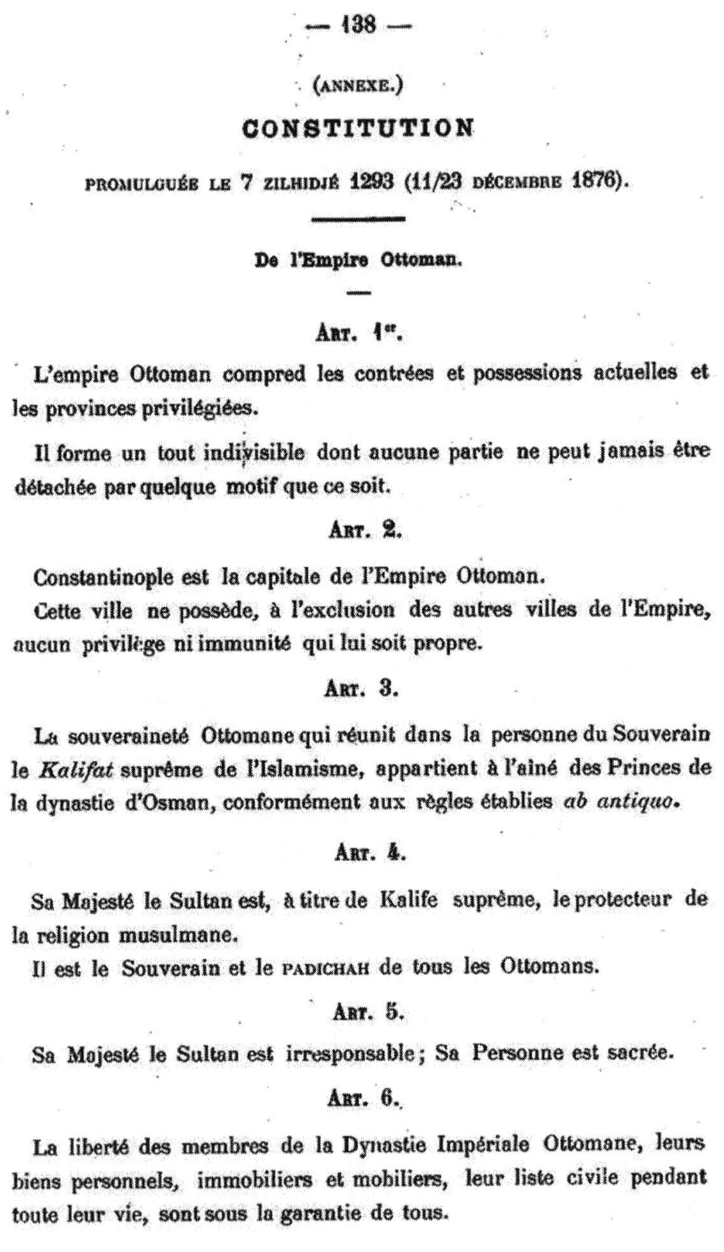

(ANNEXE.)

CONSTITUTION

PROMULGUÉE LE 7 ZILHIDJÉ 1293 (11/23 DÉCEMBRE 1876).

De l'Empire Ottoman.

ART. 1ᵉʳ.

L'empire Ottoman compred les contrées et possessions actuelles et les provinces privilégiées.

Il forme un tout indivisible dont aucune partie ne peut jamais être détachée par quelque motif que ce soit.

ART. 2.

Constantinople est la capitale de l'Empire Ottoman.

Cette ville ne possède, à l'exclusion des autres villes de l'Empire, aucun privilège ni immunité qui lui soit propre.

ART. 3.

La souveraineté Ottomane qui réunit dans la personne du Souverain le *Kalifat* suprême de l'Islamisme, appartient à l'aîné des Princes de la dynastie d'Osman, conformément aux règles établies *ab antiquo.*

ART. 4.

Sa Majesté le Sultan est, à titre de Kalife suprême, le protecteur de la religion musulmane.

Il est le Souverain et le PADICHAH de tous les Ottomans.

ART. 5.

Sa Majesté le Sultan est irresponsable; Sa Personne est sacrée.

ART. 6.

La liberté des membres de la Dynastie Impériale Ottomane, leurs biens personnels, immobiliers et mobiliers, leur liste civile pendant toute leur vie, sont sous la garantie de tous.

Figure 2.3 The official French translation of the 1876 Constitution (source: Ministere des affaires etrangeres (1877) *Documents diplomatiques*, Constantinople: Typographie et Lithographie Centrales, p. 138).

instituting a modern government with a prime minister, ministries, and a cabinet (Articles 27–38); to the legislation (Articles 42–80) restraining the power of the caliph-sultan; and to the jurisdiction (Articles 81–91), which involved a bifurcation in the legal system separating the religious courts (*Mehakim-i Şer'iyye*) from the administrative ones (*Mehakim-i Nizamiyye*). Bifurcation was also maintained in the education system, which involved, in higher education, both religious schools (*medreses*) and "secular" schools (*mektebs*). The adoption of the modern principle of the separation of powers, which had originally been put forward by Montesquieu (1834), was another important element of a modern state ("Constitutional Absolutism") characterized by the co-existence of what Max Weber (1947) calls bureaucratic or "legal-rational" and "traditional" authorities.

The constitution also maintained that the official language of the state was Turkish (Article 18), and that the state religion was Islam, but that all other beliefs and religions could also be freely practiced (Article 11). Furthermore, it was stated that "all subjects of the state have personal freedom" (Article 9), which included, in accordance with the earlier Reforms, the non-Muslims living in the Ottoman territory who were granted, together with Muslims, other rights such as equality before law (Article 17) and equality in public employment (Article 19). All these regulations amounted to the "constitutionalization" of citizenship, as anticipated in the earlier reform decrees, making the inhabitants of the empire both "subjects" of the sultan and "citizens" of the state at the same time – another indication of the hybridity of the Ottoman (traditional and legal-rational) political system.

Finally, freedom of the press (Article 12) also contributed to modernization, as both secular and religious ideas gained a ready soil for dissemination, and to the limitation of the sultan's sovereignty, especially considering the fact that the press was the main basis of the opposition and the basic tool that disseminated revolutionary ideas in the years leading up to 1908. That is why Abdülhamid II, after abolishing the parliament, censored the press and exiled the opposition leaders, who were also publishers of various newspapers, particularly in France and Macedonia. It is also why the CUP leaders added, after the 1908 Young Turk revolution, the phrase "with no censorship" to Article 12, though later (after 1913) they themselves would censor the press (Tanör 1995: 196).

The 1921 Constitution (Teşkilat-ı Esasiye)

The CUP controlled the Ottoman state from 1909 until the end of World War I, when the three leaders of the Committee, Enver Pasha, Cemal Pasha, and Talat Pasha, fled the country. But it was the CUP leaders, including also Kara Kemal, who organized the resistance movement in Anatolia by first founding an underground organization called the "Karakol," which would later turn into the "Anatolian Association of Defense of Rights," and appointed Mustafa Kemal, a mid-rank military officer and a relatively unknown member of the CUP, as its leader.[15] By the end of the war against Greece that ended in August 1922, Kemal had gradually managed to become the only leader of the movement with the help of other CUP leaders and by eliminating his rivals within the CUP (see Chapter 6 for a detailed discussion; see also Zürcher 1984).

In April 1920 the resistance proclaimed the opening of the Grand National Assembly in Ankara, which would be the center first of the movement and later of the Turkish Republic. The second constitution[16] was thus prepared during the war by the leadership of the Turkish nationalist movement headed by Mustafa Kemal. The same meta-discursive strategy of deriving legitimacy from Islam was applied throughout the text. In fact, Islam was even more emphasized here than the earlier texts we have analyzed, due to the war and the need for legitimization of the nationalist movement (initially an insurgency) and to organize the resistance against occupation. The 1921 constitution consisted only of 23 articles and was much less sophisticated compared to the earlier one. One of the reasons for this was the adoption of the principle of the unification of powers (Articles 2 and 3), including no separation between the executive and judicial branches, which also constituted an important difference between the two constitutions. The basic difference, however, was stated in the first article:

> Article 1 – Sovereignty belongs, with no restrictions and no conditions, to the nation...

Emphasizing this first article, some have claimed that this Constitution completed the change in the basis of sovereignty (e.g., Berkes 1998; Özbudun 1992; Tanör 1995). For them, it completely changed the ground of sovereignty by granting no authority to the caliph-sultan – even though the monarchy and the Caliphate had not yet been abolished – vesting it instead in the Grand National Assembly (GNA), which represented the "nation" – and, à la Rousseau, the "general will." Thus, in this narrative, the proclamation of the constitution was an important part of the process of secularization, as it curtailed the functions and power of the Caliphate in practice before it was officially ended in 1924. However, this shallow and teleological view ignores both the uncontested dominance of Islamic discourse in the rest of the text and the actual conditions upon which the new parliament and constitution were built. The constitution was proclaimed in a context in which Istanbul, the Ottoman capital, was under British occupation and the caliph-sultan and the FAP government were powerless – except that they had sent Mustafa Kemal to Anatolia and actively supported the resistance militarily and economically (Zürcher 1984, see also 1993: 141). Despite the fact that the palace had little political authority in Anatolia, the resistance leadership, including Kemal, and members of the Parliament were still loyal to the caliph-sultan until mid-1922: They conducted the "War of Independence" in the name of the caliph (Kara 2008: 24; Çarıklı 1967; Gologlu 2008a, 2008b; see also Chapter 6).

Still, the 1921 constitution did introduce a *partial* change in the basis of sovereignty, a process that had been started with earlier reforms and made explicit in the *Kanun-i Esasi*. The underlying discursive strategy in the former, unlike in the latter, which had emphasized the inseparability of the caliph-sultan and

Islam, was that the "nation" and Islam co-existed as the two bases of sovereignty. In this configuration, the GNA represented the "nation" and the caliph represented Islam – that is, the "nation" was not yet defined within an ethno-secular framework (cf. Yıldız 2001). The Islamic character of the new Turkish state would later be reinforced when the constitution was amended on the day the Republic was proclaimed (October 29, 1923) by adding a new article to it that read: "The religion of the state is Islam" (Article 2). Moreover, in the text "the nation" was not defined on the basis of (secular) ethnicity, nor did it exclude non-Turkish Muslims; the ethnic dimension would enter into the 1924 constitution, though not in an anti-religious framework.

However, the insertion of "the nation" into the constitution was still a step toward secularization, though this relatively radical change in practice was smoothly materialized at the discursive level. For the "strategic" discourse employed in the text was again that of serving Islam and the *sharia*. For instance, Article 7 regulated the GNA's authority on the "implementation of the rules of the *sharia*," as well as procedures for making, implementing and abolishing laws, and declaring war. The same article maintained that all laws and regulations must be "in accordance with the rules of *fikh* [Islamic jurisprudence] that are compatible with the needs of the time and practices of the people." This article is illustrative of the main theme of this study, as well as an important element of the secularist ideology in Turkey. As in the CUP's programs and Ziya Gökalp's discourse (see below), this text, too, employed two different discursive techniques at the same time – those of implementing the Islamic *sharia* and of addressing "the needs of the time and of the people." The discursive strategy underlying these techniques was the idea that Islam and modern civilization were compatible and that Islam only needed to accommodate modernity. It thus referred to Islam as a source of legitimization, but also limited its domain. It maintained that all laws and regulations would be in accordance with the Islamic *sharia insofar as* it was compatible with the requirements of modern life.[17] Within the intra-discursive realm, therefore, these two techniques, which were employed frequently not only by politicians but also by intellectuals, and not only by secularist actors, but by modernist Islamists, as well, share what Foucault calls a "relationship of complementarity" as part of the same discursive strategy.

The 1924 Constitution (Teşkilat-ı Esasiye)

After the independence movement defeated the Greeks, the GNA separated the Caliphate from the Sultanate and abolished the latter in November 1922. It signed the Lausanne peace treaty, in which Turkey's independence was recognized, with Western powers, including Greece, in July 1923. Then Mustafa Kemal and his newly founded party, the People's Party (PP), proclaimed the Republic on October 29, 1923; they also abolished the Caliphate and, together with it, the office of the *şeyhulislam* and all religious schools, on March 3, 1924 – though a Faculty of Theology and the Department of Religious Affairs were founded in their place – and sent the Ottoman dynasty into exile.

The 1924 constitution[18] was adopted six months after the declaration of the republic and only three weeks after the abolition of the Caliphate. By that time Mustafa Kemal had managed to become the leading power actor in Turkey, a status he later consolidated by first crushing the Kurdish opposition in 1925 and then completely eliminating his political rivals (former members of the CUP and his old friends) in 1926. His party, then the Republican People's Party, had established a single-party system and controlled every state institution in the country, including the GNA, by eliminating the pre-1923 opposition, and proclaimed a new Constitution in 1924. The basic difference between this Constitution and the earlier ones concerns the regime of the new state, which was stated in the very first article:

Article 1 – The State of Turkey is a Republic.[19]

This dictum was in fact a confirmation of the existing situation in which the monarchy had already been abolished and the republican regime declared by Mustafa Kemal and his party, but it also represented a break from the earlier regime, foreshadowing the upcoming radical secular reforms in the way of Westernization. However, as in the 1876 Constitution, it explicitly and immediately referred to Islam as the official religion of the State (Article 2).[20] The next article stated again that "sovereignty belongs, with no restrictions, to the nation," signifying its (partly) secular basis. These two articles revealed the underlying discursive strategy employed: that Islam and "the nation" co-existed as the two bases of state sovereignty, which implied, as in the previous (1921) constitution, that the state had not yet been completely secularized (this would be gradually achieved through amendments during the late 1920s and 1930s).

In addition, like the first constitution and unlike the second one, the 1924 constitution adopted the principle of the separation of powers (Articles 4–8), devoting separate sections to the legislature, which was said to belong to the GNA (Articles 9 through 30); the executive branch, which maintained the institution of a government and also – unlike the system of the first constitution – had a president as its head (Articles 31–52), rather than the office of the *sadrazam*; and the judiciary, abolishing the system of legal bifurcation (Articles 53–67). (Bifurcation in higher education had already ended on March 3, 1924 with the abolition of religious schools by the "Law of the Unification of Education.") Another indication of the incorporation of the Islamic elements in the Constitution is a familiar discursive practice: that the president and deputies would take their oaths "on [their] honor and in the name of God [*Vallahi*]," promising "loyalty to the principles of the republic" (Articles 38 and 16). Unlike the first Constitution, however, there was no mention of loyalty to "the rules of the *sharia*." Moreover, the clause "in the name of God" would, together with the Article 2, be removed in 1928 and replaced with "I promise." Similarly, another Islamic element, the clause "the application of the rules of the *sharia*" as one of the exclusive duties of the GNA (Article 26) was kept in the original version and removed in 1928.

Another important trend that went hand in hand with secularization emerged in the 1924 constitution: nationalization. Nationalism had already been underway since the Balkan War of 1912, which caused the loss of the Balkan lands occupied by Christian – and some Muslim – peoples, and accelerated with the struggle for national independence between 1919 and 1922. As a discursive strategy, "nationalization" contributed to the separation of "the nation" from Islam, implying the secularization of the new republican elite's mentality. The first *Teşkilat-ı Esasiye* of 1921 had used the word "Turkish state," and mentioned the "Grand National Assembly" as well as "the nation," but never specified their "Turkishness" due to the fact that "the nation" was not yet independent and the country was still under occupation. It was only after independence that the second *Teşkilat-ı Esasiye* (1924) could include articles on Turks, and qualified the name of the GNA as the *"Turkish* Grand National Assembly." It also stated that "the official language [of the Turkish State] is Turkish, and its capital is Ankara" (Article 2). Moreover, unlike the *Kanun-i Esasi* (1876), it exclusively talked about "the Turks" in the section devoted to individual rights, which was entitled "the Public Rights of Turks" (Articles 68–88). Article 88 maintained that "the inhabitants of Turkey, regardless of religion and race, are called Turks," which indicated the contrast between the cosmopolitanism of the first constitution that recognized the multiplicity of religions among the citizens and the nationalism of the last constitution that denied different ethnicities among the inhabitants of the country, which has been a problem to this day. In addition, as a further step toward secularism, the definition of citizenship on the basis of Turkishness stripped religion of its status as a basis for the classification of identity. In fact, this is another indication of the project of replacing religion with secular nationalism as the main source of identification for the Turkish people. Unlike the *Kanun-i Esasi*, in which the religious affiliation of "the citizens of the empire" were recognized, and they were granted autonomy accordingly, this constitution not only made nationality the basis of the categorization of citizens, which is an important strategy for instilling in them a "national consciousness," but also denied the diversity of nationalities of the country's inhabitants.

Therefore, this new discursive technique – of replacing Islam with ethnicity as the basis of identity and citizenship – that belonged to a non-Islamic (Western) framework is a reflection of the gradual influence of Western discourses, which became increasingly effective after the National Struggle, particularly after the abolition of the Caliphate in 1924. Moreover, defining citizenship on the basis of nationality constitutes another dimension of the project of state formation and nation building in modern Turkey; and this process was intensified with the incorporation in 1937 of nationalism into the Constitution as one of the basic principles of the state, which aimed to firmly establish the ethnosecular definition of Turkishness – and the exclusionary practices it implied (see Yıldız 2001).

A comparative analysis of these three constitutions indicates, therefore, that they played an important role in the process of Turkey's modernization. They were significant developments that both reflected and contributed to the transformation of an increasingly secularized state that gradually evolved into a nation-state. An important trend that we observe in the three constitutions is the fact that Islam, as in all other attempts at modernization in Turkey, was present as the fundamental source of justification – the main discursive strategy the modernizing actors employed in their projects. The secularist discourses employed in the modernizing reforms always incorporated various Islamic elements; and the underlying strategy was to better serve Islam by replacing the old institutions with new ones. We also observe, however, a discursive pattern that involves a gradual decrease in time in the extent to which Islamic elements were incorporated in the constitutions, though legitimization by Islam was always there: the three constitutions share a "relationship of presence," as the same discourse is present in all of them. Whereas the 1876 constitution gives priority to serving Islam and to the rights of the caliph-sultan, the constitution of 1924 involves much less reference to Islam and certainly no reference to the Caliphate in particular, because the institution had already been abolished. Also, it would later get rid of most of the Islamic elements in 1928 in a period in which the most radical secularizing reforms, from the famous "Hat Revolution" to the adoption of the Latin alphabet, took place. Finally, I have argued that these important texts not only contributed to the constitution of reality, but were also a reflection of it. The adoption of various articles in these constitutions, such as the institution of a modern government and bifurcation in the legal and educational systems in the constitution of 1876, and their unification in that of 1924, indicates the evolution of a discursive strategy, reflecting the changes in the contemporary socio-political conditions. However, I also argue that these texts instituted and implicated certain developments, as well, including the separation of powers in the constitutions of 1876 and 1924, their unification in the constitution of 1921, the institution of a Parliament and an election system in 1876, and various modifications in the constitutions that shaped reality in different ways. They were all justified with reference to the "exigencies of time" as well as to the Islamic *sharia*, the main discursive strategy applied in modernizing reforms.

Transformation of Islamic discourse in the public sphere

At this point, it might be useful to look at how this discursive strategy was employed by different political actors to legitimize and/or criticize existing political institutions and to reform the legal system during the First and Second Constitutional Periods. In this section, I will first analyze the relationship between the state elite (major actors in the government and opposition) and Islam. In particular, I will look at how the Ottoman Palace and then the CUP (the dominant group from 1908 to 1918), its predecessors and some of its opponents used Islamic discourse in their political projects. Then I will focus on the main ideologue of the CUP (and, later, of Kemalism), Ziya Gökalp, and his efforts to reform (secularize) the Islamic *sharia* through an Islamic discourse. Before doing that, I will discuss the important role played by the media in the secularization process.

Secularization and the press

The press was an important element of both the secularization of politics and culture *and* the dissemination of Islamic discourse in Ottoman society. It contributed to the development of secularism in at least two ways. First, it created a "language of journalism" that simplified, standardized and democratized political discourses, as well as the Turkish language writ large (Türköne 1991: 43ff.; Berkes 1998[1964]: 255ff.). The purging of Arabic and Persian words from (Ottoman) Turkish was one of the priorities of reform-minded, secularist intellectuals and statesmen (such as Ziya Gökalp and Kemal Atatürk), as many of these words were elements of the prevailing Islamic culture with their often religious connotations.[21] Second, the press made Islamic knowledge accessible to virtually everyone and thus changed its status as the "private property" of the *ulema*, opening up the domain of Islamic debates so "private individuals" (non-*ulema* intellectuals), too, found the opportunity to debate what were previously professional matters of the *ulema*, which, starting from the mid-19th century, diminished the ideological power of the *ulema* (*ilmiye*) and increased that of intellectuals and bureaucrats (*kalemiye*) – a process called "private capture" by Mardin (2005). Until the early 20th century, the *ulema* used to either look down upon the press or fear that this new, modern medium of written culture would disrupt traditional structures that were based upon verbal culture (for a discussion, see Mardin 1989: 220ff.). Their only – and highly effective – media for reaching out to the public and transmitting their knowledge were Friday sermons (*hutbe*) and conferences (*vaaz*) in mosques (Kara 2001: 84). Moreover, heavy censorship on the press decreased its effectiveness during the Hamidian period (Demirel 2007). However, with the 1908 revolution, when they realized the power of the press against the Hamidian regime that most of them resented, many of the *ulema* and Islamist intellectuals, in general, as well as more "secular" intellectuals and the CUP, embraced the new media as a tool for the dissemination of their ideas and influencing public opinion. This was facilitated by the proliferation of the press in the relatively liberal, post-revolutionary atmosphere (see Koloğlu 2010, I: 220–251). Moreover, many Islamists, such as the columnists of *Sırat-ı Müstakim* (which later became *Sebilürreşad*), a leading modernist-Islamist journal, saw the press as a useful instrument for modernization, which indicates the extent to which the secular mentality had penetrated into the Islamic society.[22]

The strategy of using the press as an instrument of modernization and "enlightenment" in Turkey would also be increasingly adopted by both the CUP and later Kemalism in the republican era with the publication of such journals as *Meşveret*, *Tanin*, *İkdam*, *Mizan* and *Işık* by the Young Turks and the *Vatan* newspaper by the Kemalist regime in the 1920s and 1930s, as well as the control and, when necessary, censorship of the dissident press. On the periphery of the Muslim world, too, the press was a highly effective tool used by both anti-Ottoman groups and Ottoman loyalists. Both Arab nationalists such as Sharif Hussein and European colonialists disseminated their propaganda via a number of newspapers and journals, such as the pro-British newspapers *Punjab Times* and *Akhbar-i Am* in India and *al-Jazeera al-Misriyya* and *al-Qahira* in Egypt, as well as such Arabist publications as Hussein's *al-Qibla*, and *al-Furat* and *al-Shahbaa'* newspapers (where Abdur-rahman al-Kawakibi [1855–1902], the father of Arab nationalism, published his articles) in Egypt (see Chapter 5). Two other Arab nationalist channels were *al-'Urwah al-Wuthqa* journal published in Paris by Muhammad Abduh (1849–1905) and Jamaluddin al-Afghani, and *al-Manar* published in Cairo for 35 years by Rashid Rida (1865–1935).

On the other hand, the press also offered a ready soil for the reproduction of Islamic discourses. It presented a valuable opportunity for Islamists who employed the printing press, newspapers, journals, and pamphlets to disseminate their ideas and to remedy the problem of the decline in their ideological power.[23] After 1908 they not only left the fear of the modern media behind, but attributed to it such "sacred" functions as being an instrument of the defense of Islam, a medium of establishing the "rapport of brotherhood" among Muslims all over the world, and a platform for the expression of the grievances of Islamic movements (see Türköne 1991: 53–54; Kara 2001: 80). Thus, in the press, the *ulema* found another medium of expressing their ideological power, in addition to weekly sermons and conferences, which continued to be what Mann (1986: 363) calls a major "ideological channel."[24] This notion is also closely connected with what Benedict Anderson (1991: 37–82) refers to as "print capitalism." In fact, such influential Islamist journals as *Beyanü'l-Hak*, *Sırat-ı Müstakim*, *Sebilürreşad*, *Volkan*, *Şura-yı Ümmet*, and *Tasavvuf*, published in Istanbul during the Second Constitutional Period, facilitated the formation of a common language and consolidated the idea of an "imagined community" – the *ummah* – for Islamists. A number of Turkist newspapers such as *Türk Yurdu* would later have the same function for nationalists, as well – in which case the Islamic *ummah* would first co-exist with, then gradually be replaced by the "Turkish nation." Though not with great success, the "language purification" movement would be promoted by such proponents of Turkish nationalism as Enver Pasha, the CUP leader, and Ziya Gökalp (1968) in the Second Constitutional Period, as well as by such republican statesmen as Kemal Atatürk and Nurullah Ataç and intellectuals such as Celal Nuri (1932) in the 1920s and 1930s, whereas many of the traditionalist and modernist Islamists and traditional statesmen such as Kazım Karabekir would oppose the language reform in both periods (see Levonian 1932; Yorulmaz 1995), which was facilitated by the expansion of the press. Finally, periodicals like *İctihad*, published by Abdullah Cevdet, *Islam* by Ziya Gökalp, and *Minber* by Mustafa Kemal and his friends, would provide a platform for secularists to disseminate their ideas – though they, too, employed a heavily Islamic discourse, as indicated by the titles of these publications.[25]

Thus, by the 1910s the status of the press had shifted from a disruptive force for Islam to a useful, even indispensable, instrument for Muslims. In sum, the press carried out a double function in the Ottoman modernization: it was both a secularizing force and a facilitator of the (re)production of Islamic discourses. This ambiguous impact of the press on the society, as indicated by the equally ambiguous appropriation of it by the *ulema*, therefore, implies the hybrid character of the secularization process in the late 19th and early 20th centuries in the Middle East, which is also visible in the discourses of leading politicians and intellectuals during this period.

The state elite, intellectuals, and Islam

The intensity of Islamic justification tended to increase as the secularization of state institutions deepened. As we shall see in Chapter 6, religious references and symbolism were used much more frequently by "secular" Turkish nationalists between 1920 and 1923 than in earlier periods. Nevertheless, Islamic justification of modernizing reforms was highly significant from the very beginning. As discussed above, the foundational texts of the *Tanzimat* reforms were full of Islamic references. The statesmen who launched these reforms, too, often resorted to religious justification, as in the case of Fuad Pasha (1815–1869), the grand vizier and one of the leading "*Tanzimat* pashas," who defended the adoption of European institutions, saying, "We need to quickly adopt these institutions, which are indispensible for the survival of any state in today's Europe, *to safeguard Islam*" (quoted in Akarlı 1978: 7). His friend and influential grand vizier Âli Pasha (1815–1871) iterated the same point: "If something undesirable happens to the sublime state, our religion and *ummah* will be left alone and unprotected, and our unity in peril" (ibid.: 12). The *Tanzimat* reformers often associated these changes with such paired concepts as "civilization and progress," "science and arts/crafts [*fünun*]," "law and order" and "liberty and consultation," all of which, they believed, were drawn from Islam (Çetinsaya 2001a: 56–71).

Sultan Abdülhamid II is already known for his policy of Islamic rapprochment in international politics, having emphasized the Caliphate much more than his predecessors (see Eraslan 1995; Çetinsaya 1999; see also Chapter 5). He also frequently resorted to Islam, in addition to creating modern institutions such as citizenship, to keep different religious and ethnic groups in unity and prevent the disintegration of his country. What is more interesting is that his opponents, both the Young Ottomans and the Young Turks, extensively used Islamic discourse to weaken his authority and justify their opposition to the caliph-sultan (see Hanioğlu 1981: 129–158; Mardin 1983a: 208; 1991a: 12). Thus, for example, while the sultan accused the CUP, which had organized an uprising in Resne (in the Balkans) in which Serbian militia also participated just before the 1908 revolution, of being "a supporter of Christianity and enemy of Islam," CUP supporters would label the sultan an "enemy of religion" whose attacks against the CUP, an "auspicious, reformist association," would harm Islam itself (Kara 2001: 38). Similarly, when the once-powerful Midhat Pasha (1822–1884) was imprisoned by Abdülhamid and labeled as the "renegade Pasha," he wrote a commentary – along the lines of the classical *tafsir* tradition – to the first chapter ("Fatiha") of the Qur'an, which was later published (in May 1910, after his death and the deportation of Abdülhamid) in *Hikmet*, a pro-CUP journal. Also, against the criticism that Midhat had behaved against the *sharia* by making anti-Islamic laws and helping the "infidels" enter parliament, the same journal introduced him as one of the Sufi leaders of the *Khalidi* order (a branch of the *Naqshibandi* order). Likewise, when in 1910 the CUP government was criticized by the *ulema*, particularly by the traditionalist journal *Beyanü'l-Hakk*, for asking people to donate the money that they had saved for pilgrimage, the Sacrifice Feast, and their alms to the Navy Foundation on the grounds that this request was against the *sharia*, the *Hikmet* journal declared the critics liars and hypocrites against the "noble *sharia*" (ibid.: 39). Finally, even the secularist intellectuals who were influenced by social Darwinist theories framed their evolutionary ideas (e.g., on the "backwardness" of the Muslim world) in Islamic terms in the late-19th and early 20th century (Doğan 2006).

Therefore, both the Palace and the opposition (and later the CUP) employed the same discursive strategy of positioning their opponents – or questioning and/ or confirming each others' positions – vis-à-vis Islam. The same strategy would be applied over and over again by all opposition groups, including such radically different figures as Derviş Vahdeti, a leading opponent of the CUP after 1908 and the alleged leader of failed counter-revolution – in the name of Islamic *sharia* – in 1909 (the March 31 Incident) who questioned the CUP leaders' loyalty to Islam (see Chapter 4) and Kemal Atatürk (then an officer in the "Action Army," which violently repressed the counter-revolution), who would later accuse his political opponents (some of whom were *ulema*) of harming the "true" Islam by mixing it with corrupt politics (see Chapter 6). He employed this strategy, as both Abdülhamid and the CUP had done before, to silence the opposition while at the same time maintaining the legitimacy of his own autocratic rule.

Moreover, in the Hamidian era, both sides tried to gain the support of the *ulema*: Sultan Abdülhamid granted titles and governmental posts to some (lower) *ulema* and Sufis, particularly some of the *Naqshibandi* sheiks, while also repressing and exiling others. Many of the higher *ulema* and Sufi groups (from among all three major Sufi orders: *Naqshibandis*, *Mevlevis*, and *Bektashis*) increasingly supported the opposition, and later the CUP when it came to power, which paralleled – but could not stop – the gradual decline in their political and ideological power (Bein 2006; Kara 2006). For the opposition, forming an alliance with the carriers of Islamic knowledge and tradition via personal and organizational networks, as a non-discursive practice, was a crucial strategy that greatly increased their political capital. A consequence of this alliance between the *ulema* and Sufis, on one hand, and the opposition movement, on the other, is the fact that "Islamism" as a politico-intellectual movement of the Second Constitutional Period was very much influenced by the Young Ottomans of the Hamidian era. Thus, for example, Namık Kemal and Ali Suavi, two leading Young Ottomans, were regarded as predecessors of the Islamists of the post-Hamidian era by Islamists themselves, in addition to being the pioneers of nationalism and even secularism in Turkey (Kara 2001: 24).

Similarly, the CUP was careful to maintain close connections with some of the *ulema* and Islamist intellectuals, who in turn put their expertise at the CUP's service. A well-known example of this is a "Declaration" published in August 1909 by *Şeyhülislam* Mehmed Sahib aimed at legitimizing the re-instituted constitution and the privileges it provided for non-Muslims and condemning the leaders of the March 31 Incident – calling them "those who waged war against God and the Prophet." The declaration triggered a great debate in the newly free press. Employing the familiar discursive strategy of drawing on sacred texts, the *şeyhülislam*, who was officially the caliph's representative in the government, also specifically praised the CUP, calling it the "Savior/Saved Group of God's warriors" (*Fırka-ı Naciye-i Mücahidin*), a direct reference to a well-known *hadith*, though the context of the *hadith* was strictly spiritual. He also cited several verses from the Qur'an and other *hadith*s – all in Arabic – to justify CUP policies in general and the violent repression of the March 31 Incident in particular. Legitimization of the new regime and CUP policies via Islamic discourse was not confined to the religious-governmental office of the *şeyhülislam*, however; many of the "civil" *ulema* and intellectuals published articles and pamphlets in the same manner. For instance, a Sufi-oriented Islamist journal, *Tasavvuf*, cited several *hadith*s that mentioned "a blessed group from within the Islamic *ummah* that will protect and restore their religion," claiming that the *hadith*s referred to the CUP. Similarly, a leading member of the anti-CUP *ulema*, Ömer Ziyaeddin Efendi (who also wrote a pamphlet on the Caliphate – see Chapter 4), wrote a 95-page pamphlet to prove that "the Constitution and each and every article and paragraph in it are compatible with the *sharia*," citing many verses and *hadith*s. A pro-CUP intellectual by the name of Doktor Hazık cited in his book, titled *Religion and Liberty*, many verses and *hadith*s, interpreting them – with no attention to their contexts – as advocating the restriction of the sultan's authority on the basis of popular sovereignty. Finally, intellectual Edhem Nejad cited the verse, "And man shall have nothing but what he strives for" (Qur'an 53/39), as advocating "individual entrepreneurship" (*teşebbüs-i şahsi*) and liberal economic policies, though the textual context of the verse is clearly about individuals being responsible for their actions in the *afterlife* due to the free will granted to humans by God. The social context of these interpretations was one of constitutionalism and liberal economic policies carried out by the CUP-dominated government, especially between 1909 and 1913.[26] These examples make clear, therefore, that the common meta-discursive strategy of deriving justification from the Islamic tradition – primarily via the strategy of freely interpreting the sacred texts – resulted in the unintended consequence of transforming the Islamic discourse itself, along with the secularization of political institutions during the First and Second Constitutional Periods (see also Chapter 4).

Let us now analyze in detail another example: Ziya Gökalp's intellectual-political project of the "Social Methodology of Islamic Jurisprudence," which was a major attempt at secularizing Islamic political and legal theory on the basis of a synthesis between Islamic *fiqh* and Durkheimian sociology.

Ziya Gökalp: Islamic discourse and modern sociology

An examination of the ideas of Ziya Gökalp's (1876–1924), one of the most important intellectual figures during the process of Ottoman-Turkish moderniza-tion, is a useful way of identifying the trend of the employment of Islamic dis-course in the ambiguous course of secularization in the Middle East.[27] For Gökalp was highly influential on the political, as well as intellectual, elite of the modernizing Turkey, both before and – shortly – after the foundation of the new republic. Many of his ideas were materialized in the policies adopted by the CUP that dominated the state from the 1908 revolution to the end of World War I, and by the Republican People's Party (RPP), which founded the new republic and ruled the country for its first 27 years. Although he never took a high political position, Gökalp influenced leading politicians (and the youth) as a public intel-lectual and ideologue, and his ideas formed the background of the programs of the CUP and RPP, and were incorporated into the 1924 constitution, as well (cf. Berkes 1959; Yağcıoğlu 1992; Davison 1998; Zürcher 2005). He is generally recognized as the leading ideologue and "father" of modern Turkish nationalism as outlined in his *Turkification, Islamization, Modernization* (1918a) and espe-cially in *The Principles of Turkism* (1968[1923]).

Gökalp is also the founder of sociology in Turkey. He followed Durkheim not only in the content and orientation of his own ideas, but also in establishing soci-ology as a discipline – he also translated Durkheim's major works into Ottoman Turkish. His interest in Durkheimian sociology and Comtean positivism coin-cided with CUP government's positivistic ideology (Kabakçı 2006) that found sociology – and particularly ethnographic studies – useful in terms of "saving" the state and modernizing society.[28] Gökalp thus emphasized sociology's signifi-cance within the context of the transformation of Ottoman society and con-sidered it indispensable for his intellectual-political project based on Turkish nationalism, which was also congruent with the CUP's Turkist cultural policy and, later, with Kemalist nationalism (Heyd 1950).[29]

Referred to (though incorrectly) as the "only systematic thinker Turkey has produced in the twentieth century" by one of his biographers (Parla 1985: 1), Gökalp is significant for his purely intellectual contributions, as well. He was born in Diyarbakır, a cosmopolitan urban center with Arab, Persian, and Turkish cultural influences felt during the 19th century, and raised in a rich intellectual environment where there was a lively debate among the late Ottoman intellectu-als that centered on the problem of the conflict between Islam and modern Western civilization. At that time there were three main currents of thought: those who argued for the compatibility of modernity with the principles of Islam and for the preservation of the traditional values (the Islamists); those who urged for a complete Westernization and rejection of the traditional order (secularists or "Westernists"); and those who longed for the romantic ideal of ethnic unity of Turks and preached a return to the pre-Islamic era (the "Turkists") (Akçura 1976[1904]). The problem of the harmonization of modernity with Islam was also Gökalp's main concern. He joined none of the above currents at the beginning, but followed a middle path, being influenced by, and subsequently influencing, all three of them (Gökalp 1918a; see also Davison 2006). Later, however, he chose Turkism and even became the intellectual leader of that ideology (Gökalp 1968[1923]).

Gökalp's ultimate aim was to synthesize Islam with Turkish nationalism on the one hand and with Western modernity on the other. This he expressed in his famous motto, "Turkification, Islamization, and Modernization" that is also the title of his major work (Gökalp 1918a) – an idea he borrowed from Dr. Hüseyinzade Ali (1864–1942) and Yusuf Akçura (1876–1935), members of the CUP and two of the founders of Turkish nationalism.[30] This evolutionist and assimilationist form of Turkism proposed that religion and the Ottoman past should be integrated into the modern Turkish identity. This idea of synthesis also constituted the background of Gökalp's crucial distinction between "culture" (*hars*) and "civilization" (*medeniyet*), which he borrowed from German philosophy, particularly Herder. He argued that a viable solution for Turkey's crisis could be found in integrating its *culture*, which would be a mixture of Islam and Turkish nationalism, into the (universal) civilization represented by modern Europe. Hence the major argument in his eclectic work: Islam, which constituted the basis of Turkish culture, could be adjusted to the exigencies of modern civilization. Here, his basic assumption was that Islam and (secular) modernity could be accommodated.[31]

Gökalp's attempt at transcending the conflict between the sacred and the profane can be examined by focusing on his views on two important issues: the debate over the social bases of Islamic law, and the Caliphate. These are the major problematic areas where he tried to solve the problem of the adaptation of Turkish society, based on an Islamic tradition, to the modern West. The evolution of his views on these issues follows the trajectory of social and political secularization in Turkey. Regarding the relationship between religion and state, he focused on the first issue between 1914 and 1917, then turned to the question of the Caliphate with the separation of the monarchy from the Caliphate in 1922 (to be discussed in Chapter 6). His emphasis on the compatibility of Islam and modernity had an important discursive function: justifying his radical project of secularizing Islamic law.

"The social methodology of jurisprudence"

Gökalp presented his views on Islamic law in a series of articles under the title "The Social Methodology of Jurisprudence" (my translation of *İctimai Usul-i Fıkıh*), published in *İslam Mecmuası* (*The Journal of Islam*), a bi-monthly journal that he founded in 1914 and issued until late 1918. The journal was sponsored by the CUP and was the main medium through which Gökalp's ideas, as well as those of the CUP, were disseminated (Berkes 1959: 318). Moreover, he published some unsigned articles possibly in co-operation with Halim Sabit, the editor of the journal, who also wrote several articles expounding Gökalp's writings on religion, which are clearer and more developed than Gökalp's ideas (see Sabit 1914a, 1914b). Gökalp's discussion of Islamic law aimed, as will be made clear below, to secularize it. In an early article (1914a) he distinguished between the two bases of Islamic *sharia* – revelation and society:

> The *shar'* [religion] determines the goodness or badness of actions using two criteria. The first is the *nass* [text] and the second is *örf* [*mores*]. The *nass* is expressed in the Book [the Qur'an] and in the *Sunna* [of the Prophet], while the *örf* is the conscience of the society expressed in the actual conduct and living of the community. [According to Islamic jurisprudence] under necessity *örf* may take the place of *nass*.... Therefore, on the one hand, *fikh* [Islamic jurisprudence] is based on revelation, and, on the other hand, on society. In other words, Islamic *sharia* is both divine and social.... The social principles of *fikh*, on the other hand, are subject to transformations taking place in the forms and structures of society, and hence are subject to changes along with society.
>
> (pp. 194–195)

Here Gökalp employed a crucial discursive strategy that laid the foundation for his entire project of transforming the bases of Islamic *fikh*: that of elevating the status of its "social basis" (*örf*) and making it equal to revelation/text (*nass*). He then used a number of discursive techniques to insert secular elements into the foundations of Islamic jurisprudence. One technique he employed involved identifying the sources of *fikh* as "traditional (*nakli*) *sharia*" and "social *sharia*" (p. 196), which was a novel idea that implied the historicization of religion – a major discursive strategy frequently employed by secularists. By doing this, he maintained the significance of social change in terms of its impact on religious practices and understanding of the sacred texts. However, he justified this (secular) claim religiously by arguing that social change and evolution were a manifestation of the "will of God" (ibid.).

In his next article (Gökalp 1914b), he made the same secular distinction, and added a further technique, arguing that the rules of *sharia* regarding worldly matters should be derived from existing socio-historical conditions and should merely be "a derivative of the *örf*." Gökalp ironically based this unusual interpretation on a Qur'anic verse that symbolically compares Islam to the "Paradise tree,"[32] a discursive technique that illustrates the nature of his (and other secularists') strategic intervention into traditional/mainstream Islamic theology – i.e., what I call their "theological engineering":

> Yes, the Islamic *sharia* is the tree of *Tuba*, which has its branches in the heavens, but the *raison d'être* of this tree is to live in an earthly environment and atmosphere, and to get its air, heat, and light from the social *örf* to satisfy civil needs.... It is evident, therefore, that there must be social fundamentals as well as dogmatic/textual fundamentals of the *fikh*.... Therefore, is it not possible to say that *the* nass *relative to* temporal *affairs and*

social life is a derivative of the örf? When we accept social determinism and the uniformity of social phenomena as the expression of the way of God, it becomes natural to regard this divine *Sunna* as the basis of the *nass* relating to social life.

(1914b: 198–199; my italics)

As discursive techniques, these arguments imply two important steps for the secularization of law. First, the distinction between the *nass* and the *örf* is not only maintained, but also emphasized. In the mainstream/traditional understanding of *fikh*, the text (the Qur'an and the *hadith*s) has an uncontestable priority over *mores*, and the *örf* is always marginal compared to the *nass* (İsmail Hakkı 1914a; Zaidan 1990). *Örf* is only one of the many secondary sources of jurisprudence, whereas in Gökalp's discourse the mainstream classification of the sources of the *sharia* was ignored and the new distinction was given a fundamental role. With this further intervention he turned the traditional hierarchy between the two sources of law upside down, but still justified it with reference to the Qur'an itself.

This strategy overall was perhaps a solution found by a concerned intellectual under the impact of the accelerated pace of social change, which created a need to make adjustments in the face of new developments. A leading member of the secularist camp, Gökalp exemplified the fact that the relationship between Islam and modernity was one of accommodation (as opposed to confrontation). Unlike Islamists, however, his main strategy was based on adapting Islam to emerging (modern) social conditions by reforming it via an instrumentally employed Islamic discourse. When the classical understanding of Islamic jurisprudence, in which the basic criteria of the *sharia* are derived from the texts rather than social practices, became an impediment in the way of adapting religion to new social conditions, he turned to highlighting the previously relatively insignificant part of the *sharia*, *örf*. Note, however, that the conceptual tool (*örf*) he used for "secular purposes" was still derived from the arsenal of the terminology of the *sharia*. Moreover, this unusual intervention – as an "invention of tradition" – was done, as we have observed before, with reference to the Qur'an itself.

The discursive strategy he employed here included three different techniques. First, the allegory of the *Tuba* tree was a direct reference to a verse in the Qur'an that describes Islam as a religion with both worldly and heavenly dimensions, which is the opposite of Gökalp's secular interpretation. Second, he interpreted the worldly dimension of Islam, again contrary to the traditional understanding, so as to limit the space of the transcendental texts in favor of social-historical context. For he first neutralized and then reversed the priority of *nass* over *örf*, and maintained that, with regard to "temporal affairs and social life the *nass* [should be] a derivative of the *örf*." Finally, Gökalp argued that this transformation in the understanding of *fikh* was necessary because changing social realities required it, and thus it helped Islamic law to better adapt to new conditions (1914b: 196), and that sociology could help *fikh* in this regard (1914b: 199). Coupled with Gökalp's secularizing policy recommendations that were taken up by the CUP government (such as bringing religious education [*medreses*], Sufi monasteries and lodges, and religious courts under state control and opening a secular appeals court in 1913), the practical consequences of his "social methodology of jurisprudence," based on a sociological interpretation of Islam, also indicate that his discourse regarding the social bases of Islamic law was of an *instrumental* nature and was consciously employed by Gökalp as part of his "theological engineering" in order to adapt religion to modernity – not necessarily to get rid of it completely – by "secularizing" it (see also Chapter 6).

The social context of these texts was one of heated intellectual debates over the relationship between Islam and modernity, and of political struggles over the future of the Ottoman state. The relationship between religion and society was a hot topic of debate among Ottoman intellectuals after the 1908 Revolution. Gökalp's ideas regarding *fikh* and the relationship between *nass* and *örf* were extensively criticized and disputed by both modernist and traditionalist intellectuals, especially from the point of view of the classical Islamic sciences (see İsmail Hakkı 1914a, 1914b; Said Halim Paşa 2000[1920]). However "weak" they may have been intellectually, Gökalp's ideas were part of a political, as well as intellectual, project that eventually won over his critics with the help of the government and political actors of the time (see also Erdem 2003, Ch. 2). The CUP's policy of interfering with religion was justified, however, as an attempt to revitalize Islam and a means of substituting true religion for superstition.

On the other hand, we see here, in terms of the formal properties of the discourse, the "relationship of presence" (Foucault 1972) between the two texts discussed above: the ideas put forward in the former were taken up and developed in the latter. Moreover, his strategy involved a reconstruction of Islamic jurisprudence as an object of knowledge in these texts with the following techniques: the *sharia* was reclassified, its components (*nass* and *örf*) were re-evaluated and had new meanings attached to them (for example, "temporal affairs" were transformed into the "divine *Sunna*" [way of God]), and, finally, the hierarchy between the two was first disturbed and then re-established in a new light, putting *örf* over *nass*. In other words, speaking from the subject position of an author(ity), Gökalp disturbed the conventional conceptual hierarchy by changing the relative positions of the objects (sacred texts and *mores*) of his discourse.[33] Another technique Gökalp employed was the introduction of a new concept, that of *İctimai Usul-i Fıkıh* (the social methodology of jurisprudence), which helped him in secularizing the nature of the Islamic law by transforming its basis to a social one. Furthermore, with his overall strategy, the author created a new subject position in the texts for himself and for others (the *ulema*) by claiming that only sociologists (or social scientists) should be concerned with those aspects of the *sharia* that applied to this world, and that the authority of the traditional *ulema* should be limited to other-worldly matters (1914b: 199). Finally, we see a familiar technique that involved the incorporation into his "Islamic" discourse of another, complementary, discourse: that of the "exigencies of life." The author wrote at the end of the first article that the "social fundamentals" of *fikh* "have to adapt themselves in accordance with the necessities of life" (1914a: 196).

Thus, Gökalp's project of "social methodology of jurisprudence" as a discursive strategy indicates a general political strategy: the adaptation of Islam to modernity by reforming its principles and institutions. The implicit presupposition in his proposal, which was based on his version of Durkheimian social theory, was that religion should function to maintain social order as simply one of the institutions constituting society, rather than as the fundamental frame of reference. This type of theological engineering (i.e., the strategy of adaptation) was based on a functionalist view of religion in society, and an evolutionist view of history, where religion was supposed to evolve, together with other institutional "parts" of society, and to adapt to new historical conditions in order to contribute to social cohesion and the better functioning of society, which was assumed to be a compact whole (see Durkheim 1915, 1947; Parsons 1951).[34]

These "background factors" are further indicated by another strategy Gökalp (1915a) employed in which he described "primitive" and "organic" societies and compared them in terms of the status of religion in each of these social formations. He argued that in primitive societies religion functioned as the source of both politics and culture whereas in organic social formations it was limited only to the spiritual domain and did not "extend over those institutions which are of a worldly and secular character." He added that "one of the greatest tasks of religion in organic society is to leave other institutions free within their own spheres" (pp. 185–186).[35]

This discursive strategy entailed the construction of religion in two different ways in two types of society: Religion played a fundamental role in the "primitive" society while occupying a much less significant place in the "organic" one. The impact of Durkheimian sociology is evident in the text not only with the designation of societies as "primitive" and "organic" as a discursive technique, but also with the rather mechanical understanding of the place of religion in these societies, as well as the functionalism of the whole text. The underlying discourse this technique was based upon was again that of the "exigencies of (modern) life," which was explicitly mentioned in the text ("adapting themselves to the expediencies of life"). In accordance with this discourse and with his earlier arguments, Gökalp made it explicit that the scope of religion was rather limited in the modern, "organic" society: Being only one of many institutions in society, it lives side-by-side with them, without encroaching onto their domains. What remained implicit, however, was the unspoken consequence of this change in the status of religion: secularization.

On the other hand, no matter how easy it was to maintain this idea theoretically, it became harder to justify it when faced with concrete reality. Thus, Gökalp tried to reconcile the theory with the reality – that of the absence of the idea of secularism in Islamic societies. Facing the problem of maintaining the dichotomy between the sacred and the profane, Gökalp resorted to another technique, pointing (in a footnote) to the absence in Islamic terminology of a word for the concept of "profane" as an antonym for "sacred," and solved the problem by introducing the Arabic word *zanim* for it (Gökalp 1915a), which apparently proved inadequate for making his case.

Therefore, Gökalp (1915b) turned to Islamic terminology to find a pair of concepts suitable for this task. He found it in the distinction between piety (*diyanet*) and jurisprudence (*kaza*) in *fikh*:

> The reason for our lagging behind other nations in religious heedfulness lies in the backwardness of our judicial methods and practices in spite of the utmost perfection of the principles of our religion. It is because of confusion of the two things that those who are dissatisfied with judicial conditions become unfaithful to religion in the long run. Whenever these two things are mixed, each becomes harmful to the other, because their respective foundations serve different purposes. When *mufti*s issue their religious judgments and *kadi*s perform their judicial functions separately both will succeed in maintaining the purity and integrity of their own fields.
>
> (p. 201)

Gökalp attempted here at a secular separation between religion and law by exploiting the already existing distinction between piety and jurisprudence in Islam, using them as main elements of his new discursive technique. Although this distinction in the *fikh* did not precisely correspond to that of the sacred and the profane, as jurisprudence was included within religion and *kadi*s were sometimes also *mufti*s, it could serve as a further step toward secularization. For, by employing these two concepts as "technical tools," he made a new distinction between the spiritual aspects of Islam and its judicial functions, where the latter were attributed to the state, which was in charge of worldly affairs. As a discursive technique, it implied that Gökalp instrumentally employed an Islamic discourse, deriving elements from it in order to legitimize his own (secularizing) project.

His discursive strategy would soon be put into action by the CUP leadership (of which Gökalp was a political advisor) that wanted to further secularize the state by removing the office of the *şeyhülislam* (*Meşihat*) from the cabinet and completely curbing its authority. It was created as a state institution in the 15th century and mostly functioned as the religious office that justified (and, theoretically, reviewed) the sultans' policies to make them compatible with the *sharia*. During the modern period (after the adoption of the cabinet system and the *Tanzimat* reforms in 1839), the *şeyhülislam* was still part of the government, enjoying some degree of political and ideological power. After 1871, however, he lost his control over "non-religious" courts (*Mehakim-i Nizamiye*) when they were attached to the Ministry of Justice, creating a bifurcation in the judiciary. Though he was tightly controlled by the powerful Sultan Abdülhamid II, the *şeyhülislam* continued to control the *medrese* system during his reign (1876–1909) (Kramers 1993; Yakut 2005; see Chapter 4 for a detailed discussion).

After the 1908 Revolution, the Unionists lowered the status of his office by first making it a ministry in the cabinet in 1911 and then removing it from the cabinet and completely abrogating its authority over the judiciary and education in 1917 (Koçer 1970: 22). This last move by the CUP was based on a report written by Gökalp (1917a), who suggested that religious courts should be administered by the Ministry of Justice and higher education by the Ministry of Education, instead of the *Meşihat* – a recommendation the CUP immediately followed through a law passed on March 12, 1917. In his report, based on the same distinction between piety (*diyanet*) and jurisprudence (*kaza*) in Islamic legal literature, Gökalp claimed that the former included the principles related to faith, worship, and morality, whereas the latter pertained to social, economic, and political affairs. Thus, he concluded, as a religious institution *par excellence*, the *şeyhülislam*'s office should be concerned with the former part of religion and have no authority over the latter, which would be taken care of by the Ministry of Justice (1915b: 48–49). This "strategic intervention" into Islamic *fiqh* by Gökalp as part of his "theological engineering" aimed to secularize the Ottoman political system by instrumentally employing an Islamic discourse, which involved as its main 'discursive technique' exploiting an already-existing distinction for secular(ist) purposes. It also exemplified how the instrumentalist discourse was – almost immediately – put into action thanks to Gökalp's political-ideological position (his being an influential advisor to the CUP), which constituted the non-discursive element in this interaction between discourse and action. Also, as mentioned, his entire project was accompanied by the discursive strategy of claiming the compatibility of modern civilization with Islamic culture.

Compatibility of Islam and modernity

Gökalp's above-mentioned "artificial" distinction had a further implication in terms of the relationship between Islam and secularism. An important presupposition in his argument was the idea that Muslims had lagged behind Westerners in terms not only of technology (which was a widespread view at that time), but also of religious life. This is significant because it implied the need for a change in the conduct of religious life and in religious institutions such as the *Meşihat* and the Caliphate (perhaps also in the nature of religion itself) in accordance with the discourse of abolishing the old order and establishing a new one, which was prevalent among secularists at that time. At the same time, however, Gökalp maintained the perfection of Islamic principles, and blamed the *ulema* and officials who were in charge of the judicial affairs. In this way he implied, however paradoxically, that making such a distinction and placing different parts of the "old" order (of religion) in their proper positions would help Islam to restore the original order of its early years.

Gökalp later clarified his view on the relationship between state and religion in two reports he wrote for the 1916 convention of the Union and Progress Party. In the first report (Gökalp 1916), which was entirely included in the party program (see Yağcıoğlu 1992), he argued that two opposite views on modernization and Westernization had emerged in the CUP's 1916 convention: "the zealots of Europeanism" and "the zealots of scholasticism" – those who believed that the principles of Islam should be dropped altogether versus those who argued that the Western civilization ought to be rejected completely. Both assumed that the principles of Islam and those of modern civilization were not compatible. The Westernists and the *Tanzimat* reformers represented the first view, and the Islamists the second. Based on the discourse of the compatibility of Islam with modernity, Gökalp criticized both views, arguing instead that it was not possible, in terms of the functioning of society, either to drop religion entirely or "dispense with the necessities of contemporary civilization." He also added that Islam, "based on reason ... and sociology," was not in conflict with modernity.[36]

In the second report (Gökalp 1917b, also referred to above), he made a comparison of Christianity and Islam, arguing again for the compatibility of Islam with modern civilization. Since Islam, unlike Christianity, included politics within religion – i.e., there was no separation between religious and secular authority (the sacred and the profane) – for him there would be no conflict between these two in the "Islamic state," and hence it was already a modern state. He argued that because "Islam had brought state, law, and court into the realm of the sacred" there was no duality of the sacred and the profane, and thus "there is only one government in Islam ... the judicial government of the caliphs" (Gökalp 1917a: 218, 221). However, the complete reversal of his position on the separation of religion and state after the abolition of the Ottoman monarchy by Mustafa Kemal in 1922, which rendered the caliph powerless, reveals the instrumental nature of his discourse.[37]

Furthermore, Gökalp explained the emergence of the modern state initially in the West, rather than in the Islamic world, with reference to the similarities between Islam and Protestantism or, rather, the putative integration of Islamic principles into Protestantism, and the imitation of the former by the latter rejecting "all institutions which had existed in [Catholic] Christianity as contrary to the principles of Islam." Protestantism for him was merely an "Islamicized form of Christianity":

> [In] the history of Christianity, we see that, following the Crusades, a new movement started in Europe which was then acquainted with Islamic culture. This movement aimed at imitating Islamic civilization and religion. It penetrated Europe with time, and finally culminated in Protestantism as a new religion entirely in contradistinction to the traditional principles of Christianity. This new religion rejected ... all institutions which had existed in Christianity as contrary to the principles of Islam. Are we not justified if we look at this religion as a more or less Islamicized form of Christianity?
>
> (1917a: 222)

In both reports, therefore, Gökalp employed two discursive strategies: maintaining that there was no conflict between the state and religion in Islamic civilization, and that the principles of Islam and those of the modern civilization were compatible. An element of the latter was based on the view that Islam did not conflict with modern science – a widespread belief held by virtually all intellectuals and politicians, secularists and Islamists alike. By "science" Gökalp meant the social sciences, in which he had an unlimited Comtean faith, particularly in sociology as the supreme positive science that could identify problems and help find their solutions (Berkes 1959: 22). The implicit presupposition here was similar to the conceptual background of earlier attempts at modernization – i.e., the need for change in the existing system – and could be seen in the integration of the discourse of "the exigencies of contemporary civilization," parallel to that of the "necessities of life," into mainstream Islamic discourse.

Gökalp was also assigned by the UPP to prepare a memorandum to be submitted to the government, in which he essentially suggested the same ideas as in his reports. He also proposed, as mentioned earlier, the transfer of the *sharia* courts from the office of the *şeyhulislam* to the administration of the Ministry of Justice, and of the schools under the *Evkaf* administration to the Ministry of Education. These proposals were accepted in the 1916 party convention (see Yağcıoğlu 1992). These were definite steps toward the secularization of religious courts and schools. Although with the fall of UPP government the old regime of the courts was restored by the last sultan, Mehmed Vahideddin VI, much more radical reforms were to be started and the process of secularization would be furthered by Mustafa Kemal with the complete abolishment of the *sharia* courts, the office of the *şeyhulislam* and the Caliphate. However, there is nothing but sympathy toward Islam in his account: the discourse Gökalp employed was that of a member of the Islamic *ummah* who was proud of his religion; and there was an emphasis on the virtues shared by Muslims, virtues that arose from the principles of Islam. In short, there was no implication of getting rid of Islam to adapt to "secular civilization." Rather, his account of the relationship between Islam and modernity implied that since the form of government in Islam was already that of the modern state, either there was no need for secularization or the Islamic state was already a secular one. However, it was not so easy to argue for the second option, given the basic argument that the "secular" institutions (state and law) were already included in the religion; for this he had to resolve the problem of the status of the Caliphate in Islam, which I will discuss in Chapter 6.

3 The Caliphate question

Historical and discursive context

Introduction

The second part of this study, containing this and the subsequent three chapters, analyzes the data specifically regarding the Caliphate. These four chapters are organized in a comparative fashion so as to compare and contrast different groups of power actors, as well as different periods and geographical regions. As discussed in the introductory chapter, I identify three main groups of actors according to the way they define and envision the future of the Caliphate: traditionalists, modernists, and secularists (as explained below). The present chapter introduces the historical and discursive context of this discussion by presenting first a brief history of the Caliphate from its beginning (632 CE) to its abolition (1924), and then a description of the actors (politicians, bureaucrats, journalists, intellectuals, and the *ulema*) who make up the three politico-ideological groups. The second part of this chapter starts with an introduction of the 20 different discursive strategies they employed in the political and discursive struggles over the Caliphate during the Second Constitutional Period up to the abolition of the Caliphate (1908–1924). This is followed by a comparative analysis of the *common* discursive strategies and "techniques" employed by all three groups. Chapter 4 focuses on the earlier phase of this process (roughly between 1908 and 1916), in which the CUP (Unionists) deposed the caliph-sultan and curbed his political authority. Here I also compare the discourses of the traditionalist and modernist Islamists that helped shape the status of the Caliphate in its center (Turkey). In Chapter 5, which covers the second phase (1914–1920), I compare and contrast the discourses of Arab nationalists and pro-Ottoman actors in the context of European colonialism on the caliphal periphery. Chapter 6 focuses on the last phase (1919–1924), in which secularist actors dominated in the center as a result of their struggle with pro-Caliphate (modernist) Islamists and ultimately brought about the end of this 1,300-year old Islamic institution. The secularists had to transform the Caliphate into a purely "spiritual" status before abolishing it, though it had combined political and religious authority when it was established in 632.

A brief history of the Caliphate

The history of the (Sunni) Caliphate reveals ongoing power struggles between Muslim leaders, vying for legitimacy and authority, as well as the overall significance of this institution and its legacy, which was heavily felt in the late Ottoman era, in terms of the relationship between Islam and politics. It reveals the shifting tensions between different figures and different political and/or religious groups, such as the Umayyads and Abbasids, throughout its history. "Caliph" is the title given to the politico-religious leaders of the Muslim society after the death of Prophet Muhammad in 632 CE. Literally meaning "successor," the term also has religious connotations, as it is mentioned in the Qur'an several times to refer to human beings as the representatives of God (2:30; 6:165; 7:69, 74; 10:14, 73; 27:62; 35:39; 38:26). The term is also used in the *hadith*s (sayings) of the Prophet, which are the second most important epistemological and legal source in the Islamic tradition, in its technical sense. In this tradition, "Caliph" has been used to refer to the leader as the representative of (i) the Prophet, (ii) God, and (iii) the Muslim community, which is itself seen in turn as God's representative. The second sense (God's representative) is, however, rare. It has largely been rejected by Islamic scholars due to its implication of divine nature, therefore denying the Caliph absolute authority.

Since the Qur'an does not contain any prescriptions about a specific political system, but rather emphasizes some general principles (such as justice, consultation, and preventing oppression), the theory of the Caliphate is derived from the practices of the Muslim society during the 50-year period (610–660 CE) of the leadership of Prophet Muhammad and the first four caliphs (Abu Bakr, Omar, Othman, and Ali), who are regarded as the "best of mankind after the prophets," especially by Sunni Muslims. The classical theory of the Caliphate, which is found in the "*Ahkam al-Sultaniyyah*" ("The Rules of Government") literature that first emerged in the 11th century (e.g., al-Māwardī 1994; al-'Amidi 1992; al-Taftazānī 1989; Ibn Qayyim 1953; Ibn Khaldūn 1957), defines the institution as "a succession of the Prophet, and as such, a general leadership/authority on matters of religion and the world" (al-Taftazānī 1989, V: 232).[1] It asserts that the caliph should be just, knowledgeable, and virtuous, and must be either elected by the *Ahl al-hal wa al-'aqd* (literally, "those who tie and untie"; terminologically, the committee in charge of the election of the caliph, consisting of several prominent members of the Muslim community) or appointed by the previous caliph, and then approved by the larger community by receiving its *bay'ah* (consent). This early literature often emphasizes the legitimacy and significance of the first four "Rightly Guided Caliphs" while maintaining the illegitimacy of the Umayyad Caliphate (661–750). Later, the Abbasid dynasty (751–1258) was usually regarded as legitimate by the *ulema*, and when the Islamic world was in chaos in the 11th and 13th centuries as a result of the Buwayhi and Mongolian invasions, respectively, some scholars viewed military force as a legitimate source of authority for the caliph (e.g., al-Ghazali 2001: 175ff.; Ibn Khaldūn 1958, I: 391ff.; see also Arnold 1965[1924]; Avcı 1998).

The history of the Caliphate started with the election of Abu Bakr (r. 632–634) with the consent of the Companions (the Prophet's friends), which then became a requirement for the legitimacy of later caliphs in the Sunni world. The Shia scholars require (i) appointment by divine will and (ii) heredity (being a descendant of the Prophet), arguing that Ali (the fourth caliph, who himself gave his consent to the succession of Abu Bakr) should have been elected as the first caliph. Unlike Sunnis, the Shia also believe that the leader of the Islamic community (*Imam*) can only be a descendant of the Prophet through Ali, the Prophet's cousin and son-in-law, and his wife Fatima, and that the *Imam* is infallible (Cleveland 2000: 34–35; cf. Crone and Hinds 2003).

At the end of his Caliphate, Abu Bakr designated his heir to be Omar (r. 634–644), who then received the Companions' consent; but this was later used by many rulers as the basis of the hereditary system of the transmission of authority (Sultanate), though scholars usually see it as nomination (which requires consent), rather than appointment. Omar, who expanded the territory of the Muslim state (*Dar al-Islam*) to all of the Arabian Peninsula and Iran, appointed a six-person committee as the *Ahl al-hal wa al-'aqd*, consisting of the most prominent Companions, who then elected Othman as the third caliph. Though he expanded the borders of the state and its power greatly during his reign, Othman (r. 644–656) also faced tribal discontent and opposition, which gradually escalated into a crisis that resulted in his murder by insurgents. The new caliph, Ali (r. 656–661), was also murdered after a chaotic reign characterized by civil war due to opposition by the Umayyad family (of which Othman was a member), whose leader, Muawiya, then came to power when Ali voluntarily stepped down from the post (Ra'if 1999).

The founding father of the Umayyad dynasty (661–750), Muawiya moved the center of the state from Karbala (the stronghold of Ali's supporters) to Damascus, and further expanded the Islamic Empire's territory. He used the title "Caliph of Allah" to ensure unconditional loyalty and legitimize the dynastic rule that he created by appointing his son, Yazid, as his heir and a committee to "elect" him. However, most of the Umayyad years were characterized by a legitimation crisis and continuous uprisings supported by the majority of (both Shia and Sunni) *ulema*, especially in Iraq, which culminated in the dynasty's overthrow by the Abbasid family, who were the relatives of the Prophet and Ali (see 'Atwan 1986). The second Abbasid caliph, Mansur, maintained dynastic rule after he founded the city of Baghdad and established it as his capital (754). Unlike the Umayyads, however, the Abbasids enjoyed a great deal of legitimacy due to their relation to the Prophet and the widespread opposition to Umayyad rule. Some Abbasids, too, kept the title "Caliph of Allah," but they also created a state system based on a large bureaucracy and a standing army. During the Abbasid era, caliphs' names were always mentioned at Friday sermons as a symbol of authority; at times when they were weak, some sultans (temporal rulers) added their own names to the caliph's to be mentioned at sermons, reflecting the shifting balance of power. Caliphs also wore the Prophet's cloak, carried his sword and minted coins as symbols of their authority. After two centuries of strong state rule, the Abbasids lost their power when the Shia Buwayhis invaded Baghdad and took control of the Caliphate (945). However, they appointed a new caliph and supported him instead of abolishing the Abbasid Caliphate, due to the high degree of ideological power it enjoyed – though this decreased gradually in the following decades. In 1055 the Seljuki Turks defeated the Buwayhis, invaded Iraq and Egypt, and took over the Caliphate. The Abbasid Caliph declared the Seljuk leader Tugrul Bey as the "partner of the Caliph" and the "leader of the East and West" and retained symbolic authority, leaving the administration of the Caliphate's entire territory to him. In return, the caliph was shown much respect, his lost prestige thus restored. Until the collapse of the Abbasid dynasty in 1258 at the hands of the Mongols, at times when the central authority was weak, many states emerged within the *Dar al-Islam*, most of them recognizing the relative authority of the Caliph, through which they gained legitimacy. Among these states, of major importance were the Murabits (1086–1146), the Muwahhids (1133–1252) and the Hafsids (1249–1277) in West Africa and Iberia, which, like most Eastern Muslim dynasties in Asia, recognized the Abbasid Caliphate, whereas the Shia Fatimids in North Africa (909–1171) and the "Andalusian Caliphate" (929–1031), founded in Iberia by survivors from the Umayyad dynasty, were rival Caliphates during the Abbasid era. When the Mongols invaded Baghdad, destroyed the city, and massacred its residents, including the Abbasid family, the Caliphate ended (1258). Three years later, however, when the Mamluks in Egypt defeated the Mongols, Abu al-Qasim Ahmad, the last Abbasid caliph's uncle, was invited to Egypt and declared caliph. Under Mamluk rule, the Abbasid Caliphate largely retained a symbolic position, but also, contrary to the claims of Arnold (1965[1924]: 98), enjoyed some degree of ideological power, as newly founded Muslim states all over the Islamic world, including the Ottomans, almost always sought the caliph's official recognition to legitimize their rule (Avcı 1998: 545). The Egyptian Abbasid Caliphate lasted for more than two centuries until the defeat of the Mamluks by the Ottoman Empire in 1517 (Arnold 1965[1924]: 55–69, 77–106; Ashmawi 1990: 206–234; Avcı 1998: 540–542; Barthold 1912: 263–301).

The Ottomans and the Caliphate

After a period of hiatus in which the Caliphate remained largely politically ineffective under the Mamluks, it regained its true power with the Ottoman rulers, who re-united the political and religious forms of power that had formed the historical basis for the classical theory of the Caliphate. When the Ottomans emerged in the 14th century as a strong state in southwest Asia, there were many Muslim rulers who called themselves "caliph" in *Dar al-Islam*. According to many historical sources, Ottoman sultans, too, had used this title at least since Murad II (r. 1421–1451),[2] though the transfer of the "Great Caliphate" is famously attributed to Selim I (r. 1512–1520) (D'Ohsson 1790, I: 269–270; see also Ata Bey 1876; Anonymous 1883; Namık Kemal 1884; Tansel 1969). According to this contested narrative, when Selim I conquered Egypt in 1517, in addition to the title of the "servant of the two holy cities" (Mecca and Medina), he also assumed the title of caliph with a ceremony that took place in Istanbul, where the last Abbasid caliph, Mutawakkil 'Alallah III (or Muhammad XII), transferred his title to the Ottoman sultan. However, since no contemporary source mentions this ceremony, some historians (e.g., Barthold 1912; Nallino 1917; Arnold 1965[1924]; İnalcık 1970; Karpat 2001) reject the possibility of the assumption of the Caliphate by Selim, arguing that this event was invented by 18th-century historian D'Ohsson, whose work was the first to mention it, and that Ottoman politicians and intellectuals took up this idea to strengthen the Ottoman Caliphate.[3] However, the debate, which is narrowly focused on whether this ceremony actually took place, does not address the real question, for a ceremony is not legally required for the transfer of the Caliphate, nor had such an event ever occurred before Selim I (Özcan 1998b: 546). Even the critics of the Ottoman caliphs, such as the Arab nationalists of the early 20th century, never attempted to delegitimize it with reference to the lack of a ceremony, but on the question of descent. As we shall discuss below, the real legal issue for the Ottomans was the problem of ethnic background: the alleged requirement that the caliph must be a member of one of the Quraysh tribes, which is mentioned in a *hadith* of the Prophet. Ottoman jurists and intellectuals, such as the historian and Grand Vizier Lütfi Pasha (see Gibb 1962), drawing on 'Ayni, Jurjani, and Baqillani's interpretation of this *hadith,* justified the absence of this condition in the Ottoman dynasty on the grounds that this requirement was limited to the first four caliphs.[4] Lütfi Pasha argued that if a ruler combines in himself the principle of the "maintenance of faith with justice, command of the good and prohibition of evil, and general leadership, then he is a sultan who has a just claim to the application of the names of *imam, khalifa, wali, amir* without contradiction" (quoted in Gibb 1962: 290).[5] Moreover, starting from Selim I, Ottoman sultans sometimes used the title of the "Great Caliph" (*Halife-i Uzma*) in official documents; some of them also asked in their letters to other Muslims rulers that they be recognized as the true caliph of the Muslim world in an attempt to revive the political power of the Caliphate (see Barthold 1912: 322; Reid 1967: 268–272; Mughul 1987: 88; Özcan 1997: 12).[6]

The argument that Ottoman sultans claimed this title only when the empire was weak (e.g., Akgün 2006) is contradicted by several pieces of historical evidence. For example, the powerful sultan Mehmed the Conquerer (r. 1451–1481) was referred to as "caliph" by contemporary sources. Similarly, Süleyman the Lawgiver (r. 1520–1566), in whose reign the Ottoman Empire was at the peak of its military and political power, was one of the sultans who most frequently used this title (İnalcık 1958: 70). In fact, in his letters to less powerful rulers he demanded recognition of his claim to the Caliphate (Gökbilgin 1992: 96–99; El-Moudden 1995b). On the other hand, various Turkish princes in Central Asia expressed their loyalty to the Ottoman caliph-sultans asking for a *berat* (certificate) as a sign of recognition by them during the 16th, 17th and 18th centuries (Yalçınkaya 1997: 222). Some princes in the Indian subcontinent, too, recognized the Ottoman caliph as their suzerain in the 18th century (İnalcık 1988: 77).[7]

Those scholars who assert that Selim I did not assume the Caliphate also argue that the first Ottoman claim for this title was the Küçük Kaynarca Treaty signed in 1774 between the Russian and Ottoman empires. However, this treaty should be seen as the first document indicating the *recognition* of the Ottoman Caliphate by a *Western* power. This common, though false, claim by many historians was actually a product of British propaganda against the Ottoman Caliphate disseminated by Orientalists and colonial administrations in the second half of the 19th century (see Özcan 1998b: 546–547). Most Ottoman sultans, both before and after 1774, did use the titles of "caliph" and "The Shadow of God on Earth," and justified their policies with reference to the Caliphate in their relations with Western and Eastern states (Syed Mahmud 1921: 77; İnalcık 1970: 320). Also, the Ottoman sultan could not have claimed this title if his predecessors had not assumed it before. Both the Ottoman claim to, and the recognition by Western powers of, the Caliphate intensified in the 19th century – both before and during the reign of Abdülhamid II – parallel to the increasing colonization of the Muslim world by Western powers. The Ottomans also staunchly defended the Caliphate against the "internal" challenges posed by Arab dissidents, such as the Wahhabis, who were supported by the influential Saudi family during the 19th century (İnalcık 1988: 72–73).

During the Reform (*Tanzimat*) era (1839–1876), the Caliphate underwent a transformation process as its authority was limited by the Reform Decree, declared under pressure by European powers, which brought equality for non-Muslims in the Empire on the basis of modern citizenship. Later, the first Constitution, proclaimed in 1876 (Articles 3, 4) stated that the sultan, as caliph, is the leader of all Muslims and, as emperor, ruler of all Ottoman citizens. The sultan's authority was thus divided into two parts, where his authority as caliph was reduced to the religious/spiritual domain. In reality, however, sultans, particularly Abdülhamid II, also made claims for *political* authority over Muslims outside the empire on the basis of the Caliphate (Türköne 1991: 186–191; Özcan 1998b: 547; see also Buzpınar 2005). During the second half of the 19th century, as expressed in official documents and intellectuals' writings (e.g., Cevdet Pasha 1960), the legitimacy of the Ottoman Caliphate was derived from its being (i) a manifestation of divine will, (ii) inherited from ancestors, (iii) based on the political and military power of the Ottoman dynasty, and (iv) the consent (*biat*) of the *ulema*, bureaucrats, and the general (Muslim) population. Thus, Şemseddin Sami, a Hamidian-era intellectual and lexicographer, defined the Caliphate as the "succession of our Lord, the last Prophet (pbuh), and the *imamate* and leadership of all people of Islam, and the sacred duty to protect the Islamic *sharia*; the Great Caliphate" (1899–1900, I: 585).

Abdülhamid II, as a devout Muslim who had received religious education, tried to revitalize the Muslim *ummah* and strengthen the Islamic character of the Ottoman state as well as to further centralize it. He thus used the Caliphate as a crucial instrument for political and administrative unity in domestic politics, and as an ideological and political source of power in international relations against the pressures of European powers (Hourani 1983: 105–107), for it had a great potential to mobilize large numbers of Muslims, particularly in the colonies of Britain, France, and Italy (Öke 1999; Smith 1974: 21). Determined to strengthen the Caliphate, Abdülhamid II sponsored the publication of many newspapers, pamphlets, and books in Britain, France, Germany, Egypt, India and Turkey in support of the Ottoman Caliphate, especially against the British propaganda that aimed to divide (by helping Arab provinces to secede from the Ottoman Empire), or at least weaken, the "Sublime State," in the last quarter of the 19th century (Buzpınar 2002, 2004; see also Chapter 5). He also politically and financially supported Islamic organizations (such as mosques and certain Sufi orders) in order to maintain the loyalty of the Muslim population to the state center (Eraslan 1995; Koloğlu 1998).

During the Second Constitutional era (1908–1918), the CUP that had deposed Abdülhamid II realized the Caliphate's international prestige and potential power and therefore tried to preserve it. At the same time, they tried – successfully – to weaken it in domestic politics in order to solidify the new constitutional system. Particularly after the failed counter-revolution, allegedly supported by Abdülhamid II, against the CUP government (the "March 31 Incident"), which then led to the dethroning of the Sultan, the Caliph's authority was further limited (e.g., his right to abolish the Parliament was curtailed) with constitutional amendments in 1909 (see Chapter 4). Among the intellectuals, politicians, and bureaucrats, those who defended the traditional, all-powerful status of the caliph were gradually weakened, while modernists, who argued that the Caliphate is only a representative form of government and that the caliph, as the representative of the "people," was not superior to them and should be held accountable for his actions, gained more power and influence with the help of the CUP government, which ruled the country in the last decade of the empire. On the other hand, the magnitude of the support that came from the Muslim world, and India in particular, made CUP leaders aware that the Caliphate could still be influential in international politics. When World War I started, the CUP decided to join the Central Powers against the Allies, relying on, among other things, the potential impact of the Caliphate on Muslims. However, Caliph Mehmed V's declaration of *jihad* was not as effective as expected, because Britain and France had already taken care of the Muslim leaders and institutions with potential for social mobilization against the Allies in their colonies. Furthermore, Britain encouraged the sharif of Mecca to revolt against the Ottomans, promising both independence and the institution of an Arab Caliphate – a problem that had been created by the British in the mid-19th century for the Ottoman Caliphate. Sharif Hussein started the Arab revolt in 1916, eventually gaining independence from the empire, and laid claim to the Caliphate in 1924 (Teitelbaum 1998). But the British denied their earlier promise due to the emergence of the "Caliphate Movement" in India that aimed to revive the Ottoman Caliphate (see below), and later because of successful resistance by the Turkish nationalist movement, led by Mustafa Kemal, against the occupation of Turkey by the Allies after World War I (Buzpınar 2002, 2005).

However, the Caliphate (and the Ottoman dynasty) emerged as a problem for Mustafa Kemal and his supporters when the British government invited the governments in both Istanbul and Ankara in Turkey to peace negotiations in Lausanne. The Turkish parliament in Ankara then separated the sultanate from the Caliphate and, after a heated debate, abolished the former on November 1, 1922. Mehmed VI, the sultan-caliph, was deposed and his nephew, Abdülmecid Efendi, was elected as the new caliph with no real political authority. However, the Caliphate's high prestige both within Turkey and in the wider Muslim world proved too much for Kemal, who was reluctant to share his power, particularly after the Republic was declared on October 29, 1923, when Abdülmecid Efendi sought to have political influence over Muslim governments and found support both inside and outside Turkey. Growing tensions between Istanbul and Ankara were deepened when the two leaders of Indian Muslims, Aga Khan and Amir Ali, sent a letter from London to the Turkish government (and the press) in support of the Caliphate, which Kemal Pasha and Prime Minister Ismet Pasha interpreted as an intervention by the British government into Turkey's internal affairs, accusing the Caliph of plotting to revive the Ottoman dynasty. The government then decided to abolish the Caliphate and, despite harsh criticism by the Istanbul media – which was not controlled by the government – and from all over the Muslim world, managed to do so relatively easily in the parliament, where the strong opposition group had been eliminated with the 1923 elections. In this process, Turkish secularists used an intense Islamic discourse to justify their radical move (see Chapter 6). The Caliphate's abolition came as a shock to most Muslims, especially those in India, who did not recognize the Turkish parliament's decision, and demanded that it be reversed. When the Turkish government stood firm, however, several attempts were made to revive the Caliphate outside Turkey. Many leaders, including the former caliphs in exile, Mehmed VI and Abdülmecid Efendi, and King Yusuf of Morocco, Sharif Hussein of Mecca, King Amanullah Khan of Afghanistan, Yahya, the (Shia) Imam of Yemen, etc. all wanted the Caliphate. None of these leaders, however, gained recognition from each other or the general public, except for Abdülmecid Efendi, who, however, lacked the necessary economic and political power as a poor exile in Switzerland and then France. In 1926 a "Caliphate Congress" convened in Cairo, where the Egyptian king, Fuad, tried to have himself elected as caliph, but failed due to negative reactions from Muslim leaders. In 1931, a second congress was held in Jerusalem, where Abdülmecid Efendi tried to gain recognition, but was unsuccessful due to political conflicts amongst the participants. After the congress was over, he was gradually forgotten (see Yıldırım 2004). Today, the Caliphate is still on the agendas of some political groups, such as the Muslim Brotherhood,[8] and of some militant groups, such as *al-Qaida*[9] and *Hizb ut-Tahrir*, as well as some more marginal ones in Pakistan (e.g., *Jamiat-ul Ansar, Tanzim-i Islami*, and *Lashkar-e Tayyiba*) and Bangladesh (*Khilafat Majlis*).[10]

Actors: three groups on three continents

The main focus of this study is on the period between 1908 and 1924, when the Caliphate was gradually weakened and came to an end with the collapse of the

Ottoman Empire following World War I. As mentioned above, I have identified three main groups of power actors who operated in Asia, Africa, and Europe in the struggle over the Caliphate: traditionalists, modernists, and secularists. *Traditionalists* (or traditionalist Islamists) were those who defined the Caliphate with a dual status, i.e., possessing both spiritual and temporal authority – and who tried to keep it in Istanbul. They were mostly traditional *ulema* (Islamic scholars), as well as some bureaucrats with middle-class backgrounds and a high level of (religious) education. *Modernist Islamists* were those who tried to transform the Caliphate into a modern, "secular" government, confining its authority to temporal affairs of the state. They were mostly *ulema* and journalists (as well as some bureaucrats) with strong religious backgrounds in terms of education and cultural milieu. A few modernists, such as Rashid Rida, were Arab nationalists who, naturally, did not want to keep the Caliphate in Istanbul, but pursued the idea of an Arab caliphate. Finally, the *secularists* were those who tried to transform the Caliphate into a purely spiritual authority, like the Papacy of the Catholic world, to render it a ceremonial and politically powerless office. They were mostly politicians, journalists, and holders of bureaucratic positions (as well as a few *ulema*) with some Western-style education and middle-class backgrounds. This last group seized state power in Turkey in 1922 and abolished the Caliphate (March 3, 1924). (Table 3.1 presents a glossary of names with a summary of the information on the actors' social backgrounds. Their detailed biographies are given in the endnotes and in subsequent chapters where their views and actions are discussed.)

Below is a description of the three groups, organized according to the center/periphery division of the Caliphate's geography. The horizontal distinction transcends the political-ideological (group) boundaries, as traditionalists and modernists were against each other in the center but worked together against Arab nationalism on the periphery. Furthermore, the set of issues surrounding the fate of the Caliphate substantially differs in the two regions. For this reason, it makes more sense to discuss traditionalists, modernists, and secularists in the caliphal center, and pro-Ottoman actors (including both traditionalists and modernists) and anti-Ottoman ones (Arab nationalists) on the periphery.

The caliphal center

In the central territory of the Caliphate, Turkey (Istanbul, in particular), the early politico-legal developments regarding the Caliphate (and the *Meşihat*) was accompanied by a discursive struggle between traditionalists and modernists. Both groups were represented primarily by the Ottoman *ulema*, who sought to increase their power by playing a crucial role (both for and against the Caliphate) as the sole carriers of Islamic knowledge and tradition, the most important source of justification in Middle Eastern politics at the time. I therefore assume that the *ulema*'s role and discourses were significant in terms of both intellectual *and* political change in the early 20th century – though they would lose all their power after 1924. This argument is not unfamiliar in the relevant literature.

Table 3.1 Glossary of names of the principal power actors

Name	Group[1]	Background	Country/province
Abdur-raziq, Ali (1888–1966)	S	Member of the *ulema*	EGYPT
Abdünnafi Efendi (?–after 1936)	S	Member of the *ulema*, bureaucrat, lawyer	TURKEY
Ali Fahmi Muhammad (1870–1926)	M	Army officer, activist (founder and leader of *al-Khizb al-Watani*, Egyptian nationalist party)	EGYPT
Ansari, Mukhtar Ahmed (1880–1936)	T	Politician, physician, educationalist (a founder of the *Jamia Millia Islamia*, member of the *Khilafat* Movement, the Indian Congress and the Muslim League)	INDIA
Atatürk, Mustafa Kemal (1881–1938)	S	First President of Turkey (1923–1938), former army officer, leader of Turkish nationalist movement (1920–1922)	TURKEY
Azad, Abu al-Kalam (1888–1958)	T	Intellectual, activist (a leader of the Indian Caliphate Movement)	INDIA
Celal Nuri (1881–1938)	S	Journalist, writer, parliament member, Turkey (1920–1935)	TURKEY
Elmalılı Muhammed Hamdi [Yazır] (1878–1942)	M	Member of the *ulema*, bureaucrat	TURKEY
Fuad Şükrü [Dilbilen] (?)	S	Intellectual, journalist, activist (a founder of the Ottoman Democratic Party, 1909)	TURKEY
Gökalp, Ziya (1876–1924)	S	Intellectual, CUP member, bureaucrat	TURKEY
Habil Adem (?–1948)	M	PhD in Philosophy, journalist, CUP secret service agent	TURKEY
Hoca Halil Hulki (1869–1940), Hoca İlyas Sami (1881–?), Hoca Rasih (1883–1952)	S	Members of the *ulema*, parliament members, Turkey (1920–1923)	TURKEY
Hoca Şükrü, İsmail (1876–1950)	M	Member of the *ulema*, politician, parliament member, Turkey (1920–1923), writer	TURKEY
Hüseyin Avni [Ulaş] (1887–1948)	S	Politician, parliament member, Turkey (1920–1923)	TURKEY
İsmail Hakkı, İzmirli (1868–1946)	T	Member of the *ulema*	TURKEY

continued

Table 3.1 Continued

Name	Group[1]	Background	Country/province
İsmet Pasha, İnönü (1876–1950)	S	Army officer, politician, parliament member, Turkey (1920–1972), Foreign Minister, Prime Minister, President	TURKEY
Jawish, Sheikh Abdulaziz (1876–1929)	M	Member of the *ulema*, politician, journalist, pro-Ottoman activist, member of the *Teşkilat-ı Mahsusa* (Ottoman secret service)	TUNISIA EGYPT TURKEY
al-Kawakibi, Abdur-rahman (1855–1902)	M	Intellectual, activist (an advocate of the Arab Caliphate movement)	EGYPT SYRIA
Khan, Hakim Ajmal (1863–1927)	T	Politician, physician, educationalist (a founder of the Jamia Millia Islamia, founding member of the *Khilafat* Movement, the Indian Congress and the Muslim League)	INDIA
Kidwai, Mushir Hussein (1878–1937)	T-M	Lawyer, politician, member of the Indian Caliphate Movement, a founder of the Muslim League of India	INDIA BRITAIN
[Ömer] Lütfi Fikri (1872–1934)	M	Jurist, lawyer, FAP member, parliament member (Turkey, 1908–1912), journalist	TURKEY
Mahmud Nedim [Maan](?)	M	Army officer, writer	TURKEY
Mehmed Tahir (1861–1925)	T	Bibliographer, army officer, a founder of the CUP, Sufi leader (The *Malamiyya* Order)	TURKEY
Muhammad Safa (1879-after 1923)	T	Egyptian journalist (founder of the Arabic-Turkish *'Adl* newspaper published in Istanbul [1908]), activist (with close ties to the *Teşkilat*)	EGYPT TURKEY
Muhyiddin Baha (1884–1954)	T	Attorney, judge, journalist, parliament member	TURKEY
Mustafa Sabri Efendi (1869–1954)	M	Member of the *ulema*, deputy in the parliament, an FAP leader, *şeyhülislam*	TURKEY EGYPT
Mustafa Zihni Pasha (1850–1929)	T	Bureaucrat, governor, member of the *ulema*	TURKEY IRAQ

Table 3.1 Continued

Name	Group[1]	Background	Country/province
Nadvi, Seyyid Suleiman (1884–1953)	T	Intellectual, activist (member of the Indian Caliphate Movement), sufi leader *(Naqshibandiyya)* member of the *ulema*, Professor of Islamic history, Arabic, Persian, history of religions and literature, educational adviser	INDIA
Ömer Lütfi (1864–1934)	T	Jurist (district attorney and high-rank judge), intellectual	TURKEY
Ömer Ziyaeddin Efendi [Dağistani] (1850–1920)	T	Member of the *ulema*, *hadith* scholar, Sufi leader *(Naqshibandiyya)*	TURKEY
Rashid Rida, Seyyid Muhammad (1865–1935)	T-M	Member of the *ulema*, intellectual (leader of Islamic Modernism in Egypt), journalist, sufi (temporary – *Naqshibandiyy*a), activist (member of the Ottoman Consultation Society, Decentralization Party and Syrian Congress), educator (founder of the Da'wa and Irshad University in Cairo)	EGYPT SYRIA
Safayihi, Sheikh Ismail (1856–1918)	T	Member of the *ulema*, jurist (chief justice of Tunisia)	TUNISIA
Said Halim Pasha (1864–1921)	T	Intellectual, royal family member, politician: grandson of Mehmed Ali of Egypt, member of the CUP, Foreign and Prime Minister during World War I	TURKEY
Seyyid Bey, Mehmed (1873–1925)	M-S	Member of the *ulema*, jurist, Minister of Justice, Turkey (1923–1924)	TURKEY
Sharif Hussein, ibn Ali (1855–1931)	S	Governor of Mecca (1908–1917), declared himself King of the Hijaz (1917–1924), proclaimed his Caliphate (1924) (not recognized)	THE *HIJAZ* (ARABIA)
Syed Mahmud (1889–1961)	T	Lawyer, activist (a leader of the Indian Caliphate Movement), Minister of Agriculture and Transportation (India, 1946–1952), parliament member (India, 1952–1957, 1961)	INDIA BRITAIN

continued

Table 3.1 Continued

Name	Group[1]	Background	Country/province
al-Tunusi, Salih Sharif (1869–1920)	T	Member of the *ulema*, journalist, pro-Ottoman activist, regional director of the *Teşkilat-ı Mahsusa* (Ottoman secret service) in North Africa	TUNISIA
al-Ubeydi, Seyyid Habib Efendi (1879–1963)	T	Member of the *ulema*, *Mufti* of Mosul (1922–1963), deputy in Iraqi parliament (1935–1945)	IRAQ
Yafi, Sheikh Salih (?)	T	Journalist (founder of the *Rashid* newspaper published in Beirut [1910])	LEBANON
al-Yemeni, Sheikh Bilal Abid (?)	T	Sufi leader (*Murghaniyya*)	YEMEN

Notes
1 Group Name: M = Modernist, S = Secularist, T = Traditionalist.

For example, Mardin (1991c: 179) argues that the *ulema* was one of the forces that balanced the sultanic absolutism and that their religiously framed political views could not be easily ignored during the Ottoman modernization. Likewise, Bein (2006) demonstrates that the *ulema* in the late Ottoman era played important and different roles, both in support of the religious establishment and in opposition to it, to avoid marginalization. He also argues that although they were all generally concerned about the institution's future, many of the *ulema* supported, intellectually and politically, the CUP's controlled reforms, which started with the Young Turk revolution of 1908 (see Chapter 4).

Following the revolution, which resulted in the deposing of the once-powerful Caliph-Sultan Abdülhamid II by the CUP, a number of constitutional changes undermined the caliph's authority. Furthermore, a debate on the status of the *şeyhülislam*, the caliph's highest religious dignitary, resulted in the removal from the government of his office, which eventually led to its demise in Turkey. In both cases, traditionalists and modernists confronted each other and tried to justify their opposing claims with reference to Islam. In the later phase of the transformation of the Caliphate, in 1922, secularists separated it from the monarchy, thereby rendering it a powerless "spiritual" institution. Then, in early 1924, they abolished the Caliphate (and the *Meşihat*), which marked the most important phase of the secularization of the Turkish state. In these two cases, the struggle was mainly between secularists and modernist Islamists, who opposed radical secularization. Both sides, however, derived justification for their respective claims from Islam. Meanwhile, traditionalists had largely disappeared from the political scene, though they were to some extent effective as political actors in the early years of the Second Constitutional Period.

This group consisted mostly of the high-ranking *ulema* of the Hamidian era, some of whom were disfranchised by the Young Turks after the revolution, in the center, and Arab and Indian activist-intellectuals struggling against European colonialism, on the periphery. It aimed at the restoration of caliphal power in Muslim society. Of the 20 traditionalist actors whose views will be discussed in this study, six were from India (Hakim Ajmal Khan, Abul Kalam Azad, Mushir Hosain Kidwai [also a modernist], Syed Mahmud, Seyyid Sulaiman Nadvi and Dr. Mukhtar Ahmed Ansari); among the Ottoman traditionalists, six were from Turkey (İsmail Hakkı [İzmirli], Ömer Ziyaeddin [Dağıstani] Efendi, Bursalı Mehmed Tahir, Ömer Lütfi, Muhyiddin Baha and Said Halim Pasha), seven were Arabs (Rashid Rida [also a modernist], Bilal Abid al-Yemeni, Ismail Safa-yihi, Salih Sharif al-Tunusi, Muhammad Safa, Habib al-Ubeydi and Salih Yafi), and one was a Kurd ([Babanzade] Mustafa Zihni Pasha, an Ottoman governor). In terms of the group's occupational structure, Islamic scholars led the tradition-alists: there were eight *ulema*, one of whom was also a bureaucrat and one a pol-itician and journalist; six politicians, two of whom were also well-known intellectuals and one a journalist; two further journalists; and four other intellec-tuals. Therefore, most group members had middle-class backgrounds. They defended the Ottoman Caliphate both in its center (against the modernists) and on the periphery (against Arab nationalists).

Modernist Islamists participated in two episodes of the struggle over the Caliphate, between 1908 and 1916 and between 1922 and 1924. In the first, where they confronted the traditionalists following the 1908 Revolution, they played a major role in terms of justifying the (secular) transformation of the Caliphate (and the *Meşihat*) by the Unionists. Consisting mostly of the *ulema* and jurists, this group lent critical support to the CUP in their attempt to under-mine the caliph's power (see Chapter 4). Moreover, ironically, it was the same group who in the second episode defended the caliph's status against the secular-ist attempts to destroy it. Although in the last analysis they were not successful in saving the Caliphate (or the *Meşihat*), they put up a formidable fight against the secularist group led by Mustafa Kemal in the 1922–1924 period (see Chapter 6). In both cases, the modernists defined the Caliphate as a temporal (as opposed to spiritual) institution, and saw the Ottoman caliph as the leader of all Otto-mans. They were fewer in numbers than the traditionalists: these politicians, scholars, and intellectuals included six Turks (Elmalılı Muhammed Hamdi, Mehmed Seyyid Bey, Lütfi Fikri, Hoca İsmail Şükrü, Habil Adem and Mahmud Nedim Maan) and three Arabs (Rashid Rida, Abdulaziz Jawish and Ali Fahmi Muhammad). All of the modernists involved in the debates in the caliphal center were Turkish; three of them were *ulema* and politicians, one was jurist, one jour-nalist, and one former army officer. Those on the periphery were all Arabs: a scholar, an intellectual-journalist, and a politician.

Finally, the anti-Caliphate, *secularist group* tried, as mentioned, first to trans-form the Caliphate into a "spiritual" institution, and then to abolish it altogether. Although they were fewer in number than others in Turkey, the political and military developments of the post-World War I period favored their position, and they were able to separate the Caliphate from the Ottoman monarchy by abolishing the latter in 1922, thereby leaving the former with no political or temporal authority. The most important figure in the secularist group was, of course, Mustafa Kemal. His closest friend, İsmet Pasha [İnönü], was also a leading politician among Turkish secularists. This group included other, less significant, political figures such as Fuad Şükrü [Dilbilen] and Hüseyin Avni [Ulaş]. The most important intellectual representative of the secularist group was Ziya Gökalp, whose intellectual formation and general views on modernization and Islam have been discussed in Chapter 2.

The caliphal periphery

On the periphery of the Caliphate, including Arabia, India, and North Africa, traditionalists and pro-Ottoman modernists worked together against British and French propaganda and Arab nationalist activities to protect the Ottoman Caliphate. Hence, their main preoccupation was with Muslim unity, which was the official foreign policy of the Ottomans under Abdülhamid II. The CUP revived this policy, epitomized by the Caliph's *jihad fatwa*, during World War I (see Chapter 5). In line with CUP policy, many Arab and Indian scholars, intellectuals, and politicians organized societies, congresses, and demonstrations, made publications and gave speeches in the Middle East and Europe to support Istanbul.

All these activities and the pro-Ottoman discourse were, as mentioned, aimed at circumventing the Arab Caliphate movement and Arab nationalism in general. Often supported by Britain and France, Arab nationalist politicians and intellectuals in the Middle East were very active. In 1913, they met in Paris at the first Arab Congress and demanded from Istanbul greater autonomy for Arab provinces, greater representation of Arabs in the Parliament, and restricting the deployment of Arab troops in the Ottoman army to Arab lands only. During and after World War I, an important part of their agenda was to get rid of the Ottoman Caliphate, as well as national independence. The main political figures were Sharif Hussein of Mecca, Abdulaziz ibn Saud of Najd (central Arabia), and Khedive Abbas Hilmi (r. 1892–1914) and King Fuad (r. 1917–36) of Egypt, following in the footsteps of Khedive Ismail of Egypt under the Hamidian regime (Teitelbaum 1998; Fromkin 2001; Goldschmidt 2005).

Among these politicians, the most troublesome for the Ottomans was Sharif Hussein ibn 'Ali (1853–1931), though Ibn Saud (1876–1953) would later prove to be the strongest leader in Arabia by defeating Hussein and his son Ali and founding Saudi Arabia (1924–1927). When Sharif Hussein published his proclamation of independence in 1916, he attacked the Young Turks but did not criticize the caliph at all or imply that he had any intentions to take over the Caliphate. His overall discourse was not explicitly Arab nationalist, either. Arab nationalism was in fact produced and disseminated mostly by intellectuals such as Abdur-rahman al-Kawakibi, Abdülhamid al-Zahrawi, and Rashid Rida. Its origins were somewhat related to the Ottoman Caliphate, as they saw the Caliphate as a "religious right" of Arabs that had been taken away by the Turks.

Finally, a secularist anti-Caliphate thinker was Ali Abdur-raziq, who, like Rida, was another disciple of Abduh, but criticized Rida and other Islamists for their political view of the Caliphate, advocating instead a complete separation of religion and politics (see Chapter 5 for a detailed discussion on Arab nationalism and the Ottoman Caliphate).

While the forerunners of Turkish nationalism (based in Istanbul), such as Yusuf Akçura and Ahmed Ağaoğlu, were Russian émigrés, those of Arab nationalism (based in Cairo), including al-Kawakibi and Rida, were Syrian émigrés. Also, while the former group had close ties to, and a certain impact on, the Unionists between 1912 and 1918, and Turkish secularists after 1922, Arab nationalists were staunch critics of the CUP, seeing it as the enemy of the Arabs and of Islam. Both groups, however, had one thing in common: their opposition to the (Ottoman) Caliphate. While Turkish nationalists supported the Unionists in their efforts to undermine the caliph's power, Arab nationalists "co-operated" with (or were "co-opted" by) European imperialists during the first quarter of the 20th century.

Arab nationalist activities on the periphery were opposed by Turkish, Arab (both traditionalist *and* modernist) and Indian supporters of the Ottomans. Arab-Ottoman traditionalists, some of whom were CUP members, operated mostly in North Africa and Syria. An early defense of the Ottoman Caliphate by an Arab traditionalist was a declaration by Sheikh Bilal Abid al-Yemeni and his students at the *al-Azhar Madrasa* in Cairo. Al-Yemeni was both an *alim* and the (Sufi) leader of the Murghaniyya order, which was strong in Yemen (Kara 2003b: 41). Written against the Zaydi (Shia) revolt in Yemen (1911), which led to its autonomy from the empire, the declaration ordered the insurgents to abort the revolt and rally behind the Ottoman Caliph, who, it argued, was the only legitimate leader of the Muslim world. The declaration, which was originally published in Arabic and distributed in Yemen, was translated into Ottoman Turkish and almost simultaneously published in the Islamist *Sırat-ı Müstakim* (February 24, 1911) and the CUP's *Tanin* (March 7, 1911) in Istanbul.

Naturally, pro-Ottoman activities and publications increased suddenly on the caliphal periphery with the start of World War I. It was not only the traditionalists who supported the Ottoman Caliphate, but also some intellectuals with a more strictly political (modernist) view of the institution, who had relations with the CUP. Two leading figures among the latter group were Ali Fahmi Muhammad, an Egyptian Islamist intellectual-politician, and Abdulaziz Jawish, a Tunisian *alim* and *Teşkilat* member. Two of the leading traditionalist activist-scholars in North Africa were Sheikh Ismail Safayihi and Sheikh Salih Sharif al-Tunusi. Both of them were among the leading *ulema* of the *Maghrib*, and both defended the Ottoman Caliphate with their writings and speeches against the British and French plans to install Arab caliphs in the *Hijaz* and the *Maghrib*, as well as against Arab nationalist propaganda. Their various writings were immediately translated into Turkish (by Mehmed Akif), French and German, and distributed by the *Teşkilat*. Another activist in North Africa working closely with the *Teşkilat* was the Egyptian journalist Muhammad Safa. He was the owner and editor of *al-'Adl* newspaper, published in Arabic and Turkish in Istanbul during the Second

Constitutional Period. His book on the *Islamic Caliphate and the Ottomans*, first published in *al-'Adl* and then translated into Ottoman Turkish in 1922, was a response to Arab nationalist writers' criticisms – published in Sharif Hussein's organ, *al-Qibla* – of the Ottoman Caliphate, particularly in relation to the charge that the Ottomans could not be legitimate caliphs because they were not Prophet Muhammad's descendants. Citing other textual (e.g., some *hadith*s) and historical evidence, Safa emphasized the legitimacy of, and the need for obedience to, the Ottoman caliph in his book, which he presented to the last caliph-sultan, Vahideddin (Kara 2005: 23–24). In the Arabian Peninsula, two important Arab traditionalist defenders of the Ottoman Caliphate include the Iraqi *alim* and politician Habib al-Ubeydi, who was very active during World War I (see also Chapter 5), and Sheikh Salih Yafi, on whose life there is no information, except that he was the founder of the *Rashîd* newspaper published in Beirut (1910), where a sizable Christian population lived and several Protestant missionary schools existed (Kara 2005: 12). Yafi's book, titled *The Caliphate and the Ottomans* (1916), was an attempt to prove the legitimacy of the Ottoman Caliphate and the necessity for all citizens to obey the sultan. Thus, he emphasized the "freedom, justice, and equality" that non-Muslims enjoyed under the Turkish caliph.

Pro-Ottoman actors were not restricted to Turkey and the Arab world. In India, the other major area within the caliphal periphery, the main issue at stake was again the Caliphate's role in Muslim unity. As a result of the close relations between the Ottomans and Indian Muslims during the 19th century (see Özcan 1997; Qureshi 1999: 25–45), the latter were among the most vocal supporters of the Ottoman Caliphate before and during World War I – they even requested from the Young Turks guarantees for the preservation of the Caliph's prestige when the latter tried to restrict the Turkish sultan's authority (Özcan 1997: 129). With the exception of Aga Khan, who was not a Sunni, all Indian-Muslim intellectuals and politicians who discussed the Caliphate voiced the traditionalist point of view, even after World War I, when the caliphal center was about to collapse. They wanted to revitalize the Ottoman Caliphate, seeing it as the only chance for the independence of the Muslim world. An immediate motive for this was their desire to get rid of the British occupation of their own country. Aware that Britain had been very much concerned about the Caliphate's ideological power, many Muslim actors in British India emphasized its religious, even metaphysical, aspects, as well as political authority. Thus, the Caliphate was at the center of the Muslim-Indian struggle for freedom from colonial rule: the national movement even adopted the name "Caliphate Movement" (1918–1924) and aimed at saving the Ottoman Empire from disintegration, as well as securing self-government for India (Qureshi 1999; Öke 1999). The aggressive pro-Caliphate action could also help them overcome the marginal position of the subcontinent (and South Asia) within the Muslim World. The movement thus mobilized "pan-Islamic" sentiment in the context of British policy toward Turkey and India. However, Muslim politics in India gradually transitioned from Islamism to territorial nationalism, particularly after the Turkish secularists abolished the Caliphate and the Indians plunged back into communal strife.

In line with the larger pattern of Western-educated intellectuals leading colonial independence movements whose nationalisms were born, as Anderson (1991: 58, 118) remarks, out of both deprivation (of independence) *and* privilege (upper-class position and elite education, which also taught them Western ideas of national independence), it was mainly Muslim (and Hindu) intellectuals who headed the resistance movement. Led by such intellectual-activists as Muhammad Ali Jouhar and his brother Shaukat Ali, Hakim Ajmal Khan, Mukhtar Ahmed Ansari, Abul Kalam Azad, Mushir Hosain Kidwai, Syed Sulaiman Nadvi and Syed Mahmud, the Indian *Khilafat* Movement allied with Hindus for independence through the Indian National Congress, the largest political party in India, and its leader, Mahatma Gandhi. They played a major role in the "noncooperation movement," a nationwide campaign of civil disobedience. The Caliphate Movement lobbied in Europe (holding two meetings with the British prime minister in 1920 and 1921) and published the *Khilafat* Manifesto in 1920, which called upon the British to protect the Caliphate (Qureshi 1999; Oliver-Dee 2009). It was also inspired by the Turkish national struggle (1919–1922) following the invasion of Istanbul and Anatolia by European states after World War I. Though the Indian resistance was largely peaceful and the Turkish one armed, both movements had strong Islamist elements (their main source of motivation and justification being Islam), but also envisioned "national" freedom from European colonialism. Moreover, a series of "All-India *Khilafat* Conferences" organized by the Muslim League openly supported the Turkish resistance led by Mustafa Kemal, and warned the British in June 1921 that their attack on Turks would mean a "war with Islam" (Sadiq 1983: 2–4, 105–108). However, the movement disintegrated after the abolition of the Caliphate by Mustafa Kemal. Then some of its leaders joined their former rival, the Muslim League, which would later found Pakistan (1947).

The elite character of the three groups

As can be seen in the above descriptions of the actors in India and elsewhere, an important aspect of the social composition of these groups is their elite character: The power struggles that shaped this process took place essentially among a relatively small group of elites, rather than on a societal level. For example, as we shall see in the next chapter, the Unionists who deposed Sultan Abdülhamid and curtailed the caliph's political authority were a small group of military officers who tried to save the state from disintegration and tyranny (of the monarch). Since they already had military (and later political) power, they did not need much support from the masses. They did, however, need the ideological support of (the modernist section of) the *ulema*. Similarly, the debate over the Caliphate between the Ottoman loyalists and Arab nationalists on the caliphal periphery was one between the elites of the two sides – though Sharif Hussein and Ibn Saud did need ordinary men in their revolts against Istanbul (see Chapter 5). Finally, the secularists in the center, led by Mustafa Kemal, greatly benefited from the masses of people during the "Independence War," but they hardly asked their opinion when abolishing the monarchy and the Caliphate, though they had to temporarily appeal to them until they became powerful enough to launch radical secular reforms (see Chapter 6). Therefore, my analysis in this study is largely confined to the intra-elite struggles (or relations between different elite groups) that by and large shaped the entire modernization process in the Middle East until the 1950s. This is hardly suprizing considering the fact that the "public opinion," which emerged with the *Tanzimat* reforms in the Ottoman Empire, consisted only of bureaucratic elites and the intelligentsia, largely excluding the ordinary people, until the end of the empire (see Kologlu 2010, III) – possibly well into the republican period.[11]

The balance of power between the traditionalists, modernists, and secularists followed a trajectory parallel to changes in political and military power relations, mainly around the central government of the Ottoman Empire. As the CUP became more modern and secular, the traditionalist group was gradually weakened, and modernist and then secularist actors came to dominate the intellectual-political debate on the nature and future of the Caliphate. On the other hand, as the Empire lost power and territory as a result of the Balkan Wars (1912–1913), World War I, domestic uprisings, including the "Great" Arab revolt (1916), and the occupation of Turkey by the Allies (1918–1922), the caliph-sultans themselves, as well as those who defended their traditional authority, lost power and status. Thus, the failure of the existing system in the face of new political and military developments opened up the way for a reconfiguration of political and ideological power relations in the public sphere, tipping the balance of power toward Western-oriented actors (bureaucrats, politicians, and journalists), and away from the Islamic *ulema* and the sultan.

Discourses: three groups, 20 strategies

As discussed in Chapter 1, the main empirical argument of this study is that despite the differences in their political-intellectual orientations, occupational backgrounds, and visions regarding the future of the Caliphate, all these actors employed the same "meta-strategy" in their discourses: deriving legitimization from Islam. This meta-strategy involved a number of "discursive strategies" in the Foucaultian sense (1972: 60), which, in turn, included many specific elements that I call "discursive techniques" (see Chapter 1). These discursive elements are important because they informed the actors' decisions to some extent by not only providing a ground for a justification of their actions but also helping them make sense of the reality that they faced. These discursive lenses helped them perceive or define the reality of the Caliphate in certain ways, which in turn shaped their actions and reactions to it.

Some of these discursive strategies (of which I discuss 20 in total) were common to all three groups; others were common to two groups only, while still others were employed by each group separately to realize their different goals mentioned above. Table 3.2 summarizes the 20 strategies employed by these actors.

Table 3.2 Discursive strategies of three groups

Groups	Different discursive strategies		Common discursive strategies
	Center	Periphery	
Traditionalists	1 Establishing the dual (temporal and spiritual) status of the caliph 2 Defining religious (as opposed to popular) legitimacy as the only basis for the caliph's authority 3 Emphasizing obedience to the caliph as a religious duty of the believer	1 Re-establishing the legitimacy of the Ottoman Caliphate 2 Emphasizing obedience to the caliph's authority 3 Promoting Islamic unity 4 Comparing and contrasting Islam with the West	1 Invoking sacred texts (Qur'anic verses and prophetic *hadiths*) 2 Invoking (early) Islamic history 3 Omitting contradictory evidence
Modernists	1 Defining the Caliphate as a temporal-political institution 2 Identifying social contract and popular legitimacy as bases for the caliph's authority 3 Emphasizing the limits of the caliph's temporal authority 4 Nationalizing the Caliphate		
Secularists	1 Reconstructing the Caliphate as a purely spiritual authority 2 Establishing the Islamic legitimacy of the Caliphate's separation from monarchy 3 Elevating the Caliphate's status vis-à-vis the "un-Islamic" monarchy 4 Relocating the Caliphate as an "un-Islamic" institution vis-à-vis the Islamic state of the Turkish parliament 5 Mixing Islamic discourse with a (Turkish) nationalist discourse 6 Adapting religion to modern conditions		

Common discursive strategies

In this section I discuss three different discursive strategies and various discursive techniques associated with them that were commonly used by all three groups. I begin with the strategy of "invoking sacred texts" (Qur'anic verses and prophetic *hadiths*) for justification of political positions and arguments, and continue with those of "invoking (early) Islamic history" and "omitting contradictory evidence." The most common *techniques* deployed as part of these strategies include emphasizing some verses of the Qur'an and sayings of the Prophet as well as certain historical events while ignoring other verses, prophetic traditions, and historical evidence. In the process of this selective reading of foundational texts of Islam and its history, a number of important themes came up repeatedly, such as the nature and basis of the caliph's authority, the number of caliphs, the significance of "consultation," etc. and different groups made their claims by deploying various strategies and techniques (often the same ones, but to different ends). Moreover, although all three groups made use of these three strategies, they did not do so to the same extent. For example, unlike traditionalists, secularists found it more difficult to draw on prophetic traditions, for reasons explained below. The discursive strategies and techniques the actors employed served political ends, making claims about legitimacy meant to strengthen the positions of each group in their ongoing power struggles.

These struggles took place in a historical context in which the Ottoman Empire was facing challenges from Arab nationalism, European imperialism, separatist movements, and economic depression. During this period, the first quarter of the 20th century, the "Sublime Porte" (Ottoman center) faced territorial problems as a result of various revolts by Arab tribes (most notably the 1916 revolt by the Hashemites in Mecca, led by Sharif Hussein, that resulted in the loss of much of the Arabian Peninsula) as well as by non-Muslim minorities (e.g., Bulgarians, Albanians and Greeks). Moreover, as the caliphal center, it felt the impact of European colonialism not only within its own territory (the Middle East and North Africa), but also in more remote parts of the Muslim world, principally in India under British rule. Finally, the empire's involvement in World War I as part of the Central Powers led to its collapse between 1918 and 1922, as a result of which many nation-states emerged in its territory (all of the current states, excluding Iran, Tunisia, and Morocco, in the Middle East and North Africa, and most of the contemporary states in the Balkans).

The Caliphate also came to an end in this process, during which its supporters and opponents alike put forward Islamic arguments. Since I will elaborate on the politico-military developments that shaped – and were partly shaped by – these discourses in the following three chapters, I will confine my analysis to the discursive struggle here. Below I discuss three common strategies, beginning with that of making references to the two fundamental sources of Islam: the Qur'an and the prophetic traditions.

Invoking sacred texts

The two commonly agreed-upon "sacred texts" of Islam are the *Qur'an* and the *hadith*s. According to the Muslim faith, the former contains the revelations of God (*wahy*), whereas the latter refer to the "traditions" (sayings, actions, and attitudes) of the Prophet Muhammad as reported by his friends (the "Companions") to subsequent generations.[12] The *hadith* is regarded as the second most important epistemological source (after the Qur'an) by Muslims because it has the status of "spoken revelation" (*wahy matluw*), that is, words indirectly revealed by God through his Prophet – a principle that is also derived from the Qur'an (53/3–4). The Prophetic traditions have been transmitted, first verbally and then in writing, since the first century of Islam up until today. There is a specific academic discipline for the study and transmission of Prophetic traditions, known as *'Ilm al-Hadith*, that is unique to Islamic civilization (Ibn Khaldūn 1957, III: 999). The scholars of *hadith* not only report the traditions but also critically analyze the authenticity of chains of narration (*isnad*) in order to eliminate those that are falsely attributed to the Prophet.[13] There are various classifications of traditions in the *hadith* literature from different angles and by different schools; but one of the most common classifications is a tripartite division: "authentic" (*sahih*), "weak" (*da'if*) and "fabricated" (*mawdu'*). A *hadith* is said to be *authentic* if it is reported by "reliable" (*thiqa*) narrators – as determined by various techniques – for every generation of scholars; it is *weak* if one or more generations of narrators is either not completely reliable or obscure (not well known by the community of scholars). Finally, *fabricated* traditions are those that are made up by different individuals and groups and falsely attributed to the Prophet, usually for political reasons, in order to legitimize their claims. These are not really *hadith*s and, therefore, not eligible as evidence for any kind of religious argument (al-Azami 1977). Of particular importance for this study is the second category; for there are few authentic *hadith*s on the Caliphate, and thus different authors cite many weak traditions. This is significant because weak *hadith*s cannot be cited as evidence in matters of faith, including the Caliphate, according to mainstream Islamic scholarly tradition. However, as we shall see below, many intellectuals and politicians, particularly the traditionalists who stressed the religious dimension of the Caliphate, often made reference to weak *hadith*s to benefit from the very high status the prophetic traditions enjoy in the Islamic faith.

The Qur'an and the *hadith* constitute two distinct sets of fundamental reference sources that have been resorted to in legitimizing theological, legal, and political positions throughout the history of Islam. In the case of the Caliphate, too, these two were the most important sources that were frequently drawn upon by different groups. For this reason, I specifically discuss in this section how textual references functioned as the primary focus of actors in terms of legitimizing their claims. The discursive strategy of invoking Qur'anic verses and prophetic traditions was both common to all three groups and the most widely used strategy during the entire period under study (1908–1924). Most political actors and intellectuals referred to the verses in the Qur'an and sayings of the Prophet

Muhammad to justify their positions in the debates over the Caliphate. More-over, though the actors classified in different groups in this study usually drew on the same verses and *hadith*s, they often interpreted them in differing, and sometimes opposing, ways by deploying different discursive techniques as part of their strategies. Among the three groups, we find that it was the traditionalists, most of whom were *ulema*, who made use of the sacred texts most. They are fol-lowed by the modernist group, which included fewer *ulema*. As for secularists, they did not cite Qur'anic verses or prophetic traditions as much as the others due to the fact that they could not easily find sayings of the Prophet that would support their position and most of them did not have a relevant educational back-ground that would allow them to effectively utilize the Islamic tradition for their political purposes. That is why they desperately needed the help of *ulema*, such as that of Seyyid Bey,[14] which proved crucial for their struggle (see Chapter 6).

This strategy of interpreting sacred texts included two common discursive *techniques*: (i) dissecting verses and *hadith*s, abstracting sentences or even phrases found in the texts from their textual and social contexts, and applying them to the solution of an emerging problem in terms of the lexicographical meaning of selected phrases – what I have called a "transformative technique"; (ii) emphasizing particular themes and giving textual references that were puta-tively associated with these themes, and ignoring others. Below I discuss how actors utilized sacred texts, focusing first on the Qur'an and then on Prophetic traditions. My discussion is organized around the primary themes that repeatedly emerged out of the data, including the nature of the caliph's authority, the unity of Muslims, "consultation," justice, multiple caliphs, etc. I also separately discuss the use of a particular verse (4/59) and a *hadith* that played a central role in the deployment of the actors' discursive techniques.

Invoking Qur'anic verses

Due to their unquestionable epistemological status, Qur'anic verses provided a solid ground for the legitimization of different positions. For this reason, adher-ents of all positions repeatedly referred to verses that could be connected to gov-ernance (or "politics") in the Qur'an. The most frequently cited verse in this regard is the command: "O ye who believe! Obey Allah, and obey the Messen-ger, and those charged with authority (*ul al-amr*) among you" (4/59). Cited by virtually every traditionalist actor as a major discursive technique, this verse formed the discursive foundation for claims about the Caliphate (its basis, legiti-macy, authority, functions, and future), as the last part of the verse regulates the relationship between the ruler and the ruled.[15] Due to its importance and popular-ity, the "*ul al-amr*" verse deserves a deeper discussion.

THE "*UL AL-AMR*" VERSE

Though cited by modernists and secularists, too, this verse was particularly popular among the traditionalists for two reasons: first, according to its mainstream interpretation, it established a clear connection between the authority of God, the Prophet, and the "ruler," locating them in an ontologically and politically hierarchical structure; second, it emphasized the necessity of obedience by believers to the authority of the caliph. To illustrate this point, we can take a pamphlet by Ömer Ziyaeddin Efendi (1908), a member of the *ulema*, a Sufi leader (*sheikh*), and a leading representative of the traditionalist group who compiled a collection of 40 *hadith*s (most of which were technically "weak" *hadith*s; see Chapter 4), titled *Hadîs-i Erbaîn fî Hukûki's-Selâtîn*, to support the traditionalist view of the Caliphate.[16] Written during the Hamidian era, the book defended Sultan Abdülhamid's rule as caliph-sultan against the Young Turks.[17] In addition to citing some (alleged) sayings of the Prophet referring to, and containing, the above-mentioned verse (p. 57), he referred, in the preface, to the religious/political hierarchy by first praising God and the Prophet, then "generously praying" for the caliph (p. 49). Referring also to some other Qur'anic verses and many *hadith*s, the author repeatedly emphasized that the (current) caliph was the "representative/agent of both Allah and of the Messenger of Allah" (pp. 49, 60, 61, 64).

For traditionalists, a common purpose of citing this (and other) verses was to establish a basis for both religious/spiritual and temporal/political authority for the Caliphate[18] and prove that his authority covered all Muslims regardless of whether they were Ottoman citizens or not. For example, Mustafa Zihni Pasha, a member of the *ulema* and a governor,[19] also drew on the same verse, as well as different *hadith*s, to establish the legitimacy of the cabinet (ministers) appointed by the caliph-sultan (1911: 109, 111, 123–132) by first discursively establishing the legitimacy of the Caliphate itself (cf. Safa 1922: 236). He also argued that since this verse called on Muslims in general to obey the *ul al-amr*, the (Ottoman) Caliph's authority covered those Muslims living outside of Ottoman territory, as well:

> all believers and Muslims on the face of the earth are obliged to obey and follow the glorious and powerful [Ottoman] dynasty, which is based on the Qur'anic verse, "Obey Allah, and obey the Messenger, and the *ul al-amr* among you," as well as countless prophetic traditions.
>
> (Mustafa Zihni 1911: 183)

Similarly, Yafi, a little-known Arab journalist from Beirut, agreed on both points, referring to the same verse as a discursive technique and arguing that since the Caliph had both spiritual and political authority over all Muslims, non-Ottoman Muslims, too, should accept the Ottoman sultan as their (religious) leader (1916: 166–167). The short book containing this argument was published in the year the Arab rebellion against the Ottomans started, which formed the social context of its publication. The author tried to support the Ottoman Caliphate (by emphasizing the need to obey it) against the danger of the territorial division of the Empire (its eventual loss of Arab provinces, including Beirut).

Moreover, the famous "*ul al-amr*" verse (4/59) had also played a central discursive role in a debate in the Ottoman parliament and the press in December 1911 on whether to limit the caliph-sultan's political authority. The debate was part of a domestic political dispute between the CUP and the liberal FAP (Freedom and Alliance Party; see Chapter 4). When the FAP's candidate won a by-election in Istanbul in 1911, the Unionists, seeing their unpopularity among the public, wanted to have an early election, which required that the caliph-sultan, Mehmed V, dissolve the parliament. But the sultan's authority to do this had previously been curbed by the CUP itself with the constitutional amendments enacted in 1909. So the CUP proposed to amend the constitution again by inserting into Article 35 the right for the sultan, whom they effectively controlled, to dissolve the parliament (Birinci 1990: 105–110). The main point of dispute between the two parties (and the independents, who supported the FAP in this case) was over the legality of this right according to Islamic principles. In this debate, Mustafa Sabri Efendi, a member of the modernist *ulema*, a deputy in parliament and a significant figure in the FAP, argued in his address in the parliament that the caliph's authority should be limited to executive affairs only (with no right to dissolve the parliament) on the grounds that the phrase "those charged with authority" in the "*ul al-amr*" verse did not refer to *umera* (administrative leaders, including the caliph), but to the community of the *ulema* – an idea he took from the 12th-century scholar Fakhruddin al-Razi's (d. 1209) commentary on the Qur'an (1938).

Critiquing Mustafa Sabri and the FAP, pro-CUP intellectual Ömer Lütfi[20] defended the sultan's status "above" the parliament on the basis of the religious and political nature of the caliph's authority, also referring to the "*ul al-amr*" verse. In his *The Caliphate in Islam* (1912), he argued that the Caliphate was sacred, its authority being spiritual as well as temporal, and that Mustafa Sabri and Razi's interpretations of both the Qur'anic verse and the historical evidence on the limited authority of the Caliphate in the early Islamic period were wrong as they were taken out of context (1912: 224–231). Effectively employing key Islamic sources, particularly Qur'anic verses, prophetic traditions, the legal (*fiqh*) literature, and examples from early Caliphs, Ömer Lütfi disproved Mustafa Sabri's claims for the religious justification of curbing the Caliph's power to dissolve the Parliament. After an extensive discussion of the (classical) theory of the Caliphate, he concluded that the caliph-sultan should not be held accountable and must have the right to dissolve the parliament (p. 252).

Though the proposal was rejected by the parliament by a slight margin, the Unionist Grand Vizier Said Pasha resigned on December 30, 1911 and the sultan dissolved the Chamber of Deputies (*Meclis-i Mebusan*), calling for elections, which the CUP would win by intimidation and violence (see Chapter 4). In this crucial development, which greatly affected the configuration of power relations in the caliphal center, the Unionists relied, among others, on a particular interpretation of the "*ul al-amr*" verse for justification. According to Lütfi, since the phrase "those charged with authority" in the verse referred to rulers (rather than the *ulema*), "obedience [required by the verse] to the *umera* and sultans is undoubtedly an integral part of obedience to Allah and His messenger" (p. 222; cf. p. 247). This also exemplifies an important aspect of the complexity of secularization in the Middle East: As in the case of Mehmed Tahir's *hadith* collection (see below), most CUP actors and pro-CUP intellectuals supported the Caliphate after the deposition of Sultan Abdülhamid, and some even employed the same traditionalist discourse as the sultan's supporters had done before, though the Young Turks who opposed the Hamidian regime had been very critical of the Caliphate before they replaced Abdülhamid with a weak caliph.[21] The defense of the traditionalist view by a CUP supporter against the liberals also indicates that my classification of the three groups cannot be read in an essentialist manner: the group boundaries are not fixed, but relatively fluid, as they change in different political contexts. That is, actors sometimes voice different arguments based on their positions in specific political-ideological struggles.[22]

Likewise, this fluid relationship between discourse and different patterns of power can also be observed on the caliphal periphery, where there was a discursive battle between Arab nationalists and Ottoman loyalists during World War I. Two North African traditionalist scholars, Ismail Safayihi and Salih Sharif al-Tunusi, pro-CUP members of the Arab *ulema*, and friends of Enver Pasha,[23] cited the "*ul al-amr*" verse and wrote in almost exactly the same words that unconditionally obeying the caliph was part and parcel of obedience to God and the Prophet prescribed in it:

> As for the Muslim world's duty [to the Caliphate], it requires every individual to obey whatever the caliph commands and forbids within the framework of his aforementioned authority, which includes the Sunna of the Prophet and the Book of Allah; in short, whatever Allah has commanded and forbidden. Obeying the Caliph is included in obedience to Allah and his Prophet. This is what is meant by the verse "O ye who believe! Obey Allah, and obey the Messenger, and the *ul al-amr* among you."
> (al-Tunusi 1916a: 148; cf. Safayihi 1915: 71)

They made this argument in a different context than Lütfi's, however: They worked – for the CUP – in North Africa, a region where the threat of secession from the Empire and of a rival Caliphate was severely felt during World War I (see also below).

Similarly, when insurgents in Yemen rebelled against Istanbul (1910–1911), a group of Yemenite scholars headed by Sheikh Bilal Abid al-Yemeni, the leader of the *Murghaniya* Sufi order, which was strong in Yemen, published an open letter in which they called on their "brethren who reside in Yemen" to immediately stop "the insurgency against his Highness Mehmed V, who is the source of religion as the leader/caliph (*Imam*) of all Muslims and the sultan of both Arabs and non-Arabs," describing the insurgency as created by "foreign powers that try to divide the Muslim *ummah*" (1911: 430). As their main discursive technique, the authors based their call on the "*ul al-amr*" verse, saying that it was all Muslims' duty to obey the caliph and fight against the insurgents according to the divine will, and if not, they would be punished in the afterlife. The authors also encouraged the Yemenite *ulema* to oppose the rebellion and disseminate their declaration, referring once again to the "*ul al-amr*" verse (p. 431). The verse, which they cited twice in a short (two-page) proclamation, was central in the arguments for the double (religious and political) authority of the caliph made by other traditionalists, as well (e.g., Yafi 1916: 165; al-Ubeydi 1916: 192, 203).

As for modernists (who defined the caliph as a strictly political ruler), they invoked Qur'anic verses less frequently than traditionalists, both because there were fewer number of *ulema* among them who could strongly claim the authority to interpret the Qur'an and because they wanted to transform the Caliphate. This was true for the "*ul al-amr*" verse, too. For example, Turkish nationalist Habil Adem (1913)[24] did not mention any verse (or prophetic tradition) in his entire book, though he strongly supported the Ottoman Caliphate, albeit in a more national and secular form. Likewise, neither Ali Fahmi Muhammad (1911), an Egyptian Islamist intellectual-politician,[25] nor Abdulaziz Jawish (1916), a Tunisian *alim* and *Teşkilat* member,[26] cited the "*ul al-amr*" verse, though they both referred to many verses in their books that they wrote to support the Ottoman Caliphate against the pressures of Britain and France, which were severely felt in North Africa during World War I. Similarly, Elmalılı Hamdi (1909), a leading member of the modernist *ulema* in Istanbul,[27] mentioned neither the "*ul al-amr*" verse nor any other (except for one verse on spiritualism in Christianity) in his critique of the traditionalist argument for upholding the *şeyhülislam*'s status (see Chapter 4). Finally, when he started the uprising against the Sublime Porte in 1916, Sharif Hussein of Mecca[28] avoided mentioning this verse – perhaps understandably – in his famous "Proclamation" (published in his organ, *Qibla*, see Chapter 5) to the Muslim world. Surprisingly, however, Mahmud Nedim Maan (1919),[29] who wrote a short pamphlet criticizing Sharif Hussein for committing a great sin by persecuting Ottoman soldiers and establishing a dynastic rule in the Holy Land, did not mention the verse, either.

One exception to this pattern among the modernists was Seyyid Bey, a member of the *ulema* and a CUP leader who played a crucial role in secularizing and then abolishing the Caliphate (see Chapters 4 and 6). Though he strongly argued for the transformation of the Caliphate into a purely temporal authority, he nevertheless cited the "*ul al-amr*" verse to emphasize the necessity of obedience to the sultan-caliph – who was for all intents and purposes controlled by the CUP at the time:

> Obeying the Caliph is mandatory both legally and religiously.... It is also religiously required because it is sanctioned by many different religious provisions. There is also the *ijma* (unanimous decision) of the *ulema*, including both jurists and theologians, on this issue. Finally, the verse that decrees "O ye who believe! Obey Allah, and obey the Messenger, and the *ul al-amr* among you" is the strongest and most conclusive evidence that it is imperative for all to obey the *ul al-amr*.
>
> (1917: 455–456)

Reflecting the typical dual orientation of modernists, he both tried to reduce the caliph's power to the politico-military level *and* urged all Muslims to obey the orders of the Ottoman caliph in the midst of World War I, when the CUP government – and the sultan – needed their support. Another leading modernist intellectual, Rashid Rida, also emphasized obedience by citing this verse (and others) (1923: 27); but since he believed that the Ottoman caliph was not a legitimate one (1922: 717), he prescribed obeying an Arab caliph only.[30]

The secularists naturally did not cite this verse as often. However, as we will discuss in Chapter 6, some of the *ulema*, whose view of the Caliphate was essentially a modernist one, sided with the secularist group for political reasons and put their "intellectual capital" at their service. A great example of this is again Seyyid Bey, who frequently helped Mustafa Kemal, the leader of this group, not only as an advisor, but as his speech writer. He also contributed to the secularist cause through his own writings. For example, following the abolition of the Ottoman monarchy in 1922, Seyyid Bey wrote an important pamphlet legitimizing the Turkish parliament's decision. He did this by portraying the Ottoman Caliphate as a "fictitious" one, and by positioning the parliament, dominated by Mustafa Kemal, as the true Islamic institution vis-à-vis the Ottoman center, for which he cited, among others, the "*ul al-amr*" verse. After citing the verse, he equated the Turkish parliament with the "*ul al-amr*" (Islamic rulers) mentioned in the verse – a discursive technique often deployed by secularists during the 1922–1924 period – and concluded that it was mandatory to obey the parliament's decisions, since God himself commanded this in the Qur'an (Seyyid Bey 1923: 46).

Other secularists did not pay much attention to the "*ul al-amr*" verse. One exception to this rule, however, was the leading secularist thinker Ziya Gökalp. He referred to this verse in a poem titled "The State," which he wrote to further support his idea of the separation of religion and "law" in the context of the CUP's curtailment of the *şeyhülislam*'s power. As discussed in Chapter 2, Gökalp suggested a series of reforms regarding the status of the religious (*şer'iye*) courts that were administered by the *şeyhülislam*'s office; he advised that this should be done by the Ministry of Justice, which was already in charge of secular (*nizamiye*) courts. He based his argument on the separation of law and religion, which he claimed was already included in Islam:

The Qur'an says: "Obey
God, then the Prophet, and the *state!*"
All my conscience feels is loyalty
To the laws, *hadith*s and verses
In worshipping and faith, always
The Book and the Sunna are my guides
If I have doubts in this business, surely
I listen to the mufti's *fatwa*s
But the law is separate from religion
Left to the "*ul al-amr*," to the *state.*
        (Gökalp 1918b: 44–45; my italics)

On Gökalp's advice, the CUP decided at its 1916 convention that the governance of religious courts would be transferred to the Ministry of Justice, curbing the *Meşihat*'s most important function (and authority), thus leaving it powerless in the government. The party justified this secular move by saying that the *şeyhülislam*'s office should focus on "sublimating" and "glorifying" Islam, rather than delving into administrative matters (see Yağcıoğlu 1992). This move, also known as the "Ziya Gökalp reform," which was legitimized with reference to Islam, was clearly based on the assumption of a dichotomy of the secular versus the spiritual that was gaining momentum at the time.[31]

Even the political leader of the secularist group, Mustafa Kemal, made use of the "*ul al-amr*" verse in a press conference he held in İzmit in early 1923. Though he did not directly quote it, he clearly referred to it when he enumerated the basic principles of Islamic government, which he did to "prove" that Islam did not approve of monarchic rule. The specific context of his remarks and the press conference was the fierce discursive battle underway between the secularists and the (modernist) Islamists in the late 1922 and early 1923 (following the abolition of the Ottoman monarchy by the secularists). The Islamist scholar-deputy İsmail Şükrü[32] had argued in a pamphlet published in January, 1923, titled "The Islamic Caliphate and the Turkish Grand National Assembly," that the current caliph, Abdülmecid Efendi, should be the head of the new state, which caused a fury among the secularists, who then started a bitter campaign against him as part of their broader press campaign against Abdülmecid. They feared that the new caliph could soon become a rival power actor posing a grave danger for Mustafa Kemal's rule. Showing a good example of how different political groups used the same Qur'anic verse for opposing purposes, Mustafa Kemal argued that the Qur'anic principle of obedience to the *ul al-amr* necessarily implied rule by the Parliament, rather than by a caliph-sultan:

> one of the [Islamic principles of government] pertains to consultation, another one to justice, and another to the *ul al-amr*.... What is meant by the *ul al-amr* is not an individual ruler, but rulers [in plural]. What is meant by the rulers is the people of specialization, the people of "*al-hall wa al-'aqd*." Therefore, a consultative body (*şura*) consisting of the persons who qualify to be the people of "*al-hall wa al-'aqd*" runs the government within the limits of justice and in accordance with the *sharia*. Our government is able to completely include these principles. For this reason, no caliph could be involved in this.
>
> (Mustafa Kemal 1923: 64)

Similar to Mustafa Kemal's strategic intervention into the theory of the Caliphate through the concepts of Islamic *fiqh*, his advisor and a famous scholar of the time, Seyyid Bey, used the "*ul al-amr*" verse in order to discursively diminish the Caliphate's significance in Islamic legal theory. In his book published by the Turkish parliament and disseminated in the Muslim world to prepare Muslim public opinion for the abolition of the Caliphate (see Chapter 6 for details),

Seyyid Bey (1923: 2) employed an interesting discursive technique using the "*ul al-amr*" verse: "In the Glorious Qur'an, there is a verse that decrees obedience to the '*ul al-amr*.' But that is all! There is no other verse, nor a prophetic *hadith*, that is related to the different aspects of the Caliphate..."

He also quoted the same verse at the end of his pamphlet to make exactly the same point that Mustafa Kemal did: the term "*ul al-amr*" did not refer to the caliph in particular but to all the rulers in general, including, particularly, the members of the Turkish parliament:

> The Glorious Qur'an tells [us] to obey the "*ul al-amr*." The "*ul al-amr*" refers to the people in charge, the rulers and commanders. It covers both the caliph and the sultan, and the governors and commanders in general.... Because the decisions taken by the current Grand National Assembly are in fact orders given by the "*ul al-amr*" and by those in charge, they are to be definitely obeyed as long as they do not violate the basic principles [of the *sharia*]. There is no need for separate approval [by the caliph].
>
> (Seyyid Bey 1923: 46)

Finally, three *ulema*-deputies, Hoca Halil Hulki, Hoca İlyas Sami, and Hoca Rasih, like Seyyid Bey, played an important role in justifying the secularist position. Being members of Mustafa Kemal's "First Group" in the GNA, they effectively employed Islamic discourse to support his cause against Islamists on the status of the new caliph vis-à-vis the Turkish parliament. Like Kemal and Seyyid Bey, the three *Hoca*s cited obedience to the true leader(ship) as one of the basic principles of Islamic government, and interpreted the "*ul al-amr*" verse as referring to the parliament rather than the caliph. But the specific discursive technique they employed was different: after citing the verse, they focused on the *grammatical* dimension of the phrase "*ul al-amr*," saying that the word "*ul*" was plural rather than singular, which for them indicated that the "*ul al-amr*" may refer to either the caliphs or to a consultative body. They thus translated this phrase, just as Mustafa Kemal did, as the people of "*al-hall wa al-'aqd*" (Hoca Halil *et al.* 1923: 12). It seems that the secularists' employment of this verse was instrumental in nature: They drew on Islamic discourse because it was politically convenient in a Muslim society. This instrumentality argument (which I will elaborate in Chapter 6) was also true for other verses, like the ones that sanction *shura* (consultation), a concept essentially associated with constitutional monarchy in the late-Ottoman context.

VERSES ON CONSULTATION

"Consultation" (*shura* in Arabic, *meşveret* in Ottoman Turkish) is a key concept in Islamic political philosophy: it is sanctioned by the Qur'an (see below) and required for caliphate; there is also a chapter in the Qur'an titled *Shura*. It has also been cited as one of basic principles of any kind of leadership throughout the Islamic history, especially in the political advice (or "mirrors for princes") literature (e.g., Nizamülmülk 1981: 133). In addition to the famous *"ul al-amr"* verse, the two most popular verses from the Qur'an that were frequently cited by traditionalists and modernists as a discursive technique were the following: "And consult them in affairs (of moment). Then, when thou hast taken a decision, put thy trust in Allah" (3/159) and "[they conduct] their affairs by mutual Consultation" (42/38). Since these verses emphasize "consultation" (*shura*), both groups drew on them to prove the legitimacy of the new political system of the empire, constitutional monarchy (*meşrutiyet*). As discussed above, with the 1908 Revolution the CUP forced Sultan Abdülhamid to re-institute the constitution and the parliament, which he had shut down in 1878, thereby opening up the "Second Constitutional Period." There was virtually no disagreement on the legitimacy of the new regime among the political actors of the time, including most, but not all, traditionalists; however, their purposes differed in referring to these two *"shura* verses." Traditionalists cited them in order to argue that the Caliphate was perfectly compatible with the modern state with its constitution and parliament, whereas modernists aimed to weaken the Caliphate by emphasizing the concept of "consultation" and its political implications, including separation of powers and the absence of absolute authority for the monarch. For, "consultation" required a consultative body (parliament) that naturally limited the Sultan's power. Secularists, on the other hand, cited these two verses because they needed to stress the religious significance of the "parliamentary state" (the Grand National Assembly) that they had founded vis-à-vis the Ottoman monarchy, which they abolished in 1922 (see Chapter 6).

A traditionalist case in point is Ömer Ziyaeddin Efendi (1908), a leading *alim* and Sufi of the time. In his 40-*hadith* compilation described above, he cited both verses twice (in the preface and at the end) in order to underline the legitimacy of the constitutional regime and its compatibility with (the traditionalist view of) the Caliphate. He also cited three prophetic traditions, as well as the sayings of historical figures (such as Ali, the fourth caliph), that emphasized the importance of consultation (pp. 65–66) – though they, like the two *"shura* verses" themselves, referred to "consultation" not necessarily as a political system, but to "affairs" in general, according to his own translation. Similarly, another traditionalist scholar-governor, Mustafa Zihni (1911), reconstructed the Sunni theory of the Caliphate in a lengthy discussion in order to prove, as he himself stated, the compatibility of the parliamentary system with Islam and to defend the Ottoman Caliphate. He gave a detailed account of these two verses, presenting different interpretations of them in the Islamic intellectual tradition, arguing that the Qur'an required consultation, which was the basis of the Caliphate in the Golden Age of Islam (pp. 180, 194). He also discussed in detail the questions of who the Caliph should consult with (members of parliament) and in what matters ("everything that is not sanctioned by the Qur'an") (pp. 195–196).

The concept of consultation and verses related to it were emphasized even more strongly by modernist Islamists who tried to adopt the (classical) Caliphate to the modern constitutional system, in which the Caliph's power was significantly limited. The two "*shura* verses" offered great help to modernists in terms of legitimating their attempt at transforming the Ottoman state by secularizing the Caliphate. Thus, for example, Seyyid Bey (1917: 467) cited both verses (3/159, 42/38), arguing that they proved "Islamic government is based on the principle of consultation (or Constitutionalism)." (Note the author's equation of the Islamic principle of consultation with the modern constitutionalist system.) Like-wise, the Egyptian intellectual-politician Ali Fahmi (1911: 81–82) argued, after citing the two verses, that Constitutionalism (*Meşrutiyet*) and the equality that it brought on the basis of citizenship were intrinsic to the Islamic "spirit" (political culture), as evidenced by the *ulema* and the *şeyhülislam*, who defended the Con-stitution and the equality of all Ottoman (Muslim and non-Muslim) citizens. Similarly, the Turkish writer Mahmud Nedim criticized Sharif Hussein (and the British who manipulated him) for creating a dynastic rule in the Holy Land on the grounds that the "Islamic religion is based on the principle of democracy" (1919: 298).

Likewise, in his critique of the Ottoman Caliphate, Rashid Rida argued that "consultation" was the Caliph's "most important duty," adding:

> The leader ... despite what many people think, is not an absolute ruler [in Islam]. Rather, he is restricted by consultation based on the evidence derived from the Book [the Qur'an], the *Sunna* [of the Prophet], and the Rightly Guided Caliphs' general principles of governance. For Muslims to under-stand this, it is enough to cite the verses "[they conduct] their affairs by mutual Consultation" [42/38] and "consult them in affairs (of moment)" [3/159].
>
> (1923a: 30)[33]

Even secularists cited these two verses to support their claims, which completely contradict those of the traditionalist and modernist Islamists. Turkish secularists, in particular, drew on the consultation verses in their discursive battle against the modernists, especially to enforce their claim that the Caliphate was useless (and thus should be abolished) because there was already a truly Islamic government: the parliamentary government of the new Turkish state (see Chapter 6 for a detailed discussion). For example, even Mustafa Kemal, the champion of secu-larism, made allusions to many verses in the Qur'an on different themes, includ-ing consultation, in a press conference he held in 1923. He explained the nature of the new Turkish state, saying that the new regime would be neither a monar-chy nor a republic ("like the American and French Republics"), but a "people's government" that would be based on the principles of "justice" and "consultation":

> Now I should make it clear that there is no clear-cut rule in the essence of the religion on the nature of government. It is only the principles on which the government is based that are explicit, clear and definite. One of these principles is consultation. Consultation is one of the most basic principles.

This principle was directly commanded by God to his messenger Muhammad Mustafa. The esteemed person who was the prophet would not do his job by himself alone. He would do it by consultation. If that is the case, then there is no doubt that those who were in charge of the leadership of the Islamic peoples after Him had to follow the same principle. For that is a divine command!

(Mustafa Kemal 1923: 102–103)

Mustafa Kemal made this remark as part of his press campaign against the modernist Islamists, represented by Hoca Şükrü Efendi in particular, who had insisted that Caliph Abdülmecid Efendi should also be the head of state after the abolition of the Ottoman monarchy (see Chapter 6). During this specific struggle, known as the "Battle of Pamphlets," Kemal received crucial assistance from the *ulema*-politicians who supported his cause. For example, in their critique of the modernist Hoca Şükrü, three *ulema*-deputies – Hoca Halil Hulki, Hoca İlyas Sami, and Hoca Rasih – cited the *shura* verses to demonstrate that the parliament was perfectly compatible with Islam because it was based on the principle of consultation (Hoca Halil *et al.* 1923: 15–16). Likewise, Seyyid Bey, who was a close associate of Mustafa Kemal between 1922 and 1924, cited the two consultation verses to emphasize that "even the Prophet, who was protected from all kinds of sins, was ordered [by God] to consult [with his aides]; therefore, each Caliph, including the 'true' [as opposed to 'fictitious'] ones, are required to practice consultation" (Seyyid Bey 1923: 28).

The main discursive technique of dissecting verses and abstracting them from their textual and social contexts can be clearly seen in how these two verses were treated. The context in which the first verse (3/159) was revealed, according to Islamic tradition, was the aftermath of the Battle of Uhud (625 CE), which Muslims had lost because some soldiers had not followed the Prophet Muhammad's orders, who then did not punish them but was nevertheless unhappy about their disobedience. The verse tells the Prophet to forgive them and keep "consulting" with them, despite this uncomfortable situation. There is some disagreement among the scholars of *tafsir* (Qur'anic interpretation) as to whether the verse sanctions consultation on military decisions only or on administrative affairs in general (Mustafa Zihni 1911: 188–193). The second verse (42/38) is about desired ethical features of an (ideal) Muslim, including observing prayers, charitable giving, and consulting with others in managing his or her affairs. Though these verses have no direct political implications, in a highly politicized environment most authors referred to them as a discursive technique and concluded that the Qur'an required a constitutional regime that was compatible with the Caliphate.

VERSES ON UNITY

The most important issue discussed in relation to the Caliphate in its periphery was Muslim unity, especially during and after World War I. By that time the

Muslim world had disintegrated as a result of European colonialism, to which the Ottoman Empire had responded, since Abdülhamid II, by pursuing a policy of "Muslim rapprochment" (see Chapter 5). During the war, this policy was adopted by the CUP, as well. The Ottomans had by then lost all their territories inhabited by non-Muslim citizens of the empire in Europe, as well as some of its Muslim territories. In this context, both traditionalist and modernist Islamists cited Qur'anic verses that emphasized the unity of Muslims, particularly the verse, "And hold fast, all together, by the rope which Allah [stretches out for you], and be not divided among yourselves…" (3/103). This theme was common to both groups (as opposed to secularists) because they both wanted to preserve the Ottoman Caliphate. Therefore, at a time when the Muslim world was being colonized by Western powers and the caliphal center faced the harsh reality of uprisings by not only non-Muslim *millet*s, but also Arab citizens of the Empire, both traditionalists (e.g., İsmail Hakkı 1910: 443; al-Yemeni 1911: 430; Mustafa Zihni 1911: 183–184; Ömer Lütfi 1912: 243; Muhyiddin Baha 1915: 383–426; al-Tunusi 1916a: 154, 157, 1916b: 429; Safayihi 1915: 76–83; Yafi 1916: 166; Kidwai 1919: 331) and modernists (e.g., Ali Fahmi 1911: 95–97; Seyyid Bey 1917: 446; Jawish 1916: 246–249 etc.) defended the Ottoman Caliphate with reference to different Qur'anic verses (see also Chapter 5). For example, in his discussion of the European assault on the Muslim world, the Egyptian politician-intellectual Ali Fahmi said:

> Their situation corresponds to the case described in the verse: "Fain would they extinguish Allah's light with their mouths, but Allah will not allow but that His light should be perfected, even though the Unbelievers may detest [it]" (9/32).… [On the other hand,] pan-Islamism resembles the pacts among contemporary Christian states, which Sultan Abdülhamid had described [in saying], "By forming political alliances, they actually engage in Crusades against us." I am not surprised that Europeans attack Islamic unity or the Caliphate, because they are obliged to pursue their own political interests. What surprises and saddens me is that when they ask some us for their help as part of their "divide and rule" strategy, those people work against their own community by forgetting the verse: "And hold fast, all together, by the rope which Allah (stretches out for you), and be not divided among yourselves."
>
> (1911: 95)

VERSES ON JUSTICE

Another theme of verses that traditionalists, modernists, and – to a lesser extent – secularists sometimes cited was the characteristics and duties of the (ideal) caliph, particularly that of "maintaining justice." The idea in the classical theory of the Caliphate that the main duty of a caliph was to maintain justice is based on a famous Qur'anic verse (16/90) that reads: "Allah commands justice, the doing of good, and liberality to kith and kin, and He forbids all shameful deeds, and injustice and rebellion." They discussed "maintaining justice" as a basic element of an Islamic government with reference to other parts of the Qur'an as well. For example, İsmail Hakkı (1910: 439),[34] a traditionalist scholar, cited a two-word phrase ("Be just...") from a verse (5/8) in order to argue that an oppressive ruler could not be a legitimate caliph. Similarly, in his discussion on the (alleged) requirement for caliphs to be a member of one of the Quraysh tribes, he cited a verse (42/13) that ordered the Muslim community not to be divided within itself to support his argument, which he derived from Ibn Khaldūn and others (see below), that the Quraysh requirement was to prevent divisions among Muslims at the time as decreed in the verse, which no longer applied under the Ottoman Caliphate.

Among the modernists, Seyyid Bey (1917: 456–457) argued that obedience to the caliph was mandatory as long as he was a just ruler. Also, in his discussion of the limits of the caliph's authority, which he constantly emphasized as a dis-cursive technique, Seyyid Bey cited a verse (26/227) that forbade oppression, stating that if the caliph acted against the rules of the *sharia* or the "interests of the public," this meant a form of oppression that required punishment by God *and* by the people he represented, and thereby necessitated dismissal from his post. (Note that the author was a top aide and advisor to the CUP leadership, which had deposed the previous caliph-sultan, Abdülhamid II.) Seyyid Bey com-plemented his modernist view of the limits of the Caliphate's power with a verse on justice:

> Obedience to him [the caliph] is absolute and general. However, this obedi-ence is not utterly and completely absolute. The caliph has a boss and a client. His boss is the *sharia*, his client the nation. [Violation of their will] is oppression; obeying the oppressor is equal to being its instrument, which is the same as oppression: "And soon will the unjust assailants know what vicissitudes their affairs will take!" [26/227].
>
> (1917: 457)

Within the secularist camp, the three *hoca*-deputies – Hoca Halil Hulki, Hoca İlyas Sami, and Hoca Rasih – who helped Mustafa Kemal and his associates win their battle against the Islamists between 1922 and 1924, made use of certain verses to prove that the Ottoman monarchy was un-Islamic. Arguing that the first principle of Islamic government was justice, they cited three verses (4/58, 16/90, 3/110) ostensibly on this subject with no attention to their textual and social con-texts, as usual (Hoca Halil *et al.* 1923: 11).

Finally, to give an example from the caliphal periphery, we can cite Sharif Hussein's use of a verse on justice. In his uprising against the caliph of Islam, which he framed exclusively in religious terms, Sharif Hussein legitimized his act with reference to a verse on "just rule": "Our Lord! Decide Thou between us and our people in truth, for Thou art the best to decide" (7/89). His "Proclama-tion" (1916) started with this verse, after which he accused the CUP (not the caliph-sultan, who he praised) of committing atrocities and oppressing Muslims in the Arabian Peninsula. He also argued that the purpose of his uprising was to save Islam and the Holy Land from oppression (see Chapter 5).

In addition to these popular verses, there are many others that were cited in the discussions on the Caliphate, though they were not necessarily directly linked to this institution. The main discursive technique deployed was again that of selecting certain phrases from verses and taking them out of their textual and social contexts to interpret them freely according to the authors' own purposes. Pro-Ottoman intellectuals usually cited verses that emphasized the significance of the Prophet as a ruler and the necessity of obedience to him and to God to imply that the (current) caliph should be obeyed by all Muslims as well – a discursive technique frequently employed by traditionalists (e.g., Ömer Ziyaeddin 1908: 49, 56–57; al-Yemeni 1911: 430; al-Tunusi 1916a: 148; Safayihi 1915: 76, 79; Yafi 1916:166–167) and by some modernists (e.g., Seyyid Bey 1917: 455; Jawish 1916: 248; Lütfi Fikri 1922: 363).

These actors also resorted to different verses for more specific purposes. For example, when reconstructing the Sunni theory of the Caliphate in order to legitimize it against claims by Shia *ulema*, traditionalist scholar-bureaucrat Mustafa Zihni (1911: 160–169) cited five different Qur'anic verses (5/54, 48/16, 24/55, 59/8, 1/6–7) that he claimed to be referring specifically to the superior personality of Abu Bakr (the first caliph of Islam) and his future Caliphate. He took these verses out of their context to argue that they clearly signaled that Abu Bakr would eventually be elected Caliph (not just by the people, but also by God), just as the Shia *ulema* had ignored their context when they had claimed that some of these verses (e.g., 48/16) actually referred to Imam Ali, a claim Mustafa Zihni rejected. Likewise, in his discussion on the cabinet, Zihni also cited two other verses (20/29–33, 25/25) to establish the Qur'anic legitimacy of the modern form of government (1911: 198–199). Here he employed the "transformative technique" of establishing semantic equality between semantically different but lexicographically similar words mentioned in verses (e.g., the word "vizier" in 20/31) – again ignoring their contexts. Thus, though the above-mentioned verses describing the status of Aaron as "vizier" ("helper") for his brother Moses are not directly linked to governance, the author argued:

> If, according to the Qur'anic verse, great prophets need to have a *vizier*, the caliph [whose status is lower than a prophet] definitely requires [a cabinet of *viziers*] in his government. [Therefore,] the cabinet system is an essential element of the Islamic Caliphate and required by the Islamic *sharia*.
>
> (1911: 198)

Similarly, against the rebellion in Yemen, the Yemenite *ulema*, led by al-Yemeni (1911: 430), cited two verses (41/33, 46/31) requiring obedience to the "Messenger of Allah" (Prophet Muhammad) who called people to God's way. They cited them to support their call for other Yemenite scholars to resist the rebellion in Yemen, therefore implying that engaging in *jihad* in the service of the Ottoman Caliphate, the only legitimate ruler of all Muslims, meant being on the way of God.

Aside from these more "popular" verses, many other Qur'anic verses were also quoted by intellectuals, especially by traditionalist and modernist Islamists with academic backgrounds, to support their arguments on different topics. Some of them were directly related to the Caliphate, while others were not, but the authors linked them to it through yet other verses.[35] In so doing, they applied the main discursive technique of taking these verses and phrases in them out of their context in order to support their political arguments. For example, in the context of the British invasion of the Middle East, Arab traditionalist scholar al-Ubeydi[36] (1916: 232) cited several verses (15/42; 5/56; 69/28–29) that were related to the transient nature of this life (as opposed to the afterlife), such as "it is the fellowship of Allah that must certainly triumph" (5/56). Though their contexts were strictly spiritual, emphasizing "working hard" for the afterlife and downplaying the significance of this world, the author referred to them to support his argument urging people to resist colonization and fight against the British.

ALLUSIONS TO VERSES

Finally, in addition to direct references to Qur'anic verses, many authors also alluded to them or to concepts and allegories contained in these verses without directly quoting them. In the caliphal center, traditionalist Mustafa Zihni (1911: 111) stated, for example, that the legitimacy of the Caliphate was based on the first three of the four fundamental sources of Islam (the Qur'an, the *Sunna*, and *Ijma'* [unanimous decision of the *ulema*]). On the periphery, the modernist Jawish (1916: 259) said, in his criticism of the Moroccan sultan, Yusuf, who had made a claim for the Caliphate with the support of the French during World War I, that the "multiplication of the Caliphate" was forbidden by "many Qur'anic verses" and prophetic traditions. Similarly, when criticizing the "oppression of Muslims by the CUP," Sharif Hussein, the Arab leader who revolted against the Ottoman Caliphate, also blamed CUP leaders for violating the "principles of the Qur'an and the *Sunna*" by allowing the publication of an article in *İctihad* (a secular journal published by Abdullah Cevdet, who was close to the CUP) that "insulted the Prophet with degrading phrases and violated the verses of the Qur'an" (1916: 420).

On the other hand, the leader of another "revolt" against the Ottoman sultan, Mustafa Kemal, toured Anatolia in mid-1923 in an effort to spread, *post facto*, the idea of a government without the sultan. During his tour he gave speeches in different cities and held press conferences, in which he often glorified Islam and smeared the monarchy. In one such event, at a Friday prayer in a mosque in Balıkesir, he delivered a sermon in which he alluded to the Qur'an and the Prophet:

O, the nation; Allah is the One and the Only; his glory is high. His peace and blessings be upon you. It is well known that the basic law that His Excellency the Prophet was sent by the Almighty God as an Ambassador and servant who explained the religious truths to the people, is stated in the Glorious Qur'an. Our religion, which has given people the spirit of blessing, is the last and the perfect religion. Because our religion fully conforms to reason, logic and truth.

(quoted in Borak 1962: 29)

Mustafa Kemal employed the same discursive technique in another speech he delivered during the same tour. In an effort to demonstrate that the Prophet of Islam had no political mission or temporal authority, he claimed: "Allah the Almighty did not bestow upon him [the Prophet] political leadership [*emaret*], monarchy, or a crown. He did not give [him] kingship" (Mustafa Kemal 1923: 101). Clearly, this implied that the caliph could have no political power or temporal authority, either, which he explicitly stated in the same speech.

An examination of the debates over the Caliphate indicates a heavy use of Qur'anic verses by most actors, especially traditionalists. They generally paid no attention to the social and textual contexts of these verses. Our survey has also shown that actors involved in the debate on the Caliphate could also be categorized as Turkish versus non-Turkish (mostly Arab) Muslim intellectuals (including the *ulema* and bureaucrats), because there was a clear distinction between them in terms of the themes they emphasized, which transcended the distinction between traditionalists and modernists (and secularists). Our analysis has shown that after the status and authority of the caliph, the most popular theme that Turkish intellectuals discussed was the constitutional system (including the parliament and elections), whereas Arab intellectuals' most popular subject was the unity of the Muslim world – and, hence, the need to preserve the Ottoman Caliphate. A similar observation in terms of the most popular topics discussed by intellectuals can also be made regarding references to the other element of the "sacred texts" of Islam, the *hadith*s of Prophet Muhammad.

Invoking prophetic traditions (hadiths)

As in the case of Qur'anic verses, we observe frequent references to prophetic traditions along with a heavy use of Islamic terminology in the sources at hand. In employing this strategy, the political actors aimed to legitimize their positions vis-à-vis their opponents based on the unquestionable authority of the Prophet Muhammad in Islam, for an authentic *hadith* on a particular matter is a binding provision for Muslims. Moreover, all traditionalists and modernists (without exception) – and some secularists – defined the caliph as representative of Prophet Muhammad. Where they disagreed was the nature of this representation: For secularists (e.g., Celal Nuri 1913: 412; Mustafa Kemal 1923: 101) the caliph represented only the spiritual aspect of the Prophet; for modernists (e.g., Elmalılı Hamdi 1909: 434–435; Seyyid Bey 1917: 445) he was a purely temporal representative of the prophet as a political leader; while traditionalists claimed that he was both (e.g., Safayihi 1915: 14; Yafi 1916: 164).

HADITH COLLECTIONS

In addition to the frequent references to individual *hadith*s, our sources also include two pamphlets that exclusively contain a list of *hadith*s specifically on the Caliphate, both written by traditionalist actors. These collections include many (alleged) *hadith*s that state that "the Caliphate is given by God" (Ömer Ziyaeddin 1908: 51) and that the "caliph-sultan is the Shadow of God on Earth" (Mehmed Tahir 1909: 70). The first of these was a 40-*hadith* collection by Ömer Ziyaeddin Efendi (1908) titled "Forty *Hadith*s on the Rights of Sultans." The author was both a respected scholar and a Sufi sheikh who had followers in Istanbul and Cairo. He presented his *hadith* compilation to Abdülhamid II in 1908, before the sultan was deposed by the CUP. After praising God, the Prophet, and the caliph (Abdülhamid II) and quoting Qur'anic verses on "consultation" in the preface, he gave translations of 40 *hadith*s (plus a few quotes from historical figures such as Ali, the fourth Caliph) regarding the Caliphate. The *hadith*s contained in the collection emphasized the necessity of obeying the caliph and of avoiding disrespect to him. Some of them also related his authority directly to that of God and the Prophet, thus giving it a sacred character, which was emphasized with the frequent use of the title "Shadow of God on Earth" (*Zillulah fil-arz*), implying the divine nature of the caliph's authority over Muslims. The idea of the caliph as a "sacred" being was shared by many traditionalists. As a discursive technique, the use of this title and other similar phrases in *hadith*s made it possible to maintain the moral supremacy of the sultan-caliph, emphasizing both the religious and political aspects of the Caliphate and defending the authority of the Ottoman caliph in particular (see also the next chapter). Moreover, the last three *hadith*s of the collection were about the importance of "consultation," after which the author cited the above-mentioned "*shura* verse" (3/159). With these, the author tried to show that the constitutional system was perfectly compatible with the caliph's Islamic government.

Yet, most of the *hadith*s he selected were "weak" (not eligible in matters of faith according to Islamic theology), which the author, as a scholar of *hadith* himself, should definitely have been aware of.[37] Despite the fact that the author knew that sound evidence could not be derived from technically weak *hadith*s, he nevertheless used them (along with a number of authentic *hadith*s) in order to help invigorate the authority of the increasingly powerless caliph-sultan in Istanbul, who, as mentioned, was about to be dethroned in 1909 by a military *coup d'état* by the CUP (see Chapter 4). Given the apparent decline of the caliph's power, Ömer Ziyaeddin desperately sought the help of the *hadith*s, which occupy the second-highest rank in the hierarchy of epistemological sources of the Muslim faith. Benefiting from the unquestionable authority and high status of the *hadith*s in general, the author employed weak *hadith*s as well, in order to make a stronger case against the modernists. Moreover, the pamphlet that he presented to the caliph was probably intended both to please the sultan and to influence the reading public outside the *ulema* circles.

The second *hadith* collection was produced by Mehmet Tahir, a former army officer and politician.[38] His collection, *el-Ehâdîsü'ş-Şerîfe fi's-Saltanati'l-Münîfe*, was actually his translation (from Arabic) of another collection by a famous Islamic scholar, Imam al-Suyuti (d. 1505). Benefiting from al-Suyuti's fame and scholarly authority in the Muslim world, the author/translator tried to support the Ottoman Caliphate with religious references. Published after Abdül-hamid II was overthrown (1909) and presented to the new caliph, Mehmed V, the collection was an example of a CUP member emphasizing the religious and political character of the Caliphate and obedience *after* the main threat (to the CUP) was gone, and of legitimating the new sultan. Similar to the first collection, the 25 *hadith*s contained in this one presented the Caliphate from a traditionalist point of view, almost as a "metaphysical" leadership that combined worldly and spiritual authority, which the Young Turks had previously completely rejected, and criticized Sultan Abdülhamid for creating such a "false" image (Kara 2003b: 11). The book emphasized the moral supremacy of the sultan, presented obeying the caliph as part of Muslim faith, and again used the title "The Shadow of God on Earth." Also like first collection, many of the *hadith*s contained in this compilation were "weak" and not valid for a theological argument. The author/translator also added an appendix at the end of the collection where he specifically emphasized that the Ottoman Caliphate was the only legitimate Caliphate (Mehmet Tahir 1909: 75). His discourse in the appendix was very similar to that of Abdülhamid's supporters during his reign (1876–1908) (see Kara 2002–2005, vols. 1–2).

In what follows I explore the use of prophetic traditions by all three groups on certain themes that come up frequently, including the legitimization of the caliph's authority, the question of multiple caliphs, consultation, and the ethnicity of the caliph. There was also an important debate that took place between Ottoman loyalists and Arab nationalists on the caliphal periphery that centered on a particular *hadith* (the famous Quraysh *hadith*), which I discuss separately. Let us start with how the caliph's authority was legitimized by different actors drawing on the *hadith*s.

LEGITIMIZATION OF THE CALIPHATE

Frequent references to prophetic traditions for legitimization purposes were found consistently in writings by traditionalists, all of whom argued that one of the (religious) foundations of the institution of the Caliphate was the *sunna* of the Prophet. As mentioned above, the traditionalists' main objective in citing these *hadith*s was to draw on the unquestionable authority of the Prophet Muhammad in Islamic theology and law. For example, in his polemic – mentioned above – with the modernist Mustafa Sabri Efendi, Ömer Lütfi (1912: 236ff.) cited many different *hadith*s – as well as the "*ul al-amr*" verse – to argue that the Caliph had both religious and temporal authority, which was rooted in the authority of God and the Prophet, and as such, could not be reduced to the status of a king. One of the *hadiths* that he cited was a famous one:

> Each one of you is shepherd. And each one of you will be asked about your flock. A ruler [*imam*] also is a shepherd and he will be asked about his flock. And every man is a shepherd to his family. And a woman is the custodian of her husband's house and his children. Thus each one of you is shepherd, and each one will be asked about his flock
> (Bukhari 1971, "Jumua" 11; Muslim, "Imara" 20; Ibn Hanbal, II: 108).

The author translated the word "ruler" mentioned in this *hadith* as "the great imam who has the full authority to administer the people's affairs." (1912: 244).

The use of this *hadith* is a good example of how different actors with opposing views employed the same discursive material and techniques to further their conflicting political interests, for some modernists also cited the same *hadith* for the purpose of *undermining* the absolute authority of the caliph-sultan, rather than supporting it. For example, Turkish modernist Seyyid Bey cited the *hadith* and highlighted the caliph's responsibility, rather than his authority. Arguing that the sultan could in no way be above the law and unaccountable, he concluded, "Just like [ordinary] individuals, the caliph, too, is responsible for his actions and decisions in terms of both legal and criminal liability" (1923: 19). Seyyid Bey made this argument following the "punishment" of the last Ottoman caliph-sultan, Vahideddin (when his temporal authority was completely purged) by the Turkish parliament in November 1922. Seyyid Bey's pamphlet was part of a debate in Istanbul on the new caliph's authority and responsibility, a debate in which he sided with the secularists, as mentioned above. In the same debate, the leading figure among the modernist Islamists was Hoca Şükrü, who cited the same *hadith* to argue that with responsibility came authority and that the new caliph should be the head of the Turkish state. Moreover, in Cairo, the anti-Ottoman, Arab nationalist intellectual Rashid Rida (1923a: 27) quoted the same *hadith* in his discussion on the duties of the caliph to underline the main assertion of his book: The Ottoman right to the caliphate should be denied, and the institution should be "returned" to Arabs.

Going back to the traditionalists, Turkish jurist Ömer Lütfi, who cited the above *hadith*, also cited six other *hadiths* to argue that obedience to the caliph – as long as he conformed to the principles of the Qur'an and the *Sunna* – was a religious duty for all Muslims (1912: 247–249). Likewise, Safayihi (1915: 69, 71, 77, 79) and Yafi (1916: 165–166) cited many *hadiths* (as well as Qur'anic verses) and discussed them in detail to argue for the necessity of a caliph with both religious and temporal power and obedience to him as the believer's religious duty.

Many traditionalists also invoked prophetic traditions in their discussions of the *limits* of the caliph's authority, which were quite broad. Mustafa Zihni (1911), like many others, determined the limits of the caliph's authority with reference to a *hadith* that stated, "There is no obedience in matters of disrespect to

Allah" (p. 131, n. 16). Similarly, Ömer Lütfi (1912: 224–225) discussed the Prophet's status in Islamic *fiqh* in detail in order to argue, with reference to the principles of *hadith* methodology, that even some of the actions and sayings of the Prophet (that were not related to his religious mission) were not mandatory to obey, as they reflected his "human side." Therefore, obedience to the *ul al-amr* (ruler) was not without its limits, either. Note that he made this argument, as discussed above, in the debate in late 1911 over the CUP's proposal that would expand the sultan's authority so as to include the dissolution of parliament, a plan the FAP opposed. Though Ömer Lütfi, a supporter of the CUP, discussed the limits of the caliph's authority, he in fact broadened them by highlighting only this particular prophetic tradition, which mentioned "disrespect to Allah" as the limit of the ruler's power, and ignoring others that further limited it. On the other hand, Seyyid Bey, the secularist, cited the same *hadith* (1923: 46) in a different context for the opposite purpose – to argue for the necessity of obedience to the parliament's decisions, including the abolition of the Ottoman monarchy, which he tried to justify in his pamphlet. He wrote it on Mustafa Kemal's request, as mentioned, to legitimize the parliament's move to strip the caliph of any temporal power before abolishing it altogether.

Modernists, too, often invoked prophetic traditions in their attempts to promote a narrower and more "this-worldly" definition of the Caliphate. Elmalılı Hamdi (1909) based his entire argument for the reduction of the caliph's authority to political affairs on a famous *hadith*: "There is no clergy in Islam" (Ibn Hanbal 1895, VI: 226). Paradoxically, however, he cited it to argue that, in contradistinction to Christianity, there was no sharp line between religion and politics in Islam, which "opposes the principles that prevent religion's intervention into worldly matters" (Elmalılı Hamdi 1909: 433). This was an example of how modernist Islamists helped secularize the Islamic discourse from within (see Chapter 4 for a detailed discussion). In this case, Elmalılı cited it to criticize the traditionalist attempt to elevate the status of the *şeyhülislam* by claiming that, as the Caliph's representative, he could not be held accountable by the parliament. Elmalılı argued, instead, that the *şeyhülislam* was no more than a civil servant working for the government. Thus, though he clearly stated that Islam should be involved in the administration of the state, he helped to diminish the power and prestige of the head of the *ulema*, of which he himself was a member, as well as the caliph's authority. Some secularists, on the other hand, cited the same *hadith* for the opposite purpose. For example, in their critical response to the modernist Hoca Şükrü, the three *hoca*-deputies (from Mustafa Kemal's group) accused Hoca Şükrü and other Islamists of attributing to the caliph spiritual functions, which, for them, Islam clearly denied. They cited this *hadith* (Hoca Halil *et al.* 1923: 9) before delving into a long discussion on how Islam, unlike Christianity, did not recognize any spiritual authority or agent who could mediate between men and God. They concluded that this principle denied any person (i.e. the caliph) or any group (i.e. the *ulema*) the right to make a claim for religious and political authority – except for the *ul al-amr* represented by the parliament in Turkey.[39] This famous *hadith* was thus used by the secularist group as a useful tool to undermine the legitimacy of the Caliph in their struggle against the modernist Islamists between 1922 and 1924.

Modernists, too, had often employed a similar strategy in their struggle against traditionalist Islamists in the previous phases of the Second Constitutional Period. For example, Seyyid Bey (when he was still in the modernist position, in 1917) made it clear that obedience to the caliph was a religious duty for every Muslim by citing two *hadith*s (as well as the "*ul al-amr*" verse), though he also opposed the definition of the Caliphate as a sacred institution (1917: 456). Accordingly, he emphasized the limits of the authority of the caliph, which he specified as the Islamic *sharia* and the "public good," with reference to two verses and three authentic *hadith*s – one of which was the same *hadith* as cited by traditionalist Mustafa Zihni, the other two being very similar in terms of their content (1917: 458). The use of these three *hadith*s indicates, then, how different groups employed the same evidence for opposite purposes: one to strengthen the caliph's position, the other to undermine it.

Secularists, on the other hand, as in the case of Qur'anic verses, did not cite too many prophetic traditions. There were two primary reasons for this: First, most of them did not have the relevant educational background in the religious sciences to allow them to effectively utilize the Islamic tradition for their political purposes; second, it was difficult for them to find *hadith*s from the Prophet that would support their positions. For this reason, they often needed to resort to the help of the (modernist) *ulema* in their quest for Islamic legitimization of their arguments. Mustafa Kemal's own strategy is a case in point. Throughout his early political career (until 1924), he often got the crucial help he needed from Seyyid Bey, who he would later appoint as his first Minister of Justice in 1923. Seyyid Bey and some other *ulema*, the three *hoca*-deputies (Hoca Halil Hulki, Hoca İlyas Sami, and Hoca Rasih) in particular, made use of a prophetic tradition known as the "30-year *Hadith*" for their secular cause. Also frequently cited by anti-Ottoman Caliphate actors, this famous *hadith* of the Prophet read, "The Caliphate will last thirty years, then will come the bitter *Sultanate*" (Ibn Hanbal 1895, V: 220, 221). Arab nationalists, as well as Turkish secularists, often referred to this *hadith* in order to justify their anti-Caliphate positions in religious terms. Both groups tried to demonstrate that the Ottoman Caliphate was illegitimate because it was not a "true" Islamic government. Though the two groups had different political ends in mind, they both used the same "evidence" to legitimize their claims, drawing on the expected influence of this prophetic saying. Turkish secularists tried to claim that, since the Ottoman Caliphate was a "fictitious" one, as demonstrated by the *hadith*, it was Islamically permissible to first separate the Caliphate from the monarchy, which would deprive it of temporal power, and then to abolish it altogether (see, e.g., Seyyid Bey 1923: 1, 8; Hoca Halil *et al.* 1923: 24). They often complemented this argument with another discursive technique: Since, as mentioned above, there was already a true Islamic government represented by the Turkish parliament, the Ottoman Caliphate was useless and even un-Islamic (see also Chapter 6). Mustafa Kemal exemplified this technique when he applied it, along with the "30-year *hadith*," to justify his claim that the Caliphate was not an Islamic institution. In the press conference mentioned above, he said:

> According to the *sharia* and religion, there is no such thing as the Caliphate. As you know, the Prophet himself said, "There will be kingdoms 30 years after me." This is a *hadith*. Therefore, to say that "there must be a Caliph, the Caliphate will exist, the Caliphate will survive" amounts to demanding something that is against the prophetic *hadith*.
>
> (Mustafa Kemal 1923: 64)

On the other hand, Arab nationalists, such as Rashid Rida (1923a), cited this *hadith* to imply that the Ottoman Caliphate, being based on dynastic power, was not legitimate anyway; therefore, it was only natural that an Arab caliph could replace the Turkish one (see Chapter 5).

MULTIPLE CALIPHS

In addition to referencing prophetic traditions to legitimize the Ottoman Caliphate, many traditionalists and modernists also invoked them to defend it against Arab nationalist criticisms by bringing up more specific themes as a discursive technique. One of the more popular themes in this context was the question of multiple caliphates. During World War I this question turned out to be a significant problem for the Ottoman political center, which by then had been greatly weakened. Some local leaders – Sharif Hussein, the sharif of Mecca, and Yusuf, the sultan of Morocco, in particular – sought to claim the caliphate based on their purported prophetic descent. To support the Ottoman Caliphate against these claims, some authors/activists who had ties to the CUP published declarations, pamphlets, and books. For example, Muhammad Safa, who was an Egyptian journalist and a member of the Ottoman secret service, the *Teşkilat-ı Mahsusa*, wrote a book, titled *The Islamic Caliphate and the Ottomans* (Safa 1922). Published in Istanbul both in Arabic and Turkish, the book was a direct critique of the Arab nationalists' Quraysh argument. The dissemination of such publications in the Middle East, North Africa, and Europe was largely funded by the CUP. These publications presented the Ottoman Empire as the "Great Caliphate" (*Hilafet-i Uzma*), emphasizing the idea of one single caliph as a religious requirement and denouncing competing claims to the caliphate as heretical and the principal cause of disunity among Muslims, the alleged "caliphs" being puppets of the imperialist powers – Britain, France, and Italy (see Chapter 5). The Islamic discourse on the question of multiple caliphs found in these publications tended to rely heavily on prophetic traditions.

This theme was particularly dominant in the writings of the North African and Arab traditionalist actors, such as Safayihi (1915: 69–70), al-Tunusi (1916a: 149) and Yafi (1916: 165), who all quoted (different versions of) the *hadith* that states that if a rival *imam* (caliph) emerges with a claim to leadership, he should be sentenced to death for violating God's command and disturbing the unity of the

Muslim *umma*. Similarly, Mukhtar Ahmad Ansari (1919: 376),[40] the president of the Muslim League of India (1918–1920), a member of the Indian National Congress, and a friend of Gandhi, cited the same *hadith* (together with a Qur'anic verse: 26/49) specifically referring to Sharif Hussein and accusing him of backstabbing the Muslim world in the midst of war by revolting against the legitimate caliph of Islam and thereby violating an important principle of the *sharia*:

> Carried away by his ambition and selfish interests, Sharif Hussein revolted against the caliph of Islam, who was to be unquestionably obeyed, as he himself admits. By doing this, he not only violated a principle of civilized ethics, but he also failed to observe a command by Allah and His Messenger as described in the Muslim faith and religious teachings.... The Prophet said: "Evil tithes will come repeatedly. But he who seeks to separate this *ummah*, which is a united community, slay him with the sword, be he who he may."
>
> (Ansari 1919: 376)

Likewise, in the last of his three pamphlets on the Caliphate, al-Tunusi (1916b: 426) criticized the Moroccan sultan, citing a different *hadith* ("Whoever creates dissension within, or tries to separate from, the *umma* is acting with Satan" [Ibn Hanbal 1895, I: 18, 26]) and accusing Sharif Hussein of committing a great sin. This discourse, then, was part of an effort to resist the apparent disintegration of the Muslim world by saving the Ottoman Caliphate at a time when the former was undergoing an intense process of colonization by the European powers. The prophetic *hadith*s that emphasized Muslim unity were thought by the pro-Ottoman actors to be effective sources against the separatist claims of would-be alternative caliphs.

THE QURAYSH *HADITH*

As part of the same effort, traditionalists and a few modernists also discussed what is known as the "Quraysh question": whether one must belong to the Quraysh tribe in Mecca, of which the Prophet Muhammad was a member, in order to be a legitimate caliph. Some of the early political theorists of Islam (e.g., al-Māwardī) had stipulated that the Caliphate had belonged to the prophetic family and that, therefore, the caliph should be a descendant of the Prophet Muhammad. This argument was based on an authentic *hadith*, known as the Quraysh *hadith*, that stated, "Imams are from the Quraysh" (Hakim 1990, IV: 76). This requirement was not a problem for the Umayyads or the Abbasids, as both of these dynasties had branched out from the prophetic family. Following the Mongolian invasions in 1258, however, the "Quraysh condition" became a problem as the Abbasid dynasty collapsed, and the descendants of the Prophet lost all their political and military power. In light of this development, a number of Sunni theorists, including 'Ayni, Jurjani, al-Baqillani, and Ibn Khaldūn (the first three being leading theologians), discarded the Quraysh condition as an element of the Sunni theory of the Caliphate (Arnold 1965[1924]: 74–76; Ashmawi 1990). They argued that the ruling contained in the Quraysh *hadith* was specific to the period of the Prophet and the first four caliphs (610–661) and that the *hadith* was no longer applicable under the new circumstances. Ibn Khaldūn, in particular, argued that the reason the Prophet Muhammad mentioned the Quraysh in the *hadith* was directly related to the Quraysh's strong *asabiyya*: It was the only polity that was strong enough to bring together all other tribes under its rule and thus unite the Muslim community. Since, he argued, the Quraysh was no longer the dominant dynastic group in the Muslim world, i.e., the power of its *asabiyya* had declined, the *hadith* was no longer applicable. Ibn Khaldūn thus argued:

> [A] direct relationship with the Prophet ... exists [in the case of Qurayshite descent], and it is a blessing. However, it is known that the religious law has not as its purpose to provide blessings. Therefore, if descent be made a condition [of the *imamate*], there must be a [public] interest which was the purpose behind making it into law. If we probe into the matter and analyze it, we find that the [public] interest is nothing else but regard for group feeling [*asabiyya*].... Therefore we consider it a [necessary] condition for the person in charge of the affairs of the Muslims that he belong to people who possess a strong group feeling, superior to that of their contemporaries, so that they can force the others to follow them and the whole thing can be united for effective protection.... Furthermore, [the world of] existence attests to [the necessity of group feeling for the caliphate]. Only he who has gained superiority over a nation or a race is able to handle affairs. The religious law would hardly ever make a requirement in contradiction to the requirements of existence. And God, He is exalted, knows better.
>
> (Ibn Khaldūn 1958, I: 399, 401–402)

Hence, for him, the Quraysh condition could be discarded as an element of Caliphate theory. Instead, Ibn Khaldūn and others emphasized political and military power as a fundamental precondition for being caliph, which was already part of the classical theory of the Caliphate. The presence of a number of *hadith*s that denied the Quraysh tribe any religious or political privilege (see below) also bolstered the Khaldūnian position.

With the decline of the Abbasid Caliphate, as discussed above, the Ottoman Empire carried the caliphal flag. Selim I (r. 1512–1520) had transferred the Caliphate from Cairo to Istanbul in 1517, after which his descendants carried the title of caliph until after the collapse of the Ottoman Empire in 1922. Obviously the Ottomans were not of prophetic descent; however, the Quraysh condition did not emerge as a major problem for them during the classical period of the empire (16th–18th centuries), as there was virtually no challenger for the Ottoman Caliphate. The Quraysh condition remained only a theoretical problem, which was relatively easily addressed by the Ottomans, often drawing on Ibn Khaldūn's interpretation of the Quraysh *hadith*.

This problem emerged as a political issue when Britain, France, and Italy began to be concerned about Ottoman Caliph Abdülhamid II's potential influence on Muslims living in their colonies in India, the Middle East, and North Africa in the last quarter of the 19th century. When Abdülhamid was deposed and replaced by a weak Caliph in 1908, after which the powerful CUP government started to pursue – however temporarily – a policy of Panturkism (unification of Turkic peoples), the European powers accelerated their efforts to undermine the Caliphate with anti-Ottoman propaganda in their colonies, claiming that the Turkish caliph, who had not come from the Quraysh tribe, could not be a true caliph and that Ottomans had seized this title by force from the true Arab (Abbasid) caliph in the 16th century. When some Arab nationalist *ulema*, led by al-Kawakibi,[41] "rediscovered" and popularized the Quraysh *hadith*, they took up the Europeans' claims and legitimized them with reference to this tradition. Arab nationalists brought up the Quraysh condition primarily to question the legitimacy of the Ottoman sultan's status as the caliph of all Muslims. They also emphasized this issue (and utilized the famous *hadith* as a basis for it) as a discursive ground on which possible claims for an alternative (Arab) caliphate could be built. In fact, later, when Sharif Hussein of Mecca and King Fuad of Egypt claimed the caliphate in 1924 and 1926, respectively, their supporters would often cite the Quraysh *hadith* to justify their otherwise unusual claims.

Thus, some Arab nationalists, including Rashid Rida, discussed this *hadith* in detail in their writings on the Caliphate. By referring to such classical theorists as al-Māwardī, al-Taftazānī, and Ibn Humam, Rida (1923a: 18–25) described in detail how being the Prophet's descendant was a fundamental prerequisite for the Caliphate. Thus, he argued, the Ottoman sultans' claim to the Caliphate clearly violated this principle:

> The Quraysh condition has been agreed upon by all *ulema*, resulting in an *ijma* [scholarly consensus]; it [the *hadith*] was reported by reliable *hadith* scholars, and all the Sunni theologians and jurists have used it as evidence. Moreover, the historical practice has always been in this line since the people of Medina accepted a Prophet from the Quraysh and obeyed him. The *ummah*, too, has always obeyed him for centuries now; so much so that nobody has ever dared to seize the Caliphate by force, other than the Turks, who forced the Abbasids to recognize their suzerainty.
>
> (Rashid Rida 1923a:19)

Pro-Ottoman actors, particularly Arab traditionalists living in the Arab provinces of the empire, such as North Africa, reacted quickly to the Arab nationalist movement, perceiving it as a significant threat to Muslim unity under the existing caliphate. Their primary discursive strategy in their response was that of invoking the sacred texts of Islam, particularly the prophetic traditions, as well as resorting to the help of the Islamic intellectual tradition, particularly the writings of Ibn Khaldūn. They applied two main discursive techniques against nationalist claims regarding the Quraysh condition. First, they re-interpreted the

Quraysh *hadith* in a way that allowed them to justify a non-Quraysh ruler's Caliphate. They derived this reinterpretation from such leading classical scholars as Ibn Khaldūn, 'Ayni, Jurjani, and Baqillani, who had argued, as mentioned, that in this *hadith* the Prophet mentioned the Quraysh not because of his ethnic identity, but because of its *asabiyya*: it was the only tribe at the time that was able to unite all tribes under its leadership due to its special political and ideological status. Thus, the strongest available state (i.e., the Ottoman Empire) could now assume this title.[42] Second, they cited several other *hadith*s that denied any ethnic requirement for the leadership of the *ummah*.

Among the pro-Ottoman traditionalists, İsmail Hakkı brought up Ibn Khaldūn's interpretation of the Quraysh question in the context of the concept of *justice* as the fundamental element of caliphal rule, which he emphasized to downplay the significance of the Quraysh condition. His view of the Quraysh issue clearly favored *asabiyya* over genealogy:

> The *ummah* has had no disagreement on the conditions [for holding the Caliphate] of wisdom, justice, competence, and physical and mental well-being. These four are commonly agreed-upon conditions. There is a disagreement only on the Quraysh condition. As Ibn Khaldūn explains, being from the Quraysh was stipulated [for the caliph] in the early [periods of] Islam in order to prevent divisions. The Quraysh had power and prestige over other nations. They had an *asabiyya* strong enough to govern other people.... Later the Quraysh lost its strong *asabiyya*. Having a strong *asabiyya* to govern the *ummah* is not confined to the Quraysh. For this reason, this condition is not required [to hold the Caliphate].
>
> (İsmail Hakkı 1910: 439)

Similarly, Sheikh Safayihi, the former chief justice of Tunisia, delved into a detailed discussion of the Quraysh *hadith* and presented a number of other *hadith*s as counter-evidence in the book he wrote titled "Warning [Muslim] Brothers against the Tactics of the Enemy" (1915: 55–60). Reviewing the relevant Islamic literature with sophisticated argumentation in the manner of a classical scholar, he argued that the "Quraysh *hadith*" was no longer applicable due to the presence of other *hadith*s that negate the notion of ethnicity as a prerequisite for being caliph. He also downplayed the role of genealogy in favor of *asabiyya*:

> Although Qurayshite descent is a precondition for the Caliphate, as stipulated by the majority of the *ulema* (*jumhur*), it is not a precondition that is always required. ... Otherwise, being a Hashemite would be required, rather than being a Quraysh member. What is necessary is the power that comes from genealogical strength. ... In the past, this [power] was found in the Quraysh [today, it is not]. Therefore, because the aim of the *hadith* is realized, it becomes valid and true for those rulers who lead Muslims after the Quraysh rule – even if they are not from the Quraysh.
>
> (Safayihi 1915: 59–60)

Citing a Qur'anic verse (49:13) that states that ethnic ties are unimportant in the eyes of God, Sheikh Safayihi concluded that the Quraysh *hadith* also justified rule by other dynasties that had enough power to unite Muslims.

al-Tunusi (1916a: 148), another North African scholar who was concerned about a rival caliph in the region claiming to be the descendant of the Prophet, cited a popular *hadith* as counter-evidence to that of the Quraysh: "Obey your leader even if he is an Abyssinian slave with a small head" (Bukhari 1971, "Adhan" 4, 5, 156; "Ahkam" 4). He repeated it in a later pamphlet (1916b: 425) in the context of preconditions for the Caliphate, the most important of which, he argued, was the ability/power to defend the rights of Muslims, which was currently enjoyed only by the Ottomans. (Obviously, he did not list the Quraysh condition as a requirement for the caliph.) Similarly, İsmail Hakkı, a prominent Turkish scholar and CUP member, cited the same *hadith* in his short discussion of the Quraysh *hadith*, adding that some of the companions of the Prophet and classical *ulema* also held his position. Finally, in his book criticizing British efforts to undermine the Ottoman Caliphate, Hussein Kidwai, a lawyer, politician, and member of the Muslim League of India and the Indian Caliphate Movement, referred to another version of the same *hadith*, saying that even if the leader was a (former) Abyssinian prisoner of war, he would enjoy the same status as a Meccan of pure Arab origin, as long as he was a *Muslim* leader (1919: 352).

After World War I was over, the Quraysh question became part of an academic, rather than political, debate in the caliphal center. Interestingly, even the secularists who wanted to get rid of the Ottoman Caliphate did not support the Arab nationalist argument for the Quraysh condition. They probably thought that a Turkish caliph with no political power would be preferable to an Arab caliph with a claim for temporal as well as religious authority. Thus, in the debate between pro-Caliphate modernists and anti-Caliphate secularists in Istanbul, only the *ulema* brought up the Quraysh question, and both groups supported the well-known Ottoman view – borrowed from Ibn Khaldūn, al-Baqillani, 'Ayni, and al-Jurjani – that what the Prophet had been referring to in the *hadith* was the Quraysh's political power rather than its high status as an ethnic group. This interpretation was one of the few points on which the Islamist Hoca Şükrü (1923: 10–11) and secularist Seyyid Bey (1923: 12) agreed regarding the Caliphate. However, Seyyid Bey was quick to add that the Ottoman Caliphate was not a "true" Caliphate, but a "fictitious" one (p. 13). This was not because the Ottoman sultans were not the Prophet's descendants, but because they were part of the illegitimate "sultanic period" that had started thirty years after the death of the Prophet, which was indicated (as discussed above) by another prophetic *hadith*.

Thus, in this specific debate on the ethnic origins of the caliph, Arab nationalists (e.g., al-Kawakibi and Rashid Rida) based their claim for the illegitimacy of the Ottoman Caliphate on the Quraysh *hadith*. In response, pro-Ottoman actors employed two discursive strategies: They first reinterpreted the Quraysh *hadith*, based primarily on the Khaldūnian approach that emphasized the *asabiyya* of the caliph rather than his ethnic/tribal background, in a way that would deny its applicability under current political circumstances and support the Ottoman cause instead. Then, they cited counter-*hadith*s that stressed the illegitimacy of making a claim for the Caliphate when there already was a caliph, and some Qur'anic verses that emphasized Muslim unity. Invoking certain prophetic traditions on the preconditions for holding the Caliphate was the primary discursive technique for both sides.

ALLUSIONS TO *HADITH*S

In addition, some authors discussed the problem of the Quraysh *hadith* without specifically referring to it or any other *hadith*, but via allusion to the debate on these traditions. For example, Said Halim Pasha[43] wrote in his memoirs (2000[1920]: 400), which were published in French and addressed to a European audience, that since Islam opposed nationalism and the Prophet had in fact reduced the significance of ethnic identity, it was impossible to derive a "theory of the Arab Caliphate" from that *hadith*. Drawing on the same arguments as other Ottoman loyalists, he stated that what the Prophet had actually been referring to was the strong organization and special status of Mecca in terms of its political and ideological influence over all Arab tribes at the time. For him, therefore, all dynastic Caliphates – from the Umayyads to the Ottomans – were legitimate, as they had the same feature as the Quraysh had possessed earlier (p. 401).

On other matters, too, allusion to prophetic traditions without citing them was a common discursive technique employed by all three groups. For example, in his discussion of the scope of the caliph's authority in the Constitution, Ömer Lütfi (1912: 243), the pro-CUP traditionalist who criticized the FAP's Mustafa Sabri in the parliamentary debate (discussed above) on the authority of the caliph, argued that even though the newly proclaimed constitution did not make the caliph-sultan accountable to anyone, the Islamic *sharia* did, and that the basis of the caliph's responsibility for his subjects consisted of the Qur'an and prophetic traditions. Based on this, he concluded that the CUP's proposal to expand Caliph-Sultan Mehmed V's authority so as to include the dissolution of the parliament should be accepted by parliament members. On the caliphal periphery, another traditionalist, Sheikh al-Tunusi (1916a: 155), referred to a *hadith* – without citing it – that compared the Muslim *umma* with the human body, in which, when one organ was hurt, all others felt the pain as well. The author alluded to the *hadith* as part of his argument for the unification of Muslims under the Ottoman Caliphate in the face of the impending Ottoman defeat in World War I and the resulting secession of Arab provinces from the empire. In a similar vein, after the war was lost, Hussein Kidwai (1919: 368), the pro-Ottoman politician and intellectual from India, referred to the life of the Prophet Muhammad, who had "refused to be crucified" and resisted the enemies of Islam, as a model for Muslims in World War I. He argued that even though the war had been lost, Muslims would soon be able to recover and defend themselves against the intrusions of the Allies. Kidwai gave a detailed account of the activities of the Indian Muslim League and other Muslim organizations and their leaders (such as Ajmal Khan) to help the Ottoman Caliphate (see Chapter 3) as a sign of this recovery.

Traditionalists also used the Ottoman dynasty's genealogy specifically to strengthen the religious legitimacy of the Ottoman Caliph. For example, at the end of his *hadith* compilation, Mehmed Tahir (1909: 75) boldly claimed that the Ottoman sultans were all descendents of the Prophet starting from the second sultan, Orhan Gazi, whose wife belonged to a *seyyid* family. He also referred to two Ottoman *vak'anuvis* (official historians) to support his claim.

Some modernists, too, employed the discursive technique of alluding to prophetic traditions without citing them. For example, in his critique of the rival caliphs in the Arab world, Tunisian-Egyptian intellectual Abdulaziz Jawish (1916: 259) argued that they ignored, just like the Fatimid and Muwahhid caliphs in their rivalry with the Abbasid Caliphate had done before, the "orders of the Qur'an and various *hadith*s on the subject," therefore leading to the disintegration of the Muslim *ummah*. Seyyid Bey (1917: 445), on the other hand, said in his discussion of the definition of the Caliphate that since the Prophet Muhammad was not only a religious leader, but also a political one, "Islam is a superior system that involves both religion and politics" (cf. Rashid Rida 1923: 9, 28). As a modernist, however, he quickly noted that the Caliph represented the Prophet's political, rather than religious, authority (see also Chapter 4). Finally, the secularist Mustafa Kemal alluded to the Prophet's life and mission many times in his speeches – e.g., in his address to the parliament on November 1, 1922 – during the debates over the abolition of the Ottoman monarchy (see below).

OTHER *HADITH*S

Another discursive technique that was widely employed by all groups as part of the strategy of invoking prophetic traditions was that of referring to specific *hadith*s on matters that were not directly related to the Ottoman Caliphate. Among the traditionalists, Mustafa Zihni, in his refutation of the Shia *ulema*'s claims for the invalidity of Abu Bakr's Caliphate, cited ten *hadith*s, most of them "weak," as well as many Qur'anic verses and sayings of the leading companions of the Prophet, in order to prove that Abu Bakr was indeed the most qualified person for the leadership of the Muslim community after the Prophet (1911: 169–179). Similarly, in their call on their "brethren who reside in Yemen" to prevent the rebellion against the Ottomans in 1911, the Yemenite scholars cited a *hadith* according to which "wisdom is from Yemen," calling on the Yemeni people to live up to this praise (al-Yemeni 1911: 431).

Among the modernists, Jawish (1916: 262), who accused the French of manipulating the Moroccan sultan to claim the Caliphate, referred to a *hadith* that orders Muslims not to collaborate with the Meccan pagans, and warned North African Muslims not to be taken in by the false promises of the French government, which was an enemy of Islam like the pagans of Mecca. Seyyid Bey, on the other hand, argued in the context of adapting Islamic law to modern conditions that "if necessary, we can make use of the Western civil code, just like we do in other sciences and techniques" (1917: 484), and justified this borrowing by quoting (in Arabic) a famous *hadith* that says, "The word of wisdom is the stray of the believer; who has the better right to it wherever it may be found" (Tirmidhi, "Ilm" 19). In a rather different context, Turkish secularists cited the same *hadith* for a different purpose. In their discursive struggle against Islamist Hoca Şükrü in early 1923, the three secularist *ulema*-deputies referred to this *hadith* to argue that under contemporary historical conditions, Muslims did not have to be "bound by what earlier authors had written" (i.e. the legacy of the Islamic legal and theological tradition) because Islam was perfect and every Muslim could pursue the core wisdom of their religion (Hoca Halil *et al.* 1923: 7).

Citing verses and *hadith*s to justify secular reforms in the process of Westernization was a very common discursive strategy employed by modernists and secularists, in particular, mostly by those who were actively involved in politics. I have already referred in the previous chapter to the example of Sultan Selim III, who, in his speech on the founding of his new, Western-style army (*Nizam-ı Cedid*) in 1796 quoted a *hadith* that read, "You can use your enemy's weapon." This technique would also be employed by CUP leaders and later by Mustafa Kemal in their various modernization projects (see Chapters 5 and 7). Moreover, Mustafa Kemal resorted to this discursive technique at a crucial point during the struggle in 1922 to separate the Caliphate from the Ottoman monarchy. In his important address to the parliament (mentioned above) on the day of the monarchy's dissolution, he not only presented a detailed discussion of Islamic history, focusing on how the Caliphate could survive without a monarchy, but he also adorned his speech with reference to a *hadith*:

> Venerable Omar remembered that the Glorious Prophet had told his leading Companions, who were the confidants of His secrets: "My followers will prevail over their enemies. They will conquer Yemen, Jerusalem and Syria, and capture the [Iranian] kings' and the [Roman] Kaiser's treasures. But then there will emerge dissension, conflict, and civil war among them, which will make them follow the footsteps of previous kings."
> (TBMMZC 1922a: 268)

In addition, both traditionalists and modernists cited prophetic traditions about "consultation" in order to prove that the (new) parliamentary system was fully compatible with the principles of Islamic government. Governor-scholar Mustafa Zihni Pasha cited four *hadith*s (all "weak") that decreed the necessity of consultation; none of which, however, was directly related to politics (1911: 194–195). He also cited another (authentic) *hadith* to support his argument for the need for a modern cabinet system (p. 198). Modernist Rashid Rida (1923a: 31–33), too, cited several prophetic traditions in which the Prophet both suggested consulting with others and did so himself as ruler. Rida cited them as part of his argument that the caliph was not to rule by his personal opinion, but had to consult with the "*Ahl al-hall wa al-'aqd*" (the committee that was in charge of the election of the Caliph, which he identified with the modern parliament), whose status was actually superior to that of the caliph, as they represented the *ummah*, which the caliph was supposed to serve (p. 23).

Finally, there were many other prophetic traditions cited by intellectuals and politicians that were not directly related to the Caliphate, as in the case of Qur'anic verses.[44] A major discursive technique employed here was again that of taking the *hadith*s out of their context and applying them directly to the current topic at hand. On the other hand, many *ulema* and intellectuals resorted to "rational/empirical" (non-textual) argumentation and observations in addition to frequently invoking sacred texts. Moreover, while traditionalists on the whole tended to emphasize textual evidence and then support their theological arguments with rational ones; e.g., by developing a social theory of collective life or political theory of the Caliphate (Safayihi 1915: 45–51), modernists and secularists tended to first make political or "rational" claims, and then justify their (sometimes unusual) arguments with reference to theological and legal sources. Thus, on the whole, for modernists and secularists rational argumentation played the primary role, whereas for most traditionalists it had a secondary role in their meta-strategy of deriving justification from sacred texts. Another discursive strategy in which rational and legal-theological arguments were mixed to varying degrees was that of invoking Islamic history.

Invoking Islamic history

Frequent references to the history of the Caliphate constituted the second major discursive strategy employed by all three groups, reflecting the contested nature of perceptions of historical facts. The main discursive technique used as part of this strategy was the selective reading of early Islamic history. While traditionalists sought to legitimize the Caliphate by emphasizing both its religious and temporal aspects, modernists tended to emphasize its political dimension and secularists focused on the spiritual dimension. On the other hand, while many early 20th-century orientalists (e.g., Barthold 1912; Nallino 1917; Samné 1919; see also Arnold 1965[1924]) writing on the Caliphate tended to de-emphasize its significance, Muslim authors, including most secularists (up until mid-1923), conversely insisted on the Caliphate's importance (see, e.g., Mustafa Kemal's address to the parliament in TBMMZC 1922a: 268). The Caliphate's significance was one of the themes in which this discursive strategy was deployed. Other themes that I discuss below include the concept of consultation, the tension between the political versus spiritual authority of the caliph, the limits of obedience to the caliph and the problem of multiple caliphs.

As in the case of invoking sacred texts, traditionalists frequently resorted to Islamic history to legitimize what they thought was the classical form of the Caliphate. Among them, Mustafa Zihni (1911: 118–160) discussed in detail the process of the election of the first caliph, Abu Bakr (r. 632–634), explaining how he was elected by all Muslims as the successor of the Prophet Muhammad and assumed both political and religious authority. Similarly, modernists Seyyid Bey (1917: 446), Hoca Şükrü (1923: 18), and Jawish (1916: 246–250), as well as traditionalists İsmail Hakkı (1910: 439–440) and Safayihi (1915: 60) summarized the debates on the election of the first caliph as part of their arguments for the invalidity of the Quraysh *hadith* against the claims of Arab nationalists.

In addition, like traditionalists, most modernists and some secularists often based their claim for the significance of the Caliphate as a fundamental Islamic institution in early Muslim history. For example, both al-Ubeydi (1916: 203), a traditionalist, and Seyyid Bey (1917: 452), a modernist, emphasized the importance of the Caliphate by referring to the fact that when the Prophet died (in 632) the early Muslims discussed the matter of the election of a caliph and finalized the election process even before his funeral ceremony. Many others also related this story, arguing that it showed the crucial significance of the Caliphate, which also implies that the actions of the Prophet's companions were taken as a basis for theological argument. Likewise, in his speech during the debates in the Turkish parliament on the abolition of the Ottoman monarchy, Mustafa Kemal (1922), a secularist, referred to early Islamic history and emphasized the significance of the Caliphate in order to de-emphasize that of the monarchy, basically arguing that the latter was not an Islamic institution and should, therefore, be separated from the former, which was the true Islamic form of government. In his speech, probably written by Seyyid Bey,[45] he even presented a kind of philosophy of history:

> O my friends! God is one and the greatest ... Allah has taken it upon himself to send some instruments to his servants from among themselves so that they can reach the point of perfection. He has sent to them a virtually countless number of messengers and prophets, known and unknown to us, since Prophet Adam. However, he has deemed it unnecessary to contact humanity via messengers after he gave us the ultimate truths of religion and civilization through our beloved Prophet. He declared that mankind's level of understanding, enlightenment, and perfection is based on every individual servant's ability to directly contact the divine inspiration. For this reason, our beloved Prophet is the last of the prophets, and his Book is the perfect book.
> (TBMMZC 1922a: 266)

Furthermore, Mustafa Kemal discussed the Caliphate's early history in detail and skillfully manipulated the controversies of Islamic history to show the necessity of separating the monarchy from the Caliphate:

> [Following the Prophet's death, there was the question of] electing a leader to succeed the Messenger of Allah.... It was very appropriate that the venerable Abu Bakr became the Caliph.... But gentlemen, as soon as the Prophet died, there emerged strife, reaction, and insurgency everywhere. The venerable Abu Bakr eliminated them and took control of the situation.... [Later,]

the venerable Omar asked the venerable Huzayfa ibn Yaman (may Allah accept his good deeds) about the [expected] "disorder that will rise like giant waves," to which he replied: "You don't have to worry about it; there is a locked door between it and you." Venerable Omar asked: Will this door be opened or broken? Huzayfa said, It will be broken![sic]

... Yes, the venerable Omar (may Allah accept his good deeds) realized that ... the political system called the "Caliphate" would no longer be enough. [Then] the venerable Othman became the caliph. But the door that had to be broken had been broken. There was gossip and displeasure in every corner of the Islamic world. Poor Othman was helpless and desperate.... The insurgent groups besieged his house and killed him in front of his beloved wife. After a lot of bloodshed and turmoil, the venerable Ali (may Allah ennoble his face) was elected caliph. Let me repeat, the door had been broken.... Muawiya did not recognize the venerable Ali's caliphate; on the contrary, he blamed him for Othman's murder. The caliph, whose main duty was to apply the Qur'anic provisions, was forced to stop the fight against the Umayyad army, whose soldiers had hoisted pages of the Qur'an on their spears.... [Muawiya] transformed the Caliphate into a dynastic rule but kept the title.... [Later,] the rulers of the Abbasid state were also called caliphs...

In the fourth century hegira, a mighty Turkish state called the Seljukids was founded [which then] dominated the Abbasid caliphs residing in Baghdad. The caliphs resided in Baghdad side by side with a person by the name of Melik Şah, who represented the Turkish dominion. Now, I'd like to briefly analyze this situation.

The Turkish sultan – who represented the sovereignty and dominion of a magnificent Turkish state – agreed to keep the Caliphate alongside his [government]. If he had wanted, he could have abolished the institution that he had controlled and incorporated all the authority and titles associated with this institution into his own title. What the [Ottoman sultan] venerable Selim did about five centuries later, Melik Şah could, if he wanted, have done at that time in Baghdad.

Now, gentlemen, it is definitely appropriate for the Caliphate to live today side by side with the institution that represents national sovereignty, which is the Turkish Grand National Assembly; and it will definitely have more dignity than the one that was helpless and powerless in relation to Melik Şah, because it is the Turkish Grand National Assembly that represents the Turkish state today. And the Turkish nation as a whole has promised and taken it upon itself as a religious duty to be the [political] basis of the Caliphate.

(TBMMZC 1922a: 267–271)

Similarly, Ziya Gökalp, the leading secularist intellectual, justified the separation of the Caliphate from the monarchy mainly with reference to the same episodes of Islamic history:

In these periods the Caliph was performing only a religious function with regard to the *ummah*. All affairs with regard to political authority were carried out by the sultans of the Seljuks in Baghdad and of the *Kölemen*s [Mamluks] in Egypt. These were the greatest periods in the history of Islam, both politically and religiously. It was only when Selim I had again unified these two offices that the decline of the Ottoman Empire ensued; its religious as well as its political life began to deteriorate.... Until now the religious authority of the Ottoman caliphs was confined to those Muslims who were their political subjects. Their religious authority over Muslims in other states was rejected by the other governments because they could not be sure that this religious authority was free from political designs. Now that the caliph will no longer be subject to the politics of any nation,... he will exercise his right of religious authority over all religious institutions [and] all Muslim states and nations will support [the Caliphate] materially and spiritually. But its real and most powerful source will be the greatness of Islam, which has today forced the European world to respect it.... We are deeply thankful to the Grand National Assembly and its famous president for their success in giving to the office of the Caliphate a character that is compatible with the principle of popular and national sovereignty, which is the foundation of modern states and through which genuine Islamic unity in religious life might be realized.

(TBMMZC 1922a: 226–227)

Thus, both Mustafa Kemal and Ziya Gökalp framed the entire operation of separating the monarchy from the Caliphate to abolish the former exclusively in religious terms and promised that the Caliphate would be better off without a dynastic base. This move in the parliament would, however, be a crucial step toward the abolition of the Caliphate, as it was greatly weakened when separated from the monarchy and, therefore, left without a basis for political power (see Chapter 6).

The abolition of the monarchy was not, of course, recognized by the Istanbul government, which continued to claim to be the only legitimate basis of the Caliphate. Against this claim, secular nationalists tried to justify their alternative regime founded with the constitution of the GNA in Ankara in 1920 also with reference to Islam. In their claim for the true political basis of the Caliphate, which assumed that the latter was a purely spiritual institution, the nationalists also invoked early Islamic history. As part of this effort, journalist and politician Fuad Şükrü[46] likened the new regime to the Caliphate of the first four caliphs, and its leader, Mustafa Kemal, to the four caliphs themselves:

O the Great Savior! You have discovered a new, independent, and free world (...) God willing; this new government will be among the world's most just governments and counted as a successor of the Rightly Guided Caliphs' period. May God's grace be with you!

(1922: 557)

In the same passage, the author also likened Mustafa Kemal to Sultan Mehmed II (the Ottoman sultan who conquered Istanbul) as well as to Laplace and Christopher Columbus – hence the phrase "a new, independent, and free world" – all of whom had, according to the author, overcome seemingly impossible obstacles. Note that these were references simultaneously made to the "heroes" of both Western and Islamic/Ottoman civilizations. This was a discursive technique that became increasingly common, especially after World War I, among secularists and some modernists, who made frequent references to the West, as well as to Islam, in a context in which the empire (and the Muslim world in general) were in a serious political and economic crisis due to major military defeat. This crisis, in turn, affected dominant cultural codes among intellectuals, as well as their perception of the world, reflecting what I call the "double-bind" – i.e., the co-existence and conflation of two different civilizational frameworks, with the Western philosophical traditions having increasingly more impact on the minds of Muslim intellectual and political elites (see also Chapter 6).

Invoking the first four Caliphs

Making references to the administration and teachings of the first four caliphs of Islam was an effective discursive technique because these early leaders of the *ummah*, known as the "Rightly Guided Caliphs," were recognized as the Prophet's greatest companions, and therefore commanded great authority. That is why, in his speech at the parliament mentioned above, Mustafa Kemal made frequent references to, and offered many quotations from, the early caliphs. This technique was, of course, deployed by the other two groups, as well. Through references to early Islamic history many modernists justified the argument that since the Caliphate involved only political authority, the caliph-sultan should not possess a more privileged status than any other head of state. This argument was made strongly during the debates in the Ottoman parliament on expanding the caliph's authority – as proposed by the CUP – in 1911 (also referred to above). The CUP tried to expand Caliph Mehmed Reşad's authority to dissolve the parliament, in which the CUP's domination had been threatened by the FAP's recent victory in by-elections. Mustafa Sabri, a member of the *ulema* and the FAP, criticized the proposal, arguing that the caliph could not have authority superior to that of the parliament because both represented "the people" and, therefore, should submit to the "national will." He supported this argument specifically with reference to the second caliph, Omar, who had admitted he was not superior to his subjects by saying, "I am like you." Against this argument, as mentioned above, pro-CUP jurist Ömer Lütfi (though not a member of the *ulema*), wrote a long pamphlet, titled "The Caliphate According to Islam," in which he said that Mustafa Sabri had completely ignored the context of this sentence and misinterpreted it; Ömer Lütfi then presented a grammatical analysis of the saying and described its historical circumstances. He also cited different *hadith*s, quoted different historically significant figures, such as Ali, the fourth caliph, and discussed the process of the election of the third caliph, Othman, to argue that the caliph should have a special status that could not be reduced to that of an ordinary member of parliament (Ömer Lütfi 1912: 210–215).

In the caliphal periphery, invoking the election processes of the first four caliphs as a discursive technique had the function of supporting/defending the Ottoman Caliphate against British propaganda and Arab nationalist activities. Many pro-Ottoman activist-authors presented two events in particular, Abu Bakr's nomination of Omar for the Caliphate and Omar's appointment of a committee to elect the next caliph, as sound evidence for the legitimacy of the Ottoman Caliphate, because Ottoman sultans from the beginning had assumed the title of caliph through nomination and appointment as heir to the throne. Many traditionalists, including Mustafa Zihni (1911: 179–181), Safayihi (1915: 87), al-Tunusi (1916a: 149) and al-Ubeydi (1916: 206–207), referred to these two events as a basis for their refutation of the "Quraysh condition" (see above) and to legitimize the existing Caliphate in Istanbul. In a pamphlet he wrote in 1913 to refute the arguments of British minister Lloyd George, who had claimed that the Caliphate was ineffective and not regarded highly by Muslims, al-Tunusi briefly referred to the Caliphate's history to argue that the Muslim world had lost the unity it possessed at the time of the first four caliphs, but was subsequently re-united thanks to the efforts of the Ottoman sultans who elevated the status of the Caliphate by supporting it with formidable political power (1913: 417).

In addition, as was the case with the first discursive strategy, both traditionalists and modernists made use of the strategy of invoking early Islamic history in their discussion of "consultation," as well. As mentioned above, they identified, as a discursive technique, the word "consultation" in the Qur'an and prophetic traditions with "constitutionalism" and the parliamentary regime that was re-established with the 1908 Revolution in the Ottoman Empire. In order to legitimize the new regime, both groups referenced Islamic history as well as the sacred texts. Thus, in his 40-*hadith* collection, Ömer Ziyaeddin (1908: 65–66) also included five aphorisms on "consultation," two of which were from Ali, the fourth caliph. Similarly, Mustafa Zihni (1911: 195) reported "seven advantages of consultation," originally attributed to Ali, one of which was "following the Prophet's path." He also described the election of all four caliphs and briefly discussed the Umayyad and Abbasid caliphates, comparing them with the Ottoman Caliphate to argue that the latter was better than both of them due to the Ottomans' better administration, superior strength, and longer reign (pp. 181–182). Likewise, in his discussion of the cabinet system, Mustafa Zihni again stated that the appointment of ministers (*vezirs*) had started with Abu Bakr and Omar and continued with the other two Caliphs, as well as during the dynastic caliphates later in Islamic history, concluding that the "cabinet system (*vezaret*) is an integral part of the Islamic government of the Caliphate and a requirement of the blessed *sharia*" (1911: 198).

Among the modernists, Seyyid Bey (1917: 446) said that during the early years of Islam caliphs were elected and given allegiance by leading companions of the Prophet that formed the *Ahl al-hall wa al-'aqd* and that this justified the election of the Ottoman caliphs by the two-tiered Ottoman parliament, which for him constituted the contemporary *Ahl al-hall wa al-'aqd*. The anti-Ottoman Rashid Rida (1923a: 30ff), too, discussed consultation as a crucial function of the *Ahl al-hall wa al-'aqd* institution in early Islam, which for him constituted the basis of Islamic Caliphate. He further claimed (pp. 11–13) that since this committee represented the "community" (Islamic *ummah*), on whose "will" the caliph's authority was based, the *Ahl al-hall wa al-'aqd* was superior to the Caliph himself. (Note the Rousseauan tone in this argument.) Rida also returned to the first four caliphs in his argument on the Quraysh condition. On this subject he asked: "Doesn't the way of the Rightly Guided Caliphs set the best example for the provisions of the Qur'an and the prophetic *sunna*?" He concluded that their Meccan origin was a significant factor in their election as caliphs, and that the same condition should be applied now, as well (p. 22).

The most important difference of opinion between traditionalists and modernists was over the scope of the caliph's authority – a disagreement that they nevertheless expressed with the same discursive strategy. Traditionalists, such as Ömer Lütfi (1912: 249) and İsmail Hakkı (1910: 442) argued that, in addition to Qur'anic verses and *hadith*s, the practices of the first four caliphs all proved that the caliph should have both political and religious authority, as they were the leaders of Islamic community in both realms. Hakkı added to this that, though the Caliphate had lost its this-worldly authority from time to time throughout history, the Ottomans restored its political authority when they assumed the title and strengthened its religious power. Modernists, on the other hand, argued, with selective references to Islamic history, that the caliph's authority should be limited to the politico-temporal realm. For example, Elmalılı Hamdi (1909: 434) said that during the reign of the Umayyads, Abbasids, and Seljuks, the caliphs would appoint two main ministers (the *sadrazam* and the *şeyhülislam*) to administer state affairs, and that neither of them had any spiritual-religious authority at all. The fact that the author "forgot" the obvious example of the first four caliphs exemplifies another discursive strategy employed not only by modernists, but by almost every actor – that of "omitting contradictory evidence" (which I discuss separately). Similarly, Seyyid Bey (1917: 458), in his attempt to discursively limit the caliph's authority with the "rules of the *sharia*" and the "public interest" (without defining the latter), argued that the caliph's actions against the interests of the public were not legally valid, because this precondition was explicitly mentioned when Othman, the third caliph, was elected – though it was never mentioned before or after his election.

Another theme that only the traditionalist Islamists emphasized with reference to Islamic history was the concept of obedience to the caliph. They argued, as already mentioned, that it was a religious duty for all Muslims to obey the (legitimate) caliph even if he was not an ideal leader. Thus, in his discussion on the conditions that necessitated the deposition of the caliph, Ömer Lütfi (1912: 246) argued that the *sharia* required Muslims to obey the leader even if he was a *fasiq* (sinner), invoking the words of one of the Prophet's companions, who said that the Prophet's leading companions used to allow a sinner to lead the (collective) prayer. He thus identified the *imam* (leader) of collective prayer with the *imam*

(caliph) of the entire Muslim *ummah*, which was a discursive technique sometimes resorted to by traditionalists to emphasize the notion of obedience to the
leader.

Political activists also employed the strategy of invoking Islamic history in
dealing with another important problem on the periphery: that of multiple/altern-
ative caliphs. As discussed in Chapter 5, both Britain and France had their own
projects of installing (Arab) caliphs in the Middle East (in the *Maghrib* and the
Arabian Peninsula, in particular) whom they could completely control. In order
to refute the claims of alternative caliphs in Morocco and the *Hijaz*, pro-Ottoman
actors declared illegitimate not only contemporary attempts to challenge the caliph's authority, but also historical incidents (*Fatimids* and *Muwahhids*) that had
posed a challenge to the mainstream Abbasid Caliphate. Thus, referring to these
alternative caliphates, both Mustafa Zihni (1911: 183) and Abdulaziz Jawish
(1916: 259), a traditionalist and a modernist, respectively, also invoked the
debate on the first caliph that took place between the *muhajirun* (Muslims of
Mecca) and the *ansar* (Muslims of Medina), in which the latter suggested electing two caliphs (one from each group), which was eventually rejected by the
majority, and Abu Bakr was ultimately elected (632 CE). Similarly, in his argument against the alternative caliphs, Arab traditionalist al-Ubeydi (1916: 209)
referred to the first civil war within the Muslim community, the "Jamal incident"
and the Battle of Siffin (657 CE), where Ali, the fourth caliph, fought against
Muawiya, then the governor of Syria and later the founder of the (Sunni)
Umayyad dynasty. The author, who was also a Sunni, interpreted this as a just
war waged by the legitimate caliph (Ali) against the illegitimate alternative
caliph, which the author justified by saying that the majority of the companions
supported Ali in the war.[47] The fact that al-Ubeydi preferred the Shia interpretation of this event was closely related to the historical context, in which he knew
that the Ottoman Caliphate was being threatened by the claims of alternative
caliphs backed by the imperialist powers during World War I. He discursively
positioned potential ccandidates for the Caliphate into the status of insurgents,
represented by Muawiya, against the legitimate caliph of Islam.

Finally, some actors also employed this same discursive strategy in their
responses to the direct challenge to Islamic law posed by Western ideologues,
who often claimed that Islam lacked such modern concepts as liberty, equality,
and justice. An early example of the response to these charges was Ali Fahmi's
book *The Ottoman Caliphate and Islamic Unity*, in which his basic argument
was that all these "virtues" assumed to belong to Western civilization were actually taken from Islam.[48] In his book, which was full of verses and prophetic traditions, Ali Fahmi (1911: 87–88) also invoked early Islamic history, giving
examples from three of the first four caliphs emphasizing their humility and sen-
sitivity to the rights of non-Muslims, as well as Muslims. He thus concluded, "If
there are such things as social and political liberty, equality, and brotherhood,
they are definitely taken from the Qur'an and Islam" (p. 88). Similar to this
reinterpretation *à la* "invention of tradition" (Hobsbawm 1992), an unsigned
editorial subtitled "Response to the British Press," which was published in

Sebilürreşad, a leading Islamist journal issued by intellectual-activist Mehmed Akif, cited an incident in which Omar as caliph had treated the prophet's son-in-law Ali and an ordinary Jewish man equally in a dispute between them, interpreting it as a sign of the significance Islam attached to equality and liberty, an argument the editorial also supported by quoting different Qur'anic verses and sayings of the Prophet (*Sebilürreşad* 1916a).

In conclusion, a survey of traditionalist, modernist, and secularist actors' discourses has shown that invoking Islamic history, especially the era of the first four "Rightly Guided Caliphs," was a discursive strategy commonly employed by all three groups. As a compliment to the strategy of invoking the fundamental sources of the Islamic faith – the Qur'an and the *Sunna* – this second strategy was instrumental in terms of providing a legitimate ground for the claims and political positions of different actors. The widespread use of this strategy suggests that the era of the first four caliphs, as part of the notion of *Asr-ı Saadet* (the Golden Age), which covers the Prophet's lifetime and the reigns of the "Rightly Guided Caliphs," has a religious (and political) significance in the eyes of Muslims. As such, perception of this part of history was one of the factors in defining the Caliphate and shaping its meaning for different groups according their diverging interpretations of this period. We have also observed that the main discursive technique used as part of the application of this strategy to different themes (such as obedience to the Caliph, the scope of his authority, multiple caliphs, and the status of the Ottoman Caliphate) was that of the selective reading of Islamic history, by interpreting certain events – sometimes unusually – in a way that would justify the claim made by the author, and by emphasizing some events and ignoring others. Furthermore, ignoring relevant information is not just confined to the interpretation of historical events, but pertains to a larger set of evidence, constituting a discursive strategy in itself.

Omitting contradictory evidence

Omitting or ignoring information relevant to a discussion can be observed among intellectuals everywhere and in every episode of history. It was a phenomenon that frequently occurred in the debates over the Caliphate, as well. However, I label it a "discursive strategy" only when the contradictory evidence that was ignored was directly related to the discussion and when there is enough circumstantial evidence to suggest that the omission was intentional. In this sense, ignoring contradictory evidence was a strategy employed by different actors from all three groups. Here I discuss the most crucial and relevant evidence relating to these arguments, including two famous *hadith*s, the "*ul al-amr*" verse, some historical facts and the quality of *hadith*s presented by some actors.

Two of the best and most obvious examples of contradictory evidence often omitted from discussions (for the purpose of defending the Ottoman Caliphate) were the Quraysh *hadith*, which required prophetic genealogy for the caliph, and the *hadith* that limited the Caliphate to 30 years after the Prophet's death, which corresponds to the period of the first four caliphs. The latter was only the traditionalists' problem. For example, neither Ömer Ziyaeddin nor Mehmed Tahir, both known as scholars of *hadith*, included in their compilations the *hadith* that stated that the true Caliphate would end after 30 years, when it would turn into a dynastic rule (which was done by Muawiya, founder of the Umayyad Caliphate, exactly 30 years after the Prophet's death). This *hadith* constituted textual evidence that directly threatened the legitimacy of the Ottoman Caliphate. Often used by some Arab nationalists and secularists (e.g., Rashid Rida, Mustafa Kemal, respectively) to discursively delegitimize Ottoman rule, this *hadith* was ignored by most of the modernist and traditionalist supporters of the Ottoman Caliphate, particularly on the caliphal periphery (e.g., al-Tunusi 1913; Safayihi 1915; Kidwai 1919; Syed Mahmud 1921).

Similarly, while initially ignored by Ottoman loyalists, the Quraysh *hadith* ("Imams are from the Quraysh") was frequently used by anti-Ottoman actors as an instrument in their attack against the Ottoman Caliphate. As discussed above, this *hadith* was popularized by Arab nationalists pursuing secession from the Ottoman Empire and the creation an Arab Caliphate; it was also used, starting in the late 19th century, by the British, French, and Italian colonial administrations in order to weaken the authority of the Ottoman caliph in the colonies (Buzpınar 2002). While this propaganda was to some extent successful in the Arabian Peninsula and North Africa (including Egypt), the British policy of undermining the legitimacy of the Ottoman Caliphate failed in the biggest colony, India, where the great majority of Muslims remained loyal to the Caliphate, even after it was abolished in 1924. Yet it was instrumental in mobilizing the Egyptian and Moroccan elites, as well as many Arab tribes that sought independence from Istanbul. Interestingly, however, the leader of the Hashemite revolt, Sharif Hussein (1916), did not mention this *hadith* in his declaration of independence. For, as mentioned above, his declaration, addressing the "Muslim *ummah*," did not present his uprising as against the Ottoman Caliph (Mehmed V), but against the CUP and its leaders' "un-Islamic actions." In order to gain legitimacy in the eyes of the elites of other Muslim countries, Hussein did not at that time make explicit his plans to pursue the Caliphate, claiming that he would remain loyal to the existing caliph (see Chapter 5).

Despite this, however, most actors were aware that he would try to declare his caliphate if he received the help he expected from the British, which they failed to materialize, largely due to disturbances among the Muslims of India. On the other hand, the French government was trying to support its own candidate for an alternative caliph, Yusuf, the sultan of Morocco, in order to both weaken the Ottoman state and counteract the British colonization of the Middle East (see Chapter 5). In this context, the Quraysh *hadith* proved useful for the plans of both Europeans and Arab nationalists. Until 1916, however, it could not be integrated into any kind of military-political action (of secession), but remained an element of the nationalist discourse of certain Arab intellectuals. Partly for this reason, the defenders of the Ottoman Caliphate, until 1916, usually preferred to ignore it. Thus, neither Ömer Ziyaeddin (1908) nor Mehmed Tahir (1909) included the Quraysh *hadith* in their collections, consisting of 40 and 25 *hadith*s, respectively, which were compiled to support the Ottoman Caliphate. Although the Quraysh *hadith* was directly related to their subject-matter, they omitted it for obvious reasons. Similarly, pro-Ottoman intellectual-politicians al-Tunusi (1913), al-Ubeydi (1916), and Seyyid Bey (1917) chose to ignore the *hadith* in their justification of the legitimacy of the Ottoman Caliphate.

In his later pamphlets, however, al-Tunusi (1916a: 148, 1916b: 425), a CUP member, and Hussein Kidwai (1919: 352), a member of the Muslim League of India, obviously aware of the *hadith*, responded to it by way of implication: They did not cite this *hadith*, but quoted another one ("Obey your leader even if he is an Abyssinian slave with a small head") as counter-evidence to it in their criticism of alternative claims for the Caliphate (see above). Others, however, took the charge head-on and discussed the Quraysh *hadith* in detail in order to prove that it was no longer applicable by presenting evidence from prophetic traditions (including the above-mentioned *hadith*) and from the Islamic intellectual tradition, as discussed above (e.g., Safayihi 1915: 55–63; Jawish 1916: 246–249; Said Halim Pasha 2000[1920]: 400; Seyyid Bey 1923: 12; Hoca Şükrü 1923: 10–11).

Another famous piece of "evidence" that was sometimes ignored was the "*ul al-amr*" verse. While traditionalists often repeated this verse to emphasize the religious character of the caliph's rule, some modernists and secularists preferred to ignore it in their discussions on the Caliphate. Moreover, on the periphery, emphasizing the spiritual leadership of the Ottoman Caliph, Sharif Hussein did not mention the "*ul al-amr*" verse for obvious reasons, while he quoted Qur'anic verses that were not directly related to the Caliphate or governance. Likewise, in the center, modernist Islamist Elmalılı Hamdi (1909) omitted the "*ul al-amr*" verse in his discussion on the status of the *şeyhülislam* (who was the head of the Ottoman *ulema*), because he did not want to stress the significance of the caliph or the *ulema*. For his aim in the text was to help downplay the *şeyhülislam*'s power by reducing the authority of the caliph (note that Elmalılı had signed the *fatwa* for Abdülhamid II's deposition), and the phrase *ul al-amr* in the verse could not be attributed to a third party. Therefore, instead of choosing one of the available interpretations, he simply chose to ignore the verse, which was central to the problem of the caliph's authority. Similarly, he ignored the mostly agreed-upon definition of the caliph as the representative of Prophet Muhammad, whose authority could not be questioned. Despite the fact that, at the time when he wrote this article, there was a critical debate underway on the scope of the caliph's authority – the article being a part of it – the author avoided explicitly stating his own definition of the Caliphate, which reduced it to a merely temporal authority. For this would be an open challenge to the dominant Islamic discourse that centered upon the assumption that the caliph filled the post of the Prophet Muhammad. He wrote the article as a polemic against another article that defended the *şeyhülislam*'s status at the time (see Chapter 4 for a detailed discussion). What Elmalılı advocated here (that the *şeyhülislam* should be a member of the cabinet, and thus held accountable by parliament members, many of whom were non-Muslim) would soon be achieved by the CUP. Moreover, the *şeyhülislam* would later (in 1916) be excluded from the cabinet as part of the "Ziya Gökalp reforms" (see Chapter 2), which further reduced his authority and status.

The strategy of omission also took the form of ignoring the *quality* of the evidence presented. For example, Ömer Ziyaeddin (1908) and Mehmed Tahir (1909) knew that most of the *hadith*s they compiled in their collections were "weak," and therefore not suitable as evidence in themselves, but did not at all address this problem. As members of the *ulema* (the former was a *hadith* scholar), it is unthinkable that they were not aware of the weakness of these *hadith*s, but they nevertheless chose to ignore the issue and refrain from acknowledging their weaknesses, which would hurt their evidence for the political and religious authority of the current sultan. This is because, as discussed above, their compilations were aimed at shaping the opinion of the reading public, rather than the *ulema*, and, in Ziyaeddin's case, impressing the sultan himself (he presented his collection to Sultan Abdülhamid).

Finally, not only textual evidence but also historical reality was often ignored. This is most obvious in the reactionary attitude of some modernists (mentioned above), who tried to defend the Islamic faith and the Ottoman Caliphate by accommodating Western concepts. In this context, both Ali Fahmi (1911) and the editorial from *Sebilurreşad* (1916a) claimed that since "liberty, equality, and brotherhood" actually originated from Islam, the non-Muslims living in the Ottoman Empire had always been equal citizens of the state. They ignored, however, the fact that, within the pluralist and hierarchical structure of the *millet* system, non-Muslims were not equal to Muslims, nor among themselves.[49] This had been the case for several centuries until the Ottoman sultan granted equality to all citizens of the empire with the declaration in 1856 of the Reform Edict, which was proclaimed under the pressures of European powers, particularly Britain (see Chapter 2).

Conclusion

The first part of this chapter introduced the historical context by presenting first a brief history of the Caliphate from its beginning (632 CE) to its dissolution (1924), and then a description of the three groups (traditionalists, modernists, and secularists) of actors (politicians, bureaucrats, journalists, intellectuals, and the *ulema*) who played different roles in the struggle over the Caliphate that took place both in its center and periphery. In the second part I analyzed the three discursive strategies commonly used by all three groups: those of "invoking sacred texts" (Qur'anic verses and prophetic *hadith*s) for justification of political positions and arguments, "invoking (early) Islamic history," and "omitting contradictory evidence." These larger strategies were employed through various discursive techniques, one of which involved focusing on certain (parts of) Qur'anic verses and prophetic traditions and often taking them out of their textual and social contexts in order to make political claims about the nature, functions, and future of the Caliphate. The second major technique that was frequently used was that of emphasizing particular themes/concepts while ignoring others (including the Caliphate's significance, the limits of the caliph's authority, the necessity of obedience to the caliph, the concept of "consultation," the question of alternative/multiple caliphs, whether or not the ethnic origins of the caliphs were significant, etc.) that came out of the selective reading of the sacred texts of Islam and Muslim history.

The third strategy, ignoring or omitting textual and historical evidence that contradicted the actors' arguments, functioned as a compliment to the first two strategies. I have also noted that the three groups in question did not make use of sacred texts and history equally, which is particularly evident in the case of prophetic traditions. As expected, these texts and historical events were drawn upon most frequently by traditionalists, and least frequently by secularists. There are two main reasons for this: First, the latter group drew its membership base mostly from bureaucrats, politicians, and journalists rather than the *ulema*, and thus lacked the necessary "cultural capital" that could be provided by qualified intellectuals who had mastery over the Islamic sciences. That is why this group always needed the assistance of the members of the *ulema*, and often got it, most notably from Seyyid Bey, who was a prominent Muslim scholar with close ties to secular politicians, including CUP leaders and Mustafa Kemal. Second, it was not easy for the secularists to find the Qur'anic verses and prophetic *hadiths* that could strongly support their arguments and positions.

The three groups also employed other discursive strategies, which were not common to all of them. The following three chapters analyze these strategies (and techniques associated with them) by locating them in their respective historical contexts. As listed above, some of these strategies were common to two groups (either traditionalists and modernists, or modernists and secularists), others were used by only one of them. In the early years of the Second Constitutional Period, the Caliphate debate, conditioned by the 1908 Revolution and subsequent attempts by the Unionists to curtail the caliph's (and the *şeyhülislam*'s) power, took place between traditionalists and modernists, which is the topic of the next chapter.

4 Secularization in the Caliphal center (1908–1916)

Introduction

This chapter examines the early debates (1908–1916) over the Caliphate between the traditionalist and modernist groups at the center of the Ottoman Caliphate, Istanbul, and the Balkans. The caliphal center witnessed a somewhat distinctive course of events regarding the Caliphate because this region constituted a different context from that of the periphery (the wider Middle East), where the debates mostly concerned the defense of the Ottoman Caliphate against the claims by alternative (Arab) caliphs supported by Britain and France during and after World War I. In the central territory of the Caliphate, however, the early debates were shaped by domestic power relations, in which the Ottoman (military and civil) bureaucratic elites, represented by the CUP, tried to curtail the powers of the Caliph and the religious establishment. (Later, when the Caliphate was extremely weakened by secularist forces between 1922 and 1924, this power struggle focused on the very survival of the Caliphate; see Chapter 6.) As already mentioned, the most powerful actor during the Second Constitutional Period was the core leadership of the CUP, led by a small group of military officers, particularly the trio of Enver Pasha, Cemal Pasha, and Talat Pasha (the latter being a civil bureaucrat). The crucial event that put the CUP in this position was the "Young Turk Revolution" of 1908, which also greatly affected the fate of the Ottoman Empire in its last decade (1908–1918), during which the caliph's authority declined steadily. During the first eight years of the Second Constitutional Period, the debate was mostly between traditionalists (represented by İsmail Hakkı, Ömer Lütfi, Mustafa Zihni, Ömer Ziyaeddin and Mehmed Tahir, among others) and modernists (represented by Elmalılı Hamdi, Seyyid Bey and Abdulaziz Jawish); secularists did not yet exist as a "group" at that time. The power struggle between the caliph and traditionalists who tried to revive the Caliphate as a political and religious institution, on the one hand, and the Ottoman bureaucracy and modernists who wanted not only to restrict its scope to temporal affairs but also to limit much of its political authority, on the other, was won by the latter. Both sides, however, derived justification from Islam for their positions and arguments.

Below I analyze this power struggle and the (Islamic) discourses that accompanied it by discussing two specific cases that represented crucial turning points in the transformation, and eventual demise, of the Caliphate. First I examine how the CUP-led bureaucratic elites weakened the Caliphate through a series of legal changes between 1908 and 1909, including a number of constitutional amendments as well as minor legal changes, which were conditioned by the 1908 Young Turk Revolution and two *coups d'état* by the Unionists in 1909 and 1913. Second, I analyze the debates over the status of the *şeyhülislam*, the caliph's religious dignitary, between 1909 and 1916. Also the head of the Ottoman *ulema*, the *şeyhülislam* had been a member of the cabinet since the early 19th century. A debate over whether to include him in the government that started in 1909 resulted in the removal of this second-highest religious authority from the cabinet and, ultimately, the curtailment of all of his powers by the CUP in 1916. This was a significant development because the decline of power of the *şeyhülislam* (and of the *ulema* in general) was accompanied by the decline of the caliph's authority and constituted an important dimension of the changing relationship between Islam and the state in the early 20th century. In my discussion of these two cases, I first present major political developments in order to contextualize my analysis of the actors' discourses, which follows this historical discussion. Finally, in addition to these two cases, I also examine an important pattern that emerges out of the data: the secularization of Islamic discourse. Though all of these actors employed an Islamic discourse, the nature of the era's political developments, which led to the secularization of the Caliphate and the *şeyhülislam*'s office, also affected the direction of this discourse. Thus, we are able to identify a pattern of partial secularization of Islamic discourse by the Islamist actors themselves.

In my analysis, I identify various discursive strategies and techniques deployed by representative actors of the period. In Case 1, traditionalists employed the strategies of

i   establishing the dual (spiritual and political) status of the Caliphate,
ii defining religious legitimacy as the only basis for the caliph's authority, and
iii emphasizing obedience to the caliph as a religious duty of the believer.

These strategies were accompanied by such discursive techniques as

i   locating the Caliphate in an ontological hierarchy involving God, the Prophet, and the caliph,
ii stressing the necessity of obeying administrators appointed by the caliph, and
iii presenting obedience to the ruler as part of one's faith.

Modernists, on the other hand, employed the strategies of

i   defining the Caliphate as a temporal-political institution,
ii identifying the social contract and popular legitimacy as bases for the caliph's authority,

iii emphasizing the limits of the caliph's temporal authority, and
iv nationalizing the Caliphate.

This group utilized such techniques as

i denying the caliph spiritual authority,
ii defining the Caliphate as a legal contract between the ruler and the ruled, and
iii upholding "public interest" and "national will" as limits to the caliph's authority.

In Case 2, the traditionalists, based on the strategy of the "dual status of the Caliphate," employed the techniques of

i presenting the *şeyhülislam* as the head of the Islamic community,
ii placing the *şeyhülislam*'s status above that of the parliament, and
iii emphasizing the preconditions and primary duties of the Caliphate.

Modernist strategies included

i invoking the sacred texts of Islam (the Qur'an and *hadiths*) and
ii designating the caliphate as a temporal institution.

Finally, with respect to the "internal secularization" (of Islamic discourse), some traditionalists adapted the (secular) distinction between the "spiritual" and "temporal" dimensions of the caliph's authority, thereby secularizing their discourse from within. Modernists, in addition to embracing this distinction, employed two other discursive strategies that contributed to the secularization of their Islamic discourse:

i selective appropriation of Western institutions, and
ii historicizing religion by stressing the primacy of (modern) social conditions and the "exigencies of contemporary civilization."

This discursive secularization, as mentioned, was shaped by the ongoing institutional secularization of the Ottoman political system as a result of the power struggle between traditionalist forces and a coalition of (secular) bureaucrats and modernist Islamists, which intensified with the 1908 Revolution.

The early transformation of the Caliphate (1908–1913)

The historical context

The debate over the Caliphate between the traditionalists and the modernist-CUP coalition was shaped by the specific political context of the 1908 Revolution and its aftermath, which included a number of secularizing legal reforms and constitutional changes. These changes helped transform the Caliphate into a more "secular" institution, which also meant the decline of the caliph's power vis-à-vis the bureaucratic elites represented by the CUP. This institutional transformation was made possible by the modernists' discursive domination over the traditionalists in terms of deriving justification from Islam. As already noted, the discursive battle both reflected and facilitated actual political developments starting from the 1908 Revolution.

The Young Turk Revolution of 1908

The CUP was the main group opposing the late Hamidian regime and had succeeded the Young Ottomans in their opposition to Abdülhamid II. Founded in 1889 and led by two influential exiles, Ahmed Rıza and Bahaeddin Şakir, the CUP consisted mostly of exiled bureaucrats and intellectuals called the "Young Turks," supported also by non-Muslim (e.g., Armenian) groups based in Europe (especially France). It also had a base in Istanbul, particularly among young military officers and medical school students, such as Enver Bey, Niyazi Bey, Abdullah Cevdet, İbrahim Temo and Ziya Gökalp. The CUP staunchly criticized

Figure 4.1 The CUP's founders. Back row (standing) left to right: İpekli Hafız İbrahim, Enver Bey, Hüseyin Kadri, Midhat Şükrü. Front row (seated), left to right: man with sword is unknown, Talat Bey, Ahmed Rıza Bey, İsmail Hakkı, Hayri Bey (picture source: Bahattin Öztuncay, 2005. *Hatıra-i Uhuvvet: Portre Fotoğrafların Cazibesi: 1846–1950*, İstanbul: Aygaz, p. 205).

Note
I thank Suat Mertoğlu for helping me with the identifications.

Hamidian "despotism," defending constitutionalism and Ottoman nationalism (Akşin 1987; Hanioğlu 1995). The 1905 Russian Revolution following the defeat of Russia by Japan in the Russo-Japanese War (see Ascher 2004) boosted the Young Turk opposition by showing both that an Eastern state with a constitution could defeat a major (non-constitutional) Western power and that a monarch could be forced to declare a constitutional regime. Moreover, the Meiji Restoration of 1868 was itself a source of inspiration for the Young Turks.[1] Such anti-monarchic feelings were further espoused by the Constitutional Revolution in Iran (1906), which the Young Turks regarded as a progressive development in a backward country (Sohrabi 2002: 53–62). Meanwhile, within the Ottoman Empire, discontented army officers in Macedonia, led by Major Enver and Mehmed Talat, who had in 1906 founded their own group, called the Ottoman Freedom Society (*Osmanlı Hürriyet Cemiyeti*), joined the CUP in 1907, and subsequently came to control it (Ramsaur 1957; Akşin 1987; Hanioğlu 2001).

Various revolts and strikes, as well as high inflation, which negatively affected their salaries, increased Ottoman military officers' discontent with the Palace in Istanbul. The tipping point, however, was the agreement in 1908 between Britain and Russia to solve the "Macedonian problem" by means of establishing a merely formal suzerainty of the Ottoman sultan over the region. The CUP interpreted this as the partition of the empire, about which the sultan had done nothing. Being "to some extent free of the reverential feelings held by their elders for the caliph, the sultan" (Karpat 2004: 204), the Unionist officers of the third (Macedonian) and second (Thracian) armies, led by Enver, took to the hills with their troops, to which Abdülhamid II responded by sending troops from Istanbul and Anatolia. Influenced by Unionist propaganda, however, many soldiers refused to fight. The sultan was therefore forced to declare the restoration of the Constitution on July 23, 1908, which marked the beginning of the Second Constitutional Period (1908–1918).

The social origins of the Unionists were rooted in the Balkans and most of them, or at least their parents, were either immigrants or from among the old Ottoman provincial elites (Karpat 2004: 208). Thus, the revolution also initiated a shift in the composition of the elite, with non-aristocratic, low-ranking army officers and low-profile intellectuals, as well as high-ranking *ulema* who had been disfranchised by Abdülhamid II, now taking over elite positions as a result of the regime change. As for the popular echoes of the event, the public reacted to the revolution with celebration in demonstrations organized by the leaders of various faith communities, as well as different CUP factions (especially in the Balkans) (Ahmad 1993: 31–32).

However, the revolution itself was not a product of a mass social movement, but of the efforts of a small group of (military) elite, the Young Turks. Some historians (e.g., Akşin 1987; Kansu 2001) have claimed that it was the result of a popular uprising, even a bourgeois revolution, caused by "tax revolts" that had started in the late 1890s. Essentially a product of Marxist nostalgia, this view is incorrect for a number of reasons. First, the social base of the revolutionaries was not the bourgeoisie – in fact there were no bourgeoisie in Turkey at the time

(Toprak 1995). Rather, the revolutionaries were military officers supported by an educated minority (journalists, bureaucrats, professionals and intellectuals) who had graduated from Western-style medical (*tıbbiye*) and administrative (*mülkiye*) schools. Second, the mass demonstrations organized by the CUP that had paved the way for the revolution did not extend beyond the borders of Macedonia, the stronghold of the opposition, and were not directly related to taxation. The revolts in East Anatolia were not controlled by the CUP, either. In fact, the Young Turks had to co-operate with *Dashnaksutiun* (Armenian socialist revolutionaries) due to their organizational weakness in the region (Hanioğlu 2001: 95–97). Third, the Young Turks were not seeking complete regime change, but a shift in the locus of political power within the existing state system – i.e., to curtail the sitting monarch's absolute power. In this sense, the revolution was no different from various Janissary revolts before the corps was abolished in 1826, or from the (successful) efforts of the military and civil bureaucrats (the Young Ottomans) to have Abdülhamid II proclaim the constitution and the parliament that had started the First Constitutional Period in 1876. A report drafted by the Young Turk central committee, dated September 27, 1907, explicitly stated that their purpose was "to bring about the implementation of the Constitution of Midhat Pasha proclaimed in 1292 [1876], and to keep it in force" (quoted in Hanioğlu 2001: 216).

Finally, the main purpose of the revolution for the CUP was to save the state from decline by preventing ethnic tensions and separatist movements, thereby restoring the old order of the glorious past, rather than establishing democracy, freedom, and civil rights (Sohrabi 2002). Therefore, though they were partly inspired by Enlightenment thought, the Young Turks' revolution was not a bourgeois, "Enlightenment revolution," but rather of a restoration that was typical of 17th-century Europe. Moreover, it was not a liberal movement that restored individual liberties and rights; rather, it emphasized the "rights of the (Ottoman) nation." Therefore, contrary to the claims of Akşin (1987) and Kansu (2001), the 1908 Revolution was not a "late bourgeois revolution."

Though the CUP had forced Abdülhamid II to reinstate the constitution and the two-tiered parliament, the sultan presented these changes to the public as if his own accomplishment. Partly because of this, the CUP did not take governmental control directly into its own hands but remained behind the scenes until 1913 (Sohrabi 2002: 50; Aydın 2001). Nevertheless, the party continued to exert influence over the central government for most of the Second Constitutional Period (Tunaya 1952: 188; see also Akşin 1987), establishing the tradition of the army's influence on politics in Turkey, which has continued through to the present.[2] The first conflict between the Sultan and the CUP occurred immediately after the Revolution, when Abdülhamid II insisted on his right to appoint the war and naval ministers, instead of merely approving the grand vizier's nominees. When Said Pasha, the grand vizier, supported the sultan, the CUP forced him to resign; the sultan then replaced him with Kamil Pasha, an anti-CUP liberal statesman, in August 1908 soon to be replaced by Unionist Hüseyin Hilmi Pasha. The next important event that helped the CUP consolidate its power was the general elections conducted through the indirect two-tier system at the end of the year.

Though the Unionists were organizationally quite weak in Anatolia before 1908 (having originated in the Balkans), they quickly organized local notables, professionals (doctors, lawyers, teachers) and tradesmen under the CUP and easily won the uncontested elections. Thus, the sultan's power was curbed – but not entirely eliminated until the middle of the next year (Zürcher 1993: 93–99).

The counter-revolution: the "March 31 Incident"

Following the revolution the CUP, though the most powerful force in the empire, encountered opposition from both liberals and pro-monarchy conservatives. The former gathered around the Ottoman Liberal Party (*Osmanlı Ahrar Fırkası*), founded in September 1908 by Prince Sabahaddin's followers, who made up the liberal (as opposed to the Unionist) faction of the Young Turks (Tunaya 1952: 189; Aydın 2001). All Young Turks opposed Hamidian absolutism, but the Unionists, consisting mostly of lower-ranking bureaucrats from the lower-middle class that had suffered most from the development of capitalism in the empire, were inspired by the strong rule and centralization policies of Germany and Japan, while the liberals, who generally had upper class (aristocratic) backgrounds, were pro-British and pro-decentralization (Hanioğlu 1995). After the elections, the latter allied with Grand Vizier Kamil Pasha, whom the CUP then replaced with Huseyin Hilmi Pasha, a Unionist, which triggered a bitter campaign by the liberal press against the Unionists. The second opposition group consisted of the conservative lower-ranking *ulema* and some Sufi leaders who were organized around the *Volkan* newspaper and the Society of Muhammedan Union (*İttihad-ı Muhammedi Cemiyeti*). Led by the *Naqshibandi* sheikh Derviş Vahdeti, they organized an armed insurrection in Istanbul on April 13, 1909 (March 31 in the Ottoman [*Rumi*] calendar) with the help of *medrese* students and the Macedonian troops originally brought to the Capital by the CUP, and demanded the "restoration of the *sharia*" and dismissal of Unionist officers and ministers, including the grand vizier and the war and naval ministers. Their demands were granted and the Unionists fled the capital. But other groups, namely the liberals and the high-ranking *ulema*, organized around the Society of Islamic Scholars (*Cemiyet-i İlmiye-i İslamiye*), did not support them. Meanwhile, the CUP organized large demonstrations in the provinces through various organizations and then launched a military campaign against the rebels. When the Unionist "Action Army," sent from Macedonia, came to Istanbul, the CUP-dominated parliament supported it and the army then occupied the city without much resistance on April 24. Three days later, Sultan-Caliph Abdülhamid II, who the CUP blamed for secretly instigating the counter-revolution, was deposed by the two chambers of parliament and replaced by his younger brother, Mehmed Reşad V. A large number of rebels, including Vahdeti, were also executed (Zürcher 1993: 100–102). The failed counter-revolution was presented as a "reactionary" uprising, backed by a "despotic" and equally "reactionary" monarch, against the (legitimate) central authority. Thus, Unionists used this incident as a justification for various secular reforms that diminished the caliph's power.[3]

Constitutional amendments and the decline of the Caliph's authority

The suppression of the counter-revolution not only crushed the opposition, but also initiated the period of "Unionism" (*İttihatçılık*), characterized by the oligarchic rule of the military and its allies in the civil bureaucracy. The Unionists' main goal was to modernize the state by replacing the old order of authoritarian monarchy with a constitutional regime, albeit based on an equally authoritarian and bureaucratic – rather than democratic – rule. With a weak sultan on the throne, the CUP immediately launched a series of legislative reforms to curb the monarch's power and consolidate the constitutional order. The reinstated constitution remained in force throughout the Young Turks' time in power, but its 119 articles were amended several times. The parliament gained sweeping control over both the Palace (the sultan) and the Porte (the cabinet) as the main source of power (Ahmad 1969: 57–64; see also Ramsaur 1957). With the constitutional amendments enacted in August 1909, legislation and the approval of treaties became the prerogative of the parliament, rather than the caliph. The caliph-sultan could only appoint the grand vizier and the *şeyhülislam* (which meant that he merely approved the CUP government's ministers and bureaucrats); also, very importantly, he had no right to dissolve parliament, which could only be done by the loss of a vote of confidence, in which case elections would have to take place within three months. Finally, the sultan-caliph would have to take an oath to obey both the *sharia* and the constitution, which formalized the limitations of his authority. These amendments marked both the reduction of the caliph-sultan's position to that of the head of the executive branch and the strengthening of the legislative branch vis-à-vis the executive. (Unionists later regretted this change and tried to weaken the legislative again when they lost the 1911 by-elections to the opposition, which gathered together under the liberal Freedom and Alliance Party; see below.)

These constitutional changes were followed by a number of new laws passed to further strengthen the (central) government. These laws restricted the freedom of press and association, also limiting public meetings, strikes, and demonstrations. Military service was also made mandatory for all male citizens, Muslim and non-Muslim alike. Moreover, both military and civil bureaucratic offices were trimmed and re-organized, eventually purging one-third (over 10,000) of the army's officers, most of them being from the Hamidian era. Finally, government expenditure on the royal family was cut by two-thirds in the new budget, indicating the clear decline of the caliph-sultan's power (Zürcher 1993: 104–105). The changes following the revolution had three main consequences: First, they strengthened the government and the parliament controlled by the CUP vis-à-vis the Caliphate and the *ulema*. Second, they also had a secularizing effect on the political structure in general, fundamentally reshaping the paths of elite formation in the empire: Whereas in previous periods, including the classical and Hamidian eras, the two major routes of upward mobility were excellence in religious education and artistic accomplishments, in addition to personal distinction in public service, under Young Turk rule "one could climb the social ladder only through association with the party and government" (Karpat 2004: 209).

Third, with the legal changes enacted in 1909, the Palace's authority was greatly weakened and the power struggle in domestic politics took place between the CUP and other parties, including the liberals, who were organized around the Freedom and Alliance Party (*Hürriyet ve İtilaf Fırkası*, or *Entente Libérale*), which also included conservatives and army officers (see Birinci 1990), and a weak Ottoman Socialist Party (*Osmanlı Sosyalist Fırkası*) (see Tunçay and Zürcher 2004). Though the opposition had been crushed in 1909, it slowly re-emerged, winning a by-election in Istanbul in late 1911. After the 1912 "elections with the stick," which the CUP had won through violence and intimidation (hence the nickname), a group of dissident soldiers calling themselves "Savior Officers" (*Halaskar Zabitan*) threatened a military coup, forcing the government to resign. The "Great Cabinet," which represented all the opposition groups, replaced the CUP government and persecuted leading Unionists, sending many of them into exile. The CUP then decided to launch its own coup and seized the opportunity offered by the Balkan War (1912–1913), which resulted in the loss of most of the empire's territory in Europe. On January 23, 1913, when Edirne, a former Ottoman capital, fell, a group of Unionist officers went to the Porte (*Bab-ı Ali*, the grand vizier's office), burst into the cabinet meeting, shot the war minister, took the rest of the cabinet prisoner, and forced the government to resign. Known as the "Bab-ı Ali Coup," this incident marked the consolidation of CUP rule, which continued until the end of World War I. After the coup, the Unionist trio of Enver Pasha, Talat Pasha, and Cemal Pasha, who had formerly ruled the country from behind the scenes, entered the cabinet. Then, following the assassination of Grand Vizier Mahmud Şevket Pasha by a FAP supporter on June 15, 1913, the CUP began persecuting the liberal and conservative opposition (Zürcher 1993: 106–108).

This violent process of the domination of domestic politics by the Unionists went hand in hand with the decline of the power of the caliph and of his religious dignitary in the government, the *şeyhülislam*, who, together with the traditionalist *ulema*, represented the religious establishment. The power struggle between the traditionalist forces and the modernist intelligentsia and bureaucrats (represented by the CUP) over the status and power of the Caliphate during the Second Constitutional Period (1908–1918) was won by the modernists. This was made possible by the formation of a coalition between secular bureaucrats and the modernist portion of the *ulema* (and a few traditionalists, such as Ömer Lütfi). Modernists set about institutionalizing secular concepts and practices to modernize the state; to this end, they drew upon the Islamic tradition's classic texts and history. Transforming the Caliphate into a secular institution by curtailing its religious/spiritual authority was also a major goal for the CUP, which did not want to share its newly acquired power with the Palace after the 1908 Revolution. For this reason, the revolutionaries made a deal with Mehmed V, who agreed to be a weaker caliph-sultan with much of his political power curtailed.

The discursive battle: traditionalists versus modernists

The traditionalist *ulema* and intellectuals, who defended the Hamidian regime, thus lost much of their influence with the 1909 Coup that saw the previous, powerful caliph-sultan dethroned by the CUP. For the modernist *ulema*, who regarded Abdülhamid's *ancien régime* as a dictatorship (*istibdad*), the idea of transforming the Caliphate was directly related to the widespread feeling that the empire's failures in the political, military, and economic arenas were to a large extent caused not only by the Hamidian regime, but also by the negative impact of the mystical teachings of the Sufi communities, which were quite well organized in the Muslim world (see Kara 1998). Modernists, who constantly emphasized the significance of such concepts as hard work and action (as opposed to more Sufi-oriented themes, like patience and *tevekkül* [resigning oneself to God's plans]) argued that Sufi doctrines had turned Muslims away from the pursuit of material success and hard work by stressing the importance of the afterlife vis-à-vis the temporal world. The modernists believed this mentality had penetrated into all major political and economic institutions, ultimately leading to the relative "backwardness" of Muslims compared to Europeans (e.g., Elmalılı 1909: 135; Rashid Rida 1923a: 9). The solution to this problem of the *ummah* laid, according to modernist Islamists, in the re-awakening of Muslims, which would start with the reformation of the Caliphate into a temporal authority. Also, the modernists proposed that social change should be started and carried out by the state, reflecting a general tendency toward top-down models of change not only among modernists, but also among other intellectuals and politicians of the time.

This political vision of the modernist *ulema* and intellectuals, as well as their view of the Caliphate, in particular, was influential during the Second Constitutional Period, as the CUP-dominated governments were sympathetic toward the modernists. CUP leaders found it useful for the continuation of their (domestic) rule to have a caliph with limited temporal power and no religious authority.[4] To curtail the caliph's spiritual authority, on which his political power was based, the CUP had to resort to religious justification, which could only be provided by the *ulema* and Islamist intellectuals. The modernist *ulema* and intellectuals, such as Seyyid Bey, who was the most important of the modernist Islamists, were willing to help the CUP for two primary reasons. First, as discussed above, they claimed that Sufi groups' over-emphasis on the spiritual aspects of Islam at the expense of the religion's material-temporal provisions led to the stagnation and, ultimately, regression of the Ottoman Empire vis-à-vis the West. They thus blamed Sufi Islam for the "moment of inertia" that the Muslim *ummah* was experiencing. Second, they also criticized Abdülhamid II for the lack of (political) freedom: The widespread impression that the reign of an all-powerful sultan was one of dictatorship was also shared by many *ulema* and Islamists, who, as we shall see below, were influenced by the modern, Western idea(l)s, particularly those of *liberté*, *égalité*, and *fraternité*, generated by the French Revolution.

Abdülhamid II had successfully emphasized the role of the Caliphate in order to consolidate his politico-ideological power domestically and internationally, and greatly modernized the Ottoman state and its infrastructure in the last quarter of the 19th century. However, he had achieved this through despotic rule, suspending the constitution and closing down the parliament at the beginning of his long reign (1878). The 1908 Revolution overthrew Abdülhamid and opened up the "period of freedom" (*hürriyet*), which was celebrated by many *ulema*, as well as most intellectuals and politicians affiliated with the Young Turks. Thus, many of the *ulema* supported the CUP in their effort to further modernize the state. For the CUP, the spiritual authority of the caliph was a great obstacle for the modernization of the political system, for which it desperately needed the help of the carriers of Islamic knowledge: the modernist Islamists. These *ulema* did not hesitate to lend the CUP their life-saving support by justifying the secularization of the Caliphate in Islamic terms. They believed that the Caliphate should be redefined as a modern political institution because only a modernized political system could "save the state,"[5] which was on the verge of collapse. Thus, the modernist *ulema*, by invoking Islamic texts, set the stage for the discursive battle over the Caliphate, which mainly centered on the institution's definition.

Definition of the Caliphate

The way traditionalists and modernists defined the Caliphate reflects the major differences between the two groups. While traditionalists applied the discursive strategy of establishing the caliph's double (spiritual and temporal) authority to their definition of the Caliphate, modernists employed the strategy of defining the Caliphate as a temporal political institution. However, most modernists (e.g., Seyyid Bey 1917: 446; Rashid Rida 1923a: 17), as well as traditionalists (e.g., Ömer Lütfi 1912: 233; Mustafa Zihni 1911: 111; al-Tunusi 1913: 416; Yafi 1916: 164), adopted definitions found in classical Sunni theology, particularly the one put forward by al-Taftazānī (d.1389), often directly quoting from him: "The Caliphate is a succession of the Prophet, and as such, a general authority on matters of religion and the world" (al-Taftazānī 1989, V: 232).

Despite their initial convergence with traditionalists regarding the definition of the Caliphate, modernist Islamists constantly emphasized its temporal dimension. Their main aim was to transform the Ottoman Empire into a modern state by isolating the Caliphate from its spiritual aspects and turning the caliph-sultan into a modern, secular ruler. Since, as mentioned above, they blamed Abdülhamid II's rule and Sufi Islam for the perceived backwardness of the Muslim world, emphasizing the this-worldly aspect of Islam and the temporal (rather than spiritual) authority of the Caliph was for them the appropriate response to the challenge posed by the modern West. They essentially held a top-down model of socio-political change and a firm belief in the (potential) transformative power of the Caliphate in terms of initiating and carrying out the wider societal transformation that they desired. Furthermore, they believed that stressing the temporal, rather than spiritual, aspect of the Caliphate would make it truly Islamic (for Islam rejected spiritual authority), in contrast to the traditionalists, who assumed that both dimensions of the Caliphate should be emphasized in order to revive the once-strong Ottoman Caliphate as the politico-religious leader of the Muslim world.

Unlike modernists, therefore, traditionalist Islamists always insisted on the dual aspect of the caliph's rule, adopting the classical definition found in the literature. Among them, for example, Ömer Lütfi quoted definitions by many classic Sunni scholars, regarding as the best a comprehensive formulation provided by Qadi Adud, which adds to al-Taftazānī's definition (quoted above) the notion of obedience by Muslims to the Caliph as a religious duty: "The Great Caliphate is a succession of the Great Prophet in administering the affairs of religion and improving and protecting Islamic lands; and obedience to the Imam is mandatory for the entire *ummah*" (Ömer Lütfi 1912: 233–234).

The context in which he produced this text was an important debate (mentioned above) in the Ottoman parliament in December 1911 on the caliph's authority (regulated by the Article 35 of the constitution) to dissolve the Parliament when necessary. During the debates on this issue, FAP member Mustafa Sabri Efendi, also a member of the *ulema* and a deputy (he would later be *şeyhülislam* in 1919–1920, and abandon his previous view completely) opposed the CUP's proposal to amend the constitution by changing Article 35 to give the sultan the right to dissolve the parliament. Making references to key Islamic sources, including the Qur'an and the early history of the Caliphate, he argued in his speech that the CUP's move was un-Islamic, for it gave the caliph unlimited authority:

> The essence of Islamic Caliphate does not envision a caliph who can do whatever he wishes, nor does it recognize him as infallible. Rather, it … places him in a high status that is bounded by the *sharia* and the law. Muslims are the followers of a prophet who taught them to mention in their prayers every night the sentence: "We depose and flee from the one who commits sins against your will." There is no doubt that our sultan has an angelic character; however, I don't think you would want to give him more rights than the second caliph, Holy Omar, would you? Do you know how many votes Omar would cast [if he was] here? Only one! He even said "*ana ka-ahadikum*" [I am like any of you]; that is, "I am no different from any of you when it comes to voting." Now we have actually given the sultan, his excellency, an authority equal to the totality of the members of both the chambers of deputies and notables; I think this is enough.
>
> (quoted in Ömer Lütfi 1912: 210)

Mustafa Sabri had also discussed the famous "*ul al-amr*" verse in the Qur'an (4/59) that commanded obedience to the ruler, interpreting the word "ruler" (*ul al-amr*) as the community of the *ulema*, rather than the caliph (see Chapter 3). Against this position, Ömer Lütfi cited the Islamic legal tradition, particularly the Hanafi school (from which he derived the above definition), and the *Tafseer* (Qur'anic commentary) literature to disprove his opponent's interpretation of the verse. Furthermore, he presented a detailed description of the early history of the Caliphate and a grammatical analysis of the saying "I am like any of you," arguing that it actually originated with Ali, the fourth Caliph, who in fact meant the opposite of what Mustafa Sabri had claimed – i.e., that he was no different than others *on matters not relating to caliphal authority* (pp. 211–213).

In another important debate between traditionalists and modernists, this time on the status of the *şeyhülislam*, Elmalılı Hamdi, a leading modernist *alim*, argued that the Caliph had only temporal, not religious, authority, and, as such, was no different from a contemporary king (1909: 435; see below for a detailed discussion). İsmail Hakkı criticized Elmalılı in an article (published in *Sırat-ı Müstakim*, a leading Islamist journal) by restating the traditionalist view. İsmail Hakkı's comprehensive definition is not particularly different from Ömer Lütfi's:

> The Islamic Caliphate is both a religious authority and a temporal rule; it is the best of governments in contemporary civilization and the highest of religious posts. It is based on justice and *taqwa* (religious wisdom), and bounded by the laws of religion and the principles of the *sharia*. The caliph is the authority over religious affairs and the ruler over temporal matters.
>
> (1910: 438)

Others (e.g., Ömer Ziyaeddin 1908: 51; al-Tunusi 1913: 416) defined the Caliphate by locating it in an ontological hierarchy that involved God, the Prophet, and the Caliph, respectively, which is implied by the *ul al-amr* verse (4/59), as discussed in the previous chapter. They argued that, since the caliph represented the Prophet, who in turn was the caliph of God in this world, the former must have naturally possessed religious authority, as well. A discursive technique deployed by the two *hadith* compilers among the traditionalists, Ömer Ziyaeddin and Mehmed Tahir, illustrates this point. This technique specifically concerns the translation of a key concept in prophetic traditions: "caliph." In their *hadith* compilations, Ziyaeddin and Tahir frequently translated the word "caliph" (or "*imam*") in prophetic traditions as "sultan" in order to more easily relate the Ottoman Empire to sacred texts and ensure loyalty to it by implying that the Ottoman dynasty, as the true embodiment of the Islamic Caliphate, had a religious significance for all Muslims rooted deeply in the sayings of the Prophet (Ömer Ziyaeddin 1908: *hadith* nos. 2, 3, 5, 7, 8, 9, 10, 14, 15; Mehmed Tahir 1909: *hadith* nos. 5, 9, 10, 11, 16, 17).

In their quest for religious justification, however, Ziyaeddin and Tahir exaggerated the "divine" basis of the Caliphate. They (Ömer Ziyaeddin 1908: 60, 61; Mehmed Tahir 1909: 70, 72) quoted "weak" *hadiths* in which caliphs are called "The Shadow of God on Earth" – an idea that is strongly rejected by the majority of Sunni *ulema* (see Chapter 3). This exaggeration becomes meaningful, however, once located in its historical context. As already mentioned, the

Ottoman Empire had been weakening and losing wars since the late 19th century, and modernist intellectuals had begun to doubt the existing government's compatibility with the modern world. For this reason, they often contrasted the Caliphate with Western forms of government during the Second Constitutional Period. Traditionalists, however, were highly self-confident, as exemplified by İsmail Hakkı and others. When they compared the Islamic government with Western monarchies and constitutional regimes, they concluded that the former was better because of its dual character (e.g., Mustafa Zihni 1911: 114–117, Safayihi 1915: 49–52). However, unconvinced modernists (such as Elmalılı) also argued that the modern caliph must not have any sacred status, fearing that if the caliph's status was assumed to be sacred, the political, economic, and military failures of the leader of the current government could imply the failure of Islam itself. Thus, their motivation could be said to be at least partly religious, stemming from the idea of protecting Islam by maintaining its "perfectness" as a religion and reducing the status of its (human) leader. Some traditionalists, however, must have felt that this would pose a grave danger for the religion itself; for them, limiting the caliph's religious authority would amount to limiting Islam's influence over politics. Therefore, both groups seemed to be reacting – albeit for different reasons – to changing political and ideological circumstances that posed a fundamental challenge to the Islamic Caliphate.

Traditionalists thus adopted the broader definition of the Caliphate, whereas modernists focused on its politico-temporal aspect. The latter emphasized this political dimension because the Caliphate's authority had putatively begun to be seen – by most Europeans as well as some Muslim observers – as purely spiritual, comparable to the Papacy of the Catholic world:

> For Muslims, the caliph is not infallible; he does not receive revelation, nor does he have a monopoly on the interpretation of the Qur'an and the Prophetic *sunna*. ... The Islamic religion grants no privilege to the caliph in terms of understanding the Book. ... Also, the caliph is obeyed only in so far as he is on the right path of the Book and the *sunna*.
> (Muhammad Abduh, quoted in Rashid Rida 1923a: 140–141; cf. Elmalılı Hamdi 1909: 433; Seyyid Bey 1917: 445; Rashid Rida 1923a: 142)

Legitimacy of the caliph's authority

Different definitions of the Caliphate by traditionalists and modernists implied different sources of legitimacy. While the former considered religious legitimization (legitimacy derived from Islamic texts) sufficient for the Caliphate, as in the classical theory, the latter added social/popular legitimacy as a *sine qua non* for the caliph's authority – without rejecting the religious basis. In other words, the modernists considered both religious and social legitimization as equally important. As a discursive strategy, their emphasis on popular legitimacy complemented their definition of the Caliphate as a purely political institution.

Together, these two strategies helped justify the secularization of the Caliphate (and of the political system in general) at the hands of the bureaucratic elite in the Ottoman Empire following the Young Turk Revolution by inserting the modern notions of strictly temporal rule and popular sovereignty into the theory of the Caliphate.

Traditionalists, by contrast, derived the Caliph's legitimacy solely from Islamic sources and the *ulema*, the carriers of knowledge of these sources. For example, Mustafa Zihni (1911: 111–112) located his definition of the Caliphate within the context of the "four fundamentals of Islam" (the Qur'an, the *Sunna* of the Prophet, the consensus of the *ummah* [*ijma'*], and analogical reasoning [*qiyas*]), arguing that the Caliphate's legitimacy was derived from the first three of these sources, after which he cited a number of Qur'anic verses and prophetic traditions, as well as the evidence for the consensus of the early Muslim community:

> [The legitimacy of] the institution of the Caliphate and the Imamate is based on both the glorious Prophet's sayings, which are the second of the "four fundamentals of religion," and the consensus of the *ummah*, which is third [of these fundamentals]; and because the virtuous [*ulema*] of Islam have clearly discerned the legitimacy of Abu Bakr's caliphate from the Qur'an, the Caliphate is also supported by the first of the four fundamentals of religion, the Qur'an. Therefore, the Caliphate is an institution built upon the most important principles and sources of our religion.
>
> (ibid.; cf. Ömer Lütfi 1912: 251)

Though Mustafa Zihni mentioned the "consensus of the *ummah*" as one of the foundations of the Caliphate, this consensus was confined, in both the classical theory and the traditionalist view, to the narrower circle of political (*umera*) and intellectual (*ulema*) elites of Islamic society in any given epoch. The implications of this traditionalist view were very different from the modernist conception of the Caliphate, which saw the institution as dependent on popular legitimacy.

As already noted, the modernists presented the Caliphate as a temporal institution in order to protect its high status in Islam, unlike the church in the Christian world, which had been greatly weakened by secular forces in Europe. This suggests that most of them were genuinely concerned about the future of the Caliphate and tried to keep it alive by emphasizing its difference from the weakened Church. Furthermore, they were also concerned that the Caliphate could be used as an instrument of oppression by a powerful tyrant – and here they certainly had Abdülhamid II in mind. For this reason, they linked the Caliphate to the parliamentary system and constitutional monarchy. Moreover, their reconstruction of the theory of the Caliphate in a way that involved popular legitimacy implied that it was based on a social contract *à la* Rousseau (1993[1762]), reflecting the influence of French political thought on the Ottoman intelligentsia (see also below). Thus, Elmalılı Hamdi, a leading modernist *alim* (and *medrese* professor) of the time, emphasized the Caliphate's social basis (contract of representation) as much as its religious grounding:

> The Caliph has the authority to represent, on the one hand, the *ummah* that has given allegiance to him, and, on the other hand, the Lawmaker[6] in terms only of practicing the law that he, too, has to obey, just like his subjects do.
>
> (1909: 434)

As we shall see below, other modernists, too, constantly emphasized the limits of the caliph's authority on the grounds that he only represented "the people" as the head of the executive branch of the government, a principle that had been formalized in the constitution.

The modernist response also entailed a strategic intervention into Islamic theology and law as part of what I have called "theological engineering": redefining the key concepts of the Islamic legal and theological traditions on the basis of the emerging exigencies of the modern historical context and using the literature in these traditions to promote their own political agenda. The way two leading modernists, Seyyid Bey and Rashid Rida, defined the Caliphate offers a good example of this intervention. While their overall argument on reviving the Caliphate was quite "Islamic," Seyyid Bey and Rashid Rida manipulated the theory of the Caliphate by positing a contractual basis for it and by inserting into it the notion of "popular sovereignty" in their discussion of the caliph's legitimacy. Seyyid Bey dismissed what I have called the traditionalist and secularist views of the Caliphate as extremist and maintained that it was no more than an executive office of the government, deriving its legitimacy from the "nation," to which it was, thus, accountable (1917: 443, 445). Similarly, Rashid Rida argued that the Caliph's legitimacy was derived from the "community," or the Muslim *ummah* (1923a: 50).[7]

An extension of this modernist argument was that the caliph needed to be elected and – if necessary – could be deposed by the representatives of "the people," i.e., parliament members. Accordingly, virtually all modernists identified the parliament (first the Ottoman *Meclis-i Mebusan*, and later the Turkish Grand National Assembly) with the *Ahl al-hal wa al-'aqd* (the committee that is in charge of the election of the Caliph) in classical theory, thereby finding an Islamic equivalent to a political institution that was imported from the West. Furthermore, some modernists (e.g., Rashid Rida 1923a: 69, 141) insisted that, since its members were direct representatives of the people, the parliament, as the *Ahl al-hal wa al-'aqd*, was more important than the Caliphate itself, and that the existing parliament, as the authorized committee, had the right not only to elect or appoint the caliph, but also to depose him (pp. 21–23). Rida thus argued that the caliph was "merely a *primus inter pares* who must seek the advice of the representatives of the community and respect their *ijma'*" (Soage 2008: 10). Seyyid Bey added that, once deposed, the caliph-sultan immediately became an ordinary Muslim and citizen with no authority over others due to the contractual nature of the Caliphate:

ازمير مبعوثى سيد بك

Figure 4.2 Seyyid Bey (source: *Osmanlı Mebusları, Birinci Devre 1324–1328*, Istanbul: Ahmed İhsan ve Şürekâsı Matbaası, n.d.).

Figure 4.3 Rashid Rida (source: Rashid Rida, *Târîkh al-Ustâdh al-Imâm Muhammad Abduh*, Cairo, 1925).

[The Caliph's authority] is given to him by the nation with a contract and *bey'at* (allegiance). For this reason, in the event of [the Caliph's] deposition or resignation their jurisdiction ceases to exist. Then they become no different from any other member of the *ummah*. Needless to say, his highness the caliph had no such authority before being a caliph, as he acquired this authority as a result of the contract of mandate/representation. Naturally, he returns to his earlier [ordinary] position in the event of deposition or resignation.

(Seyyid Bey 1917: 449–450)

These arguments make it clear that for most modernists the Caliphate had no spiritual or religious authority: Politicians or parliament members, some of whom were non-Muslims, had every right to impeach and depose the caliph if they deemed it necessary, because his office was no more than an executive one with no superiority over the legislative branch. It is also important to note the context of these arguments: they were made after the "despotic" Sultan Abdülhamid II had been deposed from the throne in 1909 by the CUP, of which Seyyid Bey was a leading member. Therefore, this discursive technique also represents an attempt at a *post facto* rationalization of a major political development (regime change) in the empire as a result of a power struggle between the Palace and the bureaucracy led by the CUP. It also exemplifies how modernist Islamists, drawing on Islam, legitimized the Unionist policies that eventually weakened both the Caliphate and – ironically – the *ulema* themselves, from which the modernist group drew most of its members. In line with CUP policies, the modernist view of the Caliphate's legitimacy as partly defined by popular sovereignty implied that the caliph's *temporal* authority was limited as well. Therefore, in addition to the nature of the Caliphate and the basis of its legitimacy, the modernist and traditionalist *ulema* also differed on a third aspect of the Caliph's status: the limits of his authority.

The scope of the caliph's temporal authority

The extent of the caliph's authority was a major point of dispute between the two groups. While traditionalists tried, as mentioned above, to reinforce the religious and temporal authority of the caliph simultaneously, modernists not only denied the institution's religious dimension, but also highlighted the limits of the caliph's *temporal* authority as a further discursive strategy. Traditionalists constantly emphasized obedience to the caliph as a religious duty in order to support the Ottoman Caliphate by reinforcing the notion that it was the only legitimate form of government in the Middle East. Therefore, emphasizing the necessity of obedience to the caliph was a major discursive technique employed by traditionalists as part of their strategy of establishing the dual status of the Caliphate. Modernists, on the other hand, deployed the technique of emphasizing the *limits* of the caliph's authority. For them, his authority was not only limited to temporal affairs (since he did not have any spiritual power), but was also confined, within the framework of these "temporal affairs," by the law (the modern constitution) and "public interest" (Elmalılı Hamdi 1909: 434, Seyyid Bey 1917: 457). For traditionalists, obedience to the caliph (and his government) was central to their understanding of this institution, which followed from the idea that he was the successor of the Prophet Muhammad in both religious and temporal leadership. Ömer Lütfi (1912: 236–238, 247–249) cited many verses and *hadiths* to justify the dual status of the Caliph and the necessity of obedience to him, and added:

> The leader of Muslims is certainly to be obeyed, because he is responsible for what he does. Responsibility must be attached to obedience, otherwise it is unacceptable. For, the command of a leader who is not obeyed [by his followers] has no validity. And the leader whose command is not effective has no power to perform the duties under his jurisdiction.
>
> (Ömer Lütfi 1912: 247)

The technique of stressing obedience was part of his above-mentioned polemic against the liberal parliament member (and modernist scholar) Mustafa Sabri over the implications of the *ul al-amr* verse. Like Ömer Lütfi, many other traditionalist *ulema* cited the same verse as part of their discursive technique when discussing obedience to the just ruler as a religious duty of the believer.

A similar technique applied to this theme involved presenting the scope of obedience in a way that included the (Ottoman) sultan's bureaucrats as well as the caliph himself. Arguing that obedience to the caliph as a religious duty implied by extension obedience to the administrators appointed by him, Ömer Lütfi concluded: "Obeying the administrators (*umera*) and sultans is without doubt a part of obedience to Allah and His Prophet" (1912: 221–222). Similarly, after establishing in religious terms the necessity of obeying the sultan-caliph in the preface to his 40-hadith collection, Ömer Ziyaeddin stated: "Just as we are required by law to respect the rights of the sultan.... We are also required by law and the *sharia* to obey all the officials [including] the ministers and viziers appointed by the sultan" (1908: 47–48). Likewise, in his discussion of the legitimacy of the modern cabinet system, Mustafa Zihni (1911: 197), who was a governor himself, argued that this system was required by both religion and "reason" and that obedience to the viziers of the caliph was also necessary.[8]

Furthermore, some took the notion of "obedience to the ruler" even further so as to make obedience part of the Muslim faith. Ömer Ziyaeddin (1908: 58) cited a *hadith* that prescribed obedience to the administrative officials appointed by the caliph even if they were slaves, and interpreted it to mean that "obeying those who are appointed by the *sultan* is a necessary consequence of one's faith" (my emphasis). Others often emphasized the idea of obedience as a fundamental requirement of Islamic *sharia* (Mustafa Zihni 1911: 111; Ömer Lütfi 1912: 247).

The modernist group, however, constantly emphasized the limits of the caliph's authority as part of their discursive strategy of transforming his office into a secular institution. This strategy entailed two main techniques: first, denying the caliph spiritual authority; second, defining the Caliphate as a legal contract between the ruler and the ruled. With the first technique, they rejected any possibility of attributing a spiritual dimension to the Caliphate, in line with the CUP's policy of limiting the caliph-sultan's power, which was justified by drawing on the Islamic theological and legal traditions. For example, Abdulaziz Jawish, a pro-CUP *alim*, North African activist and member of the *Teşkilat-ı Mahsusa* (Ottoman secret service), did not include the caliph's religious authority in his definition of the Caliphate. Though he was a staunch defender of the Ottoman Caliphate and a harsh critic of attempts in the *Maghrib* and Arabia to create alternative caliphates sponsored by the French and British governments (see Chapter 5), he carefully situated the caliph as a temporal ruler. Writing in the midst of World War I, when the CUP needed to emphasize the Caliphate's significance, Jawish glorified it, but nevertheless downplayed its religious power:

> The Caliphate is not a post with which to expect blessings and grace from the heavens; rather, it is an institution that is supposed to protect (people's) rights, carry out punishments, protect people from oppression, and make the necessary arrangements and modern (civilized) policies that are useful for the Islamic society. Being a caliph means being able to take necessary measures to conduct wars, collect and train soldiers, and to protect religion and safeguard the Muslim society. Therefore, the caliph must have the ability and power to manage the affairs of the state and the society; he must also have genius and mastery over the Islamic principles of government.
>
> (1916: 251)

It was not only Ottoman supporters who employed this discursive technique, but also anti-Ottoman activists. For example, in his book that aimed at presenting a program for reforming the Caliphate, Arab nationalist Rashid Rida (1923a: 142–143), Jawish's intellectual opponent, said the Caliphate was "sanctioned by religion" and then quickly added that the caliph did not have the kind of spiritual authority that the pope had. Therefore, he had no authority over anyone's beliefs or relationship with God. On the contrary, the caliph was responsible to the constitution and the parliament, for he was supposed to be "a modern (civilized) ruler" who ruled with "consultation" rather than despotism. Thus, according to Rashid Rida (1922: 717), since the authority of the caliph was limited to this-worldly government affairs only, he, like other rulers, was to be held accountable for his policies.

Some modernists complemented this discursive technique with a second one, which entailed the definition of the Caliphate as a legal/social contract that constrained the ruler's political power by making his legitimacy dependent on the sovereignty of "the people." Seyyid Bey's strategic intervention into Islamic law with the theory of the Caliphate as mandate and power of attorney (i.e. that the Caliphate was simply a form of legal contract between ruler and ruled) meant, in fact, delimiting the caliph's authority even within the realm of temporal affairs. By exclusively – and skillfully – employing the terminology of Islamic law,

Seyyid Bey (1917) claimed that the caliph, as the people's deputy (or "attorney"), had no authority over matters that are not useful for, or not wanted by, his "client" – i.e., the "nation" and its representatives, the members of parliament (p. 447). He added that any of the caliph's decisions that were unfavorable to the "public interest" would be legally non-binding and, moreover, that the Islamic *sharia* would not allow Muslims to obey such policies (p. 458). Finally, in his attempt to justify his idea of a Caliphate with limited power with reference to the Islamic legal tradition, he acknowledged that in the tradition the caliph's authority was "general and absolute" (see Chapter 3), but quickly moved to qualify this absoluteness:

> Though the aforementioned authority [of the caliph] is general and absolute, it is not utterly and completely absolute; [for] it has a limit.... This limit is determined by the concept of "public interest." [The Caliph's power] is thus qualified and conditioned by this.
>
> (1917: 452; cf. p. 457)

Seyyid Bey justified his apparent intervention ("engineering") into Islamic legal theory with an unusual interpretation of the theory of the Caliphate by further referencing the *sharia* and the legal provisions regarding *economic* contracts, which he transplanted into the political realm. After discussing several examples from contract law and referring to the *Mecelle*'s[9] articles related exclusively to economic concepts such as "public interest" (Article 58), compensation (Articles 33, 919) and expropriation (Articles 1216, 1217), he concluded: "The Caliph has both a boss (*amir*) and a client. His boss is the *sharia*, and his client is the nation" (p. 457).

Therefore, Seyyid Bey's intervention turned the traditional hierarchy between the caliph and his "subjects" upside down, relegating the representative of the Prophet a lower status than the "nation," which in practice meant the CUP-dominated parliament's control over the sultan's Palace. Seyyid Bey's "transformative technique," which helped him redefine the legal concept of "mandate/power of attorney" and re-interpret the centuries-long tradition of Islamic law in an unusual way, rested on his scholarly authority (his being a leading Islamic scholar of his time) as well as his close ties with the CUP. These two "non-discursive elements," then, allowed him to support the Unionists in their struggle to completely seize state power by justifying the existing situation, in which the CUP was trying to tighten its control over both the *ulema* and the already politically weak caliph, Sultan Mehmed V, by stripping him of his ideological power as well. Seyyid Bey's brand new interpretation of "representation" on the basis of his power/knowledge derived from Islamic law thus benefited the "reformist" CUP in its attempt to further modernize the state and society – and thereby weaken the Palace – by introducing modern institutions such as the parliament and citizenship. In this context, the modernists' emphasis on popular legitimacy and the superiority of the "nation" played a crucial role in terms of further limiting the authority of the caliph by trying to "nationalize" the Caliphate.

The nationalization of the Caliphate

Another element of the modernists' "theological engineering" – and a further goal of their effort to limit the Ottoman caliph's political power – was the reduction of the geo-political dimension of his authority by confining it to "national" territory. Unlike the traditionalists, who constantly emphasized the supra-national, ecumenical character of the Islamic Caliphate (see also Chapter 5), some Turkish modernists, influenced by the rise of various nationalisms and shocked by great territorial loss and widespread domestic revolts by non-Turkish Muslims, advocated turning the Caliphate into a "national" institution. Thus, the idea of the nationalization of the Caliphate was part of a larger pattern: the development of nationalism in the Ottoman Empire. In the Ottoman society, nationalist ideas disseminated by the French Revolution were first appropriated by non-Muslim groups. Various non-Muslim *millet*s had, since the early 19th century, revolted against Istanbul, eventually seceding from the empire, a process that intensified in the first quarter of the 20th century, particularly in the Balkans: The Greeks and Serbs had already gained their independence earlier in 1829 and 1878, respectively; Austria annexed Bosnia, and the Bulgarians and Cretens seceded immediately after the Young Turk revolution in 1908, followed by the Albanians, who revolted several times in 1910–1911. These revolts were followed by several Armenian uprisings in Anatolia, which led to the tragic events of 1915. Meanwhile, various Muslim groups revolted, as well: the Kurds in Anatolia (1908–1914), the Druze in Syria (1910), and the Arabs in Yemen (1911) and the *Hijaz* (1916–1918), each supported by the British, French or Russian governments. These revolts were accompanied by the Ottoman Empire's loss of territories in Africa, including Tunis (1881) to France, Cyprus (1878) and Egypt (1882) to Britain, as well as that of the European lands (except for Eastern Thrace) to Russia, the Habsburgs, and the Balkan nations, which were formerly Ottoman *millet*s, between 1853 and 1912 (Öztuna 2004; Jorga 2005, V).

This territorial loss, coupled with the sense of betrayal that came with it, affected the rise of Turkish nationalism in Anatolia. In particular, the sudden loss of much of its European territory in five years between the 1908 Revolution and the Balkan wars (1908–1913) came as a shock to the CUP-dominated political elite in Istanbul, after which some intellectuals (such as Yusuf Akçura and later Ziya Gökalp) came to advocate secular Turkish nationalism, or Panturkism (Arai 1992; Karpat 2000; Zürcher 2005).[10] The nationalist ideology had since the Hamidian period been disseminated via such periodicals as *Türk*, *Genç Kalemler*, and *Türk Yurdu*.[11] However, the CUP never fully adopted nationalism as an official policy because, as Karpat (2001: 368; cf. Kayalı 1997; Hacısalihoğlu 2008: 353–394) remarks:

> although a few of the Young Turks had begun to look upon the Ottoman Empire as a Turkish state and showed a real interest in the ethnic Turks, most were interested primarily in perpetuating the Empire's multiethnic existence, not in creating a Turkish nation.

166 Secularization in the Caliphal center

Nevertheless, the CUP's policies (and ideology) often contained Turkist overtones (Hanioğlu 2006: 18–19); this factor and the rise of nationalist sentiments
in general resulted in discrimination against, and maltreatment of, non-Muslim
Ottoman citizens, especially Armenian and Greek bureaucrats and businessmen
(Keyder 1989: 111–113; Kırmızı 2010).

After World War I, the invasion of Turkey by Britain, France, Italy, and
Greece – and the "national struggle" against this invasion – further boosted the
rise of Turkish nationalism in Anatolia. The Ottoman statesman and intellectual
Said Halim Pasha (2003: 237) observed that the idea of the "national will" as the
key to the solution of all major problems was pervasive in this period. Moreover,
Turkish nationalists, led by Mustafa Kemal, turned against not only the European imperialists, but also the Ottoman monarchy, seeing it as a major enemy to
be defeated after independence, which they finally did by abolishing it on
November 1, 1922. The ideology underlining their actions was a mixture of
Islamism and nationalism, at least until 1924, after which the Republican elite
embraced secular, ethnic nationalism as the official state ideology. The abolition
of the Caliphate on March 3, 1924 was a turning point in this respect, as the secularists had previously been extremely respectful of Islam and the Caliphate (see
Chapter 6). Their nationalism was based on the notion of "national sovereignty"
and a vaguely defined "nation," which initially did not necessarily imply ethnic
Turks, but had nonetheless strong Islamic undertones.[12] The nationalist discourse
gained momentum after each war and helped the secularists realize some of their
"reforms," especially in terms of curtailing the power of the monarchy. For
example, when the representative of the Ankara government, Refet Pasha,
visited Istanbul several weeks before the abolition of the monarchy and made a
number of public statements, he employed a very strong nationalist discourse in
his criticism of the Ottoman dynasty, expressing sentiments that were shared by
the leadership of the nationalist movement. He claimed that the monarchic
system was detrimental to the flourishing of "nationalist feelings and ideas,"
and gave the example of the war in Çaldıran (1514) between two "Turkish
rulers," Selim I and Shah İsmail, criticizing the Ottoman and Safavid sultans for
attacking each other instead of joining as brothers (quoted in Lütfi Fikri 1922:
354).[13]

The rise of nationalism in the late 19th and early 20th centuries as a result of
various revolts and wars, as well as the impact of the French Revolution, also
affected perceptions of the Caliphate, particularly among Turkish and Arab intellectuals who had received Western-style education or were influenced by modern
ideas from Europe. In addition to these two factors, the (modernist) idea that the
caliph was no different from a modern ruler espoused the perception of the
Caliphate as a "national" institution among some modernists. However, this perception was far from clear in the debates over the Caliphate. In the writings and
speeches of the modernists the Caliphate figured sometimes as a supra-national
institution and sometimes vaguely as a national one. Some modernists simultaneously utilized both the traditional, ecumenical definition of the Caliphate and its
modern, "national" definition. Seyyid Bey (1917: 444), for example, started out

with the classical definition of the Caliphate by directly quoting from leading Sunni theologians and jurists, e.g., al-Taftazānī and Ibn Humam, but then redefined it in the context of the "limits of the caliph's authority" in a very narrow way, stressing national sovereignty as a fundamental principle:

> The Caliph is the representative of the Prophet, on the one hand, and of the nation, on the other.... [He] is the representative and leader of the Islamic nation in administering the affairs of the state and observing the interests of the nation. The power and authority that he possesses are directly derived from the nation.
>
> (1917: 447, 452)

The trajectory of the nationalization of the Caliphate becomes clearer as we proceed from the early years of the Constitutional Period toward the Republican era, with World War I representing a breaking point, as indicated by the writings and speeches of many modernists and secularists, especially Turkish ones (e.g., Elmalılı 1909; Muhyiddin Baha 1915; Habil Adem 1915; Seyyid Bey 1917; Huseyin Avni in TBMMZC 1922b; Mustafa Kemal 1922; Rashid Rida 1923a). Their views of the Caliphate would increasingly fit into the nation-state form that would dominate the Middle East after World War I. Their visions of a position for the Caliphate in this modern form slightly differed, however: It implied an *Islamic* nation-state for the modernists, who saw the Caliph as a temporal ruler, and a *secular* one for the secularists, who envisioned a purely spiritual, Pope-like Caliph. The notion of nationalization was based on a triad of concepts that together comprised the modernist conception of the Caliphate: national sovereignty, popular legitimacy, and the "Caliphate as legal representation," which are all closely related to actual political developments. As discussed above, popular legitimacy appeared with the re-institution of parliament and elections held after the 1908 Revolution, while the political conception of the Caliphate (the caliph as the head of the executive) emerged with the weakening of the Caliph's authority, particularly with the 1909 amendments to the Constitution (discussed above), which curtailed the Caliph's authority to dissolve the parliament and suspend the Constitution. National sovereignty, as the third element of the definition of the Caliphate in the modernist discourse, was a result of the above-mentioned unsuccessful wars and the rise of various nationalisms in the Ottoman Empire.

In this context, national sovereignty frequently figured – implicitly or explicitly – in modernist discourse on the Caliphate. Like Seyyid Bey's emphasis on national sovereignty as an essential basis of the caliph's authority and legitimacy, Elmalılı, too, employed the strategy of nationalization as complimentary to that of transforming the Caliphate into a temporal institution. As part of this strategy, he deployed an important discursive technique: denying the caliph any authority over non-Ottoman Muslims. A significant implication of the national-political conception of the Caliphate, the idea that the Ottoman Caliph, as a "king," did not have any authority over Muslims living outside Ottoman territory, was an implicit argument, not clearly stated by other modernists, that he made explicit. After maintaining that, as the representative of the people, the caliph was bounded by the same laws (or the constitution) that he was obliged to apply, Elmalılı stated:

> He can never transgress that law with his despotic power. If he does, national sovereignty will exercise its authority/verdict. Therefore, since the Islamic Caliphate is nothing more than the executive branch of the *sharia*, it has nothing to do with spiritual authority. The Caliphate simply means the leader[ship] of the Islamic constitutional government. For this reason, it does not have any authority over the Muslims who are in foreign countries. They only have a moral sense of connection with it. [On the other hand,] the ethnic and religious diversity among the [Ottoman] citizens does not hamper this principle, either. [Likewise,] just as the titles sultan (*padişah*), emperor, and king are used by different nations, there is no harm in using the Islamic title of "caliph" in the same sense.
>
> (1909: 434–435)

The threatening tone in Elmalılı's language is directly related to the fact that he wrote his article at a time when the former caliph-sultan, Abdülhamid II, had just been deposed by the CUP and replaced by the much weaker Mehmed V. Now reduced to the head of the executive branch, the caliph's position in the state structure was further weakened in 1909 by the strengthening of the legislative branch, the curtailing of the caliph's powers with amendments to the constitution, and the reduction the status of the *şeyhülislam*'s office, which was the immediate target of Elmalılı's specific argument – the ultimate target being the Caliphate (see also below).

While Elmalılı, a supporter of the CUP, was arguing against traditional(ist) conception of politics and the status of the caliph and the *şeyhülislam* within it, another member of the modernist group, Lütfi Fikri, an anti-CUP liberal intellectual and a leading figure in the FAP,[14] would later make a similar argument against the secularists in Ankara. As mentioned above, representing the Ankara government, Refet Pasha claimed that dynastic rule (as opposed to national sovereignty) was the root of all evil and the principal cause of the calamities the Turks had experienced since 1908, implying that the caliph-sultan should have no political power. In his objection to the pasha, Lütfi Fikri defended the monarchy and the Caliphate on the basis of national sovereignty, blaming the CUP for the problems to which Refet Pasha had referred. Lütfi Fikri wrote:

> Since the beginning of the Constitutional Period, the Sultan's office has been seen as one of the greatest platforms where national sovereignty manifested itself on the basis of our constitution, and [thus] the right to appoint the cabinet to, and discharge it from, the office has been reserved for [the sultan]. ... The sultan's office was never the reason for the calamities that have troubled us for the last fourteen years since the beginning of the

Constitutional Period. Rather, the responsibility lies with the revolutionary governments [the CUP], which is a natural consequence of the historical laws of revolution.

(1922: 363–364)

An extension of the modernist argument that the Caliphate was a political authority based on national sovereignty was the idea that its status as a temporal power was "below" the national will. As mentioned earlier, in the classical theory, the caliph filled the Prophet's post and, as such, was not an ordinary Muslim. Modernists disturbed this hierarchy in the traditional theory (and practice) by equalizing the ruler and the ruled on the basis of popular legitimacy and the idea of the caliph as a dignitary of the people. Elmalılı, too, based his discussion of the *şeyhülislam*'s status in the state apparatus on popular legitimacy:

> All in all, the *şeyhülislam* is no more than a civil servant working for the government.... This is how Islam views the caliph: he is equal to any one of his poor and ordinary subjects; any other interpretation is absurd
>
> (1909: 536–537)

Seyyid Bey went further in reducing the caliph's status by suggesting that, according to Islamic contract law, the client (*müvekkil*) has authority over his representative/attorney (*vekil*) as his employer, not vice versa. Therefore, as the client of the caliph, the nation was superior to its ruler. Consequently, according to Seyyid Bey, the caliph could easily be deposed by (the representatives of) the nation:

> The Caliph is the representative of the Prophet, on the one hand, and of the nation, on the other. Since, in principle, the client has the right to dismiss his representative [attorney] ... it is therefore legally proper to depose the Caliph [if necessary]; that is to say, for his client, the nation, to dismiss him.
>
> (1917: 447)

As is clear from this passage, Seyyid Bey's discursive technique turned the traditional hierarchy between the Caliph and his "subjects" upside down by redefining this relationship as simply a legal contract between an attorney and a client. As the next step, he explored the logical consequences of this new definition in order to justify the revolutionary idea (and practice) of deposing a caliph. As mentioned earlier, this effort by Seyyid Bey for religious justification of an essentially secular notion was directly related to the social context in which he made his argument: the fact that the last caliph-sultan, Abdülhamid II, had been deposed from the throne by the CUP following the 1908 Revolution, which created disturbances within traditional circles consisting mostly of the *ulema*. As a respected member of the high-ranking *ulema* (and a well-known professor at Istanbul University), Seyyid Bey tried to help the revolutionary Unionists by strategically intervening into the theory of the Caliphate from a legal perspective, presenting the caliph as a king (of secondary importance) within the constitutional regime who could be easily displaced by the "true" owner of the regime: the nation.

In conclusion, the modernist strategy of defining the Caliphate as a (strictly) temporal institution through the technique of framing it as a legal contract between the ruler and the people was aimed at transforming the Caliphate by giving the caliph limited authority within national territories, rather than ecumenical power beyond the state's borders, and turning the traditional hierarchy between the caliph and ordinary Muslims upside down. In practice this meant the secularization of the Caliphate. As discursive techniques, these three types of intervention into Islamic theology and law (denying the caliph spiritual authority, reducing the Caliphate to "legal representation" and power of attorney, and limiting the caliph's temporal authority by "public interest" and "national will") constitute the main elements of the strategy employed by many modernists to transform the Caliphate into a secular political institution. A parallel development to this transformation of the Caliphate was the secularization of the legal and education system, a process that entailed the transformation of the office of the *şeyhülislam*, the head of the Ottoman *ulema* and the caliph's dignitary.

The decline of the *şeyhülislam*'s status

The historical context

The decline of the *şeyhülislam*'s status as a result of debates and ensuing policy changes in 1909 and 1917 marked the second major turning point in the transformation of the Caliphate during the post-revolutionary period. The *şeyhülislam*'s office, which was an Ottoman invention, emerged during the reign of Mehmed II (1451–1481) as a state institution to integrate the *ulema* into the state apparatus. The *şeyhülislam* was always appointed and dismissed directly by the caliph-sultan, representing his religious authority. During the classical period (16th–18th centuries), his office represented the leadership of the *ulema* and had under its jurisdiction the administration of both the judiciary and higher education. From the 16th century on, the office played an important role in politics, although it was not part of the *Divan* (cabinet) until the 1830s. Starting with the reign of Selim III (1789–1807), when the *şeyhülislam* acted as a member of the newly founded "Consultative Council" (*Meşveret Meclisi*), he enjoyed a certain prestige and the authority to influence (and justify) the policies and decisions of sultans and bureaucrats. His main duty was to ensure that laws and edicts were compatible with Islamic principles – or sometimes to make them *seem* to be compatible with these principles by issuing *fatwas* endorsing them. With its institutionalization (together with the development of the cabinet system) by the reformist Sultan Mahmud II, the *şeyhülislam*'s office (*Meşihat Dairesi*) functioned practically as a ministry of justice and education, being responsible for the judicial and *medrese* systems. The *şeyhülislam* himself also acted as a member of the cabinet (*Meclis-i Vükela*). During the *Tanzimat* period (1839–1876), since the *ulema* mostly supported the reforms, the *şeyhülislam* gained more power, regularly attending the highest council in the empire, the *Meclis-i Ali-i Umumi*, though, having only one vote, he was equal to council's other members. The *şeyhülislam* had full control of the judiciary between 1838 and 1871, after which a bifurcation emerged in the judiciary, with the minister of justice being made responsible for non-religious courts (*Mehakim-i Nizamiyye*). This limited the *şeyhülislam*'s jurisdiction to religious courts (*Mehakim-i Şer'iyye*). During the Hamidian era (1876–1908), he continued to enjoy his ideological power as well as his authority over the *medrese* system, but was tightly controlled by the all-powerful sultan. After the Young Turk Revolution, his status was reduced to that of a state minister, losing much of his power and prestige. During the Second Constitutional Period, the *şeyhülislam*'s status emerged as a problem for the CUP-dominated governments and parliaments, which were not always able to control the *şeyhülislam*, who was the head of the *ulema*, a group that could pose a threat to the CUP in their efforts to reshape the power structure of the Ottoman state system. Consequently, he lost his control over modern schools and religious courts in 1917 upon Ziya Gökalp's suggestion. However, when the CUP lost its power in 1918, the *Meşihat* regained control over these courts until 1924, when it was completely abolished by the new Republic's elite. The new regime created instead the Department of Religious Affairs, which had a similar status to that of the *Meşihat* under the CUP (Kramers 1993: 489; Karpat 2002: 41–43; Yakut 2005: 55–82; cf. Uzunçarşılı 1988).

The reduction of the *şeyhülislam*'s status to that of a state minister after the revolution had triggered a debate in 1909 over whether he should still be a member of the cabinet. While the CUP-led parliament kept the *şeyhülislam* in the cabinet, the traditionalist politicians and *ulema* were against this idea on the grounds that the status of the *şeyhülislam* should be *above* the cabinet so that this second-highest religious authority in Islam would not be susceptible to the demands of, or held accountable to, parliament members, some of whom were non-Muslims.[15] The conservative *Mizan* and *Volkan* newspapers were the voice of the traditionalists in this debate.

The discursive struggle: traditionalists versus modernists

The traditionalist charge: Mizan *and* Volkan

The traditionalist *ulema* made two arguments regarding the status of the *şeyhülislam*. First, they insisted that since, according to both the *sharia* and the constitution, the *şeyhülislam* was the religious dignitary of the caliph, he was to be regarded as the head of the Islamic community beyond the borders of the Ottoman state. Therefore, he could not be a member of the cabinet (*Mizan*, February 24, 1909, no. 76). Second, his status as the religious representative of the caliph also made it impossible to treat him as an ordinary minister:

The appointment of both the grand vizier and the *şeyhülislam* is under the sultan's authority. In every constitutional monarchy in the world, the monarch picks only one of them to form the cabinet; but in our system, he appoints both of them. There must be a reason for this. (...) The *şeyhülislam* is indeed a representative – but he represents the caliph, not the sultan. His main duty is to provide for the government an opinion on the matter at hand from the religious perspective. Thus, he is not responsible for the other activities of the cabinet. For this reason, he cannot have an official connection with the members of the parliament.

(Ibid.)

These two arguments implied that the *şeyhülislam* could not be held accountable by the parliament or the cabinet, which was the traditionalists' main concern, since both of these institutions opened up a space for the participation (and influence) of the Unionists *and* non-Muslims in Ottoman politics. This concern was openly expressed in the discourse of Derviş Vahdeti (the leader of the counter-revolution) in an article he published in his newspaper, *Volkan* (no. 56, February 19, 1909). Based on the strategy of the dual status of the Caliphate, he insisted that since "the constitutional regime could not be separated from religion," Islamic *sharia* was supposed to be superior to laws based on the constitution. He argued that, unlike other ministers, the *şeyhülislam* could only be appointed (or dismissed) by the caliph and, thus, could not be supervised by the parliament, which had a status was lower than that of the caliph – and, by extension, the *Meşihat*. He concluded:

It is not possible any other way. The religion of Islam cannot tolerate a situation where the *şeyhülislam* will be insulted by being exposed to the [parliament members'] handclapping and stomping of feet in protest as in theatres.

(Ibid., quoted in Yakut 2005: 97)

The traditionalists, then, tried to revive the status of the *şeyhülislam* in order to strengthen the traditional-religious power center of the Ottoman Empire, represented by the caliph and the *şeyhülislam*, vis-à-vis the CUP-modernist coalition, which had captured a significant portion of state power after the 1908 Revolution. The traditionalists' main discursive strategy was to emphasize the dual status of the Caliphate (as a spiritual and political authority), which nonetheless partly secularized their Islamic discourse by implicitly assuming the previously non-existent dichotomy of the spiritual versus the temporal (see also below). Their main discursive technique in this debate was to highlight the hierarchical relationship between the *sharia*, represented by the *şeyhülislam*, and secular politics, represented by the cabinet and the parliament. Their main aim was to elevate the status of the *şeyhülislam* and empower the increasingly powerless caliph, Abdülhamid II, by relocating the *Meşihat* outside and above the cabinet. However, with its majority in the Ottoman parliament (*Meclis-i Mebusan*), the CUP kept this highest religious office part of the cabinet, aiming to limit its independence by putting it under the control of the government and the *Meclis*. The CUP was able to achieve this with the generous help of modernist Islamists, among whom Elmalılı Hamdi played a crucial role.

The modernist response: Elmalılı Hamdi

A leading Islamic scholar and a member of the CUP's *ulema* committee, Elmalılı Hamdi published a short but crucial article in *Beyanü'l-Hak*, an important Islamist journal, in which he criticized – in religious terms – the above arguments made by the traditionalists. He justified his objection to elevating the status of the *şeyhülislam* by referring to the potential danger of raising it to the level of the infallible pope, which was strictly forbidden in Islam. He also argued that such a change in the *şeyhülislam*'s status would mean that the constitutional system was not compatible with Islam, which was unthinkable for him. To support his arguments, Elmalılı deployed a familiar discursive strategy: He cited a Qur'anic verse (57/27) that criticized the impact of spiritual authority in Christianity. He also referred to a famous *hadith* according to which "there is no clergy in Islam." Taking these two references as principles that prevented the caliph from having any religious authority, Elmalılı further claimed ironically that these principles would remove all obstacles preventing Islam from interfering in political life:

> Based on the principle of "no clergy in Islam," the religion of Islam has destroyed the philosophy of spiritualism and thus closed the door upon any factor that might prevent religions from getting involved in politics. Therefore, by abating spiritualism, [Islam] has consolidated every aspect of social life, brought an order to the [rights and] responsibilities of men, and established equality among them.
>
> (1909: 433)

Elmalılı's whole argument for lowering the status of the *şeyhülislam*, as a discourse, as well as the actual legal changes that rested on this modernist view, was made possible by a direct intervention into the theory of the Caliphate: The status of the *şeyhülislam*, the representative of the caliph, was gradually lowered in the state hierarchy by weakening the caliph's authority, thereby also reducing the caliph's power in its temporal aspect. Elmalılı clearly stated this when he said, "Islam ... requires an executive branch that will administer the affairs of the Islamic state, and [its head] is called imam and caliph" (1909: 434). In other words, Elmalılı Hamdi made his claims aimed at lowering the status of the *şeyhülislam*'s office on the basis of the same assumption of the Caliphate as temporal rule. Therefore, Elmalılı defined the former as simply a political office, or a ministry:

> Representing the Caliph is not exclusively the status of the *şeyhülislam*, nor is he in any way related to spiritual authority. For this reason, the

şeyhülislam has no place in Islamic theory other than being a member of the cabinet as part of the executive branch. Thus, he can never be seen as the spiritual leader. The special prestige he presently enjoys is only derived from the great respect that Islam has for knowledge. [Therefore] the *şeyhülislam* is responsible to the Parliament and, if necessary, has to be liable to account for his actions; treating his office as sacred and infallible like the Papacy is against the core wisdom of the Islamic *sharia*.

(1909: 436)

The traditionalist rebuttal: İsmail Hakkı

The traditionalist response to Elmalılı's strategic intervention came from an equally famous Islamic scholar and *medrese* professor, İsmail Hakkı (İzmirli). In his rebuttal in an article published in *Sırat-ı Müstakim*, another leading Islamist journal, he, knowing that the *şeyhülislam*'s status was directly related to that of the caliph, restated the traditionalist position on the latter. Like all traditionalists, İsmail Hakkı adopted the classical definition of the Caliphate, giving it an even more comprehensive meaning:

> The Islamic Caliphate is both a religious authority and a temporal rule; it is the best of governments in contemporary civilization and the highest of religious posts; it is based on justice and *taqwa* (religious wisdom), and bound by the laws of religion and the principles of the *sharia*. The caliph is the authority over religious affairs and the ruler over temporal matters.
>
> (1910: 438)

Moreover, based on this broad definition, İsmail Hakkı also rejected Elmalılı's (1909: 435) claim that "just as the titles sultan (*padişah*), emperor and king are used by different nations, there is no harm in using the Islamic title of 'caliph' in the same sense." Instead, Hakkı proposed that Muslim rulers in remote regions (relative to Istanbul) such as North Africa and India should be called "*emirs*" (governors) of the Ottoman caliph-sultan (İsmail Hakkı 1910: 443; cf. other traditionalists: Mustafa Zihni 1911: 183; Safayihi 1915: 73). Based on these arguments, İsmail Hakkı tried to help elevate the status of the *şeyhülislam*'s office by delegitimizing the CUP's policy of undermining its power along with that of the caliph.

The traditionalist strategy of establishing the dual status of the Caliphate also entailed the technique of emphasizing two other themes: the preconditions for holding the Caliphate and the main duties of the caliph. On the first theme, İsmail Hakkı and others argued that the true caliph must not only possess political and military power, but must also have mastered all religious sciences, ideally reaching the level of the *mujtahid* – the highest level of Islamic scholarship (İsmail Hakkı 1910: 438–439; Ömer Lütfi 1912: 240–243; Safayihi 1915: 54–55). Regarding the second theme traditionalists, again in line with the mainstream Sunni theology, stipulated for the caliph such functions as applying rules of the *sharia*, conducting *jihad*, and "protecting religion and people" (İsmail Hakkı 1910: 438; Mustafa Zihni 1911: 113; Safayihi 1915: 79–83). These definitely required that the caliph should possess both political and religious authority.

However, since the political and ideological power of the CUP-modernist coalition surpassed that of the traditionalists, the latter failed to achieve their goal. As discussed above, the CUP took control of the government with the suppression of the counter-revolution in 1909 (by dethroning the caliph-sultan) and later with the "Bab-ı Ali Coup" in 1913 (Tunaya 1952: 188ff; see also Akşin 1987). The Unionists then pursued further secularization of the judicial and educational systems, undermining the power of the caliph, the *şeyhülislam*, and the *ulema*. As mentioned above, the *şeyhülislam* was removed from the cabinet in 1917 as a result of the "Ziya Gökalp reforms." A leading secular(ist) intellectual, Gökalp had become an influential ideologue and policy advisor to the CUP by then. After the party's convention in 1916, following Gökalp's advice, the CUP pressed Caliph-Sultan Mehmed V to issue a decree that removed the *şeyhülislam* from the cabinet. Consequently, his authority was greatly curtailed on all three sides. The religious (*şer'i*) courts were brought under the control of the Ministry of Justice, and the *medreses* under the Ministry of Education, which modernized their curricula. Also, a new ministry was created to administer foundations (*evkaf*) in 1917. The *şeyhülislam* still controlled family law, but even that had been partly secularized when a new inheritance law, based on the German code, was enacted in 1913, further lowering the status and influence of his office. The *Meşihat* would later be abolished altogether on March 3, 1924, the same day the Caliphate was abolished. The CUP's transformation of both the Caliphate and the *Meşihat* was made possible by the crucial ideological support of the modernist *ulema*, who – based on their authority and knowledge/power – effectively used an Islamic discourse to justify the secularizing legal and political changes that weakened these two religious institutions. An unintended consequence of these efforts to secularize institutional practices by using Islamic justification, however, was the secularization of this Islamic discourse itself.

Secularization of Islamic discourse

I use this concept to refer to the – partial – transformation of Islamic discourse through the adoption of certain "secular" assumptions and redefinition of Islamic concepts for "secular" purposes within a politico-ideological context shaped by secularizing changes. In other words, I take this "secularization from within" as a reflection in the discursive sphere of the actual (institutional) secularization process. In the context of the Caliphate's evolution, the most important secular assumption that helped transform Islamic discourse was the modern distinction between the "spiritual" and "temporal" dimensions of the caliph's authority, which does not exist in the classical Islamic theory of the institution. This assumption was, as we will see in Chapter 6, most prevalent in the discourses of secularists and least prevalent among traditionalists. Some members of the latter group, however, adopted the spiritual versus temporal distinction and emphasized the former in order to help strengthen the Caliphate. Modernists, too, accepted the same distinction, but denied the spiritual authority of the Caliphate in order to emphasize its political dimension.

"Spiritual" versus "temporal" authority

In the classical theory of Islamic Caliphate, as well as in early practice, there was no distinction between the spiritual and the temporal, because the caliph's authority simultaneously entailed both political and "religious" (but not "spiritual") powers and responsibilities. As discussed in Chapter 1, the mainstream Islamic political theory does not recognize "spiritual" authority, nor does it make a distinction between religious and political authority.[16] Unlike the Shia view, the Sunni theory of the Caliphate strongly rejects the possibility of any divine basis for politico-religious power. It was the first Umayyad caliph, Muawiya, who exaggerated the religious aspect of the institution by adopting the title "Shadow of God on Earth," which was also used by some later caliphs in Islamic history. In the last decades of the Caliphate, too, some traditionalists needed to emphasize the spiritual dimension of the caliph's authority, especially in critical moments when the institution had been greatly weakened. For example, when Abdülhamid II's power was curbed after the 1908 Revolution, some traditionalists resorted to the same strategy of calling the caliph "The Shadow of God on Earth" (Ömer Ziyaeddin 1908: 60, 61; Mehmed Tahir 1909: 70, 72). Similarly, after World War I was over and just before the Caliphate was separated from the monarchy (and thus reduced to a spiritual authority) in late 1922, Syed Mahmud, an Indian Muslim intellectual and a member of the "Caliphate Movement,"[17] emphasized:

> The Khilafat implies temporal allegiance as well, because the Khalif is the heir not only to the religious but also to the temporal power of the Prophet. The Prophet united in himself the two functions of the king and the spiritual chief and this feature of the Islamic sovereignty has continued to the latest time.
>
> (Syed Mahmud 1921: 39)

This distinction between the spiritual and the temporal was a secular one, which partly secularized the traditionalists' discourse. Not all traditionalists, however, assumed such a distinction. In fact, some of them tried to emphasize the politico-religious authority of the caliph as contained within one single domain, as in the classical view. Intellectual-politician Said Halim Pasha made it explicit when he said that

> by penetrating into all human actions, [Islam] rejects the distinction between the profane and the religious. ... Since church and state constitute one single whole in Islam, it is not possible to separate them.
>
> (2000[1920]: 396)

Most modernists, on the other hand, implicitly or explicitly adopted the spiritual versus temporal distinction in order to emphasize the latter. This could be clearly seen in the definition of the Caliphate by various modernists (discussed above). For example, Abdulaziz Jawish, the pro-CUP Tunisian *alim*, defined the Caliphate by focusing on its political dimension and denying its spiritual aspect:

> The Caliphate is not a post with which to expect blessings and grace from the heavens; rather, it is an institution that is supposed to protect (people's) rights, carry out punishments, protect people from oppression, and to make necessary arrangements and modern (civilized) policies that are useful for the Islamic society.
>
> (1916: 251; cf. Elmalılı Hamdi 1909: 433, Seyyid Bey 1917: 445,
> Rashid Rida 1923a: 140, 142)

Also, Elmalılı Hamdi's religious argument for lowering the status of the *şeyhülislam* (discussed above) was based on the implicit distinction between the temporal and the spiritual. In his critique of the traditionalist view of the Caliphate, he went so far as to suggest that "the principle of spiritualism does not pertain even to worshiping and the rituals of Islam; instead, we have the principle of knowledge and science" (1909: 433). Therefore, Elmalılı's strategic interpretation of Islamic theology as part of his "theological engineering" exemplifies the secularization of Islamic discourse by an Islamist: He made an "Islamic" argument drawing exclusively on Islamic tenets, saying that the wisdom behind the principle of "no spiritual authority" was to enable Islam's involvement in politics. However, his argument was predicated upon a modern/secular dichotomy between religion and politics appropriated from the West.

This dichotomous view was essentially a reaction to two simultaneous challenges to the modernist conception of the Caliphate: On the one hand, many Orientalists and European media outlets had claimed that the caliph was no different from the pope, and therefore should not have any political power; on the other hand, some traditionalists' emphasis on the caliph's spiritual authority might have led the modernists to fear that the distorted Orientalist perception of Islamic politics would dominate the public sphere. Thus, Jawish's book on the Caliphate, which he wrote to defend the Ottoman Caliphate, was subtitled: "Against the claims made in the British and French newspapers regarding the Islamic Caliphate." Similarly, an unsigned editorial published in *Sebilürreşad*, an Islamist journal, was subtitled "A Response to the British Press," reflecting the "reactive" nature of the modernist discourse.

The previously non-existent secular dichotomy between the temporal and spiritual authority of the caliph, therefore, contributed to the secularization of Islamic discourse by the Islamists themselves as an unintended consequence of their use of this discourse. This was true for a few traditionalists as well as many modernists. Such a separation between the sacred and the profane on a more general level implies a conflation of two epistemologies, which might be called a "double-bind." That is, the Islamic epistemology was gradually "contaminated" by exposure to a secular epistemology, which was enforced by the dominance of European institutions and ways of thinking.[18] The more Islamist intellectuals were exposed to Western/secular concepts and practices, the deeper the spiritual/ temporal (or sacred/profane) distinction penetrated their mindset. This led to an ambiguity in their discourses reflecting the double-bind (co-existence of two different, or even conflicting, epistemologies) that shaped their ways of thinking. In the case of the secularists, on the other hand, this conflation and ambiguity that we observe among the Islamists would diminish and eventually be replaced by an epistemological *shift* – from an Islamic epistemology to a secular one – particularly after the abolition of the Caliphate in 1924.[19] In addition to embracing the distinction between the spiritual and temporal dimensions of the Caliphate, two other discursive strategies, employed particularly by the modernists, contributed to the secularization of their Islamic discourse: (i) selective adaptation of Western institutions, and (ii) historicizing religion by stressing the primacy of (modern) social conditions.

Selective appropriation of Western institutions

Adapting certain Western institutions, such as the modern military and the parliament, to Muslim society had already been pursued as a state policy since the 18th century.[20] Previously, in the classical period, the Ottoman elites' dominant view was that they had nothing to learn or borrow from the "infidels." During the 19th century, many bureaucrats, intellectuals, and *ulema* tried to justify the policy of adopting modern institutions with reference to Islamic sources and principles (Berkes 1957). During the Second Constitutional Period, too, modernists sometimes used this justification as a discursive technique to explain and legitimize further modernization, particularly in governmental, educational, and military institutions by importing models from European countries. As such, this technique was one of the ways that differentiated them from traditionalists; it was also a discursive element that made them similar to secularists – though the latter focused more on adapting Islam to modern conditions, rather than vice versa.

Within this framework, the modernist discourse followed a trajectory of appropriation ranging from more concrete and relatively small-scale institutions to more abstract and large-scale ones. The spectrum of appropriation is exemplified by three intellectuals' arguments: Elmalılı's view on the cabinet system, Seyyid Bey's view on certain aspects of Islamic law, and Lütfi Fikri's argument regarding the broader question of the regime of the state. First, the way Elmalılı deployed the technique of selective appropriation as part of his argument regarding the status of the *şeyhülislam* specifically drew from the composition of cabinets in European countries, which, he suggested, ought to be adopted by the Ottoman Empire. As discussed above, his main aim was to make the case for reducing the *şeyhülislam*'s power; at the end of his important article, however, Elmalılı went further and implied that the caliph's representative could be entirely removed from the cabinet, which would be achieved by the CUP in 1917 (see above). Comparing the Western cabinet system with the "Eastern" one, he proposed that the European system should be appropriated, which would reduce the *şeyhülislam*'s office to a symbolic one with no real power:

> In [Western] countries governed by constitutional monarchy, the head of state appoints the prime minister only [unlike the Ottoman sultan, who also appoints the *şeyhülislam*]. And in some countries the prime minister is also in charge of another ministry. If there is a need to make this an unchangeable law in the constitutional system in the East, thereby making it imitate the West in this respect, too, we have a solution for this, as well. For, just as there is no obstacle to the Prime Ministry and the *Meşihat* [the *şeyhülislam*'s office] living side by side, it is also entirely possible to unite them.
>
> (1909: 436)

Elmalılı justified his contention that it was possible to "unite" the two offices, i.e., to transfer the *Meşihat*'s authority to the grand vizier's office, by saying that the *şeyhülislam* "could never be seen as a spiritual leader … because the leader of the Islamic community [the caliph] could never be any more than the head of the Islamic government" (ibid.). Thus, Elmalılı deployed the technique of appropriation from the West as complimentary to his main discursive strategy (discussed above) of defining the Caliphate as a temporal authority, both of which were being gradually realized through political developments that shaped – and were shaped by – these discourses during the Second Constitutional Period. The way Elmalılı employed these two strategies together exemplifies the secularization of Islamic discourse by a modernist Islamist; for his discourse signaled the curtailing of the *şeyhülislam*'s power that would be subsumed within the Western secular institutions of the government that he wanted to adopt.

Likewise, the way Seyyid Bey deployed the technique of selective appropriation demonstrates another instance of the secularization of Islamic discourse. His use of this technique addressed a specific area of the *şeyhülislam*'s jurisdiction: family law. As mentioned above, family law based on the *sharia* had been partly secularized in 1913 when a new law of inheritance based on the German code was introduced by the CUP. This law marked a significant symbolic – and concrete – change in Islamic law because inheritance was an area in which Muslim jurists had developed a detailed and sophisticated code drawing on the principles of *fiqh* and Islamic sources (the Qur'an and the *Sunna*). The adoption of the German code of inheritance thus significantly secularized Ottoman family law. Seyyid Bey's Islamic justification of borrowing legal principles from the West (see below) was thus closely related to the legitimization of this particular change in family law. For, as a leader of the CUP, he played a role in this legal reform. Moreover, his strategic intervention not only justified an already existing situation, but also helped the Unionists enact a further change in family law: In 1917 the CUP introduced a new law regulating procedure in religious courts as a means of further modernizing the legal system, which, as mentioned, further diminished the *şeyhülislam*'s power. As part of this law, a uniform family law was decreed for all Ottoman citizens. As Zürcher notes, the law was "based on the modernist selection of regulations from all four of the orthodox Muslim schools of law" and "included a number of special arrangements for non-Muslims [as well]" (1993: 126). With his scholarly authority on Islamic law, Seyyid Bey's involvement in these two instances of legal secularization was crucial in terms of both enacting and justifying secular changes in family law. He presented his justification for these changes via the technique of selective appropriation of Western institutions.

Interestingly, Seyyid Bey did this as part of his discussion of the Caliphate: He compared Islamic and European family laws and drew an unusual parallel between the family and the (Islamic) political system in order to demonstrate the limits of the caliph's authority over the people. He maintained that in the European marriage code, the husband had absolute authority over his wife, and only he had the right to own property, which was "an irrational principle that makes the wife the husband's slave" and "not acceptable in Islamic law" (1917: 450). Islam entailed a marriage code that not only gave the wife the right to own property, but also maintained that the husband had no right over his wife's private property. Transferring this contrast onto the political domain, Seyyid Bey thus concluded that the caliph, like the Muslim husband, had no right over the "nation" except to a limited extent that was sanctioned by the Islamic *sharia* (ibid.). Therefore, his discursive reconstruction of a certain area of Islamic law via a comparison with the European marriage code exemplifies an attempt by an Islamic scholar to appropriate a modern conception of government while "demonstrating" the superiority of Islamic law over Western law.

An unintended consequence of Seyyid Bey's comparison between the Islamic and European legal systems was the secularization of his discourse. Although, as an expert on Islamic law, he maintained that "Islamic law is … better and more developed than the Western law" (1917: 484), he nevertheless advocated selective adaptation and partial synthesis between the two systems, arguing against the direct "translation of European legal codes" that had begun to be discussed in the public sphere at that time. As usual, Seyyid Bey justified his view of selective adaptation with reference to a famous *hadith*:

> If necessary, the government may also benefit/draw from the civil code of the West, just like in the case of other sciences and techniques. There is no obstacle to this in Islamic *sharia*. For, according to an authentic *hadith* that says "the word of wisdom is the stray of the believer; who has the better right to it wherever it may be found" [Tirmidhi, "Ilm" 19], wisdom is Muslims' lost property that they are looking for; thus, they deserve it more than any other nation wherever they find it…
>
> On the other hand, I would also like to point out that the Eastern science of *fiqh*, which is the Islamic law, is, as a simple comparison would make clear, better and more developed, as well as better suited to the natural laws of humanity, than the Western legal system, which is based essentially on the Roman law and partly on local customs and conditions. For this reason,

unless there is an urgent necessity for it, it would not only be unwise but also against God's will to completely abandon Islamic *fiqh* by unnecessarily translating European laws and applying them.

(1917: 484)

As an influential jurist-scholar and a member of the CUP, Seyyid Bey's suggestion of a partial synthesis between the Islamic and Western legal systems was not only a reflection of actual processes of adaptation from European legal codes, but also justified further secularization of Islamic law by CUP governments during the Second Constitutional Period. When the Ottoman Empire was defeated in World War I, he supported the Turkish nationalist movement in Anatolia and maintained close relationships with its leadership, especially Mustafa Kemal. As discussed in Chapter 3, it was Seyyid Bey who helped Mustafa Kemal on many occasions by putting his vast knowledge of Islam and scholarly authority at Kemal's service.[21] In turn, he became the first minister of justice in the Republican period (1923–1924) and played a crucial role in the abolition of the Caliphate (see Chapter 6). The new regime decided to discard Islamic law and adopt various European codes (such as Swiss civil code and the Italian penal code) as a whole, which marked a significant phase of secularization in modern Turkey. Seyyid Bey's insistence on the partial – as opposed to total – adoption of laws cost him his short career in the new regime: Mustafa Kemal dismissed him from his post as the minister of justice for resisting these radical "reforms." Such legal changes were justified with another discursive strategy that played a crucial role in the political and legal secularization of the Turkish state: "historicizing religion."

Historicizing religion

Adapting Islam to modern social conditions by historicizing it was a major strategy employed by secularists (see Chapter 6); however, a few modernists also used it in their discussions on the Caliphate. Best represented by the discourses of leading secularist thinker Ziya Gökalp (see Chapter 2) and leading modernist scholar Seyyid Bey, this strategy reflected the increasing influence of Western/ secular ideas on the Ottoman intellectuals. As such, this foreign influence helped secularize their (Islamic) discourses. The main assumption behind this strategy was that some elements of Islamic law and Caliphate-based politics were not useful or effective anymore and, therefore, Islam had to be "adjusted" to contemporary social-political conditions. The use of this strategy by some modernists also indicated the limits of their confidence in their religion: For them, Islamic law and political theory were not so perfect after all. The main discursive technique modernists deployed as part of this strategy was that of emphasizing the "exigencies of (modern) life" by giving primacy to social change over Islamic principles, or "the book."

Among the modernists, this strategy was most clearly stated by Seyyid Bey and Elmalılı Hamdi. The need to emphasize the "exigencies of contemporary life" was rooted in their concern for the perceived stagnation of Islamic law, which they felt could not provide solutions to certain modern problems. Seyyid Bey (1917) was particularly concerned about the dominance of the Hanefite school of law in the Ottoman Empire. In his discussion on the Caliphate he also extensively discussed different examples of how rigid and obsolete Hanefite rules had become and why they needed to be discarded (pp. 476–482). He justified this by claiming:

> In our time, life has been completely changed and has taken a different form. The difference between the social conditions of our time and those of the classical jurists' period is as large as the time difference between the two. And this is only natural. For, it is a social law and a divine law that every period has its own life, and every life has its own exigencies. For this reason, today, the requirements of the present civilization ... cannot be satisfied with the interpretations of the jurists of 1,000 years ago.
>
> (1917: 478)

The discursive technique deployed here involved an emphasis on the idea that legal interpretations of the sacred texts of Islam naturally changed over time, the old ones being no longer applicable to contemporary society's problems. He also applied this technique to the question of the relationship between the caliph and jurists. After discussing in detail how the legal knowledge produced by different schools of Islamic law, particularly the Hanefite school, was relative and not to be taken as unchangeable, Seyyid Bey concluded:

> In terms of legislation, the government, that is, the Caliphate, must conform either to definite textual (*nass*) rules that are permanent, fixed, and unchangeable with the change in time and social conditions, or, if such rules are unavailable, to the exigencies of the prevailing conditions of life that change over time. It cannot conform to an individual jurist's particular opinions, which were applicable to different questions of his own time. Therefore, [the caliph] is allowed to prefer any jurist's opinion if he finds it useful, i.e., "best suited to social relations and congruous with the exigencies of the time." Or, rather, he is obliged to do so according to the present circumstances of the state and society. If one does not understand this, one knows neither the *sharia* and *fiqh*, nor the art of administration.
>
> (1917: 483)

Seyyid Bey also employed the same technique of emphasizing the "exigencies of (modern) life" in his argument for limiting the caliph's authority. I have already referred above to the fact that he used the term "public interest" as a discursive tool to demonstrate – and help to realize – the limited nature of the caliph's authority. Similarly, he claimed that there were two main institutional elements that marked the limits of obedience to the caliph: Islamic law (the *sharia*) and, again, "public interest" (or collective social needs) (p. 457). He added that the second qualifying element, that is, the [caliph's] policies being incongruous with the interests of the public, is as significant as the first in terms of its incompatibility with justice and, therefore, being a sinful act.... [Thus] both elements are equally important.

(1917: 459)

However, he also knew that the classical theory of the Caliphate did not include a strong reference to "the public's interest" as a factor limiting the ruler's authority. The fact that classical Islamic legal theory did not see public interest as a major factor in governance required Seyyid Bey's further intervention through another discursive technique: transplanting a pair of familiar concepts from Islamic law, which were not directly related to his discussion, into the center of his argument:

From this perspective, since the second element [public interest] is already included in the first one [the *sharia*], it would be necessary to mention it separately.... Though both elements are related to the rights of the Law-maker [God], the first one is related to individuals' rights, and the second one to collective rights. Since the latter enjoy much significance in the Law-maker's view, collective rights are called the "rights of Allah" in the Islamic legal terminology in order to highlight their significance.

(1917: 459)

Seyyid Bey thus exploited the well-known theoretical distinction between individual and collective rights, which had nothing to do with the Caliphate, to stress the significance of public interest, which, he argued, limited the caliph's authority.[22] This technique secularized his Islamic discourse by inserting into the theory of the Caliphate the notion of the "exigencies of modern life" (socio-historical conditions) as a defining feature of Islamic law and the Caliphate. As in Göka-lp's discourse, "social conditions" became equal to, if not more significant than, the "texts" in interpreting Islamic sources and making laws.

In a similar vein, Elmalılı, too, included some elements of "contemporary civilization" as taken-for-granted assumptions in his "theological engineering." Though he did not explicitly mention the concept of the "exigencies of modern life," his discursive construction of the dichotomy of "spiritualism versus materialism" was very much influenced by the prevailing ideologies of modern Europe. Though he was a member of the *ulema*, he also learned French and studied modern French philosophy, which was dominated by positivist materialism at the time. Influenced by this philosophy, Elmalılı tried to redefine the Caliphate as what he called a purely "material" (temporal) institution that had nothing to do with religious authority. In his discussion, he categorically dismissed "spiritualism" as a Christian tradition and embraced "materialism" (though not completely) as the basis of authority in Islam (1909: 433–434). Given that he defined (political) authority narrowly as either "spiritual" or "material," embracing the latter was partly related to his unspoken assumption that the Caliphate (or Islam in general) should be adapted to the "exigencies of contemporary civilization," i.e., the prevailing positivistic social and political theories of the time. This also indicates the influence of Western modernity on Islamists during the last decades of the Caliphate, which created what I have called a double-bind, exemplified by their discursive strategy of historicizing certain aspects of Islam.

Therefore, Elmalılı and Seyyid Bey's use of the strategy of adapting Islam to modern social conditions by historicizing it demonstrates another way in which Islamic discourse was secularized by Islamic scholars themselves. However, this "internal secularization" was an unintended consequence of a defensive stance toward European orientalist views, because their main aim was to respond to the orientalist charge that the caliph was a spiritual leader. They countered this challenge by focusing on the temporal nature of the Caliphate and highlighting the superior aspects of Islam over the West. Some even believed that the modern West had discovered Islamic politics and adopted it as the best system. Elmalılı's celebration of materialism, for example, was part of his argument for the superiority of the Caliphate as a political regime. He argued that due to the very high status of spiritualist doctrines in Christianity, religious rituals were ignored by being "accepted as 'material' and thus redundant in spiritualism," and spiritual leaders (popes and saints) were seen as sacred, unlike in Islam. In modern Europe, however, "there emerged a need to terminate the influence of spiritualism on political life, with the development of civilization," which was already the case in Islam. For this reason, he said, "Today, the [European] civilization applies the religion of Islam without naming it as such" (Elmalılı Hakkı 1909: 433).

Therefore, "Islamicizing" modern institutional practices also meant secularizing Islamic discourse. Nevertheless, the need to emphasize modern social conditions ("contemporary civilization") reflects the imperfection of religion in the eyes of leading representatives of the modernist group. From this angle, Islam needed adjustments and adaptations to modern life in order to "satisfy its requirements." This strategy, which was based on the technique of emphasizing the "exigencies of modern life" and prioritizing social change over the textual Islam, was not, however, very strong in the modernist discourse, unlike in the secularist one, as we will see in Chapter 6. Ziya Gökalp's radical interpretation of the distinction in Islamic law between text (*nass*) and practice (*örf*), turning the traditional hierarchy between them upside down, is a good example of this strategy (see Chapter 2). It was also very helpful for both the CUP and the Kemalist regime in the Republican era as it provided a major venue for justifying their secular reforms.

Conclusion

In this chapter I have analyzed the transformation of, and the debates over, the Caliphate during the first eight years of the Second Constitutional Period (1908–1916). My analysis has involved a comparison between the traditionalist and modernist groups in two specific cases: (i) the power struggle between the secular bureaucratic elites of the Ottoman Empire, represented by the CUP, on the one hand, and the traditionalist establishment, represented by the caliph, on the other, which resulted in the secularization of the Caliphate through a series of constitutional changes in 1909 and 1913; and (ii) the decline of the status of the *şeyhülislam* as a result of the debates and legal changes enacted by the CUP in 1909 and 1916. These developments marked two critical milestones in the process of the secularization of the Caliphate (and the Ottoman state), as they were important steps in the transformation and, ultimately, demise, of the two highest politico-religious institutions in Islam: the Caliphate and the *Meşihat*. This was made possible by the formation of a coalition between the CUP-led bureaucracy and the modernist Islamists. The latter played a crucial role by providing religious justification for most of the secularizing reforms undertaken by the secular elites. Based on the power/knowledge that they drew from their mastery over the Islamic intellectual (theological and legal) traditions, the modernist *ulema* extended a helping hand to the Unionists, which helped solve their legitimation problem. Moreover, the modernist "intervention" into Islamic theology and legal theory not only provided a *post facto* Islamic rationalization of the CUP's secularizing policies, but also prepared the way for enacting further changes, as in the case of the removal of the *şeyhülislam* from the government in 1917, all of which gradually affected the balance of power between the religious establishment and secular forces. The traditionalist *ulema*, on the other hand, tried to revive the once-strong Ottoman Caliphate after the Young Turk Revolution of 1908, which curtailed much of Caliph-Sultan Abdülhamid II's power before replacing him with a much weaker figure, Mehmed V.

I have examined comparatively how traditionalist and modernist actors employed their major discursive strategies in these two cases. The traditionalists' main strategies included those of

i   "establishing the dual (spiritual and political) status of the Caliphate,"
ii "defining religious legitimacy as the only basis for the caliph's authority," and
iii "emphasizing obedience to the caliph as a religious duty of the believer."

Modernists used the strategies of

i   "defining the Caliphate as a temporal political institution,"
ii "asserting popular legitimacy as a basis for the caliph's authority,"
iii "emphasizing the limits of the caliph's temporal authority," and
iv "nationalizing the Caliphate."

In addition to these two cases, I have also identified a pattern of the secularization of Islamic discourse by Islamist intellectuals themselves. As we shall see in Chapter 6, this "secularization from within" was an intended consequence of the theological engineering of secularists such as Mustafa Kemal and Ziya Gökalp;

however, the strategic interventions of many modernist – and some traditionalist – Islamists also produced the same result as an *unintended* consequence of their "engineering." This is true especially for Seyyid Bey, a leading pro-CUP politician and *alim* (Islamic scholar), who was the most important representative of the modernist group. The main way this group's Islamic discourse was secularized involved their adoption of the (secular) distinction between the temporal and spiritual authority (of the caliph), which did not exist in the classical theory and practice of the Islamic Caliphate. (He would later be a leading aide to Mustafa Kemal, the leader of the secularist group – see Chapter 6.) A few traditionalists (e.g., Ömer Ziyaeddin and Mehmed Tahir), too, implicitly adopted the assumption of the distinction between the spiritual and temporal in order to emphasize the spiritual power of the caliph, e.g., by calling him "The Shadow of God on Earth." Modernists (e.g., Seyyid Bey and Elmalılı Hamdi), by contrast, de-emphasized the spiritual dimension of the dichotomy in accordance with their definition of the Caliphate as a (purely) political institution.

The secularization of the modernist Islamic discourse also involved two other discursive strategies: (i) selective appropriation of Western institutions and (ii) historicizing religion by emphasizing the "exigencies of contemporary civilization." These strategies were indicative of what I have called the double-bind – the co-existence of two conflicting (Islamic and Western) epistemologies in the intellectuals' discourse. Moreover, since the use of these discursive strategies was largely shaped by political developments, it is safe to argue that the secularization of Islamic discourse also indicates how the discourse was shaped by the "actual" process of secularization during the Second Constitutional Period, which is exemplified by the increasing references by modernists to the primacy of (modern) social conditions as a source of law over the textual sources of Islam. This is not a merely super-structural argument, however: actors' discourses (shaped by political developments) also shaped the CUP's policies and major political processes, rather than being simply a reflection of them.

My analysis so far has covered developments regarding the fate of the Caliphate in its center, namely Istanbul and the Balkans, and has focused on the debates that took place mostly among Turkish intellectuals. What happened in the "periphery" of the Islamic Caliphate, i.e., the wider Middle East, including North Africa, the Arabian Peninsula, and India, is another story – and the subject of the next chapter. The peripheral context was mainly conditioned by the effects of World War I and British and French colonialism on the Muslim world. There we see traditionalists and modernists mostly working together defending the Ottoman caliph against separatist movements and claims for alternative caliphates supported by the imperialist powers.

5 Colonization in the Caliphal periphery (1914–1920)

Introduction

This chapter examines the debates over the Caliphate and the political and military developments that affected them in the Muslim periphery, including the Middle East, north and northwest Africa, and India, between 1914 and 1920. Unlike in the caliphal center, where debates on the nature and future of the Caliphate took place in the context of domestic power relations, the discussion on the periphery was shaped by international politics. The major elements of these political developments involved World War I, colonization of the Muslim world by the European powers, including Britain, France, Italy, Spain and Germany, and the Ottoman Empire's response to these developments.

These three factors, which are also largely responsible for the formation of the modern Middle East, produced two particular challenges to the status quo surrounding the Caliphate: an attempt by France to devise a "*Maghrib* caliphate" in the western Middle East, and an "Arab caliphate" planned by Britain in the east, to which the Ottomans responded by asserting the existing Caliphate's presence and authority in the Muslim world. Therefore, the debate over the Caliphate on the periphery was not between modernists and traditionalists, as was the case in the caliphal center (Turkey) before World War I (see Chapter 4); nor was it between the modernists and secularists, as would be the case in the center after the war (see Chapter 6). Rather, the discursive and political power struggle on the periphery took place between those loyal to the Ottoman Caliphate and those who supported alternative caliphs in the Arab world, namely the European governments and media as well as Arab nationalists.

I examine this power struggle and its accompanying (Islamic) discourses through an analysis of several different cases. First, I look at the Caliphate's significance in the Middle East during the second half of the 19th century (under Abdülhamid II) and then at the role it played in World War I, as well as how it was affected by the war. I then proceed with an analysis of two specific (and failed) projects: French colonialism and its relation to an alternative caliphate in northwestern Africa, and the creation of an Arab caliphate in Arabia in the context of British colonialism. Taking these historical conditions as my point of departure, in the second part of the chapter I present a discourse analysis of the views of both Arab nationalists and Ottoman loyalists in order to discuss the role of the Caliphate and Islam in general in the legitimization of their actions. Here I first discuss the Arab nationalist discourse on the Caliphate, focusing particularly on two leading figures within the "Arab Caliphate movement," a politician (Sharif Hussein) and an intellectual (Rashid Rida), as well as other influential intellectuals. Then I examine those who defended the Ottoman caliph against his challengers. Ottoman supporters consisted both of traditionalist and modernist Islamists, who, unlike in the Caliphal center, united against the common enemy on the periphery. In my analysis, I identify five main discursive strategies that they commonly employed: re-establishing the legitimacy of the Ottoman Caliphate, emphasizing obedience to the caliph's authority, promoting Islamic unity, and comparing and contrasting Islam with the West in order to prove Islam's (and the Caliphate's) superiority over Western civilization. As usual, they also invoked the sacred texts of Islam (the Qur'an and *hadith*) as a major discursive strategy in defense of the Ottoman Caliphate. The discursive battle between the supporters and opponents of the Ottoman caliph was conditioned by the ongoing colonial activities of European powers on the caliphal periphery.

European imperialism and the Ottoman Caliphate

Starting from the 1870s, the greatest concern of the Ottoman loyalists on the periphery was the looming disintegration of the Muslim world as a result of European colonialism. For them the best way out of this crisis lay in the *ummah* coming together under the leadership of the Ottoman Caliphate, which they regarded as the last line of defense against the political and cultural onslaught of Western imperialism. They found a strong leader in the person of Sultan Abdül-hamid II, who emphasized the significance of the Caliphate during his long reign (1876–1909). As Deringil (1998) demonstrates, the Sultan employed different instruments such as education, music, coats of arms, international fairs, and propaganda efforts against foreign missionaries as well as religious institutions (e.g., the Friday prayer and the Caliphate) in order to legitimize his rule in both domestic and international contexts. The Caliphate became the basis of the sultan's grand strategy of *İttihad-ı İslam,* which shaped both his foreign and domestic policies: He tried not only to keep his Muslim citizens together under his leadership but also to reach out to other Muslim peoples outside the empire (Çetinsaya 2001b: 269–271; Landau 1990: 9–12). He also enjoyed the support of some key public figures in Istanbul. For example, Namık Kemal, an influential intellectual, wrote of the sultan's foreign policy:

> Our future is secure.... One day Muslims will definitely come together around a common word. Therefore, since the Caliphate is [seated] here, and since power is vested in this institution's capacity, and since this [country] is ahead of the rest of the Muslim countries in terms of its people's competence, its closeness to Europe, which is the center of contemporary

civilization, and even in terms of wealth and knowledge, the center of the said reunion will be this country.

(quoted in Özön 1997: 49)[1]

Similarly, Cevdet Pasha, a leading intellectual and statesman of the time, fully supported the sultan's domestic policy of privileging Muslims through the Caliphate:

> The Sublime State is a great state based on religion because it has been vested with the Caliphate since the time of Yavuz Sultan Selim.... Being composed of different nations and groups, the Sublime State is held together by the power of the Caliphate, which connects these different elements. For, it is the Islamic unity that keeps the Arab, Kurdish, Albanian, and Bosniak nations as one single body.
>
> (quoted in Özcan 1997: 137, 139)

A second element of Abdülhamid II's strategy of integrating Muslims around his leadership was the protection of the Muslim Holy Land in Arabia. Therefore, he put a special emphasis on the development of the *Hijaz* (southern Arabia, where Mecca and Medina are located) in order to establish himself as the true caliph of all Muslims and the guardian of the holy shrines in Mecca and Medina (which was one of the caliph's most important prerogatives in history and theory). As less expensive and more efficient transportation (epitomized by the *Hijaz* railway that was completed between 1900 and 1908) facilitated the pilgrimage to the holy sites and greatly increased the number of pilgrims, the Muslim Holy Land also helped the sultan legitimize his claim to universal leadership of the Muslim world (Landau 1971: 134ff.). He also used railway and telegraph technology as instruments of his centralization policies to connect the Arab territories to the caliphal center (İnalcık 1988: 75). Moreover, the availability of modern, advanced education and written information (in the form of newspapers, journals, pamphlets, and books) fostered the intellectual development and political awareness of both the pilgrims and the general population. Thus, the idea (and policy) of the political and cultural integration of Muslims (*İttihad-ı İslam*) became an important topic of discussion in every corner of the Muslim world thanks to the impact of such technologies, especially during the last quarter of the 19th century, when the *Hajj* (annual Muslim pilgrimage) became a political, as well as a religious, gathering (Karpat 2001: 244–245; cf. Çetinsaya 1999).

European (including Russian) imperialism, too, facilitated the rise of the caliph's power – and provoked the idea of Islamic unity (Eraslan 1995: 27). A specific factor that contributed to this power was the growing Russian threat against Ottoman interests in the Balkans and Caucasus. The Russian tsar's claim for the protectorate of Orthodox Slavic peoples in Eastern Europe was a direct threat to the Ottoman Empire's territorial integrity and sphere of influence during the second half of the 19th century. In response, Ottoman sultans claimed religious leadership of Muslims everywhere, including Central Asia and the Caucasus, where Muslims lived under Russian rule, as well as the Balkans and the Middle

East. In 1896, the influential Ottoman statesman Âli Pasha expressed their plans to form an "Islamic bloc" against Russian imperialism in Asia (Özcan 1997: 50). The Turco-Russian war of 1877–1878 in which the Ottoman Empire lost Serbia, Romania, and Montenegro, and the Russians threatened to invade Istanbul, further invigorated this caliphal policy: Abdülhamid II decided to focus more on the Muslim world. His policy was also affected by the large-scale migrations of Muslim populations from the Balkans and Russian-dominated areas as a result of various wars with Russia. According to the official Ottoman statistics, 1,150,015 immigrants flooded Ottoman cities between 1876 and 1894, increasing the empire's total population by 6.43 percent to 19,050 million people in 1897 (Behar 1996: 50–51)[2] – also bringing many diseases with them and putting pressure on the economy. In 1877, the representatives of Muslims from India, Afghanistan, and Central Asia convened in Istanbul and suggested to the sultan that "some sort of an Islamic league might be forged against the enemies of Islam, especially Russia, for the present" (Shukla 1973: 135). Moreover, Britain, too, initially supported Ottoman caliphal policy for two reasons: The Caliphate's sphere of influence was an obstacle to the rising Pan-Slavism and Russian ambitions that threatened British interests in Central Asia and, by supporting the Caliphate, Britain could portray itself to its Muslims subjects (especially in India) as a defender of Islam (Anonymous 1883; Shukla 1973: 124; Özcan 1997: 50). Both the Ottoman and British governments made several friendly gestures toward each other between 1869 and 1873, during which the Kashgar Muslims began to regard the Ottoman sultan as their supreme leader and their own ruler (*amir*) as simply a representative of the caliph, who sent officers to Kasghar to train the *amir*'s troops in 1867 (Shukla 1973: 126).

However, British policy toward the Ottoman Empire changed radically in the late 1870s, especially after the Liberal Party came to power under Gladstone's leadership in 1880 (Anonymous 1883; İnalcık 1988: 75). Britain occupied Cyprus in 1878 and Egypt in 1882 and the Ottomans began to see Britain as an aggressive enemy like Russia. This development led to further Ottoman emphasis on the Caliphate, which became the foundation of Sultan Abdülhamid's foreign policy (Özcan 1997). As mentioned above, he promoted Islamic unity, facilitated the *Hajj*, made investments in the Muslim Holy Land, enhanced communication and transportation between the caliphal center and the *Hijaz*, developed friendly relations with other Muslim leaders, and portrayed himself as the leader of all Muslims, the great caliph. At the same time, he mostly remained neutral in his policy toward European powers in order to avoid military conflict and consolidate Ottoman power (Eraslan 1995: 26–28).

Sultan Abdülhamid was largely successful in his two-pronged policy of manipulating tensions between European powers and promoting Islamic unity through the Caliphate. In this way, he not only kept his empire out of large-scale military conflicts with imperialist powers, but also mobilized Muslims as far away as India for the Caliphate's cause by successfully identifying Ottoman and Muslim interests, especially drawing on such symbols of Islam as the holy shrines in the *Hijaz* (Hourani 1983: 106). As Donald Smith (1974: 21) points out,

That Muslims in India, thousands of miles from Constantinople, could be moved so profoundly by the threat to these symbols (i.e., the holy places and the Caliphate) and mobilized in such large numbers for militant anti-government activity is a dramatic illustration of the potency of religion in the process of mass politicization.

The rise of the caliph's political and ideological power and the increased political consciousness of Muslim populations were alarming developments for European imperialists. In particular, Britain and France both began to see the Caliphate as the biggest threat to their colonial presence in the Muslim world in the last quarter of the 19th century (Anonymous 1883). This concern was shared by the Dutch government: The Dutch expressed their concern to the British over the growing desire among Muslims for unification, which would be "harmful for all Christian states" (Özcan 1998a: 52). The British and French foreign services sponsored various media outlets (such as the *Punjab Times* and *Akhbar-i Am* in India, and *al-Jazeera al-Misriyya* and *al-Qahira* newspapers in Egypt) to disseminate in their colonies the idea of the illegitimacy of the Ottoman Caliphate, which would also be the subject of some "academic" studies done by orientalists working for their governments (e.g., Toynbee 1920, 1927; Samné 1919). Moreover, faced with the possibility of resistance to their occupation in Libya and Central Asia, the Italian and Russian foreign services, respectively, would later join the other European imperialists in their propaganda campaign to undermine the Ottoman Caliphate through their own scholar-officials (e.g., Nallino 1917; Barthold 1912). However, due to the sheer size of the Muslim population under its administration, it was Britain that was most concerned about the Caliphate, and particularly Abdülhamid II's policies that strengthened it.

Like the European powers, the Unionists in Istanbul who dethroned Abdülhamid II in 1909 were unwilling to support the caliph and his religious dignitary, the *şeyhülislam*, in domestic politics, as discussed in Chapter 4. However, the Unionists were also aware of the significance of these figures in international politics, a reality from which they attempted to benefit when the occasion arose by claiming that the caliph and the *şeyhülislam* had religious authority over the Muslim subjects of other governments. Several such occasions arose in the aftermath of the 1908 Revolution: The agreement signed between the Ottoman government and Austria in October 1908 following the latter's invasion of Bosnia stated that the Turkish sultan would continue to be mentioned as caliph in collective prayers and that the head of the Bosnian *ulema* would still be subordinate to the *şeyhülislam* in Istanbul (Arnold 1965[1924]: 177). Likewise, the Treaty of Lausanne signed after Italy invaded Libya in 1912 stated that the Turkish caliph's name would be mentioned at Friday sermons and that the chief justice of Libya would be appointed by the Turkish *şeyhülislam*, with his salary paid by the Ottoman government (Nallino 1917: 282–283). The Treaty of Constantinople, signed with Bulgaria in 1913, and another one signed with Greece also recognized the caliph's religious authority and stated that the chief *mufti*s of the Bulgarian and Greek Muslims would receive authorization from the *şeyhülislam* in Istanbul (Arnold 1965[1924]: 178). The last attempt by the CUP to make use of the caliph's ideological power was when the Turkish sultan published a *jihad fatwa* against the Allies during World War I in which he, as caliph, called upon all Muslims to fight against the Allies.

The Great War and the Caliphate

Prior to World War I, which started on July 28, 1914, the Entente Powers (Britain, France, and Russia) were concerned that the Ottoman Empire would side with Germany – and rightly so, because Germany's Kaiser Wilhelm II had developed close relations with both Abdülhamid II and the Unionists. The Allies were particularly concerned that, as the leader of the Muslim world, Caliph-Sultan Mehmed V could declare *jihad* (holy war) against them, which could pose a great danger for Britain, France, and Russia (and Italy, which joined them in 1915) in their colonies (Monroe 1963: 24ff.). Germany and the Ottoman Empire signed a secret treaty of alliance on August 2, 1914, with which the Germans hoped to benefit from the caliph's prestige in the Muslim world (in order to prevent the Allies from consolidating the Western front with colonial troops by instigating revolts in Muslim colonies)[3] in return for military aid to the Ottomans (Fromkin 2001: 45–50; see also Trumpener 1968).

When Britain refused to deliver a warship (which the Ottomans had paid for) to the Ottoman government and instead added it to the British navy, which created a great disturbance in the Muslim world, the German navy donated two warships to Istanbul, thereby garnering much appreciation amongst Muslims. The pro-German CUP government declared war against the Allies and attacked two Russian ports in the Black Sea on October 29, 1914. Two weeks later, the caliph's *fatwa*, also signed by 29 members of the *ulema*, including the current and former *şeyhülislam*s, declared the "Great *Jihad*" (*Cihad-ı Ekber*). It stated that joining the war (on the Ottoman side) was a religious duty for Muslims, and that if a (Muslim) soldier attacked the army of the caliph of Islam or of his allies, he would be punished in the afterlife.[4] The *fatwa* was read out in mosques and disseminated all over the Muslim world. Meanwhile, the CUP started organizing various "revolutionary societies," initiated particularly by War Minister Enver Pasha via the Ottoman secret service (*Teşkilat-ı Mahsusa*) in order to instigate uprisings in the Muslim regions occupied by the Allies (see, e.g., Lal 1969).

The caliph's *fatwa* increased Germany's expectations from its Muslim ally. It was also embraced by the Ottoman loyalists who envisioned a unified Muslim *ummah* under the caliph's flag. A theatre play written by a Turkish traditionalist, Muhyiddin Baha, who was a judge during the war,[5] expressed these pro-Ottoman feelings: In addition to the heroic resistance by Turkish soldiers against British and Russian invaders in Egypt and the Caucasus, the play described how, upon hearing the caliph's call for *jihad*, Indian-Muslim soldiers in the British army and Muslim citizens of Russia happily joined the Ottoman forces (Muhyiddin Baha 1915: 402–405). In a sense, the play represents the political vision in the caliphal center of a unified Muslim *ummah* under the leadership of Turkey. The declaration of *jihad* also led to an increase in publications on the subject, particularly from a pro-Ottoman perspective. For example, the Tunisian activist-scholar al-Tunusi, who also had close ties with the CUP, wrote a pamphlet in Arabic titled "The Truth about *Jihad*" (1915), which was immediately translated into German, French, and Turkish and distributed throughout Europe and the Middle East.

The organizational network of these activities aimed at increasing the empire's political and ideological power vis-à-vis the Allies was provided by the Ottoman secret service, the *Teşkilat-ı Mahsusa* ("Special Organization"). Also known as the *Umûr-ı Şarkıyye Dairesi* (Department of Eastern Affairs), the *Teşkilat*'s center was based in Istanbul and consisted of approximately 30,000 military and civil personnel, the majority of whom were of Arab origin. The *Teşkilat* was first headed by Suleyman al-Askari, an Arab-Ottoman army officer who committed suicide after a defeat against the British in Iraq in 1915. Subsequently, a Tunisian attorney by the name of Ali Bashanba was appointed as the *Teşkilat*'s head by the Young Turks. He had previously founded the "Young Tunis" movement to organize resistance against the French occupation, for which he had been exiled by the French in 1912. Bashanba remained head of the *Teşkilat* until his death in 1918. Other prominent members of the *Teşkilat* who operated in North Africa and Arabia included Mehmed Akif, Ismail Safayihi, Salih Sharif al-Tunusi, and Bashanba's brother, Muhammad Bashanba. As mentioned above, the *Teşkilat* had a double function: to co-ordinate resistance activities in Allied-occupied Muslim territories by organizing "revolutionary societies" and to disseminate pro-Ottoman propaganda by financially and organizationally supporting various types of publications (newspapers, pamphlets, booklets, brochures). It carried out these functions in collaboration with the German "Eastern News Agency" (*Nachrichtenstelle für den Orient*), founded in Berlin by the former German council in Cairo, Max Freiherr von Oppenheim. The Germans fully supported the *Teşkilat* in hopes of instigating revolts against France and Britain in their Muslim colonies, such as India (Stoddard 1963; Landau 1990: 86–94).

Though the *Teşkilat*'s activities and the *jihad fatwa* would prove largely ineffective, the Allies were alarmed by these developments, for they were aware of the potential influence of the Turkish caliph on non-Turkish Muslims in the territory. For instance, Thomas Arnold, British academic and advisor to the Foreign Office, wrote in his memo to the FO as late as at the end of 1918 that:

> [I]f both the Sultan of Turkey and the Sheikh-ul-Islam ... renounce all authority in Mesopotamia, this will constitute no obstacle to the people of Mesopotamia praying in the mosques for the sultan as Caliph, just as present Indian Muhammadans pray for him as Caliph, even though he exercises no jurisdiction in India nor does his sheikh-ul-Islam.
>
> (IOR/L/PS/10/853/4, F202, 4; quoted in Oliver-Dee 2009: 98)

Thus, the Caliphate was once again a significant matter of discussion between Britain, France, and Russia, which is particularly evident in the two famous secret treaties signed by the Allies during the war. The first one, known as the Treaty of Constantinople, was actually a collection of correspondence between the three countries between March 4 and April 10, 1915. According to the agreement, Britain and France would accept Russia's demand to occupy Istanbul and the Turkish Straits (the Bosphorus and the Dardanelles) on seven conditions, one of which was that Islamic sacred shrines and Arabia would be governed by Muslims themselves.[6] Though the treaty was never implemented due to the Bolshevik Revolution in October 1917, both Britain and Russia agreed that the Caliphate should be "returned" to the Arabs (Nevakivi 1969: 12; Oliver-Dee 2009: 92). (A similar agreement, known as the London Treaty, was made in the same year with Italy, which promised the latter large portions of southwestern Anatolia.) The second secret treaty was the famous Sykes–Picot Agreement between Britain and France, signed in May 1916, which provided France with direct control of northern and western Syria and a sphere of influence in the Syrian hinterland. While Britain had the direct control of Iraq and indirect influence on the entire *Hijaz*, the agreement left for the Arabs only the Arabian Desert (Cleveland 2000: 159–160; Goldschmidt 2005: 213).[7] The Allies also agreed that the Ottoman Caliphate should be destroyed; the French and the British, in particular, were interested in creating an "Arab Caliphate" under their own control.

French colonialism and the "*Maghrib* Caliphate"

Britain's greatest rival in colonialism, France was also competing with Italy, Spain, and – later – Germany in colonizing Africa during the 19th and early 20th centuries. The French came to control much of northwestern Africa before World War I, though French colonialism in the region had started more than a century before: Napoleon Bonaparte had invaded Egypt for a short period (1798–1801), before being defeated by the Ottomans with British assistance. France then occupied Algeria in 1830 and Tunisia in 1881, after which it began to compete with Britain for the colonization of Egypt, and with Spain for Morocco. Confident that the Ottoman Empire would soon collapse, the British were willing to leave the French alone in western Africa if they could secure their position in the east. Lord Cromer, then consul general in Cairo, wrote in June 1903:

> The agony of these decadent Oriental States such as Turkey and Persia, is prolonged owing to the discussion and rivalries amongst the possible heirs to the succession.... I think it would be found in practice that if once the French succession were secured, the agony of Morocco would not be of long duration.
>
> (quoted in Nevakivi 1969: 1)

In 1904 the French government signed what is known as the *Entente Cordiale* with the British, who had already occupied Egypt in 1882, which ensured French control over Morocco and British control over Egypt. In the same year France reached a similar agreement with the Spanish, who had invaded northern and western Morocco, under which they partitioned the country; and another agreement with Italy, which would soon colonize Libya. France also signed a treaty with Germany in 1911, which recognized German interests in North Africa and ended its opposition to the French colonization of Morocco. France and Spain renewed their agreement in 1912 by clearly defining their respective rights and spheres of influence in Morocco (*American Journal of International Law* 1913: 357–359). Consequently, France took full control of the Moroccan government and much of its territory, as well as Algeria and Tunisia.

Previously, all of North Africa – except for Tunisia and Morocco – and the Sudan belonged formally to the Ottoman Empire. French colonial activities in the region ended the traditionally friendly relations between the two empires in the last quarter of the 19th century. Previously, Ottoman modernization, especially in the military and education, was essentially inspired by France (and French philosophy), and carried out by French military experts (see Chapter 2), but the occupation of Ottoman-Muslim territories in Africa tarnished the good relations between them and led to the replacement of France by Germany as the Ottomans' main partner – though Sultan Abdülhamid's foreign policy was mostly neutral regarding the struggle between European powers (Eraslan 1995). As the only strong Muslim state, the Ottoman Empire was an ideal partner for the Germans, who co-operated with and helped the Ottomans particularly in terms of military and economic modernization – and reaped the fruits of this co-operation in World War I. The impact of Germany's statist-nationalist model was even more visible in the modernism of the Young Turks after Abdülhamid II (Karpat 2001: 264).

On the other hand, the main factor that delayed the colonization of the *Maghrib* (northwestern Africa, including Libya) was the close co-operation between the Ottomans and the Sanusiyya, a politically oriented religious order founded by Sayyid Muhammad ibn 'Ali al-Sanusi (1787–1860) based in the *Maghrib*, against European imperialism during the last quarter of the 19th century:

> The Sanusi had acquired a pivotal role in the Ottoman strategy to defend North Africa and the Sahara against the French and Italian advance and to protect the approaches to the Hicaz. Ottoman assistance helped the Sanusi to strengthen their social position in Libya and become the dominant political group there; the Sanusi, in turn, helped the caliph-sultan [Abdülhamid II] maintain his authority in North Africa and assure Istanbul's communication with the Chad, Bornu and so on. This cooperation was based both on a mutual interest and certain ideological Islamic affinity.
>
> (Karpat 2001: 264)

This co-operation continued even after Sultan Abdülhamid was deposed by the Young Turks: the CUP's most powerful leader, Enver Pasha (who was also the commander of Ottoman forces in Libya in 1912), and the Sanusi leader Ahmad al-Sharif were good friends; and over 300 Sanusi officers were trained in Turkish military schools (Abun-Nasr 1987: 321–322).[8] The Sanusi were also active in Morocco and helped establish mutual relations between the Ottoman Caliphate and the (Shia) Sharifian dynasty (est. 1659) there. These efforts, however, were not very successful because Abdülhamid II wanted Morocco to recognize him as their caliph but the Moroccan sultans wanted to remain independent, though they would not achieve this due to the French invasion that began in 1904. Though the Young Turks sent officers to Morocco where they successfully organized a resistance against the French and Spanish armies before and during World War I, this co-operation was limited, too (El-Moudden 1995a).

The "Maghrib Caliphate"

The French protectorate in Morocco (1912–1956), established with the Treaty of Fez, preserved the position of the sultan, Yussuf ibn Hassan (1912–1927), but left him with little authority: the real ruler of the country was the French resident-general, Marshal Hubert Lyautey (1912–1925), who initiated all royal decrees and nominated all high functionaries (Abun-Nasr 1987: 373). In addition to ruling the country and exploiting its natural resources, the French also tried to create a "Caliphate" in Morocco in order to ideologically control Muslim populations in their colonies throughout Africa and the Middle East. They were aware that after Abdülhamid II the Ottoman Caliphate was weaker; at the same time, they were concerned that the British would soon have their own puppet-caliph in Arabia (see below). Therefore, the French government needed an occasion to install a caliph under their direct control; this occasion was provided by World War I, when the Ottoman Caliph's call for *jihad* largely failed and Sharif Hussein of Mecca, who would later declare himself caliph, was preparing for independence with Britain's assistance. In this context, for France King Yussuf of Morocco stood out as the best candidate for caliph, because the Sharifian ruling family (also known as the Alaouite, who still rule the country today) had been claiming since the establishment of their dynasty in the mid-17th century that they were descendants of the Prophet Muhammad through his daughter Fatima.[9]

There is little information in historical sources on the "Moroccan Caliphate"[10] largely because this project was never completed: when, as we shall see below, alternative Arab caliphs were not recognized by the wider Muslim world, and the Ottoman Caliphate was abolished in Turkey in 1924, followed by unsuccessful attempts to elect a new caliph, France and Britain would abandon their caliphate projects. Nevertheless, they did try to create their own caliphates during World War I. In the *Maghrib*, the project was carried out by the French resident-general, Lyautey, and Foreign Minister Delcassé, who anticipated in early 1915 that the ongoing Battle of the Dardanelles between Britain and the Ottoman Empire was soon to be over, resulting in an Ottoman defeat and the invasion of Istanbul by the Allies, which would then end the Ottoman Caliphate and pave the way for an alternative caliph. They knew that Britain was getting ready to nominate Sharif Hussein as caliph, which they thought was a worse possibility for France than the existing situation (Bayur 1983, III: 298). Therefore, Marshal Lyautey suggested that it was in their best interest to install the Moroccan sultan as the "caliph of the West" (*Maghrib*) who would be the head of Muslims in French colonies once the "Eastern Caliphate" (Istanbul) was gone. Aware of the difficulties involved in appointing a religious leader for Muslims, the French justified their plan by claiming that religious problems would play a significant role in shaping Muslim countries' future, which required that there be "spiritual leadership" to solve their problems. They also reasoned that the future of the French empire in North Africa, too, was closely related to their degree of control over the (future) Caliphate. They thus planned to nominate as caliph the Moroccan sultan, who they claimed was already recognized as caliph in Algeria and Tunisia as well as in his own country (Bayur 1983, III: 297–301). Once the plan was sketched out, the idea of a Moroccan caliphate was actively propagated by the French media during the autumn of 1915 (see e.g., *Le Matin de Paris* 1915).

Istanbul was apparently aware of this plan, as evidenced by the fact that some pro-Ottoman activist-intellectuals in North Africa, such as Abdulaziz Jawish (1876–1929) and Salih Sharif al-Tunusi (1869–1920), both Islamic scholars from Tunisia who had close ties to the CUP (being members of the *Teşkilat-ı Mahsusa*), immediately responded to the French propaganda by publishing articles and books reflecting the Ottoman point of view (see below). Nevertheless, Istanbul was more concerned about British plans to install an Arab caliph in the Holy Land of Islam than the French in the *Maghrib*, which was largely out of Ottoman reach. Moreover, though the Ottomans initially considered it dangerous, one year later the French gave up on their *Maghrib* caliphate plans and made a deal with the British, the secret Sykes-Picot Agreement, signed in May 1916, which provided control of Syria to France (see above) in return for giving Britain a free hand in the rest of the Arab world and in its plans for an Arab caliphate.

British colonialism and the "Arab Caliphate"

Since the late 18th century, Britain had been involved in discussions of the Caliphate, as it directly concerned Britain's Muslim colonies: the Indian subcontinent, northeast Africa, and, later, the Arabian Peninsula. British colonial administrations had been aware of the ideological power that the Ottoman caliph-sultans enjoyed both before and during the reign of Abdülhamid II (1876–1909). For example, in his resistance against the British in India, Tipu Sultan of the Mysore, who sought the Ottoman sultan's support, sent an envoy to Istanbul in 1786 declaring that he recognized the Ottoman sultan as his suzerain and the caliph of all Muslims (İnalcık 1988: 77). Britain, too, often strove to make alliances with the caliph: in 1840 London and Istanbul co-operated against Mehmed Ali of Egypt, who threatened to invade Arabia and Anatolia after the

Battle of Nizip. This alliance greatly improved Britain's position in the Middle East (Smith *et al.* 1970: 46; Kırlı 2004: 83, 87). Later, when local people revolted against the British colonial administration in India in 1857, the British government asked Ottoman Sultan Abdülmecid (r. 1839–1861) to write a letter to Indian Muslims as their caliph telling them not to join the revolt, a request that Abdülmecid accepted (Bayur 1987, III: 315–316; Eraslan 1995: 41–43). Similarly, the next sultan, Abdülaziz (1861–1876), intervened as the caliph of Muslims in the political affairs of places as far away as the Comoro islands in the Indian Ocean and Eastern Turkistan in Central Asia when the Muslim leaders, the members of the Council of Henzevan and Yakub Bey, respectively, requested his help (as the "holder of the seat of the Great Caliphate and the head and the leader of the Muslim nation") against the British and the Russians (Karpat 1987: 26–27, 2001: 56–63). Britain was thus interested in the Caliphate due to its possible positive and negative effects on social unrest among its colonial populations, particularly in India and Egypt, two of the biggest British colonies. During the early 20th century, too, the British government was concerned about the potential impact of the Ottoman Caliphate on its Muslim colonial subjects, especially after it occupied Egypt in 1882, which was an autonomous Ottoman province at the time.[11]

Britain and the Arabs

Starting in the late 1870s, British government officials (such as the foreign policy advisors George Badger and Wilfrid Blunt, colonial advisors George Campbell and George Birdwood, and Foreign Ministers Lord Granville [1870–1874 and 1880–1885] and Lord Salisbury, who was also prime minister [1886–1892 and 1895–1902]) and then the English press had already begun to propagate a view of the "illegitimacy" of the Ottoman Caliphate, which had to be "returned" to the Arabs. This was one of the basic tenets of British foreign policy and shaped its approach to the "Eastern Question." The British propaganda consisted of three arguments. First, the Ottoman claim for the Caliphate was a recent innovation; it had not existed before the reign of Abdülhamid II. Second, most Muslims did not recognize the Ottoman sultan as their true caliph because the Caliphate was supposed to belong to the descendants of Prophet Muhammad, which the Ottomans were not. The British propaganda thus focused on the "Quraysh *hadith*" (discussed in Chapter 3) that required the caliph to be a descendant of the Prophet, which would constitute the basis of the claims for an Arab Caliphate (see below). Third, the Ottomans had "captured" the Caliphate by force and transmitted it on the basis of heredity, rather than election or *bay'ah* (allegiance) of the Muslim community. For this reason, it was illegitimate from the perspective of Islamic law, as well (Özcan 1998a: 53–54). These arguments were put forward by the British foreign policy advisors and Orientalists working for the British government and disseminated throughout the Muslim world, as mentioned above, by the Publicity Bureau of the (British) Government of India and the Arab Bureau of the Foreign Office, as well as the British (and later by some Indian and Arab) press. For example, an Istanbul-based anonymous writer wrote for *The Contemporary Review* in London that:

> [Ottoman Caliphate's recognition by most Muslims] has not destroyed the rights of the family of Koreish. It only holds them in abeyance, until some one of that family is strong enough to put an end to the Turkish usurpation. The power of the Sultan does not depend upon the title, but the title depends upon his power. This is a point the political importance of which should never be overlooked ... I believe that it would be better not only for Turkey but for Islam also, if the Sultan would give up his doubtful title to the Caliphate, and pass it over to the descendant of the Prophet who is Shereef of Mecca.... In one way or another this change is sure to come, however it may be resisted by the Sultan ... The Arabs are all ready to assert their rights to the Caliphate and defend them against the Sultan. If he does not surrender the title voluntarily, sooner or later they will take it by force, and that part of the empire along with it.
>
> (Anonymous 1883)[12]

In order to benefit from the religious legitimization of the Caliphate (the Quraysh condition) and weaken the Ottoman Empire, Britain pursued a Middle East policy that favored the Arabs. Creating an Arab Caliphate was thus an integral part of British "divide and rule" policy in the region. For this purpose, British governments tried to get involved in all potential conflicts between the Ottoman sultans and Arab leaders. For instance, when the sharif of Mecca, Hussein (the famous Sharif Hussein's uncle), who had close relations with the British, was killed in 1880, the British tried to help his brother, Awnur-Rafiq, become the next sharif, though Caliph-Sultan Abdülhamid II appointed instead Abdul-Muttalib, the head of the rival Zaydi family within the Hashemite tribe (Salibi 1998: 62–66). In this conflict, James Zohrab, the British consul in Jeddah, justified British involvement in Ottoman domestic politics on the grounds that the British Empire contained the largest Muslim population in the world – an argument that was quickly echoed in the British press (Özcan 1998a: 58). Two years later, however, Awnur-Rafiq, who co-operated with the Palace in Istanbul (Salibi 1998: 67), was appointed as sharif of Mecca (1882–1905), followed by his nephew, Ali (r. 1905–1908).

Sultan Abdülhamid was always aware of the British plans to install a Hashemite caliph in the *Hijaz*, and believed that Britain was the most dangerous of all imperialists "because for them promises [had] no value." He further wrote in his memoirs in 1900 that London could also name the khedive (viceroy) of Egypt (formally an Ottoman pasha) as caliph, adding that "in case of need one would expect the English to appoint even Lord Cromer as Caliph" (quoted in Karpat 2001: 251).[13] In response to the Hamidian policy of Islamic unity, Britain supported separatist Arab movements, the Saudi family in particular, between 1880 and 1918. Though this support was not fully committed (because the British did not want to alienate the Ottomans completely), Britain was the greatest ally of Abdulaziz Ibn Saud (founder of current Saudi Arabia) and helped him emerge as the strongest leader in post-war Arabia (Bayur 1983, II: 192). The British, who had occupied Egypt in 1882 and controlled the coasts of the Red Sea, also maintained close contacts with the sharifs in the *Hijaz*, sometimes favoring them over the Saudis, until the end of World War I. The Great War created a perfect opportunity for Britain and Sharif Hussein of Mecca, who was Awnur-Rafiq's other nephew, to launch the "Great Arab revolt."

The Arab Revolt (1916–1918)

A member of the Hashemite tribe in Mecca, Hussein ibn 'Ali (1853–1931), was appointed as sharif of Mecca (1908–1916) by the Young Turks who had deposed Sultan Abdülhamid in 1909. However, the sharif, who had lived in Istanbul in exile for 15 years under Abdülhamid II's close watch, was not very loyal to the CUP, either. He was alienated by the centralization policies of the Unionists, who established their iron rule in Istanbul after 1908. These policies tended to weaken local rulers, including the sharif himself, which, coupled with Hussein's dynastic ambitions, eroded his loyalty to the imperial center (Kayalı 1997: 147ff). However, he kept his own intentions secret virtually until the last moment: In May 1915 he sent his son, Faysal, to the CUP leader and the governor and commander of Syria, Cemal Pasha (whose harsh treatment of Arab notables is the source of Arab nationalist hatred of him to this day), to declare "his family's readiness to shed its blood for the Ottoman Caliphate." The sharif himself had in February written to Enver Pasha, then the deputy commander-in-chief, to assure him that he would protect the Caliphate's rights in the Holy Land against the enemy. On July 10, just four days before he began to negotiate his independence with Britain via his infamous correspondence with McMahon (see below), the Sharif made a similar promise and requested arms and money from the government for his "*jihad*" against the British (Kayalı 1997: 190–192).

By mid-1915, then, he had planned to secede from the Ottoman Empire and to rule the Arab world by declaring himself the "king of the *Hijaz*," which he did in 1916, and ultimately as the "caliph of the Muslims," which he did in 1924 – though he was not recognized by the Muslim world. During this process, he was always in contact with the British, whose anti-Caliphate policy in the Middle East fit his plans (Westrate 1992). At the beginning of World War I, as mentioned above, Britain and the other Allies were concerned that the Ottomans would support Germany in the event of a war. When it became clear that the Ottoman Empire would indeed join the German side in the war, Sharif Hussein, who was already semi-independent, stood out as the best option for Britain's hopes of undermining the Caliphate.

Though he was officially an Ottoman dignitary in Arabia, the sharif was less powerful than the Turkish governor of the *Hijaz*. He was not able to mobilize a large portion of the population in the region against Istanbul, also because he had two contenders: (the Wahhabi leader) Abdulaziz Ibn Saud of Najd and Ibn Rashid of Jabal Shammar. With the start of World War I, Ibn Rashid sided with the Ottomans (and the Germans) and the other two supported the British. In late October 1914, when the Ottomans entered the war, British War Secretary Lord Kitchener promised Sharif Hussein independence and guaranteed him protection from "external aggression" if the Arabs supported Britain in the war (Paris 2003: 23). He also promised that the British would recognize him as caliph if he declared himself as such (Cassar 2004: 57). These promises were reiterated by the British in the sharif's correspondence with McMahon, the British high commissioner in Cairo in 1915 (Paris 2003: 29–33; Cassar 2004: 221).

In May 1916, when the British promised the French and the Jews portions of the Arabian Peninsula, a British envoy led by T. E. Lawrence ("Lawrence of Arabia") was sent to Sharif Hussein to ask him to start the uprising. Armed with British weapons and a tribalist ideology, the Sharif proclaimed independence on June 5, 1916, attacking Ottoman garrisons in the *Hijaz* and Ottoman supply routes along the *Hijaz* railroad. Jeddah surrendered on June 16, and Mecca on July 4. Medina, however, held out for the duration of the war. The last Turkish garrison holding in Yemen surrendered in December 1918. In the meantime, Ibn Saud defeated Ibn Rashid in 1918, then turned against Hussein when the latter claimed the Caliphate in 1924, ultimately defeating him and then his son Ali and taking over central and southern Arabia completely in 1925 (Teitelbaum 1998: 118–120; Fromkin 2001: 218–229; Milton-Edwards 2006: 23–28; Maisel 2007: 83–89; see also Alangari 1998).

Shortly after Sharif Hussein started his revolt, he published his "Proclamation" of independence on June 27, 1916 in his media organ, the *Qibla*, through which he disseminated propaganda supporting his bid for the Arab Caliphate from the *Hijaz* to Syria and Egypt during World War I.[14] This declaration, which was addressed to the "Muslim *ummah*," presented his uprising as one against the CUP and its leaders' "un-Islamic actions," and avoided confronting the Ottoman sultan, Mehmed V, directly, though severing the Muslim Holy Land from the caliph was clearly an act of rebellion against the caliph himself. In fact, Hussein praised and prayed for all Ottoman sultan-caliphs and squarely blamed the Unionists for both the atrocities in the Holy Land and the economic problems of the wider Muslim world:

> It is well known that of all the Moslem Rulers and Emirs, the Emirs of Mecca, the Favoured City, were the first to recognize the Turkish Government. This they did in order to unite Moslem opinion and firmly establish their community, knowing that the great Ottoman Sultans (may the dust of their tombs be blessed and may Paradise be their abode) were acting in accordance with the Book of God and the *Sunna* of his Prophet (prayers be unto him) and were zealous to enforce the ordinances of both these authorities. With this noble end in view the Emirs before mentioned observe those ordinances unceasingly. I myself, protecting the honour of the [Ottoman] State, caused Arabs to rise against their fellow Arabs in the year 1327 [1909] in order to raise the siege of Abha, and in the following year a similar movement was carried out under the leadership of one of my sons,

as is well known. The Emirs continued to support the Ottoman State until the Society of Union and Progress appeared in the State and proceeded to take over the administration thereof and all its affairs.

The result of this new administration was that the State suffered a loss of territory which quite destroyed its prestige, as the whole world knows, was plunged into the horrors of war and brought to its present perilous position, as is patent to all. This was all done for certain well-known ends, which our feelings forbid to dilate upon. They caused Moslem hearts to ache with grief for the Empire of Islam, for the destruction of the remaining inhabitants of her provinces – Moslem as well as non-Moslem – some of them hanged or otherwise done to death, others driven into exile. Add to this the losses they have sustained through the war in their persons and property, the latter especially in the Holy Land as is briefly demonstrated by the fact that in that quarter the general stress compelled even the middle classes to sell the doors of their houses, their cupboards and the wood from their ceilings, after selling all their belongings to keep life in their bodies.

(Hussein 1916: 234–235)

In order to legitimize his revolt, Hussein further discussed some more specific issues, including an article in *İctihad*, a journal published in Istanbul by a well-known secularist intellectual-politician (a founder of the CUP), Abdullah Cevdet, that the sharif argued contained outrageous ideas that were permitted by the un-Islamic Unionists:

They proceeded next to sever the essential bond between the Ottoman Sultanate and the whole Moslem community, to wit, adherence to the Koran and the *Sunna*. One of the Constantinople newspapers, called *İctihad*, actually published an article maligning (God forgive us) the life of the Prophet (on whom be the prayer and peace of God), and this under the eye of the Grand Vizier of the Ottoman Empire and its Sheikh of Islam, and all the Ulema, ministers and nobles.... It proceeds to the crowning atrocity of destroying one of the five vital precepts of Islam, the Fast of Ramadan, ordering that the troops stationed at Medina, Mecca or Damascus may break the fast in the same way as troops fighting on the Russian frontier, thereby falsifying the clear Koranic injunction, "Those of you who are sick or on a journey."

(Hussein 1916: 235)[15]

Hussein also employed a further discursive technique whereby he directly linked his critique of the Ottoman government to the Caliphate. According to the Sharif, the despotic CUP leadership had committed crimes against the Islamic Caliphate by:

destroying the Sultan's power, robbing him even of the right to choose the chief of his Imperial Cabinet or the private minister of his august person, and breaking the constitution of the Caliphate of which Moslems demand the observance.

In spite of all, we have accepted these innovations in order to give no cause for dissension and schism. But at last the veil was removed and it became apparent that the Empire was in the hands of Enver Pasha, Djemal Pasha and Talat Bey, who were administering it just as they liked and treating it according to their own sweet will.

(Hussein 1916: 235–236)

Sharif Hussein then went on to enumerate the Unionists' other grave mistakes, including the hanging of 21 leading Arab *ulema* and noble men, and their families (including their children) as well as the confiscation of their property. He also claimed that by the order of Istanbul, troops had bombed the Ka'ba, the most sacred shrine for Muslims. For him, all this was enough to justify his revolt against the Ottoman Caliphate, with which he actually aimed to restore the *sharia* and protect the Holy Land:

We leave the whole Mohammedan world from East to West to pass judgment on this contempt and profanation of the Sacred House. But we are determined not to leave our religious and national rights as a plaything in the hands of the Union and Progress Party.

God (blessed and exalted be He) has vouchsafed the land an opportunity to rise in revolt, has enabled her by His power and might to seize her independence.... She stands quite apart and distinct from countries that still groan under the yoke of the Union and Progress Government. She is independent in the fullest sense of the word, freed from the rule of strangers and purged of every foreign influence. Her principles are to defend the faith of Islam, to elevate the Moslem people, to found their conduct on Holy Law, to build up the code of justice on the same foundation in harmony with the principles of religion, to practice its ceremonies in accordance with modern progress, and make a genuine revolution by sparing no pains in spreading education among all classes according to their station and their needs...

We raise our hands humbly to the Lord of Lords for the sake of the Prophet of the All-Bountiful King that we may be granted success and guidance in whatsoever is for the good of Islam and the Moslems. We rely upon Almighty God, who is our Sufficiency and the best Defender.

(Hussein 1916: 237–238)

Interestingly, apart from the reference to the "land" and its independence, the Proclamation contained few Arab nationalist undertones; rather, it derived justification almost exclusively from Islam. This is related to the fact that, prior to the revolt, Arab nationalism had not found a ready soil in the *Hijaz*, mainly because of the lack of secular education and the professional groups it helped create and the absence of media to spread the nationalist message (Ochsenwald 1993). During the revolt, too, "Arabism was not espoused by the Hashemites until it became of particular use to them," that is, until the Arab forces led by Hussein's sons Faysal and Abdullah moved northward into Syria in 1916 and into Transjordan in 1921, where, unlike in the *Hijaz*, they tried to appeal to the elites through a nationalist discourse (Wilson 1993: 214–215).

Thus, Sharif Hussein's stated ideology in his declaration was essentially a mixture of Islamism and tribalism – though he also resorted to nationalism when necessary. In addition to his religious justification of his – normally unacceptable – action against the existing Caliphate, two more discursive techniques stood out in Hussein's proclamation. First, parallel to his careful language and respectful attitude toward Ottoman sultans, he never mentioned the "Arab Caliphate": He was not yet making explicit his plans to pursue the Caliphate in order to gain legitimacy in the eyes of the elites of other Muslim countries. Second, by claiming that the Holy Land would remain "independent in the fullest sense of the word, freed from the rule of strangers and purged of every foreign influence," he implied that as the new guardian of the holy shrines, he would allow neither the Turks nor the Europeans (Britain, in particular) to interfere in the affairs of the *Hijaz*. This message was clearly intended to further justify his revolt in the eyes of the Muslim public, who would not approve of any foreign influence in the Holy Land.

Yet, it was clear that Britain had an immense influence on Hussein and played a decisive role in the success of the Arab Revolt by not only arming the sharif's militia, but also preparing the ground for the uprising through propaganda against the Ottoman Caliphate. The British propaganda was disseminated in the Middle East through different media outlets, such as the *Al-Haqiqah* newspaper and the Arab Bulletin, a "secret" publication circulated by the (British) Arab Bureau established in Cairo, between 1916 and 1919. The Arab Bureau, a branch of the British intelligence service that was popularized by "Lawrence of Arabia," was set up in 1916 to further the British interests in the Middle East at the expense of the Ottomans (and the French) by supporting Arab separatist movements (Fromkin 2001: 168–172). Sharif Hussein's revolt in 1916 provided an opportunity for the British agents, who "viewed the Arab Revolt as the vehicle by which both to hasten the eviction of the Turks and to provide Britain with a relationship to the Arabs that would ensure its postwar dominance" (Westrate 1992: 205, cf. Oliver-Dee 2009: 101).[16] The British, however, supported only a limited Arab movement: they aimed to restrain Sharif Hussein's movement from merging with the other significant one, the Wahhabis led by Ibn Saud, who would later take over the "Kingdom of (Saudi) Arabia," overthrowing Hussein's son Ali in 1925. The British Foreign Office thus supported the two groups against each other as well as against the Ottomans militarily and politically – using different "mechanisms of artifice and manipulation that would bestow on the necessary flexibility to confront the rising tide of Arab nationalism and extend Britain's stay in both India and Egypt" (ibid.). One element of this manipulation was the British promise to the sharif of the creation of an Arab Caliphate.

The "Arab Caliphate"

As a politico-ideological project, the "Arab Caliphate" was a product of both emerging Arab nationalism and the ongoing British colonialism in the Ottoman periphery. In more strategic terms, this was a project launched by Britain's Foreign Office as part of the wartime British operation in colloboration with the Arab insurgents in the *Hijaz*. As mentioned above, Britain had long been disseminating the idea of the "Arab Caliphate" in the Muslim world in order to reduce the political and ideological influence of Sultan Abdülhamid II on Muslims during the last quarter of the 19th century, and later to colonize the Middle East. As early as 1876, Britain financed the Arabic language newspapers *Mir'at al-Ahwal* and *Al-Nahla* (both published in London, starting from 1876 and 1877, respectively), and France *Al-Sada* newspaper, published in Paris, all propagating an Arab caliphate (Kramer 1989: 771; Koloğlu 2010, I: 100). Similar views were voiced in the British press, including particularly *The Times* and *The Contemporary Review* (see, e.g., Anonymous 1883). This propaganda influenced a number of Muslim-Arab rulers, such as Khedive Ismail of Egypt and Khedive Abbas II, as well as Sharif Hussein of Mecca. Long before Hussein's revolt, Khedive Ismail, who had been dismissed from the post by Abdülhamid II, challenged the sultan's caliphate in 1879 through two publications that he sponsored: *Al-ittihad*, published in Paris, and *Al-khilafah*, published in Naples. Unlike Hussein, who eventually made a claim for the Caliphate, Ismail did not propose an alternative caliph but still co-operated with the British in undermining the Ottoman Caliphate (Karpat 2001: 246). His grandson, Khedive Abbas, who was under British control after the occupation of Egypt in 1882, tried to claim his own Caliphate, for which he sent his representative, Abdurrahman al-Kawakibi, to different Muslim countries in 1901 to gain the support of local Muslim leaders, though this proved unsuccessful (Kedourie 1972: 227ff.; Haim 1962: 42; Teitelbaum 1998). Al-Kawakibi (1991) advocated the political unification of Arab peoples as alternative to Abdülhamid II's "universalistic Islamism" and acted as the intellectual leader of the Arab Caliphate movement (as well as Arab nationalism) until his death in 1902 (Saint-Prot 1995). Meanwhile, Britain and France intensified their support for the Arab-caliphate campaign, by sponsoring two more newspapers, *Al-Hilafa* (published in London), which would later change its title with the Ottoman pressure to *Al-Ittihad al-Arabi*, and *Al-Baseer* (published in Paris), beginning from 1881 (Koloğlu 2010, I: 101).

During the Second Constitutional Period, the Unionists usually pursued a policy of administrative centralization, as Sultan Abdülhamid had done before. But, unlike the sultan, the CUP failed (or was reluctant) to support the centralization program with a strong discourse of Islamic unity, but instead promoted an ideology of Ottomanism with Turkish nationalist overtones, which created an image of Turkification, alienating many Arab notables and intellectuals. Therefore, many CUP policies in the Arab world were perceived by Arab political and cultural elites as motivated by ethnic Turkish nationalism, which in turn boosted

Arab nationalist feelings, especially in Syria and, later, Egypt (Khalidi 1993: 53; see also Dawn 1973, 1993a; Kayalı 1997).[17] Arab nationalist activities were supported by some local rulers, such as Khedive Abbas Hilmi of Egypt (1892–1914). Nationalists also operated freely in Europe with the support of the British and French governments. An "Arab Congress" convened in Paris in June 1913 to demand administrative autonomy for the Arab provinces of the Ottoman Empire. One of the organizers of the congress, Abdülhamid al-Zahrawi, who represented the Syrian Decentralization Party, told *Le Temps* newspaper:

> This Arab race has its characteristics in the unity of language, customs, interest, and tendencies that have emphasized Arab rights still ignored to this hour. For that reason, we, as Ottomans, demanded to have an effective share in the administration of the affairs of the empire, and to expose, as Arabs, special demands with reference to our nationalism and status.
>
> (quoted in Tarabein 1993: 103)

A number of Muslim Arab nationalists, led by al-Kawakibi, also advocated the Arabs' "religious right" to the Caliphate (Moaddel 2002: 15). The Arab Caliphate movement and the nationalist ideology espoused by al-Kawakibi that supported independence from Turkish rule, however, "mattered more as a power ploy for diplomats, khedives, and *Amir*s than for its popular following" (Goldschmidt 2005: 208). This movement, which culminated in Hussein's rebellion, was supported by Britain throughout the last quarter of the 19th century and the first quarter of the 20th. European powers also supported the Saudi-Wahhabi revolt in Najd (central Arabia) in 1902, which was justified by Arab nationalists as an attempt at the reformation (*islah*) of religion by returning to the "original" Islam (this is still the main ideological tenet of the Wahhabi regime in Saudi Arabia). Following the Wahhabis, who did not make a claim for the Caliphate, the Shia Zaydis in Yemen revolted in 1904 against the Ottoman sultan-caliph, eventually gaining their autonomy, but the two Zaydi leaders, Imam Yahya and Sheikh Said Dahiani, both claimed their own caliphate and thus failed to gain the recognition of any Muslim country (Eraslan 1995: 191).

While Sharif Hussein did not, as mentioned above, make a claim for the Caliphate until 1924, there is evidence that he was preparing to do so after his revolt in 1916, when his alliance with Britain successfully led him to his independence – though only for a short period. After independence, he called himself "Hussein the First, King of *Hijaz* and Hereditary Custodian of the Holy Cities" (Horne 1923: 233), obviously aware that being the guardian of holy shrines in the *Hijaz* was an important prerogative of the caliph. Also, about nine months after he revolted he had a group of *Hijaz ulema* loyal to him publish another "Proclamation to the Faithful" (March 1917) in support of his kingship (and potential caliphate). Based on their knowledge/power derived from their scholarly authority and status as the carriers of Islamic knowledge, the aim of the *ulema*'s declaration was to defend Hussein against widespread criticism for his rebellion against the Ottoman caliph by justifying it in religious terms. Similar to Hussein's own Proclamation, the Meccan *ulema* first blamed the CUP for oppressing Muslims and disobeying God:

> We, the elders and lawyers of the House of God [Ka'ba], are among those whom God has permitted to serve the faith and defend its truths...
>
> We have discerned the hearts of the usurpers of Osman's empire. We have learned their evil purpose with regard to our faith, we have beheld their crimes and wickedness in this our Holy Land.... [W]e are absolutely certain that the secret committee of the Young Turk Party has notoriously disobeyed God.... Now we content ourselves with begging those of our brethren who oppose us to send some reliable person or persons to Constantinople, the capital of the Unionists, and there witness personally, as we have ourselves witnessed, Moslem women employed by the Government and exposed in public places unveiled before men of strange nations...
>
> Would the obedience of people who do such a thing (and it is the least of their crimes against Islam and Moslems) be a true obedience or would it be disobedience to God? Never, by the God of the "Kaaba," never. To obey them is to disobey God.
>
> *(Proclamation*, pp. 238–239)

Second, these Arab *ulema* supporting Hussein also employed, just as the sharif had done earlier, a discursive technique whereby they presented his revolt as an attempt to serve Islam and restore the *sharia* in the Holy Land:

> We endeavoured to please God and avoid a rebellion so long as it was possible. We rebelled in order to please God, and He gave us victory and stood by us in support of His law and religion, and in accordance with a wisdom known to Him which would lead to the uplifting of this people. Every Moslem heart in the Ottoman Empire, even among the Turks in Anatolia and among the members of the Turkish royal family in the palaces, prays to God for our success, and God always answers the prayers of the oppressed and the righteous...
>
> We have done what we ought to do. We have cleansed our country from the germs of atheism and evil. The best course for those Moslems who still side with and defend this notorious gang of Unionists, is to submit to the will of God before their tongues, hands, and feet give witness against them [in the afterlife].
>
> *(Proclamation*, pp. 239–240)

Unlike what Hussein had said a year earlier, however, the Meccan *ulema* also claimed that the Ottoman caliph-sultans were far from qualifying as the leaders of the *ummah*, for in reality they were puppets of despotic bureaucrats ruling the empire:

It is a great mistake to suppose that in rising against this party [the CUP] we are rising against a legitimate Caliph possessing all the legal or, at least, some of the conditions qualifying him to be such.

What does the Mohammedan world say of the Beni Osman who pretend to be Caliphs of Islam, while for many years they were like puppets in the hands of the Janissaries.... To those Janissaries, grandsons [Unionists] have appeared in these days who are repeating the acts enacted in the days of Abdul Aziz, Murad, and Abdul Hamid...

Those who oppose us and side with the Beni Osman should do one of two things: (1) Consider the Janissaries and their grandsons as the final authority on the question of the Caliphate, which we do not think any reasonable man would do, because it is against the laws of religion; or (2) consider those Janissaries and their grandsons as void of authority on the Caliphate question...

(*Proclamation*, pp. 240–241)

Finally, having attacked the legitimacy of the Ottoman Caliphate, the Arab *ulema* described the person who was most qualified for the leadership of the Muslim world: King Hussein. Though they could not explicitly nominate him for caliph (for, even his status as the local ruler of the *Hijaz* had not been established yet), they implied that he was the only viable candidate:

We want those who are present here to tell you who are far away that we shall confess before Almighty God, on the last day, that today we do not know of any Moslem ruler more righteous and fearing God than the son of His Prophet who is now on the throne of the Arab country. We do not know any one more zealous than he in religion, more observant of the law of God in words and deeds, and more capable of managing our affairs in such a way as would please God. The people of the Holy Land have proclaimed him their King simply because, in so doing, they would be serving their religion and country.

As to the question of the Caliphate, in spite of all that is known of the deplorable condition in which it is situated at the present moment, we have not interfered with it at all and it will remain as it is pending the final decision of the whole Mohammedan world.

(*Proclamation*, p. 241)

These arguments, all framed in religious terms, were very much in line with the British strategy of undermining the Ottoman Caliphate pursued during the late 19th and early 20th centuries. The British anti-Ottoman propaganda also influenced some reformist Arab intellectuals, especially in Egypt, including Muhammad Abduh, Jamaluddin al-Afghani (who was originally from Iran), and Ali Abdur-raziq, as well as Abdur-rahman al-Kawakibi and Rashid Rida, who were leading Arab nationalists (see Khoury 1983; Khalidi *et al.* 1993). Most of these intellectuals lived in Egypt, which was "the largest Arabic-speaking country and an influential center of Arabist publishing and thinking among émigré Syrians"

(Khalidi 1993: xvi), including al-Kawakibi and Rida. They were also the founders of the "modernist movement" that proposed to "reform" Islam by criticizing the Islamic intellectual tradition and "returning to the fundamental sources" of Islam (the Qur'an, in particular).[18] Their ideas also carried the seeds of modern Arab nationalism, which has been substantially influenced by Islamic modernism since the mid-19th century; this influence intensified following World War I, especially in Egypt (Dawn 1993b: 6–12). They organized various clubs and associations such as *al-Jam'iyya al-'Arabiyya* (the Arab Society), founded in Cairo by Rida, and *al-Khilafa al-'Arabiyya* (the Arab Caliphate) (Kutay 1998: 154), and disseminated their ideas through different publications, such as *al-Furat*, *al-Shahbaa'*, and *al-Qibla*. They all argued that an Arab leader should be elected caliph, and, with the exception of al-Kawakibi and Abdur-raziq, who conceived the caliph as a spiritual leader, that the Caliphate was a strictly political institution. The main discursive strategy they employed was to draw on the sacred texts of Islam, particularly the "Quraysh *hadith*" (the prophetic tradition that stated that "*Imam*s are from the Quraysh" [Hakim 1990, IV: 76]), implying that only an Arab could be the true caliph (see Chapter 3 for details).

Among these intellectuals, the most influential were al-Afghani (1839–1897), his disciple Abduh (1849–1905), who published their famous journal, *Al-'Urwah al-Wuthqa* in Paris, and Rashid Rida (1865–1935), who published his *Al-Manar* in Cairo for 35 years. Their ideas still continue to inspire many political movements, such as the Muslim Brotherhood of Egypt and Syria, as well as many Islamist intellectuals today. Though al-Afghani was explicitly anti-imperialist and "pan-Islamist," Abdülhamid II suspected him of co-operating with the British in creating an Arab Caliphate, and kept him under house arrest in Istanbul during the last five years of his life (see Keddie 1972) due to his close relationship with the British diplomat Wilfrid Blunt, a strong advocate of the Arab Caliphate who admired al-Afghani as a "liberal" Muslim intellectual (Blunt 1907: 100; al-Afghani n.d.). Muhammad Abduh, who was very much influenced by al-Afghani, expanded his emphasis on rationality and Islam's compatibility with modernity so as to reform all aspects of Islamic law (Hourani 1983: 104 ff). He also made the familiar argument that the Turks had illegally seized the Caliphate by force and, unlike Arabs, distorted the true teachings of Islam without properly understanding them.[19] Finally, influenced by both al-Afghani and Abduh, Rashid Rida (1923a) similarly attacked the legality of the Ottoman Caliphate, arguing that the Turks not only lacked the Quraysh condition but that they had also turned the Caliphate into a repressive institution. Believing that Arabs, representing the "authentic" Islam, should hold the role of leadership of Islam, he advocated the Arab Caliphate and nominated the Sunni Sharif Hussein, the Wahhabi Ibn Saud, and the Shia Imam Yahya (of Yemen) as caliphs. Rida also met with Sharif Hussein in Mecca during his pilgrimage in 1916, the year the latter declared his independence; his visit was on behalf of prominent Arab leaders in Egypt to show their solidarity (Kayalı 1997: 198; see also the memoirs of Hussein's son, King Abdullah 1950). Rida's arguments were countered by another Arab nationalist, Abdur-raziq the secularist, who – like Rida – wrote a book specifically on the Caliphate.

Arab nationalism and the Islamic Caliphate: Rashid Rida versus Ali Abdur-raziq

The status of the caliph in the age of national states was one of the central issues in the emergence of Arab nationalism following World War I. Rida and Abdur-raziq represented two versions of the Arab nationalist view of the Caliphate: while the latter voiced the secularist conception of the caliph as a spiritual leader, the former spoke for the Islamic-modernist view of the caliph as a political ruler. Rashid Rida's ideas on the Caliphate in general, and on the Arab Caliphate in particular, do not constitute a set of coherent arguments, as they changed over time (see Chapter 3 above) – though he took a largely modernist position in his book on the subject (1923a). Throughout his life, he believed in the significance of the Caliphate, seeing it as the center of Islamic unity and politics – and the best form of government that humankind had ever seen (1923a: 70, 115–116; see also Kerr 1966: 153–186). He argued that it was the main duty of the caliph to fight against the archaic and dogmatic traditions that obliterated the true religion of Islam and created various divisions within the Muslim *ummah* – such as the division between the Sunnis and the Shia. His pro-Arab/anti-Turkish attitude was also related to the political atmosphere of the time: He wrote his book (a collection of a series of articles, beginning from December 1922) right after the Ottoman monarchy was abolished by the Ankara government, which then appointed Abdülmecid Efendi as a ceremonial caliph with no political power (see Chapter 6). Rashid Rida, rejecting the idea of a "spiritual caliph," criticized Mustafa Kemal and nationalists in Ankara, maintaining that Abdülmecid was not a real caliph (Mertoğlu 2005: 53).[20] Therefore, his disappointment, first with CUP leadership, who he thought used the Ottoman Caliph as their puppet, and then with the Turkish nationalists, must have driven him toward Arab nationalism. The superiority of Arabs was for him related directly to their privileged position in terms of understanding and living Islam, which was rooted in two advantages they had as Arabs: first, *ijtihad* (religious innovation based on novel interpretations of key Islamic sources) was dependent on mastery of Arabic; and second, the holy shrines of Islam were in the Arabian Peninsula (1923: 70, 73).[21]

Consequently, though he criticized al-Kawakibi's reduction of the caliph to a mere spiritual authority with no political power, he nevertheless shared his Arab nationalist outlook and the idea that the caliph must be an Arab scholar and descendent of the Prophet Muhammad – and, preferably, also a politically independent leader. Extensively discussing the Quraysh *hadith* and examples from early Islamic history (see Chapter 3), he concluded that Qurayshite descent was a fundamental precondition for being caliph (1923: 19–24). He further claimed that, though Sharif Hussein (who had already declared his independence) fulfilled this condition, he failed to have the next important qualification: mastery over religious sciences. Therefore, Rashid Rida nominated Imam Yahya, the Shia leader of the Zaydi family in Yemen, as the only appropriate person for the Caliphate, for he was both a descendant of the Prophetic family and an Islamic scholar. He also proposed that a new committee be formed as the *Ahl al-hal wa al-'aqd* to elect the new caliph, which would be composed of a "reformist group" of Muslim scholars who had "truly understood the essence of European civilization," but also a group that would not blindly imitate Westerners or the degenerated Islamic "tradition" (1923: 62). For him, the Ahl al-hal wa al-'aqd is ideally the same as the elected Parliament in a given epoch, which implies, however, quite a weak caliph to be elected, supervised, constrained and – if necessary – deposed by deputies. Furthermore, he proposed that the center of the Caliphate should also be moved from Istanbul to Mosul; for the latter was under the influence of neither the "Westernist elite" (like Istanbul), nor British colonialism (like the *Hijaz*). Finally, though he did not like the new, Western-oriented government in Ankara, Rashid Rida did not completely give up on the Turks. He proposed that Turkey, as the strongest independent Muslim state, be the politico-military bastion of the Caliphate, which would in turn be represented by an Arab elected by leading Islamic scholars from all over the Muslim world (1923a: 73).

The anti-Ottoman and modernist view of Rashid Rida and others grew popular in Egypt and the wider Arab world and was influential for a short period of time following the abolition of the Caliphate in 1924 (Lapidus 1988: 666ff.; Moaddel 2005: 125ff.; see also Moaddel 2002; Kavak 2011; Mertoğlu 2011). This was closely related to the efforts by local rulers, such as Khedive Abbas Hilmi and his son, King Fuad of Egypt, to declare their own right to the Caliphate (Mitchell 1969: 39). When they failed, however, Rida's view was quickly discarded. Instead, the secularist view became dominant. This angle was represented by an Egyptian intellectual, Ali Abdur-raziq (1888–1966), who criticized Rida and other Islamists on the problem of state-religion relations. He argued that Islam already included secular politics and that the Caliphate, being originally a strictly religious institution, should have no more than a spiritual function in the modern national state. He framed his whole argument in religious terms, however. He claimed that the Caliphate had no basis in the Qur'an, the *Sunna* of the Prophet, or consensus (*ijma*) among the *ulema*, arguing that the Prophet had only religious authority and that his prophetic mission was purely spiritual, with no intention to create a state: "If we were to collect all [the Prophet's] direct teachings on the question of government, we would get little more than a fraction of the principle of law and organizations needed for maintaining a state" (Abdur-raziq 1925: 110).[22] In his attack on the traditional view of the Caliphate, Abdur-raziq claimed that throughout Islamic history sultans had propagated the wrong idea that the Caliphate was a politico-religious institution "so that they could use religion as a shield protecting their crowns against the attacks of rebels" (Abdur-raziq 1925: 111). For him, unlike Rashid Rida, the Caliphate was merely a spiritual institution with no say in politics, and its politicization had been a major cause of Muslim backwardness in history. The Ottoman sultans, like other dynastic rulers, had usurped the Caliphate to justify their secular governments. Thus, he concluded, the Caliphate as a dynastic rule had always hindered Muslims' progress, and must retreat to its "proper" (non-political) position:

The complete separation of religion and politics is to be achieved in the interest of Islam as a universal faith. The faith could then be released free from the contingencies of history and power politics. This device can also be instrumental in furnishing the basis of the modern state. It thus keeps the option open as to whether we want to hold onto the archaic and cumbersome regime, or the time has come to lay the foundation for a new political organization according to the latest progress of human spirit.

(Abdur-raziq 1925: 103)[23]

In spite of their divergence on the nature of the Caliphate, Rida and Abdur-raziq agreed on the "Arab right" to Muslim leadership. However, despite the efforts of Arab nationalist intellectuals, the success of the Sharifian and Wahhabi revolts in Arabia, and Egypt's complete independence from the Ottoman Empire, the "Arab Caliphate" project was never realized. The collapse of the Ottoman Empire did not help it, either. It failed because Britain did not keep its promise to the Arabs after the war, and local Arab leaders could not elect a caliph who would be recognized by the Muslim world. The Indian Muslims, in particular, strongly rejected any claim to the Caliphate other than that of the Ottomans. Britain abandoned its plans because after the war it found a new leadership in Turkey that was happy to abolish the Ottoman Caliphate (see Chapter 6). Therefore, it was too late when Sharif Hussein and other Arab leaders realized that the Allies had secretly partitioned Arabia with the Sykes–Picot agreement (signed in May 1916), after which they tried to restart negotiations with Istanbul, hoping to put up a united Muslim front against colonialism (Kayalı 1997: 203–204). During the process leading up to this failure, however, the Arab Caliphate movement was increasingly a matter of concern for Istanbul. Against both the secularist and Islamic modernist versions of Arab criticism (and the nationalist politics that it supported), many Arab, Turkish, and Indian intellectuals loyal to Istanbul defended the Ottoman sultan and his right to the Caliphate.

The defense of the Ottoman Caliphate from the periphery

During World War I, the Ottoman Empire could not prevent the loss of its Arabian territories and North Africa because, following the Balkan Wars (1912–1913) and various domestic revolts, which led to a lack of human resources, the Ottoman army was already stretched too thin to fight on several fronts simultaneously, from Galicia and Libya to the Caucasus and Yemen. Therefore, Arab insurgents, backed by Britain and France, won their independence from the empire by 1918, when the Allies occupied much of the Middle East and North Africa, and left a small portion for Arabs. However, many Arab Ottomans and Muslim Indians in the Caliphate's periphery, including intellectuals and politicians, were loyal to the caliphal center. They saw the Ottoman sultan as the only legitimate caliph and, given the magnitude of the crisis caused by the colonization of the Muslim world and by the Great War, they were very much concerned about the unity and independence of the Muslim *ummah*.

Nevertheless, in line with the greater emphasis put on Islam by the Young Turks in the political ideology of the state in Turkey during both the war and the ensuing resistance against the Allied occupation (Kayalı 1997: 200, 203), they were hopeful that the Caliphate could save the *ummah*. This, they reasoned, was dependent on the rallying of Muslims against European colonialism around the Ottoman Caliphate (Shakib Arslan 2005). Therefore, disobedience and uprising against the legitimate caliph, such as Sharif Hussein and others had engaged in, was a major mistake both religiously and politically. Further, claiming the Caliphate when there already was a caliph was not only a grave sin but also meant the betrayal of the Muslim *ummah* for parochial political ambitions in the service of European colonialism. For this reason, the defenders of the Ottoman Caliphate considered those who made claims to the Caliphate as puppets of Britain and France (e.g., Ansari 1919: 376).

Moreover, both traditionalists and pro-Ottoman modernists shared this view. As discussed in Chapter 4, the two groups differed in terms of how they defined the Caliphate and the specific focus of their loyalty (most modernists had close ties to the CUP that had rendered the Caliphate powerless, whereas traditionalists were loyal to the caliph himself); they were nevertheless united, unlike in the center, against the common enemy on the periphery: European colonialism and the Arab Caliphate movement. Thus, for example, Abdulaziz Jawish, a pro-CUP, modernist *alim*, member of the *Teşkilat-ı Mahsusa* and activist in North Africa, argued that the Ottoman Caliphate was the only legitimate Islamic government in the Middle East, adding:

> Being a caliph means being able to take necessary measures to conduct wars, collect and train soldiers, and to protect religion and safeguard Muslim society. Therefore, the caliph must have the ability and power to manage the affairs of the state and the society; he must also have genius and mastery over the Islamic principles of government.
>
> (1916: 251)

Jawish's insistence on the caliph's independence and power to "protect religion and safeguard Muslim society," was a direct critique of the claims by alternative caliphs, particularly Sharif Hussein, whom he saw as a puppet of the British government with no real authority over Arabs, let alone over the whole Muslim world. This view was shared by all other pro-Ottoman actors, as well. Many traditionalists, too, stipulated that the true caliph must have the power to "protect religion and people," conduct wars independently and maintain the rule of law, which only the Ottoman sultan was able to do (Mustafa Zihni 1911: 113; İsmail Hakkı 1910: 438; Safayihi 1915: 79–83).

Moreover, as discussed in Chapter 4, the defenders of the Ottoman Caliphate often resorted to the sacred texts of Islam to respond to the allegations of the European and Muslim advocates of an Arab Caliphate. Against the prophetic tradition, exploited by the latter group, which stated that "*Imam*s are from the Quraysh" (i.e. the caliph must be an Arab), pro-Ottoman intellectuals quoted several other *hadith*s as counter-evidence, one of which read: "Obey your leader even if he is an Abyssinian slave with a small head" (Bukhari 1971, II: "Adhan" 4, 5, 156, IV: "Ahkam" 4). The Quraysh *hadith* is technically an "authentic" (*sahih*) report, and therefore non-refutable on the grounds of authenticity, which is the only way to refute a *hadith* in the Islamic tradition. Unable to do this, they thus interpreted the former Quraysh *hadith* as no longer being applicable, because the Quraysh tribes now did not have the necessary political and military power to support the Caliphate (e.g., Jawish 1916: 246–251; see Chapter 3 for details). In addition to making use of sacred texts, the defenders of the Ottoman Caliphate employed four discursive strategies:

i   emphasizing the legitimacy of the Ottoman Caliph,
ii stressing the religious and political necessity of recognizing the caliph's authority,
iii promoting Islamic unity, and
iv contrasting Islam with the West.

They deployed these strategies through various discursive techniques, such as relating the Ottoman Caliphate to the Holy Land, celebrating its historical achievements, and making references to the Islamic legal-theological tradition in order to establish its legitimacy vis-à-vis alternative caliphs.

Legitimacy of the Ottoman caliph

Emphasizing the legitimacy of the Ottoman Caliphate vis-à-vis would-be challengers was a major discursive strategy employed by both traditionalists and pro-Ottoman modernists, for regardless of how they conceived of the Caliphate (i.e. whether it was only a political or both a political and a religious institution), both groups saw the Ottoman leadership as the only way out of the current political turmoil and an essential element of the revival of the Muslim *ummah*. As part of this strategy, they used the above-mentioned discursive techniques. In deploying these techniques, the pro-Ottoman intellectuals' main aim was to counter the allegations made by the European press and colonial administrations, as well as Arab nationalists, regarding the "illegitimate foundations" of the Ottoman Caliphate and the alleged "religious right" of Arabs to the leadership of the Muslim world. As already mentioned, these allegations were directly related to the emergence of Arab nationalism and the retreat of the Ottoman Caliphate with a series of wars in Libya (1911–1912) and the Balkans (1912–1913) and World War I (1914–1918). More specifically, the *Maghrib* and Hashemite caliphate projects designed by France and Britain between 1914 and 1918 were an immediate threat to the status of the Ottoman caliph.

In this context, both traditionalists and modernists often made references to the Islamic legal-theological tradition to prove the legitimacy of the Ottoman Caliphate. An important theme through which they applied this discursive technique was the question of the preconditions for becoming caliph. They emphasized these conditions because neither Sharif Hussein nor Yussuf of Morocco possessed them, which undermined their legitimacy as potential caliphs. Traditionalist intellectuals, in line with the classical theory (al-Māwardī 1994; al-Taftazānī 1989), commonly stipulated four main preconditions for the Caliphate: "wisdom," "competence," "physical and mental well-being," and "justice."[24] They usually explained these preconditions by invoking the two major Sunni theological schools (*Maturidiyya* and *Ash'ariyya*) and the *Hanefite* legal school. Based on this tradition, they required both political and religious competence in the leader by arguing that the true caliph must not only possess political and military power, but must also have mastered all religious sciences, ideally reaching the level of the *mujtahid* – the highest level of Islamic scholarship (Safayihi 1915: 54–55; cf. Turkish traditionalists, İsmail Hakkı 1910: 438–439; Ömer Lütfi 1912: 240–243).

A related theme traditionalist intellectuals frequently raised as part of the technique of referencing the Islamic legal-theological tradition was the main duties of the caliph. Again following mainstream Sunni theology, they attributed to the *imam* some crucial functions, including "protecting religion and people," conducting *jihad*, and applying the *sharia* (Safayihi 1915: 79–83; cf. Mustafa Zihni 1911: 113; İsmail Hakkı 1910: 438). Clearly, for them, local Arab leaders – including Hussein – lacked the political and military power necessary to carry out these duties. Moreover, assuming that Arab contenders for the Caliphate also lacked ideological power, pro-Ottoman actors presented these duties as the natural implication of the dual authority of the caliph-sultan, often emphasizing his religious status. For example, some traditionalists argued that the Ottoman Caliphate itself had religious significance due to a famous *hadith* that praised the Muslim community and its leader who would conquer Constantinople, which implied that the Ottomans were blessed directly by the Prophet himself (Ömer Ziyaeddin 1908: 63).[25]

In some instances, however, this emphasis was taken much further. For example, al-Tunusi (1913: 416) maintained that caliphs' main function was the same as that of prophets, including "leading people to the righteous path." Moreover, in a book he wrote to refute claims about the Ottoman Caliphate made by the French newspaper *Le Matin*[26] in an effort to legitimize the "*Maghrib* Caliphate," al-Tunusi defined the authority and duties of the caliph in a manner that went well beyond the classical view:

> The duties of the caliph of Islam in this world include spreading the principle of the unity of Allah as prescribed by the Prophet (peace be upon him); limiting worship to Him only; directing reason to the true philosophy, and particularly clearing off the false philosophy that leads to worshiping any being other than Allah; embellishing ethics; bringing perfection and dignity to souls and protecting them from moral decadence; promoting social solidarity and co-operation and educating individuals in a way that gives them happiness, security, peace, and purity; providing legitimate ways of accumulating wealth based on honesty, contentment, and fairness, staying away

from greed, lies, and deception; maintaining and distributing justice, and giving everyone their due; protecting the rights of the powerless against oppressors without regard to the power of the powerful and the weakness of the weak as well as kinship relations; improving all branches of sciences and arts; managing the affairs of the *umma* with utmost attention and effort; preparing for emergency with everything that is humanly possible; uniting the world of Islam under the Muhammadan flag in order to achieve happiness in this world and in the afterlife; establishing alliance and signing treaties with friendly nations; co-operating with them in a way that benefits humanity and wards off negativities; maintaining mutual interests based on fairness, trust, honesty, and justice; waging war against those who assault the Islamic world or any part of it. All these are the caliph's duties.

(1916a: 147–148)

Such an exaggerated list was nowhere to be found in the classical sources on the Caliphate – nor in contemporary ones.[27] The high degree of authority and responsibility attributed to the caliph was directly related to the context in which the author, a pro-Ottoman North African scholar, wrote his book. As mentioned, Algeria and Tunisia had already been invaded by France in 1831 and 1881, Egypt by Britain in 1882 and Libya by Italy in 1912. Having close ties to the CUP and the Porte, al-Tunusi was also very politically active in the region against British, Italian, French, and Arab nationalist propaganda, which, as discussed above, aimed to separate all of North Africa and Arabia from the Ottoman Empire. Such activities intensified during World War I, when the Arab Caliphate movement, led by Sharif Hussein in the east and Morocco's Sultan Yussuf in the west, was strongest. In the midst of this discursive – as well as military – war, al-Tunusi must have felt the grave danger posed to the Caliphate and needed to help solidify the Ottoman rule by strongly emphasizing the caliph's dual authority. The best way to do this was to justify it in religious terms and present it as the only chance for reviving a unified Muslim *ummah*.

As a further discursive technique, Ottomanists argued that the Ottoman Caliphate was the only legitimate leadership of Muslim society because it fulfilled the necessary political and historical conditions. In fact, they argued, the Ottoman Caliphate was the best of its kind since the time of the Four Caliphs (al-Tunusi 1916a: 149; cf. Mehmed Tahir 1909: 74) because it was endorsed not only by the representatives of Ottoman Muslims (parliament members), but also by the those of the entire *ummah* from all over the world, and their allegiance was renewed every year with the sultans' annual ascension ceremonies (*cülus bayramı*) (al-Ubeydi 1916: 208–209). Moreover, according to this narrative, the Ottoman Caliphate had established its legitimacy historically, too. Ottoman sultans had neither seized the Caliphate by war nor in fact wanted to possess it, but it was voluntarily given to them by Muslims on meritocratic grounds, and they had carried this title with dignity and competence by serving the interests of the Muslim world and not waging war against other Muslim states. In the words of Ismail Safayihi, an Arab jurist:

The last Abbasid caliph in Egypt, who only nominally possessed this title, saw the Ottoman sultan's [Selim I] power and competence to protect the Caliphate, and therefore stepped down from the post in his favor, entrusting to him the Holy Prophet's relics, including his flag, sword, and his glorious cloak. Then, every Ottoman sultan became the "leader of the believers and the caliph of the Prophet of the Lord of the universe." They did not fight to secure the Caliphate, nor did they demand it. By taking up this post, they have become glorified. And all Muslims have embraced them for their just practices as caliphs. For this reason, since then, no Muslim has ever disputed their Caliphate.

(Safayihi 1915: 87; cf. al-Tunusi 1916a: 149, 1916b: 426; Ansari 1919: 376;
    Said Halim Pasha 2000[1920]: 403; Azad 1920: 103; Nadvi 1921: 154;
                        Safa 1922: 241–242)

In addition to historical references, the Caliph's supporters also made, as a further discursive technique, a connection between the Ottoman Caliphate and the cultural-geographical dimension of Islam by relating its legitimacy to the Holy Land: the Ottomans held the custody of the holy shrines (in Mecca, Medina, Jerusalem, and Karbala) and the role of protectors of the sacred relics (personal belongings of the Prophet), which made them the true leaders of Muslim society (Syed Mahmud 1921: 37). The guardianship of the holy shrines was not only one of the essential duties of the caliph in classical Islamic theory, but it also became an important sign of the Caliphate's sovereignty and prestige in the context of World War I and the Arab revolt (Margoliouth 1924: 335). At the end of the Great War, when the Arabian Peninsula was invaded by the British and seceded from the Ottoman Empire, many Muslim organizations in the Caliphate's periphery, including the Muslim League of India, protested Britain. Its president, Dr. Mukhtar Ahmed Ansari, said in his address at the League's 1919 convention in Delhi that the caliph's most important responsibility was to protect the holy shrines in the Arabian Peninsula (especially Mecca and Medina), and that all believers were mandated by God to help their leader in this crucial task (1919: 377). He added that Sharif Hussein had committed a grave sin by revolting against the Ottoman sultan and co-operating with the British, which was against the will of God and His Prophet:

The [first] Sharif of Mecca, Barakat, recognized Sultan Selim as the true Caliph and saw to it that the Turkish sultan's name was mentioned in prayers. Since then, none of the Sharifs has objected to the status of Turkish sultans. Even Sharif Hussein himself recognized the sultan as the "true Caliph" and became subject to his religious authority. Despite this, being a slave of his ambitions and [short-term] interests, Sharif Hussein revolted against the Caliph, who was to be unquestionably obeyed. By doing this, he not only violated a principle of civilized ethics, but he also failed to observe a clear command of Allah and his Prophet.

(1919: 376)

Likewise, Hakim Ajmal Khan, the Muslim President of the Indian National Congress,[28] made a similar comment in his address to the congress, saying that guarding the holy shrines was the first priority of the Caliphate and that Britain should end the occupation of the *Hijaz*:

> The safety and independence of the Holy Shrines is a question that deeply concerns Muslims. These places ... enjoy a very high status in their social, political and religious lives. The current situation is a source of great concern and deep sorrow for them. As Muslims want to see these places as a completely independent land, I suggested that the government [of British India] should fully understand their highest and deepest religious meaning. The question of the Caliphate is also closely related to this. It is a purely religious question that concerns only Muslims. It is also an integral part of Islamic religion; therefore, Muslims never want to let anyone else to get involved in solving this question. Even if all the governments in the world came together to pick a Caliph for Muslims, they would never follow such a Caliph.
>
> (Ajmal Khan at the Indian National Congress, December 26, 1919,
> Session 33, quoted in Kidwai 1919: 385)

After the conventions, the Muslim League of India formed a "Caliphate committee" and sent it to Europe, where it requested, particularly from Britain, that the Ottoman Caliphate be left alone and the Arabian Peninsula set free due to their sacred status (Qureshi 1999; Oliver-Dee 2009). They made this request on the basis of the assumption that the Ottoman caliph had political authority over all Muslims, which was built upon his religious/ideological power.

Emphasizing the ideological power of the Caliphate and connecting this to its political authority was another discursive technique that traditionalists deployed as part of the strategy of emphasizing the legitimacy of the Ottoman caliph, particularly during and after World War I. During this devastating war that would bring about the end of the Ottoman Empire, they tried both to resist the influential imperialist propaganda and to ensure the loyalty of Muslims living outside the territories of the empire by presenting the caliph-sultan as having the religious right to leadership. Addressed to both European, and Arab and Indian Muslim audiences, this discourse was harmonious with the policies the CUP followed during the Second Constitutional Period, which aimed to secure recognition of the Ottoman caliph's religious authority over the Muslim subjects of other governments. Thus, in their response to the claim by the Publicity Bureau of the Indian government that Indian Muslims had only recently recognized the (Ottoman) Caliphate, two leaders of the Indian Caliphate movement, Syed Nadvi[29] (1921: 141ff.) and Syed Mahmud (1921: 49–51), argued that not only did the subcontinent's relationship with the Caliphate go back to the very first Muslim state in India (the Ghaznivites), but also the Abbasid Caliphs, even when they were politically extremely weak, had a strong authority over local rulers in India:

Those who have a narrow perspective suppose that the excitement and debates created by the Caliphate are only a product of today's political turmoil and [Indian Muslims'] demand for freedom. This study will demonstrate how deep and pristine the Islamic Caliphate's connection with India is, how deeply attached this country has been to the Porte of the Caliphate, and how important and precious the latter is for Indian rulers.

(Nadvi 1921: 141)

They also argued that Indian Muslims had from the beginning recognized the Ottoman caliphs as the true *imam*s of the Muslims, as evidenced by the fact that Indian rulers had always minted coins for Ottoman sultans and their names had been mentioned in Friday sermons (Kidwai 1919: 351; Nadvi 1921: 152–153).

Likewise, in the context of French colonialism in North Africa, and more specifically against the claim by the *Matin* article that the "Turkish sultan" had no authority over non-Turkish Muslims, particularly in the *Maghrib*, al-Tunusi (1916b: 427) argued that the Ottoman caliph had power and recognition not only in the Muslim world, but also in the West, and that the alliance between Germany and the Ottoman Empire against the Allies in the war was the best evidence for this. He added that the caliph's authority over Muslims was not only spiritual, but also political, as evidenced by non-Turkish Muslims' loyalty to the empire during World War I. Therefore, according to traditionalist supporters of the Ottoman Caliphate, the politico-legal authority of the caliph over all Muslims was directly related to his ideological power:

In the eye of the Muslim law the Khalif ... is the only legal authority in the matters of innovation [in religion]. He is competent enough to bring about any political, legal and social reform on the authority of the Qur'an.

(Syed Mahmud 1921: 38)

More specifically, traditionalists often presented the caliph's ideological power as the driving force of his political authority in order to stress the (desired) influence of the Ottoman Caliphate in the Muslim world, arguing that since the Caliphate was ecumenical, the Ottoman sultan's authority exceeded the boundaries of the empire, reaching the frontiers of the Muslim world (e.g., Yafi 1916: 166; cf. Said Halim Pasha 2000[1920]: 398). Consequently, they further argued, local Muslim rulers' status was nothing more than that of governors of the caliph, the true Muslim ruler (Azad 1920: 150). Therefore, the legitimacy of local rulers (such as Sharif Hussein) was conditioned upon the approval of the caliph. Moreover, the authority of local rulers – Muslim and non-Muslim alike – was legitimate as long as they were loyal to the (Ottoman) Caliphate:

A Muslim or a non-Muslim ruler cannot command the loyalty of the faithful living under him if that loyalty is at variance with his loyalty to his Imam. The principle is clear and simple. The loyalty to one's God and faith should always take precedence over his loyalty to a purely secular ruler. Among the Mussalmans ... loyalty and obedience to the Khalif means loyalty and obedience to God.

(Syed Mahmud 1921: 47; cf. Nadvi 1921: 150)

Some Indian Muslim intellectuals tried to stress the ecumenical character of the religious and temporal authority of the caliph even after World War I had been lost and the Ottoman Empire was about to collapse. They were temporarily optimistic about the 1919 Paris Peace Conference and Wilsonian principles, hoping that the Ottoman claim for self-determination would be accepted by Western imperialists. Within this context, a representative committee of the Muslim League of India, led by its president, Aga Khan III, gave a memorandum to the British prime minister and foreign minister requesting that the Ottoman government be granted the right of self-determination.[30] The Indian intellectual and activist Mushir H. Kidwai[31] (1919: 355), who served on this committee, also suggested in his book (writing in London for the British audience) that the Caliphate should be re-organized under the auspices of the newly founded League of Nations as a Muslim confederation that would consist of all Muslim-majority regions, including Albania, Thrace, Tripoli, Egypt, Tunis, Crimea and those of Turkish-speaking Muslims in the pre-Berlin Treaty (1878) era whose lands had been annexed by Russia in 1877.[32] All these arguments were based on the (traditionalist) assumption of the dual authority of the sultan-caliph, which covered all Muslim populations regardless of their national-political affiliations. A natural implication of the dual authority of the caliph was the necessity of unconditional obedience to his authority, which was the next traditionalist discursive strategy.

Obedience to the caliph's authority

Since the term "obedience" (*itaat*) has many religious connotations (e.g., the *ul al-amr* verse in the Qur'an [4/59] prescribes obedience as the believers' responsibility in their relationship with God, the Prophet, and "those vested with authority"), and since it concerns primarily the caliph's personality (as opposed to his government), the modernist supporters of the Ottoman Empire did not emphasize it. Instead, they supported the Ottoman Caliphate in the context of Islamic unity (see next section). Therefore, it was the traditionalists who constantly stressed the necessity of obedience to the Caliph's authority as a religious and political duty of all Muslims. This discursive strategy worked as complementary to the earlier one that highlighted the legitimacy of the Ottoman Caliphate vis-à-vis alternative caliphs.

Champions of the Ottoman Caliphate worked the concept of obedience into their overall discourse through various techniques. One such technique was presenting obedience as a direct consequence of the ontological hierarchy that they constructed when defining the Caliphate: Both al-Tunusi (1916b: 424), an Arab scholar, and Azad (1920: 99), an Indian politician,[33] wrote that obeying the caliph meant obeying the Prophet, and thus God. Similarly, disobedience to the caliph would be equal to failure to comply with God's orders. Thus, Indian intellectual Syed Mahmud stated:

> Islam compels obedience to the Khalif as much as it does to the word of Allah [the Qur'an] and to the Prophet.... Disobedience to the Khalif is the source of displeasure of God and his Prophet.
>
> (1921: 45)

Others often emphasized the idea of obedience as a fundamental requirement of the *sharia*:

> God has also made the following mandatory for all Muslims: after the death of our Prophet (peace be upon him) they would definitely give allegiance (*bay'ah*) to a person who is to be recognized as the caliph of the Prophet (peace be upon him) who in turn is the caliph of Allah.... For every member of the Islamic nation, obeying the caliph and following his commands is mandated by the *sharia*; whoever disobeys [him] will be punished by the *sharia*.
>
> (al-Tunusi 1913: 416; cf. Mustafa Zihni 1911: 111;
> Ömer Lütfi 1912: 227, 247; Safayihi 1915: 76)

Furthermore, Yafi, the journalist from Beirut, elevated obedience to the caliph to the status of worship, labeling disobedience as forbidden by God and the Prophet, which he supported by citing the "*ul al-amr*" verse and some *hadith*s (Yafi 1916: 165). Similarly, al-Tunusi's (1916a: 148) discussion on the "believers' responsibility towards the caliph," which he defined as unconditional loyalty to the caliph's religious and political decisions that were in line with the *sharia*, was mostly focused on the "*ul al-amr*" verse and certain *hadith*s that decreed obedience. Moreover, Tunisian jurist Safayihi (1915: 83) combined the two techniques in his discussion of the indispensability of the Caliphate, arguing that both the Qur'an and the Prophet's legacy required having a just ruler with dual authority who must be obeyed by Muslims.

Moreover, in addition to relating obedience to faith, some traditionalists deployed more "sociological" techniques, as well. The Indian intellectual and politician Azad argued that since the Caliphate was the center of the socio-political system in Islam, obedience to the caliph was naturally the basis of social life in the Muslim community:

> Following [the death of] the Holy Prophet, the Caliphate has had two different forms: during the period of the Rightly Guided Caliphs, it was the real practice of the Caliphate.... The second period is the era of absolute monarchy and dynasty, which started after the first four Caliphs, and is still going on. In this period, the Caliphate has gained a somewhat different form. [However,] the Islamic order based on the *sharia* compels every Muslim to

obey the caliph in every epoch. A Muslim must obey the caliph just like obeying Allah and his Prophet. This is a central principle.

(Azad 1920: 99)

The Arab scholar Safayihi (1915: 74) echoed this view and added that obedience on the part of Muslims was essentially a voluntary act, rather than something mandated by established legal rules.

Other traditionalists mixed the caliph's religious and political functions in their discussion on obedience – a discursive technique that worked as a compliment to their strategy of establishing the dual status of the institution. Among them, the Indian Muslim intellectual Syed Mahmud (2005: 192; cf. Kidwai 1919: 352) said it was only the caliph who had the authority to declare *jihad* against enemies and, when he did so, it was imperative according to Islamic theology that all Muslims obey him, which indicated his crucial religious (and political) status. It is intriguing that Syed Mahmud (and Kidwai) made this argument for the caliph's political power *after* the Ottoman Empire was defeated in World War I (in which the imperial call for *jihad* had not worked) and the caliphal center was occupied by the Allies. This shows that they believed the Caliphate was still the only institution with enough potential (ideological) power to unite the various Muslim peoples. In order to underscore this ideological power, Syed Mahmud (1921: 38) also claimed that the Turkish sultan, as caliph, had the authority to choose the opinions of some jurists over others, which would then be a binding resolution for all Muslims, thereby directly intervening into the realm of the *ulema*. He cited the example of Süleyman the Lawgiver (r. 1520–1566), who had sometimes preferred the opinions of non-Hanefite jurists, though the Hanefite school was the official *madhab* (school of law) of the empire.

Furthermore, some traditionalists related the caliph's status to the legitimacy of certain religious rituals, arguing that the Caliphate was a precondition for the validity of collective rituals. Thus, Egyptian journalist Muhammad Safa (1922: 234–236; cf. Syed Mahmud 1921: 46) stated that, from a theological point of view, believers were not allowed to perform such collective forms of worship as the Friday prayer, the Pilgrimage or Eid prayers without an independent caliph, because these collective rituals had political, as well as religious, significance: They signified the political sovereignty of the Caliphate.[34] This argument, which is also made by many Salafi groups today, indicates the extent to which traditionalists were concerned about the future of the Caliphate in a context in which Istanbul, the center of the Caliphate, was occupied by the British army and Caliph Mehmed Vahideddin himself was practically a prisoner of war with no real political power or religious authority. It was, therefore, a discursive technique employed by traditionalists who were in desperate need of the Muslim world's help at a time when the Caliphate was coming to an end. Equally important to their concern for the future of the Caliphate was the problem of the disintegration of the Muslim world due to colonization by European powers and internal divisions created by Arab revolts. For this reason, both traditionalists and pro-Ottoman modernists on the caliphal periphery often resorted to the strategy of Islamic unity around the Ottoman flag.

Promoting Islamic unity (İttihad-ı İslam)

The first half of the 19th century had been a period when the economic, military, and political challenges posed by European powers were intensely felt by Istanbul, which then had to start many secularizing reforms as concessions to Europeans, such as the *Tanzimat* Reforms (see Chapter 2). Abdülhamid II emphasized economic modernization to centralize the state; in fact, his reign witnessed the fastest and most fundamental economic and technological transformation in the Middle East until the 1950s. He also de-emphasized secular reforms, slowing down the pace of secularization. At the beginning of his reign, the Ottoman Empire lost the western Balkans (Serbia, Romania and Montenegro) and some of eastern Anatolia, as well as Cyprus (1878). He also had to deal with many domestic uprisings, most of which were started by non-Muslim minorities within the empire, such as Armenians (1894) and Cretans (1896). He therefore tried to keep the territories inhabited by Muslim populations, pursuing the policy of appealing to non-Turkish Muslims emphasizing the Ottoman Caliphate (Eraslan 1995). To achieve this, he not only developed good relations with the leaders of other countries with large Muslim populations, such as India, but also emphasized the development of the Holy Land (the *Hijaz*) and facilitated the annual pilgrimage, which made him popular among the Muslim public (Öke 1999: 12–13; Karpat 2001: 230–231). He successfully used, as mentioned above, transportation technology (i.e., the *Hijaz* railway), making it possible for millions of Muslims to come together and witness the caliph's services to holy shrines. Moreover, by facilitating communication (via telegraph lines) and transportation between Istanbul and the *Hijaz*, he intended to further centralize the empire. He also made use of the media, financing many publications (journals, books, newspapers, etc.) in Turkish, Arabic, Urdu and French to elevate the political awareness of Muslims against European imperialism and foster the Caliphate's public image (Landau 1990: 55–64).

During the post-Hamidian period (1908–1922), when the CUP was mostly in power, Islamic unity was not emphasized; but the CUP leadership tried, though unsuccessfully, to revive it during World War I. Accordingly, many Ottoman politicians and intellectuals stressed the significance of allying Muslims around the Caliphate, which they conceived as the only solution to one of the biggest crises in the history of the *ummah*. For them, the Caliphate represented the only institution that was capable of uniting diverse Muslim peoples. Thus, as in Abdülhamid II's time, they insisted that *İttihad-ı İslam* was possible only through the revival of a strong Caliphate. However, unlike Abdülhamid II, who had not had significant problems with the empire's Muslim subjects, this time the Sublime Porte also had to deal with domestic problems caused by Arab revolts pursuing secession from the empire, most notably by the Hashemite revolt led by Sharif Hussein (1916–1918), as well as the European occupation of Muslim-populated territories in North Africa.

Therefore, the main factor that created the discourse of Muslim rapprochment in this period was World War I, which also led to territorial divisions within the empire. Before the crisis reached its peak with the Great War, domestic revolts were not a major source of concern in terms of Islamic unity. For example, when the Zaydi revolt against Istanbul started in Yemen in 1911, a group of pro-Ottoman Yemeni *ulema* published a declaration that was disseminated by the government in Istanbul against the insurgent tribes. The declaration did not mention Islamic unity, but instead downplayed the revolt as a local problem: "No doubt our powerful Ottoman state is able to put out the fire of disorder in Yemen with a slight effort today. Yet [the caliph] is generously showing mercy and compassion for you" (al-Yemeni 1911: 430). This indicates that the disintegration of the Middle East was not perceived as a serious problem until a major shock came in the form of the Great War; instead, the Ottomans were mostly busy with the loss of European territories between 1912 and 1914. With the start of the war, however, they immediately began to spread the message of unity all over the Arab world with financial and media support provided by the CUP government. Like Abdülhamid II, the CUP sponsored the publication and dissemination of journals, pamphlets and books in the Muslim world and even in Europe as of early 1915. This production and dissemination of the Ottomanist message was developed mostly in response to British, French, Italian, and Arab nationalist propaganda, spread mainly by newspapers and publicity bureaus, in the Muslim world (see above).

Pro-Ottoman actors employed four primary discursive techniques in their discussions regarding the unity of the Muslim world in relation to their view of the Caliphate. First, the traditionalists made a connection between the theological principle of God's oneness/unity (*tawhid*) and the political unity of Muslims. The second technique, employed by both traditionalists and modernists, entailed presenting Islamic unity as dependent on the well being of the Ottoman Empire. The third, also deployed by both groups, involved questioning the role of European imperialists, particularly that of Britain, in the disintegration of the Muslim polity and possible solutions to this problem. Finally, some intellectuals compared and contrasted the Sunni and Shia theological traditions within the context of Islamic unity (this also has implications for recent debates concerning divisions between Sunni and Shia Muslims, which has become a major political problem as a result of the ongoing Iraq war).

The discursive technique of relating Muslims' unity to Islamic theology constituted the religious dimension of traditionalists' strategy of *İttihad-ı İslam*. In the context of World War I, they all argued that the political unity of the Muslim world was a situation that was desired, even commanded, by God (e.g., Yafi 1916: 165). They maintained that the notion of *tawhid*, the most important theological principle in Islam, directly implied the necessity of the political unity of Muslim peoples (al-Tunusi 1916a: 152; al-Ubeydi 1916: 179–180; Azad 1920: 120). Within this framework, al-Tunusi (1916a: 153–155) formulated eight principles of Islamic unity:

1 believing in and surrendering to the will of one single God (Allah);
2 internalizing the same set of moral principles;

3   showing respect to all prophets of God without any distinction;

4   coming together under the authority of the legitimate caliph, which was mandatory for all believers;

5   making alliances with non-Muslims on the basis of justice and mutual interest;

6   defending Islam and Muslims against enemies;

7   firmly believing that obedience to the caliph ("who is now his Excellency Ghazi Mehmed Resad V") was mandated by God and that disobedience to him would mean disrespect for Allah and His Messenger;

8   believing that Muslims were like an organic body which would suffer as a whole when one of its organs suffered.[35]

Furthermore, as mentioned above, the Indian traditionalists, who were alarmed by the British invasion of the *Hijaz* at the end of World War I, emphasized the significance of the holy shrines, particularly the Ka'ba and the pilgrimage to it, as symbols of Islamic unity, which could only be protected by the (Ottoman) Caliphate (Ansari 1919: 376; Ajmal Khan, quoted in Kidwai 1919: 385; Azad 1920: 121).

Traditionalists also often drew attention to the *theoretical* inter-relationships between Islamic unity and the Caliphate. They argued that maintaining and protecting the political unity of Muslims was one of the major duties of the Caliph (Safayihi 1915: 73), and at the same time it was the only institution that could perform this duty. Thus, they frequently linked Islamic unity to the survival of the existing Caliphate, arguing that a unified Muslim polity, which was required by Islam, required the existence of one single caliph (Safayihi 1915: 79; al-Tunusi 1916a: 154; al-Ubeydi 1916: 180; Kidwai 1919: 352). The message here was clearly addressed to the British, French, and Italian authorities, as well as Arab nationalists, who were attempting to weaken the Ottoman Caliphate:

> As for the wisdom behind religion's decree for the necessity of a sultan, this implies, first of all, the existence and unity of Allah. [Similarly,] the impossibility of safety and order in a country under two rulers also indicates the fallacy of the idea of the universe being governed by multiple gods. Likewise, Muslims' general interest and prosperity depend upon their ability to come together around one single caliph, and upon much needed mutual cooperation. The multiplicity [of caliphs] will destroy this order. Without a caliph, none of the conditions necessary to maintain order will suffice.
>
> (Safayihi 1915: 79)

The second major technique employed by the modernists involved connecting Islamic unity directly to the Ottoman Empire: the former, they argued, could only be achieved under the auspices of the Turkish empire, which was the protector of the Islamic Caliphate. Abdülhamid II's somewhat influential pursuit of Islamic unity that had fundamentally shaped Ottoman foreign policy for approximately 30 years formed the background of this argument for some modernists – as well as for all traditionalists. For example, Ali Fahmi Muhammad (1870–1926), an Egyptian politician (a founder of the pro-Ottoman "Homeland Party"), wrote a series of articles in 1910 and 1911 that would later be published in book form by the "Egyptian Ottoman Club" (*Club Ottoman Caire*) to defend the Ottoman Caliphate and Islamic unity, even though Abdülhamid II was no longer on the throne (Kara 2003b: 13). Despite his being an anti-CUP intellectual (he opposed the Young Turks over their deposition of Abdülhamid), he nevertheless defended the existing Ottoman government against both British and Arab nationalist propaganda in Egypt. Ali Fahmi maintained that Islamic unity was for him a policy that did not have any aspirations against non-Muslim populations or European states, but rather aimed to improve the political and economic conditions of Muslims.[36] This was only possible through a strong Ottoman Caliphate. In order to explain the "true nature" of Islamic unity, he described the activities of the London-based "Association of Islamic Unity," the first organization in Europe (founded in 1903) under this name, which mainly worked toward economic and cultural co-operation among Muslim countries (Kara 2003b: 14). After discussing its peaceful principles, Ali Fahmi said the organization should be politicized by adding a few more principles, particularly "supporting the Ottoman Caliphate," "recognition of it by Muslim governments as the leader of the Muslim world and as the 'Great Caliphate'," and "the Ottoman Empire being responsible to work against the oppression of Muslims by European colonizers" (1911: 94). Moreover, arguing that non-Turkish Muslims all had a sense of loyalty to the Ottoman Empire ("the state that belongs to us and we to it"), being linked to it through the Caliphate, he listed the reasons the Ottoman Caliphate was indispensible for Islamic unity:

> The Ottoman State is the strongest of all Muslim states today, and it will remain so in the future as well. Also, it is the protector of the Holy Land and shrines (*al-Haramayn*) and *Bayt al-Maqdis* ["House of the Holiness," i.e., Jerusalem]. The Ottomans also had the right to inherit the Caliphate from their ancestors; it must remain in their hands for the sake of public interest as well.
>
> (Ali Fahmi 1911: 96–97)[37]

A similar argument was made by another North African intellectual (and Islamic scholar), Abdulaziz Jawish (1876–1929), who was also an activist on behalf of the Ottoman government during World War I in North Africa and Germany, publishing books and journals in favor of rallying Muslims around the Ottoman sultan-caliph. Defending the Ottoman Caliphate "against the claims made in the British and French newspapers regarding the Islamic Caliphate," he wrote a book on the subject in the same year that Sharif Hussein's Arab revolt started. The first topic he discussed in his book was Islamic unity, which he quickly tied to the Ottoman Empire, arguing that the former was predicated upon the leadership (and survival) of the latter. He then called his fellow Muslims to "wake up" and support the Ottomans in the ongoing war:

The people of Muslim countries [should] wake up from the deep sleep that they have been in by realizing the fact that if it was not for the Ottomans, their political existence would come to an end and sink into oblivion, just like the past generations that are gone now. They [have to] unite around the principle of holding fast to this solid rope that is the Ottoman Caliphate.

(1916: 245)

The activities and publications of all traditionalists (and most modernists) were implicitly or explicitly aimed at supporting the Ottoman Caliphate. Many of them did this by making explicit connections between the Caliphate and the Ottoman Empire, as its embodiment. According to many Ottoman supporters, just as the integration of the Muslim world depended on the Caliphate, the survival of the latter was predicated upon the existence of the Ottoman Empire. This view was shared by both Arab and Indian Muslim intellectuals:

The Islamic Caliphate is the religious spirit in a political body. And this body is the Ottoman Empire. [It follows that] if, God forbid, the empire was destroyed, the Caliphate would cease to exist, too.

(al-Ubeydi 1916: 211)

Turkey's future is an extremely important matter that directly concerns us, Indian Muslims, because both the Caliphate and the guardianship of the holy shrines of Islam are closely related to it.

(Ansari 1919: 388)

Furthermore, he argued, the claim made by imperialists and Arab nationalists that the Ottoman Caliphate was illegitimate had no grounds because the latter was based on all four of the legitimate methods of becoming caliph, though even one would have been sufficient: election (by the *Ahl al-hal wa al-'aqd*), appointment (by the previous Caliph), receiving the allegiance of the *ummah*, and political power. These were the exact same preconditions stipulated by the Turkish traditionalists (e.g., İsmail Hakkı 1910: 438; Mustafa Zihni 1911: 113; see Chapter 4).

Having established the legitimacy and religious significance of the Ottoman Caliphate, traditionalists went on to condemn the Arab rebels (and imperialist powers) that were working to divide and destroy the empire. They warned that attacking the Ottomans would mean attacking the Caliphate, and thus assaulting Islam itself, which would not be accepted by Muslims around the world (Said Halim Pasha 2000[1920]: 404). Likewise, it was a religious duty of every Muslim to resist both colonization and insurgence (by Sharif Hussein and others) by responding to the caliph-sultan's call for *jihad* and joining the Caliphate's army (Safayihi 1915: 140; al-Tunusi 1916a: 150, 1916b: 426; Azad 1920: 105). In fact, that Muslims from different parts of the world had politically and financially supported the empire during World War I (even after the war had been lost) showed that they saw the Ottoman caliph as their true leader (Muhyiddin

Baha 1915: 403; al-Tunusi 1916b: 426; Said Halim Pasha 2000[1920]: 406). These arguments indicate that the Caliphate to some extent enjoyed its ideological power vis-à-vis Arab separatism and European imperialism, even though its political, economic, and military power was far from being strong.

A third pro-Ottoman discursive technique entailed questioning the role of European imperialists, particularly that of Britain, in creating obstacles to Islamic unity. This technique, deployed by both traditionalists and modernists, constituted the second element of the political dimension of their discourse on the relationship between Muslim unity and the Caliphate. While they saw the lack of political unity among Muslim states as the most important reason for the "backwardness" of the Muslim world (e.g., al-Ubeydi 1916: 178; Jawish 1916: 245), they did not blame the Caliphate for this development. Instead, they blamed European intruders, particularly Britain, for dividing Muslim governments and turning them against each other and Arab nationalists for their separatist ambitions (see Ali Fahmi 1911: 96–97; Kidwai 1919: 347–349; Ajmal Khan, quoted in Kidwai 1919: 385; Said Halim Pasha 2000[1920]: 405).[38]

Many Ottoman loyalists focused on how Britain and other European powers had not kept their promises to the Ottomans and other Muslims. For example, in his call for the British government to respect the territorial integrity of the Ottoman Empire at the end of World War I, the Indian Muslim intellectual Mushir Kidwai (1919: 347–349) argued that Europeans and Britain had long pressured Ottoman Empire for reforms (regarding the constitutional regime, equality for Christians, accommodating Jews, etc.) but then tried to divide and destroy it (by encouraging Arabs and Christians to rise up against the empire) instead of supporting its reforms. The president of the Muslim League of India, Dr. Mukhtar Ansari, was much more critical of European imperialism. In his address at the League's 1919 convention, he harshly criticized British policy in the Middle East:

> Now is the time for us Muslims to demand from the nation's representatives, in whose hands the fate of the British Empire has been entrusted, to perform their duties for Indian Muslims. We all know how Islam lost much of its material power in the second half of the 19th century. Each new generation has witnessed the gradual disintegration of the Islamic lands. To justify this, [the imperialists] have put forward a number of excuses, and tried to present reasonable explanations. They invented grand principles of politics to cover up their hostile and intrusive ambitions, and instrumentally used basic principles of humanity in order to justify their acts of aggression and usurpation in the Muslim world. They even employed the [idea of] "white man's burden" to oppress innocent Muslims. However, these seemingly harmless beliefs and high principles, when insulated from all the grandiose discourse, will reveal the fact that [our] calamities are created either by the general hatred towards the people of Islam or by the animosity and rapacity of European statesmen.
>
> (Ansari 1919: 375)

Most Islamic governments of the world today have fallen prey for the imperialist Christian states of Europe, despite the latter's earlier promise that they would respect and recognize the freedom of small countries. Muslim countries like Morocco, Tunisia, Algeria and even Egypt and Iran exemplify the inauspicious and unjustified aggression of the powerful against the powerless.

(p. 388)

Similarly, the entire concluding chapter of Arab scholar al-Ubeydi's book on the Caliphate discussed how Britain was leading other Western countries in hatred and enmity towards Muslims. The author enumerated fourteen different "acts of aggression and deception by the British government," which, he argued, had resulted in the political, ideological, and economic exploitation of the Muslim world (1916: 218–226).

Supporters of the caliphal center on the periphery also saw the rise of Arab nationalism (and separatist movements) as a direct consequence of European imperialism. When the Zaydi (Shia) governor Yahya started his revolt in Yemen in 1911, which resulted in concessions by Istanbul that practically made Yemen an autonomous region, the Egyptian politician Ali Fahmi said the British government was behind the revolt, arguing that this was part of the British "divide and rule" policy in the Middle East. He also blamed the British for the emergence of the Arab Caliphate movement and for seducing its intellectual leader Abdurrahman al-Kawakibi (d. 1902), otherwise "an independent thinker and a respected scholar":

Had this independent thinker thoroughly reviewed his political vision, he would have seen that the application of his efforts would deeply harm the Muslim world in general and the Middle East in particular. The British are [very good] at seducing naïve scholars like him, who did not have a sound political judgment and was not familiar with particular conditions [of the region].... [The Ottoman Caliphate] has no rival to fear today. But foreign governments create divisions among us and agitate us against each other in order to undermine the central authority and disrupt our unity.

(Ali Fahmi 1911: 96–97)

Therefore, a major source of concern – and an important target – for many pro-Ottoman actors was Arab nationalism in general, and the Arab Caliphate movement in particular. They believed that the separatist movements in the Middle East were agitated by Britain, France, and Italy and essentially intended to undermine the integration of the Muslim *ummah* beyond the Ottoman Empire. When the Arab revolt was started by Sharif Hussein in 1916, Abdulaziz Jawish, a modernist, reacted like many traditionalists of the time by accusing the British of agitating Arab Muslims to rebel illegally against their own government. Seeing the leaders of the revolt as puppets of the imperialists, he argued that both the principle of Islamic unity and various prophetic *hadith*s required that

Muslims unite under the leadership of the legitimate caliph, who, at the time, was Ottoman Sultan Mehmed V (1916: 245). Jawish further claimed that the alternative caliphs, Sharif Hussein and King Yussuf, who claimed to be descendants of the Prophet, were actually the imperialists' puppets. He concluded that the only legitimate Caliphate was that of the Ottoman sultan, who was politically and militarily powerful enough to unite the Muslim world:

> Muslims know that Mehmed V is not like the puppets appointed and protected by France in the West [Northern Africa] and Britain in Egypt as caliphs of Muslims; rather, he is the sultan son of sultans and the king of all Muslims. The enemy does not know that the real descendants of the Prophet are those who know best who is the well-deserved caliph on earth.
>
> (1916: 255)

Similarly, when Sharif Hussein, who was preparing to declare his independence from the Ottoman Empire after the war was over, was invited to the Paris Peace Conference (1919) as the "King of the *Hijaz*," Mahmud Nedim Maan, a former Ottoman army officer in *Hijaz*, wrote a short pamphlet protesting Hussein's aspirations for creating a "dynastic kingdom" in the Arabian Peninsula. Without defending the Ottoman dynasty (for he was a supporter of democracy and opposed monarchy), Mahmud Nedim argued that Sharif Hussein had been deceived by the British into attempting to establish an Arab kingdom in the Holy Land, which constituted a great sin, for all dynastic regimes were built upon oppression, and the existence of an oppressive regime in the Holy Land was unacceptable for Muslims. Moreover, the fact that Hussein had prosecuted the Ottoman soldiers fighting in the Holy Land against the imperialists during World War I (which he himself had witnessed) was concrete evidence of such oppression (Mahmud Nedim 1919: 297–299).

The Ottoman loyalists thus believed that the Arab Caliphate movement was part of an imperialist plan designed to destroy Islamic unity and the Caliphate. Some of them, such as the Indian intellectual and activist Syed Mahmud (1921: 61–62), argued that weakening the Caliphate and thereby dividing the Muslim world was the main purpose of the infamous "Eastern Question" that had formed the basis of the foreign policies of European powers since the mid-19th century. However, they also claimed that the Ottoman Caliphate, particularly during the reign of Abdülhamid II, had awakened Muslims against the intrusions of the colonialists (al-Tunusi 1913: 417; al-Ubeydi 1916: 180; Said Halim Pasha 2000[1920]: 405). For example, the loyalty of non-Turkish (Indian and Arab) Muslims to the Ottoman Caliphate was not diminished by the impact of the Greek insurgency that had led to the secession of Greece with Britain's support in 1896 (Nadvi 1921: 170), nor by World War I despite the efforts by the British government and Sharif Hussein, and that it was the British government itself that had irreversibly united Muslims by invading Istanbul in 1918 (Said Halim Pasha 2000[1920]: 407). The most recent example of Muslim loyalty to the Ottoman sultan was the fact that Amanullah Khan, the sultan of Afghanistan, had rejected the title of caliph offered by the British and instead strongly voiced his support and loyalty to the Ottoman Caliphate (Syed Mahmud 1921: 55–56). Therefore, the desired Islamic unity was only possible through the survival and strengthening of the Ottoman Caliphate: "The Islamic Caliphate is dependent on the Ottoman Empire, both religiously and politically" (al-Ubeydi 1916: 206; cf. Ansari 1919: 388). Moreover, supporters of the Caliphate who strongly opposed the claims of alternative caliphs such as Sharif Hussein, who were agitated by European imperialists, proposed that Muslim rulers in remote regions such as North Africa and India be called "emirs" (governors) of the Ottoman caliph-sultan:

The caliph's only concern is the unity of Muslims. And without him, local rulers cannot come together. He himself is not supposed to rule such a broad territory. [By] necessity,... we have had many honorable rulers ... appointed by caliphs since the beginning of Islam. Now, rulers are appointed by the people, which is also acceptable. But there can only be one single Caliph...

(Safayihi 1915: 73; cf. Mustafa Zihni 1911: 183)

As for the local Islamic rulers, they are called commander (*emir*), ruler (*melik*), sultan, monarch (*hükümdar*) or king (*padişah*), but not caliph. There is only one single caliph; and there may be multiple leaders, rulers, monarchs, and kings.

(İsmail Hakkı 1910: 443)[39]

A final traditionalist technique deployed as an element of the discourse of *İttihad-ı İslam* involved comparing the views on the Caliphate of the two major theological traditions within Islamic civilization, the Sunni and Shia schools. As mentioned in Chapter 3, both Iran and the Ottoman Empire experienced constitutional revolutions almost simultaneously – in 1906 and 1908, respectively. Both before and after the revolutions, the Sunni and Shia *ulema*/intellectuals were aware of the developments in each other's countries and, therefore, influenced each other (Cleveland 2000: 125–139; Sohrabi 1995). In particular, the Iranian constitutionalist movement had largely been inspired by the Ottoman constitution of 1876 and the Young Turks of the Hamidian era (Afary 2005: 346; cf. Lambton 1993). In a context in which the Qajar government in Iran was greatly weakened by both Russian imperialism and the Shia *ulema* (Algar 1969), some of the pro-Ottoman traditionalists also discussed the need for unity between the two countries by addressing their counterparts in Iran. Though they called for political unity between the two largest sects of Islam on the basis of being part of the same *ummah*, they stipulated that this was only possible under the leadership of the Ottoman Caliphate (Mustafa Zihni 1911: 152; Syed Mahmud 1921: 45).

Some traditionalists' comparisons between the Sunni and Shia schools were critical of the latter (e.g., Mustafa Zihni 1911; Ömer Lütfi 1912) whereas others were more tolerant and inclusive (e.g., Syed Mahmud 1921). Mahmud argued that there were no real differences between the two schools in terms of their views of the Caliphate, except for the method of the election of caliphs (1921: 44). He added, however, that though Ali, the fourth caliph, and his supporters had not agreed with the way Abu Bakr and others were elected or appointed, they nevertheless had given their allegiance to them, which had made them legitimate for all the Shia. He thus concluded that "there can be no question of difference between these two great sects of Islam as to the established fact of the Ottoman Khilafat" (p. 45). Mahmud's more inclusive approach toward the Shia was also reflected in the fact that in his discussion on the preconditions for the Caliphate, the third and fifth requirements (guardianship of holy shrines and possession of the sacred relics) also included Karbala, the third city of pilgrimage for the Shia (in addition to Mecca and Medina), and Ali's flag, also sacred for the Shia (pp. 34–37). Some traditionalists, on the other hand, were more critical of the Shia: while Ömer Lütfi (1912: 234) pointed to the doctrinal differences between the Sunni and Shia theories of the Caliphate, Mustafa Zihni (1911: 136–151) argued that the historical sectarian disputes that had divided Muslims were actually political (as opposed to doctrinal) differences, and that the Shia had used religion as a tool in these political disputes and thereby politicized it. This difference of attitude between the Turkish critics and the Indian intellectual Syed Mahmud was probably related to the political context of the period of their writing and the change in the (Ottoman) Caliphate's power: Those critical of the Shia's reluctance to recognize the Sunni Caliphate were both Turkish bureaucrats working (in 1909) for Abdülhamid II, who still enjoyed some power despite the Young Turk revolution, whereas Syed Mahmud wrote his book primarily for the British audience and in the desperate context (for Muslims) of the post-World War I period.

In conclusion, in the discursive struggle between the supporters of the Ottoman Caliphate and the institution's European and Arab nationalist critics, one of the most important problems for the former group was Islamic unity, which became an urgent matter during World War I. In order to defend the Caliphate, pro-Ottoman actors argued that the *İttihad-ı İslam*, which they connected with theological principle of God's unity (*tawhid*), was only possible under the Ottoman Caliphate, and blamed European imperialism for the existing challenges that Muslims faced. What is significant in these arguments regarding Islamic (dis)unity is that Ottomanist intellectuals and politicians never blamed Islam or the caliph for the disintegration of the Muslim world. This implies a widespread and strong confidence, especially among traditionalists, in their own world view and the traditional institutions of Islamic civilization, particularly the Caliphate. This self-confidenceformed the background of their attitude not only toward the issue of Islamic unity, but also to all other political problems. It was also one of the traditionalists' most distinguishing features, particularly vis-à-vis secularists, whose discourses demonstrate, as we shall see in the next chapter, a relative lack of self-confidence in their comparisons between Islamic and Western civilizations. Anti-secularists thus often compared Islam with the West to demonstrate the superiority of Islam over Western values and institutions.

Contrasting Islam with the West

The traditionalist and modernist Islamist strategy of contrasting Western and Islamic civilizations was aimed at defending Islam in general and the Ottoman Caliphate in particular. I have already referred in Chapter 2 to the fact that, as the pace of modernization increased in the 18th and 19th centuries, along with more military defeats and local revolts as well as growing economic problems, the Ottoman political and intellectual elites increasingly made references to the West. The main discursive technique employed in these references was that of "adopting only what is good, and therefore Islamic, from the West." This was also the main technique used by Islamists during the Second Constitutional Period. The idea of selective appropriation, i.e., receiving only what is good and leaving what is bad, implied that there were a lot of culturally inappropriate things in the West that should be avoided. Moreover, they used this technique with a twist: They emphasized the superiority of Islamic civilization over the West more than they identified what was good in the latter. A second discursive technique Islamists deployed was to make selective references to Western/European intellectuals who had made positive remarks about Muslims in order to universalize their own arguments. These two techniques functioned complimentarily and were often deployed as part of the same specific arguments to defend the Ottoman Caliphate. Arab scholars such as Safayihi and al-Ubeydi sometimes employed these techniques to reassure their fellow Muslims that the causes of these challenges had nothing to do with Islam, but that the solutions had to be derived from Islam. At other times they targeted European critics to counter their allegations, as did Ali Fahmi Muhammad, by showing that it was actually the West that should be blamed for creating problems for Muslims. This was part of their effort to maintain the perfection and purity of their religion despite the many challenges that the Muslim world faced militarily, politically, and economically.

Superiority of Islam over the West

Islamists assumed that, since Islam was perfect, it did not need a major revision or novel forms of religious or political principles. However, given the challenging circumstances, they also saw the need for new institutions, such as the constitution and parliament, though they framed this need in Islamic terms, a strategy that was more apparent among modernist Islamists. Furthermore, unlike secularists, Islamists never agreed to replace Islamic institutions *in toto*, including, first and foremost, the Caliphate.

Within this framework, they compared Islam with the West in terms of both the theoretical and practical aspects of political institutions. On the theoretical level, Tunisian traditionalist Safayihi (1915: 49–52), for example, classified existing regimes into two categories: despotic and political. The former (*mulk al-ghaleb wa al-qahr*) was based on the personal power and will of a single tyrant, who often experienced problems keeping his subjects together due to the oppressive nature of his regime. The latter (*mulk al-siyasi*) was based on "rational laws" obeyed by all citizens. However, since most political regimes were based on laws made by human beings, they were necessarily imperfect. The Caliphate, on the other hand, was a "political" regime that was based on laws created by God. Therefore, unlike both despotic and political regimes in the West, which were all defective, the Caliphate was a perfect form of government that helped its citizens live in peace and harmony:

> The rules of the *sharia* are never in conflict with rational laws, nor is it possible, if *sharia* rules are applied properly, to suffer division, tension, or disintegration. For these rules are both suitable for their [the believers'] societies, and approved by them.... Such a society does not need anything other than a leader who applies these rules with justice, who is the caliph and his administrators, such as judges.
>
> (Safayihi 1915: 50)

Modernist intellectual and politician Ali Fahmi Muhammad's less abstract comparison between Islamic and Western civilizations was related to war and peace. He maintained that, unlike Europe, Islam was a religion of peace, with no colonial history of which to be ashamed (1911: 84). He also argued, referring to the French Revolution's slogans of *liberté*, *égalité*, and *fraternité*, that these democratic principles actually had their roots in Islam:

> [Islam is] a religion that makes a king and his subjects equal to one another.... If today we have religious, political, or social liberties, equality, and brotherhood, that is because they are taken from the Qur'an and Islam.... We cannot deny, however, that some Muslims do inappropriate things; these must be seen as stemming from their own personal moral decadence, rather than their faith.
>
> (1911: 88–89; cf. Kidwai 1919: 350)

Ali Fahmi also referred to the Lahey Conference and the Permanent Court of International Justice (founded in 1921 at The Hague, predecessor of the current International Court of Justice) that European countries were trying to establish, saying that the principles declared by the conference were "still not as progressive as the civilizing and humane principles that Islam brought 13 centuries ago" (p. 85). He then cited several Qur'anic verses and *hadith*s about love, brotherhood and peace (pp. 86–87). Moreover, citing several examples of religious wars in the West and atrocities committed by the Catholic and Protestant churches against each other's adherents, as well as non-Christians, he concluded that "the best religion is Islam" (p. 92) – which is also an allusion to a Qur'anic verse (3/19).

Similarly, traditionalist Mustafa Zihni (1911: 114–117) argued that Europeans had only recently discovered democracy and that the establishment of constitutional and parliamentary regimes in the West was only possible through a long and violent process of wars and massacres. Islam, on the other hand, already included the principle of "consultation" (*meşveret*), and since Islamic government was also based on the fundamental principle of justice, despotic regimes did not last long in Islamic history. Unlike in the West, he argued, in Muslim history there had not been much need for continuous uprisings and bloodbaths to get rid of tyrannical rulers and return to Islamic governments based on the principles of consultation and justice. Therefore, Islam naturally included the necessary mechanisms to prevent despotism (Mustafa Zihni 1911: 115). He added that the parliamentary system, as it was found in Europe, had its own pitfalls in terms of adequately reflecting the will of "the people" in politics, but that it was nevertheless useful in terms of pre-empting the potential tyranny of individual rulers (p. 116). While in the West this system was justified only on such rational/political grounds, Islam required a constitutional system both religiously and politically:

> In the Islamic religion, the Caliphate is an important and sacred institution established by the Holy Prophet (peace be upon him) in order to protect and manage the collective and individual rights of the members of the Islamic *ummah* in line with the divine laws [of God]. And since it [the Caliphate] is based on the principle of consultation, establishing this principle is a central religious requirement for us. [Therefore,] it is not for us simply a necessity derived from rational considerations – as in Europe.
>
> (Mustafa Zihni 1911: 117)

Likewise, Syed Mahmud (1921: 38) compared the Caliphate to the Roman Empire in that within both systems "each successor [is] chosen from amongst the people by common consent." He criticized Rome, however, for separating religion and politics: "Early Greek thought or early Roman thought would never have comprehended [the unity of Church and state]" (p. 40). For him, the best system, exemplified by the Caliphate, was one that included the unification of powers, rather than their separation. On a more empirical level, Yafi, a journalist living in Beirut, where there was a large non-Muslim minority, argued that throughout Ottoman and Islamic history non-Muslims had always been treated with dignity and respect and protected by Muslim administrations, unlike Western governments that oppressed Muslim minorities and tortured prisoners of war during World War I (1916: 168–170). The Indian intellectual Azad (1920: 106) repeated the view that until the end of the 16th century the Turks were far superior to Europeans in science, transportation, military technology, security, health administration etc. though he acknowledged that the situation had since changed.[40] As already implied, it was both traditionalist and modernist Islamists who emphasized the superiority of Islamic institutions over Western ones. Similar to the traditionalists and modernist Ali Fahmi, who all defended the Ottoman Caliphate, one of its most vocal opponents, Rashid Rida, too, emphasized the Islamic Caliphate's superiority over Western parliamentary democracy, arguing that the former was the best form of government the humanity had ever known, and that Europeans had learned the bases of constitutional government from Saladin (Soage 2008: 14, 20).

Selective references to Western intelligentsia

In addition to comparing Islam and the West, traditionalists and modernists also deployed the discursive technique of making selective references to the Western intelligentsia, which they thought was useful because it helped to universalize their views on politics in Islam in general, and the Ottoman Caliphate, in particular. This is a technique to which virtually all actors involved in this political struggle would resort, and Islamists were no exception. Targeting the European audience in particular, they often made references to certain Western authors and newspapers when they found an argument that was supportive of their own views. They usually employed this technique as a compliment to the first one, i.e., either when criticizing European imperialism or proving the superiority of Islamic civilization over the West. For example, Safayihi (1915: 135) referred to the French historian and politician Gabriel Hanatoux's book (*Turkey and the Upcoming War*), in which the author "confessed" that the main purpose of European politicians was to divide the Muslim world. Similarly, Azad (1920: 106) referred to four Western historians (Draper, Edward Creasy, Kingendom, and Clifford) to prove the superior qualities of the Turks in relation to their above-mentioned scientific, administrative, and organizational skills. Likewise, while Nadvi (1921: 152) thanked historian Edward Thomas for stressing the importance of the Caliphate for Indian Muslims, Syed Mahmud (1921: 46), in his criticism of Sharif Hussein, quoted the British diplomat Wilfred S. Blunt, who had said that Muslims would never follow a ruler who was a puppet of non-Muslim states. He also quoted Lane-Poole, "the well-known British historian," to support his claim that the entire Muslim world, including the Far East, had recognized the Caliphate of Selim I in the 16th century (p. 51).

Similarly, modernist Ali Fahmi Muhammad (1911) cited in his book, which he wrote to defend Islam and the Ottoman Caliphate, several leading orientalists of the time, including John Davenport, Edward Gibbon, and "another scholar" who had written an article titled "East and West," all of whom had said that Islam was the most advanced religion because it encouraged equality, science, and progress, as well as governance based on consultation (1911: 80–81). He also referred to the tripartite motto of the French Revolution, *liberté, égalité*, and *fraternité*, saying that the origins of these ideas were actually to be found in Islam, citing the British orientalist E. Bosworth-Smith and the Scottish William and Robert Chambers' *Chambers's Encyclopaedia* to prove this claim (pp. 88–89). Moreover, he quoted several European authors, including Ernest Renan, a certain Bishop Goodman, Robert N. Cust, and others to demonstrate with historical examples that it was Christianity, not Islam, that produced religious intolerance, hatred, and persecution (pp. 89–91):

> [Christians, unlike Muslims,] consider it legitimate to use every means that will bring them victory in converting other religions' followers through their missionary activities. Because this mission is obligatory for them, when their peaceful methods of spreading their faith fail, they try to realize their

aim by relying on Christian states' weapons and forces. It is with these heinous methods that they "sublimate" the glory of Christian civilization.

(Ali Fahmi 1911: 91)

Finally, he also cited some negative views on Islam by European authors, including "Daniel, Luther, Melanchthon, and Herbold," as well as Gabriel Hanatoux (also referred to by Safayihi; see above) and the British politician Lord Cromer, who all blamed Islam for "Muslim backwardness." He added that such remarks from these figures (who were all somehow linked to politics, some of them being colonial administrators) were not a surprise for him, except for Martin Luther, who must have known what religious persecution really was; however, for Ali Fahmi, Luther's indulgence in politics made him attack Islam for political purposes, rather than speak the truth:

None of the critics of Islam – past or present – such as Hanatoux and Lord Cromer – have surprised me as much as Martin Luther did. For he was an independent-minded and honored thinker, and the founder of the Protestant religion under the Vatican's oppression in the Middle Ages. Yet, many intellectuals like him are blinded by political ambitions, which have penetrated their souls and inspired their [anti-Islamic] writings. Despite this, however, there are also those who admit the truth, whose views on Islam and the Holy Prophet (peace be upon him) I will quote below so that Arabic-speaking people can see that there are some honest people among our enemies as well.

(Ali Fahmi 1911: 80)

Finally, Arab nationalist Rashid Rida quoted several unnamed Europeans, who supported his conviction that Islam was superior to the West, including an English teacher who had been expelled from an Egyptian school for suggesting the compulsory teaching of Islam to all students, a German intellectual who had said that Europeans should erect the statues of Muawiya, who had prevented the Muslim conquest of the entire Euorope by deviating from the Rightly Guided Caliphs' path, and a British scholar who had suggested that if there were one single language for humanity, that would be Arabic (Soage 2008: 14–15). All these examples show how Islamists made selective references to Western sources in order to derive support from the "opposite side" for their comparisons between Islam and the West and make a stronger case for their own arguments.

Conclusion

The topic of this chapter has been the pro-Ottoman response to the challenge posed by Arab nationalism and alternative caliphate projects supported by European powers, as well as the military and political power relations that conditioned this challenge for the Caliphate before and during World War I. The debates over the Caliphate between pro-Ottoman actors and their Arab and

European opponents took place mainly on the caliphal periphery, i.e., the wider Middle East, including North Africa, the Arabian Peninsula, and India. Here both the parties of the political-ideological struggle and its themes and related discursive strategies were different from those in the caliphal center. In Istanbul, as discussed in Chapter 4, the power struggle was between the coalition of the secular bureaucracy and modernist Islamists, on the one hand, and the religious establishment, consisting of the caliph's Palace and the traditionalist *ulema*, on the other. On the periphery, however, the pro-CUP modernist intellectuals and politicians joined the traditionalist *ulema* in their fight against Arab nationalists and European imperialists. For this reason, they employed a different set of discursive strategies, such as emphasizing the legitimacy of the Ottoman caliph and the necessity of obedience to him, promoting Islamic unity and "demonstrating" Islam's (and the Caliphate's) superiority over the West, as well as more familiar strategies such as invoking the Qur'an and prophetic traditions. Their opponents, too, resorted to similar strategies, particularly making references to the sacred texts and history of Islam.

In my examination of this struggle, I have first presented the historical background of the relationship between European imperialism and the Caliphate from the beginning of the 19th century, including the role played by the latter during World War I (1914–1918), in which the Ottoman Empire sided with Germany and Austria against the Entente Powers (Britain, France, Russia, and Italy). I then discussed two specific cases in which European powers and Arab nationalist movements challenged the political and religious authority of the Ottoman Caliphate. First, I examined the "*Maghrib* Caliphate" in the context of French colonialism in North Africa, which was an incomplete project created by the French Foreign Ministry and its colonial administration in Morocco attempting to install an alternative, "Western" caliphate, for which they nominated Morocco's Sultan Yussuf (r. 1912–1927), against both the Ottoman caliph and potential Arab caliphates in the East. Second, as part of their colonial activities in the Middle East (and India), the British tried to install Sharif Hussein of Mecca (r. 1916–1924) as alternative to the 400-year old Ottoman Caliphate. Both projects were also rooted in the rising tide of Arab nationalism before and during World War I, as well as European imperialism in the region.

Historically, though Britain had initially supported the rise of Ottoman caliphal power throughout much of the 19th century (particularly against the imperialist ambitions of Russia and in order to portray itself as a defender of Islam), it turned against the Ottoman Caliphate beginning in 1877, seeing it as the biggest threat to its interests in colonies such as Egypt and India. Likewise, France severed its previously friendly relations with the Ottomans when it occupied Algeria in 1830, Tunisia in 1881 and Morocco in 1904. In response, both Abdülhamid II (r. 1876–1909) and the Young Turks (1908–1918) who deposed him co-operated with local resistance movements in North Africa, such as the Sanusi who fought against the Italians in Libya and against the French in Algeria and Morocco. In these power struggles Istanbul's main aim was to solidify its position as the center of the Caliphate and the protector of shrines in the Holy

Land. In World War I, too, the Ottomans used the caliph's ideological power – though not with much success – upon the request of Germany's Kaiser Wilhelm II, who offered them military and political aid in return for using the caliph's religious influence over Muslims in the British and French colonies.

Therefore, the Caliphate was at the center of the military, political, and ideological struggles in the Middle East between European imperialists and Arab nationalists, on the one hand, and the Ottoman Empire and its local supporters, on the other, during the last quarter of the 19th century and the first quarter of the 20th. European states, and Britain in particular, tried to get involved in every conflict between the caliphal center and the Arabs, always supporting one or another local Arab ruler (such as Ibn Saud and Sharif Hussein) against each other, as well as against the Ottoman sultan. At the end of these struggles, epitomized by World War I, the Ottoman Empire reached the verge of collapse, losing all of its territories in the Balkans and the Middle East – except for Anatolia – including the *Hijaz*, where Sharif Hussein ruled for a few years before he was defeated by Ibn Saud, who then founded Saudi Arabia.

During this process, in order to delegitimize the Ottoman Caliphate, its opponents put forward several arguments: that the Ottoman claim for the Caliphate was a recent phenomenon and was not recognized by most Muslims, and that the Ottomans had captured the Caliphate by force rather than consent. However, the Ottomans easily refuted these historical claims. The strongest anti-Ottoman argument was that they were not descendants of the Prophet Muhammad, which for Arab nationalists and Europeans was required for the Caliphate. In order to reinforce this argument, they used different discursive strategies, including, first and foremost, the use of sacred texts for justification. In particular, they invoked a prophetic tradition that mentioned the Quraysh tribe (to which the Prophet had belonged). The Ottomans responded to this by invoking other traditions that explicitly rejected any ethnic dimension to the Caliphate and by making references to Qur'anic verses. British and French propaganda, disseminated throughout the Middle East and India in many newspapers and books, influenced some local rulers (e.g., Khedive Ismail and Abbas II of Egypt, and Sharif Hussein) and modernist Muslim intellectuals (e.g., Abdur-rahman al-Kawakibi, Jamaluddin al-Afghani, Muhammad Abduh, Rashid Rida, and Ali Abdur-raziq), some of whom were leading Arab nationalists. Among the critics of the Ottoman Caliphate, two figures were particularly influential: Hussein and Rida. Neither of them, however, targeted the Ottoman Caliphate itself; rather, they blamed the Unionists for corrupting this highest politico-religious office in Islam. They agreed, however, that the Ottoman Caliphate, as a form of dynastic rule, was not a truly Islamic institution, and thus should be "returned" to Arabs, who had the religious right to it.

In defense of the existing Caliphate, Ottoman loyalists countered these attacks by employing different discursive strategies. They first established the legitimacy and religious significance of the Ottoman Caliphate with reference to Islamic texts, history, and intellectual tradition. They also insisted on obedience to the caliph-sultan as a religious duty of all believers, and then condemned the

Arab rebels and imperialist powers for plotting to divide and destroy the Caliphate. Third, they promoted Islamic unity in line with Sultan Abdülhamid's foreign policy strategy of *İttihad-ı İslam*, which they saw as the only way out of the crisis that had been undermining the integration of the Muslim world. Therefore, they presented the Ottoman Caliphate as their only chance against the looming disintegration of the *ummah*. Finally, they also compared and contrasted Islam with the West in order to defend the Ottoman Caliphate by selectively invoking European intellectuals and statesmen and demonstrating the superiority of Islam over the West.

Unlike in the debates in the caliphal center, as mentioned, traditionalist and modernist Islamists were not on the opposite sides in this debate: The two groups united against Europeans and Arab nationalists on the periphery in defense of the Ottoman Caliphate. Thus, unlike many Turkish modernists who tried to undermine the authority of the caliph in the center, many Arab modernists, such as Ali Fahmi and Abdulaziz Jawish, sided with Turkish, Arab, and Indian traditionalists, such as Mustafa Zihni, İsmail Hakkı, al-Tunusi, Safayihi, Nadvi, Kidwai, Ansari, and Syed Mahmud on the periphery. Their efforts to save the Caliphate failed, however. Following World War I, secularists, led by Mustafa Kemal, politically and militarily dominated the caliphal center and further undermined the caliph-sultan's power, ultimately destroying it completely. This was not, however, an easy process, for they faced a great opposition – both domestic and international – in their efforts to secularize the state and religion. The next episode of the power struggle over the Caliphate in the center was, therefore, between secularists and modernist Islamists.

6   Abolition of the Caliphate
Secular reform, religious justification (1919–1924)

Introduction

This chapter examines the process through which the Caliphate was brought to an end following the collapse of the Ottoman Empire in World War I. Here I focus on domestic political struggles within the caliphal center, Turkey, analyzing two cases in particular: the abolition of the Ottoman monarchy (1922) and that of the Caliphate itself (1924). After discussing the post-war politico-military context of the collapsing empire, I locate these two crucial events in their historical context and present a discourse analysis of the political struggle between the pro-Caliphate group (mostly consisting of modernist Islamists) and the anti-Caliphate, secularist group led by Mustafa Kemal, who emerged as the leader of the Turkish resistance against the Greek invasion of Anatolia between 1919 and 1922. I demonstrate that, though the secularists won the political and legal battle by destroying both Ottoman rule and the caliph's power, both groups extensively resorted to the meta-discursive strategy of deriving justification from Islam. In fact, the frequency and intensity of such Islamic legitimization could be said to be equal to, or at times even higher than, earlier periods.

Religious symbolism and rhetoric was extremely visible and abundant during the 1920–1923 period, when Turkish nationalists, who would later abolish the Caliphate, as well as Islamic law and institutions, needed to legitimize themselves in a struggle that the caliph (Mehmed VI) did not approve of and to receive financial, medical, and military help from the Muslim world. As Kara (2008) observes, one of the famous "consultation verses" (3/159) was inscribed behind the seat of the Turkish Grand National Assembly's (GNA) president, which was not the case in the *Meşrutiyet* era, and the *ulema* and sheikhs constituted the highest percentage of the deputies in the GNA's first term, which lasted three years and four months. The GNA president, Mustafa Kemal, also appointed two Sufi sheikhs as his vice presidents. His – and other secularists' – political discourse was truly "Islamic," albeit instrumentally, until at least mid-1923, less than a year before they abolished the Caliphate. During this time, they extensively deployed such familiar discursive strategies as invoking the sacred texts of Islam (the Qur'an and the prophetic traditions), and making references to Islamic history. They also enjoyed the strategic support, as Midhat Pasha had in the debates over the 1876 Constitution (see Chapter 2), of some of the *ulema*, particularly Seyyid Bey, who was a deputy between 1920 and 1923 and the minister of justice between 1923 and 1924, and Vehbi Efendi, who was the minister of religious affairs when the Ottoman monarchy was abolished. It was also a Sufi sheikh, Safvet Efendi, who prepared the proposal of the law that abolished the Caliphate. In both cases, Seyyid Bey was especially instrumental in framing Mustafa Kemal's secular moves in religious terms, using his extensive knowledge of Islamic law and theology.

The secularists' main discursive strategy was

i   reconstructing the Caliphate as a purely religious/spiritual authority; but they also employed several complementary strategies, including
ii   establishing the Islamicity of a two-tiered political system in which the Caliphate was separated from the monarchy,
iii elevating the Caliphate's status vis-à-vis the "un-Islamic" monarchy,
iv   redefining the Caliphate as an "un-Islamic" institution in contrast to the Islamic state of the GNA,
v   mixing an Islamic discourse with a (Turkish) nationalist one, and
vi   adapting religion to modern conditions.

In addition to their frequent use of Islamic discourse, however, we also observe the rise of nationalism as an alternative source of legitimization for the secularists. Though not as extensively as Islamic justification, they employed a nationalist discourse, which particularly centered on the concept of national sovereignty, in such a way as to complement their Islamic discourse, rather than oppose it. That is, they often resorted to a mixture of Islamic and nationalist rhetoric in order to justify their politico-religious arguments and ideological positions. This, of course, created contradictions within their discourses stemming from the deep tension between the universalism of Islamic teachings and nationalism's limited character. These contradictions were particularly visible in the rhetoric of Mustafa Kemal, who tried to impose his biggest secular reform, the abolition of the 1,300-year-old Caliphate, on a war-torn Muslim society. The gradual rise of nationalist discourse among the Turkish secularists was a product of the change in historical conditions, i.e., the shift from a multi-ethnic religious empire to a secularizing nation-state. This historical shift also conditioned their view of the Caliphate: both secularists and their opponents (modernist Islamists) imagined the future of the Caliphate within the emerging nation-state form. This nation-state was itself a product of the military and political developments that constituted the post-war crisis of the Ottoman Empire.

Therefore, this chapter will first discuss the politico-military and economic conditions of the Ottoman Empire in its last years and describe how a national resistance movement emerged and conducted the Turkish "independence war" in Anatolia. It will then analyze two specific cases: the transformation of the Caliphate into a "spiritual" status without temporal power as a result of the abolition of the Ottoman monarchy in 1922, and the end of the Caliphate itself. It will present a discourse analysis of the ideological struggle between pro- and anti-Caliphate groups in the context of the political and military power relations that characterized the Caliphate's final years.

End of the Ottoman Empire (1918–1922)

As discussed in Chapter 5, World War I was disastrous for the Ottoman Empire, leading to its disintegration together with that of the Habsburg, German, Russian, and Iranian empires. During the war, the Allies occupied the entire Middle East, including much of Turkey and Arabia. Though at first Sharif Hussein's rebellion was a success, much of the Arabian Peninsula ended up under British and French mandate, while Anatolia and Thrace were also partitioned by the victors. The ensuing Turkish resistance successfully retook control of much of Anatolia and Eastern Thrace, after which Turkish nationalists created a new national state in Ankara. Though founded as an "Islamic state," the new Turkey developed an increasingly secular character. The two crucial steps on this path of political secularization (and nation-state formation) were the abolition of first the Ottoman monarchy (1922), and then the Caliphate (1924), which took place as a result of political and military developments in the chaotic atmosphere of the post-World War I context.

The post-war crisis of the Empire

World War I ended for the Ottomans with the Armistice of Mudros, signed with Britain on October 31, 1918. Its 25 articles entailed such provisions as the disarmament of the Ottoman army, the Allied occupation of Istanbul and the Dardanelle Straits, and the freeing of all Allied (but not Ottoman) prisoners of war. Two crucial provisions in the armistice provided the Allies with the right to occupy any place within the empire that was considered a security threat (Article 7), and to intervene in the "Armenian provinces" should order break down there (Article 24). In practice, these articles allowed the Allies to use military force anywhere they wanted (Zürcher 1993: 138).

Soon 50,000 British and French troops occupied Istanbul. This was supposedly to execute the armistice terms, but the Allied high commissioners also had to help with the actual administration of the war-torn city, including the provision of food, health services, and security, as well as shelter for the large numbers of refugees. (Apart from the displaced masses who had landed in Istanbul during the war, there were also 150,000 anti-Bolshevik White Russians who fled from the revolution.) Prices had gone up 400 percent during the war and after the war ended they quadrupled again, which created a major burden for the economy, particularly when coupled with a shortage of wheat and coal (Zürcher 1993: 146).

On the other hand, British and French officials tried to influence domestic politics as well. Sultan Vahideddin Mehmed VI (Mehmed V had died in July 1918) tried to get a favorable peace treaty by appeasing the Allies. Unlike his predecessor, who was mostly under the CUP's influence, he intervened in domestic politics by pursuing anti-Unionist and pro-British policies. Like his predecessors, he was concerned with the well-being of the Caliphate and the fate of his Muslim subjects in the Middle East (for whom he felt a strong sense of responsibility), as well as his own dynasty, rather than only preserving Turkish Anatolia (Zürcher 1993: 142). He dissolved the parliament in December, replacing the Unionist cabinet with a liberal one led by Tevfik Pasha. Due to pressure by the Allies, the government changed several times, each time led by a member of the Freedom and Alliance Party (FAP), mostly by Damad Ferid Pasha. The main opposition included the Ottoman Liberal People's Party (*Osmanlı Hürriyetperver Avam Fırkası*) and the unionist Renovation Party (*Teceddüt Fırkası*), which replaced the CUP in 1918 (Shaw 2000, II: 432ff.).

Top CUP leaders, including Bahaeddin Şakir and Dr. Nazım, as well as Enver Pasha, Cemal Pasha, and Talat Pasha, who had ruled the Empire for much of the Second Constitutional Period, fled the country aboard a German submarine in early October because the Allies had declared that they would prosecute them for the Armenian massacres during the war. Other CUP leaders were tried and exiled to Malta until 1921, after which most of them, including four of the five top leaders (except Enver), were killed by Armenian assassins. Convinced that only the first phase of the war was over, just like in the 1912–1913 Balkan war, Enver had ordered the troops that had returned from Europe to eastern Anatolia, and he himself went to Azerbaijan and Central Asia (where he presented himself as "the caliph's son-in-law") with the hope of uniting all Turks. Meanwhile, though their leaders had left and the CUP dissolved itself in November, the Unionists in Istanbul still controlled much of the government, including the parliament, the army, the police, and the communication infrastructure. They also prepared the ground for resistance in Anatolia by smuggling people, arms, and information to the nationalist forces led first by local CUP leaders and then by Mustafa Kemal; various "defense of rights" societies they created formed the organizational backbone of the resistance (Zürcher 1984: 73ff.; see also below).

Meanwhile, the Allies convened in Paris on January 12, 1919 to sort out their disagreements on the partitioning of the Middle East and to prepare a peace treaty for the Ottoman Empire. As discussed in the previous chapter, during the war Britain, France, Russia, and Italy had made secret agreements to partition the empire, including the Constantinople and Sykes-Picot treaties, which the Russians had made public after the 1917 Revolution. This made it clear that Britain's promises to Sharif Hussein for independence and support for his bid for the Caliphate would not be honored and that, despite Hussein's protest, Northern Arabia would be occupied by France, Britain, and Jewish settlers. Moreover, Greece joined the Entente powers at the end of the war with the intention of invading southwestern Anatolia and Thrace, which created a conflict of interest with Italy. At the end of the Paris Conference, Greece received permission to occupy Izmir and its vicinity in the West, and the Armenians to establish their own state in the East, both of which were rejected by the Ottoman delegation. There was also a request to create an American mandate for Armenia, which then turned into a mandate for all of Anatolia by the American Harbord Commission. This appealed to many Turkish intellectuals, who feared the total occupation of their country. They even founded a "Wilsonian League" to promote the idea, but it was never accepted by the resistance or the occupying powers (Zürcher 1993: 152).

Britain also decided to completely occupy Istanbul and end the Ottoman Caliphate, but could not do so due to great resistance by the Muslims of India (Özcan 1997; Qureshi 1999). Already stirred to action by the *Teşkilat-ı Mahsusa* (the Ottoman secret service) and the caliph's *jihad fatwa* during the war, Muslim and Hindu nationalists protested Britain both in India and in London. Three days after the Allied occupation began in Istanbul, the *Khilafat* Movement sent a delegation to Prime Minister Lloyd George.[1] The Head of the Delegation, Muhammad Ali [Jinnah], voiced the traditionalist understanding of the Caliphate's theological foundations as a basis for their political requests:

> Islam as we understand it, is not a set of doctrines or dogmas; it is a complete outlook on life, a moral code and a social polity. It recognises no lacerating and devitalising distinctions between things spiritual and things temporal, between church and state ... The personal centre [of Islam] is the Caliph, or the Khalifa, as we call him, the successor of the Prophet. Because the Prophet was the personal centre of Islam, his successors ... continue his tradition to this day. The Khalifa is the Commander of the Faithful in all matters for which Islam provides divine guidance, and his orders are to be obeyed by all Mussalmans as long as they do not conflict with the Commandments of God and the Traditions of the Prophet.
>
> (quoted in Oliver-Dee 2009: 110)

Lloyd George's reluctance to respond positively implied that both Istanbul and the *Hijaz* would be taken from the Ottomans. In response, the *Khilafat* leadership declared:

> The *Khilafat* [Caliphate] must be preserved with adequate temporal power. After the various wars in which Turkey has recently been engaged, Moslems consider that the irreducible minimum of temporal power adequate for the defence of the Faith to be the restoration of the *status quo ante bellum* subject to guarantees for security of life, property, and opportunities of autonomous development for all communities. Muhammad Ali therefore was unable to agree to the independence of Arabia.... No control by mandate or other means should be exercised over Arabia. And the Khalifa [caliph] must continue to be the warden of the Sacred Harems of Mecca, Medina and Jerusalem. The retention of Constantinople is a point of overwhelming sentiment. To drive the Turks thence would constitute a challenge of the Modern Crusaders to Islam and European domination of the entire East.... The whole of the above ... may be reduced to a short sentence: "Restore Turkey to her pre-war status with certain guarantees, otherwise you will evoke the hostility of the whole Moslem world and the East generally."
>
> (quoted in Shaw 2000, II: 839)

Similarly, they also wrote to US President Wilson appealing to his "Fourteen Points":

> The Indian Khilafat delegation have learned with profound alarm of the forcible Allied occupation of the seat of the Khilafat and the use of Muslim troops against the commander of the faithful. The delegation['s] mission of peace and reconciliation ... on behalf of these people of India will be frustrated if a policy so aggressive and humiliating to Islam is pursued. The delegation urge that protection of Christian populations in Asia Minor does not necessitate or justify an affront to the conscience of Islam, which ... will have the most unfortunate effect possible upon feeling in India already too gravely exasperated by suggestion of dismemberment of Khilafat.
>
> (Syed Sulaiman Nadvi) (quoted in Shaw 2000, II: 839)

Though the British government first ignored the warnings by Sir Edwin Montagu, secretary of state for India, the Muslim opposition (mainly represented by Muhammad Pickthall, a British Muslim intellectual, Ameer Ali, a London-based Indian attorney, and Mushir Hosain Kidwai, an Indian politician and lawyer) sent letters to the British press and petitions to the government demanding that the Allies treat the Ottomans fairly, though this met with little response. Finally, Muslims in Algeria and Morocco (under French colonial rule) pressured Paris to ease their relationship with Ankara, which might have influenced the French decision to sign the Treaty of Ankara in October 1921, with which France agreed to end the occupation in Anatolia (Shaw 2000, II: 841).

But the real impact came from India. The *Khilafat* Movement not only lobbied in London and published five proclamations in Europe, but also organized demonstrations and a general strike in India, in which more than 1,000,000 Muslims and a large number of Hindus participated. Gandhi himself gave a speech in Bombay threatening to separate from Britain "unless Britain ended its efforts to attack Islam" (Shaw 2000, II: 840). Moreover, on March 5, 1922, they presented a formal protest to the Allies that Muslim and Hindu peoples of India considered the Sèvres Treaty (imposed on the Ottoman Empire; see below) a "crime against Islam," urging them to pull the Greeks out of Turkey. They also made substantial financial contributions to the resistance in Anatolia: Mustafa Kemal reported that the Indians sent £110,000 between November 1921 and May 1922, and smaller, similar contributions were made by the Egyptian Muslims as well (Shaw 2000, II: 840).

In the end, with the warning from the India Office of a possible violent reaction by Indian Muslims, the Lloyd George government decided not to sever Istanbul from the empire or declare a non-Turkish caliph in the peace treaty, which nevertheless contained extremely harsh provisions for the Ottomans. The Treaty of Sèvres, signed on August 10, 1920, left for them only a small territory in northern Anatolia; Britain established mandates in Iraq, Palestine, and Trans-jordan; France in Lebanon, Syria, and southern Anatolia; and Italy received southwestern Anatolia. Also, Greece was given Izmir and its vicinity, as well as eastern Thrace, and the Armenians received eastern Anatolia. The Treaty also aimed to effectively abolish the Caliphate:

> *Article 139*: Turkey formally renounces any rights of suzerainty or jurisdiction of any kind over Muslims who are subject to the sovereignty or protectorate of any other state.
>
> No power shall be exercised directly or indirectly by any Turkish authority whatever in any territory detached from Turkey...[2]

Though the Ottoman Sultan was forced to sign the treaty, it was not ratified by the last Ottoman parliament, which had prorogued itself in protest against the arrest of Unionist leaders after the formal occupation of Istanbul by Britain on March 16, 1920. This ended all political activity in Istanbul; the power struggle would subsequently take the form of military resistance organized in Anatolia.

National resistance in Anatolia

As mentioned above, the resistance in Anatolia against the Allied occupation following the war had been started by the CUP. Enver Pasha and Talat Pasha had ordered the *Teşkilat-ı Mahsusa* to store arms and ammunition in Anatolian cities; they then reconstituted the *Teşkilat* as the "General Revolutionary Organization of the Islamic World" to start guerilla bands and resistance efforts not only in Anatolia, but also in North Africa and Arabia. Moreover, they created a specific underground organization, called *Karakol* (The Guard), to protect Unionists from retaliation by Christian communities and Allied forces and to support the resistance in Anatolia and the Caucasus by sending people, money, arms, and information through its vast espionage network (Zürcher 1984: 73–82). Between November 1918 and March 1920, *Karakol* smuggled a large number of unionist officers, and at least 56,000 gun locks, 320 machine guns, 1,500 rifles, 2,000 boxes of ammunition, and 10,000 uniforms to Anatolia (Zürcher 1993: 147).

In addition, CUP branches in provincial capitals founded a number of "defense of rights" societies, as well as many smaller organizations, to provide both a public façade for underground resistance and political agitation to influence public opinion. They also specifically aimed to counter Armenian and Greek claims to land in Anatolia. While the Unionists acted underground, they elected local notables and religious dignitaries as formal heads of these organizations, which were also supported by landowners and merchants, some of whom had taken over the property of deported or emigrated Armenians and Greeks (Zürcher 1993: 154). The occupation of Izmir by the Greeks in May 1919 created a great sense of injustice and thus boosted the resistance. The Unionists organized many regional congresses to garner public support and bring these diverse communities together. They also organized two national congresses in Erzurum and Sivas in 1919, which then formed the basis of the Grand National Assembly (GNA) that would conduct the resistance as of April 1920. Though the resistance did not yet have a regular army, there were 35,000 troops in western Anatolia, 26,000 in the south and 30,000 in the east, controlled by Young Turk officers such as the commander of the 15th army corps, Kazım Karabekir, who uniformly supported the resistance (see below).

In Istanbul, when the Unionist leaders Kara Kemal and Kara Vasıf (*Karakol*'s founders), needed someone to organize the dispersed resistance, they first approached former Grand Vizier Ahmed İzzet Pasha, who was not a Unionist. When they could not reach an agreement with him, they turned to Mustafa Kemal Pasha, a lesser-known CUP member. Due to his personal problems with Enver Pasha, who had constantly undermined him, he had not been able to make a name for himself until the Dardanelles campaign (1915), where he was still a division commander under Enver. He was a viable candidate for the resistance leadership because he was not held accountable for the Armenian massacres by the Allies. Also, his unsuccessful attempts to enter politics in Istanbul after the war made him consider leaving for Anatolia, as many other Unionist officers had done (Zürcher 1993: 148). With the sultan's permission (and money), Mustafa Kemal was appointed as inspector of the Third Army and sent to Anatolia with a staff of 18 and very wide powers in May 1919. Upon his arrival, he contacted all commanders, after which he and three pashas (Rauf, Ali Fuat, and Refet) drafted a statement in Amasya, called the "Amasya Circular," which stated that the country was in danger and the Istanbul government could not protect it. It also stated that only the "national will" could save the country, which necessitated the organization of a national congress in Sivas, the safest place in Anatolia. Concerned about his activities in Anatolia, Britain forced the Istanbul government to recall and fire Mustafa Kemal, who then refused and resigned from the army. This could have jeopardized the resistance, but he was saved by Kazım Karabekir, who refused to arrest him despite having received instructions to do so. Then the majority of commanders followed him in recognizing Mustafa Kemal as the resistance leader. Before the Sivas congress, a regional congress headed by Mustafa Kemal was held in Erzurum (in the east) on July 23, the eleventh anniversary of the 1908 Young Turk Revolution, to declare that Eastern Anatolia could not be left to Armenians. It also demanded the sovereignty of Muslim-majority provinces in Turkey, and that the Caliphate and the sultan be left alone by the Allies, and reaffirmed the nationalist movement's loyalty to the caliph-sultan (Articles 2 and 4).[3] The national congress in Sivas, held between September 4 and 11, was opened with a long speech by Mustafa Kemal and affirmed the principles adopted in Erzurum, including the nationalists' adherence to the Caliphate and the monarchy (Articles 2, 3, and 4). The congress formed the Anatolia and Rumelia Defense of Rights Society, and elected a 15-person Representative Committee, headed by Mustafa Kemal (who was aided by Kara Vasıf Bey), which then functioned as the executive committee of the resistance (Shaw 2000, II: 674–716; see also Gologlu 2008a, 2008b). The committee then moved to Ankara, which was chosen because it was at the head of a railway linked directly to Istanbul (Zürcher 1993: 157).

Meanwhile, a change in the government in Istanbul resulted in a pro-nationalist cabinet headed by Ali Rıza Pasha, but co-operation between Istanbul and Ankara remained limited – though the new government adopted the nationalist program as formulated in Erzurum and Sivas. Later, when the Unionist Renovation Party was closed down in May, the resistance pressed for new elections, which the Unionists overwhelmingly won. The new deputies, mostly nominated by the Defense of Rights Society and always in touch with Ankara, then came together in the new parliament in Istanbul as the "Salvation of the Motherland Group" and published a manifesto called the National Pact (*Misak-ı Milli*) in February 1920, which constituted the program of the nationalist resistance:

1. The territories inhabited by the Muslim majority form an indivisible whole...
4. The security of Istanbul, the Ottoman capital, and the seat of the Islamic Caliphate and the glorious Sultanate, and of the Sea of Marmara must be assured...
6. The economic, financial, and judicial independence of the empire should be assured and free from restrictions [i.e. from capitulations].
(Mustafa Kemal 1961[1927], I: 363)

This document, which demanded the independence of Muslim Ottomans (i.e. Turks and Kurds), rather than Turks only, acted as the mouthpiece of the resistance until the proclamation of the Constitution in 1921.

However, the new grand vizier in Istanbul, Damad Ferid Pasha, was pressured by the occupation forces to ask *şeyhülislam* Dürrizade Abdullah for a *fatwa* condemning the nationalists, which was granted. The *fatwa* read:

Is the following a duty prescribed by religion and is it legal: namely to kill and put out of the way certain criminal persons who have leagued together and attributed to themselves leadership in the lands of Islam which are under the sovereign authority of the Muslim Caliph, who is the fountain of universal order and whom may God protect until the day of the resurrection;... persons who without any sovereign orders have raised troops and, pretending that it was to feed and arm them but really desiring to enrich themselves, have levied and shared out among themselves contributions and taxes, contrary to the sacred precepts and to the laws;

...persons who by their own authority have deposed the religious, military and civil functionaries nominated by the Commander of the Faithful and have replaced them by their sycophants;

persons who have cut the communications between the seat of the Caliphate and the rest of the Empire;

persons who have prevented the execution of the Government's orders and, with the object of striking at the prestige of the Caliphate, have isolated the central seat of the Government from the other parts of the country, thus rendering themselves culpable of treason against the Caliphate from which they have separated themselves;...

God knows better than we do: yes.

Therefore is it an action approved by the Sacred Law of the *sharia* for all Muslims of the Empire capable of bearing arms and fighting to gather round the Caliph the Just, His Majesty the Sultan Mehmed Vahdettin and to answer his appeal to struggle and fight against the persons aforesaid?

God knows better than we do: yes.

...Is it true that those among the soldiers of the Caliph who shall kill these rebels will be Ghazis, and those who shall be killed by the rebels will be martyrs?

God knows better than we do: yes.

(quoted in Shaw 2000, II: 846–847)

The *fatwa* was published in major Istanbul newspapers, including *Tasvir-i Efkar, İleri, Yenigün, Vakit, Peyam-ı Sabah*, and *İkdam*, on April 10. On that same day, Damad Ferid was forced to publish his own proclamation condemning those who, "under the false cloak of nationalism," were following the disastrous Unionist policies that "had dragged the nation into war, threatening Anatolia with occupation and troubling the state, turning America and Europe against the Ottoman Empire and causing the occupation of Istanbul" (Shaw 2000, II: 847). The grand vizier also had the Istanbul Court Martial pronounce death sentences against Mustafa Kemal and his senior colleagues *in absentia* for treason against the sultan and causing rebellion. The sultan then issued an order that dissolved the parliament, promising to hold new elections within four months, as prescribed by the constitution. When the Allies started the official occupation of Istanbul on March 16, 1920 they immediately arrested 150 prominent Turks, 14 of whom were nationalist leaders in the parliament, including Rauf Bey and Kara Vasıf Bey. Most deputies then moved to Ankara to form – with new deputies elected by the Defense of Rights Society – a parliament called the "Grand National Assembly" (*Büyük Millet Meclisi*), which met on April 23, 1920. The GNA opened with public Qur'an recitations and prayers and a number of religious dignitaries in attendance. The GNA stressed its loyalty to the caliph-sultan, but declared the Istanbul government's acts under occupation void, effectively forming a new provisional government in Ankara (Zürcher 1993: 159).

The next day, in his inauguration speech as the head of the Turkish Grand National Assembly, Mustafa Kemal said, "I wish from God's grace that our Lord, the Ruler of the Universe, will forever remain in his crown in good health and free of any foreign intrusion" (April 24, 1920: Mustafa Kemal 1945: 64). Likewise, in his telegraph to express his loyalty on behalf of the GNA to the sultan against British propaganda, he said:

Our most sacred Emperor and Caliph!... We will continue our jihad as long as foreign soldiers stay in our homeland and the enemy walks around the mosques of Istanbul, every corner of which is the shining symbol of our great emperor's love of religion and Islam...

Our Sultan! Our hearts being filled with the sense of loyalty and servitude, we have gathered around your throne connected to it tighter than ever.

Loyalty to its sultan and caliph is the first promise of the Grand National Assembly; it also declares with great respect and pleasure that its last word will be the same.

(April 28, 1920: Mustafa Kemal 1964: 307)

This telegraph was published in *İrade-i Milliye*, the GNA's semi-official gazette, on the same day as the Resistance's public view of the monarchy and the Caliphate. The GNA members' oath contained the words "the only goal I will pursue is the independence of the Caliphate, the Sultanate, the homeland, and the nation" (TBMMZC quoted in Satan 2008: 117).

Also, stressing the Islamic character of their struggle, Mustafa Kemal carefully rallied the support of the local religious dignitaries in Anatolia. He then requested a *fatwa* from the *mufti* (jurisconsult) of Ankara in response to that of the *şeyhülislam*, which had greatly disturbed him due to its demoralization of the Resistance troops (Mustafa Kemal 1929[1927]: 401). In a very similar style, the *fatwa*, also signed by 153 Anatolian *Mufti*s and scholars at Kemal's request (because the Ankara *mufti*'s opinion could not possibly match the *şeyhülislam*'s great prestige), declared the members of the Istanbul government traitors while still remaining loyal to the caliph-sultan, emphasizing that the nationalists were fighting to protect the Caliphate and the Ottoman monarchy.[4] He also requested a second *fatwa* from the Bursa *ulema*, according to which:

[It was] the duty of all Muslims to help rescue the Caliph from captivity in Istanbul by the enemies of Islam, who had killed Muslim soldiers and innocent Muslim civilians, who had tried and convicted Muslims in Christian courts according to Christian law, and who were striving to destroy Islam by invading different parts of the country and massacring their inhabitants. [Moreover,] any *fatwa*s issued by Muslims who were captives of Christians, such as that of the *Şeyhülislam*, did not have to be obeyed.

(Shaw 2000, III: 968)

The discursive and legal battle between Istanbul and Ankara turned into a civil war when the former sent troops – armed by the British – to suppress the nationalist "revolt." But the nationalists successfully fought against the forces sent by Istanbul, both irregular bands (most notably the Circassian Anzavur forces, beaten by bands of Edhem Bey, who was himself Circassian) and then a regular army (the "Disciplinary Forces," also known as "the Caliph's Army")[5] as well against several local rebellions between 1920 and 1921. They also adopted a High Treason Law that charged members of the Istanbul government who signed or approved the Sèvres Treaty with treason, and instituted extraordinary courts, the so-called "Independence Tribunals," which severely punished rebels and deserters. The civil war constituted one of the two dimensions of what is called the "national struggle," and was responsible for the majority of the death toll of 8,000–9,000 people between 1919 and 1922.

Apart from these domestic conflicts, the nationalists waged a war against Armenians in the East and Greeks in the West – the second dimension of the national struggle. A few small-scale and intermittent clashes with the French in the south were conducted by urban guerilla forces and did not turn into a war. After Kazım Karabekir's forces decisively beat the Armenians by the end of October 1920, the nationalists signed a friendship treaty with the Bolsheviks (who had overthrown the Armenian *Dashnaksutiun* government), which provided vital diplomatic, military, and financial support for the Turkish resistance. Meanwhile, the Greeks had been pushing forward from Izmir since May 1919; it was not until January 1921 that the Turkish army was able to stop them near Eskişehir, very close to Ankara. At this point, the Allies invited all sides of the Sèvres Treaty for a conference to revise it. The Greeks could not reach an agreement with the Turks, but the French and the Italians (who were concerned that Britain was trying to establish a vassal state with the Greeks in the West) did: on March 11 and 13, respectively, they agreed to leave south and southwest Anatolia in exchange for certain economic concessions (though these were first rejected by Ankara, they would later be renewed). With the negotiations broken down, the Greeks restarted their offensive near Eskişehir; though they were beaten at first, they slowly occupied most of western Anatolia during the summer, and came to Sakarya, 50 miles west of Ankara. This caused a panic among GNA members, who discussed a possible relocation to Sivas in the east. Moreover, to resist the Greek army, the GNA requisitioned one-third of all food-stuffs and farm animals, as well as arms, in Anatolia. At Sakarya, Turkish forces won the battle in mid-September, but were too exhausted to pursue the enemy. The Greek army withdrew but remained in west Anatolia for one more year, during which Britain declared its neutrality and tried to re-open negotiations, but failed to do so. Now recovered and rearmed with Russian and Muslim (from India, Egypt and elsewhere) aid, the Turkish army started its final attack against the Greeks, and drove them entirely from western Anatolia in four days (August 26–30), entering Izmir on September 9. The Ankara government then signed an armistice in Mudanya with the British on October 10, in which the Turks received eastern Thrace and Britain still occupied Istanbul and the Straits (Shaw 2000, II: 919–949, III: 1256–1358, IV: 1687–1867; Zürcher 1993: 159–163).

Mustafa Kemal and his opponents

Between 1920 and 1922, Mustafa Kemal emerged as the strongest leader of the resistance in Anatolia. The influence of Unionist leaders, who had started the resistance, gradually diminished, particularly after the Allies had invaded Istanbul and exiled many of them to Malta. During the Greek offensive in the summer of 1921, the GNA gave Mustafa Kemal personal command of all forces and invested in him all of its powers – a turning point for his accumulation of power in such a way as to make him rule the government with an iron fist. Despite the opposition by the "Second Group" (see below), who were very much concerned about what they saw as Mustafa Kemal's dictatorial tendencies, Kemal refused to give back this total authority, pressing the Assembly to extend it several times until July 1922; that is, shortly before he overthrew the Ottoman monarchy.

Following the regime change in 1922, he would rule Turkey with increasingly authoritarian methods until his death in 1938.

However, though all commanders were loyal to Mustafa Kemal during the national struggle, his political authority was far from uncontested. He was frequently challenged by two kinds of opposition: conservative Islamists and "socialist Islamists" (Zürcher 1993: 164–166). Armed with a mix of Islamic, corporatist, and socialist ideologies, the latter were organized, with Mustafa Kemal's approval, in a political group called the "Green Army" ("green" referring to Islam) in May 1920 to counter Istanbul's propaganda and its "Caliphal Army." But when Çerkez Edhem, the leader of a large Circassian band that had been crucial in fighting against Istanbul's forces and local revolts mentioned above, joined the Green Army, Mustafa Kemal dissolved it, perceiving it as a threat to his personal rule. When they reorganized as the "People's Faction," he had a few of its members that he trusted found the Communist Party of Turkey. The Third International did not recognize it because there was already a Turkish communist party founded in Baku in 1920. Its leader was Mustafa Suphi, a former teacher and Unionist who had fled to Russia in 1914 and helped propagate communism among Turkish prisoners after the Bolshevik Revolution. His supporters and the People's Faction formed an alternative party in Ankara, called the "People's Socialist Party," in November. Determined to crush this movement, Mustafa Kemal first ordered Çerkez Edhem to disband his forces in January 1921; when he refused, Kemal sent his troops on him and took many of his men prisoner; he himself escaped to the Greek side. Then Mustafa Kemal dissolved the Socialist Party. When Mustafa Suphi tried to enter Anatolia to reorganize it, he and his supporters were denied entry and drowned by local nationalist militia in the Black Sea off the Trabzon coast (Shaw 2000, III: 1092–1114).

The leftist opposition would not have posed a real threat to Mustafa Kemal by itself if Enver Pasha had not posed as a left-wing alternative to him for the Bolsheviks, whose help he needed desperately. Enver attended the Soviet-sponsored "Congress of the Peoples of the East" in Baku in September 1920, where he founded the "People's Soviets Party," which was based on a partly Islamic, partly socialist program that he had drafted. His aim was to raise an army with Soviet money and enter Anatolia to take over the leadership of the resistance. But when the Bolsheviks chose Mustafa Kemal with the friendship treaty, Enver attempted to go to Anatolia alone, relying on the Unionists within the resistance. When he was denied entry, Enver held a congress in Baku under the name of the Union and Progress Party. But with the nationalist victory at Sakarya that solidified Kemal's position, he left to pursue his dream of a Turkish-Islamic empire in Afghanistan, where he died fighting the Red Army at the head of the Turkish guerilla forces (June 1922) (Zürcher 1993: 165–166).

The second major opposition to Mustafa Kemal came from conservative circles organized around the "Association for the Preservation of Sacred Institutions" in March 1921. Led by Unionist *alim* Hoca Raif, this group stressed the significance of the Caliphate and the monarchy. It also constituted the majority of the opposition group in the GNA, which was heterogeneous and very active in terms of political participation. Mustafa Kemal organized his followers around the "Defense of Rights Group" in the GNA; the unionist opposition founded the "Second Group" in early 1922, when the unionist leaders, including Kara Vasıf, returned from exile in Malta. This group was also heterogeneous, but unified against what they perceived as Mustafa Kemal's dictatorial desires (Demirel 1994). These they would test when he decided to end the Ottoman monarchy after the victory against the Greeks in September.

The Caliphate and the end of monarchy

The abolition of the Ottoman monarchy

The historical context of the post-World War I era was very conducive to the abolition of the monarchy. The collapse of the Russian, German, Habsburg, and Iranian monarchies between 1917 and 1921 created favorable conditions for Republican regimes; moreover, most of the Young Turks who conducted the "National Struggle" in Turkey had been raised under the "despotic" regime of Sultan Abdülhamid II and despised absolute monarchy as a political institution; and, finally, the current sultan's generally negative attitude toward the nationalist resistance in Anatolia led to a fierce reaction among the nationalists against the Sultan. They voiced their dislike of the Palace strongly after the victory over the Greeks in August 1922. For example, after the Armistice of Mudanya between Britain and the Anatolian resistance, Mustafa Kemal's close friend Refet Pasha went to Istanbul in late October 1922 as the governor of Thrace. He was welcomed and cheered by people in Istanbul, where he met with British high commissioners to plan an orderly transition of power (from the Greeks) in Thrace. He also visited monumental mosques and attended prayers there as well as giving speeches in which he strongly criticized the monarchy as an oppressive system that had to be abolished, but he was careful to use a religious discourse. In one of these speeches, in the Hagia Sophia mosque, Refet Pasha spoke of the Greek war:

> This victory was born out of belief in national sovereignty, national power, national strength and [belief] in almighty God! This place will remain Muslim for all time!
>
> ("Stamboul Celebrates" *The Orient*, IX/11, November 8, 1922; quoted in Shaw 2000, IV: 1874)

Following the war against the Greeks, Mustafa Kemal, who had by this time solidified his position as the leader of the resistance, decided to abolish the monarchy and declare the GNA, which he would later fully control, as the sole sovereign body in Turkey. He did not have any plans to restore the imperial order, as the Ottoman Empire had lost its Arab territories anyway. However, he could not make his plans explicit due to pro-monarchy, unionist opposition in the GNA. After all, he himself had many times expressed the Resistance's loyalty to the sultan (see above), and the Constitution that he had drafted in 1921 explicitly stated that their primary aim was to protect the Caliphate and serve the sultan, though it also made clear that "sovereignty belongs, with no restrictions and no conditions, to the nation" (Article 1; see Chapter 2 for a detailed discussion). Even Rauf [Orbay] Bey, one of Kemal's close friends and the head of the GNA's "executive committee" (there was no formal government within the GNA; the executive committee effectively acted as the cabinet), said in July 1922:

> It is hard for us to control the general situation. This can only be secured by an authority that everyone is accustomed to regard as unapproachably high. Such is the office of the Sultanate and the Caliphate. To abolish this office and try to set up an entity of a different character in its place would lead to failure and disaster. It is quite inadmissible.
>
> (quoted in Ahmad 1993: 15)

In October 1922, however, there were rumors that Mustafa Kemal had plans to abolish the monarchy. Upon the request of some of his closest friends, including Rauf Pasha, Fuad Pasha, and Refet Pasha, he explicitly denied these allegations before the GNA members, deeming it a political move necessitated by his "general and historic duty" (Mustafa Kemal 1961[1927], II: 685).

The opportunity that Kemal was waiting for came with the peace treaty offered by the Allies to Turkey after the latter's victory. Britain, France, Italy, and Greece, as hosts, invited both the Istanbul and Ankara governments to Lausanne for negotiations. Grand Vizier Tevfik Pasha in Istanbul then sent a message to Ankara suggesting that a joint delegation represent the Turks in Lausanne. This caused a fury among GNA members – including, first and fore-most, Mustafa Kemal – who thought that Istanbul had no right to represent the country. Hamid Bey, Ankara's representative in Istanbul, criticized the Allies for their double invitation, and Kemal immediately ordered Rauf Bey (effectively prime minister) to declare the necessity of separating the Caliphate from the monarchy and abolishing the latter. For Mustafa Kemal,

> the abolition of the Sultanate was necessitated by the fact that [Sultan] Vahideddin and Tevfik Pasha and his colleagues had accepted the invitation [by the Allies] to the Lausanne Conference at the expense of the advantages that the nation had gained at the price of so many efforts and sacrifices.
>
> (1961[1927], II: 687)

In the closed sitting of the GNA, on October 30, Rauf Bey proposed, on behalf of the executive committee, a move to this effect. In this sitting, Kemal, who did not allow much discussion, declared the end of the empire, but used, as usual, careful language regarding the Caliphate:

> Whereas the Ottoman Empire has collapsed, the Government of the Grand National Assembly has been organized,... whereas by the Constitution, the

nation has given it the right to rule, and whereas the Sultanate in Istanbul
has passed into history, and there is no legitimate government in Istanbul, it
therefore has been decided that Istanbul and its area must be transferred to
the officials of the Grand National Assembly, and that the Place [Seat] of
the Caliphate, which is the legal right of the Turkish Government, is imprisoned and must be rescued from foreigners.

(TBMMZC XXIV: 311; quoted in Shaw 2000, IV: 1883)

The committee's proposal was accepted by 132 votes, with two deputies abstain-
ing and two (Colonel Sabahaddin Bey and Ziya Hurşid) objecting – arguing that
the people would never approve this with no discussion in the assembly.
However, the results left the GNA without a quorum and no final decision could
be reached. The next day, the Defense of Rights Group convened to discuss how
to proceed and Mustafa Kemal reiterated his earlier views on the necessity of
abolishing the monarchy (Mustafa Kemal 1961[1927], II: 689). On the same
day, the two groups resolved their conflict at the suggestion of Education Minister Rıza Nur that the Caliphate should be retained by the royal family, with the
caliph to be chosen by the GNA (Shaw 2000, IV: 1883). On November 1, 1922,
the GNA met again and voted to abolish monarchy. During the debates, Mustafa
Kemal not only attacked Sultan Vahideddin as an incompetent leader, but also
presented, employing a strong Islamic discourse, an unusual reinterpretation of
the Caliphate's history (see Chapter 4 and below). The GNA accepted the executive committee's move and the Ottoman Sultanate was officially abolished. The
law had two articles:

1. Since the people of Turkey have decided with the *Teşkilat-ı Esasiye*
   [the 1921 Constitution] that their sovereign rights be represented and
   practiced – with no limits or partition – by the Grand National Assembly of Turkey, which is their real representative, and that no force or
   committee that is not based on the national will be recognized, they do
   not recognize any form of government other than the government of the
   Grand National Assembly of Turkey, within the borders specified by
   the National Pact. Therefore, the people of Turkey have buried in
   history the government in Istanbul, which was based on individual sovereignty, as of March 16, 1336 [1920].
2. The Caliphate belongs to the Ottoman dynasty; the best qualified
   [member] within this dynasty in character and wisdom is elected caliph
   by the Grand National Assembly of Turkey. The State of Turkey is the
   basis of the Caliphate

(TBMMZC 1922a: 279).[6]

The law also declared all the laws, decrees, and treaties made by the sultan's government null and void as of March 16, 1920, the day Istanbul was occupied and
the parliament dissolved (see Toynbee 1927: 50–51). The GNA also declared
November 1, said – by Kemal – to be the Prophet's birthday, a national holiday.

Figure 6.1 The GNA motion to abolish the Ottoman monarchy (source: *TBMM Arşivi C*, Devre 1, Dosya 308).

Islamic Caliphate, un-Islamic sultanate

The pro-monarchy opposition was quite weak in the GNA during the debate over its abolition. What was really at stake, however, was the Caliphate, as indicated by long and heated debates on the deposition of Vahideddin from the Caliphate and the election of a new caliph on November 18, 1922 (see below). Many deputies, especially in the "Second Group," but also in the first one, did not want the Caliphate to be left without political power. That is why they demanded guarantees from Mustafa Kemal, who agreed with their concerns, instrumentally. But the future of the Caliphate was also the real source of concern for many during the earlier debate over its separation from the Ottoman Sultanate on November 1.

As mentioned, the tipping point for the abolition of the monarchy was Grand Vizier Tevfik Pasha's request from Ankara to send a joint delegation to Lausanne for the peace conference. During parliamentary debates on November 1, although the topic of discussion on the agenda was this request and the proper response to be given to Istanbul, the deputies focused on the Caliphate and its status and meaning for the GNA government in Ankara. Rasih Efendi of Antalya, a member of the *ulema* and an influential deputy from Mustafa Kemal's First Group, claimed that the Muslim world did not recognize the sultan as their caliph anymore; instead, they considered the GNA the "only savior of Islam," as evidenced by the fact that they had sent their delegations to Ankara rather than Istanbul. He complemented his argument with two discursive techniques – by comparing Islam with the West on the origins of monarchy, and by alluding to a famous *hadith* of the Prophet Muhammad. He said the principle of hereditary rule, which was inserted into this "rag called the *Kanun-i Esasi* [Ottoman Constitution]," had been "literally copied from the constitutions that belonged to the popes and kings of the old Europe [and] conformed to neither the *sharia* nor truth and reason." Criticizing Article 5 of the *Kanun-i Esasi*, which designated the sultan as "sacred" (see Chapter 2), Rasih Efendi also argued: "Our *sharia* requires that every leader is a shepherd and responsible for his herd. The word 'sacred,' which is diametrically opposed to our *sharia*, could only be used for Allah the Greatest and the Most Exalted" (TBMMZC 1922a: 257–258). Note that the shepherd-herd metaphor here was directly taken from a famous prophetic *hadith* that emphasizes the responsibility of leaders – a *hadith* that was frequently used by not only traditionalists and modernists, but also secularists (see Chapter 4).

Similarly, in his passionate speech, Hüseyin Avni of Erzurum, a leader of the "Second Group," but also a harsh critic of Sultan Vahideddin,[7] said the "great Turkish nation" had already awakened and realized its exploitation by the sultans, and then "seized its destiny" with the Anatolian resistance (TBMMZC 1922a: 258). For this reason, he continued:

> The Turkish Grand National Assembly has combined everything in itself and will safeguard that which is entrusted to it [i.e., the Caliphate].... The Turkish Grand National Assembly will never let the door open to the

monarchy's murders under the guise of the Caliphate [and] never allow them to assume certain illegitimate titles. Its [the Caliphate's] religious status is explained in the Book. It is the Turkish Grand National Assembly that will determine its legal status and entrust it to the qualified people. We have sworn since the very beginning: We are the true defender of the Caliphate and we are its protector; and the [GNA's] legal personality is its manifestation.

(TBMMZC 1922a: 261)

Likewise, Feyzi Bey, a deputy from Diyarbekir and minister of public works, spoke after Hüseyin Avni and recalled that the caliph was effectively a prisoner of war, declaring, "Despite the Caliphate's captive status, only the Turkish Grand National Assembly can protect it" (TBMMZC 1922a: 263). The discursive technique deployed by both Hüseyin Avni and Feyzi Bey (as well as many others) involved positioning the GNA, dominated by Mustafa Kemal and his friends, as the protector of Islamic Caliphate. This "benevolent" technique was aimed to help the secularists legitimize their claim for the GNA's right – on behalf of the "Turkish nation" –not only to abolish the Ottoman Sultanate and banish the current sultan-caliph, but also to appoint the next caliph, which they would soon accomplish by picking a docile member of the Ottoman dynasty (see below). For this, they first had to delegitimize the status of the current caliph-sultan, Vahideddin. In the same speech, Feyzi Bey chose an interesting discursive technique, again with reference to Islam, to prove the legal-religious invalidity of Vahideddin's claim to the Caliphate. Referring to the rule in classical *fiqh* according to which a "great *imam*" was required for the validity of collective prayers, which in earlier debates traditionalist Islamists had used to establish the dual (political and religious) status of the caliph against the claims of the modernists (see Chapter 4), Feyzi Bey said:

> I have visited every inch of Anatolia this time and witnessed that all people and the *ulema*, even those raised during the Sultanate period, agree that the [collective] Friday prayer is illegitimate now. Everybody has understood this fact today.... There is only a small group of people gathered around the Sultanate. Apart from these few people, the view of the majority is with the Grand National Assembly.
>
> (TBMMZC 1922a: 263)

After these speeches, Mustafa Kemal ascended to the podium as the chair of the GNA to give his famous – and long – speech on the necessity of abolishing the monarchy. In his speech he not only emphasized the un-Islamic nature of monarchy, but also presented a sophisticated account of the Caliphate, supporting and glorifying it. Fortified by two familiar discursive strategies of referencing sacred texts and invoking Islamic history, as discussed in Chapter 3, Kemal's speech first presented a kind of Islamic philosophy of history, where he argued that humanity had had a childhood and an adolescent stage from which it had reached adulthood only with the help of the prophets sent by God. At this point, interestingly, Kemal skillfully related the GNA's motion to separate the Caliphate from the monarchy to the Prophet Muhammad's life story:

> For this reason, the Great Prophet is the last prophet and his book is the Perfect Book. Muhammad Mustafa – peace and blessings be upon him – who was the last of the prophets, was born 1,394 years ago, in the dawn – before the sunrise – of Monday morning on the 12th of the [Hijra] month of Rabi' al-Awwal, or the *Rumi* April. Today is that day. May God make this a useful coincidence.
>
> (TBMMZC 1922a: 266–267)

He then talked more about the Prophet's life story, including his childhood and the hardships he had encountered during his mission as a prophet. Then Kemal proceeded to discuss in detail how, after the Prophet's death, the first four caliphs of Islam were elected and how the true Caliphate later turned into a monarchic system, which was not intended by God or the Prophet:

> [Following the Prophet's death, there was the question of] electing a leader to succeed the Messenger of Allah.... It was very appropriate that the venerable Abu Bakr became the caliph.... But, gentlemen, as soon as the Prophet died, there emerged strife, reaction, and insurgency everywhere. Venerable Abu Bakr eliminated them and took control of the situation.... [Later, the second Caliph], venerable Omar, once asked venerable Huzayfa ibn Yaman (may Allah accept his good deeds) about the [expected] "disorder that will rise like giant waves," to which he replied, "You don't have to worry about it; there is a locked door between it and you." Venerable Omar asked: Will this door be opened or broken? Huzayfa said, It will be broken!...
>
> Yes, venerable Omar (may Allah accept his good deeds) realized that ... the political system called the "Caliphate" would no longer be enough. [Then] venerable Othman became the caliph. But the door that had to be broken had been broken. There was gossip and displeasure in every corner of the Islamic world. Poor Othman was helpless and desperate.... The insurgent groups besieged his house and killed him in front of his beloved wife. After a lot of bloodshed and turmoil, venerable Ali (may Allah ennoble his face) was elected caliph. Let me repeat, the door had been broken.... Muawiya did not recognize Venerable Ali's Caliphate; on the contrary, he blamed him for Othman's murder. The caliph, whose main duty was to apply the Qur'anic provisions, was forced to stop the fight against the Umayyad army, whose soldiers had stuck pages of the Qur'an onto the ends of their spears.... [Muawiya] transformed the Caliphate into dynastic rule but kept the title.... [Later,] the rulers of the Abbasid state were also called caliphs.
>
> (TBMMZC 1922a: 267–271)

After this long introduction, Kemal focused on the Seljukid period (11th century), in which the Caliphate and monarchy were separate, in order to make his major point – that the former could survive if separated from the latter. He then jumped to 1922 to argue that a two-tiered system consisting of the GNA government and the Caliphate (with no political power) was perfectly compatible with Islam:

> In the fourth century hijra, a mighty Turkish state called the Seljukids was founded [which then] dominated the Abbasid caliphs residing in Baghdad. The caliphs resided in Baghdad side by side with a person by the name of Melik Şah, who represented the Turkish dominion. Now, I'd like to briefly analyze this situation.
>
> The Turkish sultan – who represented the sovereignty and dominion of a magnificent Turkish state – agreed to keep the Caliphate outside his [government]. If he had wanted, he could have abolished the institution that he had controlled and incorporated all the authority and titles associated with this institution into his own title. What venerable Selim did about five centuries later, Melik Şah could, if he had wanted, have done at that time in Baghdad…
>
> Now, gentlemen, it is definitely appropriate for the Caliphate to live today side by side with the institution that represents national sovereignty, which is the Turkish Grand National Assembly; and it will definitely have more dignity than the one that was helpless and powerless vis-à-vis Melik Şah; because it is the Turkish Grand National Assembly that represents the Turkish state today. And the Turkish nation as a whole has promised and taken it upon itself as a religious duty to be the [political] basis of the Caliphate.
>
> (TBMMZC 1922a: 271)

Mustafa Kemal then briefly recounted the history of the Caliphate from the first four caliphs to the 20th century in order to demonstrate "how natural, necessary and useful the current form of our government is for both Turkey and the entire Muslim World" (TBMMZC 1922a: 271–274). He noted that "venerable Yavuz" (Selim I) had re-united the Caliphate with political power "in order to revive and glorify" it, but the last sultan, Vahideddin, had betrayed the Turkish nation by "ending the independence of the Turkish state," and therefore prepared the end of his own rule.

Selective appropriation of Islamic history (supported by the detailed – though essentially unrelated – discussion of the Prophet's life story) and the subsequent Islamic justification of the separation of the monarchy and the Caliphate as discursive techniques were "instrumental" – in the double sense of the word – in terms of legitimizing the radical move to deprive the Islamic Caliphate of its political infrastructure, though Kemal claimed that from then on the GNA would constitute its "basis." His Islamic discourse was "instrumental" both in the sense that it gave skeptical deputies the assurance that the Caliphate would still survive

within the new system (side by side with the GNA), and in that later developments (i.e., the abolition of the Caliphate) would prove that this assurance was
not "sincere." That is, this Islamic discourse seems to be used by Mustafa Kemal
instrumentally as part of his "grand strategy" of becoming the head of the secular
Turkish nation-state, which would not tolerate an ecumenical religious leader
(see also below).

Moreover, his critical speech contained a discursive strategy that would
become an increasingly visible and significant feature of the secularist actors'
rhetoric: mixing the Islamic and (Turkish) nationalist discourses. We have
already detected this strategy in the earlier speeches given by Kemal's two
deputy friends, Hüseyin Avni and Feyzi Bey; Mustafa Kemal made it more
explicit in his address to the GNA by discursively locating the "nation" in the
subject position in this secular move:

> The Turkish nation, which has founded the Mongol, Seljuk, and Ottoman
> empires, trying all of them in the face of various events, has this time
> founded a state by its own name, and managed, with the ability and power
> with which it was born, to stand up to all the calamities it has faced.
>
> Now the nation has seized its destiny with its own hands and chosen to
> represent its national monarchy and sovereignty not through an individual,
> but by an assembly that consists of deputies elected by all of its members.
> That assembly is this high assembly of yours, the Turkish Grand National
> Assembly; and the government of this sovereign institution is called the
> Turkish Grand National Assembly government. There is no other institution
> of monarchy/power, and no other government.
>
> (TBMMZC 1922a: 274)

Toward the end of his speech, Mustafa Kemal reiterated his view on the
Caliphate – that it would survive alongside the GNA government, which would
function as its basis, and that this system was more Islamic than a dynastic rule.
What he "omitted" in his speech as a discursive practice was, however, the fact
that his view clearly implied a spiritual form of the Caliphate devoid of any
politico-military power, which would fit into a secular Republican rule. Redefining the Caliphate as a purely spiritual institution was another discursive strategy
he employed:

> There is the question of what will happen when this personal status (the
> monarchy) that attributes to itself the title of the Caliphate is gone!
>
> Gentlemen, we have seen that the Caliphate remained side by side with,
> but separate from, the monarchy for centuries in Baghdad during the time of
> Abbasid caliphs and then in Egypt. Today, too, it is only natural that the
> institution of monarchy and sovereignty and the institution of the Caliphate
> will live side by side. The difference is that in Baghdad and Egypt, there
> was an individual sitting on the seat of the monarchy. In Turkey, the nation
> itself is now sitting on that seat. The Caliphate's seat will be occupied by a

venerable individual whose basis will be the Turkish state, unlike in Baghdad and Egypt, where there was a powerless and desperate person [sitting on the seat]. This way, on the one hand, the people of Turkey will be ... happier and more affluent as a modern civilized state, and on the other hand, the Caliphate will function as the connecting point for the spirit, conscience, and faith of the entire Islamic world and as an exalted and honorable source [of inspiration] for Islamic hearts.

Gentlemen!... From now on, the future will clearly show how useful the Caliphate is for the Turkish State and for the entire world of Islam.

The Islamic Turkish state will be the happiest state in the world as the source of this double happiness...

(TBMMZC 1922a: 274–275)

After Kemal's speech, a heated debate took place in the assembly and several motions were proposed by GNA members, especially by conservative deputies such as [Hoca] İsmail Şükrü of Karahisar and Yusuf Ziya of Bitlis, regarding the separation of the Caliphate from the monarchy. These proposals were then referred to a joint committee that consisted of the *ulema* deputies to be discussed by them in terms of their compatibility with the *sharia*. The committee initially agreed that the Caliphate and the Sultanate could not be separated according to the Islamic *sharia*. Mustafa Kemal, who had so far been listening to the discussions quietly, stood on the bench in front of him and was very angry:

"Gentlemen," I declared, "neither the sovereignty nor the right to govern can be transferred by one person to anybody else by an academic debate. Sovereignty is acquired by force, by power and by violence. It was by violence that the sons of Osman acquired the power to rule over the Turkish nation and to maintain their rule for more than six centuries. It is now the nation that revolts against these usurpers, puts them in their right place and actually carries on their sovereignty. This is an actual fact. It is no longer a question of knowing whether we want to leave this sovereignty in the hands of the nation or not. It is simply a question of stating an actuality, something which is an already accomplished fact and which must be accepted unconditionally as such. And this must be done at any price. If those who are assembled here, the Assembly and everybody else would find this quite natural, it would be very appropriate from my point of view. Conversely, the reality will nevertheless be manifested in the necessary form, but in that event it is possible that some heads will be cut off!"

(Mustafa Kemal 1929[1927]: 578, 1961[1927], II: 690–691)

This explicitly threatening tone, which was symptomatic of the violence that accompanied the secularization of the Turkish political system between 1920 and 1930, worked well with the committee members: Kemal ended the discussion by warning the deputies of dire consequences should they refuse his view. Also, he once again mixed his nationalist discourse with an Islamic one as a discursive strategy. He employed this strategy through an influential technique: He identified himself with the "nation" and placed himself in a position where he could speak in the name of the "nation." This discursive technique, which he would often apply throughout his career, aimed at deriving justification from the widespread legitimacy of the idea of popular sovereignty that the conditions of national resistance against "European enemies" had created. It did not, however, exclude Islamic justification; rather, as was the case with the 1921 constitution that he had drafted and many of Kemal's other remarks, it was a mixture of national(ist) and religious references:

> "With regard to the theological aspect of the matter, the anxieties and the alarm on the part of the hoca gentlemen are quite unjustified. I will explain this to you," I said, and then I made a long statement. "Pardon me," responded Hoca Mustafa Efendi, deputy for Ankara, "we had regarded the question from another perspective. Now we are enlightened."
>
> (Mustafa Kemal 1961[1927], II: 691)

The joint commission's proposal containing the above-mentioned two articles was then brought to the Assembly and, after two short speeches by Mustafa Kemal and Hüseyin Avni in the same manner as the ones quoted above, it was accepted by majority vote on November 1, 1922. The Turkish GNA then declared the end of the Ottoman monarchy both in Turkey and the wider Muslim world. Although this decision meant the formalization of a regime change through a military and legal *coup d'état*, it did not, as mentioned, encounter strong opposition within the GNA. However, there was a reaction both within and outside the assembly, not particularly against the regime change itself, but against the change in the caliph's status from a temporal office to a spiritual one.

The major reaction to the law passed by the assembly led by Mustafa Kemal on November 1 came especially from the caliphal periphery. For instance, influential scholar and former *şeyhülislam* Mustafa Sabri Efendi, who lived in Egypt at the time, strongly criticized the GNA's move to separate the two offices by referring – as usual – to Islamic history. He argued that it had always been the norm that the caliph would appoint local rulers (sultans and *amir*s), but that, for the first time in Islamic history, a "sultan" (the Ankara government) appointed the caliph, which was unacceptable from an Islamic point of view (Mustafa Sabri 1924). Likewise, the GNA was criticized by another scholar and a leading modernist intellectual in Egypt, Rashid Rida, whose ideas have been discussed in Chapter 5. He had previously called Mustafa Kemal a "*ghazi*" (Islamic warrior) and "the servant of Islam and Muslims, a hero who is against the Unionist ideology of Turanism" (Rashid Rida 1921: 743ff.), but this time protested Kemal's decision. For Rida, this move, which separated the Caliphate from the monarchy and abolished the latter, thereby curtailing whatever was left of the political power of the caliph, produced a Caliphate with no political authority, and this was not acceptable according to Islam. He also argued that since the Islamic

Caliphate should not have spiritual authority (*sultah ruhaniyya*), the last two (Ottoman) caliphs, Sultan Vahideddin and Abdülmecid Efendi, were not eligible to be caliphs because they did not possess any real (political) power, being only "spiritual caliphs," which did not exist in Islam (Rashid Rida 1922). Instead, he proposed, as discussed in Chapter 5, the election of a Caliph from among the Arab *ulema* equipped with political power, and the recognition of the new Turkish state as the Caliphate's basis.[8] The election of a new caliph by the GNA following the motion on November 1 proved Mustafa Sabri and Rashid Rida right about the transformation of the Caliphate into a completely powerless office.

Election of the new caliph

The official transfer of power from Istanbul to Ankara following the abolition of the Ottoman monarchy was a peaceful procedure. Four days after the GNA's decision, Grand Vizier Tevfik Pasha in Istanbul handed over his seal of office to Ankara's representative Refet Pasha; on November 17, 1922, Sultan Vahideddin left the Palace and took refuge on board a British warship, fearing for his freedom and even for his life.[9] The next day, the GNA unanimously voted for, and published, a *fatwa* removing the ex-sultan from the Caliphate.[10] The same day, the deputies debated the election of the new caliph and how it should be done. İsmail Şükrü, a modernist scholar and one of Mustafa Kemal's staunch opponents, suggested that, in terms of procedure, a mere election was not enough; the entire GNA should give allegiance (*biat*) to the new caliph, which would formalize the caliph's (political) leadership. In response, Hacı Mustafa Efendi of Ankara, a scholar and member of Kemal's "First Group," suggested that allegiance by "a committee of five to ten people" representing the GNA would be sufficient (TBMMZC 1922b: 1057–1058). A few conservatives (e.g., Hafız Mehmed Bey of Trabzon) claimed that the GNA did not qualify as the *ahl al-hall wa al-'aqd* (the committee for electing the caliph) and that the caliph should have temporal authority, but they were ignored (TBMMZC 1922b: 1060). Following the debates, the deputies elected Abdülmecid Efendi, Vahideddin's cousin and the heir to the throne, as caliph by 148 out of 163 votes (TBMMZC 1922b: 1063). The sitting was closed with a prayer performed by a scholar-deputy, Alim Efendi of Kayseri.

During the election process, although most deputies agreed with Mustafa Kemal, who severely criticized the ex-sultan and proclaimed him a traitor,[11] on deposing Sultan Vahideddin, the assembly's decision to elect Abdülmecid, as mentioned, came after a heated debate over the new caliph's status. Many conservative (and "modernist") deputies, especially some *Hoca*s (*ulema*), wanted to see him as the head of the assembly and the leader of the Muslim world armed with political power, which Mustafa Kemal and his friends could not tolerate. The secularists, particularly Kemal himself, put forward exactly the same religious arguments using similar discursive techniques as they had three weeks earlier during the debates over the abolition of the monarchy.

CABINET - PORTRAIT

Figure 6.2 Sultan Vahideddin (source: Bahattin Öztuncay, 2005. *Hatıra-i Uhuvvet: Portre Fotoğrafların Cazibesi: 1846–1950*, Istanbul: Aygaz, p. 243).

Figure 6.3 Fatwa deposing Sultan Vahideddin, 1922 (source: *TBMM Arşivi C*, Devre 1, Dosya 308).

Figure 6.4 Abdülmecid Efendi, the last caliph (source: Bahattin Öztuncay, 2005. *Hatıra-i Uhuvvet: Portre Fotoğrafların Cazibesi: 1846–1950*, Istanbul: Aygaz, p. 282).

Against the opposition's charges, Kemal reiterated his earlier claim that the "Turkish state and people are the basis of the Caliphate," but this time he added a twist by making this assumption a justification for the claim that the caliph as an individual could not exercise the whole spectrum of the Caliphate's authority given the existence of an institution (the GNA) that was already equipped with political power. This idea, carefully framed in religious terms, was a crucial discursive technique because it would later be used by secularists as the most important argument for the abolition of the Caliphate itself (see below). Kemal complemented this technique with another by juxtaposing the ecumenical nature of the Caliphate with the national scope of the new Turkish state bounded by nation-state boundaries:

> This Assembly belongs to Turkey, to the Turkish people. Its authority and mandate belong only to the feelings and destiny of the Turkish state and Turkish people. Gentlemen, this assembly cannot assign to itself a power that embraces the whole Islamic world. Therefore, what the person who serves as the head of this assembly represents can belong only to Turkey. This is something limited. The noble office of the Caliphate is, on the other hand, a sacred institution that embraces the entire Muslim world. The religious and conscientious mission of the Turkish state and people at this point is to be the basis of this sacred office until the rest of the Muslim world reaches the same point [of independence]. [Our mission] is to protect ... the Caliphate's power and honor in the eyes of both the whole Muslim world and the non-Muslim world. But, gentlemen, it does not, cannot, and will not surrender its own existence to a caliph's whims and jurisdiction!
>
> (TBMMZC 1922b: 1051)

One specific aim of the secularist group was to keep caliph-elect Abdülmecid Efendi in Istanbul rather than invite him to Ankara, because Istanbul was still under British occupation, which made it impossible for the caliph to exercise any temporal power over the GNA. Against the modernists' argument that, according to Islamic *sharia*, the caliph could not be a prisoner of war (see e.g., speeches by Necati Bey, Hoca Şükrü, and Yusuf Ziya Bey, TBMMZC 1922b: 1048–1052), Mustafa Kemal instrumentally made an equally Islamic argument referring to Istanbul's special status as the "seat of the Caliphate" and the GNA's (and the nationalists') declared mission of "saving the Caliphate":

> We have started to exert some influence on [occupied] Istanbul without using any [military] power. [However,] the seat of the Caliphate has not yet become completely independent. But it is Turkey's duty to save the Caliphate. This is a special responsibility upon us.... This is also a mission that strongly supports us in the eyes of the Muslim world. It would be inappropriate to disturb this [image]. That is, it would not be appropriate to relocate the seat of the Caliphate to a different place given today's special circumstances.
>
> (TBMMZC 1922b: 1052)

In enacting the law (and *fatwa*) that deposed Vahideddin and elected Abdülmecid as the new caliph, Mustafa Kemal received crucial assistance from some of the *ulema* deputies in the assembly. As discussed above, Rasih Efendi of Antalya had skillfully provided Islamic justification for the abolition of the Ottoman monarchy on November 1, just like Seyyid Bey, who had helped Kemal prepare his important speech on the same day. This time, Minister of *Sharia* Mehmed Vehbi Efendi, previously a member of the low-rank *ulema*, played a crucial role in silencing the conservative opposition to the way the new caliph was elected and his status, determined on November 18. He not only signed the *fatwa* that deposed Sultan Vahideddin from the caliph's office, but also legitimized Mustafa Kemal's requests for electing the new caliph. As both a scholar and the *Sharia* minister, he spoke authoritatively on Vahideddin's – normally unlawful – deposition only on the grounds of "seeking refuge from the enemy" and on the necessity of electing a new caliph, which was mandated by the *sharia* (TBMMZC 1922b: 1046). Also, immediately after Mustafa Kemal's speech he ascended to the podium and made a crucial intervention into Islamic political theory: The caliph had to have all of the conditions enumerated in the classical theory, including being a *mujtahid*, the highest level of Islamic scholarship, and political and military strength, in order to exercise political authority; but since this was not possible today, it would be necessary to transfer this authority to an already existing institution that had political power. Vehbi Efendi's theological engineering somewhat lacked internal coherence, but it was nonetheless effective:

> Gentlemen, Allah the Almighty decrees that he made venerable Adam a caliph. But, gentlemen, the Caliphate means trying to build up the world until it comes to an end. Therefore, the person called the caliph must be in charge of executing the provisions of the glorious *sharia*. The person called the caliph must then be ... powerful. But, gentlemen, the caliph must [also] be a scholar, a *mujtahid*, and must possess vision and strength. This includes courage, bravery, and the rest. But is it possible to combine all these features in one single person? The answer is no! If not, then, according to the *sharia*, every task must be performed by its expert...
>
> Now, gentlemen, as for our current situation: Yes, we give allegiance to the caliph. This is a religious mandate for Muslims; besides, delaying it is not permitted, either. And [in return] this caliph leaves his responsibilities to the assembly; he can perform them through the assembly.
>
> (TBMMZC 1922b: 1053)

Mustafa Kemal also received the support of a number of secular intellectuals in the aftermath of the monarchy's abolition. Of particular importance among them was Ziya Gökalp, the leading ideologue of the secular-nationalist group, who wrote a series of articles soon after the GNA's decision in early November. In his first article, Gökalp explained the separation of religious and temporal authorities with reference to the "expediencies of life," i.e., the newly emerging political conditions after World War I:

Formerly, the religious head of an *ummah* could, to some extent, be the political head of an empire comprising several nations. When these nations emerged as separate states [following the defeat of the empires in World War I], the religious head of the *ummah* could not be the political head of only one of these nations. The function of the head of the [Islamic] *ummah* is to serve the religious life of the Muslims. The function of the state, on the other hand, is to serve national life. *When the two are united in one person, there may be occasions on which either the general interests of the* ummah *will be sacrificed for the sake of the particular interest of one nation* or the political aims of a nation for the sake of the *ummah's* ideals.

(Gökalp 1922a: 224; my italics)

Juxtaposing the ecumenical status of the Caliphate with the limited (national) and territorial nature of the Turkish state was a discursive technique frequently adopted by secularists following November 1 as part of their "theological engineering" (Mustafa Kemal himself had done it in the GNA on the day the new caliph was elected, as mentioned above). Gökalp also justified this separation with reference to Islamic history, praising the nature of the relationship between religious and temporal authority in the late Abbasid and early Seljukid period, and in that of the Mamluks in Egypt, where the authority of the caliph was submitted to that of the sultan. He called these times "the greatest periods in the history of Islam, both politically and religiously," and identified later periods (the Ottomans) as times of decline and degeneration (1922a: 226–227; see also below).

An important assumption underlying Gökalp's argument was the distinction between, or rather the dichotomy of, the *ummah* and the nation. For him, religion was the only common element between different societies comprising the *ummah*, whereas the common elements of a nation included language, morals, law, and political institutions, as well as religion (p. 223). Therefore, religion was only one of the elements that comprised a nation, having a much less significant status in modern society (cf. Gökalp 1915a). Relying on this distinction, he maintained the separation of the sacred and the profane, and emphasized, contrary to his earlier views (cf. Gökalp 1917a, 1917b), the separation of religion and politics. He justified his argument with reference to history and to current socio-political circumstances, but the ultimate source of justification was the idea of protecting the integrity of each of these two spheres. He insisted on the need to avoid mutual harm through the fusion of religion and politics.

In his next articles, Gökalp (1922b, 1922c) went on to maintain the idea of the separation of religious and temporal authority by claiming that it would give religion independence from politics.

The Caliphate, before now, has not been able to create such an organization, because it was not independent. When the Caliphate and the Sultanate were united in one person, one of the two dominated the other.... The Turkish revolution of today has assured the complete independence and freedom of these two powers. As the right of sovereignty of the Turks has passed to the people, *the Caliphate, too, has its independence by being separated from the Sultanate.* [Thanks to this separation] *our religious life, which has been for many centuries in a state of lethargic slumber, will re-awaken,* and, in accordance with the promise of our Prophet, the splendor of Islam will shine in much the same way as it shone in its Golden Age.

(1922b: 229; my italics)

Again, in the rest of the article, Gökalp justified his view by deploying familiar discursive strategies, with references to Islamic history, the Qur'an, and a *hadith* of the Prophet, all interpreted in a heterodox way. He attributed an exceptional status to the unification of religious and temporal authority in one person, which was in fact the rule in much of Islamic history, including the periods of the Prophet Muhammad, the first four Caliphs, the Umayyads, much of the Abbasids, and the Ottoman Empire.

We also witness here the crystallization of another secularist discursive strategy: that of adopting religion to modern conditions. Gökalp employed it via the technique of instrumentally stressing the need to protect the authenticity of Islam. (This technique would also characterize many secular reforms following the Caliphate's abolition.) He argued that separating the Caliphate from the Sultanate under the new system would bring a "complete independence" to the former assuring "religious freedom," i.e., freedom of the religious sphere from politics. Thus the discourse employed in the texts located both realms in their respective positions, where religion was not immune to the possible harmful effects of politics (and politicians), and therefore was in need of protection. It is obvious, however, that what provided religion with protection was nothing but (secular) politics itself, which implied the superiority of the political realm over religion.

Though framed mostly in religious terms, Abdülmecid Efendi's election (or appointment) as new caliph was clearly an important step in the way of secularization. For, since the last Abbasid caliph, Mutawakkil III, the Caliphate had never – at least formally – been deprived of political power and temporal authority. Led by Mustafa Kemal, the GNA's decision formalized the weak status of the Islamic caliph. Following the election process, a committee representing the GNA went to Istanbul to give allegiance to the new caliph in a ceremony, which was as grandiose as the sultans' accession ceremonies, but lacked the elements that symbolized temporal power, such as sitting on the throne and the procession of the sword. Abdülmecid Efendi accepted visitors for more than a month, in addition to many congratulatory messages from Muslim and non-Muslim leaders abroad. The first congratulatory telegram from the Muslim world came from India's Caliphate Committee; it was followed by the leaders of Muslim minorities in Europe, Russia, and China. Also, the Istanbul press immediately started quoting letters and articles published in the Arab media, all approving the new caliph and congratulating him (see Satan 2008: 161–162 for details).

On the other hand, after leaving Istanbul, deposed Caliph-Sultan Vahideddin went first to Malta and then to the *Hijaz* to be hosted by King Hussein, who had revolted against the Ottomans during World War I. In Mecca Vahideddin published a proclamation denouncing the GNA's election of a new caliph on the grounds that the Caliphate concerned the "entire Muslim world of three-hundred million, rather than the five-six million Turkish people." He also argued that, since the Caliphate meant both a political and religious succession of the Prophet, the GNA's earlier decision to separate the two was unacceptable, as well. Moreover, using the strategy of invoking Islamic history, Vahideddin defined his Caliphate as the "Muhammadan government" (*saltanat-ı Muhammediyye*) by saying that "from my grandfather Osman Ghazi to Selim I there was Turkish rule in the name of the Ottoman state; after Selim I, this rule turned into the Muhammadan government with the addition of the Caliphate" (Vahideddin 1923: 4). The former sultan then severely criticized Mustafa Kemal and his friends for accusing him of high treason:

> Those who are wrongfully accusing me of high treason have destroyed the Muhammadan government by isolating the Caliphate from its rights and power, thereby committing treason against not only their own homeland, but also the entire Islamic world. Having suffered the consequences of extreme actions in our involvement in the Great War, I acted with caution and continence – or, cowardice, according to my opponents – in foreign policy in order to protect the state. In fact, I was determined to sacrifice myself, if necessary, to buy time. In contrast to this moderate policy, if my opponents' extreme and imprudent actions were successful, I would personally lose, but the state would win; however, they have made the state lose its Islamic government.
>
> (Vahideddin 1923: 5)[12]

Meanwhile, the election in Ankara of the new caliph would be a turning point in terms of the weakening of the Caliphate, because the caliph would have no politico-military power, as his status was designed by Mustafa Kemal as that of a "spiritual caliph." With a message he sent to the caliph via Refet Pasha, Kemal made this explicit by ordering the caliph to publish a declaration to the Muslim world, in which he would

> particularly disapprove of the way Vahideddin Efendi acted,... declare that the regime of the new Turkish State [was] the most suitable and useful for the whole Muslim world,... admire and appreciate the celebrated efforts of [the nationalists], [and] not mention or propose any idea – other than those mentioned above – that could be deemed political in this proclamation.
>
> (Mustafa Kemal 1961[1927], II: 695–696)

Ordered to submit to Ankara's will, Abdülmecid Efendi was practically under house arrest in Istanbul, forbidden to speak to the press, publicly express any binding opinion on any religious or political matter, or to appoint religious dignitaries. He did not even have any authority over his family's property. As such, his election would turn out to be the first step in abolishing the Caliphate – though for the majority of the assembly members this does not seem to have been the intention at the time. Even Kemal's closest friends, and the leaders of the nationalist movement at the time, including Kazım Karabekir, Rauf Bey, and Refet Pasha, were pro-Caliphate and would remain so even after the institution was abolished in 1924. For Kemal, however, the Caliphate's final demise would be an *intended* consequence of its transformation into a purely "spiritual" institution (see Mustafa Kemal 1961[1927], II: 685).

The abolition of the Caliphate

The last caliph had very little, if any, political power during the period between November 1922 and March 1924, which rendered his office what Jaschke (1972: 115) calls a "pseudo-Caliphate." However, the Caliphate's abolition was not as smooth and easy process as its suddenness may suggest. Though Mustafa Kemal, who increasingly perceived the caliph (who he himself had elected) as a threat to his single-party rule, wanted to get rid of the Caliphate as soon as possible, he could not do it immediately due to the caliph's high level of ideological power both in Turkey and in the wider Muslim world – as evidenced by the fact that it took Caliph Abdülmecid Efendi more than a month to accept visitors and congratulatory messages from all over the world. This was despite the fact that the abolition of the Ottoman monarchy by the GNA on November 1, 1922 meant, as mentioned, the "deactivation" of the Caliphate, since it was turned into a "spiritual" institution with no temporal authority. However, there were still some actors, both in the GNA and the media, who wanted to see the caliph as the leader of the GNA and head of the new Turkish state. Though he publicly denounced it several times, Abdülmecid Efendi himself was probably willing to support such a plan, which obviously disturbed Mustafa Kemal and his friends. The tension between Istanbul and Ankara surfaced following the election of the new caliph with what Tunçay (2005: 53) calls "a war of pamphlets."

The battle of the pamphlets

The discursive confrontation between the secularists and modernist Islamists in early 1923, which I prefer to call the "battle of the pamphlets," is significant because it both represents the religious justification by *secularists* of the secular reform that curbed the caliph's temporal power in November 1922, on the one hand, and epitomizes the process in which secular nationalism increasingly gained the status of a source of legitimation, on the other. That is to say, though secularists still drew heavily on Islam, deploying such discursive strategies as invoking the sacred texts of Islam and the history of the Caliphate, they also used, by insisting on the principle of national sovereignty as the basis of the new Turkish state, a secular-nationalist repertoire as an alternative framework for Islam. This process (of the rise of modern nationalism as a source of legitimation) had started in 1919–1920 during the early phases of the "Turkish national struggle," but it was crystallized during the debates in the public sphere on the Caliphate after the abolition of the Ottoman monarchy in November 1922.

What really triggered the discursive battle between the pro- and anti-Caliphate groups was an essential tension between the universal/ecumenical nature of the Islamic Caliphate and the territorially-limited, national character of the new "GNA state." The shift from the multi-ethnic and multi-religious Ottoman Empire to the Turkish nation-state based on the modern principle of national sovereignty produced a profound tension between the two institutions. This tension was reflected not only in the content of some 35 publications (pamphlets, articles, letters, politicians' declarations) involved in the debate, but also in their titles: Many of them contained one or both of the phrases "national sovereignty" and "Islamic Caliphate." Modernist Islamists (e.g., Hoca Şükrü 1923; Mustafa Sabri 1924) tried to solve this tension in favor of the Caliphate, the secularists (e.g., Ziya Gökalp 1922a, 1922b; Hoca Halil *et al.* 1923; Ağaoğlu 1923a, 1923b) in favor of the Turkish Grand National Assembly headed by Mustafa Kemal Pasha.

The "battle of the pamphlets" was begun symbolically by Yunus Nadi, a friend of Mustafa Kemal and the editor of *Yeni Gün*, who criticized the Caliphate in an article titled "A New Era of Battle" on November 26, 1922. This was followed by several other articles published in *Yeni Gün* and other "Kemalist" newspapers, such as Celal Nuri's *İleri*. What really stirred the action, though, was the publication of a 28-page pamphlet by deputy İsmail Şükrü Efendi (also known as Hoca Şükrü) titled "Islamic Caliphate and the Grand National Assembly," which was distributed to the deputies in the GNA on January 15, 1923.[13] The short book alarmed Mustafa Kemal and other secularists because it voiced the concerns and demands of the pro-Caliphate group. It was also significant as the major text outlining the modernist-Islamist view of the Caliphate, on the basis of its definition as a political institution, between 1922 and 1924. Hoca Şükrü started out by observing that the GNA's November 1 decision to abolish the Ottoman monarchy may have created the "confused" belief in some circles that the Caliphate had become a spiritual institution. On the contrary, he argued, the caliph's primary responsibility was to "administer worldly affairs and represent the Prophet in politics and protecting religion." He noted that the caliph and the GNA were in different cities, which might have caused this confusion:

> But all Muslims would admit that we are in critical and abnormal times. No doubt this is a temporary situation, and, God willing, it will soon return to its original and natural condition. Islamic public opinion must know that there is no cleavage between the Grand National Assembly and the caliph of the Muslims, who the Assembly has elected and given its allegiance. The caliph belongs to the assembly; the assembly belongs to the caliph!
>
> (Hoca Şükrü 1923: 4)

In order to support his claim that the caliph should be the head of the GNA because he was supposed to be a political ruler, Hoca Şükrü advanced a series of religious arguments and discursive techniques drawing on Islamic political theory and history. He argued that Islamic unity required the presence of a strong caliph with political power, and that whenever the Caliphate had turned into a spiritual institution in the past, the Islamic state faced demise and destruction, as was the case with the Abbasids and the Andalusian Caliphate. Then it was the Ottomans who had unified the Caliphate with state power, which created the strongest Muslim empire in history (pp. 6, 12–14). Furthermore, according to *sharia*, the "Islamic law" (*ahkam-ı İslamiye*) included both "religious" and "this-worldly" rules (p. 7), and the laws issued by local rulers and parliaments should be approved by the caliph as the supreme leader, whose authorization was, more-over, required for the legitimacy of local Muslim rulers (pp. 9, 27). Finally, that the Caliph should be the head of the parliament was a religious mandate, which was also implied by the fact that his presence was required by religion for the validity of collective prayers (including the Friday and annual festival prayers), the annual pilgrimage (*hajj*), and for the maintenance of holy shrines and their guardianship (pp. 26–27). Hoca Şükrü concluded that if the government kept the Caliphate while abolishing the monarchy, then it should respect the caliph's rights and his status in the Islamic *sharia* as outlined here.

Hoca Şükrü's pamphlet outraged Mustafa Kemal, who interpreted it as an assault on "national sovereignty" by "a reactionary group" that wanted to bring the monarchy back under a caliphal guise:

> The absurd ideas which ignorant people like Şükrü Hoca and his compan-ions were disseminating about the actual conditions prevailing in the world under the power of "religious prescriptions" with the intention of abusing our nation, are not worthy of being repeated here. In the course of centuries there have been people and there are still people today in the interior as well as in foreign countries who profited by the ignorance and fanaticism of the nations and try *to make use of religion as a tool to help them in their polit-ical plans and personal interests.*
>
> (Mustafa Kemal 1929[1927]: 591; my italics)

He was particularly angry because he was concerned that Hoca Şükrü's "idea would penetrate into the nation's mind" (Mustafa Kemal 1923: 62). The GNA's attorney general requested that Hoca's immunity be suspended, but failed (Toynbee 1927: 55). Mustafa Kemal himself held a press conference to respond to him in İzmit on January 16, where he called those who supported Hoca "igno-rant" and accused them of demanding the return of the old order of constitutional monarchy. He claimed that the GNA government was based on both the *sharia* and national sovereignty, and that "the Caliphate has no official status" in the Turkish state (p. 63).[14] He also responded to most of Hoca Şükrü's claims one by one through a series of religious and political arguments. He said Islamic unity around a caliph was not possible given the existing situation of Muslim countries (p. 64) and that Muslims would never recognize the superiority of the Caliphate anyway, because the latter was ecumenical (p. 65). Its ecumenical nature clearly indicated, moreover, that the Caliphate was not compatible with the basic principle of national sovereignty (p. 68). He added that the Caliphate would be a liability for the new Turkish state because it would bring the responsibility of "saving" the Muslim world, which Turkey clearly was not able to do (p. 70). However, he was careful to justify his unusual claims:

> Another principle, according to the *sharia* and religion, there is no such thing as the Caliphate. As you know, the Prophet himself said "there will be kingdoms 30 years after me." This is a *hadith*. Therefore, to say that "there must be a Caliph, the Caliphate will exist, the Caliphate will survive" amounts to demanding something that is against the prophetic *hadith*.
>
> Another thing; for example, when Omar was elected Caliph, they called him the Caliph of the Prophet. He said in his address, "I don't have such a title, and I can't. There is no such title. There is no Caliph. You are the believers, and I'm your leader." Also, when the Prophet died, nobody thought of electing a Caliph; [it is] leadership, leader (*emir*). What was formed under the name of the Caliphate was leadership, which is only a government. That is to say, the Caliphate means the government.
>
> (Mustafa Kemal 1923: 64)

This last sentence is a perfect example of how secularists exploited modernist (Islamist) arguments: Kemal reversed the modernist formula (as expressed by Hoca Şükrü) that "the Caliphate means the government," which originally meant that the caliph must be a temporal ruler, to turn it into the secularist claim that the Caliphate was just a religious guise for secular rule. The implication was that it was not an essential institution in Islam and thus could be abolished. In addition, Kemal's "strange" way of applying the strategy of invoking Islamic history (his discursive technique) involved presenting a well-known historical event in a completely incorrect manner: By claiming that "when the Prophet died, nobody thought of electing a caliph," he reversed the fact that electing their first caliph was the first thing the early Muslims had done (even *before* they buried the Prophet). In fact, this event had frequently been used as evidence for the Caliphate's significance, even by Kemal himself.[15] Furthermore, the way he invoked what Omar, the second caliph, had said about not being a "caliph" exemplifies another secularist discursive technique: taking historical events out of their context and freely interpreting them as the "expediencies of time" require. In this case, Kemal interpreted Omar's remark as evidence to negate the Caliphate's existence, while in fact he had objected to attributing any divine component to his caliphate, because some had called him the "caliph of Allah." Needless to say, in reality this "evidence" directly contradicted the secularist conception of the Caliphate as a spiritual institution, which is why modernists frequently made use of this historical reference.

Another discursive technique through which Kemal invoked history was his interpretation of the relationship between the Ottoman Empire and the Caliphate. Contrary to the pro-Caliphate (modernist and traditionalist) argument on the (positive) impact of the latter on the Ottomans' power and prestige, Kemal said off the record:

> Gentlemen! The Caliphate is a big trouble for our nation. Before assuming the Caliphate, the Ottoman Empire had its strongest period. But a few years after assuming this status, it began to decline. It was of no use. Ottoman sultans, rulers, leaders were most powerful and prestigious when they were isolated from the Caliphate. That is, the Caliphate did not help in any way. [On the contrary,] it brought many troubles
>
> (Mustafa Kemal 1923: 70)[16]

He concluded:

> This state has nothing to do with the Caliph. To tell you the truth, it has been necessary to make the revolution that we want gradually. We have divided it into two [phases]; first [we have completed] the first one, then the second one...
>
> To say that the state is secular (*la-dini*) is to tell the people to attack the state.
>
> MÜŞTAK BEY [*Tanin* columnist]: Mr. Hüseyin Cahit called it "secular" in his letter.
>
> GAZI PAŞA [*Mustafa Kemal*]: One must say "material," or "temporal"; and these words must not be replaced by "secular."
>
> MÜŞTAK BEY: No sir, they still understand it that way. Because they interpret it that way, we censor ourselves. What is truly scary is our self-censorship...
>
> GAZI PAŞA: Gentlemen, to say unnecessary things may produce unwanted results, but for positive results, one should not remain completely silent, either.
>
> (Mustafa Kemal 1923: 67, 75)

Two days later, Mustafa Kemal held another meeting, this time open to the public, in İzmit. He declared that the new regime was neither a monarchy nor a Republic:

> Gentlemen! Our government is no longer a despotic government; nor is it an absolutist or constitutional monarchy. Our government is not like the French or American Republics, either. Our government is a people's government. It is fully based on consultation. It is the people who have power in the new Turkish state.
>
> (Mustafa Kemal 1923: 97)

Furthermore, he assured the people that there would be no conflict between the Caliphate's new status and the GNA government. To support this claim, he discussed the status of the Prophet of Islam, saying that the Prophet was neither a king nor a temporal ruler; rather, his primary mission was to carry God's message to humanity, which was a religious/spiritual one. Though the Prophet intended no regime change in Arabia and neighboring countries, such as the "Iranian State" (Sassanids) and the Roman Empire, due to the existing situation in the *Hijaz*, he was obliged to take up political and military power as his secondary mission (p. 102). Kemal concluded that the new state, which already included all the basic principles of Islamic government such as justice and consultation, was the best possible Islamic state; therefore, there was no need for the Caliphate:

> Our Assembly and the government consisting of its noble members fully conform to the requirements of the *sharia*. Why, then, do we still need the office of the Caliphate?... The assembly does not belong to the Caliph; it never will. The Assembly belongs to the nation.
>
> (Mustafa Kemal 1923: 102–103)

In 1923, the discursive technique of presenting the Caliphate as "useless" when there was already an Islamic state (the GNA) constituted the essence of the secularist argument to abolish the institution and would be increasingly repeated until March 1924. As we have seen, Kemal often complemented this claim with his specific discursive technique of identifying his own political interests with those of the "nation." To support this claim in his address, Kemal reiterated his earlier argument that Islamic unity around the Caliphate was utopic and dangerous and, because all Muslim countries had been colonized by the West, the Caliphate was useless anyway. He completed his speech by calling the Caliphate's supporters "reactionaries" and by openly threatening the caliph in Istanbul:

> The Caliphate's existence is not regarded as a source of conflict by the nation. Unless it is forced [to be one]! But it must certainly be known that when there is a conflict in any shape or form, then discourse ends and practice starts.
>
> (Mustafa Kemal 1923: 109)

This kind of language constituted a pre-emptive strike against reactionaries like Hoca Şükrü who wished to see the caliph as the head of the Turkish state. Mustafa Kemal then ordered the journalists and scholar-deputies in the GNA (Seyyid Bey, in particular) to prepare public opinion for the Caliphate's abolition (Ahmed Emin 1970: 31).

Mustafa Kemal's "First Group" then appointed a research committee to respond to Hoca's arguments (and those of the pro-caliph group), with the resulting work being published as a book (Toynbee 1927: 55). Titled "The Caliphate and National Sovereignty," the 240-page book contained 28 short articles by secularist intellectuals and some *ulema* and six declarations (by Caliph Abdülmecid, Mustafa Kemal, Ismet Pasha, Refet Pasha and Sheikh Sanusi) in favor of the GNA's two decisions made in November 1922. The book included Ziya Gökalp's three articles discussed above (1922a, 1922b, 1922c), as well as those written, by, among others, Ahmed Ağaoğlu (whose five articles were included), Ahmed Emin, Hoca Rasih Efendi and Celal Nuri, all of whom defended the decision to deprive the Caliphate of temporal power by advancing religious arguments. Also, in order to resolve the tension between the principle of national sovereignty and the universal Caliphate, they employed, in different degrees, major discursive strategies and techniques as applied by the two leaders of the secularist group, Mustafa Kemal and Ziya Gökalp, particularly those of invoking sacred texts (the Qur'an and prophetic traditions) and referencing different episodes of Islamic history (see *Hilafet ve Milli Hakimiyet* 1923: 5–207). The book also contained an open letter (by Ağaoğlu) to the Indian Caliphate Committee and Indian Muslim leaders Amir Ali and Aga Khan (Ağaoğlu 1923b), and two reports on how Arab Muslims perceived the Caliphate's current status.

In the collection, there was only one article that directly addressed Hoca Şükrü's pamphlet: "A Response to Hoca Şükrü Efendi" by a certain "F. C." (1923). Basically repeating Mustafa Kemal's arguments, the author accused Hoca Şükrü of "using religion as an instrument of politics" and labeled him as the representative of a reactionary group that was trying to reverse the advancement of the Turkish nation. He accused him of creating the false image of an illegitimate GNA by claiming that the caliph should have approved its decisions for the last four years and of provoking people to revolt against the GNA (*Hilafet ve Milli Hakimiyet* 1923: 178–180). The author also accused Hoca Şükrü of justifying the essentially illegitimate Sultanate system by equating it with the Caliphate, which was supposed to be independent of dynastic power:

> The likes of Şükrü Efendi, who claim to be a guide to the ordinary people, do not see any difference between the hereditary system and [the system based on] election. They perceive both to be equally legitimate sources of the Caliphate['s authority].
>
> (*Hilafet ve Milli Hakimiyet* 1923: 185)

Finally, just one day after the publication of Hoca Şükrü's pamphlet, another pamphlet that directly criticized him, titled "National Sovereignty and the Islamic Caliphate," was written by three *ulema*-deputies. They were all from Mustafa Kemal's First Group: Hoca Halil Hulki (1869–1940) was elected deputy six times from Siirt during his lifetime; Hoca [el-Hac] İlyas Sami (1881–?) was elected deputy three times from Muş, Bitlis, and Çoruh; Hoca Rasih (1883–1952) was elected deputy seven times from Antalya and once from Maraş (Tunçay 2005: 68). The authors declared, "Armed with the glorious Qur'an, we will respond to the reactionary view in [Hoca Şükrü's] pamphlet" (Hoca Halil *et al.* 1923: 3). In fact, they quoted many Qur'anic verses (12 in total) and prophetic *hadiths* as well as making historical references. Since they applied modernist-Islamist strategies and techniques to support the secularist position, however, they often contradicted themselves. Drawing on their intellectual formation, which was similar to Hoca Şükrü's, they defined the Caliphate as the "same as government" and as a "contract" and "power of attorney" (p. 14), arguing that there was no distinction between the political and the spiritual in Islam (p. 24). But the authors still accused Hoca Şükrü of supporting a reactionary group that was trying to bring the monarchy back. They accused him of using religion as a tool for the monarchy (p. 27), of trying to transfer the GNA's authority to the caliph (p. 33) and trying to create a kingdom under the caliphal guise, while Turkey could not be a kingdom or a republic (p. 35).

The three Hocas also claimed that the principle of national sovereignty was fully compatible with Islam, because its embodiment, the parliament, corresponded to the principle of "consultation" decreed by the Qur'an, which they supported by citing the two *shura* verses (4/144, 3/159). Based on this argument, they further claimed that the Turkish GNA was not only to function practically as a modern Caliphate, but that it was also the best form of government since the time of the four "rightly guided" caliphs of Islam:

> Muslims have formed a government in light of Islamic principles. This government was formed to maintain justice. It was based on consultation. It has appointed its administrators (*ul al-amr*).
>
> Ministries have been formed to perform the duties mentioned in the *sharia* documents under the title of the Caliphate's responsibilities.... It is clear that our government has acted by the rules of the *sharia*, and never deviated from them. This is the government that conforms to the *sharia* the most after our rightly guided Caliphs. It is for this reason that Allah the Almighty has given this government and its armies his grace.
>
> (Hoca Halil *et al.* 1923: 15–16)

They also added, as a new discursive technique, that since the first four Caliphs had come to power in different ways (by election and appointment), it was now possible to make a new *ijtihad* in order to have a new form of Islamic government that was compatible with current circumstances (p. 6). Moreover, since the GNA was the only authority able to perform *ijtihad*, its members were free to make the necessary adjustments in the government in light of new developments. In such a government, they concluded, the caliph should have no say either in religious affairs (such as appointing *imams* to mosques) or in the administration of the state, not only because there would be a conflict between his ecumenical authority and the individual Muslim state's national mandate, but also because his status was too high to deal with these mundane affairs:

> Hoca Şükrü Efendi must know that the caliph is not the head of a particular Islamic state. ... The caliph's status is very high, and it is only the common Muslim affairs that are included within his jurisdiction. We will be relieved of our religious responsibility if we are satisfied with this [definition].
>
> (Hoca Halil *et al.* 1923: 28)

The three Hocas' essentially religious justification of a secular reform in response to the modernist scholar-deputy Hoca Şükrü exemplifies yet another instance of the secularists receiving crucial support from the *ulema* in legitimizing their political positions and actions. However, neither the *ulema*'s nor secular intellectuals' discursive rebuttals to the modernist Islamists represented by Hoca Şükrü would be enough for Mustafa Kemal and his friends to win the "battle of the pamphlets." They needed some further pro-Islamic action to prepare the Muslim public for their ultimate secular reform.

Preparing Muslim public opinion

The secularists made certain symbolic gestures to counteract the possible negative reactions that the GNA's decision to curb the Ottoman caliph's temporal authority, as well as Islamist critiques such as Hoca Şükrü's pamphlet, might have triggered in the Muslim world. One such gesture was the establishment of a "scientific committee" led by Abdulaziz Jawish, a Tunisian scholar, politician, and journalist who lived in Cairo and Istanbul as a member of the CUP's *Teşkilat-ı Mahsusa* (secret service) and was very politically active against the British occupation of Egypt during World War I. Founded by the Ankara government, this committee was supposed to organize religious affairs in Turkey and maintain its connections with other Muslim countries. Likewise, Ankara also revitalized the former Islamic Society (*Jamiat al-Islam*) under the leadership of Mehmed Akif, a deputy from Burdur, former *Teşkilat-ı Mahsusa* member, and important figure both within the CUP and the nationalist movement in Anatolia. The society had played a key role in getting funds and public support from Muslims in India, Afghanistan, Iran, and North Africa for the Turkish resistance. Its new aim was to strengthen links between Turkey and other Muslim societies, especially in the Arab world, particularly against the expansion of the forces of Ibn Saud. Because of Jawish and Mehmed Akif's earlier "Pan-Islamic" activities in the Middle East and Europe, the British interpreted these two bodies as an attempt by Mustafa Kemal to revitalize Pan-Islamism (FO's Report, 371/9290, quoted in Satan 2008: 163–165). Also, upon a request from non-Turkish Muslims, Ankara decided to organize a "Congress of Islamic Unity" through these two institutions after the Lausanne peace negotiations in Anatolia.

Still, Mustafa Kemal must have known that abolishing the Islamic Caliphate would result in a far greater reaction than had deposing the Ottoman sultan. Therefore, this action, which concerned the entire Muslim *ummah*, rather than just the Turks, and which was directly connected to the essential principles of the Islamic religion, would require more time and better preparation. The move to reactivate the Islamic Society and organize a large-scale congress that would represent the majority of the Muslim world was a significant act on the part of Ankara to preserve its image in Muslim public opinion and the high level of ideological power that it had enjoyed during the national struggle. In this context, another gesture the GNA made after limiting the caliph's authority was the publication in early 1923 of a semi-official, unsigned pamphlet titled "The Caliphate and National Sovereignty," which legitimized the separation of the Caliphate from political power exclusively with reference to canonical arguments. It was actually written by Seyyid Bey at Mustafa Kemal's above-mentioned request.[17] Aimed at preparing Muslim public opinion for the deposition of the caliph, this influential document was distributed to the media and within the GNA. Also, an authorized translation into Arabic by Abdulghani Sani (1871–1951), the Turkish Consul in Beirut and the GNA's spokesperson, was published in *al-Ahram* in 1924 in order to "win the hearts and minds" of the Arab public. Sani added to it as a preface a short article that he had originally published in *al-Ahram* in 1923, in which he presented a summary of the GNA's longer text arguing that (i) the Caliphate was a matter of law rather than theology, (ii) that it was a purely political authority, and (iii) that there were no precise rules in the Qur'an or the *Sunna* of the Prophet regarding its organization (quoted in Haim 1965: 210–211).

The significance of Seyyid Bey's text lies in the fact that it outlined and justified the secularists' view of the Caliphate, which they would soon materialize, and that it was backed by the GNA's institutional endorsement and disseminated widely in the Middle East. In terms of textual characteristics, the document contained many instances of familiar discursive strategies, such as invoking Qur'anic verses and prophetic traditions, as well as referencing early Islamic history and the Islamic intellectual tradition. For example, in the author's own preface there was a reference to a verse that stated that the "religion has been completed" (5/3) as well as to the "*ul al-amr*" verse and the famous *hadith* that limited the Caliphate to the first 30 years of Islam was quoted (p. 1). The author also discussed the election of the first four Caliphs and quoted al-Taftāzānī and Ibn Humam, two great scholars of theology and law, respectively (pp. 2–3).

The document also functioned as the First Group's response to Hoca Şükrü's pamphlet which, as discussed above, had alarmed Mustafa Kemal and the secularists by calling on the GNA to elect Caliph Abdülmecid as the head of the new state. The document's author, Seyyid Bey, skillfully rallied his vast knowledge of Islamic terminology and history to "prove" that what Hoca Şükrü and other conservatives had said about the Caliphate could not be supported by evidence from Islamic law or theology. That is, the caliph could no longer be a temporal ruler due to existing circumstances, but he should remain as the spiritual leader of the Muslim world (Seyyid Bey 1923: 6–7, 43–46). This specific argument actually contradicted both Seyyid Bey's earlier writings on the Caliphate and some of the arguments developed in this text itself (see below).

The text was divided into two main parts, discussing the history of the Caliphate in the first, and the question of separating it from the monarchy in the second. To provide a theoretical and historical background to this question, Seyyid Bey made a series of religious arguments in the first section. He began by saying that Islam was sublime and that it recognized no spiritual authority attached to any individual. Second, implying Seyyid Bey's essentially modernist view, since the caliph was not like the Catholic Pope, he must have necessarily resembled a modern king or republican president:

> In the Catholic religion, the pope is the infallible representative of the Christ in establishing religion. He issues orders in Christ's name.... Islam is

perfect and free from these kinds of superstitions.... Therefore, in Islam, unlike in Christianity, there is no clergy, nor succession [of the Prophet] in establishing religion. In Islam, there is no church as in Christianity. The offices of the *müfti* and of the *şeyhülislam* are not organizations established by Islam.... They are administrative offices. [Therefore,] the caliph, or the imam, is the leader of the Islamic community. The "general authority" that he possesses is never spiritual, as is the case with the pope; rather, it is administrative and political just like a president or monarch's general authority.

(Seyyid Bey 1923: 5, 7)

Third, the author again employed the familiar discursive technique of defining the Caliphate as a kind of mandate entrusted to the caliph by the "nation," which was the basis of Seyyid Bey's alternative theory of the Caliphate, as discussed in Chapter 4. He argued that it was a contract offered by the nation and concluded by both parties, which was no different from the power of attorney. Thus, all the rules of mandate should apply to this contract, including the fact that the nation (as the "mandatory") could depose the caliph from his post. (This was an argument that Seyyid Bey had developed earlier – when he was a CUP leader – to justify the deposition of Abdülhamid II by the CUP; see Seyyid Bey 1917.) As a further discursive technique, the author equated the allegiance (*biat*) of the nation (or its representatives) with the power of attorney given to the caliph, which was, as discussed in Chapter 4, very unusual given the traditional/mainstream conception of *biat* (see also Arnold 1965[1924]: 70–71):

The Caliphate is like a contract signed between the nation and the caliph. It is an agreement for a kind of mandate or power of attorney [*akd-i vekâlet*].... The duties which the Caliph is responsible for are in fact the nation's own responsibilities; they are collective national duties. If in a particular way the nation offers and allocates them to a person deemed eligible and suitable [for the post], and if that person accepts the offer, then he becomes the caliph. And this agreement, concluded by an offer and acceptance, is called the "Caliphate" ... Since the Caliphate is a kind of mandate agreement, the majority of the Sunni *ulema* says that "the basic principle of Caliphate agreement is consultation. In other words, it is election and allegiance [*bey'at*]."

(Seyyid Bey 1923: 14–15)

The fact that the caliph's authority was no more than a kind of power of attorney implied, Seyyid Bey claimed, that the Caliphate was not an end in itself, but a means to proper Islamic government, which consisted of such virtues as justice, happiness, and order – i.e., the caliph's main responsibilities.

Fourth, as a further discursive technique, Seyyid Bey made a distinction between the "true" and the "fictitious" Caliphate. Referring to the familiar *hadith* of the Prophet, which reads, "The Caliphate will last thirty years, then will come the bitter *Sultanate*,"[18] he repeatedly stated that the period of the first four caliphs, which had indeed lasted 30 years, had been followed by the era of oppressive regimes, including the Umayyads, Abbasids, and Ottomans (pp. 8–9). Thus, the author implied that the separation of the Caliphate from the "despotic" Ottoman monarchy made the former even more authentically religious:

> In terms of its true nature and ostensible form, the Caliphate is divided into two: the perfect or true Caliphate and the formal or fictitious Caliphate.... The true Caliphate is the one which contains the characteristics and necessary conditions that will be explained below, established by the nation's will and consent and through election and allegiance. The fictitious Caliphate is the one which does not include the necessary conditions but is acquired by force through domination and invasion, rather than the nation's election and allegiance; it is an *imamate* that is based on a dynastic and monarchic system and kingdom.... Though this looks like the Caliphate in appearance and form, in reality it is not the Caliphate; rather, it is a kind of dynasty and sultanate, domination and oppression; it is kingship.... As all the leading Sunni scholars unanimously agreed, the Umayyad and Abbasid Caliphates were of this kind. As explained in the most prestigious books in the literature of theology and law, such as the *Müsâyera* and *Ta'dîlu'l-ulûm*, they were in reality not caliphs, but only sultans and kings.... The Islamic *shariah* does not approve or accept this kind of sultanate based on oppressive rule. To attribute it to Islam means insulting and deriding this exalted religion.
>
> (Seyyid Bey 1923: 8–9)

The document concluded that since the Caliphate of the despotic Ottoman caliphs was "fictitious," the power these sultans had exercised was illegal from an Islamic point of view. Therefore, it was a religious duty of the believer *not* to obey the authority of these oppressive tyrants.

Seyyid Bey supported this claim with reference to his theory of the Caliphate as a mandate of power of attorney entrusted by the nation to the caliph. He argued that, according to Islamic contract law, all the rules of mandate should apply here, including the authority of the nation to depose the caliph and the rule that mandate (the Caliphate) could not be inherited (p. 17). Furthermore, though he admitted that, according to the *sharia*, the caliph's mandate over the nation was "general and absolute," he claimed that this authority actually belonged to the nation and could not be exercised as a despotic power over the people. Here Seyyid Bey deviated from his earlier theory of the Caliphate (1917) in that he had previously claimed that the caliph's "general and absolute" authority was not "utterly and completely absolute" (Seyyid Bey 1917: 452), i.e., his authority could be limited, as the CUP (of which Seyyid Bey was a leader) had done after the 1908 Revolution. This time he claimed that the caliph's "general and absolute" authority actually belonged to the "nation" rather than a single individual, and could not be divided or monopolized. Moreover, in order to justify the nation-state form that the GNA had adopted by abolishing the Ottoman monarchy, he made another crucial intervention into the theory of the Caliphate by equating the Islamic concept of "general and absolute authority" (*velayet-i amme*) with the Western concept of "national sovereignty":

> Therefore, the conclusion drawn from truths of *fiqh* is that the general authority and sovereignty that the caliph possesses is the totality of individual authorities and sovereignties. It is directly taken from the nation. And in essence it is the nation's right and its property. It does not belong to any individual per se, but to the Islamic society as a whole.... It is collective, common to all individuals, and not exclusive or peculiar to any individual or community. This is the essence of the concept of "national sovereignty," that is, it is the nation's *general authority*, and nothing else.
>
> (Seyyid Bey 1923: 22)

In other words, Seyyid Bey's "theological engineering" as applied here implied another instance of the secularization of Islamic discourse, because it involved reconstructing the Caliphate on the basis of a completely modern (and newly emerged) concept of "national sovereignty" by "Islamicizing" it under the guise of a term well known in Islamic literature. Given the pragmatic nature of most of what Mustafa Kemal and his friends did to transform the state, it is safe to argue that this discursive "relocation" of national sovereignty under a religious guise was a quick yet useful solution to the tension between the Caliphate's ecumenical nature and the new state's limited/national form. It thus helped legitimize the Kemalist policy of getting rid of a supreme religious authority that could limit Kemal's power in Turkey. Moreover, at the macro level, this discursive shift was clearly a product of the transformation of the Ottoman Empire into a national state owned by Turks (and Kurds) in Anatolia.[19]

A final discursive technique was put forward in the text against the possible objection that the newly elected Caliph (Abdülmecid Efendi), who had no temporal power, looked more like a fake caliph than a true *imam*. The author listed a number of qualifications that a true caliph should possess, such as being a *mujtahid* (the highest level of Islamic scholarship), justice, power, and physical health. He concluded that unless it was possible to elect a caliph with all these qualifications, there was no religious requirement to elect one at all (p. 13). He further argued that the "Quraysh condition" was not required today and that it was best to keep the Caliphate within the Ottoman dynasty instead of transferring it to a powerless ruler like Sharif Hussein. Moreover, by discussing different ways of electing a caliph, Seyyid Bey concluded that the GNA's election of Caliph Abdülmecid was the one that best fit the *sharia*:

> When there are numerous candidates, age cannot be a criterion for selection [of the caliph]. It is necessary to prefer and elect the most faithful and the most mature one among them. And the Caliphate is never inherited by heredity, because power of attorney cannot be inherited. Therefore, the decisions recently taken by the Turkish Grand National Assembly to appoint

the caliph by election and allegiance, and to prefer and pick the wisest and the most suitable member of the Ottoman dynasty, deserve celebration and congratulations, because they meant the revitalization of the *sharia* principles that had not been put into practice for centuries.

(Seyyid Bey 1923: 16)

The second part of the document discussed the separation in November of the Caliphate from the monarchy. It included a series of religious arguments to defend the GNA's decision to restrict the Caliphate's temporal power. To do this, the author first tackled a crucial obstacle: the consensus among the earlier *ulema* that it was mandatory to have a caliph as a temporal ruler. Against this consensus, which was supposed to be a binding resolution, as Hoca Şükrü had emphasized, Seyyid Bey resorted to his own distinction between the "true" and "fictitious" Caliphate, arguing that it was not religiously permissible to have a monarch-caliph, let alone mandatory:

When the evidence is carefully scrutinized, one sees that what is required is establishing a government. What is not permissible is the lack of government, and to leave the members of the nation in an unregulated, chaotic situation…. Then, is it necessary to appoint an imam who has absolute authority, in a situation where there already is, or it is possible to form, a stable and just government, in whatever shape or form?… In other words, could the evidence, which points to the necessity of appointing an imam who is just and with a mature personality and the necessary conditions, also imply appointing an ignorant sultan who is overwhelmed by his ambitions and, to say the least, someone who wastes the state treasury?

(Seyyid Bey 1923: 24–25)

Seyyid Bey then proceeded to argue that Islam did not accept absolute rulers and that even the first four caliphs' authority was restricted during the Islamic Golden Age. He maintained that Islam imposed restrictions on rulers' power based on two sources: consultation and contract law. For him, the fundamental political principle of consultation (*şura*) in Islam was required by God even for the Prophet himself, which was naturally true for his successors and other rulers as well. Moreover, the fact that the Caliphate was a kind of mandate entrusted by the "nation" necessarily made the ruler subordinate to the will of the nation, which was reflected in the parliament. Seyyid Bey concluded that putting restrictions on the caliphs' authority was not only permissible, but in fact required by Islam. Furthermore, against the possible objection that it would have been enough just to depose the former sultan instead of abolishing the monarchy itself, he argued that, historically, changing persons on the throne did not work, as it was the institution of the Sultanate itself that produced an unjust and oppressive system:

There is no need to hesitate to approve limiting the authority and rights of the Sultanate, which is nothing more than despotism and ambition. Because limiting it means reducing public loss, oppression, and domination.... Experience and historical events have shown us that in replacing sultans, the successor is not better than the incumbent.... For this reason, the best and healthiest way in this context is to put the caliph in a position where he cannot cause any damage.

(Seyyid Bey 1923: 32–33)

To reiterate this point, Seyyid Bey explicitly stated that the former sultan, Vahideddin, had abused his power derived from the Caliphate and "committed high treason," which made it necessary to "return" his political authority to the "nation" that actually owned it.[20] To support this claim, he went back to the historical argument by saying that never in Islamic history, except for the period of the first four caliphs, had the rulers been "true" caliphs: All sultanic Caliphates were fictitious. He further argued, as part of the same discursive strategy, that in Egypt the Abbasid caliphs' authority was separated from the temporal authority of the Mamluk sultans for 250 years (pp. 34–35). He concluded that, since the separation of religious and temporal authorities had been approved by the "respected Egyptian *ulema*" at that time, it should now be admitted that the existing situation created by the GNA was also genuinely Islamic:

It is well known how Vahidüddin acted and how he used the Islamic *sharia* as an evil tool for his own ambitions. Thus, instead of leaving it to the people who are known to misuse this kind of force, isn't it more appropriate to take it back from them and give it to the nation, its real owner, and to form, whenever possible, a government that serves the realization of the aims of God? There is no doubt that the government of a national assembly, whose only concern is the nation's happiness, is more acceptable in God's view than a sultan who values nothing but his own crown and throne.

(Seyyid Bey 1923: 38)

Seyyid Bey complemented this argument with the strategy of invoking Qur'anic verses, particularly the famous "*ul al-amr*" verse (4/59). After citing the verse, he equated the Turkish GNA with the "*ul al-amr*" (Islamic rulers) mentioned in the verse – a discursive technique often deployed by secularists between 1922 and 1924 – and concluded that it was mandatory to obey the GNA's decisions, since God himself commanded this in the Qur'an (Seyyid Bey 1923: 46). He added that what the GNA had done was simply return the Caliphate to the legitimate form it had taken in Egypt previously.

Finally, to further reinforce his defense of the curbing of caliphal authority by Mustafa Kemal and his friends, Seyyid Bey argued that Islam was "a democratic religion" and that the form of government was not one of religious fundamentals, but a matter of changing historical circumstances: People chose their own government "in accordance with the expediencies of time." Thus, using the techniques of historicizing religion and prioritizing social change, Seyyid Bey claimed:

What we need is to establish a just government, rather than to appoint a person as monarch and endow him with some holy rights like former European monarchs. Islam is a completely democratic religion, a populist *sharia*. It does not involve any traces of aristocracy, [which is indicated by] the verse "*Verily the most honoured of you in the sight of Allah is (he who is) the most righteous of you*" [49/13]. The question of the form of government is a matter of the exigencies of time. The [legal] rulings on these kinds of matters are determined in accordance with the exigencies of time, the requirements of the public interest, and the social conditions of the people. And, as these conditions and exigencies change [over time], the rulings change as well.

(Seyyid Bey 1923: 39)

Thus, this crucial document exemplifies how Islamic discourse was further secularized after the caliph's temporal power had been purged at the end of 1922: Certain secular notions, such as national sovereignty, democracy as the best political system, the primacy of social-historical context (the "expediencies of time"), and an increasingly secular/ethnic definition of the "nation," were inserted into the Islamic discourse of political actors. This trend, which was increasingly visible in the discourse of the secularist group, was clearly related to the institutional secularization forged by the Turkish GNA between 1920 and 1923.

Furthermore, the GNA's document is also a good example of how the secularists made use of historical information and fragments of (religious) argumentation from the literature on Islamic political theory as a tactical device to justify their claims, even though sometimes they might have contradicted themselves. For example, as demonstrated above, in the text Seyyid Bey ambiguously claimed both that the Caliphate was a strictly temporal authority and that it should have no political power. This apparent contradiction within the text, which was in fact a contradiction between Seyyid Bey's modernist view and Kemal's secularist one, stems from the fact that the secularists, who first turned the Caliphate into a powerless, ceremonial institution and then destroyed it, mostly started out with a *modernist* argument (that the "Caliphate was the same as the government" [i.e. political rule]), because they could not directly derive a secularist argument from Islamic traditions. As much as indicating their pragmatism, this contradiction also implies, as Haim (1965: 213) observes, that Mustafa Kemal had in mind the idea of abolishing the Caliphate itself as early as in 1922, as he himself would later claim:

To labour for the maintenance of the Ottoman dynasty and its sovereign would have been to inflict the greatest injustice upon the Turkish nation.... As for the Caliphate, it could only have been a laughing-stock in the eyes of the really civilized and cultured people of the world.

(Mustafa Kemal 1929[1927]: 18)

The Caliphate at Lausanne

The Lausanne Peace Conference, which started on November 20, 1922 and ended on July 24, 1923 with the Treaty of Lausanne, resulted in Turkey's recognition by European powers as an independent state. Turkey was represented by a delegation headed by Foreign Minister İsmet Pasha[21] – Mustafa Kemal's most loyal friend – in the conference, which was organized by the Allies (Britain, France, and Italy, in particular) following the Turkish victory over the Greeks in August 1922. As discussed above, Mustafa Kemal had used the Allies' invitation to the Istanbul government to attend the conference as an excuse to abolish the Ottoman monarchy in early November. What was left of the Ottoman-Islamic order was the Caliphate. Though it was not directly part of the official agenda of the peace negotiations because the British saw it, at least publicly, as Turkey's internal problem, Article 27 of the treaty, which was very similar to the Article 139 of the Treaty of Sèvres (1920), directly concerned the Caliphate:

> *Article 27*: No power or jurisdiction in political, legislative or administrative matters shall be exercised outside Turkish territory by the Turkish Government or authorities, for any reason whatsoever, over the nationals of a territory placed under the sovereignty or protectorate of the other Powers signatory of the present Treaty, or over the nationals of a territory detached from Turkey.
>
> It is understood that the spiritual attributions of the Moslem religious authorities are in no way infringed.[22]

This last sentence, however, reserved room for the Caliphate as a spiritual authority, unlike the Sèvres Treaty that had effectively abolished it. As such, the article reflected (and reinforced) the existing status quo wherein the Caliphate was stripped of its temporal power by the Turkish GNA. It thus seems that the question was resolved in favor of the Turkish delegation because the Treaty attributed to the Caliph the spiritual authority that Britain and its Allies (seemed to have) wanted to remove from him (Oliver-Dee 2009: 136).

The Caliphate also came up – indirectly – on two more occasions. First, Articles 17 and 22 specifically mentioned Egypt, Sudan, and Libya in the context of Turkey having no political or legal rights over the people and property of its former territories. Second, the Allies requested that the "Medina treasury" (Prophet Muhammad's personal belongings) that the Ottoman army had taken to Istanbul when leaving the *Hijaz* at the end of 1918 be returned to Arabia. İsmet Pasha refused this by saying, "Legally, these items are the caliph's property" (LBKTB 1971, I: 68). Third, the Turkish delegation also refused to give the Orthodox Patriarch in Istanbul any political privileges (which he had enjoyed during the Ottoman period) on the grounds that religious leaders could have only "spiritual titles" in the new Turkish state after the separation of the Caliphate from monarchy (LBKTB 1971, II: 327).

Although the Caliphate was not openly discussed during the negotiations, there are some indications and claims that Britain required its abolition as a condition for recognizing Turkish independence (discussed in Satan 2008: 185–186). First, though the Lausanne Treaty was signed on July 24, 1923 and ratified by the GNA on August 23, the British parliament did not ratify it until April 15, 1924, that is, after the Caliphate was abolished. Second, during the discussions on the conference in the British parliament, Foreign Minister Lord Curzon stated that the government would have left the Turks alone had they been willing to confine their country "as an Asian state surrounded by other Asian kingdoms," rather than "returning to Europe." He added that he had told the Turks "since they came back to Europe, they would have to adopt Western administrative and governmental standards" (quoted in Satan 2008: 180). Third, on March 5, the British Foreign Office declared, in response to a question in the parliament, that there was no implicit or explicit indication in the Lausanne Treaty of recognizing the existence of the Turkish Caliphate (ibid.: 237). Fourth, when the peace negotiations were broken off in February 1923, İsmet Pasha returned to Turkey to meet with Mustafa Kemal. They met alone in Eskişehir, rather than Ankara: Turkish Prime Minister Rauf Bey wrote in his memoirs that the negotiations had broken down over the Caliphate question and that İsmet had convinced Kemal that abolishing it was necessary for peace with the British. Fifth, Kazım Karebekir Pasha, one of the leaders of the Anatolian resistance, also said that an anti-Caliphate atmosphere dominated Ankara upon İsmet's return from Lausanne. Sixth, Mushir H. Kidwai, a leader of the Indian Caliphate movement (whose ideas on the Caliphate have been discussed in Chapter 5), wrote an article in July 1923 claiming that Britain had required the abolition of the Caliphate (and of the Indian Caliphate Committee) as a condition for signing the treaty. Finally, according to a secret British report, after signing the treaty, İsmet Pasha told Turkish generals that abolishing the Caliphate and exiling the Ottoman royal family may have helped Ankara on the Mosul question by convincing the British that Turkey would not pursue Pan-Islamist policies in the Middle East (ibid: 237).[23]

Regardless of any British influence on Ankara, it is clear that the Caliphate's demise was an extremely "positive" development for Britain. Some British bureaucrats in the Foreign Office reported that by abolishing the Caliphate and thus getting rid of a great source of Muslim opposition, Turkey had done the British Empire a "great favor" and that Turkey had undermined its own power in Middle Eastern politics (Tunçay 2005: 82–83).[24] Again, whether Britain had demanded it or not, a bitter anti-Caliphate campaign began in Ankara and Istanbul following the peace negotiations, especially after the proclamation of the Turkish Republic on October 29, 1923. The campaign's discourse was dominated by the claim that the new Turkish state was already an Islamic state and thus there was no need for the Caliphate, which had lost its true Islamic character.

Islamic state, un-Islamic Caliphate

Though members of the GNA in Ankara called the regime of the new Turkish state the "GNA government" after November 1922, the Ankara government had secretly ordered its representatives abroad to refer to their state as the "Republic of Turkey" (*Türkiye Cumhuriyeti*) as early as May 1922 (Shaw 2000, IV: 1875). However, perhaps because the republican regime was perceived to be vulnerable to dictatorship, they never pronounced the republic until after the Lausanne Treaty; instead, they stressed Turkey's uniqueness, which was part of the nationalist discourse they often employed. For example, as mentioned above, when in October 1922 Kemal's friend Refet Pasha went to Istanbul as the representative of the Ankara government, he harshly criticized the sultan (Mehmed VI) and his regime. But he also argued against the idea of a republic, seeing it as "harmful" as a constitutional monarchy:

> We have never thought about a republic. It has always been away from us. I do not see any difference between the republic and constitutional monarchy, and perhaps the former would be more harmful for our country. As I said before, the only difference between constitutional monarchy and a republican presidency is that in one of them the leadership is hereditary. Ultimately, however, they are same. The style we have found is different; it perfectly fits to our nation's character. [It is based on] the Grand National Assembly. The cabinet is composed of the members of the Assembly.
>
> (quoted in Lütfi Fikri 1922: 357)

Modernist Islamists considered this "regime" to be a temporary situation and a pragmatic solution, as exemplified by Hoca Şükrü's famous pamphlet discussed above. Some modernists also regarded it as a form of dictatorship because it involved the unification – rather than separation – of powers and was vulnerable to domination by powerful politicians. For example, the liberal intellectual (and modernist Islamist) Lütfi Fikri, who was the head of the Istanbul Bar Association, wrote a pamphlet criticizing the Ankara government and Refet Pasha's comments discussed above. Against Refet's unusual "theory," Lütfi Fikri remarked that he had just invented a new category (the third way) that was not found in the literature on regime types, then cited a certain legal scholar, "F. Brantano" for the established classification. His critique of Refet Pasha centered on the fact that it excluded the principle of the separation of powers. The 1908 Young Turk Revolution had re-established this principle after the Hamidian regime, but the nationalists had blamed the constitutional monarchy for the military and political problems of the *Meşrutiyet* era, and thus abrogated this principle with the new Constitution (1921) that united the executive, legislative, and judicial branches – all undertaken by the GNA under Mustafa Kemal's increasingly powerful leadership. Fearing the possible rise of a dictatorship, Lütfi Fikri remarked that in a government consisting of the entire parliament (as suggested by Refet Pasha) the legislature could not be endowed with powers to check the executive branch:

> Turning a Parliament that contains hundreds of members into a cabinet would create imbalance and instability within the state.... But since, according to Refet Pasha, these deputies will always have to get permission from

the parliament to do anything, they will gradually turn into puppets with no individual initiative...

On the other hand, how do we know that "the parliament that continuously governs as the only sovereign" will not make any mistake? Who will check it? Nothing exists in this world that is without any limits. Constitutional principles are not supposed to be arbitrary; they are the products of the centuries of common experience. Though both represent the national sovereignty, the executive and legislative branches check and balance each other. If the executive cannot fulfill its duties, the parliament removes it from power.... In Refet Pasha's system ... what will prevent the dictatorship of the Parliament? Who will force it to be responsible to the nation?

(1922: 360–361; cf. Lütfi Fikri 1923a)

Lütfi Fikri's critique, which was published before Hoca Şükrü's pamphlet, similarly angered the secularists, who responded with several pamphlets (e.g., Celâleddin Feyyaz 1922; Fuad Şükrü 1922; Süleyman Nazif 1922) to influence public opinion. Mustafa Kemal himself would later harshly criticize Lütfi Fikri in 1925 for being pro-Caliphate (Kara 2005: 41).

Such pro-monarchy and pro-Caliphate opposition to the secularists might have delayed the proclamation of republic. In order to eliminate the opposition, Kemal had the GNA renew national elections, and turned his Defense of Rights Group into a political party called the "People's Party." In this process, Kemal emphasized the Caliphate's importance as part of the foundations of his party's program and even made the "protection of the Caliphate" one of its foundational "Nine Principles." On April 8, 1923, shortly before he officially founded the party, Kemal said:

The office of the Caliphate, whose basis is [now] the Grand National Assembly, is a supreme institution with a high status among Muslims. In the Islamic religion, all prayers are performed collectively. And this congregation has a leader [*imam*] on whom all the members of the congregation depend. For this reason, the leader is the representative of the congregation.... In addition to this, Islam involves strong solidarity, which unites the entire *ummah* on a single spirit. The way this occurs is through the spiritual obedience of all leaders to the greatest leader [*imam-ı ekber*]. And this leader is called the caliph.... For this reason, the entire Muslim world is concerned with the question of the Caliphate. If there is no Caliphate on earth, the Muslim world will be distraught and miserable.... Therefore, the Grand National Assembly has made his highness the caliph himself the basis of this venerable and supreme office.

(quoted in Karabekir 1991: 136–137)

In early 1923, Mustafa Kemal had gone on a country-wide tour to consolidate his prestige in Anatolia. In February 1923, he delivered a speech/sermon in a mosque in Balıkesir, where he said:

O, the nation; Allah is the One and the Only; his glory is high. His peace and blessings be upon you. It is well known that the basic law that His Excellency the Prophet was sent by the Almighty God as an Ambassador and servant who explained the religious truths to the people, is stated in the Glorious Qur'an. Our religion, which has given people the spirit of blessing, is the last and the perfect religion. Because our religion fully conforms to reason, logic and truth.

(quoted in Borak 1962: 29)

He also repeated the same speech in other places encouraging the audience to openly express their views, saying that the mosques were not only for worship, but also forums where public/worldly matters and the issues of the state should be discussed freely. The instrumental nature of his discursive strategy is apparent in his attitude toward the role of Islam in the public sphere, which was in direct contradiction with his later views, which centered on the idea that religion was "a matter of conscience" and should therefore be kept in the private sphere.

In order to cleanse the opposition from the parliament and have the latter ratify the Lausanne Treaty, Kemal decided to hold national elections. Held in July 1923, the elections were conducted in conformity with the Ottoman electoral law of 1877: one deputy was to be elected for every 20,000 men, and every male over 18 now had the right to vote; the old condition of having to pay an electoral tax had been lifted. In order to be elected, one had to be a male Turkish citizen over 30 years of age. However, parliamentary elections were still held in two rounds, as had been the case during the Ottoman period, and a second "voter" was to be elected for every 200 people (Demirel 1994: 511–521). Once a person was a candidate on the People's Party's list, he would definitely be elected as a deputy, even with a single vote. In 1923, the second-round candidates, selected by the party, were presented to the first-round voters, who had no alternative to this list. Secondary candidates (themselves party members), also had no choice but to vote for the candidates nominated by the party (ibid.: 584–597).[25]

In the elections, 52 percent of the elected deputies were bureaucrats (including government and military officials and educators), 20 percent were professionals (lawyers, doctors, and engineers), 12 percent were traders, agriculturalists, and industrialists, 2 percent were *ulema*, and 5 percent were journalists (Frey 1965: 210). As a result of the elections, the opposition was completely eliminated from the GNA: 290 of the 437 deputies of the previous term, including all 63 members of the Second Group, were not elected; there was only one deputy (Zeki Bey) who was not from Kemal's party (Demirel 1994: 571–584). Kemal made the idea of a republic public in an interview, which was also published in Turkish, with a French newspaper in September. While much of the Istanbul press criticized this decision, the two Ankara newspapers supported it. Kemal also made his party's name the *Republican* People's Party (RPP), appointed İsmet Pasha as the new prime minister, and moved the state capital from Istanbul to Ankara. Istanbul still remained as the seat of the Caliphate. On October 29, 158 out of 287 members of the GNA who were present on that day unanimously voted to change the regime into a republic and elect Mustafa Kemal as its first president. Caliph Abdülmecid was one of the first to congratulate him.

The proclamation of the republic restarted the debates over the Caliphate in the press. Toward the end of 1923, there were rumors everywhere that Mustafa Kemal and the GNA would abolish the Caliphate. Necmeddin Sadak, an RPP deputy and journalist, suggested that the caliph should resign and a new caliph be elected by all Muslims in a Caliphate congress to be held in Istanbul. Caliph Abdülmecid Efendi refused to resign, insisting on the legitimacy of his status and adding that he had no plans to get involved in politics. The head of the GNA, Fethi Bey, similarly denied the allegation that they had plans to abolish the Caliphate (Uluğ 1975: 128). Lütfi Fikri (1923b) also wrote an "open letter" to the caliph asking him not to resign, adding that these allegations were fabricated on purpose, implying that Ankara was behind them (see Gümüşoğlu 2004: 90–93 for debates in Turkish press). The British press, too, often published news and comments on this issue. The press commented on November 4 that the Caliphate was an impediment for Mustafa Kemal and that he needed to get rid of it; it could be either destroyed entirely, or turned into a harmless institution. Later the press reported that the "secular trend" was getting stronger in Turkey, which would help Kemal, who believed that the new republic would never be safe until it completely cleansed itself of religion and from the influence and prestige of the Ottoman dynasty (Kürkçüoğlu 1978: 306–307).

Meanwhile, in Istanbul, there were rumors that an opposition movement was being formed around Caliph Abdülmecid. When a group of former nationalist leaders, including former Prime Minister Rauf Bey, Kazım Karabekir, Refet Pasha and Adnan [Adıvar] visited the caliph, Ankara interpreted the move as an attempt to revive the Ottoman monarchy and condemned it. Also, the fact that the caliph had accepted Muslim statesmen as official visitors/delegations angered the Republicans even more. İsmet Pasha, the vice chairman of the RPP and the prime minister, responded to this development as well as to the opposition's criticisms on behalf of his party with very harsh language, which was yet another indication of violence (symbolic and otherwise) as an essential component of Turkish secularism:

> If at any time a Caliph takes it into his head to interfere with the destiny of this country we shall not fail to cut his head off. If, for reasons of tradition, be it implicitly or explicitly, any Caliph should assume the attitude of a man who seems to interest himself in the destinies of Turkey, or should have views which could raise the belief in him that he could treat Turkish statesmen in a benevolent or protecting manner, we should regard such conduct as being in absolute contradiction of the principles of the existence of this State. We should consider his attitude an act of high treason.
>
> (quoted in Mustafa Kemal 1929[1927]: 679)

By the end of 1923, Mustafa Kemal and the party bosses were looking for an excuse to abolish the Caliphate, but the caliph's public declarations in support of the GNA and his careful avoidance of politics made it difficult to realize this plan. The opportunity they had been waiting for came with a letter written by Indian Muslim leader Aga Khan and London Islamic Society President Amir Ali to İsmet Pasha, which was published in three Istanbul newspapers on December 5 – before it arrived in Ankara. It requested on behalf of Indian Muslims that the caliph's official status be clearly defined after the October 29 amendments, and that it should be protected as a religious connection between Muslim peoples. Though the letter attributed no political functions to the caliph, and its authors were known to be of the opinion that the caliph should only be a spiritual leader, Ankara interpreted it as part of a plot to bring back the Ottoman monarchy in Istanbul and an intrusion in domestic politics by a foreign country – since its authors were also British citizens – accusing them of being British agents.[26] Aga Khan and Amir Ali denied the allegations.

In January 1924, the government leaders went to İzmir to watch a combat exercise, where they firmly decided to abolish the Caliphate. In a series of secret meetings, Mustafa Kemal first convinced the top military personnel, then met with leading journalists, and finally the president and deans of Istanbul University and received their support (Satan 2008: 206–207). This way he made sure that both the military and civil society would accept his radical move. The next month, the GNA reduced the expenditures of the caliph's office (including allocations for royal family members) to 0.3 percent of the government budget (331,000 lira), though the caliph had requested an increase. During the discussions on the budget, some deputies proposed that the Caliphate be abolished and the royal family exiled. In response, Caliph Abdülmecid said in his telegraph that he had never deviated from the path determined for him by the GNA, and that abolishing the Caliphate would harm Turkey's relations with the Muslim world (ibid.: 208).

On March 1, Mustafa Kemal gave the inauguration speech for the GNA's new working year, where he insisted that "the nation" wanted the unification of education (which meant that the *medrese* system would be abolished) and that it was necessary to separate Islam from politics for the sake the religion itself. This was an early example of the secularist deployment of the discursive strategy of protecting the authenticity of religion by keeping it away from the corruption of politics, which is still common in contemporary Turkish politics. In his address, Kemal described politics as "vague and slippery" and "a stage of selfish interests and passion." He concluded:

> It is indispensable *in order to secure the revival of the Islamic faith*, of which we are happy and satisfied to be a member, to disengage it from the condition of being a political instrument, which it has been for centuries through habit.
>
> (Mustafa Kemal 1929[1927]: 684; my italics)

The next day in the RPP's meeting, a group of deputies led by Sheikh Safvet Efendi of Urfa, a scholar and Sufi leader, proposed that the Caliphate be abolished and the royal family exiled. In its introduction, the proposal claimed that in essence the Caliphate was the same as the government, and that there was no need for a Caliphate in addition to the "present Islamic government that is responsible for both this-worldly and other-worldly functions" (quoted in Satan 2008: 210). Some deputies, like Hoca Rasih of Antalya, Musa Kazım of Konya, and Yahya Galip of Kırşehir, also proposed that Mustafa Kemal be the caliph, but he refused this. Some, such as Azmi Efendi of Eskişehir and Halid Bey of Kastamonu, however, objected to the idea of abolishing the Caliphate. Finally, Minister of Justice Seyyid Bey gave a speech on the necessity of abolishing the Caliphate, framing it exclusively in Islamic terms. Essentially reiterating his earlier views in his pamphlet discussed above, he argued that the Caliphate was a kind of mandate given by the nation to a person, and that it was up to the nation to decide whether it was necessary to appoint a representative at all. He concluded that the nation (represented by the GNA) had the right not to have any caliph if deemed necessary, an authority which the Qur'an also recognized (see Erdem 1996). After these speeches, the articles in the proposal were put to a vote; only six deputies objected to the first article (Satan 2008: 216).

The next day, on March 3, three proposals were brought to the GNA to be discussed: the unification of education (banning religious schools), the abolition of the Ministry of War (removing the military from the cabinet), and the abolition of the Caliphate. While the first two laws passed in less than 40 minutes, discussions over the latter lasted for three hours and twenty minutes (Satan 2008: 222). It was proposed by Sheikh Safvet and 50 other deputies. The original proposal discussed in the RPP meeting had stated, "The Caliphate is abolished"; this sentence was modified so as to transfer the functions and powers of the Caliphate to the GNA: "Because the Caliphate is essentially intrinsic to the concept and purview of the government and the republic, the office of the Caliphate is abolished."

Only two deputies spoke against the proposal. One of them, liberal Zeki Bey of Gümüşhane, the only independent deputy in the GNA, stressed two points. First, he referred to the November 1, 1922 law that abolished the monarchy, noting that the same law established the office of the Caliphate as part of the new Turkish state, and that because the GNA had not abolished this law, the proposal contradicted it. He added that the RPP had promised to keep the Caliphate during the election season, and the people had voted for them based on that promise. Second, he argued that the Caliphate was essential for Islamic unity, and abolishing it would thus "leave this enormous power to the enemy." Tunalı Hilmi of Zonguldak objected, saying: "It is not the Caliphate itself that is being abolished; it is the office of the Caliphate. The Caliphate still exists, my friends! The imamate is here [at the GNA], the Caliphate is here!" Then Sheikh Safvet repeated the same point, saying that the Caliphate would "become manifest in the Turkish GNA's collective personality." He added that protecting Islam was the GNA's first and most important duty. Halid Bey of Kastamonu was the second deputy and the only RPP member to criticize the proposal. He said the 1,300-year old institution should not be destroyed, and that they had conducted the "national struggle" to save the Caliphate. Like Zeki Bey, he added that the Muslim world had helped them because of the Turkish Caliphate, and that the RPP had made protecting the institution one of its essential principles before the elections (TBMMZC 1924, VII: 32–41).

Finally, Seyyid Bey, as Minister of Justice and deputy from İzmir, gave a long speech that was instrumental in convincing hesitant deputies (Erdem 1995: 37) – just like *Kadıasker* Seyfeddin Efendi had done half a century ago in 1876 (see Chapter 2). The speech was very similar to both his pamphlet published by the GNA in 1923 and his previous address to the RPP group. Based on his scholarly authority and political position, he repeated the same points, arguing that the Caliphate was a matter of law rather than theology, i.e., it was a secular and not a religious institution (Seyyid Bey 1924: 4–5). For this reason, it was to change according to the "expediencies of time," which was why the Prophet had not established a Caliphate for himself. The Qur'an did not specify a political system, either: All it decreed was the principles of consultation and obedience to the *ul al-amr* (p. 7). Like the Umayyads and Abbasids, the Ottoman Caliphate was a fictitious one; that is, what the Prophet had called the "bitter sultanate." The Prophet had also decreed that Islam did not recognize any spiritual authority. Therefore, unlike the Christian Pope, the caliph had no other authority than power of attorney, as the Caliphate was a mandate entrusted to him by the nation (pp. 33–45).[27]

After Seyyid Bey's influential speech, which was full of familiar discursive strategies such as referencing the sacred texts of Islam and invoking Islamic history and the relevant traditional literature, as well as redefining the Caliphate itself, Prime Minister İsmet Pasha assured the GNA members that "there will not be any defects in the protection and full application of Islamic principles after the abolition of the Caliphate" (Satan 2008: 219). Then the articles of the proposal were put to a vote by GNA President Fethi Bey and all passed into law. The introductory part and 11 of the 13 articles of the proposal previously discussed in the party meeting remained the same in the text of the law; the first two articles were slightly modified. These two crucial articles of the law read:

1. The caliph has been deposed. Because the Caliphate is essentially intrinsic to the concept and purview of the government and the republic, the office of the Caliphate is abolished.
2. The deposed caliph and all male and female members and sons-in-law of the previously abolished Ottoman dynasty are permanently banned from residing within the territory of the Republic of Turkey. Those who are born of the female members of this dynasty are also considered to belong to the Ottoman family.

(TBMMZC 1924, VII: 62–64)

President Mustafa Kemal approved the law on the same day and it was quickly published in the official gazette as Law 431.[28] On that night, the Dolmabahçe Palace, the caliph's residence, was surrounded by military and police forces

آبونه شرائطى

سنه لكى ٣٩٠ غروش
آلتى آيلغى ١٩٥ ﻩ
طائره ايجون سنه لكى پوسته اجرتى
داخل اولديغى حالده ٤٦٥ غروشدر
آلتى آيلغى ٢٣٥ ﻩ
بهر نسخه سى ﻩ ١٠٠ ﻩ پاره در

بازار ايرتسى

٤ رمضان ١٣٤٢
٧ نيسان ١٣٤٠

تأسيس تاريخى :
٧ تشرين اول ١٣٣٦

مقتدم او چ دفعه نشر اولنور

سنه : ٢

توركيه جمهوريتنك رسمى غزته سيدر

نومرو : ٦٨

(رسمى جريده)

نومروسى : ٤٣١

خلافتك الغاسنه وخاندان عثمانينك توركيه
جمهورى ممالكى خارجنه چيقار لمسنه دائر قانون

ماده ١ — خليفه خلع ايدلمشدر. خلافت ،
حكومت وجمهوريت معنا ومفهومنده اساساً مندمج
اولديغندن خلافت مقامى ملغادر .

ماده ٢ — مخلوع خليفه وعثمانلى سلطنت
منقرضه سى خانداننك اركك، قادين بالجمله اعضاسى
وداماد لرى، توركيه جمهورى ممالكى داخلنده اقامت
اتمك حقندن ابداً ممنوعدرلر. بو خاندانه منسوب
قادينلردن متولد كيمسه لرده بوماده حكمنه تابعدرلر .

ماده ٣ — ايكنجى ماده ده مذكور كيمسه لر
اشبو قانونك اعلانى تاريخندن اعتباراً اعظمى اون
كون ظرفنده توركيه جمهورى اراضيسنى ترك
مجبوردرلر .

ماده ٤ — ايكنجى ماده ده مذكور كيمسه لرك
تورك وطنداشلق صفتى وحقوقى مرفوعدر .

Figure 6.5 The first four articles of the GNA Law no. 431 that abolished the Caliphate
(source: *Resmi Ceride* [The Official Gazette], April 7, 1924, p. 3).

before Caliph Abdülmecid was told to leave the country. The next day, the caliph and royal family members were paid approximately 100,000 lira before they left for Switzerland under strict police surveillance. Upon his arrival in Switzerland, Abdülmecid Efendi issued a press release in response to the many telegraphs he had received regarding the future of the Caliphate. Refusing to recognize the GNA's decision, he said the GNA could not abolish the Caliphate, which belonged to the entire Muslim world, and added that the Turkish people were loyal to their caliph. Moreover, he stressed that the GNA's decision was invalid because it had violated its promise to the Turkish nation, and thus its decision was against the principles of national sovereignty and political representation, as well. He also called upon other Muslim countries to convene a Caliphate congress. Furthermore, Abdülmecid Efendi sent a letter to the GNA repeating the same points and asking the deputies to reverse their decision. Meanwhile, in Turkey, the GNA's decision was disseminated to the people through the press and mosques; the muftis and *imams* were forced to sign a document promising to not mention the caliph's name in Friday sermons but, instead, pray for the republic's safety (Satan 2008: 222–226).

After the Caliphate

The reactions to the GNA's decision from within Turkey were mostly positive: President Mustafa Kemal and Prime Minister İsmet Pasha received many congratulatory telegraphs. For the most part, this was due to fear: In mid-1923 Kemal and İsmet had modified the existing High Treason Law so as to include any expressed opposition to the GNA's decisions, including particularly the 1922 decision to abolish the Ottoman monarchy. In fact, the Independence Tribunal had convicted and punished Lütfi Fikri for his "open letter" to the caliph and several other journalists for publishing the letter of Aga Khan and Amir Ali. Both the High Treason Law and the abolition of the Caliphate, then, played an important role in consolidating Kemal and İsmet's iron rule in Turkey. Moreover, at the same sitting on March 3, the GNA also abolished the Ministry of Religious Affairs and Foundations and established in its stead the Department of Religious Affairs (DRA), which was merely an office working directly under the prime minister. The GNA also abolished the religious school system on the same day, effectively banning Islamic education. Supported by the High Treason Law, these two laws silenced the *ulema*, who had a long history of influencing politics in Turkey. Moreover, the government tried to control religion through the DRA by monopolizing the appointment of religious personnel, the ownership of mosques and other religious property, and the content of Friday sermons.[29] Thus, the abolition of the Caliphate in 1924 did not, nor was it meant to, result in the separation of the state from religion, but instead led to the *domination* of religion by the state. Many of the scholars I have classified under the "conflict paradigm" in the literature have ignored this crucial point, simply claiming instead that the Caliphate's end signified the separation of mosque and state in Turkey (e.g., Tunaya 1962; Lewis 1961; Berkes 1998[1964]; Akgün 2006).

Reactions from the wider Muslim world were mixed, but mostly negative: While the Mufti of Turkistan supported the GNA's decision, some of the Azhar *ulema* in Egypt, the Indian Caliphate Committee, and the Berlin Islamic Society, representing delegations from 41 Muslim countries, protested it. Indian Muslims also asked Ankara to review its decision, but received a negative response (Toynbee 1927: 80–81). On the other hand, Sharif Hussein, who had already begun to prepare for his own caliphate by calling Muslim countries to organize a Caliphate congress in 1923, declared his caliphate on March 5. In his proclamation, Hussein criticized the Ankara government for destroying the Caliphate and praised the Ottoman sultans. He claimed that he was only responding to the requests of many Muslims, and that his only purpose was to serve Islam (Hussein 1916: 234–235). Hussein then organized a congress in Mecca in July, but could not gain the Muslim public's recognition, except for a few Hashemite tribes. He was protested by most participants, especially those from India and Egypt (Kramer 1986: 83–85). He did not have enough political power to consolidate his own small kingdom, anyway: Soon he was driven out of Arabia by Abdulaziz ibn Saud, the Wahhabi leader who then founded the current Saudi Arabia (Teitelbaum 2001: 243ff).

Ibn Saud was reluctant to take up the Caliphate: He first declared himself king of the *Hijaz* in early 1925, then organized a congress in Mecca the next year in order to gain Muslims' recognition as king of the Arabs and to discuss the regulation of the annual Muslim pilgrimage to the *Hijaz*. Rashid Rida, one of the organizers, tried to turn the congress into a political conference for Islamic unification, which was protested by Turkey and Egypt, for King Fuad of Egypt wanted to claim the Caliphate for himself, for which he organized his own congress in Cairo in May 1926 (Hourani 1983: 184; Kramer 1986: 86–105). But this was a failure, too. Originally planned to be held in 1925, the congress was first delayed because of the charge that it was not legitimate to elect a caliph under foreign occupation and Egypt was still under British mandate at the time. Furthermore, the ambitious organizers of the 1926 congress, including Rashid Rida, planned it to be all inclusive: They invited delegations from all Muslim countries and theological schools, including Zaydis and other Shia sects, Aga Khan, and the Wahhabis (Bruinessen 1995: 126ff.).[30] Sunnis did not like the idea and protested it. Moreover, the Indian Caliphate Committee was against Fuad's claim to the Caliphate – they saw him as a British puppet. Instead, they wanted to convince the Turks to reverse their decision. Also, the fact that the delegations from Syria and Tunisia were selected by the French government made others suspicious of the congress (Kedourie 1963: 225–227; Bruinessen 1995: 140; Yıldırım 2004: 212–225). Former Caliph-Sultan Vahideddin, too, protested the congress by sending a letter in which he said that he himself was the only legitimate caliph and that it was not permissible to elect a new one (see Vahideddin 1926). Finally, as mentioned above, some al-Azhar *ulema* declared their support for and allegiance to Caliph Abdülmecid in 1924, which indicates the internal division among the Egyptian elite.[31] All these factors led to the failure of the Cairo Congress, where the discussions were limited to whether a caliph was needed; in the end, King Fuad could not be elected.

A final congress was held in Jerusalem (under the British mandate) in 1931, to which Abdülmecid Efendi was also invited; but he failed to gain Muslim leaders' support due to various political conflicts among them. Turkey, Egypt, and Sharif Hussein's sons (Faysal and Abdullah) protested the congress, whose principal aim was then changed to cement Muslim solidarity against Zionism and establish a Muslim university in Jerusalem (Toynbee 1927: 99–109; Kramer 1986: 125–126). Back in Egypt, the next king, Faruq, also tried in vain to make a claim for the Caliphate during his reign (1936–1952) before he was deposed by a *coup d'état* led by Nasser and Nagib (Kedourie 1963: 239–242). Throughout this process, the intellectual debates over the Caliphate took place between (modernist) Islamists and secularists and were very similar to the debates in Turkey between 1920 and 1924.[32]

As for the reactions from the West, the GNA's decision to end the Caliphate created surprise and joy. In the European press, there were hundreds of news pieces and articles on the abolition of the Caliphate (see Şimşir 1981: 341–858). Orientalist Margoliouth (1924: 335) summarized how most of the press – and politicians – saw the event: "From the European point of view Mustafa Kemal in abolishing the Caliphate was depriving his government of an effective weapon." The *Daily Telegraph* wrote that, previously the leader of the Muslim world, Turkey had turned itself into a small Tatar republic. It added that by finishing off the Pan-Islamic movement, Ankara made France happy as the latter could embark on its own Caliphate project in the *Maghrib*. On the other hand, the Paris-based *Le Journal* commented that Britain could not even have imagined such a favorable result for its long-pursued policy of creating an Arab Caliphate and destroying Turkey's power and prestige.[33] Likewise, the *New York Times* said a Turkey without the caliph would make Britain especially happy, while the *New York Tribune* noted that Turkey had proven its pro-Western orientation by abolishing the Caliphate (Satan 2008: 234, 238). As for European orientalists, unlike the press – and most Muslims – they saw it more as a frank recognition of a *fait accompli* than the infliction of a blow on Islam:

> Since the Caliph de facto is the ruler who is in possession of the Sanctuaries and can maintain the Pilgrimage, the loss of Arabia terminated the Ottoman Caliphate, which thereby became a title similar to "King of France," which the English sovereigns retained more than a century after the last of their French possessions had been lost.
>
> (Margoliouth 1924: 335)

But since "the Oriental frequently confuses semblance with reality [and] in religious matters he is sometimes too serious" (p. 336), Muslims were unable to comprehend the reality of the Caliphate and therefore demanded an explanation from Turkey for abolishing it. The orientalist view also applauded Mustafa Kemal's decision and expected Muslims to realize that "since where Islam has held undisputed sway civilization has not advanced a step, it is a reasonable supposition that a necessary condition of advance is emancipation from Islam" (p. 337; see also Toynbee 1927).

The instrumental nature of the secularist discourse

Karl Marx once spoke of an "[i]nnate human casuistry to seek to change things by changing their names! And to find loopholes for breaking through tradition within tradition itself, wherever a direct interest provided a sufficient motive!" (quoted in Engels 2004[1844]: 66–67). I have argued that the way secularists dissected Qur'anic verses and prophetic traditions, selectively drew upon certain episodes of Islamic history and particular elements of the Islamic intellectual tradition while ignoring others and claimed to be protecting Islam's authenticity – in short, their "theological engineering" – was part of what seems to be an essentially *instrumental* discourse. In other words, they seem to have exploited the possibilities of deriving justification from Islam as their "meta-discursive strategy," which they shared with their opponents, for secular political purposes by strategically intervening into Islamic theology and law.[34] This intervention was part of their attempt at an "invention of tradition" (Hobsbawm 1992) whereby many Islamic elements (e.g., the concept of *örf*, or a particular historical event) were reframed, exaggerated, biased, or distorted toward the secularist interpretation. As is the case with many "reformist" movements, the Turkish secularists resorted to theological engineering as a form of the invention of tradition for their own politico-ideological ends.

That this discursive in(ter)vention or "tactic" (de Certeau 1984, 1994) was instrumental makes much sense when one considers the pragmatist nature of the modernizing reforms during much of the Second Constitutional Period and (later) the early Republican Era. Most of these reforms (particularly political and legal ones) in both periods took the form of a pragmatic adoption of the European institutions that were perceived to have offered immediate solutions to the elites for emergent practical problems. Moreover, as discussed in Chapter 2, most of the challenges in the way of "modernization" were perceived as technical problems, and the reforms launched to solve them aimed at (or were justified with reference to the higher purpose of) "saving the state."[35]

The idea of "saving the state" was complemented by that of "protecting the religion," as indicated by the frequent equation of the two and by the oft-used phrase "*din ü devlet.*" The discourse of protecting Islam positioned its subjects (the modernist elite) as the guardians of religion, whereby they placed themselves in a dominant position where they had the power to protect Islam – but also to shape, constrain, and expand the limits of it. This was a fundamental challenge to the "old" order of things where Islam was the single most important force that to a large extent determined the boundaries of political life, as well as the border between the public and private spheres. Thus, this discourse ultimately helped undermine the dominant position of the religion vis-à-vis all other – potential or actual – institutions and actors, including the new elite. By effectively employing this discourse of protecting Islam from corruption and exploitation, the secular elite tried to reconfigure the existing balance of power, placing themselves (and secular institutions) in a dominant position vis-à-vis religion. This is why it is basically a secularist discourse: it was ultimately aimed at secularizing the structure of poltical life and the public sphere by "privatizing" Islam, i.e., reducing it to a private matter between the individual and God. The incorporation in their secularist project of this seemingly ambiguous discourse was thus the best option for them.

The secularists in general and Mustafa Kemal in particular do seem to have a paradoxical attitude toward Islam: they both had a very negative, "positivistic" view of religion that saw it as obsolete in the modern world, and tried to pragmatically "use" it for legitimization purposes. This ambiguity is also a reason for the polarization among both scholars and the general public in contemporary Turkey regarding Atatürk's position vis-à-vis Islam. The source of the secularists' ambiguous attitude lies, as Hanioğlu (2011: 48ff.) stresses, in the idea that "religion is a guide for the lay people while science is the religion of the elites," which they learned from the secular-positivistic, *fin de siècle* intellectuals such as Abdullah Cevdet and Gustave Le Bon. This belief was one of the ideological continuities between the Ottoman and Kemalist-Republican periods, which created both a "scientistic"-Comtean discourse and an "accommodative" and pragmatic attitude toward Islam, which still prevails among Kemalist-nationalists in Turkey.

The secularist instrumentality is further implied by several other factors. One is the "gap" between what the actors said and did – i.e., the discrepancy between their discourse and their actions. A second sign of instrumentality comes from what they themselves later "confessed" regarding their earlier actions. Finally, analyzing the differences between what they said in different time periods and in different contexts also imply instrumentality of their discursive formation. In terms of the first factor, one sometimes finds significant differences and discrepancies between what the secularists said and how they acted. I have already mentioned above how Mustafa Kemal glorified Sultan Vahideddin and offered his loyalty to him in 1919 and 1920 but then abolished the Ottoman monarchy as soon as he found an opportunity to do so in 1922. More generally, as I have discussed, the secularist leadership of the Anatolian resistance, represented by Mustafa Kemal, started out by claiming that their sole purpose was to protect the Ottoman sultan's rights and save the Caliphate from the enemy, but they ended up abolishing both the monarchy and the Caliphate. In terms of the second sign of instrumentality, Mustafa Kemal's own words provide the best evidence. In his famous *Speech* in the 1927 convention of his party, the Republican People's Party, Kemal spoke of their strategy in destroying the Ottoman religious order as follows:

> It was necessary to proceed by stages, to prepare the feeling and the spirit of the nation and to try to reach our aims by degrees, profiting meanwhile by our experience. This is actually what happened. If our attitude and our actions during these nine years are examined in their logical sequence, it is evident from the very first day that our general behavior has never deviated from the line laid down in our original resolution, nor from the purpose we had set out to achieve.... We never disclosed the views we held. If we had

done so we would have been looked upon as dreamers and illusionists. If we had offered explanations we might from the outset have alienated those who ... were fearful of eventual revolutionary changes which would be contrary to their tradition, their way of thinking and their psychology.... This is how I acted, [trying] to develop our entire social organization, step by step, until it corresponded to the great capability of progress [our nation had,] which I kept to myself and in my own consciousness as a national secret.

(Mustafa Kemal 1929[1927]: 19–20)[36]

Therefore, Kemal's own justification for deploying an instrumental discourse reveals the fact that the secularists' main concern was, in addition to the obvious legitimization problem, to avoid "alienating" their comrades in their struggle for political power. Despite this, Kemal said, they (in fact, he) could not avoid the "dissension which was observable from time to time between us and our most intimate co-workers" (ibid.).[37]

Finally, in terms of understanding the instrumentality of their theological engineering by looking at their discourse in different contexts, we can cite again Mustafa Kemal's own words. As mentioned above, in a press conference he held in January 1923, he critized the pro-Caliphate politicians and told (the distorted versions of) two historical narratives. In the first one Caliph Omar had purportedly said: "I don't have such a title. ... There is no Caliph. You are the believers, and I'm your leader." The second one was about the death of the Prophet Muhammad, after which "nobody thought of electing a Caliph" (Mustafa Kemal 1923: 64). Only three-and-one-half months before this conference, however, he had cited (the "correct" versions of) the same stories to make precisely the opposite argument to glorify the Caliphate vis-à-vis the "un-Islamic" monarchy.

A second example of instrumentality is provided by an intellectual leader of the secularist group, Ziya Gökalp. There are great discrepancies between what he said about the Caliphate during World War I and after the GNA's decision in 1922. In other words, Gökalp's view of the relationship between religion and politics suddenly shifted following the separation of the Caliphate from the monarchy. Earlier, when the CUP needed the caliph's religious authority in the midst of the war, he, being an influential advisor to the Unionists, had described the unified form of the Caliphate as a perfect type of government:

It was because Islam had brought state, law, and court into the realm of the sacred that those traits such as loyalty to the secular ruler, genuine fraternity and solidarity among the believers, sacrifice of interests and life for the sake of *jihad*, tolerance and respect toward the opinions of others, which are the very basis of a permanent order in society, were cultivated among all Muslims as common virtues ... the Caliph, although having judicial authority, lacks any authority over matters of piety such as the Catholic pope or the Russian tsar enjoyed. However, the *mufti* does not have any authority over matters of piety, either.... The fact that the *mufti* has no authority over matters of piety shows that there is no *ifta* government of the *mufti*s in

addition to the judicial government of the caliphs. There is only one government in Islam ... [and that is] the judicial government of the caliphs.

(Gökalp 1917: 218, 221)

When the Caliphate was separated from the state, however, Gökalp praised the
move:

> In these periods [during the Seljukid and Mamluk eras] the caliph was per-
> forming only a religious function with regard to the *ummah*. All affairs with
> regard to political authority were carried out by the Sultans of the Seljuks in
> Baghdad and of the *Kölemen*s [Mamluks] in Egypt. These were the greatest
> periods in the history of Islam, both politically and religiously. It was only
> when Selim I had again unified these two offices that the decline of the
> Ottoman Empire ensued; its religious as well as political life began to dete-
> riorate.... Until now the religious authority of the Ottoman Caliphs was
> confined to those Muslims who were their political subjects. Their religious
> authority over Muslims in other states was rejected by the other govern-
> ments because they could not be sure that this religious authority was free
> from political designs. Now that the caliph will no longer be subject to the
> politics of any nation,... he will exercise his right of religious authority over
> all religious institutions [and] all Muslim states and nations will support [the
> Caliphate] materially and spiritually. But its real and most powerful source
> will be the greatness of Islam which has today forced the European world to
> respect it.... We are deeply thankful to the Grand National Assembly and
> its famous president for their success in giving to the office of the Caliphate
> a character that is compatible with the principle of popular and national sov-
> ereignty, which is the foundation of modern states and through which
> genuine Islamic unity in religious life might be realized.

(1922a: 226–227)

> When the Caliphate and the Sultanate were united in one person, either one
> of the two dominated the other.... The Turkish revolution of today has
> assured the complete independence and freedom of these two powers.

(1922b: 229)

Such a sudden change in the direction of Gökalp's ideas on the Caliphate, which
is also observable in the ideas of Mustafa Kemal, as discussed above, was
closely related to political changes that took place between 1918 and 1922. This
was the principal reason for the many contradictions within their often-confusing
Islamic discourse. However, by emphasizing such an "invention of tradition," I
do not mean to propose a kind of conspiracy theory here. The secularists were
not a clandestine society with secret plans to overthrow the caliph. Whatever
their intentions may have been, they were *obliged* to employ a religious discourse as Islam was the sole source of legimacy before they completely seized
the state power at the end of 1922. Also, the intensity of the Islamic justifications

offered by the secularists implies that they had to draw on Islam in order to legitimize their actions and their political positions in a Muslim society. In fact, as quoted above, Mustafa Kemal himself said this was the case (1929[1927]: 19–20) because they knew that they had to play the game by the rules laid down by the centuries-long presence and the enormous influence of religion in Turkey. For the same reason, moreover, the secularists resorted to a similar Islamic justification by employing any number of expedient and convenient discursive tools in 1923 and 1924, too, though they were politically more powerful than before – powerful enough to abolish the Caliphate itself on March 3, 1924.

Conclusion

The tragic demise of the Caliphate marked a significant milestone in the history of Muslim societies for, in addition to representing strong Islamic political leadership throughout much of its history, the Caliphate also symbolized Islamic unity and religious connection among Muslim peoples. Thus, caliphs enjoyed a certain degree of ideological power even in those periods when they were quite weak politically and militarily. The Turkish "national struggle" was one of those moments when Muslims (from India and Egypt in particular) financially and otherwise supported the Anatolian resistance movement; and the nationalists fighting against Europeans conducted their struggle in the name of the caliph and to protect the "seat of the Caliphate," Istanbul.

The Caliphate's abolition in 1924 was related more to the concrete political struggles that followed the collapse of the Ottoman Empire than its religious status: the new republic's leader, Mustafa Kemal, was concerned that the royal family (represented by Caliph Abdülmecid Efendi) could be the carriers and/or patrons of opposition to the new regime and that Istanbul could turn into a center of attraction for the opposition. In fact, those who opposed single-party rule following the declaration of the republic in October 1923 had often approached the caliph to express their disturbance, and used the press in Istanbul for political propaganda. Kemal thus wanted to repress a potential *political* challenge to his rule by destroying a "spiritual" institution that he saw as a potential locus of opposition. (This is also evident in the fact that he would shut down the Progressive Republican Party [founded with his approval by Rauf Pasha and Refet Pasha] on June 5, 1925 after violently repressing the Kurdish Sheikh Said Rebellion, on the grounds that its members were trying to "bring the Caliphate back" as well supporting the rebellion.) Three years after the abolition of the Caliphate, in his famous *Speech* in 1927, Kemal was still concerned about a possible return of the Caliphate:

> Gentlemen, I must frankly and categorically declare that those who continue to occupy themselves with the chimera of the Caliphate and thereby mislead the Muslim world are nothing but enemies of the Muslim world, and especially of Turkey. They are only ignorant or blind men who could attach hopes to such jugglery. ... From now onwards it will not be so easy to

suppose that the people of Islam and the Turkish nation would have fallen to
such a low level as to continue in the abuse of the purity of the conscience
and the tenderness of the sentiments of the Muslim world to criminal aims.

(Mustafa Kemal 1929[1927]: 686)

Also, according to Tunçay (2005: 71), Mustafa Kemal may have thought of
abolishing the Caliphate as a "show of force" to gain the society's approval for
his personal rule and as "part of the process in which he tried to identify the
Republic and the reforms with his own personality."

On the other hand, the new Turkish elite probably also wanted to send a
powerful message to the West that the new Turkey would not be a threat to their
interests in the Muslim world, unlike the Ottoman Empire, by abolishing the latter's important institution, the Caliphate. This act thus signified an assurance by
Mustafa Kemal and his friends to Britain and the Allies, which needed a suitable
gesture in that regard: The "provision adopted [was] that of casting the new state
in a European mould; hoping to inspire confidence in Europe by abandoning its
power of menacing Europe" (Margoliouth 1924: 337–338).

Of course, the secularists did not achieve the abolition of the Ottoman monarchy in November 1922 or of the Caliphate in March 1924 through ideological
struggle alone. As I have tried to demonstrate, their struggle was conditioned by
both political and military power relations. They first won the "national struggle" against the Greeks and the civil war against the Istanbul government, and
then seized state power – just as the CUP had done in 1908 and 1909 – by overthrowing the Ottoman sultan. All this made it possible to enforce what I call
their "theological engineering." Mustafa Kemal in particular often made use of
military power resources in his personal struggle to control the political system
in the new Turkey. In November 1922, for instance, he threatened violence in
the GNA to get the law abolishing the monarchy passed. He specifically said
"sovereignty is acquired by force, by power, and by violence" and that he had
already done it. He then added that "some heads will be cut off" if the parliament members did not acquiesce in his proposal. Less than a year later, he tight-
ened the High Treason Law, with which the opposition had been severely
punished between 1920 and 1922, so as to include any opposition to the GNA.
This helped him tighten his control over the GNA and other components of the
new Turkish state. Therefore, the secularist theological engineering was enforced
with power resources (politics and military), beyond its Islamic discourse.

The destruction of the monarchy and the Caliphate were also important
turning points in terms of Turkey's domestic politics and the secularization of
the Turkish state. Following the elimination of Islamic education and the *ulema*
in 1924, as mentioned, the Republican elite crushed the Kurdish opposition in
1925 and in 1926 silenced all pro-Caliphate politicians, some of whom were sentenced to death, others either sent to jail or kept under house arrest. Then, the
iron rule of the single-party regime initiated a number of significant changes in
social and political life, including the abolition of Ottoman law (including some
legal codes that had been taken from Europe, such as the Commercial Code,

since the *Tanzimat* Reforms in 1839), the Islamic calendar, the Arabic alphabet, religious titles, Turkish attire for men, the veil, Friday as a day of rest, and non-Turkish words. The secularization of the constitutional basis for the Kemalist regime was completed in 1928 by the elimination from the constitution of Article 2, which read "the religion of the State is that of Islam," and later consolidated and given a formal expression in the revised constitution in 1937 by explicitly stating that "the Turkish Republic is a ... secular state" (Article 2) (see Davison 1988: 128–143; Ahmad 1993: 52–71; Berkes 1998[1964]: 430–499). Constituting the backbone of the "Turkish revolution," all these later (post-1924) reforms were a reflection of the idea of (and a desire for) a "civilizational change," rather than practical and pragmatist solutions to emergent challenges in the way of modernization. For they directly targeted Islamic customs and institutions, aiming to cleanse Islam from the public sphere. The method through which these changes took place was a top-down, Jacobin enforcement of new laws and regulations (along with a frequent use of physical and symbolic violence) by the state in order to "modernize the people, despite their resistance."

7   Islam and modernity

Confrontation or accommodation?

Aristotle once said that if there can be no authority without tradition, there can be no tradition without authority (quoted in Friedrich 1958: 56). With its long history, the Caliphate was one of the highest political authorities in the Muslim world, and the most important symbol of the "tradition" that was to be destroyed for secularists. It represented the fusion of, or at least the interconnection between, Islam and politics for both "traditionalists" and secularists. Its abolition thus symbolized the end of Islamic politics and the victory of secularist politics in the post-World War I period. Moreover, for many, political actors and intellectuals alike, it also represented the essential tension and confrontation between Islamic tradition and (secular) modernity.

But, in truth, the issue is more complicated than this: The transformation and eventual demise of the Caliphate in the first quarter of the 20th century demonstrate more compatibility and accommodation than simply conflict and confrontation between Islam and modernity. This is the main theoretical argument of this study. Of course, I do not deny the existence of some degree of conflict between the two (particularly on the philosophical level). But I argue that the *dominant* feature of their relationship during this period (up until 1924) was accommodation rather than confrontation. Clearly, this does not fit well with conventional wisdom. The sociological literature on the process of secularization, which has mostly been limited in its scope to the Western/Christian world, has for a long time assumed an essential tension between religion and secular politics. Similarly, the historical literature on the modernization of the Middle East, which was for too long dominated by what I have called the "conflict paradigm," also held the same assumption of a dichotomous relationship between religion and politics and religion and modernity. This study contributes to both of these literatures by helping correct the conflict-based view of these relationships in the Middle East, broadening the scope of secularization theory, and refining it in its application to Islamic-Middle Eastern cases.

Talal Asad (1993) has remarked that the idea of religion as a "bounded entity" naturally distinct from other social institutions, such as politics, is itself a modern, secular assumption, which may not hold true in "traditional" societies. This study has tried to decipher the complexities of the relationship between Islam and secular politics (and modernity at large) using the case of the

Caliphate as a window through which to analyze them. My examination of this phenomenon is based on two main methods: comparative-historical analysis and discourse analysis. The former has three dimensions: inter-group, temporal, and spatial comparisons. First, I have identified three groups of actors involved within the debates over the Caliphate and in the wider process of secularization: the "secularists" were those who wished to destroy the Caliphate and who initially defined it as a purely spiritual institution; the "modernists" were those who defined the Caliphate as a strictly temporal-political institution and wanted to keep it alive; and "traditionalists" were those who saw the Caliphate as both a spiritual and political authority and who obviously wanted to see the caliph on top of the Islamic political establishment and as the religious leader of all Muslims. Second, in terms of temporal comparison, I have divided the period under study (1908–1924) into three phases: the pre-World War I part of what is called the "Second Constitutional Period" (i.e., the period of constitutional monarchy in the Ottoman Empire) covered the years 1908–1916; the middle phase roughly consisted of the war years and after (1914–1920); the last phase involved the last few years of the Caliphate in the post-World War I period (1919–1924). Though these periods were not mutually exclusive, they witnessed somewhat different sets of issues and debates related to the Caliphate. Third, in terms of spatial comparison, I have divided the geography of the Muslim world into two parts: the caliphal center and the caliphal periphery. The former included present-day Turkey, the latter India, the Arabian Peninsula, Egypt, and the rest of the North Africa. This spatial distinction overlaps with the temporal one: the issues debated by different groups in the first and third phases mostly took place in the center of the Caliphate, whereas those that emerged in the middle phase occurred on the caliphal periphery more than in the center. In other words, different politico-military developments conditioned different discursive struggles in the center and the periphery (see also below).

The second method I have employed, discourse analysis, is based on Foucault's approach, though in a limited manner. Rather than fully applying Foucaultian discourse analysis, I have selectively drawn upon it. In particular, I have borrowed his concept of "discursive strategy" as a major tool as well as using some of his other, related concepts. In order to apply his concepts in a more refined way, I have added my own two terms as derivatives: "discursive technique" and "meta-discursive strategy." The former refers to a discursive strategy at a more focused, micro level, the latter at the broader, macro level. Thus, I have argued that during the period under study deriving justification from Islam was the single most important "meta-discursive strategy" employed by all three groups. The actors also deployed various discursive techniques (e.g., emphasizing certain Qur'anic verses, such as the famous "*ul al-amr*" verse [4/59], or prophetic traditions and historical events while ignoring others, and reinterpreting certain rules, events, and sources of knowledge in an unorthodox way, etc.) as part of their discursive strategies (e.g., invoking sacred texts of Islam and its history). All these were useful "tools" or "lenses" with which they made sense of the reality of the Caliphate and acted accordingly in a modernizing and secularizing historical context. I have further argued that the modernist and secularist groups often had to intervene – as a "tactic" (de Certeau 1984, 1994) – into Islamic theology and law with unusual interpretations because their political positions were usually in conflict with the traditional understanding of Islamic politics. This I have called their "theological engineering": they redefined key Islamic concepts in legal and theological theory to adopt them to a specific situation conditioned by the modern-secular historical context and used the literature in the Islamic intellectual tradition to justify their own political claims and positions. This helped them frame the "definition of the situation" (Thomas 2002) in which they struggled to transform and abolish Caliphate.

Islamic discourse and institutional secularization

Though the debates over the Caliphate during the Second Constitutional Period (up to 1924) constitute the main topic of my study, I have also devoted a chapter to the examination of the wider process of modernization before and after this period in order to demonstrate that what I have argued for the case of the Caliphate is also true for Middle Eastern modernization in general. I have demonstrated that the secularization of political institutions in this process was always accompanied by an Islamic discourse, as actors constantly tried to derive justification from Islam as a dominant and hegemonic "strategy" (de Certeau 1984, 1994), from the late 18th century to the 1930s. To do this, I have analyzed the Islamic discourse produced in the early reform projects and in important texts, including the two Ottoman reform decrees (in 1839 and 1856) and three constitutions (1876, 1921 and 1924) as well as the discourses of the political elites attempting to limit the Ottoman caliph-monarch's authority. I have observed, for example, that during the debates on the first constitution, proclaimed in 1876 by the Ottomans, the modernizing elite often cited Qur'anic verses; however, these verses were often transformed through a brand new and – given the centuries-long tradition of *tafsir* (Qur'anic commentary) in Islam – unusual interpretation. This "transformative technique," by which the meanings of verses as objects of knowledge were transformed, signified a common pattern, particularly among the secularists, throughout the entire modernization process: Their "theological engineering" involved, as mentioned above, an act of redefining certain Islamic concepts in light of the "exigencies of the modern life"; the new meanings attributed to key concepts were then reproduced in many attempts at secularizing the political sphere.

I have also examined the transformation of the press and its interaction with the secularization process as well as the writings of certain intellectuals. I have discussed in more detail the ideas of a leading ideologue of Ottoman-Turkish secularism, Ziya Gökalp, who tried to synthesize Islamic law with Durkheimian social theory in an attempt to secularize the former – a project he called the "Social Methodology of Jurisprudence" (*İctimai Usul-i Fıkıh*). I have demonstrated how a secularist intellectual, who was also very influential in politics, made use of an Islamic discourse for secular purposes using various techniques, such as redefining key Islamic concepts, disturbing the conceptual hierarchy of Islamic *fiqh*, and creating different subject positions for secular intellectuals and the *ulema*, whose status was in decline during the 19th century.

In my examination of the transformation of, and debates over, the Caliphate, I have first presented a short history of the institution and introduced my three groups of actors and the major discursive strategies that they employed. Then I discussed in detail the three major strategies that all three groups commonly and most frequently employed: invoking sacred Islamic texts (the Qur'an and the *hadith*s of the Prophet) and referencing Islamic history, particularly the era of the first four ("rightly guided") caliphs, and ignoring contradictory evidence, such as the famous "Quraysh *hadith*," which was often ignored by pro-Ottoman actors because it allegedly required the caliph to be an Arab (see also below).

Let me now briefly review my discussion on the transformation of the Caliphate in its three phases, focusing particularly on the major issues around which the actors debated the caliph's status. In my analysis of these three phases, I focused on two cases in each phase, which represented the crucial turning points within it. In the first phase, I analyzed the power struggle in the center of the Caliphate between the bureaucratic elite, represented by the CUP in coalition with the high-ranking modernist *ulema* (who were previously disfranchised by Abdülhamid II), and the religious establishment, represented by the Ottoman Palace in co-operation with the traditionalist Islamists, consisting mostly of low-ranking *ulema*. As my first case, I examined the decline of the caliph's authority in Ottoman domestic politics as a result of the 1908 Young Turk Revolution and subsequent developments, including the failed attempt at counter-revolution known as the "March 31 Incident" and the constitutional amendments that followed it. Then I focused on the second case, the decline of the status of the *şeyhulislam*, who was the caliph's highest religious dignitary, through a series of laws enacted by the CUP. In both cases I have analyzed how in their discursive battle the modernist and traditionalist Islamists, most of them *ulema*, made use of different discursive strategies and techniques, drawing on Islamic history, theology, and law to support the contradictory claims of the two opposing political blocks they represented.

The major issues debated by the two groups around the Caliphate in this phase included the definition of the Caliphate, the scope of the caliph's authority, the source of his authority, and the Caliphate's nationalization. Each of these elements led to the gradual secularization of the Caliphate through the interaction of discourse and political action: The intellectuals and *ulema* Islamically justified the Young Turks' secular policies, which were also shaped by this Islamic discourse. While the traditionalists defined the Caliphate as both a temporal and spiritual authority, the modernists saw it as a strictly temporal ("secular") institution. Accordingly, the latter helped the CUP legitimize curbing the caliph's religious authority, whereas the former unsuccessfully tried to preserve the religious power of the Caliphate. Moreover, the modernists also tried to limit the caliph's temporal authority as the head of the executive branch of a modern government, which was completely in line with the CUP's fundamental policy of seizing state power by rendering the caliph powerless and ceremonial. This act of limitation was directly copied in the case of the *şeyhulislam* as well: the modernist *ulema*, again in line with CUP policies, defined him as merely a "civil servant" working for the government (the *şeyhulislam* was a member of the cabinet at the time) who had no religious or spiritual authority. The traditionalists, who saw the *şeyhulislam* as the head of the Muslim community and the supreme leader of the Islamic *ulema*, failed to elevate his status. Furthermore, the modernist group also intervened in Islamic political theory by partitioning the source of the caliph's authority: Unlike the traditionalists, such as Ömer Ziyaeddin, Mehmed Tahir, and Mustafa Zihni, who confined the source of Islamic legitimacy to the "texts" (fundamental sources of Islam, i.e., the Qur'an and the *hadith*), the modernist *ulema*, such as Elmalılı Hamdi and Seyyid Bey, did not settle for strictly religious legitimization but added a secular element, popular sovereignty, as an integral part of the legitimacy of the caliph's authority. In particular, Seyyid Bey, an influential scholar and politician (a leader of the CUP), strategically intervened in Islamic political philosophy with his alternative – and quite secular – theory of the Caliphate, which constituted the bulk of his "theological engineering." He posited a contractual basis for the Caliphate by redefining it as a kind of mandate given by the "nation" to the caliph through a social contract of representation, in which the people were the "boss" and the latter had only the power of attorney. Accordingly, the "nation," represented by the CUP-controlled parliament, could elect and depose a caliph in any way it wished – or not elect one at all. This theory, which was quickly adopted by most modernists, was quite useful in justifying the deposition of the once strong (and "despotic") Caliph-Sultan Abdülhamid II by the Young Turks in 1909, and would later be used by secularists, led by Mustafa Kemal, in abolishing the Caliphate itself. This modernist emphasis on the "nation" and popular sovereignty also led to the discursive nationalization of the Caliphate: They increasingly saw the Caliph as the head of the executive branch of a territorially shrinking empire whose collapse would pave the way for many nation-states in the Middle East after World War I.

As discussed so far, all these discursive strategies shaped, and were shaped by, the institutional secularization of the Caliphate. But I have also argued for the secularization of the Islamic discourse itself, which was caused by Islamist intellectuals themselves as an unintended consequence of their discursive strategies. This kind of "secularization from within" implied what I have called the "double-bind," i.e., the co-existence and conflation of two different civilizational epistemologies, with Western philosophical traditions gaining an increasing impact on the mentality of Muslim intellectuals and political elites. The secular transformation of Islamic discourse took place in three distinct ways. First, both modernists *and* traditionalists made a previously unpopular, secular distinction between the spiritual and temporal authority of the caliph. There was no such distinction in the classical theory of the Islamic Caliphate, nor in the early practice of it, because the caliph's authority simultaneously entailed both political and "religious" (but not "spiritual") powers and responsibilities. Traditionalist

Islamists attributed to the caliph spiritual authority in an attempt to elevate his status and strengthen his office, whereas the modernists sharply rejected this idea, emphasizing the argument that Islam did not recognize any spiritual authority as in the Catholic Papacy. However, their view of the Caliphate as strictly a temporal rule was based on the modern/secular dichotomy between religion and politics appropriated from the West, i.e., Enlightenment philosophy

A second way in which Islamic discourse was secularized was through the discursive strategy of appropriation, albeit selective, of Western institutions. Only the modernists employed this strategy, and they did so in order to justify the ongoing process of adopting European institutions, especially in government, military, legal, and educational systems. For example, Elmalılı Hamdi suggested completely adopting the modern cabinet system, under which the *şeyhulislam* would be no different from a minister, and the caliph a king, as a measure *against* the obstacles facing Islam's involvement in politics. Likewise, Seyyid Bey suggested a partial adoption of civil code and family law from Europe in order to modernize the legal system (i.e. to adapt Islamic law to modern conditions) but justified it with reference to a *hadith* that advocated "receiving" the "word of wisdom" wherever it was found. Third, Islamic discourse was also secularized, as an unintended consequence, via the strategy of historicizing religion. The modernist emphasis on the "exigencies of (modern) life" and prioritizing social change over the textual sources of Islam were the main discursive techniques in this context, both of which were based on their concern for the perceived stagnation of Islamic law. Thus, in order to develop new responses to the problems of "modern" civilization, they discarded some of the essential features of the Islamic legal tradition in favor of European solutions that they still framed in religious terms. Their main assumption in this form of theological engineering was the historicity of Islamic rules and sources, including some of the fundamental principles of Islamic law, and it is with this that they justified new developments and the "need to modernize" imposed by the emerging political conditions.

The secularization of Islamic discourse would be more visible in the third phase, in accordance with the pace of institutional secularization. The ways in which this discursive transformation occurred included the insertion into the actors' discourses of particular secular notions, such as national sovereignty, democracy as the best political system, the primacy of social-historical context (reference to the "expediencies of time") and an increasingly secular/ethnic definition of the "nation." This kind of "contamination" was particularly apparent in the discourses of the two leaders of the secularist group, Mustafa Kemal and Ziya Gökalp – and in that of Seyyid Bey, who was of great help to them with his power/knowledge as a leading Islamic scholar and influential political figure.

In the second phase, which included the World War I years and their immediate aftermath, I have focused on the debates over the Caliphate in its periphery, for there was not much discussion on the institution in the center, where the docile Caliph Mehmed V had little power in domestic politics, but the CUP tried to use his ideological power in international relations as a weapon against

European imperialists who had millions of Muslims under their colonial rule. Instead, the center of gravity for these debates had shifted to the caliphal periphery, especially the Arab Middle East. In this context, I have first discussed the Caliphate's significance in Middle Eastern politics and then specifically analyzed two cases: the French project of a Caliphate in North Africa to be filled by Morocco's King Yusuf and the British project of an Arab Caliphate to be claimed by Sharif Hussein, formerly the Ottoman caliph's religious dignitary in the Holy Land (the *Hijaz*) and then the leader of the "Arab revolt." For French and British foreign policy in the Muslim world, the Ottoman caliph's power and influence on their Muslim colonies, which they had witnessed throughout the 19th century, was an important concern. Thus, for them, the "Eastern Question" also entailed measures to curb the Turkish caliph's ideological power in the Muslim world. This led them to plan installing Arab caliphs, who were supposedly descendants of the Prophetic family, to replace the Ottoman caliph. Arab nationalists, including intellectuals such as Rashid Rida, passionately supported these projects while pro-Ottoman politicians and intellectuals, including Arab and Indian as well as Turkish figures, traditionalists and modernists alike, fought against them. Both of these projects failed, not only because they encountered great resistance from Muslims in the colonies and in the center, but also because they became unnecessary when the Ottomans lost World War I.

The major issues around which the Caliphate was debated on the periphery included the legitimacy of the Ottoman caliph vis-à-vis its alternatives, Arab nationalism, the significance of Muslim unity, and comparisons between Islam and the West. I have argued that the Caliphate question was one of the significant elements of the rise of Arab nationalism. An "Arab Caliphate movement," led by the Syrian-Egyptian intellectual Abdur-rahman al-Kawakibi, had already emerged in the late 1890s and had questioned the legitimacy of Caliph-Sultan Abdülhamid II's authority. Following the 1908 Revolution in Istanbul, many Young Turk policies in the Arab world were perceived as motivated by Turkish nationalism, which further triggered nationalist sentiments among Arab notables and intellectuals such as Rashid Rida and Ali Abdur-raziq. They claimed that the Ottoman Caliphate was illegitimate and that having an Arab origin, coming from the prophetic genealogy in particular, was a fundamental requirement of being a caliph. They often justified this claim with reference to Islamic texts, particularly a prophetic *hadith*, known as the "Quraysh *hadith*," which says, "Imams are from the Quraysh [the Prophet's tribe]." Arab nationalist activities, also backed up by British policies, were accelerated during and after World War I. Against this nationalist challenge, and British and French propaganda, the Ottoman government organized its own propaganda activities, particularly through the *Teşkilat-ı Mahsusa* (secret service), and financed the dissemination of pro-Ottoman views in Europe and the Middle East. Many Indian and Ottoman (Turkish, Kurdish, *and* Arab) intellectuals and *ulema*, such as Ismail Safayihi, Salih al-Tunusi, and Abdulaziz Jawish from Tunisia; Ali Fahmi and Muhammad Safa from Egypt; Habib al-Ubeydi from Iraq; and Mukhtar Ansari, Ajmal Khan, Mushir Kidwai, Abul Kalam Azad, and Syed Mahmud from India, supported the

Ottoman Caliphate. They emphasized its legitimacy with reference to Islamic sources and history and tried to delegitimize Arab claims to the Caliphate by arguing that Sharif Hussein and King Yusuf were no more than puppets of European imperialism. They also strongly emphasized the importance of political and cultural unity among Muslim countries, which they believed could only be achieved under the auspices of the Ottoman Caliphate. Since Islam required Islamic unity (*İttihad-ı İslam*), they reasoned, the claims of alternative caliphs not only hurt Muslims politically, but also violated some of the fundamental principles of Islam. Finally, as another major discursive strategy, the pro-Ottoman intellectuals often compared and contrasted Islamic institutions with European ones, arguing for the superiority of Islamic civilization. They claimed that, throughout history, it had been superior over the West in terms of political institutions, including, first and foremost, the Caliphate, but also equality, freedom, and human rights; what the West had produced in contrast was colonialism, wars, and economic backwardness for the rest of the world. They also often made references, as a discursive technique, to European intelligentsia to prove their claims about the superiority of Islamic civilization.

Finally, in the third phase, I examined the Caliphate's transformation and demise in Turkey during the post-World War I years. Here, too, I analyzed two cases in particular: the abolition of the Ottoman monarchy (1922) and that of the Caliphate (1924). I first discussed how the partitioning of the Ottoman Empire and the invasion of Anatolia, the last piece of territory left for the Turks, by European powers led to the emergence of an insurgency, which then turned into an organized resistance movement supported by other Muslim countries, particularly India and Egypt, as well as Bolshevik Russia. I have also discussed how Mustafa Kemal, a former Unionist army officer, gradually managed to become the leader of the resistance movement conducting *jihad* against the "infidel" Greeks, and then founded, with his friends, the new Turkish state (as an "Islamic State"), which then overthrew the Ottoman government and deposed the caliph in 1922. Until then the nationalist leadership had always been loyal to Caliph-Sultan Vahideddin. They justified their abolition of the Ottoman monarchy with reference to the Caliphate's religious significance, claiming that sultanic rule was un-Islamic and that separation of the Caliphate from temporal rule was most suitable to Islam. Curbing the temporal authority of the Caliphate and turning it into a purely spiritual institution was the first step in the process of its abolition, which was finally achieved by the secularists in March 1924. The power struggle in this phase mostly took place between the secularists and modernist Islamists.

The major issues discussed by political actors and intellectuals regarding the Caliphate during this period included the Islamic legitimacy of monarchy and the Caliphate, the tension between the Caliphate's universal character and the modern principle of national sovereignty, and the Islamic status of the Caliphate with regard to the Turkish Grand National Assembly. During the entire period between 1919 and 1924, the secularists framed virtually every secular move they made in religious terms. As mentioned, the secularist group, particularly Mustafa Kemal and Ziya Gökalp, justified their *coup d'état* against the Ottoman monarchy and the caliph with reference the high status of the caliph's office in Islam, claiming that the dynastic system was in conflict with Islamic principles, and that those periods of Islamic history where the Caliph had no political power were the "greatest periods in the history of Islam." In this process, the secularists received crucial support from the *ulema*, particularly Seyyid Bey, Rasih Efendi, and Minister of *Sharia* Vehbi Efendi, who all justified the claim that the Caliphate was being separated from temporal authority for its own sake with reference to Islamic sources and by manipulating key Islamic concepts through their own theological engineering. Seyyid Bey, in particular, emphasized that the Ottoman Caliphate was already illegitimate because, unlike the original Caliphate of early Islam, it was a "fictitious" institution.

The GNA's move to render the caliph powerless did not eradicate, however, the essential tension between the ecumenical nature of the Caliphate and the territorially limited nature of the nation-state and the principle of national sovereignty on which the new Turkish state was founded. For there were still many people, both inside and outside the GNA, who wanted to see the caliph as the head of state. Besides, the new caliph, Abdülmecid Efendi, still had some degree of ideological power as he enjoyed great prestige both in Turkey and in the wider Muslim world. In this context, the debates between the modernists, who wished to see the caliph as the executive leader of the new republic, and the secularists, who aimed to destroy the Caliphate, also revealed the fact that the secularist discourse simultaneously entailed a mixture both Islamic and secular-nationalist elements. Though Islam was still dominant in their rhetoric, secular notions such as the "sacred" status of national sovereignty and the GNA that represented it gradually entered their discourse.

The Caliphate's demise was not an easy process for secularists. They had to frame everything they did in religious terms and find a way to transcend the tension between the universal Islamic institution and the national power base (the GNA) they controlled in Ankara. In late 1922 and throughout 1923, on the one hand, they had to prepare the Muslim public in Turkey and abroad, for which they again used the power/knowledge capacity of famous scholar Seyyid Bey; on the other hand, they had to fight against modernist Islamists such as politician Hoca Şükrü and intellectual Lütfi Fikri. I have called the discursive struggle between these two groups the "battle of the pamphlets," after which the secularists seized state power and abolished the Caliphate. It was still a shock to virtually everyone, however. Even the European press was very surprised. There are claims and indications that the Lausanne peace negotiations with the Allies might have influenced the secularists' decision to get rid of the Caliphate. Its relatively sudden demise after the proclamation of the Turkish Republic in October 1923 following the Lausanne Treaty was also related to concrete power struggles between Ankara and Istanbul. The secularist leadership, represented by President Mustafa Kemal and Prime Minister İsmet Pasha, perceived the caliph in Istanbul as a real threat when the modernists, including such figures as Rauf Bey, Hoca Şükrü and Lütfi Fikri, started to gather around him. When they decided to do away with the Caliphate, they had to resort to an intensely Islamic discourse for propaganda. The major discursive strategy they employed was emphasizing the un-Islamic nature of the Caliphate in its existing form (as a spiritual institution, which ironically they themselves had created in 1922) vis-à-vis the truly Islamic character of the Turkish GNA. They thus claimed that since there was already an institution (the GNA) that represented the true Islamic government, there was no need for a separate institution called the Caliphate. Here, too, Seyyid Bey played a crucial role – this time as minister of justice – in legitimizing the secularist policy, especially by convincing hesitant deputies – through his speeches both in the party group and the GNA meeting on March 3, the day the Caliphate was abolished – that this act had to be done for the sake of Islam itself.

I also argued, finally, that the Islamic discourse employed by the secularists was essentially "instrumental": They used Islamic elements in their political rhetoric in order to achieve their secular aims. For the most part, I have argued, they were *obliged* to do this because Islamic legitimization was the only way to justify their arguments and political positions. In other words, Islam was the only source of legitimacy in Muslim-Turkish society at the time. Moreover, the religious form of justification was a necessity for social mobilization; without it they could not harness enough political support for their leadership in the Anatolian resistance movement and then in the Turkish GNA. It also proved useful for mobilizing non-Turkish Muslims to support the Turkish resistance financially, militarily, and politically. Furthermore, Islamic legitimization was also indispensable due to the fact that there was no viable alternative: Islamic discourse was the most powerful linguistic framework, or "strategy" in Turkey between 1918 and 1924. As mentioned above, a somewhat secular nationalist discourse also emerged (as a "tactic") and gradually entered the secularist discourse, but it was far from challenging the Islamic one. (Turkish nationalism would gradually transform into a dominant "strategy" after the abolition of the Caliphate and other secularist reforms launched during the late 1920s and 1930s.)

The instrumental nature of the secularist discourse was apparent in actions, writings, and speeches of Mustafa Kemal and Ziya Gökalp. Their earlier (Islamic) discourses were contradicted both by their subsequent actions (or policy recommendations, in Gökalp's case) and by what they said to justify these actions. For example, Mustafa Kemal discursively elevated the status of the Caliphate in his attempt at overthrowing the Ottoman monarchy in late 1922; but in less than a year he became a staunch critic of the Caliphate as an "un-Islamic" institution, and of the caliph he himself had appointed. Moreover, he said in his famous 1927 *Speech* that previously he had to hide his real views due to unsuitable political climate and unfavorable circumstances – i.e., when he was not yet the single ruler of the country. The secularist intellectual Gökalp, too, often resorted to this instrumentalist discourse. For example, in 1917, when the CUP needed the caliph's ideological power in the midst of World War I, he had praised the unification of temporal and religious authority in one person, the Ottoman caliph, with reference to Islamic sources and history; however, in 1922 he celebrated the abolition of the Ottoman monarchy, again with reference to

Islamic sources and history, by claiming that the separation of religious and temporal powers was the basis of the true Islamic government. Moreover, his political project of secularizing Islamic law, which he called the "Social Methodology of Jurisprudence," was a prime example of the instrumental use of Islamic discourse for secular purposes.

Thus, the secularization of Islamic discourse by secularists was an *intended* consequence of their theological engineering, unlike the modernist Islamists and traditionalists, for whom the internal secularization of their discourse was largely an unintended consequence. In either case, committed or instrumental, deriving justification from Islam was still the only "meta-discursive strategy" for all three groups. Whether to counter or support secular reforms and policies (the latter was witnessed more than the former), Islamic discourse was almost always employed, which opened up a social space for the very possibility of these reforms. Therefore, it was accommodation that mostly characterized the relationship between Islam and secularism in the modernization of the Middle East.

I have thus tried to demonstrate that during much of the secularization process, which was a significant dimension of Middle Eastern modernization, Islam was central to all political positions and political actors invoked Islam in different ways to legitimize their claims. This applies as much to Islamists (both traditionalists and modernists) as – paradoxically – to secularists. The instrumental use of a dominant discourse may not be unique to Turkey's modernization process, however. The invocation of democracy, for example, was essential to socialist transformation in the Soviet world in the early years. This was indicated most clearly by Ceausescu's use of "democratic" rhetoric to justify the transformation to National Socialism in Romania (see Verdery 1995).

The substantive analyses in this book have tried to demonstrate this pattern in the Middle Eastern context. Obviously, this study is limited in terms of its temporal and spatial dimensions, as well as its focus. First of all, it does not include Iran, which is an important region within the Middle East, though the relevance of my analysis is limited in the Shia context because they do not recognize the (Sunni) Caliphate. Still, it would be very useful to compare the Ottoman-Sunni world with Iran, where there was also a constitutionalist movement that launched a revolution in 1905 similar to the 1908 Young Turk Revolution (see Keddie 1993; Sohrabi 1995; Afary 2005). Second, this study is confined to the analysis of the political aspect of the secularization process, which needs to be expanded to include other dimensions, such as education, culture, manners, etc. Third, a comparative-historical analysis of Middle Eastern modernization within a larger time frame, from the late 18th to the early 21st centuries, is necessary in order to reach a broader understanding of this topic. Fourth, this large-scale examination also requires a comparative analysis of the Muslim countries that were founded during the 20th century as a result of anti-colonial struggles, including those in Southeast Asia (Indonesia and Malaysia). This would help complete the larger picture of the Muslim world in terms of the development of secularism and its relationship with Islam. Fifth, as the next step, the nature of this relationship must be compared with Christian countries, particularly in the Balkans, where the Orthodox Church played a role in the modernization process. Finally, the Islamic case must be compared with Russian modernization, which was contemporaneous to, and interacted with, the process in Ottoman society. Many scholars have so far examined different parts of these large and complex processes; my study, too, can hopefully be considered as a contribution to this conversation.

Notes

1 Islam, politics, and secularization

1 The "Circle of Justice" (or the "Circle of Equity"), whose roots go back to ancient civilizations in Mesopotamia and Egypt, is a famous saying found in the Islamic wisdom literature that emphasizes the interconnectedness of political, economic, legal, and moral values and institutions. As such, it represents a model for achieving a "just society" and political stability. It has different versions attributed to different thinkers and statesmen from Aristotle to Noushirwan; the saying is usually in the form of a circle with no definite beginning or end. This model deeply influenced Islamic political thought, including the Ottoman milieu. (See, e.g., Ibn Khaldūn 1958, I: 80–82; see Darling 2002 for a discussion on the pre-Ottoman uses of the Circle.) The Ottoman "Circle of Equity," as reported by 16th-century scholar Kınalızade (2007), goes like this:

> *Adldir mucib-i salah-ı cihan*
> *Cihan bir bağdır divarı devlet*
> *Devletin nazımı şeriattır*
> *Şeriata olamaz hiç haris illa mülk*
> *Mülk zabt eylemez illa leşker*
> *Leşkeri cem edemez illa mal*
> *Malı kesb eyleyen raiyettir*
> *Raiyeti kul eder padişah-ı aleme adl*
> *Adldir mucib-i salah-ı cihan...*

2 The title of the journal – *İctihad* – where he wrote this and which was published by Cevdet himself is also telling, in that it is a term derived from Islamic *fıqh*, which means "applying Islamic principles to new situations by way of reasoning." It also became one of the key concepts widely used in that period by both "secular" and Islamist intellectuals to justify their respective positions regarding the role of Islam in the public sphere (see Erdem 2003). For a study on the rather weak socialist movement of the time, see Tunçay (1967).

3 Historically, there have been several "great awakenings" in the US since the 1730s, and perhaps we have been experiencing a new one at the turn of the 21st century. What is unusual – and significant – this time is that it has influenced federal politics with the Bush administration (2000–2008) with significant consequences in both domestic and international politics (see Wallis 2008).

4 Keddie, too, takes the state-religion confrontation as an unquestioned premise, however.

5 There is no independent "secularization literature" on the Middle East, but many studies on modernization also touch – often superficially – upon the elements of secularization in the region. For this reason, here I review a limited sample of studies that represent what I see as the two contending broad perspectives in the literature:

"conflict" and "accommodation" paradigms (see below). In my review I focus more on the literature on Ottoman-Turkish modernization because (i) my main empirical case (the Caliphate) has been discussed more in this literature than others; (ii) I am more familiar with the former; and (iii) the general literature on the Middle East often ignores or overlooks the Ottoman-Turkish case.

6 The idea that all Republican reforms in Turkey were opposed by "reactionary conservatives" was produced by the early Republican elite and the press to silence the opposition – and has since been widely used in Turkish politics, particularly to justify *coups d'état* by the army. Tunaya played a crucial role in transferring the ideological concept of "religious reaction" (*irtica*) into the academic field, which for a long time was not questioned by many academics, especially by Turkish ones with strong Kemalist/secularist inclanations (e.g., Berkes 1998[1964]; Karal 1968; Toprak 1981; Akgün 2006). For a recent critique of the (mis)use of this term in the literature, see Brockett (2006).

7 Sabri Ülgener, an economic historian, investigated the connections between Islam, especially Sufism, and social and economic change in the Ottoman and modern Turkish society from a Weberian perspective (Ülgener 2006[1951]). His sophisticated analyses were largely ignored by scholars until the 1980s because of the above-mentioned hegemony of the Kemalist discourse in Turkey. For a nice intellectual biography of Ülgener, see Sayar (1998).

8 For a useful study on a more recent revival of debates on, and demands for, the *sharia* in the Muslim world, and its relationship with "rule of law," see Feldman (2008).

9 An exception to this is Ahmet Kuru's recent study on the relationship between secularism and state policies in Turkey, France and the US (Kuru 2009). Kuru locates the three countries on an axis based on the concepts of "assertive" vs. "passive" secularisms: Turkey and France, both of which had a republican movement against monarchical rule allied with religious establishment in the past, falls into the first category while the US, lacking such a history of confrontation, has produced the passive version. On the other hand, Browers (2009) focuses on the Arab world examining how contemporary political (opposition) groups have produced a moderate Islamist discourse (associated with the *wasatiyya* movement) by combining Islamic and modern elements in the context of the retreat of secularist ideologies and post-colonial regimes, particularly in Egypt and Yemen.

10 See also Wodak (2001) for a summary of CDA's central assumptions and analytical procedures. Discourse analysis as a method and theoretical perspective has also affinities with narratology, the study of narratives, which has been influenced by Straussian structuralism, and more recently, by semiology (Bal 1997). Certain variants of the narrative theory, such as positioning theory (see, e.g., Davies and Harré 1990; Benwell and Stokoe 2006) share a number of methodological concepts (e.g., "subject positions") with the (Foucaultian) discourse analysis.

11 I also thank Professor Kara for lending me the unedited copies of some unpublished pamphlets for the 1922–1924 period.

2 Modernization, religion, and the Ottomans

1 Traditional scholarship sees the transformation of the Ottoman Empire in terms of a linear sequence of "birth-rise-stagnation-decline-collapse." The "decline" of Ottoman (military) power is often seen as symptomatic of the decline of "Islamic civilization" in general (e.g., Gibb and Bowen 1950: 173–199; Lewis 1961: 21–39). This (false) periodization was unquestionably repeated in the literature on Ottoman-Turkish modernization as well (e.g., Berkes 1969, I: 17). However, the "decline literature" has recently been highly criticized for ignoring the complexities of historical patterns, such as the sophistication of the Ottoman bureaucracy during the 19th century (see Hathaway 1996; Kafadar 1993, 1997–1998; Grant 1999).

2 Although the *Nizam-ı Cedid* is treated mostly as a military reform in the literature (e.g., Berkes 1998[1964]: 71–85; see also Karal 1998[1947]), recent research has shown that it was actually a broader program that entailed political, economic, financial and educational reforms (e.g., Beydilli 1999). Aksan (1993: 63) argues that this period contained the seeds of a significant change in the Islamic-Ottoman political philosophy; Şakül (2005: 117–121) adds to this that there emerged a kind of "proto-citizenship" as a result of this reform program.

3 I use the term *İttihad-ı İslam* in a neutral sense to refer to the idea(l) and policy of Muslim rapprochment in the late 19th and early 20th centuries. As such, it is different from "Pan-Islamism," which was coined by 19th-century British diplomats, and used as a value-laden, ideological concept to accuse the Ottomans, particularly Sultan Abdülhamid II, of aggressive imperialism. For instance, an anonymous reporter in Istanbul wrote an article titled "Panislamism and the Caliphate" for the London-based *The Contemporary Review* in 1883, in which he stated that the term was "designed to express the idea that the scattered fragments of the Mohammedan world have all rallied around the Caliph to join in a new attack upon Christendom" (Anonymous 1883). It has also been used to describe the political activism of anti-imperialist intellectuals, especially in India (e.g., Qureshi 1999). Many scholars have used this concept without questioning it (e.g., Vambéry 1906: 547–558; Toynbee 1954: 692–695); but such usage is partial and exeggerated (Yalçınkaya 1997: 142–146; cf. Landau 1990: 3–7). Some contemporary scholars who rely heavily on British archives, too, over-emphasize its significance (see Karpat 1987 for a critique).

4 Some historians disagree on the year the CUP was founded; among leading Ottomanists, Tunaya (1952) and Hanioğlu (1986) argue that it was founded in 1889 whereas Birinci (1988) sets 1895 as the true date.

5 Rıza Tahsin, *Mir'at-ı Mekteb-i Tıbbiye* (Istanbul, 1906), I: 18 (quoted in Berkes 1998: 113).

6 The original Turkish text of the *Tanzimat Fermanı* was published in *Takvim-i Vekayi*, no. 187 (15 Ramadan 1255/1839); see also *Tanzimat Fermanı* (1940, I: 48ff.); Alkan (2001: 449–451). For English translations, see Hertslet (1875, II: 1002–1005); Bailey (1942: 277–729).

7 Quoted in Berkes 1998[1964]: 145. The complete text of the protocol can be found in Reşat Kaynar, *Mustafa Reşit Paşa ve Tanzimat* (Ankara, 1954) pp. 172–173.

8 For the full text of the Edict in Turkish, see Karal (1988[1947], V: 266–272); Alkan (2001: 451–454); for the English version, Bailey (1942: 287–291).

9 The modern-secular notion of citizenship would be formalized with the *Tabiiyyet-i Osmaniyye Kanunnamesi* (Ottoman Citizenship Law) in 1869; it would be included in the 1876 Constitution as well. The development of citizenship in the Ottoman Empire followed a similar trajectory to the one in the Habsburgs and Tsarist Russia during the 19th century; it was also more "liberal" reserving a greater room for social and political liberties, especially for non-Muslims, than in the latter two (Adanır 2009: 61; see also Davison 1954: 845–848, Akarlı 1978).

10 *Düstur* (1876) *Birinci Tertip*, vol. 4, p. 3; my italics (see also Ahmed Midhat 1878, II: 281; Feridun 1962: 13).

11 Mahmud Celaleddin, *Mir'at-ı Hakikat* (Istanbul, 1910), I: 189 (quoted in Berkes 1998[1964]: 233). As we shall see in the following chapters, the Qur'anic concepts of *şura* and *meşveret* (consultation) were frequently employed by all three groups in debates over the Caliphate, as well. More recently, they were also interpreted as "democracy" and "Parliament" by a member of the so-called Islamist Welfare Party in the early 1990s, indicating the continuity of the same trend in contemporary Turkey. Mardin (1989) analyzes how the Islamic "idiom" was used by Said Nursi, a leading Islamic figure in the early Republican period, for cultural and religious mobilization of the masses in Turkey. For accounts of the use of the Qur'anic idiom in political discourses in different secularized contexts – in contemporary Yemen, Iran,

and Egypt, see Messick 1996; Mohammadi and Mohammadi 1994; and Starrett 1998, respectively.

12 The interpretation of the Qur'anic verses in unusual ways became a very widespread discursive technique, especially after 1908, in accordance with the pace of modernization in the Ottoman Empire (see Mertoğlu 2001).

13 An important topic of discussions on the 1876 Constitution was the expected presence of non-Muslim deputies in the Parliament, who would be able to limit the caliph-sultan's authority, which was problematic in terms of Islamic law and philosophy. The constitutionalist intellectuals (e.g., Namık Kemal 1867) put a great deal of effort to find a religious solution to this problem (see Oktay 1991 for a useful discussion on this).

14 See *Düstur* (1876) *Birinci Tertip*, vol. IV, pp. 1–40; see also Erdem (1982: 3–26); Kili (1982), Feridun (1962).

15 Born in Salonika, near the Ottoman border with Eastern Europe, Mustafa Kemal grew up observing the decline of Ottoman power in the Balkans. He went to a military high school in Manastır (in modern-day Macedonia), then to the *Mekteb-i Harbiye-i Şahane* (Royal War College) and the *Erkân-ı Harbiye Mektebi* (War Academy) in Istanbul, graduating in 1905. As a young army officer (captain), he joined the Young Turks, who tried to stop the loss of territory in Europe and the Middle East, in addition to getting rid of the "despotic" Sultan Abdülhamid II. However, he was never able to get a leadership position in the CUP partly due to his personal conflict with Enver Pasha, who was younger than himself and favored by the palace after 1909. Mustafa Kemal joined the Ottoman army (led by Enver) in Tripoli (Libya) to resist the Italian invasion in 1911; then he fought against the Bulgarians in Gallipoli during the First Balkan War (1912). During World War I, he was a division commander of the 5th Army in the Battle of Gallipoli (1915), and fought against the Russians in Eastern Anatolia (1916–1917) and on the Palestinian front (1918) (Kinross 1964: 100ff). After the war, he was appointed as an inspector to oversee the demobilization of the remaining Ottoman troops in Anatolia, where the Unionists made a deal with him for the organization of a resistance against the Allied occupation (Zürcher 1993: 148). When an arrest warrant was issued for Mustafa Kemal, he resigned from the army. Then he and his unionist friends organized two congresses in Erzurum and Sivas to prepare for the national liberation struggle (1919). When the British dissolved the Ottoman parliament in Istanbul, they moved it to Ankara as the Grand National Assembly (GNA), which convened on April 23, 1920, with Mustafa Kemal as the speaker of parliament. In the ensuing struggle, the Turkish nationalists defeated the Greek army; the Allies then decided to end the occupation in light of Turkish resistance and loss of lives in urban warfare. The only power center left in Turkey, the GNA led by Mustafa Kemal, abolished the Ottoman monarchy on November 1, 1922; the following year, he founded the People's Party, won the elections and declared the Republic on October 29, 1923. Elected president of the new regime, he then abolished the Caliphate (March 3, 1924), and curbed the *ulema*'s and Sufi sheiks' power before crushing the Kurdish opposition in 1925. He then started a series of radical reforms, including the formation of a single-party system, a new constitution, the adoption of civil and penal codes from Europe, and changes in dress code, the alphabet (its Latinization) and education. He also undertook a thorough secularization of the political system and banned religious orders and schools. He was idolized as Turkey's "Eternal Chief" during much of his presidency – and even after he died of cirrhosis in 1938.

16 This Constitution was published in *Resmi Gazete* on February 7, 1921. See *Düstur* (1921) *Üçüncü Tertip*, vol. I, p. 196; see also Erdem (1982: 27–30); Kili (1982).

17 Mustafa Kemal would later (in 1927) claim that he had influenced the content of the Constitution and that the direction of the developments in his mind at that time was toward the secular West (1961[1927], II: 445ff.).

18 See *Düstur* (1924) *Üçüncü Tertip*, vol. V, pp. 576–585; see also Erdem (1982: 31–45); Kili (1982).

19 The 1921 Constitution had also been amended with a similar sentence when the Republic was declared in October 1923.

20 This sentence would, however, be removed from the constitution in 1928 and the principle of secularism would enter it in 1937. Secularism was one of the six principles of Kemalism, which are also called the "six arrows of the RPP"; it entered the Constitution together with others, including republicanism, nationalism, populism, etatism, and "revolutionism." That the article stating the official religion of the Turkish State was replaced by Atatürk's (or the RPP's) principles is another indication of the fact that Kemalism was perceived among the state elite as a "secular religion" with its own sacred book (*The Speech*), the idea of a Golden Age, salvation, and a savior (Atatürk). This is also evident in the RPP's programs (see, for example, CHP 1931, 1935).

21 Simplification and/or purification of the Ottoman-Turkish language has always been a hot topic and continues to be such to this day. The first attempts at simplification were started in the *Tanzimat* era (1838–1876) by the Young Ottomans, and later promoted by the Young Turks and – after the 1908 Revolution – by the CUP. The leading CUP ideologue, Ziya Gökalp, actually prepared a program for language reform (see Gökalp 1968[1923]: Ch. 2). However, it was the Kemalist regime that in 1928 instituted a language reform (called the "Turkish language revolution") that was even more radical than Gökalp's, as it included the adoption of the Latin alphabet and the banning of Arabic letters. For discussions on language reforms, see Heyd (1954); Levend (1972); Yorulmaz (1995); for the Republican era, see G. Lewis (2002); Çolak (2004).

22 Kara (2001: 80–81) shows how in 1909 *Sırat-ı Müstakim* celebrated the publication by the CUP of a journal titled *Işık* (*Light*) targeting especially rural areas as a propaganda tool for the post-revolutionary regime, which would educate the public about the newly found "liberty" and "enlighten the peasantry" in the countryside. The *SM*'s embracing of the press as a modernizer emphasizing its "enlightenment function" indicates the gradual fusion of Enlightenment philosophy and Islamic elements in the "background" of their discourses.

23 Despite some exceptions, the political and cultural modernization of the Middle East resulted in the gradual rise of "civil" intellectuals and decline of the *ulema*'s power and their influence over politics and the everyday practices of masses. This is particularly visible in the retreat of the *şeyhülislam*, the head of the *ulema* and the caliph's religious dignitary, and the decline in his status during the 19th and early 20th centuries, before it was abolished altogether by Turkish secularists in 1924 (see Chapter 5 for a detailed discussion).

24 Though Mann applies his concept of "ideological power" principally to Europe and does not discuss the Ottoman Empire in this respect, his theory has recently been applied to the Ottoman-Turkish context (Jacoby 2004), particularly centering on his concept of the "tracklaying achievements of ideological power" (Mann 1986: 364ff.). Though successful in general, Jacoby's account of secularization in Turkey is too linear, and could not explain, for example, the fact that sermons and conferences by the *ulema* were the main medium of ideological power until 1924 (see Chapter 4 for further discussion).

25 The term "*ictihad*" means religious innovation based on novel interpretations of key Islamic sources; and the "*minber*" is the high pulpit where imams give their sermons in mosques. Mustafa Kemal's column in *Minber* was titled "*Hutbe*" (Friday sermon) (see Tevetoğlu 1988).

26 Examples taken from Kara 2001: 37–45. For a discussion of how Qur'anic verses were used to explain specific events and legitimize certain policies in this period, see Mertoğlu (2001).

27 Gökalp was born in Diyarbakır in southeastern Turkey, which was a cosmopolitan urban center with Arab and Persian as well as Kurdish and Turkish influence in the mid-19th century. His father was an editor for a government-sponsored newspaper.

Though he was of Kurdish origin, he would ironically become one of the leading ideologues of Turkish nationalism, and his *The Principles of Turkism* a major outline of this ideology. At the age of 20 he migrated to Istanbul, where he attended the Veterinary College, but also got involved in the underground revolutionary society, which would later become the CUP, for which he was jailed for one year and then exiled to Diyarbakır in 1899. After the 1908 revolution, he first worked as the CUP's representative in Diyarbakır and was later elected to the CUP's central committee in Salonika as the head of the propaganda division. In 1910 he started teaching sociology in this city. Five years later, he founded the first sociology department at Istanbul University (*Darülfünun*). Following World War I, he was exiled to Malta with other CUP leaders until 1921, when he returned to Diyarbakır and supported the Turkish nationalist movement led by Mustafa Kemal. Here he published his articles on sociology, Turkish nationalism, and the Caliphate in his *Küçük Mecmua* (*The Little Journal*). One year later, he was appointed to Istanbul as the head of the cultural publications and translations department of the Ministry of Education. His ideas were a synthesis of Islamic *fiqh*, Turkish nationalism, and Durkheimian sociology, as he believed that the Turkish nation simultaneously belonged to the Islamic *ummah* and European civilization. In 1924 he was elected as deputy for Diyarbakır but soon died at the age of 48 (for Gökalp's biography and main ideas, see, among others, Heyd 1950; Berkes 1959; Parla 1985; Davison 1998; Zürcher 2005).

28 Gökalp's corporatism, which he borrowed from Durkheim again, was not only influential on the CUP, but was also adopted after 1923 as the official social policy of the Kemalist regime (see Parla 1985). Though not as strong any longer, this corporatist ideology still exists in the Turkish constitution and is reflected in the organization of state institutions today.

29 An interesting consequence of the overlap between Gökalp's ideas and the CUP's and Kemalists' cultural-political agenda was the development of Kurdology as a scientific study of Kurds living in the Ottoman Empire, which was also founded at the *Darülfünun* by Gökalp himself and financially and legally supported by CUP governments. Also, he wrote a book in this area, titled *Sociological Analyses on Kurdish Tribes* (1992), which he initially wrote in 1922 as a report for the nationalist government in Ankara. For a discussion of the origins of Kurdology in Turkey, see Dündar (2006).

30 Other founders of Turkish nationalism, including Ahmet Ağaoğlu, İsmail Gaspıralı and Mehmet Emin were all Russian émigrés. (Another important figure, Moiz Cohen [Tekin Alp] was a Jew from Salonika.) Escaping from oppression by the Russian government, these intellectuals of Turkish origin came to Istanbul and founded the "Turkish Homeland Society" (*Türk Yurdu Derneği*) in 1911 and published their journal, *Turkish Homeland* (*Türk Yurdu*), which disseminated propaganda in support of the unification of all Turks (Turanism) under the leadership of the Ottoman Empire, which they saw as the only option for the liberation of Turks living under Russian rule. They also influenced the CUP leadership (Enver Pasha, Talat Pasha, and Cemal Pasha) but could not have them adopt Turkish nationalism as the empire's official policy (Kushner 1977; Kayalı 1997). Gökalp was very much influenced by them, particularly Hüseyinzade and Akçura (1976[1904]), who advocated synthesizing Islam with nationalism and "Europeanization." They were also influential for the post-1923 Kemalist regime, which emphasized the more nationalist overtones of their ideas (see Ülken 1994[1966]; Arai 1992; Hanioğlu 1997; Zürcher 2005; for biographies of some of them, see Shissler 2003; Georgeon 1980). To this day, these figures have been regarded as founding fathers of Turkish nationalism and as true heroes in nationalist circles in Turkey.

31 For general (and somewhat conflicting) discussions on Gökalp's view on religion, see Heyd (1950: 82–103); Berkes (1954: 380–385); Dodd (1979: 83–85); Parla (1985: 38–41); and Arai (1992: 91–97). For a more detailed discussion, see Davison (1998: 110–133).

32 A Qur'anic verse in the Chapter of Abraham (14/24) reads:

> Seest thou not how Allah sets forth a parable? – A goodly word like a goodly tree, whose root is firmly fixed, and its branches (reach) to the heavens, – of its Lord. So Allah sets forth parables for men, in order that they may receive admonition.

33 Disturbing traditional conceptual and institutional hierarchies as a discursive strategy was also applied by modernist Islamists and secularists in the case of the Caliphate. The status of this institution in Islamic political theory was gradually lowered using similar discursive techniques (see Chapters 5 and 7).

34 Sociology entered the Ottoman Empire in the second half of the 19th century and evolved as an alternative to Islamic *fikh*. It became part of the school curriculum in 1914 in the Istanbul *Darulfünun* (University), though it had been taught in some Western-style high schools before that. The first Institute of Sociology (*İctimaiyat Darul Mesaisi*) was founded in 1915, and it started the publication of the first sociological journal, *İctimaiyat Mecmuası*, in 1917. Other, quasi-academic, journals such as Abdullah Cevdet's (the first socialist thinker in Turkey) *İctihad*, also published social-science related articles in the Second Constitutional Period. Starting from this period, the development of sociology over the next several decades was heavily influenced by 19th-century French positivism, particularly by Le Bon, Comte and Durkheim, as in the case of Gökalp and others such as Ahmed Riza, Mehmed İzzet, M. Ali Şevki, and I. Hakkı Baltacıoğlu (see Ülken 1994[1966]; Kaçmazoğlu 2001; Zürcher 2005). (In a letter to Mustafa Reşit Pasha, first the ambassador to Paris and then the Grand Vizier of the *Tanzimat* period, Comte himself had expressed his support and made suggestions for the modernizing efforts of the Young Ottomans [Ortaylı 1985].) Prince Sabahaddin, the second most important name in the first phase of sociology's development in the Ottoman society, followed the Le Play school. Sabahaddin, whose mother was a member of the royal family, opposed the Hamidian monarchy as a Young Turk, but was also a founder of the liberal Freedom and Alliance Party (FAP), the main opposition group to the CUP, with which Gökalp had close ties (see Akşin 1987: 43–53). The influence of French sociology would later be replaced by that of Jewish German refugees in the 1930s and 1940s, and then by the Anglo-American tradition in the 1950s up until today. This course of development closely followed – and is to some extent a reflection of – the evolution of Turkey's political relations with these countries, except for the dominance of Germany as the principal ally of the Ottoman Empire during World War I. For a collection of articles on the development and various aspects of sociology in Turkey, see *TALİD*, vol. 6, no. 11 (2008), special issue on the history of Turkish sociology.

35 Here Gökalp sounded as if he was quoting from Durkheim's *The Elementary Forms of the Religious Life* and *The Division of Labor in Society*:

> In primitive societies, the religious institutions perform the functions of the other two institutions [politics and culture] because these societies do not have political and cultural organs.... All institutions of primitive societies, therefore, necessarily spring from religion and acquired their power and value from this source of sacredness.... This power [in the modern world] becomes harmful when it is extended to worldly or secular, and especially to material, institutions because it prevents these institutions from adapting themselves to the expediencies of life. Therefore, the predominance of religious *mores* over all institutions is not something to be desired for organic societies.
>
> In organic societies religious *mores* still exist, but they cover only those ideals and sentiments which have to remain spiritual and sacred. They do not extend over those institutions which are of a worldly and secular character. (...) One of the greatest tasks of religion in organic society is to leave other institutions [including the state] free within their own spheres.
>
> (1915a: 185–186)

Cf. Durkheim (1915, 1947):

> At the roots of all our judgments there are a certain number of essential ideas which dominate all our intellectual life; they are what philosophers since Aristotle have called the categories of the understanding.... Now when primitive religious beliefs are systematically analyzed, the principle [*sic*] categories are naturally found. They are born in religion and of religion; they are a product of religious thought.
>
> (1915: 9)

> It is an historical law that mechanical solidarity which first stands alone, or nearly so, progressively loses ground, and that organic solidarity becomes, little by little, preponderant.... If we try to construct intellectually the ideal type of a society whose cohesion was exclusively the result of resemblances [mechanical solidarity], we should have to conceive it as an absolutely homogenous mass whose parts are not distinguished from one another
>
> (1947: 174).

> It is quite otherwise with the solidarity which the division of labour produces. Whereas the previous type [mechanical solidarity] implies that individuals resemble each other, this type [organic solidarity] presumes their difference ... This solidarity resembles that which we observe among the higher animals. Each organ, in effect, has its special physiognomy, its autonomy. And, moreover, the unity of the organism is as great as the individuation of the parts is more marked. Because of his analogy, we propose to call the solidarity which is due to the division of labour, organic
>
> (1947: 131)

> [In modern society] (t)here is, above all, an organ upon which we are tending to depend more and more; this is the State.
>
> (1947: 227)

36 It is obvious that both views are entirely blind to the facts. People can neither entirely drop the religion they hold sacred, nor can they dispense with the necessities of contemporary civilization. Reason demands, not that one be sacrificed at the expense of the other, but that an attempt be made to reconcile the two.... A religion like Islam, which is based on reason in metaphysics and on *'urf* in sociology, cannot be in conflict with positive sciences

> (1916: 202, 212)

Note the emphasis on "reason" (rationality) as the "background" of this discourse particle, which is in fact implicit in Gökalp's entire project.

37 Gökalp celebrated the separation of the Caliphate from the monarchy, but still embraced the Caliphate, claiming that this (secular) move would both protect Islam and glorify the Caliph's position (see Chapter 6 for a detailed discussion).

3 The Caliphate question: historical and discursive context

1 Another leading classical scholar, al-Māwardī (d. 1058), defines the Caliphate as follows:

> God, may His power be exalted, ordained for the community (*ummah*) a leader through whom He provided for the vicegerency of the prophet and ... protected the religion (*millah*), and He entrusted to him authority (*siyasah*) so that the management of affairs should proceed [on the basis of] legitimate religion ... and the Caliphate [*Imamate*] became the principle upon which the bases of the community were founded, by which the wellbeing of the community was regulated and affairs of general interest were made stable, and from which particular public functions (*al-wilayāt al-khassah*) emanated.
>
> (al-Māwardī 1994: 3)

2 For a discussion of these sources, see Özcan (1998b: 546).

3 For discussions on this debate, see Asrar 1983, Sümer 1992.

4 The debate over the "Quraysh condition" for the Caliphate was revived in the late-Ottoman era when Arab nationalists, with the "encouragement" of the British and the French, made a claim for an Arab Caliphate. I discuss this in detail in Chapter 5.

5 This notion of the sultan's centrality in the Ottoman socio-political system is reflected in the Divan literature as well. During the classical and early modern periods (14th to 18th centuries), the Ottoman sultan, who is "always likened to the Four Caliphs of Islam in terms of their religiosity and fairness," was at the center of the linguistic-symbolic, aesthetic and imaginative worlds of the Divan poetry (Tanpınar 1997: 5–7).

6 Özcan (1997) documents the intimate and complex relations between the Ottoman Caliphate and Indian Muslims, as well as Britain's role in them during the colonial period. Also, recent research has shown that starting from Selim I and throughout the 16th century the Ottomans were very active in and around the Indian Ocean, rivaling the Portuguese Empire and challenging it ideologically as well as commercially and militarily (Casale 2010). In fact, Casale argues that there was a "century-long struggle for global dominance" between the two empires that took place in a vast expanse from Western Africa to the steppes of Central Asia (pp. 34ff.).

7 An extension of this false claim is another argument that it was only Abdulhamid II who capitalized on the power of the Caliphate in international relations (e.g., Berkes 1957; Lewis 1961; Akgün 2006). Although it is true that the Ottoman Caliphate played a very significant role in the Hamidian-era foreign policy, this does not mean that it had no influence in previous periods. For example Sultan Abdülmecid (r. 1839–1861) as the caliph of Muslims intervened, per British request, into the Indian revolt against the British colonial administration in 1857 (Bayur 1987, III: 315–316; Eraslan 1995: 41–43), and Sultan Abdülaziz (1861–1876) in the Comoro Islands in the Indian Ocean and Eastern Turkistan in Central Asia when the Muslim leaders requested his help against the British and the Russians (Karpat 2001: 56–63). See Chapter 5 for more discussion.

8 The Muslim Brotherhood (*al-Ikhvan al-Muslimeen*), the largest opposition group in many autocratic Arab countries, particularly in Egypt, Jordan and Syria, was founded by Hassan al-Banna in Cairo in 1928. As the "General Guide of the Muslim Brotherhood," al-Banna sent a letter to various Muslim leaders, including the Egyptian King Faruq I, in 1936. Titled "Towards the Light" (and published as a book in 1947), this long letter outlined the Brotherhood's political philosophy and main objectives, one of which was "Strengthening the ties between all the Islamic countries, especially the Arab countries, to pave the way for a practical and serious consideration concerning the departed Caliphate" (al-Banna 1936: 10). This piece was until recently posted on the *Ikhvan* website in the "Messages of Imam" section (Muslim Brotherhood 2010b). Although the Brotherhood's official Bylaws do not include a direct reference to the Caliphate, Article 2 of the bylaws mentions as one of its objectives "The need to work on establishing the Islamic State, which seeks to effectively implement the provisions of Islam and its teachings (Muslim Brotherhood 2010a)

9 Usama bin Laden and his aide Aiman al-Zawahiri declared the creation of a caliphate as their ultimate goal, and even nominated the Iraqi city of Ramadi, then under their control, as its capital in 2006. But bin Laden and, now, al-Zawahiri have not been able to get the recognition of the Muslim World (Liebl 2009: 373, 379).

10 *Hizb ut-Tahrir* is a Syria-based international group founded in 1952 by a Taqiuddin al-Nabhani, which also operates in Europe and is banned in some Muslim countries, including Turkey, Lebanon, Egypt and Syria (see *Hizb ut-Tahrir* 2010). The *Khilafat Majlis* is a legal political party in Bangladesh, others are banned by Pakistan and the US (see the American Foreign Policy Council's *World Almanac of Islamism*, online at: http://almanac.afpc.org/Bangladesh).

11 Here I use the term in its more political sense, to refer to the capacity of social groups

to influence power relations in a polity. It is also slightly different from the concept of the "public sphere" in the Habermasian sense – the abstract space in which free individuals have a rational discussion on social issues, which Habermas argues emerged in 18th century Western Europe (Habermas 1991). On the other hand, Kafadar criticizes Habermas arguing that a public sphere as a site of political negotiation and even resistance (to the state center) had emerged in the Ottoman Empire, starting from the mid-16th century (Kafadar 1994).

12 Therefore, it is the Prophetic traditions (*hadith*s), not the Qur'an, that corresponds to the Bible in the Judeo-Christian tradition, as the Word of God (*al-Qur'an*) is directly revealed by Allah in the Muslim faith.

13 For a recent study on the multiple networks of *hadith* transmission, which constitute the largest known set of social networks that covers a span of approximately 1,000 years (from 610 to 1505 CE) involving 1,226 prominent *hadith* scholars, see Şentürk 2005.

14 A famous scholar of his time, Mehmed Seyyid Bey's (1873–1925) religious justification – through a series of crucial interventions into Islamic theology and legal theory – of limiting the caliph-sultan's authority was quite comprehensive and influential. He had theorized the modernist view of the Caliphate in a number of books (Seyyid Bey 1917, 1923, 1924) before he took up an essentially secularist position in Kemal Atatürk's service (see Chapter 6). He received education both in the *medrese* and *Dârülfünûn*'s Law School, where he subsequently taught Islamic law and methodology. He was politically very active as well: he worked in both chambers of the parliament – elected three times to the Chamber of Deputies in 1908, 1912, and 1914, and then appointed to the Chamber of Notables in 1916. He also acted as chairman of the parliamentary committee to prepare a modern civil code (1924). Moreover, he was not only a leading ideologue of the CUP, but was also elected as the vice-president (1910) and then president (1911) of the party. Later, he became a member of the executive committee of the Renewal Party (*Teceddüd Fırkası*) that was created by the Unionists when they dissolved the CUP in 1918. Following the war, Seyyid Bey was exiled, like other CUP leaders, to Malta by the British (1919–1921), after which he returned to Istanbul to enter the Chamber of Deputies and to teach at *Dârülfünûn*. Before the proclamation of the republic in 1923, he developed good relations with Mustafa Kemal, was elected as a deputy, and became Turkey's first Minister of Justice (August 1923–March 1924). He was also one of the authors of the 1924 Constitution. On the day the Caliphate was abolished (March 3, 1924), he gave a long speech as minister in the parliament that justified the secular move by effectively utilizing key Islamic sources, which broke down the opposition in the parliament (see Chapter 6). Despite his crucial role, however, he soon fell from favor and resigned from the government to return to the university because he opposed the aim of Mustafa Kemal and Prime Minister İsmet İnönü to adopt the Swiss code completely (he supported a partial transfer of it), and of giving the president the right to abolish the parliament in the Constitution (Art. 25) (Erdem 1995, 1996).

15 The signification of the term *ul al-amr* shifts depending on the user's intellectual and/ or political position and historical context: it may refer to the caliph, or to the group of *umera* (administrative leaders and/or parliament members), or the community of the *ulema*, or both groups in the Sunni tradition. (In the mainstream Shia tradition, it refers exclusively to the *imams* who have prophetic descent.) For an investigation of the meanings and history of this concept, see Kavak (2011: Ch. 3).

16 Collections of 40 prophetic *hadith*s are a scholarly and literary form based on a longstanding tradition, which goes back to the second century of Islam. It is rooted in a *hadith* of the Prophet Muhammad, who said, "Whosoever memorizes and preserves for my followers forty *hadith*s relating to their religion, Allah will resurrect him on the Day of Judgment in the company of great men of wisdom and learning" (al-Nawawi 1997). Since then it has been customary to compile different sets of 40 (and

sometimes 25 or 100) *hadith*s, usually on a particular topic, such as prayers, ethics, spiritual improvement, and, of course, the Caliphate. General 40 *hadith* compilations (as opposed to specific ones) have usually been aimed at educating the general public and students about the basic teachings of Islam, and functioned as a significant medium of the socialization/popularization of Islamic knowledge. This popular form acted as a channel through which religious knowledge produced by intellectual elites was transmitted to the masses. One of the most popular general anthologies is the compilation by Imam al-Nawawi (d. 1278 CE), which contains *hadith*s about Islamic faith, ethics, and *fiqh*. Furthermore, the tradition has been widely practiced throughout Islamic history by both Sunni and Shia Muslims. (For example, Ayatollah Khomeini compiled a set of forty *hadith*s, too.)

In the case of the Caliphate, 40 *hadith* compilations were used as a discursive technique (what I call the technique of "justification by form") as this format itself has – independently of its content – religious implications (due to the above-mentioned popular *hadith* and the existence of the strong tradition based upon it), which were drawn upon by traditionalist intellectuals.

17 An émigré from northern Caucasus, Ömer Ziyaeddin [Dağıstani] Efendi (1850–1920), received his *medrese* education in Istanbul, worked as the *müfti* (chaplain) of the second army in Edirne (1878–1892), and then as the *kadı* (judge) in Malkara, Jerusalem, and Tekirdağ. He republished his famous *hadith* compilation immediately after the 1908 Revolution while the Sultan was still on the throne. This angered the Unionists, who later exiled him to Medina under the pretext that he had participated in the March 31 Incident (1909). During World War I, he lived under the protection of the khedive of Egypt, Abbas Hilmi Pasha, in Cairo, where he was later temporarily arrested by the British. Then he returned to Istanbul, where he taught at the *Dârü'l-Hilâfeti'l-Aliyye Medresesi*. Ömer Ziyaeddin was a well-known *hadith* scholar. In addition to his *hadith* compilation mentioned above, he published several other books, including *Zubdat al-Bukhārī* (Cairo, 1330/1914), a famous commentary – published in both Arabic and Turkish – on the most important *hadith* collection, *al-Bukhārī's Sahīh*. He was also a Sufi leader and in 1919 he succeeded Ahmed Ziyâeddîn Gümüşhânevî, a well-known leader of the local *Naqshi* order, as the sheikh of the Gümüşhânevî lodge in Istanbul until his death in November 1920 (Binatlı 1993: 406–407).

18 This is another discursive strategy, used only by traditionalists, that was frequently employed in the debates over the Caliphate (see Chapters 5, 6).

19 Mustafa Zihni Pasha (1850–1929) was a high-rank bureaucrat. He worked under Sultan Abdülhamid as the governor of Yanya, the *Hijaz*, and Adana (1909). Previously, he had worked in different bureaucratic positions, such as the "seal holder" (*mühürdar*), correspondence officer (*mektupçu*), and city administrator (*mutasarrıf*), in Iraq and Anatolia. Born in Süleymaniye (northern Iraq), he was a member of an influential Kurdish clan, the Baban family. Educated in the *medrese*, he was knowledgeable in Islamic sciences, and wrote several books in Islamic theology and ethics (Kara 2003b: 23). His book on *The Caliphate in Islam* (1911) is relevant to the Caliphate debates both in the center and the periphery: Being a governor in Iraq and southern Anatolia (near Syria), he was aware of the nationalist challenges to Islamic unity and the Caliphate, which is reflected in his book. It also speaks directly to the early debates in Istanbul over the limits of the Caliph's authority. The book is a very comprehensive account of Islamic political theory and a scholarly defense of the traditionalist view. It also includes a critique of the Shia view of the early Islamic Caliphate, which was probably addressed to the Shia literati in Iraq, where he was born, educated, and employed.

20 Though a descendant of a line of military and administrative Pashas, Ömer Lütfi (1864–1934) went to law school after attending a military high school in Istanbul. Throughout his life, he worked as a public prosecutor, district attorney, lawyer and

judge (including various courts of appeal) in Anatolia, Syria and Istanbul. He was also the first chief justice at the court of appeal of Turkish Republic (1920–1925). He wrote his pamphlet on the Caliphate when he was the judicial administrator for Salonika, where he also taught Islamic law at the Salonika Law School (Erk 1961: 495–496).

21 See Kara (2002–2005, vols. 1–2) for a collection of writings on the Caliphate during the Hamidian era (1876–1909).

22 Another indication of the fluidity of group boundaries is the change in Seyyid Bey's politico-ideological position: during much of the Second Constitutional Period (until 1918), he voiced the modernist-Islamist arguments in a sophisticated manner (see Chapter 5); but once he became an advisor to Mustafa Kemal in 1922, he began to defend the secularist position, though he did not completely give up his modernist arguments (see Chapter 6). This mixture of his secularist political position with a modernist scholarly viewpoint caused some inconsistencies in his discourse, which are particularly visible in his later writings on the Caliphate (Seyyid Bey 1923, 1924).

23 Both Safayihi and al-Tunusi received their education at the famous Zaytuna *madrasa* in Tunisia. Safayihi worked as a *madrasa* professor and administrator in Tunisia; he was also the chief judge of the *Hanafi* school there under Sultan Abdülhamid. In 1906 he moved to Istanbul where he stayed until his death in December 1918. al-Tunusi, too, went to Istanbul the same year after teaching at the Zaytuna *madrasa* for 12 years, during which time he entered a heated debate with the two leading Islamic modernists, Muhammad Abduh and Rashid Rida, accusing them of propagating fundamentalist Wahhabism. From Istanbul, he went to Libya with Enver Pasha, then commander-in-chief of the Ottoman forces in Africa, who organized the resistance against the Italians there in 1911. (Though al-Tunusi had opposed the CUP for deposing Sultan Abdülhamid, he later made peace with the Unionists due to Arab nationalist activities, such as the Arab Congress convened in Paris in 1913.) al-Tunusi also acted as the North African regional director of the *Teşkilat-ı Mahsusa* and organized various pro-Ottoman activities with Mehmed Akif, a leading Islamist thinker, poet, CUP member and activist of the time, in Germany and Arabia. After the Ottoman defeat in the war, al-Tunusi escaped to Berlin with his activist friends (such as Abdulaziz Jawish) from Tunisia, and then at the end of 1918 moved to Switzerland, where he died two years later (Commins 1990: 106; Kara 2004: 8, 12).

24 A rather obscure character, "Habil Adem" was actually a pseudonym used by Naci İsmail Pelister, who also signed his writings with various foreign names such as "Dr. Fritz" and "Professor White." Albanian by birth, he had a PhD in philosophy and was a journalist during the Second Constitutional Period. He worked with Ziya Gökalp as an ethnographer to map out information on Turcoman and Kurdish tribes in Eastern Anatolia in an anthropological project that shaped the CUP's population policy (see Chapter 2, note 29). He also worked for the *Teşkilat-ı Mahsusa* as a secret agent (Birinci 2001). His book on *The Politics of the Caliphate and the Politics of Turkishness after the War* (1913), which was immediately translated by Muhammad Safa (see below) into Arabic, presented a sketch of the Muslim countries following the Ottoman defeat in the Balkan War (1912–1913) and advocated a confederation of Muslim nation-states headed by Turkey. Given the loss of the Balkans, populated mostly by non-Muslim citizens of the Empire, which resulted in the virtual Islamization of the Ottoman population, Habil Adem suggested supporting various Muslim nationalisms against European intrusions and uniting them under the Turkish caliph's leadership.

25 Born in Egypt, Ali Fahmi Muhammad (1870–1926) graduated from the military school before he entered politics. He was the famous Egyptian nationalist Mustafa Kamil's older brother and helped him found *al-Hizb al-Watani* (the Homeland Party) in 1894, later leading the party after his brother died. He was a staunch critic of Britain. For this reason, he was arrested several times and even sentenced to death, but eventually pardoned (Kara 2003b: 16). Though he never liked the CUP (as he

blamed the Unionists for undermining the Caliphate by deposing Sultan Abdülhamid), he nevertheless supported Istanbul's control over Arabia. He wrote several books, including his brother's biography and others on Egyptian politics and the Caliphate, in which he harshly criticized British plans to install an Arab caliph, i.e., Sharif Hussein (Ali Fahmi 1911).

26 Abdulaziz Jawish (1876–1929) was born in Alexandria to a Tunisian father and a Turkish mother, and died in Cairo, having spent most of his life in Egypt and Istanbul. He was educated at *al-Azhar* and *Dar al-Ulum* in Cairo, and at the Borough Road Teacher's Training College in London, and taught Arabic at Cambridge. In Egypt he was both a well-known journalist and an active politician. A leader of the National Party together with Muhammad Farid Bey, he was also the editor of the party's daily, *Liwa'*, both of which were a major platform for struggle against the British occupation of Egypt and its supporters, particularly the *Watan* newspaper. (*Liwa'* reached a circulation of 18,000 and employed 162 staff.) He was arrested four times and served two prison sentences, after which he was exiled to Istanbul, where he became the editor of *al-Hilal* and *al-Hidaya*, the CUP's Arabic-language newspapers. Jawish was also the editor of *Die islamische Welt* and *al-'Alam al-Islami*, published in Berlin by the German Foreign Office during World War I. After the war, he worked for Mustafa Kemal, the leader of the Turkish nationalist movement, but broke with him toward the end of 1923, when the latter decided to abolish the Caliphate. Upon returning to Egypt, he worked for the Education Ministry and was elected vice president of the Muslim Youth Association before his death in Cairo (Goldschmidt 2000: 96–97). He wrote books on education, Islam, and the Caliphate. His critique of the British, French, and Arab nationalist press on the Caliphate (1916) was published in Istanbul by the *Teşkilat-ı Mahsusa* (Ottoman secret service) in Arabic and translated into Turkish the same year (Kara 2004: 19). The book included a harsh criticism of the Arab Caliphate project, trying to disprove the nationalist anti-Ottoman claim that the caliph should be a descendant of the Prophet and that there could be multiple caliphs at the same time.

27 Scholar and politician Elmalılı Muhammed Hamdi [Yazır] (1878–1942) was born in Elmalı, a small town in Anatolia. He was educated and then taught at different *medreses* in Istanbul, including *Mekteb-i Nuvvab, Süleymaniye*, and *Medresetu'l Vaizin*, as well as at the School of Political Science (*Mülkiye Mektebi*). He worked in the *şeyhülislam*'s office before being elected as a parliament member following the 1908 Revolution. He was one of the *ulema* who wrote and signed the juridical decision (*fatwa*) in support of deposing Sultan Abdülhamid at the CUP's request. He also acted as a member of the CUP's *ulema* committee, and of the Council of Islamic Wisdom (*Dârü'l-Hikmeti'l İslamiye*), eventually becoming its chairman. After 1919 he entered the Chamber of Notables (*Ayân*) and then the government as the minister of charities. In the Republican period, he was tried for not supporting the nationalist resistance and sentenced to death by an "Independence Tribunal," but saved from execution. With the abolition of the Caliphate and the *medreses*, he went into seclusion for 20 years, during which he wrote his monumental Qur'anic commentary (1935). In the debates over the *şeyhülislam*'s status between 1909 and 1911, he strongly voiced the modernist argument that it was no more than that of a civil servant working for the government (Elmalılı Hamdi 1909), which eventually won over the traditionalist argument as the CUP removed the *şeyhülislam* from the cabinet in 1916 (see Chapter 4).

28 Hussein was a member of the Hashemite tribe in Mecca, to which the Prophet had belonged (hence the title "sharif"). Because of its history, Ottoman sultans always appointed a member of this tribe as the "sharif" (religious dignitary) of Mecca, whose status was more ideological than political, as the Turkish governor was the real administrator of the region. Hussein was born in Istanbul, where his family lived under Abdülhamid II's close watch. After 15 years of forced residence in the capital,

he was appointed as sharif of Mecca (1908–1916) by the Young Turks who deposed Sultan Abdülhamid. During World War I, though initially loyal to the center, he co-operated with the British and declared war against the Ottomans (the "Arab revolt"), eventually gaining independence. He then declared himself "king of the *Hijaz*" (1916) and then "king of all Arabs," which triggered Ibn Saud's hostility toward the Hashemites. Two days after the Caliphate was abolished by the parliament in Ankara, Hussein declared himself the "caliph of all Muslims," but he was soon driven out of Arabia by the Saudi army, forcing him to flee Mecca and live the rest of his life with his son Abdullah, the Emir of Transjordan (1924). Hussein's son Ali succeeded him as king of the *Hijaz*, only to be defeated by Ibn Saud next year. Hussein's youngest son, Faysal, was briefly made king of Syria (shortly before it was occupied by France), and then king of Iraq (1921–1933) by the British colonial administration (Teitelbaum 1998, 2001).

29 Mahmud Nedim [Maan] was a former army officer, on whose life there is very little information. He fought in the *Hijaz* during World War I as an army commander against the British in 1915. After retirement, he wrote several short books on politics, including Russian politics (1918), the Wilsnonian principles (1920), and Mustafa Kemal's activities during the resistance (1922) (Kara 2004: 26–27). He also wrote a short pamphlet – examined in Chapter 5 – criticizing Sharif Hussein's declaration of himself as the "king of *Hijaz*" on the grounds that the British would control the holy shrines through Hussein, who was their puppet, and that Islam banned any dynastic regime in the Holy Land and required democracy instead (Mahmud Nedim 1919).

30 One of the most influential Arab-nationalist intellectuals during the Second Constitutional Period, Rashid Rida (1865–1935) was born and raised in Syria, where he received his higher education in classical Islamic sciences and was temporarily a Sufi as a member of the *Naqshibandi* order, which was (and still is) the biggest Sufi group in the Muslim world (see Algar 1976). During the Hamidian era he was a member of the "Ottoman Consultation Society" in Syria that supported Abdülhamid II's caliphate; after the 1908 Revolution, he joined the anti-CUP "Decentralization Party" and the Arab nationalist "Syrian Congress." In 1898 he moved to Egypt, where he published *al-Manar* (1898–1935), a weekly and then monthly journal (Tauber 1989; Soage 2008). Rida criticized al-Kawakibi's view of the Caliphate for reducing it to a mere spiritual authority with no political power, but nevertheless shared his Arab nationalist views (Kerr 1966: 153–186). Though at first he was against the "Arab caliphate" project designed by Britain during World War I (see Chapter 5), harshly criticizing its proponents, he later supported that project – and Sharif Hussein (Mertoğlu 2005: 46). During and after World War I, he was a vocal member of the Arab Caliphate Movement. As of 1924, however, he withdrew his support for Hussein (accusing him of "stealing" the Caliphate and calling him "Satan's caliph" [Mertoğlu 2005: 88]) and nominated instead Imam Yahya of Yemen as caliph, retaining his Arab nationalist views. Toward the end of his life he supported the Wahhabi Abdulaziz ibn Saud who was the most powerful leader in the Arab world at the time. (For a detailed examination of his intellectual biography and ideas, see Kavak 2007: 1–61.)

31 I have already discussed in Chapter 2 how Gökalp referred to a Qur'anic verse that symbolically compares Islam to the "Paradise tree" (14/24) in order to justify his very unusual (secular) distinction between *mores* (*örf*) and text (*nass*), and between law and religion in general, which was clearly against the mainstream legal (*fiqh*) tradition. He argued that "to satisfy civil needs," Islamic law should be based on both "social fundamentals" (*mores*) and "textual fundamentals" (the Qur'an and *hadith*), and that the former should have priority over the texts when it came to "temporal affairs and social life" as a source of law, because *mores*, or the "exigencies of contemporary life," were the "expression of the way of God" and God's "divine *Sunna*" (Gökalp 1914b: 199).

32 İsmail Şükrü Hoca [Efendi] (1876–1950) was very active in the last two years of the Caliphate against the secularists, though Mustafa Kemal had had good relations with him earlier during the national struggle (1919–1922). A son of İzzet Efendi, a famous *alim* and *medrese* professor in Afyon (Karahisar-ı Sahib), Hoca Şükrü was born and raised in the same city. He received a formal *medrese* education and informal training in agricultural science. He taught at the Afyon *medrese* before he joined the Anatolian resistance when the Greeks occupied İzmir in May 1919. He not only acted as a propagandist for the nationalist cause but also fought against the Greeks. The Turkish regimen under his command stopped the Greeks in Dumlupınar for nine months, after which he became a war hero and was awarded an honorary medal by Mustafa Kemal. In 1920 he was elected as deputy from Afyon in the parliament's first term. He was one of the most active members of the parliament: He had 103 motions to censure during this term, which lasted three years and four months. He also acted as the secretary of the *sharia* commission at the GNA (Sarıkoyuncu 1995: 11–12). Though he supported the abolition of the Ottoman monarchy in 1922, Hoca Şükrü strongly opposed ending the Caliphate. He acted as a leading representative of modernist Islamists during the debates over the Caliphate's abolition, particularly in what is called the "Battle of Pamphlets" (see Chapter 6). With the 1923 elections, the opposition in the parliament was eliminated by Mustafa Kemal, who did not allow anyone who was not a member of his People's Party to be elected. Hoca Şükrü was among those who could not be elected for the parliament's second term (1923–1927). He thus lost much of his political influence and worked as a preacher and writer for the rest of his life.

33 For a fresh study on Rashid Rida's general understanding and use of Qur'anic verses, see Mertoğlu forthcoming.

34 İsmail Hakkı [İzmirli] (1868–1946) was a leading member of the Turkish traditionalist *ulema* in Istanbul. He was born in İzmir and received his higher education in both the *medrese* and the modern *Rüşdiye* (high school) in İzmir. He graduated from the Fatih *medrese* and then the Istanbul *Dârülfünun* (University) in 1892, to which he would later return to teach Islamic sciences, including law, theology, Arabic, history of religions, and philosophy. He also taught at the Süleymaniye *medrese* in Istanbul until 1923, when he began to work at the School of Letters and the School of Theology at the *Dârülfünun*. Formerly, he was a member of the CUP and traveled in Anatolia to propagate the new constitutional regime in religious terms following the 1908 Revolution. His important article (published in *Sırat-ı Müstakim*, a leading Islamist journal) on the Caliphate, however, was a restatement by a respected scholar of the traditionalist position in response to a modernist critique (published in *Beyanu'l-Hak*, another Islamist journal) by Elmalılı Hamdi of the statuses of the caliph and the *şeyhülislam* (see Chapter 4 for a detailed discussion). İsmail Hakkı also worked for the Ottoman Ministry of Education as an inspector, and acted as a member of the *Dârü'l-Hikmeti'l İslamiye* (Council of Islamic Wisdom), a prestigious high council of Islamic scholars attached to the *şeyhülislam*'s office. During the Republican period, he was tried for his relation to the CUP and was nearly executed by the Kemalist regime, but was pardoned and promoted to dean of the Theology School at *Dârülfünun* in 1931. During this period he co-authored a report for the government that justified the policy of changing the language of worship from Arabic to Turkish (Çetinkaya 2000).

35 Caliphate-related themes include: the necessity of a Caliph and rule by God's commands (e.g., Chapter 2, verse 246 by Safayihi 1915: 66; 33/62 by Yafi 1916: 165; 5/44, 45, 47 by SR: 1916a: 435), the necessity of a *single* Caliph (21/22 and 2/246–47 by Safayihi 1915: 79, 83), the unity of Muslims (2/136–37 by al-Tunusi 1916a: 154; 42/3 by Yafi 1916: 166; 8/46 and 3/103 by al-Ubeydi 1916: 179–80; 6/153 by Jawish 1916: 246), the uses of the word "Caliph" in the Qur'an (38/26 and 2/30, 33 by al-Ubeydi 1916: 187; 38/26 by al-Tunusi 1913: 416), monarchy as an un-Islamic

institution (2/124 by Seyyid Bey 1923: 10 and by Hoca Halil *et al.* 1923: 13), and common features of Muslims (49/10 by al-Tunusi 1916a: 154).

Other themes include: virtues of the Prophet Muhammad (53/3–4; 68/4 by Mustafa Zihni 1911: 187–188; and 21/107; 68/4; 3/159 by Ali Fahmi 1911: 82; 33/6 by Jawish 1916: 248), the human side of the Prophet (18/110; 41/6 by Ömer Lütfi 1912: 214), the significance of the two holy cities (Mecca and Medina) and of Jerusalem (Ansari 1919: 379, 380), Islam as a perfect religion (3/19; 5/3 by Ali Fahmi 1911: 82; 5/3 by Seyyid Bey 1923: 1; 6/59 by Hoca Halil *et al.* 1923: 4), spiritualism in Christianity (57/27 by Elmalılı Hamdi 1909: 433), the illegitimacy of forced conversion into Islam (60/89; 2/256; 28/56; 10/99 by Ali Fahmi 1911: 86–87), the many convenient aspects of Islam (2/256, 60/8 by SR: 1916a: 434; 2/185, 22/78 by Seyyid Bey 1917: 482; 2/185 by Hoca Halil *et al.* 1923: 10), tolerance and peace (42/40, 41/34, 6/160 by Ali Fahmi 1911: 87), patience (26/227 by Safayihi 1915: 137), charitable giving (9/60 by Seyyid Bey 1923: 37), *jihad* (9/24 by Safayihi 1915: 140; 2/190–191 by al-lTunusi 1916a: 157), the illegitimacy of waging war except for self-defense (2/194 by Ali Fahmi 1911: 87), resisting colonialism (26/227 and 2/193 by Safayihi 1915: 137, 142; 37/173 by Jawish 1916: 263), measures to be taken against the British (4/71 and 2/194 by al-Ubeydi 1916: 227; 4/144 by Hoca Halil *et al.* 1923: 20), the status of non-Muslims in the Ottoman Empire (8/61 by Yafi 1916: 169), relations with Jews and Christians (2/135–136 by Ali Fahmi 1911: 92), the insignificance of ethnic ties (49/13 by Safayihi 1915: 65), Islam prohibiting dynastic and absolute power (33/40, 4/58, 42/15 by Mahmud Nedim 1919: 98–99), the principle of no double-punishment for one crime (6/164 by Sharif Hussein 1916: 421), the legitimate forms of (economic) transaction (4/29 by Seyyid Bey 1917: 479), marriage and sexual intercourse between spouses (4/3, 2/222 by Seyyid Bey 1917: 471; 4/3, 4/129 by Ali Fahmi 1911: 83), inheritance law (4/11 by Sharif Hussein 1916: 420), sources of Islamic *sharia* (59/7, 3/31, 4/115, and 4/83 by al-Ubeydi 1916: 200–201), *ijtihad* (legal reasoning) (9/122 by al-Ubeydi 1916: 192), disagreement among scholars (4/59 by Ömer Lütfi 1912: 222), equality and individual freedom in Islam (42/13 by Ali Fahmi 1911: 87; 18/110 by Hoca Halil *et al.* 1923: 12), human free will and responsibility associated with it (21/23 by Ömer Lütfi 1912: 244), honoring contracts and promises (3/1, 17/34, 23/8, 2/177 by Seyyid Bey 1917: 479–480), "enjoining the good and forbidding the evil" (3/110 by Seyyid Bey 1917: 466), the creation of man and evolution (30/20–21, 38/71–72, 76/3, 2/33 by al-Ubeydi 1916: 184–186) and death (62/8 by al-Ubeydi 1916: 228), etc.

36 Al-Ubeydi (1879–1963) was born and educated in Mosul and lived in Istanbul (1910–1912) and Syria (1914). During World War I, he went to Istanbul and had ties to *Şeyhülislam* Musa Kazım Efendi. He wrote books on the Balkan War (1913), the Dardanelles War (1916), Britain's atrocities in the Muslim world (1916), and the Caliphate (1916). This last book, titled *The Rope of Unity and the Necessity of the Caliphate in the Islamic Religion*, discussed the Caliphate's significance and presented the Ottoman state as the embodiment of it. Addressing the Arab nationalists in Syria and Egypt, he emphasized that the Caliphate and Muslim unity were dependent on the Ottoman Empire. He dedicated his book to Cemal Pasha, one of the CUP leaders known for his harsh treatment of Arab nobility in Syria and hated by Arab nationalists, and presented it to the Turkish *şeyhülislam* in Istanbul. At the end of the war, he was arrested twice by the British, in India and Egypt, and was active in the Iraqi independence movement's resistance against Britain in 1920. He was then appointed *mufti* of Mosul (1922) and remained in that office until his death in 1963. In 1935 he was also elected as deputy in the Iraqi parliament (Kara 2004: 18).

37 In addition to being a Sufi sheikh, Ömer Ziyaeddin is the author of a famous commentary (*Zübdetü'l-Buhari*) on al-Bukhārī's *Sahīh* (1971), the most important *hadith* collection in the Islamic tradition.

38 Bursalı Mehmed Tahir (1861–1925) was not only a high-ranking army officer and a founder of the CUP, but also a Sufi, a biographer, and a bibliographer. He worked in

the Ottoman army as teacher and military judge, and retired from the army as colonel in 1914. As a CUP member, he was a deputy from Bursa in the first Parliament (1908–1911). He was also a prolific writer: He wrote several books containing detailed information on biographies and works of Ottoman scientists, poets, jurists, and Sufi sheikhs (Akün 1992).

39 Some actors preferred to allude to this *hadith* instead of directly citing it (e.g., Hoca Şükrü 1923: 11; Seyyid Bey 1923: 5; Mustafa Kemal 1923: 66). See below for a discussion of making allusions to prophetic traditions as a discursive technique in itself.

40 Dr. Mukhtar Ahmed Ansari (1880–1936), who was also a physician, politician and educationalist, succeeded Ajmal Khan as the leader of the Caliphate movement. Like Khan, he was a founder of the Jamia Millia Islamia (JMI) and served as its chancellor following Khan's death (1928–1936). Unlike Khan, he received a complete English education in India and Britain, and practiced medicine in London. He returned to Delhi to join the *Khilafat* Movement, the Indian Congress and the Muslim League, serving as the latter's president between 1918 and 1920. He also participated in the *Khilafat* delegation to London (1920), led by the Muslim League's president, Aga Khan III, to lobby for the protection of the Ottoman right to self-determination, which was highlighted by the Wilsonian Principles and the 1919 Paris Peace Conference. In 1922 he brought the Congress, the League, and the *Khilafat* together to protest Mustafa Kemal, who had exiled the Ottoman caliph-sultan, and the British, who had recognized Turkey's independence. Later, due to conflicts with the separatist Muslim League led by Muhammad Ali Jinnah, he sided with Gandhi and acted as a member of the Congress Party's central committee for the rest of his life (see JMI 2011b).

41 Abdur-rahman al-Kawakibi (1855–1902) was perhaps the first influential nationalist thinker, along with Najib Azoury (a Christian intellectual), and a leading ideologue of the Arab Caliphate movement. He was a staunch critic of the Ottoman Empire also because he saw it as a despotic regime that prevented the development of science and rationality in the Arab world. He expressed his idea of seceding from the Ottoman Empire and establishing an independent Arab caliphate in the two Arabic-language newspapers of the time: *al-Furat* and *al-Shahbaa'*. He was arrested several times and exiled to Egypt, where he met with other Arab modernists, including Rashid Rida (who, together with his mentor, Muhammad Abduh, was the most important name in Egyptian intellectual modernism, see Chapter 5) and continued to criticize the Ottomans and advocate a unified Arab-Islamic state led by an Arab caliph, a theory he elucidated in his two books: *Tabaye' al-Istibdad* (*Characteristics of Despotism*) and *Umm al-Qura* (*Mother of Towns*, 1991) (see Kedourie 1972; Saint-Prot 1995; see also Tauber 1993).

42 Interestingly, while pro-Ottoman actors tried to dismiss the "Quraysh argument," writer Kadir Mısıroğlu, a representative of the "Islamist" camp in present-day literature on the Caliphate, claims that the Ottomans were actually descendants of the Prophet Muhammad (Mısıroğlu 1993: 138). This he cites as yet another "evidence" that what Turkish secularists did by abolishing the Caliphate was disrespectful to the principles of Islam, which makes sense only in the context of the discursive struggle among contemporary writers.

43 Said Halim Pasha (1864–1921) was not only a leading intellectual of the time, but also an influential politician: A member of the CUP, he was first the Minister of Foreign Affairs (1913–1915), then the Grand Vizier (Prime Minister) (1913–1917) of the Ottoman Empire during World War I. He was also a member of the royal family: a grandson of Mehmed Ali of Egypt and son of Vizier Halim Pasha. He received his higher education in political science in Switzerland, then returned to Istanbul and was appointed by Abdülhamid II first as a member of the Ottoman Council of State (*Şûrâ-yı Devlet*), then as the commander-in-chief (*beylerbeyi*) of Rumelia (1900). Later, he was exiled by Abdülhamid to Egypt and Europe, where he met with the Young Turks. After the 1908 Revolution, he became a member of the Ottoman senate (*Meclis-i*

Ayan) and the secretary (and later chairman) of the CUP. In 1913 he first became the Minister of Foreign Affairs and then – when Mahmud Şevket Pasha was killed – the Grand Vizier; his surfacing disagreements with the CUP trio (Enver Pasha, Cemal Pasha and Talat Pasha), who were the real patrons of the government, led him to resign from the former office in 1915, and from the latter in 1917, being replaced by Talat Pasha. At the end of the war he was exiled by the British to Malta for two years (1919–1921) and killed by a member of the *Dashnaksutiun* (Armenian socialist party) in Rome in 1921. In his memoirs he wrote in Malta, titled *L'Empire Ottoman et la Guerre Mondiale* (1920), he elaborated on the Caliphate, arguing that Islamic politics required the caliphal rule and that it was the strongest bond that could bring diverse Muslim countries together. He also wrote long letters to British Prime Minister Lloyd George, French Prime Minister Georges Clemenceau and American President Woodrow Wilson in this manner. Similarly, in his earlier writings (2003) he had suggested, from a traditionalist viewpoint, a Caliphate-centered solution to the current crisis of the Muslim *ummah*.

44 Some of these include *hadith*s on the importance of the *Ansar* (early Muslims of Medina) (Mustafa Zihni 1911: 133; Safayihi 1915: 56), the importance of the Prophet's family (Safayihi 1915: 63), the significance of the two holy cities (Ansari 1919: 379), the significance of Northern Africa (Ansari 1919: 378), the conquest of Istanbul (Kidwai 1919: 351), features of a good believer (Safayihi 1915: 74–75; Seyyid Bey 1923: 40, 41), love and brotherhood (Ali Fahmi 1911: 86), solidarity among Muslims (Safayihi 1915: 133, 144), the prohibition of inflicting damage on one another (Seyyid Bey 1923: 32–33), convenient aspects of Islam (Seyyid Bey 1923: 40), *rukhsah* (relief or dispensation) and *'azimah* (obligation) in *fiqh* (Seyyid Bey 1917: 473, 480;), *ijtihad* (al-Ubeydi 1916: 192; Rashid Rida 1923a: 94), *jihad* (al-Tunusi 1916a: 157), respecting the boundaries determined by God (Seyyid Bey 1923: 41), etc.

45 Apart from the fact that such a speech required an extensive knowledge of Islamic history and law, which Mustafa Kemal did not have, Rashid Rida, who translated this speech and published it in his *Al-Manar* ("Khutbatu al-Mustafa Kamal Basha," vol. XXIII, no. 10, December 18, 1922), stated that Kemal's speech had been written by Seyyid Bey (see Kara 2005: 30).

46 A little-known secularist intellectual, Fuad Şükrü [Dilbilen] was a relatively significant politician in the early years of the Second Constitutional Period. After the first elections (December 1908) in this period, he founded the Ottoman Democratic Party (together with İbrahim Temo and Abdullah Cevdet) in February 1909 and then the Ottoman Unity Society (*Osmanlı İttihadı Cemiyeti*). He would later write ultra-nationalist poems (collected and published under the title *Turan ve Türkler* (Istanbul, 1931) (Tunaya 1952: 171).

47 I have already discussed above how in a different context Mustafa Kemal interpreted the same series of events differently, because his purpose was to justify the separation of monarchy from the Caliphate.

48 This typical modernist "reactionary" attitude toward modern notions popularized by the French Revolution was expressed through another discursive technique, "selective appropriation of Western concepts," which will be analyzed in Chapter 5.

49 The *millet* system, which had a long history in the Middle East, consisted of confessional communities based on religious affiliation (as opposed to ethnic identity). As a *legal* system, however, it is ambigious and still debated in the literature. In the Ottoman context, according to the mainstream narrative, it referred to the separate legal courts pertaining to personal law under which minorities were allowed to rule themselves with little interference from the central government. The *millet*s enjoyed a high degree of autonomy, as they independently set their own laws, had their own educational and religious institutions, and collected their own taxes. It was a system the Ottoman elite successfully manipulated to prevent competition between different ethnic and religious groups and confine it within groups instead (see Davison 1954).

Though it is usually the non-Muslim communities that are regarded as *millet*s in the literature, Karpat (2001:126) argues that Muslims, too, should be considered a *millet*. The Muslim *millet*, including both Sunni and Shia groups, had some privileges while the rest (Jews, Orthodox Christians – i.e., Greeks and Armenians – Catholics, Assyrians, etc.) were basically autonomous in terms of legal and social status. On the other hand, Kenanoğlu (2004) contests this mainstream narrative, arguing that the system did not imply legal pluralism but the domination of one single (Islamic) law that also reserved room for non-Muslims' rights.

4 Secularization in the Caliphal center (1908–1916)

1 The Japanese victory in 1905 was crucial for the Ottoman revolutionaries. The Young Turks were convinced that a constitutional regime, even an Oriental one, could prevail over a monarchical European state (Russia), which made the idea of "freedom" and of the parliamentary regime all the more desirable for them, and they came to regard Japan as a main role model for the post-revolutionary Ottoman Empire. In fact, "the CUP had so thoroughly appropriated Japan as the symbol of its state vision after 1909" that the conservative critics of the CUP also targeted Japan in their bitter criticisms of the Unionist policies (Worringer 2004: 217). Throughout much of the 20th century, too, Japanese modernization was taken in the Turkish popular imagination as a model to be emulated, especially in terms of rapid economic development and "indigenous modernization" by a non-Western society. For a collection of articles comparing various aspects of Japanese and Turkish modernizations, see Ward and Rustow (1968); see also Hayashi (1983).

2 During Turkey's last 100 years, including both "unionist" and "democratic" (post-1950) periods, bureaucratic elites have always been more powerful than either politicians or civil society. In particular, following CUP tradition, the military bureaucracy, which saw itself as the "guardian of the state" against both external *and* internal enemies, has always been the dominant actor in Turkish politics setting the agenda for, and the limits of, the rather narrow political sphere. While mostly acting unofficially, it has sometimes directly intervened into politics, as exemplified by a series of *coups d'état* that occurred in 1960, 1971, 1980, and 1997, implying a lack of confidence in civil society. The army has often enjoyed the judiciary's support for justifying their privileged status and interventions throughout the Republican period. The 1908–1909 interventions were crucial turning points in terms of the relationship between civil politics and (military) bureaucracy, which started the modern "tradition" of interventionism. This was further solidified by the fact that many army officers, who were members of the – still secret – CUP, were allowed not only to hold key positions in the government, but also to serve as deputies in the Parliament during the Second Constitutional Period.

3 Throughout the Republican period, too, bureaucratic elites used the March 31 "reaction" to suppress the civil liberties of religious groups in Turkey. Similarly, the conventional scholarship, heavily influenced by the Kemalist ideology, has presented this event as a "reactionary uprising" against the enlightened government to restore the *sharia* (see, e.g., Akşin 1994).

4 However, the CUP needed this religious authority during World War I in order to mobilize other Muslim countries, which was reflected by Caliph Mehmed Reşad's famous – but relatively unsuccessful – call for *jihad* against the Allies (see Chapter 5). This call was not successful in rallying the Muslim world partly because CUP policies had by then greatly weakened the Caliphate by stripping it of much of its political power, a process that began with the amendments to the Constitution in 1909 (see also Chapter 2).

5 "Saving the state" was, according to many scholars (e.g., Karpat 2001; Kara 2003a), the main motive behind virtually every reform undertaken by the Ottoman elites since

the late 18th century because they believed that the state could be saved by modernizing it through a series of technical improvements, especially in military technology and political institutions. The Young Turks' political culture, too, entailed a top-down and elitist, positivistic, and pragmatic attitude toward politics and religion (see Zürcher 2005; Kabakçı 2006).

6 Note that the "Lawmaker" here may refer to both God and the Constitution. It was a widespread tendency at the time to identify the Qur'an with the (existing) constitution, the *Kanun-i Esasi*. Elmalılı himself called it the "Kanun-i Esasi of Islam."

7 Seyyid Bey used the term "nation" in a more secular (ethnic) sense than Rashid Rida's "community," which referred to the inhabitants of the "just land" where the "true imam is elected in order to maintain justice" (1923a: 50) whereas the "nation" in Seyyid Bey vaguely referred to the Ottoman nation with an ethnic tone. See below for further discussion on the national conception of the Caliphate.

8 Though Mustafa Zihni's book on the Caliphate and Islamic government was mostly theoretical, he put a footnote at the end of his discussion on the cabinet system in which he touched upon Sultan Abdulhamid II's "reign of despotism," saying that it was actually the high-ranking bureaucrats that were to be blamed for oppression, rather than the sultan himself, who was deceived by the corrupt bureaucrats around him (p. 203). This view reflects the general attitude among traditionalists toward the Hamidian regime.

9 The *Mecelle* is the text of codified laws in the Ottoman Empire. As such, it represents the first-ever codification of law in Islamic history. It was prepared by a committee of scholars, led by Ahmed Cevdet Pasha, an intellectual and statesman of the Hamidian era, in order to systematically establish the Islamic law in a modern form, which was a part of the attempt, started by the Young Ottomans and carried on by the CUP, to reform the Ottoman legal system. On the preparation of, and amendments to, the *Mecelle*, see Kaşıkçı (1997).

10 On Akçura's nationalism and its influence, see Georgeon (1980); on Gökalp, see Chapter 2 above.

11 This propaganda was hardly effective on state policies, however. Although some historians (e.g., Deringil 1998: 11) argue that the Ottoman identity had been assuming an increasingly "Turkish character" since the mid-19th century, this view is not substantiated with sound evidence.

12 This Islamic discourse can be clearly seen in the 1921 Constitution, which I have demonstrated in Chapter 2, and in the speeches by leading (secular) politicians between 1920 and 1923, which I discuss in Chapter 6.

13 The Çaldıran war between the Ottomans and Safavids is still regretfully presented by Turkish official historiography in school textbooks as an unnecessary war between two Turkish states, causing loss of life and waste of energy that could have been spent against common enemies.

14 The son of a rich landowner, Ömer Lütfi Fikri (1872–1934) was born in Istanbul and went to the School of Political Science (*Mekteb-i Mülkiye*) and then to law school in Paris (1894). Upon his return to Istanbul, he was first jailed over his ties to the Young Turks in Paris and then exiled to Konya, where he worked as a city administrator and teacher until 1901, when he escaped to Paris. Later he worked as a lawyer in Egypt. With the 1908 Revolution he returned to Istanbul and was elected as a parliament member and participated in the liberal opposition against the CUP. He also published the *Tanzimat* newspaper (1911–1913), which was closed down 16 times by the Unionists. After World War I, Lütfi Fikri worked as a lawyer and served as the president of the Istanbul bar association (1920–1925). He also tried – though unsuccessfully – to bring together the Istanbul government and the nationalist resistance in Anatolia in 1922. Between 1922 and 1923 he harshly criticized Mustafa Kemal for what he perceived as dictatorial tendencies and advocated the continuation of the constitutional monarchy, opposing the idea of a republic with a weak parliament (see Lütfi Fikri

1922, 1923a; see also Chapter 6). For this reason, he was arrested and sentenced to hard labor by the Istanbul Independence Tribunal, but was pardoned by the parliament (Demirel 1991: 171ff.; see also Çulcu 1992).

15 The ethnic distribution of the deputies in the first-term Parliament (1908–1912) in the Second Constitutional Period was as follows: Turks: 156, Arabs: 56, Albanians: 25, Greeks: 21, Armenians: 11, Jews: 4, Bulgarians: 4, Vlachs: 1. This ethno-religious plurality continued until the end of World War I (1918). During this period, there were almost always a few non-Muslim (usually Greek and Armenian) ministers in the cabinet (see Güneş 1990).

16 Cf. al-Māwardī's definition of the Caliphate:

> God, may His power be exalted, ortained for the community (*ummah*) a leader through whom He provided for the vicegerency of the prophet and … protected the religion (*millah*), and He entrusted to him authority (*siyasah*) so that the management of affairs should proceed [on the basis of] legitimate religion … and the Caliphate [*Imamate*] became the principle upon which the bases of the community were founded, by which the well-being of the community was regulated and affairs of general interest were made stable, and from which particular public functions (*al-wilayāt al-khassah*) emanated.
>
> (al-Māwardī 1994: 3; cf. al-Taftazānī, 1989, V: 232)

17 Syed Mahmud (1889–1961) was an intellectual, politician, and jurist who strongly advocated Muslim unification under the Ottoman leadership after the Paris Peace Conference following World War I. He had received an education in law at the Aligarh College, Cambridge University, and Munster University; he then returned to Patna, India, to work as a lawyer. In 1917 he joined the *Khilafat* Movement and acted as the secretary of its central committee between 1921 and 1926. In the split between the Indian National Congress and the Muslim League, he sided with Gandhi's Congress, becoming a member of its working committee (1940–1945), and then minister of agriculture and transportation in the Indian government (1946–1952). He also served in the parliament in 1952–1957 and 1961. He wrote several books and many articles on the past and present situation of Muslims in India and on Hindu-Muslim unity (Kara 2005: 22). His influential book, titled *The Khilafat and England* (1921), was both an exposition of the traditionalist view of the Caliphate as a temporal and spiritual institution, and a critique of British policy toward India, Muslims, and the Ottoman Caliphate. The book was published twice in English and once in Urdu within two years (1921–1922).

18 I borrow the term "double-bind" as a metaphor from anthropologist Gregory Bateson (1972) and use it in its basic, communicative sense but also on a more abstract level. Simply put, double-bind refers to a contradictory situation in which the victim is trapped by two conflicting demands, causing confusion on his part. Bateson and others use it to understand schizophrenic cases, but also argue that confused communication often occurs in "normal" situations as well. Here I do not mean, of course, that it implies a pathological situation in the case of Islamist intellectuals.

19 Jale Parla (1993) traces the roots of such an epistemological shift in the Ottoman novel during the Tanzimat period (1839–1876) demonstrating how European, secular epistemologies increasingly influenced Ottoman novelists who imported this literary form from the West.

20 In Chapter 2, where I discussed the early modernizing reforms, I gave the example of Sultan Selim III (1789–1807), who justified his military reforms (inviting European experts and founding a new, Western-style army) with reference to a prophetic *hadith*: "You can use your enemy's weapon."

21 For example, Mustafa Kemal's famous speech in the parliament on November 1, 1922 on the abolition of the Ottoman monarchy, which will be analyzed in Chapter 6, was written in its entirety by Seyyid Bey.

22 As discussed in Chapter 2, Ziya Gökalp (1915 b) employed the same technique with another pair of legal concepts (*kaza* and *diyanet*) in his effort to open up a secular space within the Islamic *sharia*.

5 Colonization in the Caliphal periphery (1914–1920)

1 Like Namık Kemal, other "Young Ottomans" (e.g., Ziya Pasha, Mustafa Nuri) had also been espousing the idea of *İttihad-ı İslam*, particularly in their periodical *İbret*, since the early 1860s (Mardin 1962: 60).

2 The Ottoman population had experienced a sharp decline during the 1870s: it was estimated to be 40 million in 1867 and had dropped to 17,388,604 by 1881 (Behar 1996: 29, 39), mostly due to territorial losses in the European provinces.

3 In a top-secret telegraph to Ottoman Grand Vizier Said Halim Pasha on August 5, 1914, Wilhelm II assured the Ottomans of a definite victory, and added: "The Caliphate's power is big enough to incite all the Muslims of the world to rise up [against the Allies]" (quoted in Satan 2008: 41).

4 Technically, the *jihad fatwa* actually consisted of five separate *fatwa*s; the first one contained a general ruling that ordered all Muslims, "young and old," to join the great *jihad*; the others elaborated on this ruling. The *fatwa*'s text was published in the official gazette *Takvim-i Vekayi*, November 23, 1330 [1914] and in the *Meşihat*'s official journal, *Ceride-i İlmiyye* ("Cihad-ı Ekber" vol. 1, no 7, pp. 437–439).

5 Muhyiddin Baha (1884–1954) came from a long line of Sufis: His grandfather, father and brother were all local Sufi (*Naqshi*) sheikhs in the Ahmed Baba lodge in Bursa. He himself graduated from the Law School and worked as an attorney, judge, and teacher during the Second Constitutional Period. After World War I, he worked as a journalist and member of parliament from Bursa in the first Grand National Assembly (1920–1923); later he acted as judge in the "Independence Tribunals" in Eskişehir and Konya (Kara 2003b: 37). His work on the Caliphate, titled *The Caliph's Army in Egypt and the Caucasus* (1915), is a five-act theatre play that dramatizes the heroism of Turkish, Arab, and Indian soldiers who come together under the caliphal flag against the British and Russian armies in Egypt and the Caucasus during World War I. According to the author, the play was staged in Bursa before being published by the request of the audience (Muhyiddin Baha 1915: 426).

6 The same year, Russian and British embassies in Istanbul even discussed the possibility of transforming the Caliphate into a Vatican-like city-state, based in either Istanbul or Damascus, with no temporal authority over Muslims (FO/141/587/2, F72; quoted Oliver-Dee 2009: 54).

7 To appeal to American, Russian, and German Jewry, the British also promised the establishment of a Jewish settlement in Palestine with the famous Balfour Declaration in 1917. Britain and France later formalized their agreement in San Remo on April 25, 1920 whereby France had the mandate over Syria and Lebanon, and Britain over Iraq and Palestine (Nevakivi 1969: 260).

8 The Sanusi, who fought against the Italians before and during World War I, also took control of Libya after independence, with Muhammad al-Sanusi's grandson Idris I becoming king in 1951; he was overthrown by a military coup led by Muammar al-Qaddafi in 1969.

9 For an examination of Ottoman-Moroccan relations and the Caliphate during the 16th and 17th centuries, see El-Moudden (1995b).

10 Many local rulers also carried the title of "caliph" in the *Maghrib*; but in the North African context it means viceroy (or deputy), and only refers to the sultan's regional governors. In pre-colonial Morocco it was particularly used for the formal representatives of the sultan in Marrakech, Fès and Meknès, the old "imperial" capitals.

11 For an extensive examination of the Ottoman-Egyptian relations during the 19th and early 20th centuries, see Kedourie 1970.

12 See also British Foreign Office Advisor Wilfred Blunt's view in his *The Future of Islam* (1882: 51–88).
13 One should note that among Turkish historians it is highly disputed if these "memoirs" were actually written by Sultan Abdülhamid himself. While most historians involved in the debate reject the possibility of him writing these memoirs, Karpat is one of the few who believe they are authentic and uses them. See Birinci (2005) for details of the debate.
14 Hussein's "Proclamation" was later reprinted in Egypt in the *al-Manar* journal (vol. xix), published by Rashid Rida, a leading member of the Arab caliphate movement (see below).
15 The second part of the last sentence refers to a Qur'anic verse (2/184) that allows Muslims to not perform the – otherwise mandatory – Ramadan fasting under certain circumstances, i.e., when they are sick or on a journey. Sharif Hussein thus criticizes here the (mis)use of the Qur'an for secular purposes by the *İctihad* article, which originally referred to this verse.
16 Following the collapse of the Ottoman Empire, Britain created many small kingdoms in the Arabian Peninsula, which have made up the contemporary configuration of Arab nation-states in the region. The "constructed" nature of these states with "unnatural" borders separating them is also evident in the fact that it was Sharif Hussein's sons, chosen by the British, who ruled some of them: following the Sharif's death in 1924, his biggest son Ali became the "King of the *Hijaz*" (1924–1925), Abdullah the "King of Jordan" (1921–1951) [the current King Abdullah's grandfather], and Sharif's youngest son Faysal I the "King of Iraq" (1920–1933).
17 The CUP's policies had an alienating impact not only on Arab elites but also in the Balkan provinces of the empire, especially among the Albanians and Greeks (Hacısalihoğlu 2008: 246, 373).
18 "Islamic modernism," which first emerged in the late 19th century and was led by Rashid Rida and his two mentors, Jamaluddin al-Afghani and Muhammad Abduh, is a general name given to the modernist Islamist movements and their unifying political ideology, which was influential across the Muslim world, particularly in Turkey, Egypt, Syria, Pakistan, and Iran, during the 20th century (see Donohue and Esposito 1982; Moaddel 2002, 2005; Mertoğlu forthcoming). The "modernist" group in this study covers only those advocates of Islamic modernism who produced a political discourse on the Caliphate during the period between 1908 and 1924, rather than all of the leading representatives of these movements.
19 Like Rida's, Abduh's view of the Caliphate was influenced by changing political conditions and thus lacked consistency. In his *Al-Islam wa-l-Nasraniyya*, he likened the Caliphate to parliamentary democracy and argued that the Caliph was a secular ruler; in *Al-A'mal al-Kamila*, he called for a restoration of the Caliphate "on a more spiritual basis." He also both suggested the rule by a "benevolent dictator," and that a republic was the best possible regime for Muslims (see Kerr 1966: 146–152; see also Soage 2008: 19).
20 Although some scholars (Sayyid 2003: 61; Zubaida 2004: 411) claim that Rida's view of the Caliphate is similar to the Catholic Papacy, this fits neither to his own writings, nor many other scholars' interpretations (e.g., Mertoğlu 2005; Soage 2008; Kavak 2011). Rida only stated in passing that Muslims would rally around the Caliphate, just like the Catholics did around the Pope (*Al-Manar*, XXIV: 198).
21 Rida also "quoted" an unnamed (or imaginary) British scholar who had affirmed that if one single language were to be chosen for the entire humanity, that language would have to be Arabic (Soage 2008: 15).
22 As we shall see below, Abdur-raziq's secularist view of the Caliphate was very similar to that of Turkish politician Mustafa Kemal (Atatürk), who had abolished the Caliphate a year before Abdur-raziq published his book. For instance, Kemal had argued that the Prophet had intended no regime change in Arabia as he was not

actually interested in politics, but eventually he had become "obliged" to take up political and military power as his "secondary" mission due to political circumstances of the time (Mustafa Kemal 1923: 102–103).

23 A graduate of al-Azhar, a centuries-old *madrasa* and the center of traditional Islam in Egypt, Abdur-raziq was strongly condemned by the al-Azhar *ulema*, who revoked his diploma and requested that the book (*Islam wa Usul al-Hukm*, 1925) be banned. He later renounced his book and publicly apologized; nevertheless, his book was published and disseminated widely, opening up a channel for the secularist argument for the separation of religion and politics, which other Egyptian nationalists such as Lütfi al-Sayyid (1965) and Taha Hussein (1947) also voiced following Abdur-raziq. Rida himself criticized these intellectuals for being anti-Islamic (see 1925a: 100–104, 1925b: 230–232, 1928: 619–627).

24 There were other preconditions that were classified as sub-elements of the four main features, rather than separate conditions. They included being Muslim, adult, male, and free (as part of "justice") as well as courage and military power (as part of "competence"). Furthermore, two additional preconditions that were not required by the mainstream Sunni scholarship were ethnicity (membership in the Quraysh tribes) or direct relation to (being a descendant of) the Prophet (required only by the Shia) and infallibility (also required by the Shia). These were naturally rejected by pro-Ottoman intellectuals either implicitly – by ignoring them (e.g., al-Tunusi 1913; al-Ubeydi 1916) – or by explicitly discussing and refuting the evidence for them in detail with reference to Sunni-*Hanefite* scholarship, including Ibn Khaldūn (e.g., Ömer Lütfi 1912: 241–242; Safayihi 1915: 55–67; Jawish 1916: 246–249) (see Chapter 4 for details.)

25 As discussed in Chapter 4, Ömer Ziyaeddin and Mehmed Tahir specifically deployed another discursive technique that was related to the translation of a key concept in prophetic traditions. In their *hadith* compilations, Ziyaeddin and Tahir frequently translated the word "caliph" (or *imam*) mentioned in these traditions as "sultan" in order to more easily relate the Ottoman Empire to sacred texts and ensure loyalty to it by implying that the Ottoman dynasty, as the true embodiment of the Islamic Caliphate, had a religious significance for all Muslims that was rooted deeply in the sayings of the Prophet of Islam. See Ömer Ziyaeddin (1908: *hadith* nos. 2, 3, 5, 7, 8, 9, 10, 14, 15), Mehmed Tahir (1909: *hadith* nos. 5, 9, 10, 11, 16, 17).

26 "Islam et la Guerre" *Le Matin de Paris*, November 10, 1915.

27 Interestingly, a British Foreign Office document, dated January 1919, would come close to the traditionalist view of the Caliphate in its own version of the Caliph's duties, which included "defense of the faith, legal dispute settling, preservation of public safety, punishment of wrongdoing, defense of frontiers, warring against those who refuse to accept Islam or to submit to Muslim rule, payment of salaries, appointment of officials and attention to the detail of government" (FO 141/587/2, F43; quoted in Oliver-Dee 2009: 106).

28 Hakim Ajmal Khan (1863–1927), a medical doctor, politician, and educationalist, was a leading Muslim actor in India. Receiving both Islamic and medical education, he was a trustee of the Aligarh College and founded the *Jamia Millia Islamia* (Islamic National University) in Aligarh in 1920 (see JMI 2011a). His family established the *Tibbia* College in Delhi to support research on alternative medicine. He also contributed to the Urdu weekly newspaper, *Akmal-ul-Akhbar*, which had been founded by his family (1865). He was politically very active as well: He was a founding member of the Muslim League, the Indian Congress (being the only person to be president of both of them), and the Caliphate movement. A close friend of Gandhi, he also played a leading role in the Indian independence movement, in addition to supporting the Ottoman Caliphate during World War I (Haq 2008a).

29 Syed Sulaiman Nadvi (1884–1953) was one of the *Khilafat* Movement's strongest intellectual leaders, though not as politically active as others. A descendant of Prophet

Muhammad (hence the title, "Syed"), he was born into a Sufi family and received both *madrasa* and Sufi education. Becoming a disciple of the famous scholar and Sufi leader Shibli Numani (1857–1914), he both taught at Shibli's *madrasa Nadvat-ul Ulema*, and acted as the deputy editor of his influential journal, *al-Nadva* (1906–1911), and as the editor of the *Maarif* journal in Azamgarh. He also wrote in Abul Kalam Azad's *al-Hilal* (see below) and taught at Bombay University and later at the *Ahmadiyya* University in India. Nadvi authored many books on different subjects, including history, geography, biography, and literature. His *opus magnum*, co-authored with his mentor Shibli, was the six-volume *Sirat-un-Nabi* (biography of Prophet Muhammad in Urdu). He also wrote on *The Caliphate and India* (1921) – first published as a series of articles in *Maarif* (1920–1921) – in which he criticized the British colonial government and the pro-British Indian press, which had claimed that there was no real connection between the Ottoman Caliphate and Indian Muslims. He argued instead that the latter recognized the Turkish caliph as their religious leader and offered historical evidence of the connection between India and the caliphs both before and during the Ottoman period. Nadvi's work on the Caliphate indicates his interest in politics. He was a member of the Caliphate committee that traveled to Europe to lobby on behalf of the Ottoman caliph in 1922 (see above). In 1926 he led the Indian delegation to the *Mu'tamar Islami*, an international congress organized in Mecca by the Saudi king, Abdulaziz, to discuss Muslims' problems in the post-Caliphate world. In 1933 he went to Afghanistan as consultant to King Nadir Khan on educational and cultural policies. Later he immigrated to Pakistan after the partition in 1947, and worked there as the chair of the committee to oversee the Islamic aspects of the new constitution before he died in Karachi in 1953 (Özşenel 2006).

30 The text of the memorandum is quoted in Kidwai (1919: 363–366). The League had also published a similar memorandum on the status of Palestine in 1917.

31 Mushir Hosain Kidwai (1878–1937), an intellectual, politician, and jurist, advocated Muslim unity under the Ottoman Caliphate and criticized Britain and Arab nationalists for their anti-Caliphate strategy. He visited Istanbul and met with Ottoman statesmen in 1906 (Kidwai 1919: 326); two years later, he published (in English) a book titled *Pan-Islamism* in which he supported the Hamidian policy of Muslim unification. In his later books, *The Future of the Muslim Empire-Turkey* and *The Sword against Islam or a Defence of Islam's Standard Bearers*, both published in London in 1919, he strongly restated his pan-Islamic views and criticized both Arab nationalists and the CUP for undermining the Caliphate. Addressing the British audience, he also advocated that a Muslim federation be established under the auspices of the League of Nations and led by the Ottoman caliph in accordance with the Wilsonian principle of self-determination. The former book on Turkey was translated into Ottoman Turkish and published in Istanbul the same year (1908).

32 Azad (1920) and Syed Mahmud's (1921) views (mentioned earlier), however, reflect the frustration among Muslim intellectuals that was created by the failure of the Paris Peace Conference to acknowledge the Muslim right of self-determination, which led to the re-emergence of the strong anti-Western and anti-imperialist discourse that had been dominant before and during World War I.

33 Another Muslim leader who opposed India's partition and remained at the Congress with Gandhi was Abul Kalam Azad (1888–1958), who was also a leader of the Caliphate Movement. He worked with Gandhi and others for *Swara* (self-rule) for India, became the youngest president of the Congress in 1923, and the first Minister of Education after India's independence. Coming from a family of traditional *ulema*, he studied both Islamic sciences and Western philosophy and actively participated in politics as a journalist and politician advocating Muslim–Hindu unity. In 1912 he founded an Urdu weekly called *Al-Hilal* in which he harshly criticized British policies in India and abroad. When his newspaper was outlawed by the British, he established a new one, *Al-Balagh*, which became very popular and played an instrumental role in

disseminating the pro-Caliphate propaganda by the *Khilafat* movement in India during World War I. For this reason, he was put in jail (1915–1920) and his newspaper banned by the government (Haq 2008b). Later, Azad worked closely with Gandhi to prepare a program for non-co-operation and *ahimsa* (non-violence); he was also elected president of the All-India *Khilafat* Committee, and founded the JMI with Khan and Ansari. Later, as president of the congress for six years, he was one of the leaders of the Indian independence movement (1947) together with Gandhi and Patel (Islam 2006). In his major work on the Caliphate, *Khilafat and Jaziratul Arab* (Bombay, 1920), which he wrote in jail, he strongly supported the revival of the Ottoman Caliphate after the war, and sharply criticized Sharif Hussein and the British government for undermining Muslim unity.

34 He took this claim further by also arguing that the latter was required for the validity of legal contracts and economic transactions as well (ibid.).

35 This last principle was an allusion to a *hadith* (discussed in Chapter 4), while principles (1), (3) and (7) alluded to different Qur'anic verses.

36 He added that as the leader of the Muslim *ummah*, the Ottoman caliph was also the protector of non-Muslims, granting them many rights and freedoms (p. 97). This "careful" language, which presented Pan-Islamism as a policy that would not constitute a threat to Western powers, was a widespread discourse at the time, as it had been in the Hamidian era (Kara 2003b: 14). Soon, however, this would change as colonization of the Middle East accelerated. For the radicalized, anti-Western discourse, see, e.g., Safayihi (1915), al-Tunusi (1916a, 1916b).

37 When the author's book was originally published as a series of three articles in Rashid Rida's *al-Manar* (1910–1911, vol. 13, no. 9, 11, 12), Rida, an Arab nationalist, added several footnotes objecting to the author's positive view of the Ottoman Caliphate.

38 Although they all agreed that the major responsibility for the disintegration of the Muslim world rested with European colonialists, some, particularly the Indian Islamists who were still hoping the British would support the Ottomans after World War I, also argued that the CUP had made a mistake by entering the war and joining the Central Powers (e.g., Ajmal Khan, quoted in Kidwai 1919: 385).

39 This was also a response to the charge by some Turkish modernists (e.g., Elmalılı 1909: 436) that the caliph was no different from a contemporary (secular) king (see Chapter 4).

40 This was one of several instances of Indian Muslim intellectuals praising the Turks, seeing the Ottoman Empire as the only potential savior of the Muslim world at a time of great crisis accelerated by World War I. In a similar fashion, the epigraph of Syed Mahmud's book on the Caliphate, which was dedicated "to the Turkish nationalists," praised the "rule of the Turks, [which] has been pronounced by wise prophets." The dedication was complemented with a quote from Mustafa Kemal that explained the author's sympathy toward the Turkish nationalist movement: "My friends and myself are going to stand up for the cause of old Islam to the last drop of blood" (*Evening News*, London, April 29, 1910). This also exemplifies the secularists' meta-discursive strategy of deriving justification from Islam (see Chapter 6).

6 Abolition of the Caliphate: secular reform, religious justification (1919–1924)

1 For a detailed description of the Delegation and its members, see Qureshi 1999: 462–475.

2 For the full text of the Treaty, see *The American Journal of International Law* 1920; for the online version, see www.hri.org/docs/sevres.

3 Similar declarations expressing Anatolia's loyalty to the sultan-caliph were also made by the two other local congresses during June–August 1919 in Balıkesir and Alaşehir (see Çarıklı 1967).

4 See Mustafa Kemal (1964: 298) for the full text of the *fatwa*.

5 This army was sent to Anatolia under British pressure, but its commanders secretly promised nationalist commander Ali Fuad Pasha that they would switch sides with all their men and arms in case of any encounter between the two armies (quoted from Ali Fuad Pasha's memoirs in Satan 2008: 119–120, n. 357).

6 For the original texts of the motion and the law, see TBMM *Arşivi C*, Devre 1, Dosya 308, 1922.

7 Hüseyin Avni [Ulaş] was a deputy in the last Ottoman Parliament (*Meclis-i Mebusan*) and the GNA's first term. Though not very close to Mustafa Kemal, he was nevertheless a staunch critic of the Ottoman monarchy. Born in Erzurum in 1887, Hüseyin Avni was educated in the law school at the Istanbul *Darülfünun*. He participated in the Erzurum and Sivas Congresses during the Turkish national struggle in 1919. In January 1920, he was elected deputy at the Ottoman Parliament, which was soon shut down by the sultan under British pressure. Then he went to Ankara to join the newly opened Turkish Grand National Assembly, and acted as the leader of the "Second Group" in the GNA, which was the main opposition to Mustafa Kemal's increasingly authoritarian rule. He was elected vice chairman of the GNA with his group's support (Mustafa Kemal was the chairman). Like other opposition members, however, he was not allowed to be elected in the 1923 elections. Outside the parliament, he remained mostly silent until his death in 1948, except that he was a founder of the short-lived and insignificant National Development Party, founded in 1945 with the return to a multi-party system in Turkey.

8 As noted in Chapter 3, after the abolition of the Caliphate Rida would participate in the organization of the (first) Caliphate congress in Cairo (May 13–23, 1926), and publish its proceedings in his *al-Manar* (see Rashid Rida 1926). However, he would be disappointed by the congress' failure due to lack of any Turkish support, which he saw as essential for the Caliphate's revival (Mertoğlu 2005: 58). I discuss the failed Caliphate congresses, including the one in Cairo, in more detail below (under "After the Caliphate").

9 See the "Declaration" by General Sir Charles Harrington, the commander of British occupation forces in Istanbul, in a letter from Harrington to Refet Pasha (quoted in TBMMZC 1922b: 282). Vahideddin first went to Malta and then to Mecca as a guest of King Hussein.

10 For the text of the *fatwa* signed by Vehbi Efendi, the Minister of *Sharia* and a deputy from Konya, see TBMM *Arşivi C*, Devre 1, Dosya 308, 1922; see also TBMMZC 1922b: 1053.

11 As usual, İsmail Şükrü of Karahisar and Yusuf Ziya of Bitlis were the most outspoken members of the "Second Group" (conservatives) who opposed calling Vahideddin a traitor (see TBMMZC 1922b: 296ff.). The secularists also tried to disseminate propaganda, suggesting that the ex-caliph had betrayed the Turkish people and the Muslim world, outside the GNA, mainly through journal articles and pamphlets written specifically on the "fugitive" Vahideddin (see, e.g., Abdünnafi 1922).

12 A summary of this proclamation was later translated into Arabic to be published in *al-Ahram* (in Egypt) on April 16, 1923, but it did not have a significant impact on Muslim public opinion. The British government invited Vahideddin to live in Switzerland, but he refused to live under British mandate and went to Italy instead. He could not realize his plans to launch a Caliphate campaign due to the lack of an effective Muslim organization there.

13 Eşref Edib (1882–1971), an Islamist intellectual and the editor of *Sebilürreşad*, said that it was he who had actually written the pamphlet, but published it under deputy Hoca Şükrü's name because the latter had parliamentary immunity (see Mısıroğlu 1993: 295).

14 One of the journalists who attended the press conference, Ahmed Emin [Yalman], would later write in his memoirs that at the beginning of the conference, after listening

to the journalists, Mustafa Kemal explicitly said: "You're all wrong. The Caliphate must definitely be abolished altogether," which was a great surprise to them (Ahmed Emin 1970: 29).

15 Only three-and-a-half months before this press conference, in his address to the GNA during the debates on the abolition of the monarchy, Kemal had cited this historical example to stress the importance of the Caliphate vis-à-vis the Sultanate (TBMMZC 1922a: 266; see also above). This is yet more evidence for the instrumental nature of Kemal's discourse (see also below).

16 Note the impact of Ziya Gökalp's view of the rise and fall of Islamic empires (discussed above) on Kemal's discourse.

17 Though some historians (e.g., Haim 1965: 210) claim, following the GNA's official view, that this document was "prepared by a group of *ulema* under the direction of a member of parliament," Sami Erdem (1995: 81) has demonstrated that it was Seyyid Bey who wrote the text. Himself a deputy in the GNA at the time, Seyyid Bey later said (in 1924) that he had written it. This argument is supported by both the incredible similarity between this text and Seyyid Bey's other writings (Seyyid Bey 1917, 1924) *and* by journalist Ahmed Emin's and Arnold Toynbee's observations mentioned above. Ahmed Emin (1970: 31) also said that thanks to this pamphlet by Seyyid Bey and conferences organized at Kemal's request, most skeptics were convinced to accept the abolition of the Caliphate. This important document was soon translated into French and published in *Revue du Monde Musulman*, vol. 59 (1925): 3–81.

18 As discussed in Chapter 3, the word originally included at the end of the *hadith* is *mulk*, which means "power," but modernist Islamists have always translated it (till today) as "monarchy/sultanate" in order to emphasize that a monarchical regime cannot be a true Caliphate.

19 Further evidence for Seyyid Bey's secularization of Islamic discourse was his definition of the caliph's status and main duties: Though Seyyid Bey admitted that "Islam is an advanced religion that involves both religious and political affairs" and that the Prophet Muhammad's mission was both religious and administrative (1923: 4), he insisted that the caliph represented only the political/administrative dimension of the prophetic mission (p. 5). However, he also ambiguously categorized the responsibilities of the caliph as "religious" (such as "working for the advancement of Islam") and "secular/worldly" or "civil" (p. 18).

20 This accusation by Seyyid Bey was closely related to a particular development at the time: on April 15, 1923, Mustafa Kemal had the GNA modify the High Treason Law expanding it to include any opposition to the GNA. Initially the aim was to prosecute those who would support the return of the Ottoman monarchy; the law would also prove useful in silencing all kinds of opposition (see below).

21 Born in İzmir, İsmet Pasha [İnönü] (1884–1973) received his secondary and higher education in military schools. He graduated from the Military Academy in 1906 and fought against the insurgency in Yemen between 1910 and 1913. During World War I he was a division commander under Mustafa Kemal in the Caucasus and Syria, where their friendship, which had started in the military school, matured. He was also one of Kemal's closest friends and commanders during the national struggle (1920–1922). He was the commander of the Western front until the final victory over the Greeks in August 1922. İsmet Pasha also acted as a deputy from Edirne and minister of foreign affairs during the same period. He then became prime minister after the establishment of the Turkish Republic in October 1923, and remained in the post until 1937, during which he was Kemal's most important aide in realizing secular reforms, from the abolition of the Caliphate to that of the Arabic alphabet, religious education, and law. Together they kept the country under tight control through the single-party system that they controlled via Republican People's Party (RPP) and the army. However, toward the end of this period he opposed some of Kemal Atatürk's policies, which cost him his status as the republic's second man. After Atatürk's death in 1938, he

became Turkey's second president. As President, he first continued "Eternal Chief" Atatürk's iron rule, declaring himself Turkey's "National Chief" and the RPP's "Permanent Chairman," but then started, under European and American pressure, the return to a multi-party system. After winning fraudulent elections in 1946, he lost the first free elections since 1911 to Adnan Menderes' Democratic Party in 1950, when his presidency ended and democracy was re-established in Turkey. Ten years later, however, it was suspended again by a military *coup d'état* that resulted in the execution of Menderes and two of his ministers, after which İnönü once again became prime minister (1961–1965). In 1972 he resigned from his posts as parliament member and RPP chairman; he died one year later on December 25, 1973 (Heper 1998).

22 For text of the Treaty of Lausanne, see *League of Nations Treaty Series* 1924.

23 At Lausanne, Turkey claimed the province of Mosul, which was under British mandate, as part of the "National Pact." After negotiations, the future of Mosul was left to be determined through the League of Nations; later, despite Ankara's hopes, Britain left it to Iraq in 1926.

24 Some contemporary scholars, too, think that the British should have been "very pleased with [Mustafa Kemal] for doing the work of dismantling the Caliphate that they were not able to do" (Oliver-Dee 2009: 136).

25 The "party" here should be understood as its head, Mustafa Kemal, who, after the elections, had full control over it – and the Parliament. By having the latter elect himself as the President of the newborn Republic, Kemal also moved the "locus of stateness" (the ability to fully control state power) from the GNA to the Presidency (Heper 1985: 58). In fact, during the entire single-party period in Turkey (the first 23 years of the Republic), the president had the sole authority to pick every party member for parliament. Political competition was thus extremely restricted, for both two short-lived opposition parties (the Progressive Republican Party and the Liberal Party, founded and shut down in 1925 and 1930, respectively) and few independent candidates. In selecting the candidates, certain social classes, including high-ranking officers and bureaucrats, were privileged, but sometimes rural notables with close ties to party headquarters were easily elected (Koçak 2005).

26 Though this was clearly a pragmatic maneuver by Mustafa Kemal, some Turkish historians (e.g., Berkes 1998[1964]; Bayur 1983), who were also among the makers of the official historiography, took this argument seriously and reproduced it. Many contemporary authors also followed suit (e.g., Uluğ 1975; Akgün 2006). Serious scholars, however, did not buy the official justification, calling it "absurd" (Toynbee 1927: 59), "weak, even ridiculous" (Benoist-Mechin 1984: 154), and "wrong" (Tunçay 2005: 82).

27 Seyyid Bey's parliamentary address was subsequently published, and 10,000 copies of it were distributed in Turkey (Satan 2008: 234, n. 704). When Seyyid Bey finished his speech, Mustafa Kemal, who was present at the GNA, reportedly said: "Seyyid Bey has done his final job" (quoted in Atay 1968: 388). Two days later, he was removed from his post as minister of justice because Kemal did not agree with him on the transfer of the civil code from the West: He favored the full translation of European laws without making any adjustments in light of Turkey's local customs, which Seyyid Bey had suggested to make at the end of his parliamentary address.

28 TBMM *Arşivi A*, Devre 2, Dosya 431, 1924. See also *Resmi Ceride*, April 7, 1924, p. 3; and *Düstur* (1924) *Üçüncü Tertip*, vol. 5, p. 665.

29 In Turkey, the state still controls, though not completely, the content of Friday sermons: Officially, *imams* have to read the sermons sent by the DRA every week from Ankara.

30 See, e.g., TBMM *Arşivi A*, Devre 2, Dosya 431 (1924) for the originals of invitations sent to the Turkish GNA members by the Al-Azhar Sheikh and Congress Chairman Muhammad Abu'l-Fadl.

31 A third trend in Egypt was the policy of indifference adopted by the ruling *Wafd* Party led by nationalist leader and Prime Minister Saad Zaghlul Pasha. The constitutionalist liberals supported nationalists on this policy (Toynbee 1927: 82).

32 For a collection of articles that discuss the impact of Kemalism on Muslim countries, including the reception of the Caliphate's abolition in the Islamic world, see Georgeon and Gökalp (2007).

33 I have discussed in Chapter 5 how France made plans for a "*Maghrib* Caliphate" and Britain for an "Arab Caliphate" during World War I to replace the Ottoman Caliphate, and how both projects failed (or were abandoned by the Europeans).

34 I have already mentioned above how in a press conference in early 1923 Mustafa Kemal advised off the record not to use the word "secular" or "non-religious" (*la-dini*) in describing his government, and how a journalist (Müştak Bey) complained about self-censorship on this issue. On the other hand, my argument for an instrumental use of Islamic discourse is not unfamiliar in the literature. Several leading scholars on Turkish modernization (e.g., Mardin 1971, 2003; Karpat 2004; and Kara 2003a, among others) agree with me on the fact that the early-Republican secular elites (a group that roughly corresponds to my "secularists") tended to view religion in an instrumental manner. Mardin (1971: 210) also argues that the roots of this "manipulative attitude" lie in the modernist education these elites had received in the late 19th century. Karpat (2004: 201) extends this argument further back arguing that all ideologies (and not just Islam) were used instrumentally by political elites between 1876 and 1945 in Turkey.

35 Although this pragmatic attitude can be said to have dominated the first quarter of the 20th century, I limit my argument for secularist instrumentality to one of the three groups, to one of the three periods (1919–1924) and to Turkey only.

36 Although Mustafa Kemal's clarity and decisiveness in his discourse in 1927 do not necessarily mean that his actions were characterized by the same features to the same degree between 1920 and 1924, we must assume (cf. Haim 1965: 222) that he actually did plan – or at least had a rough image in his mind – for different stages of secularization, due to the way the subsequent events unfolded and the lack of evidence to counter what he later claimed.

37 These "co-workers" included Ahmed İzzet Pasha, Rauf Bey, Fethi Bey, and İsmail Canbolat, with whom Kemal conducted the "National Struggle" between 1919 and 1922. Before that he had also unsuccessfully tried to convince Sultan Vahideddin to form a cabinet with these figures (led by Ahmed İzzet as Grand Vizier, and Kemal himself as War Minister) in Istanbul after the war was over in November 1918 (Akşin 1983: 70ff.). Refet and Rauf later founded the first opposition party to Kemal's Republican People's Party in 1924, though it was soon to be shut down by Kemal; also, Ahmed İzzet and Rauf were two of the most heavily criticized figures in Kemal's *Speech*; Canbolat, former Finance Minister Cavit Bey (who had sponsored the *Minber* newspaper that Kemal and Rauf had published in Istanbul after the war) and former Minister of Public Works Kara Kemal (one of the Unionist leaders who initially organized the Anatolian resistance) were all accused of playing a role in the attempted assassination of Mustafa Kemal in 1926. The first two were executed and the third committed suicide before being arrested.

References

Primary sources

Abdur-raziq, A. (1925) *Islam wa Usul al-Hukm*, Cairo: n.p.

Abdullah [King of Jordan] (1950) *Memoirs of King Abdullah of Transjordan*, London: Cape.

Abdünnafi (1922) *Firari Vahideddin Halife Değil İdi, Alem-i İslam'ın Dikkatine*, Istanbul: Şehzadebaşı Evkaf-ı İslamiye Matbaası. [Published in *Hilafet Risaleleri*, vol. 5, Istanbul: Klasik, 2005.]

al-Afghani, J. (n.d.) *al-Radd 'ala al-Dahriyyin*, Beirut, n.p.

Ağaoğlu, A. (1923a) "Tarihi Celse" in *Hilafet ve Milli Hakimiyet*, Ankara: İstihbarat Matbaası (1339), pp. 11–32.

Ağaoğlu, A. (1923b) "Açık Mektup" in *Hilafet ve Milli Hakimiyet*, Ankara: İstihbarat Matbaası (1339), pp. 142–148.

Ahmed Emin [Yalman] (1970) *Yakın Tarihte Gördüklerim ve Geçirdiklerim*, vol. 3, Istanbul: Rey.

Akçura, Y. (1976[1904]) *Üç Tarz-ı Siyaset*, Ankara: Türk Tarih Kurumu Basımevi.

al-'Amidi, S. (1992) *al-Ihkam fi al-Usul al-Ahkam* vol. 4, Beirut, n.p.

Anonymous (1883) "Panislamism and the Caliphate" in *The Contemporary Review*, vol. XLIII, online, available at: www.munseys.com/diskseven/cotre.htm#1_0_6, (retrieved February 26, 2011).

Ali Fahmi Muhammad (1911) *Al-Khilafa al-Islamiyya wa al-Jamia al-Uthmaniyya*. [Published in *Hilafet Risaleleri*, vol. 3, Istanbul: Klasik, 2003.]

The American Foreign Policy Council (2010) *World Almanac of Islamism: Bangladesh*, http://almanac.afpc.org/Bangladesh (retrieved March 4, 2010).

The American Journal of International Law (1913) "The Treaty of November 27, 1912, Between France and Spain Concerning Morocco" vol. 7, no. 2 (April).

The American Journal of International Law (1920) "The Treaty of Sèvres" vol. 15, supp. 79.

Ansari, Mukhtar Ahmed (1919) *Umum Hindistan Cemiyet-i İslamiyesi Kabul Heyeti*. [Published in *Hilafet Risaleleri*, vol. 4, Istanbul: Klasik, 2004.]

Atay, F. R. (1968) *Çankaya*, Istanbul: n.p.

Azad, A. (1920) *Hilafet Meselesi, İngiltere, Arap Yarımadası ve Osmanlı Hilafeti*. [Published in *Hilafet Risaleleri*, vol. 5, Istanbul: Klasik, 2005.]

al-Banna, H. (1936) *Toward the Light*, online, available at: www.kalamullah.com/ Books/ Towards%20the%20Light.pdf (retrieved December 14, 2010).

Barthold, V. (1912) "Halife ve Sultan" *Mir Islama*. [Published in *Hilafet Risaleleri*, vol. 3, Istanbul: Klasik, 2003.]

Blunt, W. S. (1882) *The Future of Islam*, London: Kegan Paul.

Blunt, W. S. (1907) *Secret History of the English Occupation of Egypt*, London: Unwin.

Bukhari, M. (1971) *Sahîh Al-Bukharî, vols. II, IV* (5 vols.) Gujranwala: Taleem-ul-Qur'an Trust.

Celal Nuri, İ. (1913) *Mesele-i Hilafet*. [Published in *Hilafet Risaleleri*, vol. 4, Istanbul: Klasik, 2004.]

Celal Nuri, İ. (1932) "A New Phase of the Turkish Revolution" in *The Turkish Press 1925–1932*, L. Levonian (trans. and ed.), Athens: School of Religion.

Celâleddin Feyyaz (1922) *Hâkimiyet-i Milliye ile Saltanat-ı Şahsiyenin Mukâyesesine Dâir Bir İki Söz ve Lütfi Fikri Beyin Hükümdarlık Karşısında Nam Risalesine Cevâb*, Istanbul, n.p. (1338).

Ceride-i İlmiyye [*Meşihat*'s official journal] vol. 1, no 7, Istanbul: Evail-i Muharrem (1333).

Cevdet Pasha (1960) *Tezakir*, 4 vols., Ankara: TTK.

CHP (1931) *Cumhuriyet Halk Fırkası Nizamname ve Programı*, Ankara: TBMM Matbaası.

CHP (1935) *CHP Tüzüğü, 1935*, Ankara: Ulus Basımevi.

D'Ohsson, I. (1790) *Tableau general de l'empire othoman, vol. 1* (3 vols.) Paris: Didot.

Düstur (1876) *Birinci Tertip* [Records of the Ottoman Parliament] vol. 4 [4 vols.], Istanbul: Matbaa-i Âmire.

Düstur (1908–1918) *İkinci Tertip* [Records of the Ottoman Parliament] vols. 1–3 [18 vols.], Dersaadet: Matbaa-i Osmani.

Düstur (1921) *Üçüncü Tertip* [Records of the Turkish GNA], vol. 1, Istanbul: Evkaf-ı İslamiye Matbaası.

Düstur (1924) *Üçüncü Tertip* [Records of the Turkish GNA], vol. 5, Istanbul: Matbaa-i Âmire.

Edib (Adıvar), H. (1930) *Turkey Faces West: A Turkish View of Recent Changes and their Origin*, New Haven, CT: Yale University Press.

Elmalılı Hamdi, [Yazır] (1909) "İslamiyet ve Hilafet ve Meşihat-ı İslamiye" *Beyanu'l-Hak*, vol. I, no. 22, February 16, 1324. [Published in *Hilafet Risaleleri*, vol. 3, Istanbul: Klasik, 2003.]

Elmalılı Hamdi [Yazır] (1935) *Hak Dini Kur'ân Dili*, vol. 1, Istanbul: Matbaa-i Ebüzziya.

F. C. (1923) "Hoca Şükrü Efendiye Cevab" in *Hilafet ve Milli Hakimiyet*, Ankara: İstihbarat Matbaası (1339), pp. 177–185.

Feridun, S. (1962) *Anayasalar ve Siyasal Belgeler*, Istanbul: Aydın Güler Kitabevi.

Fuad Şükrü (1922) *Halk Slatanatı: Lütfi Fikri Bey'in "Hükümdarlık Karşısında Milliyet ve Mesuliyet ve Tefrik-i Kuva Mesaili" Hakkındaki Risalesine Cevap*. [Published in *Hilafet Risaleleri*, vol. 5, Istanbul: Klasik, 2005.]

al-Ghazali, M. (2001) *Fada'ih al-Batiniyya wa Fada'il al-Mustazhiriyya*, Beirut: al-Maktaba al-'Asriyya.

Gökalp, Z. (1989[1912]) "Asker Duası" in *Ziya Gökalp Külliyatı*, F. A. Tansel (ed.), Istanbul: Türk Tarih Kurumu.

Gökalp, Z. (1914a) "Fıkh ve İctimaiyyat" *İslam Mecmuası*, vol. I, no. 2, Istanbul. English translation: "Islamic Jurisprudence and Sociology" in Z. Gökalp (1959) *Turkish Nationalism and Western Civilization: Selected Essays of Ziya Gökalp*, trans. and ed. Niyazi Berkes, London: George Allen and Unwin.

Gökalp, Z. (1914b) "İctimai Usul-i Fıkh" *İslam Mecmuası*, vol. I, no. 2 Istanbul. English translation: "The Social Sources of Islamic Jurisprudence" in Z. Gökalp (1959) *Turkish Nationalism and Western Civilization: Selected Essays of Ziya Gökalp*, trans. and ed. Niyazi Berkes, London: George Allen and Unwin.

Gökalp, Z. (1915a) "Dinin İctimai Vazifeleri" *İslam Mecmuası*, I vol. I, nos. 34, 36, Istanbul. English translation: "Social Functions of Religion" in Z. Gökalp (1959) *Turkish Nationalism and Western Civilization: Selected Essays of Ziya Gökalp*, trans. and ed. Niyazi Berkes, London: George Allen and Unwin.

Gökalp, Z. (1915b) "Diyanet ve Kaza" *İslam Mecmuası*, vol. II, no. 35, Istanbul. English translation: "Religion and Law" in Z. Gökalp (1959) *Turkish Nationalism and Western Civilization: Selected Essays of Ziya Gökalp*, trans. and ed. Niyazi Berkes, London: George Allen and Unwin.

Gökalp, Z. (1916) "İttihat ve Terakki Kongresi Münasebetiyle" *İslam Mecmuası*, vol. IV, no. 48, Istanbul. English translation: "State and Religion" in Z. Gökalp (1959) *Turkish Nationalism and Western Civilization: Selected Essays of Ziya Gökalp*, trans. and ed. Niyazi Berkes, London: George Allen and Unwin.

Gökalp, Z. (1917a) "İslamiyet ve Asri Medeniyet" *İslam Mecmuası*, vol. V, nos. 51–52, Istanbul. English translation: "Islam and Modern Civilization" in Z. Gökalp (1959) *Turkish Nationalism and Western Civilization: Selected Essays of Ziya Gökalp*, trans. and ed. Niyazi Berkes, London: George Allen and Unwin.

Gökalp, Z. (1917b) "İslamiyet ve Asri Medeniyet -II" *İslam Mecmuası*, vol. V, no. 52, Istanbul.

Gökalp, Z. (1918a) *Türkleşmek, İslamlaşmak, Muasırlaşmak*, Istanbul: Yeni Mecmua.

Gökalp, Z. (1918b) *Yeni Hayat*, Istanbul: Evkaf-ı İslamiye Matbaası.

Gökalp, Z. (1922a) "Hilafetin Hakiki Mahiyeti" *Küçük Mecmua*, no. 24, Diyarbakır. English translation: "Caliphate" in Z. Gökalp (1959) *Turkish Nationalism and Western Civilization: Selected Essays of Ziya Gökalp*, trans. and ed. Niyazi Berkes, London: George Allen and Unwin.

Gökalp, Z. (1922b) "Hilafetin İstiklali" *Küçük Mecmua*, no. 25, Diyarbakır. English translation: "Caliphate" in Z. Gökalp (1959) *Turkish Nationalism and Western Civilization: Selected Essays of Ziya Gökalp*, trans. and ed. Niyazi Berkes, London: George Allen and Unwin.

Gökalp, Z. (1922c) "Hilafetin Vazifeleri" *Küçük Mecmua*, no. 26, Diyarbakır. English translation: "Caliphate" in Z. Gökalp (1959) *Turkish Nationalism and Western Civilization: Selected Essays of Ziya Gökalp*, trans. and ed. Niyazi Berkes, London: George Allen and Unwin.

Gökalp, Z. (1968[1923]) *The Principles of Turkism*, trans. R. Devereux, Leiden: E. J. Brill.

Gökalp, Z. (1992) *Kürt Aşiretleri Hakkında Sosyolojik Tetkikler*, Istanbul: Sosyal.

Güneş, İ. (1990) "II. Meşrutiyet Dönemi Hükümet Programları" *OTAM*, no. 1: 171–290.

Habil Adem [Profesör Vayt] (1913) *Muharebeden Sonra: Hilafet Siyaseti ve Türklük Siyaseti*, Istanbul: Şems Matbaası (1331). [Published in *Hilafet Risaleleri*, vol. 3, Istanbul: Klasik, 2003.]

Hakim al-Nishaburî (1990) *al-Mustadrak 'ala al-Sahîhayn, vol. IV* (5 vols.), Beirut: Dar al-Kutub al-'Ilmiyya (1411).

Halim Sabit (1914a) "Örf-Ma'ruf-1" *İslam Mecmuası*, vol. I, no. 10, Istanbul.

Halim Sabit (1914b) "Örf-Ma'ruf-2" *İslam Mecmuası*, vol. I, no. 11, Istanbul.

Hertslet, E. (1875) *The Map of Europe by Treaty*, vol. II, London: Harrison and Sons.

Hilafet ve Milli Hakimiyet (1923) Ankara: İstihbarat Matbaası (1339). [Süleymaniye Kütüphanesi İhsan Mahvi, 000210.]

Hizb ut-Tahrir (2010) Official website of *Hizb ut-Tahrir*: www.hizbuttahrir.org (retrieved March 13, 2010).

Hoca Halil Hulki, Hoca İlyas Sami and Hoca Rasih (1923) *Hakimiyet-i Milliye ve Hilafet-i İslamiye* 2nd ed. Ankara: Yenigün Matbaası (1341).

Hoca Şükrü (1923) *Hilafet-i İslamiye ve Büyük Millet Meclisi*, Ankara: Ali Şükrü Matbaası (1339).

Hussein [Sharif] (1916) *Proclamation of the Sherif of Mecca*, in C. Horne (ed.) (1923) *Source Records of the Great War*, vol. IV, London: National Alumni: 234–238.

Ibn Hanbal, A. (1895) *Musnad*, 6 vols. Cairo, n.p. (1312–1313).

Ibn Khaldūn, A. (1957) *Muqaddimat Ibn Khaldūn*, 4 vols., ed. 'Ali 'Abd al-Wāḥid Wāfī, Cairo: Lajna al-Bayān al-'Arabi.

Ibn Khaldūn, A. (1958) *The Muqaddimah: An Introduction to History*, 3 vols., trans. F. Rosenthal, Princeton, NJ: Princeton University Press.

Ibn Qayyim, al-Jawziyah M. (1953) *Al-Ṭuruq al-Hukmīyah fī al-Siyāsah al-Shar'iah*, Cairo: Maṭba'at al-Sunnah al-Muḥammadīyah.

İsmail Hakkı [İzmirli] (1910) "Hilafet-i İslamiye" *Sırat-ı Müstakim*, vol. III, no. 56, September 17 (1325). [Published in *Hilafet Risaleleri*, vol. 3, Istanbul: Klasik, 2003.]

İsmail Hakkı (1914a) "Örfün Nazar-ı Şer'ideki Mevkii" *Sebilürreşad Mecmuası*, no. 293, Istanbul.

İsmail Hakkı (1914b) "İctimai Usul-i Fıkh'a İhtiyaç Var mı?" *Sebilürreşad Mecmuası*, no. 298, Istanbul.

Jawish, A. (1916) *Hilafet-i İslamiye*, Istanbul: el-Adl Matbaası (1334). [Published in *Hilafet Risaleleri*, vol. 4, Istanbul: Klasik, 2004.]

Karabekir, K. (1991) *Paşaların Kavgası: Atatürk-Karabekir* (ed. by İ. Bozdağ), Istanbul: Emre.

al-Kawakibi, A. (1991) *Umm al-Qura*, Beirut: Dar al-Shuruq al-'Arabi.

Kınalızade, A. (2007) *Ahlak-ı Alai*, Istanbul: Klasik.

Kidwai, M. H. (1919) *Türkiya İslam İmparatorluğu'nun İstikbali*. [Published in *Hilafet Risaleleri*, vol. 4, Istanbul: Klasik, 2004.]

Koçi Bey (1860[1631]) *Koçi Bey Risalesi*, Istanbul, n.p.

LBKTB (1971) *Lozan Barış Konferansı, Tutanak-Belgeler*, ed. S. Meray, Set 1, vol. 2, Ankara.

Le Matin de Paris (1915) "Islam et la Guerre" November 10.

League of Nations Treaty Series (1924) no. 701, online, available at: http:// untreaty.un. org/unts/60001_120000/14/30/00027480.pdf (retrieved October 13, 2008).

Levonian, L. (ed.) (1932) *The Turkish Press 1925–1932*, Athens: School of Religion.

Lütfi al-Sayyid (1965) *Ta'ammulāt fī al-falsafah wa-al-adab wa-al-siyāsah wa-al-ijtimā'*, Cairo: Dar al-Ma'ārif.

Lütfi Fikri (1922) *Hükümdarlık Karşısında Milliyet ve Mesuliyet ve Tefrik-i Kuva Mesaili*, Istanbul: Akşam Teşebbüs Matbaası (1338). [Published in *Hilafet Risaleleri*, vol. 5, Istanbul: Klasik, 2005.]

Lütfi Fikri (1923a) *Meşrutiyet ve Cumhuriyet*, Istanbul: Ahmed İhsan ve Şürekası Matbaacılık Osmanlı Şirketi (1339).

Lütfi Fikri (1923b) "Huzur-ı Hazreti Hilafet-Penâhîye-Açık Arîza-" *Tanin*, 10 Teşrin-i sâni (1339), p. 1.

Mahmud Nedim [Maan] (1919) *Hicaz'da Saltanat Tesisini Din-i İslam Men Eder*. [Published in *Hilafet Risaleleri*, vol. 4, Istanbul: Klasik, 2004.]

al-Māwardī, A. (1994) *Ahkam al-Sultaniyyah wa al-Wilayat al-Diniyyah*, 2nd ed., Beirut: Dar al-Kitab al-'Arabi.

Mehmed Tahir (1909) *El-Ehadisü'ş-Şerife fi's-Saltanati'l-Münife*, Topkapı Sarayı Kütüphanesi, MR 915. [Published in *Hilafet Risaleleri*, vol. 3, Istanbul: Klasik, 2003.]

Ministere des affaires etrangeres (1877) *Documents diplomatiques*, Constantinople: Typographie et Lithographie Centrales.

Mizan (1909) "Şeyhülislam Meclis-i Mebusan'a Gelmeli mi Gelmemeli mi.?" *Mizan*, February 24, no. 76 (1324).

Muhyiddin Baha (1915) *Halife Ordusu Mısır ve Kafkas'da*, Bursa: Muin-i Hilal Matbaası, May (1331). [Published in *Hilafet Risaleleri*, vol. 3, Istanbul: Klasik, 2003.]

The Muslim Brotherhood (2010a) "Bylaws of the International Muslim Brotherhood," online, available at: http://grendelreport.posterous.com/missing-bylaws-of-the-international-muslim-br (retrieved September 29, 2011).

The Muslim Brotherhood (2010b) "Messages of Imam," online, available at: http://ikhwanweb.com/article.php?id=802 (retrieved December 14, 2010).

Mustafa Kemal (1922) "Türk ve İslam Tarihine Kısa Bir Bakış" in E. Z. Ökte (ed.) (1968) *Atatürk, Din ve Laiklik*, Istanbul: Menteş Matbaası.

Mustafa Kemal (1923) *Gazi Mustafa Kemal Atatürk'ün 1923 Eskişehir-İzmit Konuşmaları*, Arı İnan (ed.) 2nd ed. Ankara: TTK, 1996.

Mustafa Kemal (1929[1927]) *A Speech Delivered by Ghazi Mustapha Kemal*, Leipzig: K. F. Koehler.

Mustafa Kemal (1945) *Atatürk'ün Söylev ve Demeçleri, vol. I*, Ankara: Türk İnkılâp Tarihi Enstitüsü.

Mustafa Kemal (1961[1927]) *Nutuk*, 3 vols. Istanbul: Milli Eğitim Basımevi.

Mustafa Kemal (1964) *Atatürk'ün Tamim, Telgraf ve Beyannameleri*, Ankara: Türk İnkılâp Tarihi Enstitüsü.

Mustafa Sabri [Efendi] (1924) *al-Nakîr alâ Munkir al-ni'ma min al-Dîn wa al-Khilâfah wa al-Ummah*, Beirut: Matba'ah al-'Abbasiya (1342).

Mustafa Zihni (1911) *İslam'da Hilafet*, Konstantiniyye: Matbaa-i Ebüzziya (1327). [Published in *Hilafet Risaleleri*, vol. 3, Istanbul: Klasik, 2003.]

Nadvi, S. Suleyman (1920–1921) *Hilafet ve Hindistan*. [Published in *Hilafet Risaleleri*, vol. 5, Istanbul: Klasik, 2005.]

Nallino, C. A. (1917) *Hilafet*. [Published in *Hilafet Risaleleri*, vol. 4, Istanbul: Klasik, 2004.]

Namık Kemal (1867) "Usul-ü Meşveret Hakkında Mektuplar-6" *Hürriyet*, 26 Eylül (1285).

Namık Kemal (1884) *Evrak-ı Perişan*, Istanbul: Matbaa-i Osmaniye (1301).

Nizamülmülk (1981) *Siyasetname*, Istanbul: Dergah.

Ömer Lütfi (1912) *Nazar-ı İslam'da Makam-ı Hilafet*, Selanik: Asır Matbaası (1330). [Published in *Hilafet Risaleleri*, vol. 3, Istanbul: Klasik, 2003.]

Ömer Ziyaeddin (1908) *Hukuk-ı Selatin: Hadis-i Erbain fi Hukuki's-Selatin*, Istanbul (1326). [Published in *Hilafet Risaleleri*, vol. 3, Istanbul: Klasik, 2003.]

Proclamation of March, 1917, by the Ulema or Body of Priests of Mecca, in C. Horne (ed.) (1923) *Source Records of the Great War*, vol. IV, London: National Alumni, pp. 238–241.

al-Razi, F. (1938) *al-Tafsir al-Kabir*, Cairo: al-Matba'at al-Bahiyyah al-Misriyyah, 32 vols.

Rashid Rida, M. (1921) "Tafsir al-Qur'an al-Hakim" *al-Manar*, vol. XXII, no. 10, October 31.

Rashid Rida, M. (1922) "Zafar al-Turk bi al-Yunan wa Salluhum 'Arsha Dawlat Othman wa Ja'luhum al-Khilafah al-Islamiyya Sultah Ruhaniyya Adabiyya" *al-Manar*, vol. XXIII, no. 9, November 19.

Rashid Rida, M. (1923a) *al-Khilafa aw al-Imama al-'Uzma*, Cairo: Matba'at al-Manar (1341).

Rashid Rida, M. (1923b) "al-Khilafa al-Islamiyya (4)" *al-Manar*, vol. XXIV, no. 3, March 18.

Rashid Rida, M. (1925) "al-Islâm wa Usûl al-hukm [I]" *al-Manar*, vol. XXVI, no. 2, June 21.

Rashid Rida, M. (1925) "al-Islâm wa Usûl al-hukm [II]" *al-Manar*, vol. XXVI/3, July 21.

Rashid Rida, M. (1926) "Mudhakkarat al-Mu'tamar al-Khilafa al-Islamiyya" *al-Manar*, vol. XXVII, no. 3, June 11.

Rashid Rida, M. (1928) "Anbâu-l-âlem al-Islâmiyya" *al-Manar*, vol. XXIX, no. 8, December 1.

Resmi Ceride [The Official Gazette] (1924), April 7.

Safa, M. (1922) *Hilafet-i İslamiye ve Al-i Osman*. [Published in *Hilafet Risaleleri*, vol. 5, Istanbul: Klasik, 2005.]

Safayihi, I. (1915) *Iqaz al-Ikhwan li-Dasais al-A'da wa Ma Yaqtadhih Hal al-Zaman*, Istanbul: Matbaa-i Askeriye (1331). [Published in *Hilafet Risaleleri*, vol. 4, Istanbul: Klasik, 2004.]

Said Halim Pasha (2000[1920]) *L'Empire Ottoman et la Guerre Mondiale*, Istanbul: Isis.

Said Halim Pasha (2003) *Bütün Eserleri*, Istanbul: Anka Yayınları.

Samné, G. (1919) *Hilafet ve Panislamizm*. [Published in *Hilafet Risaleleri*, vol. 4, Istanbul: Klasik, 2004.]

Sebilürreşad (1916a) "Din ve Devet Yahut Hilafet ve Saltanat" vol. 21, no. 359 (6 Teşrin-i Evvel 1332/October 19, 1916). [Published in *Hilafet Risaleleri*, vol. 4, Istanbul: Klasik, 2004.]

Sebilürreşad (1916b) "Sabık Mekke Emiri Hüseyin ve Hint Matbuatı" vol. 21, no. 359 (6 Teşrin-i Evvel 1332/October 19, 1916). [Published in *Hilafet Risaleleri*, vol. 4, Istanbul: Klasik, 2004.]

Seyyid Bey, M. (1917) "Hilafet" in *Idem, Usul-i Fıkıh – Medhal*, Istanbul: Matbaa-i Amire (1333). [Published in *Hilafet Risaleleri*, vol. 4, Istanbul: Klasik, 2004.]

Seyyid Bey, M. (1923) *Hilafet ve Hakimiyet-i Milliye*, Ankara: Türkiye Büyük Millet Meclisi Matbaası [originally undated but subsequent scholarship has fixed the date of publication as 1923/1339].

Seyyid Bey, M. (1924) *Hilafetün Mahiyet-i Şer'iyyesi*, Ankara: Türkiye Büyük Millet Meclisi Matbaası.

Shakib Arslan (2005) *İttihatçı Bir Arap Aydınının Anıları*, Istanbul: Klasik.

Süleyman Nazif (1922) *Lütfi Fikri Bey'e Cevap: Hilafet, Milliyet ve Tefrik-i Kuva Mesaili*. [Published in *Hilafet Risaleleri*, vol. 5, Istanbul: Klasik, 2005.]

Syed Mahmud (1921) *The Khilafat and England*, Patna: Imtyaz.

Syed Mahmud (2005) *Hilafet ve İngiltere*. [Published in *Hilafet Risaleleri*, vol. 5, Istanbul: Klasik, 2005.]

Şemseddin Sami (1899–1900) *Kamus-ı Türkî*, 2 vols., Dersaadet: İkdam Matbaası (1317–1318).

al-Taftazānī, S. (1989) *Sharh al-Maqasid*, 5 vols., Beirut: 'Alam al-Kutub.

Taha Hussein (1947) *Al-Fitna al-Kubrā*, Cairo: n.p.

Takvim-i Vekayi, May 30, 1329; November 23, 1330.

Tanzimat Fermanı (1940) *Tanzimat* vol I, Istanbul: Maarif Matbaası.

TBMMZC (Grand National Assembly Records) (1922a) *Türkiya Büyük Millet Meclisi'nde 30 Teşrin-i Evvel ve 1 Teşrin-i Sani 338 Tarihli Mühim ve Tarihi Celseler ve Karar*, Dersaadet: Akşam-Teşebbüs Matbaası. [Published as "Hilafetin Saltanattan Tefriki" in *Hilafet Risaleleri*, vol. 5, Istanbul: Klasik, 2005.]

TBMMZC (Grand National Assembly Records) (1922b) *TBMM Gizli Celse Zabıtları*, vol. III, Ankara: İş Bankası (1985).

TBMMZC (Grand National Assembly Records) (1924) *TBMM Zabıt Ceridesi*, Devre 2, vol. VII. Ankara: T. B. M. Meclisi Matbaası (1968).

TBMM *Arşivi A* (1924), Devre 2, Dosya 431.

TBMM *Arşivi C* (1922), Devre 1, Dosya 308.

Toynbee, A. (1920) "The Question of the Caliphate" *The Contemporary Review*, February, pp. 192–196.

Toynbee, A. (1927) *Survey of International Affairs, 1925, vol. 1: The Islamic World since the Peace Settlement*, London: Oxford University Press.

Toynbee, A. (1954) "The Ineffectiveness of Pan-islamism" in A. Toynbee, *A Study of History*, vol. 8, London: Oxford University Press, pp. 692–695.

al-Tunusi, S. (1913) "Hilafet-i Muazzama-i İslamiye Hakkında İngilizlerin Hezeyanları," *Sebilürreşad*, vol. XIII no. 333, April 1 (1333) [Published in *Hilafet Risaleleri*, vol. 4, Istanbul: Klasik, 2004.]

al-Tunusi, S. (1915) "Fi-sebilillah Cihadın Hakikati, Gayesi, Hükmü, Mücahidinin Vezaifi" *Sebilürreşad*, vol. 13, no. 315.

al-Tunusi, S. (1916a) *Sharkhu Dasais al-Fransees Zidda al-Islam wa Khalifatih*. [Published in *Hilafet Risaleleri*, vol. 4, Istanbul: Klasik, 2004.]

al-Tunusi, S. (1916b) *Hilafet-i Muazzama-i İslamiye*. [Published in *Hilafet Risaleleri*, vol. 4, Istanbul: Klasik, 2004.]

al-Ubeydi, M. H. (1916) *Habl al-I'tisam wa Wujub al-Khilafah fi Din al-Islam*. [Published in *Hilafet Risaleleri*, vol. 4, Istanbul: Klasik, 2004.]

Vahideddin [Sultan] (1923) *Şevketlü Sultan Mehmed Vahîdeddîn Efendimiz Hazretlerinin Beyannâme-i Hümâyunlarıdır*, in Kadir Mısıroğlu (1993) *Geçmişi ve Geleceği ile Hilafet*, Istanbul: Sebil Yay, pp. 185–203.

Vahideddin [Sultan] (1926) *Kahire'de Camiu'l-Ezher Şeyhi ve Hilafet Mu'temeri Reisi Ulema-yı Benâmdan Muhammed Ebu'l-Fazl Efendi'ye*.

Volkan (1909) no. 56, February 19 (1324).

Yafi, S. (1916) *Hilafet ve Osmaniyet*, Beirut: Matbaa al-Iqbal (1334). [Published in *Hilafet Risaleleri*, vol. 4, Istanbul: Klasik, 2004.]

Yağcıoğlu, E. (ed.) (1992) *İttihat ve Terakki'nin Son Yılları: 1916 Kongre Zabıtları*, Istanbul: Nehir.

al-Yemeni, Ş. B. (1911) *Al-Nasiha al-Shar'iyya li al-Qabail al-Yemeniyya*. [Published in *Hilafet Risaleleri*, vol. 3, Istanbul: Klasik, 2003.]

Secondary literature

Abun-Nasr, J. (1987) *A History of the Maghrib in the Islamic Period*, Cambridge: Cambridge University Press.

Adanır, F. (2009) "Çarlık Rusya'sı ve Habsburg İmparatorluğu Arasında Osmanlı'da Vatandaşlık: Karşılaştırmalı Bir Değerlendirme" *Toplumsal Tarih*, no. 182.

Afary, J. (2005) "Civil Liberties and the Making of Iran's First Constitution" *Comparative Studies of South Asia, Africa and the Middle East*, vol. 25, no. 2.

Ahmad, F. (1969) *The Young Turks: The Committee of Union and Progress in Turkish Politics, 1908–1914*, Oxford: Clarendon Press.

Ahmad, F. (1993) *The Making of Modern Turkey*, London: Routledge.

Ahmed Midhat (1878) *Üss-i İnkılab*, Istanbul: Takvimhâne-i Amire (1294).

AJS (1998) Symposium on Historical Sociology, *American Journal of Sociology*, vol. 104, no. 3.

Akarlı, E. D. (1978) *Belgelerle Tanzimat: Osmanlı Sadrazamlarından Âli ve Fuad Paşaların Vasiyyetnameleri*, Istanbul: Boğaziçi Üniversitesi Yayınları.

Akarlı, E. D. (2002) "The Tangled End of Istanbul's Imperial Supremacy," in L. Fawaz and C. A. Bayly (eds.) *Modernity and Culture from the Mediterranean to the Indian Ocean, 1890–1920*, New York: Columbia University Press.

Akgün, S. (2006) *Halifeliğin Kaldırılması ve Laiklik*, Istanbul: Temel.

Aksan, V. (1993) "Ottoman Political Writing, 1768–1808" *International Journal of Middle East Studies*, no. 25.

Akşin, S. (1983) *Istanbul Hükümetleri ve Mill Mücadele*, Istanbul: Cem.

Akşin, S. (1987) *Jön Türkler ve İttihat ve Terakki*, Istanbul: Remzi.

Akşin, S. (1994) *Şeriatçı Bir Ayaklanma: 31 Mart Olayı*, Istanbul: İmge.

Aktay, Y. (1997) "Body, Text, Identitiy: The Islamist Discourse of Authenticity in Modern Turkey" unpublished PhD thesis, Ankara: METU.

Aktay, Y. (1999) *Türk Dininin Sosyolojik İmkanı*, Istanbul: İletişim.

Akün, Ö. F. (1992) "Bursalı Mehmed Tahir" *TDV İslam Ansiklopedisi*, vol. 6. Istanbul: TDV.

Akyıldız, A. (2004) *Osmanlı Bürokrasisi ve Modernleşme*, Istanbul: İletişim.

Alangari, H. (1998) *The Struggle for Power in Arabia: Ibn Saud, Hussein and Great Britain, 1914–1924*, Reading: Ithaca Press.

Albayrak, S. (1992) *Hilafet ve Halifesiz Müslümanlar*, Istanbul: Araştırma Yayınları.

Algar, H. (1969) *Religion and State in Iran, 1785–1906: The Role of the Ulama in the Qajar Period*, Berkeley/Los Angeles, CA: University of California Press.

Algar, H. (1976) "The Naqshbandi Order: A Preliminary Survey of its History and Significance" *Studia Islamica*, no. 44: 123–152.

Alkan, M. Ö. (ed.) (2001) *Modern Türkiye'de Siyasi Düşünce I: Tanzimat ve Meşrutiyet'in Birikimi*, Istanbul: İletişim.

Anderson, B. (1991) *Imagined Communities: Reflections on the Origin and Spread of Nationalism*, 2nd ed. New York: Verso.

Arai, M. (1992) *Turkish Nationalism in the Young Turk Era*, Leiden: E. J. Brill.

Arnold, T. W. (1965) *The Caliphate*, London: Routledge & Kegan Paul.

Armstrong, H. C. (1938) *Grey Wolf: Mustafa Kemal: An Intimate Study of a Dictator*, London: Baker.

Asad, T. (1993) *Genealogies of Religion: Discipline and Reasons of Power in Christianity and Islam*, Baltimore, MD: Johns Hopkins University Press.

Asad, T. (2002) "Muslims and European Identity: Can Europe Represent Islam?" in A. Pagden (ed.) *The Idea of Europe: From Antiquity to the European Union*, Cambridge: Cambridge University Press.

Ascher, A. (2004) *The Revolution of 1905: A Short History*, Stanford, CA: Stanford University Press.

Ashmawi, M. S. (1990) *Al-Khilafa al-Islamiyya*, Cairo: Sina li-l-Nashr.

Asrar, N. A. (1983) "Hilafetin Osmanlılara Geçişi İle İlgili Rivayetler" *Türk Dünyası Araştırmaları*, no. 22 (February).

Ata Bey, T. A. (1876) *Târih-i Ata*, Istanbul, n.p. (1293).

'Atwan, H. (1986) *Al-Amawiyyûn wa al-Khilafa*, Amman: Dar al-Jil.

Avcı, C. (1998) "Hilafet" *TDV İslam Ansiklopedisi*, vol. 17, Istanbul: TDV.

Aydın, C. (2006) "Between Occidentalism and the Global Left: Islamist Critiques of the West in Turkey" *Comparative Studies of South Asia, Africa and the Middle East* vol. 26, no. 3: 446–461.

Aydın, S. (2001) "İki İttihat-Terakki: İki Ayrı Zihniyet, İki Ayrı Siyaset" in M. Ö. Alkan (ed.) *Modern Türkiye'de Siyasi Düşünce I: Tanzimat ve Cumhuriyet'in Birikimi*, Istanbul: İletişim.

al-Azami, M. M. (1977) *Studies in Hadith Methodology and Literature*, Indianapolis, IN: American Trust Publications.

Bailey, F. E. (1942) *British Policy and the Turkish Reform Movement*, Cambridge, MA: Harvard University Press.

Bal, M. (1997) *Narratology: Introduction to the Theory of Narrative*, 2nd ed., Toronto: University of Toronto Press.

Bateson, G. (1972) *Steps to an Ecology of Mind: Collected Essays in Anthropology, Psychiatry, Evolution, and Epistemology*, Chicago, IL: University of Chicago Press.

Bayur, Y. H. (1983) *Türk İnkılabı Tarihi*, 3 vols., Ankara: TTK.

Bayur, Y. H. (1987) *Hindistan Tarihi, vol. III*, 3 vols., Ankara: TTK.

Behar, C. (1996) *Osmanlı İmparatorluğu'nun ve Türkiye'nin Nüfusu, 1500–1927*, Ankara: DİE.

Bein, A. (2006) "The Ulema, Their Institutions, and Politics in the Late Ottoman Empire (1876–1924)" unpublished PhD dissertation, Princeton University, NJ.

Bell, D. (1977), "The Return of the Sacred? The Argument on the Future of Religion" *British Journal of Sociology*, no. 88: 419–449.

Bellah, R. (1970) *Beyond Belief: Essays on Religion in a Post-Traditional World*, New York: Harper & Row.

Bellah, R. (1975) *The Broken Covenant: American Civil Religion in Time of Trial*, New York: The Seabury Press.

Benoist-Mechin, J. (1984) *Mustapha Kemal: le loup et le leopard*, Paris: Editions Albin Michel.

Benwell, B. and Stokoe, E. (2006) *Discourse and Identity*, Edinburgh: Edinburgh University Press.

Berger, P. (1967) *The Sacred Canopy: Elements of a Sociological Theory of Religion*, New York: Anchor Books.

Berger, P. (ed.) (1999a) *The Desecularization of the World: Resurgent Religion and World Politics*, Washington, DC: Ethics and Public Policy Center.

Berger, P. (1999b) "The Desecularization of the World: A Global Overview" in P. Berger (ed.) *The Desecularization of the World: Resurgent Religion and World Politics*, Washington, DC: Ethics and Public Policy Center.

Berger, P. (2000) "Secularism in Retreat" in A. Tamimi and J. Esposito (eds.), *Islam and Secularism in the Middle East*, New York: New York University Press.

Berger, P. and Luckman, T. (1966) *The Social Construction of Reality*, New York: Doubleday.

Berkes, N. (1954) "Ziya Gökalp: His Contribution to Turkish Nationalism" *Middle East Journal*, vol. 8, no. 4: 375–390.

Berkes, N. (1957) "Historical Background of Turkish Secularism" in R. Frye (ed.) *Islam and the West*, The Hague: Mouton.

Berkes, N. (1959) "Introduction" in Z. Gökalp, *Turkish Nationalism and Western Civilization: Selected Essays of Ziya Gökalp*, London: George Allen and Unwin.

Berkes, N. (1969) *100 Soruda Türkiye İktisat Tarihi*, 2 vols., Istanbul: Gercek.

Berkes, N. (1998[1964]) *The Development of Secularism in Turkey*, New York: Routledge.

Beydilli, K. (1999) "Küçük Kaynarca'dan Tanzimat'a Islahat Düşünceleri" *İlmi Araştırmalar: Dil, Edebiyat, Tarih İncelemeleri*, no. 8.

Binatlı, Y. Z. (1993) "Dağıstani, Ömer Ziyaeddin" *TDV İslam Ansiklopedisi*, vol. 8. Istanbul: TDV.

Birinci, A. (1988) "İttihad ve Terakki Cemiyeti, Kuruluşu ve İlk Nizamnâmesi" *Tarih ve Toplum*, no. 52.

Birinci, A. (1990) *Hürriyet ve İtilaf Fırkası*, Istanbul: Dergah.

Birinci, A. (2001) "Habil Adem Pelister Hakkında" in *Idem, Tarihin Gölgesinde*, Istanbul: Dergah.

Birinci, A. (2005) "Sultan Abdülhamid'in Hatıra Defteri Meselesi" *Divan: İlmi Araştırmalar*, vol. 10, no. 2.

Borak, S. (ed.) (1962) *Atatürk ve Din*, Istanbul: Anıl.

Bourdieu, P. (1984) *Distinction: A Social Critique of the Judgment of Taste*, London: Routledge & Kegan Paul.

Bourdieu, P. (1989) "Social Space and Symbolic Power" *Sociological Theory*, vol. 7, no. 1: 14–25.

Bozarslan, M. E. (1969) *Hilafet ve Ümmetçilik Sorunu*, Istanbul: Ant Yay.

Brockett, G. (2006) "Revisiting the Turkish Revolution, 1923–1938: Secular Reform and Religious 'Reaction'" *History Compass* vol. 4, no. 6: 1060–1072.

Browers, M. (2009) *Political Ideology in the Arab World: Accommodation and Transformation*, Cambridge: Cambridge University Press.

Bruinessen, M. V. (1995) "Muslims of the Dutch East Indies and the Caliphate Question" *Studia Islamica*, vol. 2, no. 3.

Budd, S. (1973) *Sociologists and Religion*, London: Collier-Macmillan.

Buzpınar, Ş. T. (2002) "II. Abdülhamid Döneminde Osmanlı Hilafetine Muhalafetin Ortaya Çıkışı" in İ. Kara (ed.) *Hilafet Risaleleri* vol. 1, Istanbul: Klasik.

Buzpınar, Ş. T. (2004) "Osmanlı Hilafeti Meselesi: Bir Literatür Değerlendirmesi" *Türkiye Araştırmaları Literatür Dergisi*, vol. 2, no. 1.

Buzpınar, Ş. T. (2005) "The Question of Caliphate under the Last Ottoman Sultans" in I. Weismann and F. Zachs (eds.) *Ottoman Reform and Muslim Regeneration*, London: I. B. Tauris.

Calhoun, C. (1987) "History and Sociology in Britain: A Review Article" *Comparative Studies in Society and History*, vol. 29, no. 3: 615–625.

Calhoun, C. (1998) "Explanation in Historical Sociology: Narrative, General Theory, and Historically Specific Theory" *American Journal of Sociology*, vol. 104, no. 3: 846–871.

Casale, G. (2010) *The Ottoman Age of Exploration*, New York: Oxford University Press.

Casanova, J. (1994) *Public Religions in the Modern World*, Chicago, IL: University of Chicago Press.

Cassar, G. (2004) *Kitchener's War: British Strategy from 1914 to 1916*, Dulles, VA: Brassey's Inc.

Certeau, M. de (1984) *The Practice of Everyday Life*, trans. S. Rendail, Berkeley, CA: University of California Press.

Certeau, M. de (1994) "The Practice of Everyday Life" in J. Storey (ed.) *Cultural Theory and Popular Culture: A Reader*, New York: Harvester Wheatsheaf.

Cleveland, W. (2000) *A History of the Modern Middle East*, 2nd ed., San Fransisco, CA: Westiew Press.

Commins, D. (1990) *Islamic Reform: Politics and Social Change in Late Ottoman Syria*, New York: Oxford University Press.

Comte, A. (1969) *Cours de philosophie positive*. 4 vols., Paris: Anthropos.

Cox, H. (1965) *The Secular City*, New York: Macmillan.

Cox, H. (1984) *Religion in the Secular City: Toward a Postmodern Theology*, New York: Simon & Schuster.

Crone, P. and Hinds, M. (2003) *God's Caliph: Religious Authority in the First Centuries of Islam*, New York: Cambridge University Press.

362   *References*

50

300

Çakır, C. (2001) *Tanzimat Dönemi Osmanlı Maliyesi*, Istanbul: Küre.

Çarıklı, H. M. (1967) *Balıkesir ve Alaşehir Kongreleri ve Kuvayi Milliye Hatıraları (1919–1920)*, ed. Ş. Turan, Ankara: Türk İnkılâp Tarihi Enstitüsü.

Çetinkaya, B. A. (2000) *İzmirli İsmail Hakkı: Hayatı, Eserleri, Görüşleri*, Istanbul: İnsan.

Çetinsaya, G. (1999) "'İsmi Olup da Cismi Olmayan Kuvvet': II. Abdülhamid'in Pan-İslamizm Politikası Üzerine Bir Deneme" *Osmanlı* vol. 2, Ankara: Yeni Türkiye.

Çetinsaya, G. (2001a) "Kalemiye'den Mülkiye'ye Tanzimat Zihniyeti" in M. Ö. Alkan (ed.) *Modern Türkiye'de Siyasi Düşünce I: Tanzimat ve Meşrutiyet'in Birikimi*, Istanbul: İletişim.

Çetinsaya, G. (2001b) "İslami Vatanseverlikten İslam Siyasetine" in M. Ö. Alkan (ed.) *Modern Türkiye'de Siyasi Düşünce I: Tanzimat ve Meşrutiyet'in Birikimi*, Istanbul: İletişim.

Çolak, Y. (2004) "Language Policy and Official Ideology in Early Republican Turkey" *Middle Eastern Studies*, vol. 40, no. 6: 67–91.

Çulcu, M. (1992) *Hilafetin Kaldırılması Sürecinde Cumhuriyetin İlanı ve Lütfi Fikri Davası*, 2 vols., Istanbul: Kastaş.

Darling, L. (2002) "'Do Justice, Do Justice, for That is Paradise': Middle Eastern Advice for Indian Muslim Rulers" *Comparative Studies on South Asia, Africa, and the Middle East*, vol. 22, nos. 1–2: 3–19.

Davie, G. (2000) *Religion in Modern Europe: A Memory Mutates*, Oxford: Oxford University Press.

Davie, G. (2002) *Europe: the Exceptional Case. Parameters of Faith in the Modern World*, London: Darton, Longman and Todd.

Davie, G. (2006) "Is Europe an Exceptional Case?" *The Hedgehog Review*, no. 8: 23–34.

Davie, G., Berger, P. and Fokas, E. (2008) *Religious America, Secular Europe: A Theme and Variations*, Aldershot: Ashgate.

Davies, B. and Harré, R. (1990) "Positioning: The Discursive Production of Selves" *Journal for the Theory of Social Behaviour*, vol. 20, no. 1: 43–63.

Davison, A. (1998) *Secularism and Revivalism in Turkey: A Hermeneutic Reconsideration*, New Haven, CT/London: Yale University Press.

Davison, A. (2006) "Ziya Gökalp and Provincializing Europe" *Comparative Studies of South Asia, Africa and the Middle East*, vol. 26, no. 3: 377–390.

Davison, R. H. (1954) "Turkish Attitudes Concerning Christian-Muslim Equality in the Nineteenth Century" *American Historical Review*, vol. 59, no. 4: 844–864.

Davison, R. H (1963) *Reform in the Ottoman Empire 1856–1876*, Princeton, NJ: Princeton University Press.

Davison, R. H (1988) *Turkey: A Short History*, Walkington: The Eothen Press.

Davutoğlu, A. (1994a) *Alternative Paradigms: The Impact of Islamic and Western Weltanschauungs on Political Theory*, Lanham, MD: University Press of America.

Davutoğlu, A (1994b) *Civilizational Transformation and the Muslim World*, Kuala Lumpur: Quill.

Davutoğlu, A (2000) "Philosophical and Institutional Dimensions of Secularization: A Comparative Analysis" in A. Tamimi and J. Esposito (eds.) *Islam and Secularism in the Middle East*, New York: New York University Press.

Dawn, C. E. (1973) "The Rise of Arabism in Syria" in C. E. Dawn, *From Ottomanism to Arabism: Essays on the Origins of Arab Nationalism*, Urbana, IL: University of Illinois Press.

Dawn, C. E. (1993a) "From Ottomanism to Arabism: The Origin of an Ideology" in A.

Hourani, P. Khoury and M. Wilson (eds.) *The Modern Middle East*, Berkeley/Los Angeles, CA: University of California Press.

Dawn, C. E. (1993b) "The Origins of Arab Nationalism" in R. Khalidi, L. Anderson, M. Muslih and R. Simon (eds.) *The Origins of Arab Nationalism*, New York: Columbia University Press.

Delanty, G. (2006) "Modernity and the Escape from Eurocentrism" in G. Delanty (ed.) *Handbook of Contemporary European Social Theory*, London: Routledge.

Demirel, A. (1994) *Birinci Meclis'te Muhalefet: İkinci Grup*, Istanbul: İletişim.

Demirel, F. (2007) *II. Abdülhamid Döneminde Sansür*, Istanbul: Bağlam.

Demirel, Y. (ed.) (1991) *Lütfi Fikri Beyin Günlüğü (Dersim Mebusu) Daima Muhalefet*, Istanbul: Arma Yayınları.

Deringil, S. (1998) *The Well-Protected Domains: Ideology and the Legitimation of Power in the Ottoman Empire, 1876–1909*, London: I. B. Tauris.

Dilipak, A. (1988) *Bir Başka Açıdan Kemalizm*, Istanbul: Beyan.

Dobbelaere, K. (1981) "Secularization: A Multi-Dimensional Concept" *Current Sociology*, vol. 29, no. 2: 1–216.

Dobbelaere K. (1985) "Secularization Theories and Sociological Paradigms: A Reformulation of The Private–Public Dichotomy and the Problem of Social Integration" *Sociological Analysis*, vol. 46, no. 4: 377–387.

Dodd, C. H. (1979) *Democracy and Development in Turkey*, Walkington: The Eothen Press.

Doğan, A. (2006) *Osmanlı Aydınları ve Sosyal Darwinizm*, Istanbul: Bilgi University.

Donohue, J. and Esposito, J. (1982) *Islam in Transition: Muslim Perspectives*, Oxford: Oxford University Press.

Douglas, M. (1970) *Natural Symbols*, New York: Vintage Books.

Durkheim, E. (1915) *The Elementary Forms of the Religious Life*, London: George Allen & Unwin.

Durkheim, E. (1947) *The Division of Labor in Society*, New York: The Free Press.

Dündar, F. (2006) "La fondation de la kurdologie turque et Ziya Gökalp" *European Journal of Turkish Studies*, no. 5.

Eisenstadt, S. (2000) "Multiple Modernities" *Daedalus*, vol. 129, no. 1: 1–29.

El-Moudden, A. (1995a) *Le Maghreb à l'époque ottomane*, Rabat: Royaume du Maroc.

El-Moudden, A. (1995b) "The Idea of the Caliphate between Moroccans and Ottomans: Political and Symbolic Stakes in the 16th and 17th Century-Maghrib" *Studia Islamica*, no. 82: 103–112.

Engels, F. (2004[1844]), *The Origin of the Family, Private Property and the State*, Broadway, New South Wales: Resistance Books.

Engin, A. (1955) *Atatürkçülük'te Dil ve Din*, Istanbul: Özyürek Basımevi.

Eraslan, C. (1995) *II. Abdülhamid ve İslam Birliği*, Istanbul: Ötüken Neşriyat.

Erdem, S. (1995) "Hilafetin Kaldırılması Sürecinde Teorik Tartışmalar ve Adliye Vekili Seyyid Bey'in Katkısı" unpublished MA thesis, Istanbul: Bogazici University.

Erdem, S. (1996) "Cumhuriyet'e Geçiş Sürecinde Hilâfet Teorisine Alternatif Yaklaşımlar: Seyyid Bey Örneği (1922–1924)" *Divan: Disiplinlerarası Çalışmalar Dergisi*, no. 2.

Erdem, S. (2003) "Tanzimat Sonrası Osmanlı Hukuk Düşüncesinde Fıkıh Usulü Kavramları ve Modern Yaklaşımlar" unpublished PhD dissertation, Istanbul: Marmara University.

Erdem, T. (1982) *Anayasalar ve Seçim Kanunları 1876–1982*, Istanbul: Milliyet.

Erk, H. B. (1961) *Meşhur Türk Hukukçuları*, Adana: Varol Matbaası.

Eroğlu, H. (1982) *Türk İnkılap Tarihi*, Istanbul: Milli Eğitim Basımevi.

Esposito, J. (2000) "Islam and Secularism in the Twenty-First Century" in A. Tamimi and J. Esposito (eds.), *Islam and Secularism in the Middle East*, New York: New York University Press.

Fairclough, N. (1992) *Discourse and Social Change*, Cambridge: Polity Press.

Fairclough, N. (1995) *Critical Discourse Analysis*, London: Longman.

Fairclough, N. (2001a) "Critical Discourse Analysis as a Method in Social Scientific Research" in R. Wodak and M. Meyer, *Methods of Critical Discourse Analysis*, London: Sage.

Fairclough, N. (2001b) *Language and Power*, 2nd ed., London: Longman.

Fairclough, N. (2003) *Analysing Discourse: Textual Analysis for Social Research*, London/New York: Routledge.

Feldman, N. (2008) *The Fall and Rise of the Islamic State*, Princeton, NJ: Princeton University Press.

Fenn, R. (1978) *Toward a Theory of Secularization*, Storrs, CT: Society for the Scientific Study of Religion.

Findley, C. V. (1994) *Osmanlı Devletinde Bürokratik Reform: Babıali (1789–1922)*, Istanbul: İz.

Finke, R. (1992) "An Unsecular America" in S. Bruce (ed.) *Religion and Modernization: Sociologists and Historians Debate the Secularization Thesis*, Oxford: Clarendon Press.

Finke, R. (1997) "The Consequences of Religious Competition: Supply-side Explanations for Religious Change" in L. A. Young (ed.) *Rational Choice Theory and Religion: Summary and Assessment*, New York: Routledge.

Finke, R. and Iannaccone, L. R. (1993) "Supply-side Explanations for Religious Change" *The Annals of the American Association for Political and Social Science*, vol. 527, no. 1: 27–39.

Finke, R. and Stark, R. (1988) "Religious Economies and Sacred Canopies: Religious Mobilization in American Cities, 1906" *American Sociological Review*, vol. 53, no. 1: 41–59.

Finke, R. and Stark, R. (1992) *The Churching of America, 1776–1990: Winners and Losers in our Religious Economy*, New Brunswick, NJ: Rutgers University Press.

Fortna, B. C. (2002) *Imperial Classroom: Islam, the State, and Education in the Late Ottoman Empire*, Oxford: Oxford University Press.

Foucault, M. (1972) *The Archaeology of Knowledge*, trans. S. Smith, London: Tavistock.

Foucault, M. (1979a) *Discipline and Punish: The Birth of the Prison*, New York: Random House.

Foucault, M. (1979b) "Powers and Strategies: Interview between Michel Foucault and *Revoltes Logiques* Collective" in M. Morris and P. Patton (eds.) *Michel Foucault: Power/Truth/Strategy*, Sydney: Feral Publications, pp. 48–58.

Foucault, M. (1979c) "Truth and Power: an Interview with Alessandro Fontano and Pasquel Pasquino" in M. Morris and P. Patton (eds.) *Michel Foucault: Power/Truth/Strategy*, Sydney: Feral Publications.

Fowden, G. (1993) *Empire to Commonwealth: Consequences of Monotheism in Late Antiquity*, Princeton, NJ: Princeton University Press.

Fowler, R. (1996) *Linguistic Criticism*, 2nd ed., Oxford: Oxford University Press.

Fowler, R., Hodge, B., Kress, G. and Trew, T. (1979) *Language and Control*, London: Routledge.

Fox, J. (2008) *A World Survey of Religion and the State*, New York: Cambridge University Press.

Frey, F. W. (1965) *The Turkish Political Elite*, Cambridge: MIT Press.

Friedrich, C. J. (1958) "The Rational Ground of Authority" in C. J. Friedrich (ed.) *Tradition and Authority*, Cambridge, MA: Harvard University Press.

Fromkin, D. (2001) *A Peace to End All Peace: The Fall of the Ottoman Empire and the Creation of the Modern Middle East*, New York: Macmillan.

Gauchet, M. (1997) *The Disenchantment of the World: A Political History of Religion*, Princeton, NJ: Princeton University Press.

Geertz, C. (1966) "Religion as a Cultural System" in Michael Banton (ed.) *Anthropological Approaches to the Study of Religion*, London: Tavistock.

Geertz, C. (1973) *The Interpretation of Cultures*, New York: Basic Books.

Genç, M. (2000) *Osmanlı İmparatorluğu'nda Devlet ve Ekonomi*, Istanbul: Ötüken.

Georgeon, F. (1980) *Aux origines du nationalisme Turc: Yusuf Akcura, 1876–1935*, Paris: Institut d'edutes Anatoliennes.

Georgeon, F. and Gökalp, İ. (eds.) (2007) *Kemalizm ve İslam Dünyası*, Istanbul: Kaynak.

al-Ghannouchi, R. (2000) "Secularism in the Arab Maghreb" in A. Tamimi and J. Esposito (eds.), *Islam and Secularism in the Middle East*, New York: New York University Press.

Gibb, H. A. R. (1962) "Lütfi Pasha on the Ottoman Caliphate" *Oriens*, no. 15: 287–95.

Gibb, H. A. R. and Bowen, H. (1950) *Islamic Society and the West, vol. 1*, London: Oxford University Press.

Glasner, P. (1977) *The Sociology of Secularisation*, London: Routledge.

Goankar D. P. (ed.) (2001) *Alternative Modernities*, Durham, NC/London: Duke University Press.

Goldschmidt, A. (2000) *Biographical Dictionary of Modern Egypt*, Boulder, CO: Lynne Rienner.

Goldschmidt, A. (2005) *A Concise History of the Middle East*, 8th ed. London: Westview Press.

Goloğlu, M. (1973) *Halifelik Ne İdi? Nasıl Alındı? Ne İçin Kaldırıldı?* Ankara: Kalite Matbaası.

Goloğlu, M. (2008a) *Erzurum Kongresi*, Istanbul: Türkiye İş Bankası Kültür Yayınları.

Goloğlu, M. (2008b) *Sivas Kongresi*, Istanbul: Türkiye İş Bankası Kültür Yayınları.

Gorski, P. (2000) "Historicizing the Secularization Debate: Church, State, and Society in Late Medieval and Early Modern Europe, ca 1300 to 1700" *American Sociological Review*, vol. 65, no. 1: 138–167.

Gökbilgin, M. T. (1992) *Kanuni Sultan Süleyman*, Istanbul: MEB.

Grant, J. (1999) "Rethinking the Ottoman "Decline": Military Technology Diffusion in the Ottoman Empire, Fifteenth to Eighteenth Centuries" *Journal of World History*, vol. 10, no. 1: 179–201.

Gümüşoğlu, H. (2004) *Osmanlı'da Hilafet ve Halifeliğin Kaldırılması*, Istanbul: Kayıhan.

Gündüz, M. (2007) *II. Meşrutiyet'in Klasik Paradigmaları: İçtihad, Sebilü'r-Reşad ve Türk Yurdu'nda Toplumsal Tezler*, Ankara: Lotus.

Habermas, J. (1991) *The Structural Transformation of the Public Sphere: An Inquiry into a Category of Bourgeois Society*, Cambridge, MA: MIT Press.

Hacısalihoğlu, M. (2008) *Jön Türkler ve Makedonya Sorunu*, Istanbul: Tarih Vakfı.

Haim, S. (1965) "The Abolition of the Caliphate and its Aftermath" in T. W. Arnold, *The Caliphate*, London: Routledge & Kegan Paul.

Haim, S. (ed.) (1962) *Arab Nationalism: An Anthology*, Berkeley, CA: University of California Press.

Hanioğlu, M. Ş. (1981) *Bir Siyasal Düşünür Olarak Abdullah Cevdet ve Dönemi*, Istanbul: Üçdal Neşriyat.

Hanioğlu, M. Ş. (1986) *Bir Siyasal Örgüt Olarak Osmanlı İttihat ve Terakki Cemiyeti ve Jön Türklük (1889–1902)*, Istanbul: İletişim.

Hanioğlu, M. Ş. (1995) *The Young Turks in Opposition*, New York/Oxford: Oxford University Press.

Hanioğlu, M. Ş. (1997) "Garbcılar: Their Attitudes toward Religion and their Impact on the Official Ideology of the Turkish Republic" *Studia Islamica*, vol. 86, no. 2: 150–158.

Hanioğlu, M. Ş. (2001) *Preparation for Revolution: The Young Turks, 1902–1908*, New York/Oxford: Oxford University Press.

Hanioğlu, M. Ş. (2006) "Turkism and the Young Turks, 1889–1908" in H. L. Kieser (ed.) *Turkey Beyond Nationalism: Towards Post-Nationalist Identities*, London: I. B. Tauris.

Hanioğlu, M. Ş. (2011) *Atatürk: An Intellectual Biography*, Princeton, NJ: Princeton University Press.

Haq, M. (2008a) "Hakim Ajmal Khan" on *All India Congress Committee*'s website, available at: www.aicc.org.in/new/past-president-detail.php?id=35 (retrieved September 13, 2011).

Haq, M. (2008b) "Maulana Abul Kalam Azad" on *All India Congress Committee*'s website: www.aicc.org.in/maulana_abul_kalam_azad.htm (retrieved July 12, 2008).

Hathaway, J. (1996) "Problems of Periodization in Ottoman History: The Fifteenth through the Eighteenth Centuries" *The Turkish Studies Association Bulletin*, vol. 20, no.2: 25–31.

Hawthorn, J. (1992) *Concise Glossary of Contemporary Literary Theory*, London: Edward Arnold.

Hayashi, T. (1983) "The Modernization of Japan and Turkey: Some Comparisons" in Kazancıgil and E. Özbudun (eds.) *Atatürk: Founder of a Modern State*, London: A. C. Hurst and Company.

Heper, M. (1985) *The State Tradition in Turkey*, Walkington: The Eothen Press.

Heper, M. (1998) *İsmet İnönü: The Making of a Turkish Statesman*, Leiden: E. J. Brill.

Heyd, U. (1950) *Foundations of Turkish Nationalism: The Life and Teachings of Ziya Gökalp*, London: Luzac.

Heyd, U. (1954) *Language Reform in Modern Turkey*, Jerusalem: The Israel Oriental Society.

Hill, M. (1973) *A Sociology of Religion*, New York: Basic Books.

Hobsbawm, E. (1992) "Introduction: Inventing Traditions" in E. Hobsbawm and T. Ranger (eds.) *The Invention of Tradition*, Cambridge: Cambridge University Press.

Hodgson, M. (1974) *The Venture of Islam, vol. I: The Classical Age of Islam*, Chicago, IL: University of Chicago Press.

Horne, C. (1923) "Arab Independence Proclaimed" in C. Horne (ed.) *Source Records of the Great War*, vol. IV, London: National Alumni.

Hourani, A. (1983) *Arabic Thought in the Liberal Age*, Cambridge: Cambridge University Press.

Hourani, A., P. Khoury and M. Wilson (eds.) (1993) *The Modern Middle East*, Berkeley/Los Angeles, CA: University of California Press.

Huntington, S. P. (1993) "The Clash of Civilizations?" *Foreign Affairs*, vol. 72, no. 3: 22–49.

Iannaccone, L. (1997) "Rational Choice: Framework for the Scientific Study of Religion" in L. A. Young (ed.), *Rational Choice Theory and Religion: Summary and Assessment*, New York: Routledge, pp. 25–42.

Introvigne, M. (2006) "Turkish Religious Market(s): A View Based on the Religious Economy Theory" in H. Yavuz (ed.) *The Emergence of a New Turkey: Democracy and the AK Parti*, Salt Lake City, UT: University of Utah Press.

Islam, S. (2006) "Azad, (Maulana) Abul Kalam" *Banglapedia*, online, available at: www. banglapedia.org/httpdocs/HT/A_0376.HTM (retrieved 13 July 2008).

Issawi, C. (1966) *The Economic History of the Middle East, 1800–1914*, Chicago, IL: University of Chicago Press.

İnalcık, H. (1958) "Osmanlı Padişahı" *AÜSBF Dergisi*, vol. 13, no. 4: 68–79.

İnalcık, H. (1968) "The Nature of the Traditional Society: Turkey" in E. Ward and D. Rustow (eds.) *Political Modernization in Japan and Turkey*, Princeton, NJ: Princeton University Press.

İnalcık, H. (1970) "The Ottomans and the Caliphate" in P. M. Holt, A. Lambton, and B. Lewis (eds.) *The Cambridge History of Islam, vol. 1A*, Cambridge: Cambridge University Press.

İnalcık, H. (1988) "Recession of the Ottoman Empire and the Rise of the Saudi State" *Studies on Turkish-Arab Relations*, no. 3: 69–85.

İnalcık, H. (1998) "Büyük Devrim: Hilafetin Kaldırılması ve Laikleşme" *Doğu Batı*, vol. 1, no. 3: 71–88.

İnalcık, H. and Quataert, D. (eds.) (1994) *An Economic and Social History of the Ottoman Empire, 1300–1914*, 2 vols., New York: Cambridge University Press.

Jacoby, T. (2004) *Social Power and the Turkish State*, London/New York: Frank Cass.

Jaschke, G. (1972) *Yeni Türkiye'de İslamlık*, trans. H. Örs, Ankara: Bilgi.

Jenkins, P. (2007) *God's Continent: Christianity, Islam, and Europe's Religious Crisis*, New York: Oxford University Press.

JMI (2011a) "Hakim Ajmal Khan" on *Jamia Millia Islamia*'s website http://jmi.ac.in/ aboutjamia/profile/history/Founders-14/Hakim_Ajmal_Khan-2150 (retrieved September 29, 2011).

JMI (2011b) "Dr. Mukhtar Ahmed Ansari" on *Jamia Millia Islamia*'s website http://jmi. ac.in/aboutjamia/profile/history/Past_Chancellors_Profile-15/Dr_   Mukhtar_Ahmad_ Ansari-2178 (retrieved September 29, 2011).

Jorga, N. (2005) *Osmanlı İmparatorluğu Tarihi*, 5 vols., Istanbul: Yeditepe.

Kabakçı, E. (2006) "Sauver l'Empire. Modernisation, positivisme et formation de la culture politique des Jeunes-Turcs (1895–1908)" unpublished PhD thesis, Université Sorbonne (Paris I Panthéon).

Kaçmazoğlu, B. (2001) *Türk Sosyoloji Tarihine Giriş*, Istanbul: Birey.

Kafadar, C. (1993) in "The Myth of the Golden Age: Ottoman Historical Consciousness in the post-Suleymanic Era" H. Inalcik and C. Kafadar (eds.) *Suleiman the Second and His Time*, Istanbul: Isis Press.

Kafadar, C. (1994) "The Ottomans and Europe" in T. A. Brady (ed.) *Handbook of European History, 1400–1600, Vol. 1*, Leiden: E. J. Brill.

Kafadar, C. (1997–1998) "The Question of Ottoman Decline" *Harvard Middle Eastern and Islamic Review*, vol. 4, nos. 1–2: 30–75.

Kansu, A. (2001) *1908 Devrimi*, Istanbul: İletişim.

Kara, İ. (1991) "Müslüman Kardeşler Türkçe'ye Tercüme Edildi mi?" *Dergah*, vol. 2, no. 21: 14–15.

Kara, İ. (1998) *Biraz Yakın Tarih, Biraz Uzak Hurafe*, Istanbul: Kitabevi.

Kara, İ. (2001) *İslamcıların Siyasi Görüşleri, vol. 1: Hilafet ve Meşrutiyet*, 2nd ed., Istanbul: Dergah.

Kara, İ. (ed.) (2002–2005) *Hilafet Risaleleri*, 5 vols., Istanbul: Klasik.

368   *References*

Kara, İ. (2003a) *Din ile Modernleşme Arasında*, Istanbul: Dergah.

Kara, İ. (2003b) "Giriş" *Hilafet Risaleleri*, vol. 3, Istanbul: Klasik.

Kara, İ. (2004) "Giriş" *Hilafet Risaleleri*, vol. 4, Istanbul: Klasik.

Kara, İ. (2005) "Giriş" *Hilafet Risaleleri*, vol. 5, Istanbul: Klasik.

Kara, İ. (2006) "Modernleşme Döneminde Dini Otorite Meselesinin Ele Alınışı ve Problemleri, veya 'İslam'da Ruhbanlık Vardır'" in A. İ. Demir (ed.) *Dini Otorite*, Istanbul: Ensar Neşriyat.

Kara, İ. (2008) *Cumhuriyet Türkiyesi'nde Bir Mesele Olarak İslam*, Istanbul: Dergah.

Karal, E. Z. (1940) "Tanzimattan Evvel Garplılaşma Hareketleri" in *Tanzimat I*, Istanbul: Maarif Matbaası.

Karal, E. Z. (1968) "Devrim ve Laiklik" in E. Z. Ökte (ed.) *Atatürk, Din ve Laiklik*, Istanbul: Menteş Matbaası.

Karal, E. Z. (1988[1947]) *Osmanlı Tarihi V: Nizam-ı Cedid ve Tanzimat Devirleri (1789–1856)*, Ankara: TTK.

Karpat, K. (1987) "Panislamizm ve II. Abdülhamid, Yanlış Bir Görüşün Düzeltilmesi" *Türk Dünyası Araştırmaları Dergisi*, no. 48.

Karpat, K. (2000) "Historical Continuity and Identity Change or How to be Modern Muslim, Ottoman and Turk" in K. Karpat (ed.) *Ottoman Past and Today's Turkey*, Leiden: E. J. Brill.

Karpat, K. (2001) *The Politicization of Islam: Reconstructing Identity, State, Faith, and Community in the Late Ottoman State*, New York: Oxford University Press.

Karpat, K. (2002) "The Transformation of the Ottoman State, 1789–1908" in K. Karpat, *Studies on Ottoman Social and Political History*, Leiden: E. J. Brill.

Karpat, K. (2004) "The Evolution of the Turkish Political System and the Changing Meaning of Modernity, Secularism and Islam (1876–1945)" in K. Karpat, *Studies on Turkish Politics and Society*, Leiden: E. J. Brill.

Kaşıkçı, O. (1997) *İslam ve Osmanlı Hukukunda Mecelle: Hazırlanışı, Hükümlerinin Tahlili, Tadil ve Tamamlama Çalışmaları*, Istanbul: Osmanlı Araştırmaları Vakfı.

Kavak, Ö. (2007) "Reşid Rıza'nın Hayatı ve Eserleri" in Reşid Rıza, *İttihad-i Osmanî'den Arap İsyanına*, Istanbul: Klasik.

Kavak, Ö. (2011) *Modern İslam Hukuk Düşüncesi: Reşid Rıza Örneği*, Istanbul: Klasik.

Kayalı, H. (1997) *Arabs and Young Turks: Ottomanism, Arabism and Islamism in the Ottoman Empire, 1908–1918*, Berkeley, CA: University of California Press.

Keane, J. (2000) "The Limits of Secularism" in A. Tamimi and J. Esposito (eds.), *Islam and Secularism in the Middle East*, New York: New York University Press.

Keddie, N. (1972) *Sayyid Jamal ad-Din "al-Afghani": A Political Biography*, Berkeley/Los Angeles, CA: University of California Press.

Keddie, N. (1993) "Iranian Revolutions in Comparative Perspective" in A. Hourani, P. Khoury and M. Wilson (eds.) *The Modern Middle East* Berkeley/Los Angeles, CA: University of California Press.

Keddie, N. (1997) "Secularism and the State: Towards Clarity and Global Comparison" *New Left Review*, vol. I, no. 226.

Kedourie, E. (1963) "Egypt and the Caliphate 1915–1946" *Journal of the Royal Asiatic Society*, no. 3/4: 208–248.

Kedourie, E. (1970) *The Chatham House Version and Other Middle Eastern Studies*. London: Weidenfeld and Nicholson.

Kedourie, E. (1972) "The Politics of Political Literature: Kawakabi, Azouri and Jung" *Middle Eastern Studies*, vol. 8, no. 2: 227–240.

Kenanoğlu, M. (2004) *Osmanlı Millet Sistemi: Mit ve Gerçek*, Istanbul: Klasik.

Kennedy, H. (2004) *The Prophet and the Age of the Caliphates: The Islamic Near East from the 6th to the 11th Century*, 2nd ed., London: Longman.

Kerr, M. H. (1966) *Islamic Reform: The Political and Legal Theories of Muhammad 'Abduh and Rashid Rida*, Berkeley, CA: University of California Press.

Keyder, Ç. (1989) *Türkiye'de Devlet ve Sınıflar*, Istanbul: İletişim.

Khalidi, R. (1993) "Ottomanism and Arabism in Syria before 1914: A Reassessment" in R. Khalidi, L. Anderson, M. Muslih and R. Simon (eds.) *The Origins of Arab Nationalism*, New York: Columbia University Press.

Khalidi, R., Anderson, L., Muslih, M. and Simon, R. (eds.) (1993) *The Origins of Arab Nationalism*, New York: Columbia University Press.

Khoury, P. (1983) *Urban Notables and Arab Nationalism: The Politics of Damascus, 1860–1920*, New York: Cambridge University Press.

Kili, S. (1982) *Türk Anayasaları*, Istanbul: Tekin.

Kinross, P. (1964) *Atatürk: The Rebirth of a Nation*, London: Weidenfeld and Nicholson.

Kırlı, C. (2004) "Coffeehouses: Public Opinion in the Nineteenth-century Ottoman Empire" in A. Salvatore and D. Eickelman (eds.) *Public Islam and the Common Good*, Leiden: E. J. Brill.

Kırmızı, A. (2010) "Meşrutiyette İstibdat Kadroları: 1908 İhtilali'nin Bürokraside Tasfiye ve İkame Kabiliyeti" in S. Akşin, S. Balcı and B. Ünlü (eds.), *100. Yılında Jön Türk Devrimi*, Istanbul: Türkiye İş Bankası Yayınları.

Kiser, E. and Hechter, M. (1991) "The Role of General Theory in Comparative-Historical Sociology" *American Journal of Sociology*, vol. 97, no. 1: 1–30.

Kiser, E. and Hechter, M. (1998) "The Debate on Historical Sociology: Rational Choice Theory and Its Critics" *American Journal of Sociology*, vol. 104, no. 3: 785–816.

Koçak, C. (2005) "Parliament Membership during the Single-Party System in Turkey (1925–1945)" *European Journal of Turkish Studies*, Thematic Issue No. 3.

Koçer, H. A. (1970) *Türkiye'de Modern Eğitimin Doğuşu*, Ankara: Uzman Yayınları.

Koloğlu, O. (1998) *Avrupa'nýn Kýskacýnda Abdülhamit*, Istanbul: İletişim.

Koloğlu, O. (2010) *Osmanlı Dönemi Basınının İçeriği, vol. 1* (3 vols.), Istanbul: İÜ İletişim Fakültesi Yayınları.

Korlaelçi, M. (2002) *Pozitivizmin Türkiye'ye Girişi*, Istanbul: Hece.

Koloğlu, O. (1986) *Islam Assembled: The Advent of Muslim Congresses*, New York: Columbia University Press.

Koloğlu, O. (1989) "Pen and Purse: Sabunji and Blunt" in C. E. Bosworth, C. Issawi, R. Savory and A. L. Udovitch (eds.) *The Islamic World From Classical to Modern Times: Essays in Honor of Bernard Lewis*, Princeton, NJ: Darwin Press.

Kramers, J. (1993) "Şeyh-ül-İslam" *İslam Ansiklopedisi*, vol. 11, Istanbul: Milli Eğitim Basımevi.

Kuru, A. (2009) *Secularism and State Policies toward Religion: The United States, France, and Turkey*, Cambridge/New York: Cambridge University Press.

Kushner, D. (1977) *The Rise of Turkish Nationalism: 1876–1908*, London: Frank Cass.

Kutay, C. (1998) *Tarihte Türkler, Araplar, Hilafet Meselesi*, Istanbul: Aksoy.

Kürkçüoğlu, Ö. (1978) *Türk-İngiliz İlişkileri (1919–1926)*, Ankara: Ankara Üniversitesi.

Lal, B. (1969) "Activities of Turkish Agents in Khyber During World War I" *Journal of Asiatic Society of Pakistan*, vol. 14, no. 2: 185–192.

Lambert, Y. (2004) "A Turning Point in Religious Evolution in Europe" *Journal of Contemporary Religion*, vol. 19, no. 1: 29–45.

Lambton, A. (1993) "Social Change in Persia in the Nineteenth Century" in A. Hourani,

P. Khoury and M. Wilson (eds.) *The Modern Middle East*, Berkeley/Los Angeles, CA: University of California Press.

Landau, J. (1971) *The Hejaz Railway and the Muslim Pilgrimage: A Case of Ottoman Political Propaganda*, Detroit, MI: Wayne University Press.

Landau, J. (1990) *The Politics of Pan-Islam: Ideology and Organization*, London: Clarendon Press.

Lapidus, I. M. (1988) *A History of Islamic Societies*, Cambridge/New York: Cambridge University Press.

Latimer, F. P. (1960) "The Political Philosophy of Mustapha Kemal Atatürk: As Evidenced in His Published Speeches and Interviews" unpublished PhD dissertation, Princeton, NJ: Princeton University.

Lee, R. D. (2009) *Religion and Politics in the Middle East: Identity, Ideology, Institutions, and Attitudes*, Boulder, CO: Westview Press.

Lerner, D. (1958) *The Passing of Traditional Society: Modernizing the Middle East*, Glencoe, IL: The Free Press of Glencoe.

Levend, A. S. (1972) *Türk Dilinde Gelişme ve Sadeleşme Evreleri*, Ankara: TDK.

Lewis, B. (1961) *The Emergence of Modern Turkey*, London/New York: Oxford University Press.

Lewis, B. (2002) *What Went Wrong? The Clash between Islam and Modernity in the Middle East*, New York: Oxford University Press.

Lewis, G. (2002) *The Turkish Language Reform: A Catastrophic Success*, London/New York: Oxford University Press.

Liebl, V. (2009) "The Caliphate" *Middle Eastern Studies*, vol. 45 no. 3: 373–391.

Lombard, M. (2003) *The Golden Age of Islam*, Princeton, NJ: Markus Wiener Publishers.

Luckmann, T. (1967) *The Invisible Religion: The Problem of Religion in Modern Societies*, New York: Macmillan.

Maisel, S. (2007) "Kingdom of Saudi Arabia" in D. Long, B. Reich, and M. Gasiorowski (eds.) *The Government and Politics of the Middle East and North Africa*, Boulder, CO/London: Westview Press.

Mann, M. (1986) *The Sources of Social Power. Vol I: A History of Power from the Beginning to A.D. 1760*, Cambridge: Cambridge University Press.

Mann, M. (1993) *The Sources of Social Power Vol. II: The Rise of Classes and Nation-States, 1760–1914*, New York: Cambridge University Press.

Mardin, Ş. (1962) *The Genesis of Young Ottoman Thought*, Princeton, NJ: Princeton University Press.

Mardin, Ş. (1971) "Ideology and Religion in the Turkish Revolution" *International Journal of Middle Eastern Studies*, vol. 2, no. 3: 197–211.

Mardin, Ş. (1983a) *Jön Türklerin Siyasi Fikirleri 1895–1908*, Istanbul: İletişim.

Mardin, Ş. (1983b) *Din ve İdeoloji*, Istanbul: İletişim.

Mardin, Ş. (1983c) "Religion and Secularism in Turkey" in A. Kazancıgil and E. Özbudun (eds.) *Atatürk: Founder of a Modern State*, London: A. C. Hurst and Company.

Mardin, Ş. (1989) *Religion and Social Change in Modern Turkey: The Case of Bediuzzaman Said Nursi*, Albany, NY: State University of New York Press.

Mardin, Ş. (1991a) *Türkiye'de Din ve Siyaset*, Istanbul: İletişim.

Mardin, Ş. (1991b) "The Just and the Unjust" *Daedalus*, vol. 120, no. 3: 113–129.

Mardin, Ş. (1991c) *Türk Modernleşmesi*, Istanbul: İletişim.

Mardin, Ş. (2003) "Türkiye Cumhuriyeti'nde Laik Modelin Oluşumu" in *Devlet ve Din İlişkileri: Farklı Modeller, Konseptler ve Tecrübeler*, Ankara: Konrad Adenauer Vakfı.

Mardin, Ş. (2005) "Turkish Islamic Exceptionalism Yesterday and Today: Continuity, Rupture and Reconstruction in Operational Codes" *Turkish Studies*, vol. 6, no. 2: 145–165.

Margoliouth, D. (1924) "The Latest Developments of the Caliphate Question" *The Muslim World*, vol. 14, no. 4: 334–341.

Martin, D. (1969) *The Religious and the Secular: Studies in Secularization*, London: Routledge and Kegan Paul.

Martin, D. (1978) *A General Theory of Secularization*, Oxford: Blackwell.

Mawdudi, A. A. (1965) *Caliphate and Kingship*, New Delhi: Markazi Maktaba Islami.

Menteş, S. (ed.) (1969) *Hilafetin Mahiyet-i Şer'iyesi*, Istanbul: Menteş Matbaası.

Mert, N. (1994) *Laiklik Tartışmasına Kavramsal Bir Bakış: Cumhuriyet Kurulurken Laik Düşünce*, Istanbul: Bağlam.

Mertoğlu, S. (2001) "Osmanlı'da II. Meşrutiyet Sonrası Modern Tefsir Anlayışı (Sırat-ı Müstakim/Sebilürreşad Dergisi Örneği: 1908–1914)" unpublished PhD dissertation, Istanbul: Marmara University.

Mertoğlu, S. (2005) "Reşid Rıza'da Hilafet Düşüncesi: Bir Kronoloji ve Tahlil Denemesi" in İ. Kara (ed.) *Hilafet Risaleleri*, vol. 5, Istanbul: Klasik.

Mertoğlu, S. (forthcoming) *Reşid Rıza'nın Kur'an Yorumu*, Istanbul: Klasik.

Messick, B. (1996) *The Calligraphic State: Textual Domination and History in a Muslim Society*, Berkeley/Los Angeles, CA: University of California Press.

Mills, S. (1997) *Discourse*, London/New York: Routledge.

Milton-Edwards, B. (2006) *Contemporary Politics in the Middle East*, Cambridge: Polity Press.

Mısıroğlu, K. (1993) *Geçmişi ve Geleceği ile Hilafet*, Istanbul: Sebil.

Mitchell, R. (1969) *The Society of the Muslim Brothers*, London: Oxford University Press.

Moaddel, M. (2002) "Discursive Pluralism and Islamic Modernism in Egypt" *Arab Studies Quarterly*, vol. 24, no. 1: 1–29.

Moaddel, M. (2005) *Islamic Modernism, Nationalism, and Fundamentalism: Episode and Discourse*, Chicago, IL: University of Chicago Press.

Mohammadi, A. S. and Mohammadi, A. (1994) *Small Media, Big Revolution: Communication, Culture, and the Iranian Revolution*, Minneapolis, MN: University of Minnesota Press.

Monroe, E. (1963) *Britain's Moment in the Middle East, 1914–1956*, Baltimore, MD: Johns Hopkins Press.

Montesquieu, C. S. (1834) *De l'esprit de lois*, Paris: Didot.

Moore, B. (1958) *Political Power and Social Theory*, Cambridge, MA: Harvard University Press.

Mughul, M. Y. (1987) *Kanuni Devri*, Ankara: Kültür ve Turizm Bakanlığı.

Muslim, H. (1955–1956) *Sahih al-Muslim*, ed. A. F. Abdulbaqi, Cairo: Dar Ihya al-Kutub al-Arabiyya.

al-Nawawi, Y. (1997) *Al-Nawawi's Forty Hadith*, London: Islamic Texts Society.

Nevakivi, J. (1969) *Britain, France and the Arab Middle East 1914–1920*, London: Athlone Press.

Ochsenwald, W. (1993) "Ironic Origins: Arab Nationalism in the Hijaz, 1882–1914" in R. Khalidi, L. Anderson, M. Muslih and R. Simon (eds.) *The Origins of Arab Nationalism*, New York: Columbia University Press.

Oktay, C. (1991) "Hum Zamirinin Serencamı: Kanun-ı Esasi İlanına Muhalefet Üzerine Bir Deneme" in C. Oktay, *Hum Zamirinin Serencamı*, Istanbul: Bağlam.

Oliver-Dee, S. (2009) *The Caliphate Question: the British Government and Islamic Governance*, Lanham, MD: Lexington Books.

Ortaylı, İ. (1983) *İmparatorluğun En Uzun Yüzyılı*, Istanbul: Hil.

Ortaylı, İ. (1985) "Mustafa Reşit ve Midhat Paşalarla A. Comte ve Pozitivistler" *Tarih ve Toplum* vol. 3, no. 14: 30–34.

Owen, R. (1981) *The Middle East in World Economy, 1800–1914*, London: Methuen.

Öke, M. K. (1999) *Mustafa Kemal Paşa ve İslam Dünyası: Hilafet Hareketi*, Istanbul: Aksoy.

Öklem, N. (1981) *Hilafetin Sonu*, İzmir: Ege University.

Ökte, E. Z. (ed.) (1968) *Atatürk, Din ve Laiklik*, Istanbul: Menteş Matbaası.

Önelçin, H. A. (ed.) (1970) *Şeriat Açısından Halifeliğin İç Yüzü*, Istanbul: Ekin Basım.

Özbudun, E. (1992) *1921 Anayasası*, Ankara: Atatürk Araştırma Merkezi Yayınları.

Özcan, A. (1997) *Pan-İslamizm: Osmanlı Devleti, Hindistan Müslümanları ve İngiltere (1877–1924)*, Istanbul: İSAM.

Özcan, A. (1998a) "İngiltere'de Hilafet Tartışmaları" *İslam Araştırmaları Dergisi*, no. 2: 49–71.

Özcan, A. (1998b) "Hilafet – Osmanlılar" *TDV İslam Ansiklopedisi*, vol. 17, Istanbul: TDV.

Özön, M. N. (1997) *Namık Kemal ve İbret Gazetesi*, Istanbul: YKY.

Özşenel, M. (2006) "Gelenek ile Modernite Arasında Bir Sentez Denemesi: Seyyid Süleyman Nedvi (1884–1953)" *Divan: Disiplinlerarası Çalışmalar Dergisi*, vol. 11, no. 21.

Öztuna, Y. (2004) *Osmanlı Devleti Tarihi I*, Istanbul: Ötüken.

Öztuncay, B. (2005) *Hatıra-i Uhuvvet: Portre Fotoğrafların Cazibesi: 1846–1950*, Istanbul: Aygaz.

Paris, T. (2003) *Britain, the Hashemites and Arab Rule, 1920–1925: The Sherifian Solution*, London: Routledge.

Parla, J. (1993) *Babalar ve Oğullar: Tanzimat Romanının Epistemolojik Temelleri*, Istanbul: İletişim.

Parla, T. (1985) *Social and Political Thought of Ziya Gökalp, 1876–1924*, Leiden: E. J. Brill.

Parsons, T. (1951) *The Social System*, New York: Free Press.

Parsons, T. (1977) *Social Systems and the Evolution of Action Theory*, New York: Free Press.

Pêcheux, M. (1982) *Language, Semantics and Ideology: Stating the Obvious*, London: Macmillan.

al-Qadi, W. (1988) "The Term 'Khalifa' in Early Exegetical Literature" *Die Welt des Islams*, no. 28: 392–411.

Quataert, D. (1994) "The Age of Reforms; 1812–1914" in H. İnalcik and D. Quataert (eds.) *An Economic and Social History of the Ottoman Empire, 1300–1914, Vol. 2*, New York: Cambridge University Press.

Qureshi, M. N. (1999) *Pan-Islam in British Indian Politics: A Study of the Khilafat Movement, 1918–1924*, Leiden: E. J. Brill.

Ra'if, A. (1999) *al-Khilafah min al-Saqifah ilá Karbala*, Cairo: al-Zahra lil-I'lām al-'Arabī.

Ramsaur, E. E. (1957) *The Young Turks: Prelude to the Revolution of 1908*, Princeton, NJ: Princeton University Press.

Reid, A. (1967) "Nineteenth Century Pan-Islam in Indonesia and Malaysia" *The Journal of Asian Studies*, vol. 26, no. 2: 267–283.

Rousseau, J. J. (1993[1762]) *Du contrat social ou principes du droit politique*, Paris: Garnier Flammarion.

Rustow, D. A. (1973) "The Modernization of Turkey in Historical and Comparative Perspective" in K. Karpat (ed.), *Social Change and Politics in Turkey: A Structural-Historical Analysis*, Leiden: E. J. Brill.

Sadiq, M. (1983) *The Turkish Revolution and the Indian Freedom Movement*, New Delhi: Macmillan India.

Sadiq, M. (1991) "The Turkish Revolution and the Abolition of the Caliphate" *International Studies*, vol. 28, no. 1: 25–40.

Saint-Prot, C. (1995) *Le nationalisme arabe: Alternative à l'intégrisme*, Paris: Ellipses.

Saint-Simon, H. (1975[1832]) *Nouveau christianisme*, Paris: Au bureau du Globe.

Salibi, K. (1998) *The Modern History of Jordan*, London: I. B. Tauris.

Sanhoury, A. (1926) *Le Califat: son Évolution vers une Société des Nations Orientale*, Paris: Le Séminaire Oriental d'Etudes Juridiques et Sociales.

Sarıkoyuncu, A. (1995) *Milli Mücadele'de Din Adamları*, vol. I, Ankara: Diyanet İşleri Başkanlığı.

Sasaki, M. and Suzuki, T. (1987) "Changes in Religious Commitment in the United States, Holland, and Japan" *The American Journal of Sociology*, vol. 92, no. 5: 1055–1076.

Satan, A. (2008) *Halifeliğin Kaldırılması*, Istanbul: Gökkubbe.

Sayar, A. G. (1998) *Bir İktisatçının Entellektüel Portresi – Sabri F. Ülgener*, Istanbul: Eren.

Sayyid, B. (2003) *A Fundamental Fear: Eurocentrism and the Emergence of Islamism*, London/New York: Zed Books.

Shaw, S. J. (1971) *Between Old and New: The Ottoman Empire under Sultan Selim III 1789–1807*, Cambridge, MA: Harvard University Press.

Shaw, S. J. (2000) *From Empire to Republic: The Turkish War of National Liberation, 1918–1923*, Ankara: TTK/Turkish Historical Society.

Shaw, S. J. and Shaw, E. (1977) *History of the Ottoman Empire and Modern Turkey, vol. 2*, New York: Cambridge University Press.

Sherrill, C. H. (1934) *A Year's Embassy to Mustafa Kemal*, New York/London: C. Scribner's Sons.

Shissler, H. (2003) *Between Two Empires: Ahmet Ağaoğlu and the New Turkey*, London: I. B. Tauris.

Shukla, R. (1973) *Britain, India and the Turkish Empire, 1853–1882*, New Delhi: People's Publishing House.

Silverstein, B. (2003) "Islam and Modernity in Turkey: Power, Tradition and Historicity in the European Provinces of the Muslim World" *Anthropological Quarterly*, vol. 76, no. 3: 497–517.

Silverstein, B. (2008) "Disciplines of Presence in Modern Turkey: Discourse, Companionship and the Mass Mediation of Islamic Practice" *Cultural Anthropology*, vol. 23, no. 1: 118–153.

Skocpol, T. (1984) "Emerging Agendas and Recurrent Strategies in Historical Sociology" in T. Skocpol (ed.) *Vision and Method in Historical Sociology*, New York: Cambridge University Press.

Smith, C. (2003) "Introduction: Rethinking the Secularization of American Public Life" in C. Smith (ed.) *The Secular Revolution: Power, Interests, and Conflict in the Secularization of American Public Life*, Berkeley/Los Angeles, CA: University of California Press.

Smith, D. E. (1970) *Religion and Political Development*, Boston, MA: Little Brown.

Smith, D. E. (1974) "Religion and Political Modernization: Comparative Perspectives," in D. E. Smith (ed.) *Religion and Political Modernization*, New Haven, CT: Yale University Press.

Smith, H. H. *et al.* (1970) *Area Handbook for the United Arab Republic (Egypt)*, Washington, DC: Superintendent of Documents, US Government Printing Office.

Soage, A. B. (2008) "Rashid Rida's Legacy" *The Muslim World*, vol. 98, no. 1: 1–23.

Sohrabi, N. (1995) "Historicizing Revolutions: Constitutional Revolutions in the Ottoman Empire, Iran, and Russia, 1905–1908" *The American Journal of Sociology*, vol. 100, no. 6: 1383–1447.

Sohrabi, N. (2002) "Global Waves, Local Actors: What the Young Turks Knew about Other Revolutions and Why It Mattered" *Comparative Studies in Society and History*, vol. 44, no. 1: 45–79.

Somel, S. A. (2001a) *The Modernization of Public Education in the Ottoman Empire, 1839–1908: Islamization, Autocracy, and Discipline*, Leiden: E. J. Brill.

Somel, S. A. (2001b) "Osmanlı Reform Çağında Osmanlıcılık Düşüncesi (1839–1913)" in M. Ö. Alkan (ed.) *Modern Türkiye'de Siyasi Düşünce I: Tanzimat ve Meşrutiyet'in Birikimi*, Istanbul: İletişim.

Somers, M. (1998) "'We're No Angels': Realism, Rational Choice, and Relationality in Social Science" *American Journal of Sociology*, vol. 104, no. 3: 722–784.

Spickard, V. (1998) "Rethinking Religious Social Action: What Is 'Rational' about Rational-Choice Theory?" *Sociology of Religion*, vol. 59, no. 2: 99–115.

Stark, R. and Iannaccone, L. R. (1993) "Rational Choice Propositions about Religious Movements" *Religion and the Social Order*, vol. 3A: 241–261.

Stark, R. and Finke, R. (2000) *Acts of Faith: Explaining the Human Side of Religion*, Berkeley/Los Angeles, CA: University of California Press.

Starrett, G. (1998) *Putting Islam to Work: Education, Politics, and Religious Transformation in Egypt*, Berkeley, CA: University of California Press.

Stinchcombe, A. (1978) *Theoretical Methods in Social History*, New York: Academic Press.

Stoddard, P. (1963) *The Ottoman Government and the Arabs, 1911 to 1918: A Study of the* Teskilat-i Mahsusa, Princeton, NJ: Princeton University Press.

Sümer, F. (1992) "Yavuz Selim Halifeliği Devraldı mı?" TTK, *Belleten*, LVI/217.

Şakül, K. (2005) "Nizam-ı Cedid Düşüncesinde Batılılaşma ve İslami Modernleşme" *Divan: İlmi Araştırmalar*, no. 19: 117–150.

Şentürk, R. (1996) *İslam Dünyasında Modernleşme ve Toplumbilim*, Istanbul: İz.

Şentürk, R. (2005) *Narrative Social Structure: Anatomy of the Hadith Transmission Network, 610–1505*, Stanford, CA: Stanford University Press.

Şimşir, B. N. (1981) *Dış Basında Atatürk ve Türk Devrimi, vol. I: 1922–1924*, Ankara: TTK.

TALİD (Turkish Studies Review) (2008) *Special Issue on the History of Turkish Sociology*, vol. 6, no. 11.

Tamimi, A. (2000) "The Origins of Arab Secularism" in A. Tamimi and J. Esposito (eds.) *Islam and Secularism in the Middle East*, New York: New York University Press.

Tanör, B. (1995) *Osmanlı-Türk Anayasal Gelişmeleri (1789–1980)*, Istanbul: AFA.

Tanpınar, A. H. (1997) *19uncu Asır Türk Edebiyatı Tarihi*, 8th ed., Istanbul: Çağlayan Basımevi.

Tansel, S. (1969) *Yavuz Sultan Selim*, Ankara: Milli Eğitim Bakanlığı.

Tarabein, A. (1993) "'Abd al-Hamid al-Zahrawi: The Career and Thought of an Arab

Nationalist" in R. Khalidi, L. Anderson, M. Muslih and R. Simon (eds.) *The Origins of Arab Nationalism*, New York: Columbia University Press.

Tauber, E. (1989) "Rashid Rida as Pan-Arabist before World War I" *Muslim World*, vol. 79, no. 2: 102–112.

Tauber, E. (1993) *The Arab Movements in World War I*, London: Frank Cass.

Taylor, A. R. (1988) *The Islamic Question in Middle East Politics*, Boulder, CO/London: Westview Press.

Taylor, C. (2001) "Two Theories of Modernity" in D. P. Goankar (ed.) *Alternative Modernities*, Durham, NC/London: Duke University Press.

Taylor, C. (2007) *A Secular Age*, Cambridge, MA: Harvard University Press.

Teitelbaum, J. (1998) "Sharif Husayn ibn Ali and the Hashemite Vision of the Post-Ottoman Order: From Chieftaincy to Suzerainty" *Middle Eastern Studies*, vol. 34 no. 1: 103–121.

Teitelbaum, J. (2001) *The Rise and Fall of the Hashemite Kingdom of the Hijaz*, London: C. Hurst & Co. Publishers.

Tevetoğlu, F. (1988) "Atatürk'ün Minber Gazetesi'nde Kullandığı Takma Adı: Hatib" *Milli Kültür*, Aralık 1988.

Thomas W. I. (2002) "The Definition of the Situation" in N. Rousseau (ed.) *Self, Symbols, and Society: Classic Readings in Social Psychology*, Lanham, MD: Rowman & Littlefield.

Thompson, E. P. (1978) "The Poverty of Theory or An Orrery of Errors" in E. P. Thompson (ed.) *The Poverty of Theory and Other Essays*, New York: Monthly Review Press.

Tilly, C. (1981) *As Sociology Meets History*, New York: Academic Press.

Tilly, C. (1984) *Big Structures, Large Processes, Huge Comparisons*, New York: Russell Sage Foundation.

Toprak, B. (1981) *Islam and Political Development in Turkey*, Leiden: E. J. Brill.

Toprak, Z. (1995) *İttihat-Terakki ve Devletçilik*, Istanbul: Tarih Vakfı.

Towler, R. (1974) *Homo Religiosus: Sociological Problems in the Study of Religion*, New York: St. Martin's Press.

Trumpener, U. (1968) *Germany and the Ottoman Empire, 1914–1918*, Princeton, NJ: Princeton University Press.

Tschannen, O. (1991) "The Secularization Paradigm: A Systematization" *Journal for the Scientific Study of Religion*, vol. 30, no. 4: 395–415.

Tunaya, T. Z. (1952) *Türkiye'de Siyasi Partiler, 1859–1952*, Istanbul: n.p.

Tunaya, T. Z. (1962) *İslamcılık Cereyanı*, Istanbul: Baha Matbaası.

Tunaya, T. Z. (1981) *Devrim Hareketleri İçinde Atatürk ve Atatürkçülük*, Istanbul: Turhan.

Tunçay, M. (1967) *Türkiye'de Sol Akımlar 1 (1908-1925)*, Ankara: BDS Yayınları.

Tunçay, M. (2005), *Türkiye Cumhuriyeti'nde Tek-Parti Yönetiminin Kurulması (1923–1931)*, 4th ed., Istanbul: Tarih Vakfı.

Tunçay, M. and E. J. Zürcher (eds.) (2004) *Socialism and Nationalism in the Ottoman Empire 1876–1923*, London: I. B. Tauris.

Türköne, M. (1991) *Siyasi İdeoloji Olarak İslamcılığın Doğuşu*, Istanbul: İletişim.

Tyan, E. (1954) *Institutions du droit public musulman. Tome premiere: Le califat*, Paris: Recueil Sirey.

Tyan, E. (1956) *Institutions du droit public musulman. Tome deuxième: Sultanat et califat*, Paris: Recueil Sirey.

Uluğ, N. H. (1975) *Halifeliğin Sonu*, Istanbul: T. İş Bankası Kültür Yayınları.

Uzunçarşılı, İ. H. (1988) *Osmanlı Devleti'nin İlmiye Teşkilatı*, Ankara: TTK.

Ülgener, S. (2006 [1951]) *İktisadî Çözülmenin Ahlâk ve Zihniyet Dünyası*, Istanbul: Derin.

Ülken, H. Z. (1994[1966]) *Türkiye'de Çağdaş Düşünce Tarihi*, Istanbul: Ülken Yayınları.

Vambéry, A. (1906) "Pan-Islamism" *Nineteenth Century and After*, no. 60: 547–558.

Vatikiotis, P. (1980) *The History of Egypt*, 2nd ed., Baltimore, MD: Johns Hopkins University Press.

Verdery, K. (1995) *National Ideology under Socialism: Identity and Cultural Politics in Ceausescu's Romania*, Berkeley/Los Angeles: University of California Press.

Wallis, J. (2008) *The Great Awakening: Reviving Faith and Politics in a Post-Religious Right America*, New York: Harper Collins.

Ward, E. and Rustow, D. (eds.) (1968) *Political Modernization in Japan and Turkey*, Princeton, NJ: Princeton University Press.

Warner, S. (1993) "Work in Progress Toward a New Paradigm for the Sociological Study of Religion in the United States" *The American Journal of Sociology*, Vol. 98, No. 5: 1044–1093.

Warner, M., Vanantwerpen, J. and Calhoun, C. (eds.) (2010) *Varieties of Secularism in a Secular Age*, Cambridge, MA: Harvard University Press.

Weber, M. (1947) *The Theory of Social and Economic Organization*, New York: Oxford University Press.

Weber, M. (1949) *The Methodology of the Social Sciences*, Glencoe, IL: Free Press.

Weber, M. (1963) *The Sociology of Religion*, Boston, MA: Beacon.

Wegner, M. (2001) "Islamic Government: The Medieval Sunni Islamic Theory of the Caliphate and the Debate over the Revival of the Caliphate in Egypt, 1924–1926" unpublished PhD dissertation, Chicago, IL: University of Chicago.

Westrate, B. (1992) *The Arab Bureau: British Policy in the Middle East, 1916–1920*, University Park, PA: Pennsylvania State University Press.

Wilkinson, S. and Kitzinger, C. (1995) *Feminism and Discourse: Psychological Perspectives*, London: Sage.

Wilson, B. (1966) *Religion in Secular Society: A Sociological Comment*, London: C. A. Watts.

Wilson, M. (1993) "The Hashemites, the Arab Revolt, and Arab Nationalism" in R. Khalidi, L. Anderson, M. Muslih and R. Simon (eds.) *The Origins of Arab Nationalism*, New York: Columbia University Press.

Wodak, R. and Meyer, M. (2001) *Methods of Critical Discourse Analysis*, London: Sage.

Wodak, R. (2001) "What CDA is About – A Summary of its History, Important Concepts and its Developments" in R. Wodak and M. Meyer, *Methods of Critical Discourse Analysis*, London: Sage.

Worringer, R. (2004) "'Sick Man of Europe' or 'Japan of the Near East'?: Constructing Ottoman Modernity in the Hamidian and Young Turk Eras" *International Journal of Middle East Studies*, vol. 36, no. 2: 207–230.

Wuthnow, R. (1987) *Meaning and Moral Order: Explorations in Cultural Analysis*, Berkeley/Los Angeles, CA: University of California Press.

Yakut, E. (2005) *Şeyhülislamlık: Yenileşme Döneminde Devlet ve Din*, Ankara: Kitap Yayınevi.

Yalçınkaya, A. (1997) *Sömürgecilik - Panislamizm Işığında Türkistan (1856'dan Günümüze)*, Istanbul: Timaş.

Yıldırım, R. (2004) *20. Yüzyıl İslam Dünyasında Hilafet Tartışmaları*, Istanbul: Anka.

Yıldız, A. (2001) *"Ne Mutlu Türküm Diyebilene": Türk Ulusal Kimliğinin Etno-Seküler Sınırları (1919–1938)*, Istanbul: İletişim.

Yorulmaz, H. (ed.) (1995) *Tanzimattan Cumhuriyete Alfabe Tartışmaları*, Istanbul: Kitabevi.

Yücesoy, H. (2007) "Allah'ın Halifesi ve Dünyanın Kadısı: Bir Dünya İmparatorluğu Olarak Hilafet" *Divan: Disiplinlerarası Çalışmalar Dergisi*, no. 22.

Zaidan, A. (1990) *al-Wajez fi Usul al-Fiqh* 3rd ed., Muassasa al-Risalah: Maktabah al-Bashair.

Zallum, A. (2002) *How the Khilafah was Destroyed*, New Delhi: Milli Publications.

Zubaida, S. (2004) "Islam and Nationalism: Continuities and Contradictions" *Nations and Nationalism*, vol. 10, no. 4: 407–420.

Zürcher, E. J. (1984) *The Unionist Factor: The Role of the Committee of Union and Progress in the Turkish National Movement, 1905–1926*, Leiden: E. J. Brill.

Zürcher, E. J. (1993) *Turkey: A Modern History*, London: I. B. Tauris.

Zürcher, E. J. (2000) "Young Turks, Ottoman Muslims and Turkish Nationalists: Identity Politics 1908–1938" in K. Karpat (ed.) *Ottoman Past and Today's Turkey*, Leiden: E. J. Brill.

Zürcher, E. J. (2005) "The Ottoman Sources of Kemalist Thought" in E. Özdalga (ed.) *Late Ottoman Society: the Intellectual Legacy*, London: Routledge-Curzon.

Index

380 *Index*

Cairo 28, 64, 85, 89, 93, 116, 118, 123, 193–4, 201, 204, 209, 282, 301, 330, 332, 334, 348; commission 29

Caliph: as supreme leader 190, 276, 286, 293; as head of state 29, 106, 110, 118, 134, 150, 158, 167–8, 179, 271, 274–6, 279, 281, 283, 313–14, 318; of Allah 6, 80, 101, 221, 277; -sultan 54, 57–8, 62, 65, 78, 82, 90, 94, 96, 101–2, 106, 112, 116, 118, 127, 134, 150–3, 158, 163, 168–70, 174–5, 185, 192, 195, 197, 199, 208, 215, 218, 228, 231, 240, 248, 250–1, 259, 272, 301, 314, 316–17, 325, 331, 338; authority of 8, 33, 39, 58, 65, 79–84, 86, 90, 96–8, 100–4, 112, 115–20, 127, 134, 136–45, 150–6, 158, 161–5, 167–8, 170–7, 180, 182–3, 185, 187–8, 193, 195, 208, 214–16, 220, 225, 229, 240, 247, 249, 255, 269–71, 273, 280–2, 284–5, 287–8, 298, 312–16, 325, 331–2; religious authority of 31, 141, 155–6, 161, 163, 170, 172–7, 186, 191, 217–23, 238, 242, 305, 313–14, 340; temporal authority of 97, 101–2, 104, 115–18, 130, 136, 140, 143, 145, 152–4, 161, 169–70, 172, 174–7, 179, 185–6, 218–21, 238, 264–5, 270, 274, 282–3, 288–9, 311, 313–14, 317–18, 343

caliphal: center 4–5, 20, 26, 32–3, 37, 39, 78, 86, 91, 94–5, 97–8, 102, 111, 114, 126, 140, 141, 143, 186–90, 192, 211, 213, 222, 229, 238–41, 311, 313, 315–16, 332; periphery 4–5, 20, 26, 32–3, 37, 39, 63, 78, 86, 91–5, 97, 103, 110, 112, 114, 117, 127, 135, 137, 139–41, 148, 186–8, 205, 212–13, 217, 223, 229, 238, 240, 264, 311, 315–16, 332

Caliphate: abolition of 3, 5, 7–8, 16, 18, 23–9, 33, 44–5, 58–62, 78, 85–6, 90–1, 94–6, 104, 106, 109, 120, 133, 166, 175, 178, 196, 241–2, 247, 255, 262, 269, 274, 277, 279, 282, 289–91, 295–302, 304, 307–8, 310, 312, 314, 317–19, 325–6, 331, 334–6, 338, 344, 348–9, 351; Arab 32, 39, 84, 86, 92–3, 105, 121, 126–7, 139, 187, 194, 196–9, 201, 204–5, 209–10, 212, 214, 238, 302, 316, 330, 334–5, 338, 351; as a legal/social contract (mandate) 97, 144–5, 157–8, 161, 163–4, 169–70, 270, 276, 280, 284–6, 287, 297–8, 314; as useless 29, 109, 120, 279; Committee 218, 220, 272, 280, 291, 301, 346–7; Congress(es)

28, 85, 282, 295, 300–2, 346, 348, 350; deactivation of 274; definition of 31, 78–9, 83, 86, 91, 96, 104, 115, 119–20, 128, 140, 153–7, 163, 166–7, 169, 174–5, 177, 183, 213, 215, 273, 275, 280–1, 296, 311, 313, 329; demise of 1, 24, 32, 38, 90, 144, 185, 274, 276, 291, 307, 310, 317–18; destruction of 9, 27, 31–3, 37, 39, 91, 194, 230, 240–1, 276, 289, 295, 297, 301, 304, 307–8, 310–11, 318; ecumenical (universal) nature of 7, 165–6, 170, 189, 219–20, 242, 262, 269, 271, 275–6, 280–1, 286, 317–18; emergence/expansion of 8, 79–81; movement 188, 205–6, 212–13, 216, 229–30, 316, 335, 338, 344 nationalization of 97, 145, 165–7, 185, 313–14; obedience to 94, 97, 101–7, 112–13, 117–20, 130, 136–8, 142, 144, 154, 161–2, 182, 185, 188, 207, 213, 220–5, 238, 240, 293, 298; pseudo- 274; significance of 5, 79, 106, 130–1, 138, 140, 142, 155, 163, 187–8, 193, 210, 215, 223, 227, 236, 240, 253, 277, 293, 316–17, 324, 330, 337, 345, 349; transformation of 83, 90–1, 104, 144–6, 170, 175, 184–5, 242, 265, 274, 310, 313, 317; "true" versus "fictitious" 105, 110, 120, 126, 284–5, 287–8, 298, 318

Post-Caliphate period 22, 300–2, 346

Calvinism 12

Celal Nuri 64, 87, 115, 275, 280

Cemal Pasha 43, 57, 143, 151, 200, 244, 327, 337, 339

Central Powers 84, 98, 347

Cevdet Pasha 83, 189, 341

China 14, 272

Christian(s), 'Christianization' 2, 10, 12–13, 15, 17, 42, 49, 61, 94, 111, 157, 183, 191, 228–9, 235, 237, 246–7, 251, 298, 310, 320, 331, 337–8, 340

Christianity 6, 13, 65, 76, 104, 119, 184, 237, 284, 337; authority of 12, 173; Eastern 10; 'Islamicized' 76; Western 10

Church: authority of 10–11, 15, 157; -state duality 12–13, 15, 235, 245; Catholic 235; Orthodox 321; state- 10; separation from state 10, 14, 16, 176

"Church model" 6

Citizenship 42, 234; proto- 47, 324; identity and 61; Ottoman 44, 49, 57, 65, 83, 101, 109, 111, 141, 150, 164, 166, 168, 179, 188, 324

UPP (Union and Progress Party) 77
Urdu 38, 223, 342, 345–6
al-'Urwah al-Wuthqa journal 64, 209

vaaz 63
Vahideddin (Mehmed VI), Sultan 77, 85,
　94, 118, 222, 241, 243, 255–6, 258–9,
　261, 265–7, 270, 272–3, 288, 292, 301,
　304, 317, 348, 351
Vatan newspaper 63
vekil (representative) 41, 169
verse(s) *see* Qur'an
verstehen 31
Volkan journal 64, 149, 171–2

Wafd (party) 29, 351
Wahhabis 83, 201, 204, 206, 210, 212,
　301, 333, 335
wahy see God: revelations
"War of Independence" (Turkish) 45, 58,
　61, 95, 242
Weber, Max 4, 10–12, 20, 24, 30–1, 57,
　323
Westernization 15, 41, 44, 46, 53, 60, 68,
　75, 129
Westphalia 10
Wilhelm II, Kaiser 192, 239, 343
World War I 8, 28, 39, 44–5, 57, 68, 84,
　86, 91–6, 98, 103–5, 110, 114, 121,
　126–7, 134, 137, 143, 151, 163, 166–7,
　176, 181, 187, 192–6, 200–2, 209–32,
　235, 238–40, 243, 254, 270–3, 282,

　305, 310–11, 314–19, 328, 340, 342–3,
　347

Yafi, Sheikh Salih 90–1, 94, 101, 104, 111,
　113, 116, 118, 121, 153, 219, 221, 224,
　235, 336–7
Yahya (Imam of Yemen) 85, 206, 210,
　229, 335
Yazid 80
Yemen 211–12, 224, 229, 323, 325, 335,
　349
al-Yemeni, Sheikh Bilal Abid 90–1, 93,
　103–4, 111, 113–14, 128, 224
Young Italy (*Giovine Italia*) Movement 43
Young Ottomans 42–3, 52–3, 65–6, 146,
　148, 326, 328, 341, 343
Young Turks 8, 20, 43, 63, 65, 91–2, 94,
　101, 103, 117, 146–50, 153, 165, 193,
　195–6, 200, 207, 213, 226, 231, 239,
　248, 254, 313–14, 316, 325–6, 328, 335,
　338, 340–1; Revolution (1908) 32, 39,
　57, 63, 65, 68, 72, 74, 90–1, 108, 135,
　142–51, 153, 157, 165, 167, 169, 171–2,
　176, 185, 191, 232, 248, 285, 292, 313,
　316, 320, 326–7, 332, 334–6, 338, 341
Yunus Nadi 275
Yusuf Akçura 20, 68–9, 93, 165, 327, 341
Yusuf, Sultan of Morocco 44, 85, 114,
　121, 139, 316–17

Ziya Pasha 42, 343
al-Zahrawi, Abdülhamid 92, 206